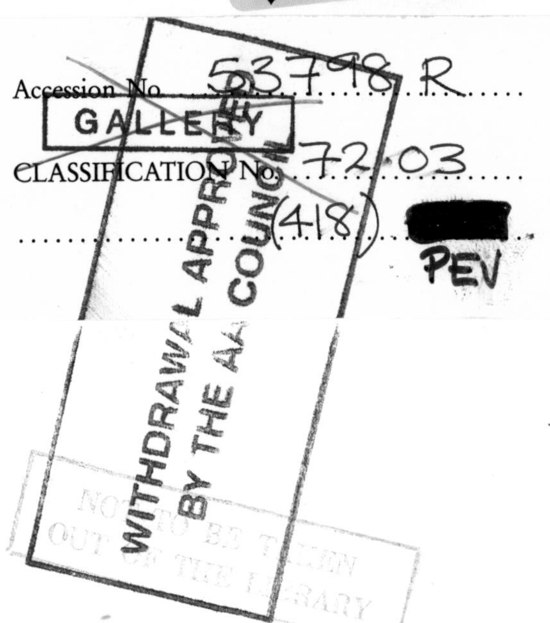
Accession No. 53798 R
GALLERY
CLASSIFICATION No. 72.03
(418)
PEV
WITHDRAWAL APPROVED BY THE AA COUNCIL
NOT TO BE TAKEN OUT OF THE LIBRARY

WITHDRAWN BY ORDER OF THE A.A. COUNCIL

KU-769-478

70
80
90
00
10
20
N
ARMAGH
MONAGHAN
LOUTH
MEATH
KILDARE
Dundalk Bay
Omeath
Ravensdale
Carlingford
Greenore
Kilcurry
Ballymascanlon
Grange
Dundalk
Gyles Quay
Blackrock
Knockbridge
Louth
Readypenny Crossroads
Dromiskin
Tallanstown
Castlebellingham
Charlestown
Stabannan
Drumcar
Ardee
Dunleer
Togher
Barmeath Castle
Drumcondrath
Whitewood Lodge
Nobber
Rokeby Hall
Clogher Head
Tinure Cross
Round Tower
Collon
Lobinstown
Monasterboice
Moynalty
Robertstown Castle
Castletown
Carstown
Termonfeckin
Mellifont Abbey
Lough Ramor
Headfort House
Clongill Crossroads
Rathkenny
Townley Hall
Beaulieu
Mornington
Kells
Arch Hall
Slane Castle
Slane
Oldbridge
Drogheda
Crossakiel
Stackallen House
Dowth Hall
Donaghpatrick
Donaghmore
Beauparc
Julianstown
Kilskyre
Liscarton
Fordstown Crossroads
Ardmulchan Castle
Clonmellon
Drewstown House
Ardbraccan
Navan
Duleek
Gormanston Castle
Bellewstown
Stamullen
Ballinlough Castle
Rathmore
Cannistown
Kentstown
Balrath Crossroads
Athboy
Castletown Delvin
R. Boyne
Bellinter
Skreen
Moymet
Tara
Bective Abbey
Kildalkey
Kilmessan
Trimlestown Castle
Newtown Trim
Trim
Ballivor
Killeen
Dunsany
Dunshaughlin
Ashbourne
Ratoath
Dangan Castle
Galtrim House
Rathmoylan
Summerhill
Longwood
Clonard
Enfield
Royal Canal
Dunboyne
Hamwood
Moyglare
Dublin

The publication of this, the second volume of *The Buildings of Ireland*, has been made possible through the generosity and sustained support of
THE LILA ACHESON WALLACE FUND

P. J. CARROLL & COMPANY
have contributed substantially towards the costs of research in the field

North Leinster

The counties of Longford,
Louth, Meath and Westmeath

BY

CHRISTINE CASEY
AND ALISTAIR ROWAN

THE BUILDINGS OF IRELAND

PENGUIN BOOKS

PENGUIN BOOKS
Published by the Penguin Group
27 Wrights Lane, London W8 5TZ, England

Viking Penguin, a division of Penguin Books USA Inc.,
375 Hudson Street, New York, New York 10014, USA
Penguin Books Australia Ltd, Ringwood, Victoria, Australia
Penguin Books Canada Ltd, 10 Alcorn Avenue, Toronto, Ontario, Canada M4V 3B2
Penguin Books (NZ) Ltd, 182–190 Wairau Road, Auckland 10, New Zealand

Penguin Books Ltd, Registered Offices: Harmondsworth, Middlesex, England

First published 1993

ISBN 0 14 071085 X

Copyright © Christine Casey, George Eogan
and Alistair Rowan, 1993

All rights reserved

Made and printed in Great Britain
by Butler & Tanner Ltd, Frome and London
Set in Monotype Plantin by Selwood Systems, Midsomer Norton

Except in the United States of America,
this book is sold subject to the condition
that it shall not, by way of trade or otherwise,
be lent, re-sold, hired out, or otherwise circulated
without the publisher's prior consent in any form of
binding or cover other than that in which it is
published and without a similar condition
including this condition being imposed
on the subsequent purchaser

For

ANN MARTHA and MICHAEL,

our respective spouses,

who sharing all the anxieties of this series

have had very little of the fun

MAP REFERENCES

The map on pp. 2–3 shows all those places, whether towns, villages, or isolated buildings, which are the subject of separate entries in the text. References to the map square in which each place mentioned will be found are given in italic type in the margins of the gazetteer. The first two numbers of each reference indicate the *western* boundary, and the last two the *southern* boundary, of the 10-mile square in which the place in question is situated. For example, Athlone, reference *0040*, will be found in the 10-mile square bounded by grid lines 00 and 10 on the west and 40 and 50 on the south; Navan, reference *8060*, in the square bounded by grid lines 80 and 90 on the west and 60 and 70 on the south.

CONTENTS

LIST OF TEXT FIGURES AND MAPS

MAPS

The authors and publishers are grateful to Reginald and Marjorie Piggott and Richard Andrews for their work on the maps and plans.

FOREWORD

The first volume of this series, on North West Ulster, is dedicated to the late Sir Nikolaus Pevsner, founder of the Buildings of England *series, whose lectures in Belfast in 1955 awakened the interest of one of us in the history of architecture and whose enthusiasm and encouragement turned a rash notion into the reality of a printed book. With the publication of this second volume, devoted to the architecture of North Leinster and including the four counties of Louth, Meath, Westmeath and Longford,* The Buildings of Ireland, *as a series, may be said to have come of age. Both authors are still convinced that it is rash for a small team to attempt to catalogue the entire architecture of a nation, yet all our experience – whether it is in the field, in libraries and archival collections or in composing the description of buildings at our respective wordprocessors – has served only to reinforce the conviction that Irish buildings matter and that a huge resource for pleasure and instruction – perhaps even for inspiration – lies almost at the door of every Irish person. Our architectural heritage is here to be enjoyed and, if properly respected (which is not always the case today), must illuminate and enrich our understanding of the course of Irish history and should make us proud of the ingenuity and creativity of earlier generations of builders and architects. It is our hope that this book and this series as a whole may encourage others to look with greater curiosity, with more pleasure, and perhaps even with more sympathy, at the buildings which surround them.*

The layout of this volume and the arrangement and sequence of the individual entries follow the pattern established by the first Pevsner volumes on the Buildings of England *over forty-five years ago, which was copied for the first volume of the* Buildings of Ireland *series in 1979. In its shape this volume adopts the taller format of recent publications in the Penguin series on the* Buildings of England, Scotland *and* Wales, *but in other respects the pattern is unchanged. The Introduction is intended to provide an overview of architectural development within the four counties, an historical context for the types of buildings and, in the later periods, some information on the principal architects who worked in this part of Ireland. Detailed information on particular buildings is given in the gazetteer, where the entries deal either with single sites – such as country houses or monasteries – or are devoted to a whole town or village, with the descriptions for a range of individual buildings grouped under the one place-name. The map on pp. 2–3 shows the approximate location of each place which has an entry in the gazetteer: entries for single buildings are marked with a small open square, those for a group of buildings with a dot. The numbered references printed in the margin opposite each place-name in the gazet-*

teer refer to this map, while the letters LF, LO, ME *and* WM, *printed on the right, stand respectively for Longford, Louth, Meath and Westmeath and indicate the county in which the place is situated. The scattered settlements of rural Ireland quickly pose problems to anyone attempting to give a simple yet precise location for an individual site, and it should be noted that the references given after the names of many buildings, as for example '2.5 km* NE' *or '4 km* SW', *are at best approximate. These distances are 'as the crow flies' and ignore the pattern of the roads. Returning to a structure whose architecture seemed to us to merit a second visit has sometimes proved less easy than it should have been: we have at times got lost, and it is inevitable that architecturally curious people who roam in North Leinster will do the same. The serious visitor should procure a good map.*

As with the first volume it will be noted that a place or the name of a parish has sometimes been selected as a gazetteer heading – Readypenny Crossroads and Kilcurry are examples – simply to provide the focus for a quantity of modest buildings which could not easily be included under any other heading. Minor houses, farms and the ruins of churches or castles may thus not necessarily be included under the place-name that would immediately occur to local people. We hope that most of the buildings of architectural interest in these four counties will be found somewhere in these pages. In the countryside there are a great many pleasant, ordinary old farmhouses, vernacular mills and C 19 *industrial or agricultural stores, many of which are briefly noted as good examples of a common type. It must be emphasized, however, that the omission of a building cannot be taken to imply that it lacks interest or quality, and though we have explored many lanes and have tried to visit all the antiquities recorded in Ordnance Survey maps, fragmentary ruins of medieval castles or of small churches have sometimes been omitted. These must await the more particular description of the* Archaeological Survey of Ireland, *currently in progress under the Office of Public Works.*

In most cases the descriptions of buildings given under towns or villages begin with churches, though when particular buildings are of outstanding importance, as for example the de Lacy castle at Trim, the entry will start with them. In the Irish Republic, where 96.2 per cent of the population is at least nominally Roman Catholic, it seems unnecessary to indicate that a church belongs to this denomination: thus churches which are entered solely under the name of their dedication, or by a place-name, are all Roman Catholic. Protestant churches are noted as Church of Ireland (C of I), Presbyterian, Methodist or other denomination. As the Church of Ireland was the established church until 1869, the name of the Protestant parish is also included, for this can often be quite different from the name of the place where a church is situated, and for an historian it is the parish name which can provide immediate access to further references in C 19 *directories, gazetteers and official publications. Frequently the Catholic parish will have the same name, though its boundaries were not necessarily co-extensive.*

The four counties whose buildings are recorded here cover an area of some 2,215 square miles (574,090 hectares), which is just under 30 per cent of the whole of the Province of Leinster. Visiting this large area has taken a number of years and was begun by Christine Casey in her native county, Louth, in 1982, extending to Meath in 1983, and to Westmeath and Longford in 1984. The initial survey both of the published literature and of the countryside was her responsibility, with return joint visits organized to check any buildings whose history or interpretation seemed to present problems. We should record our particular thanks to Desmond and Mary Casey for the numerous occasions on which the family car was borrowed for days on end. Later we made highly entertaining trips together in an elderly Saab, whose passenger window had to be wedged shut in wintertime, and we know at first hand the pleasures of a minor discovery, the disappointment of having to examine a really good building in torrential rain, and the horrid anxiety induced by bovine creatures of steamy breath and indeterminate sex, whose interest in ourselves became at times intolerable. We have each demonstrated a remarkable ability to get through hedges quickly, and to climb up walls. Only Christine had to endure the fangs of an Alsatian dog in Longford town! Bernadette Goslin shared some of the visiting in 1983 and 1984, and we spent an enjoyable week with the Sisters of Sion at Bellinter House which, coupled with bright sunshine and high skies, made the routine of investigating the southern corner of Co. Meath particularly enjoyable. The Bellinter kitchen produces a wonderfully sustaining wheaten bread.

In the Preface to his Topographical Dictionary *of 1837, Samuel Lewis remarks on 'the extreme paucity' in Ireland of 'county histories and local descriptions of cities, towns and districts', which in England and Wales were already widely available. The lack of published material imposed on him 'the necessity of greater assiduity in the personal survey' and increased the extent to which he depended on the assistance of his contemporaries. The same is true today. Irish architectural history has seen a remarkable expansion in activity in the past ten or twelve years, yet it is still the case that anyone who attempts something of a comprehensive survey of the buildings of the country must rely on the help of others. It is also impossible to accumulate information simply on a regional basis. Most Irish topographical writing and administrative records are centralized, covering the country as a whole, so that the business of extracting information for one province or county necessarily involves a survey of literature that covers Ireland as a whole. When work on this series began in 1970 a large number of research assistants – Hugh Dixon, Peter Lamb, Veronica Aliaga Kelly, Lucy Anne Hunt, Alban Reade, Anne Simpson, Jackie Chadwick, Neil Burton, Rebecca Bodmer, James Lawson and Frances Law – read and noted a large quantity of antiquarian and architectural literature relating to Ireland as a whole. Their transcriptions have provided the basis for much of the information contained in this volume, and their particular contribution is acknowledged in more detail in the foreword to the first volume of this series. The notes on sources and further reading on pp. 102–3 provide detailed information on what has been read specifically for this volume. Bernadette Goslin helped with the survey of some of this material and also with information on the Murray Collection of architectural drawings; Rebecca Minch carried out specific pieces of research in the later stages of work on the book.*

As authors we have benefited much from the specialist knowledge and local expertise of many people who have contributed quite particularly to this volume. We would like to thank John Bradley of the Urban Archaeology Survey of Ireland for information on medieval architecture in the area; Ray Refausse of the Representative Church Body Library; Noel Ross, Secretary of the Co. Louth Archaeological and Historical Society, for a wealth of detail on the history of that county; Maureen Wilson and Paul Gosling for Dundalk; Maura Cochrane and John McCullen for Drogheda; Gearoid O'Brien for Westmeath; Terry Trench for Co. Meath, particularly Slane; Harold O'Sullivan for Beaulieu; Larry Conlon for Collon; John Corfield for Thomas Smith; Hugh Dixon for Thomas Duff; and Dr Emmett O'Brien for information on Irish bank architecture. We are particularly grateful to David Griffin and Frederick O'Dwyer, who kindly undertook to read the manuscript of the gazetteer section and who have suggested several corrections and additions. A word should also be said about the prompt and practical help of Honora Ni Chriógáin of University College, Dublin, who typed a great many of the gazetteer entries before the purchase of two Buildings of Ireland wordprocessors removed the need for this type of work. It was she who encouraged us to 'go modern'.

When *North West Ulster* was published in 1979, the Irish Architectural Archive had only recently been established. It is now located permanently at 73 Merrion Square, Dublin, where its holdings and records, which are available for consultation by the public, provide an essential resource for the study of Irish historic buildings of all periods. It is a pleasure for us to record both the very great use which we have made of the Archive and our indebtedness to its staff. Dr Edward McParland, Secretary to the Archive Board since its inception, has contributed much to our work; David Griffin, who has read the text, is the Archive Director, and Ann Simmons and Sean O'Reilly have helped with many requests.

The illustrations for this volume come from several sources. Much medieval architecture is now in the care of the Parks and Monuments Branch of the Office of Public Works, whose photographer John Scarry has been especially helpful and prompt in supplying excellent prints of some of the best architecture in these four counties. We have also been helped by the staff of the photographic library of the Irish Tourist Board, *Bord Fáilte*, and have selected further illustrations from the collection of photographs taken by William Garner, which are now the property of the Irish Architectural Archive. Mr Hugh Doran possesses an admirable collection of photographs of Irish country houses which he has recorded over many years, and we are particularly grateful to him for permission to use his photographs of a number of important houses in North Leinster. Dr David Sweetman has kindly contributed the illustration of Carstown. The balance of the photographs which illustrate this volume comes from the many rolls of record film which we have exposed in the course of examining and exploring the buildings themselves. We owe a particular debt to Patrick Nolan of the photographic unit of the Royal College of Surgeons in Ireland, whose scrupulous printing has done much to enhance the quality of those which are published here. The negatives and printed contact sheets of all the photographs taken in the four counties are now deposited in the Irish Architectural Archive. The figures in the text have been drawn either from plans made available through the Office of Public Works, from *plans published in the* Archaeological Survey of Co. Louth, *or, in the case of post-medieval architecture, by David Griffin and from surveys made by Alistair Rowan. The two illustrations showing conjectural reconstructions of medieval buildings represent a new departure in architectural graphics and have been drawn by Alistair Rowan on the basis of computer projections by students in the School of Architecture, the Edinburgh College of Art: Jonathan Dames constructed the view of the lavabo at Mellifont and Catherine Best the interior of the choir at Newtown Trim Cathedral.*

The text for this volume has been written, as time allows, over a number of years and is very much a joint production. Most of the gazetteer entries were written by Christine Casey, and have been edited and in certain cases expanded by Alistair Rowan, who is responsible for the description of the major early Christian sites, some of the medieval buildings and the principal country houses. All the text has been agreed between both authors and it has also benefited from the careful scrutiny of the Penguin Buildings of England *team: John Newman, advisory editor for the whole series; Bridget Cherry who, mixing kind encouragement with immoveable practical demands, has mastered the art of nudging her authors; Stephany Ungless whose imperturbability and quiet competence is wonderful; and Judith Wardman, to whom, as copy-editor, a very special debt is owed. Without their work and care many a blunder and textual inconsistency would have survived to the printed page.*

Inevitably, as the funding for the Buildings of Ireland *is modest, the completion of the volume has been carried out in our spare time and has had to take second place to our other commitments and responsibilities. As a result there is now a considerable time-lag between the date when some places were visited and the appearance of their description in print. While we have tried to ensure that the accounts of the buildings in principal towns have kept pace with recent changes, it must happen – particularly in the countryside – that several buildings have been altered or lost altogether since our accounts of their architecture were written. Others may now be in a better state of repair than when we visited them. It must also be evident that the inclusion of any building in this volume does not and cannot imply any right of access to the public. We have been kindly received and are most grateful to the many owners who made us welcome to their property or made arrangements for us to examine buildings in their care. Without their co-operation a book like this would not have been possible. We trust that this account of the architecture of North Leinster may prove interesting and generally acceptable, and we hope that readers who become aware of any omissions, factual errors or misinterpretations will be good enough to draw them to our attention.*

CHRISTINE CASEY
ALISTAIR ROWAN

Dublin, January 1993

June 1993. We are greatly indebted to Kevin O'Brien for new information on Trim Castle supplied while this book was in proof.

INTRODUCTION

Leinster is Ireland's central province, the heart of the country, and much of its ancient history lies here in a band of four counties – Louth, Meath, Westmeath and Longford – that run from the coastline on the E far into the Irish midlands. These four counties border Ulster to the N, Connacht to the W; and in early Irish history two of them – Meath and Westmeath – formed a separate province or kingdom on their own, Meath or Meáin, the middle kingdom whose dominance and central position are marked by the prehistoric and legendary importance of Tara, the hill-top place of assembly and coronation site of Ireland's High Kings. It was from Tara that Gráinne, the grand-daughter of the High King Art, promised in marriage to Fionn Mac Chumhaill, eloped with the ill-starred Dermot; while the great Irish saga, the *Táin Bó Cúailnge*, recounts the course of an epic cattle raid, pursued by Queen Maeve of Connacht, across the counties of North Leinster to the Cooley peninsula in Louth with a final dénouement and last battle in the plain of Meath.

One of Ireland's major rivers, the Boyne, rises in Co. Kildare and soon becomes the boundary between Kildare and Meath. Then it turns NE to flow in ample curves through the centre of Meáin until, just before it reaches the sea at Drogheda, its course becomes a boundary once again, now between Meath and Louth. The Boyne is the key to North Leinster. On its northern bank near Slane are the three great burial mounds of Dowth, Knowth and Newgrange which, with other archaeological sites, provide impressive evidence of man's earliest social activity in Ireland and of the Boyne valley civilization, which dates from *c.* 4000 B.C. Archaeology is not normally a part of the *Buildings of Ireland* volumes, yet these great monuments, more ancient than the pyramids, are where the history of Irish buildings must truly begin; they are discussed below in a separate chapter (pp. 91–101) by Professor George Eogan, who has excavated the burial mound and passage graves at Knowth for many years.

When, with the advent of Christianity and St Patrick's mission to Ireland, building in the accepted sense of architecture begins, it is the Boyne which once again provides the central location. It was on Slane hill that St Patrick lit the first Easter fire, reputedly in the year 432, and anyone who climbs the winding stair of the ruined late medieval church that marks the place will appreciate at once the wisdom of his choice, for this modestly elevated point commands a view seemingly of all Ireland, with gently folded hills stretching to infinity: the Mountains of Mourne a blue mass in the distant N, the Wicklow Hills far in the S, and the Boyne flowing towards Drogheda on the eastern skyline. Some seven hundred years later, when the Cistercians first introduced continental patterns of monasticism to Ireland, the site chosen by St Malachy for their abbey, Mellifont, was barely three miles from the Boyne. Some thirty years later the Norman baron Hugh de Lacy, to whom King Henry II granted the whole of Meath, made his capital on the banks of the river at Trim, and soon afterwards a new cathedral was founded at Newtown Trim just a little downstream. In the C14, when the Black Death and political instability in Britain brought Norman control in Ireland to its lowest ebb, the Pale, which marked the limits of English jurisdiction, extended only a little further than the valley of the Boyne, with Ardee in Co. Louth as very much a border town and the Abbey of Fore in Westmeath fortified against the native Irish. The Boyne leaps to significance again in 1690 when the army of William of Orange defeated the forces of James II in a battle fought across the river on 1 July, a victory which spelt the end of Catholic and Stuart hopes in Ireland and ushered in more than two centuries of rule by the Protestant Ascendancy. In the C18 the river was put to profitable commercial use: mills grew up along its length, and it was made navigable as far as Navan, over twenty miles upstream, which became the county town. Even in recent times, the Boyne has had a part to play in Leinster politics, latterly as the focus of an unpopular and ill-considered drainage scheme that has left its upper reaches scarred and ugly, with the river almost invisible between high earthen banks.

Drainage, or the drainage pattern, is probably the most distinguishable difference between the four counties which make up this volume, as most of North Leinster is fertile and highly productive agricultural land, with few distinctive natural features to separate one part from another. The buildings that served this rural society – castles, tower houses, monasteries, churches and farms – take their place, for the most part, in uneventful pastoral landscapes. Much of Meath is flat, and it is only where improvement agriculture has intervened with large plantations, creating stands of beeches and mature deciduous woods, that views can build up into impressive scenery. At its northern limit, where Leinster touches the Ulster counties of Monaghan and Cavan, the landscape changes to a succession of many little hills, none of great height but large enough to dictate the zig-zag line that the provincial boundary follows. Much of Louth and the northern part of Meath has this character. Westmeath and Longford are different: these inland counties are part of a huge catchment area that drains, not towards the E and into the Irish Sea, but W through a succession of loughs and tiny lakes into the Shannon, Ireland's longest river, which marks the division between Leinster and Connacht and is the western boundary of the area covered in this volume.

In this western part of North Leinster it is the Inny River, very different from the Boyne, that drains from Lough Sheelin, flows to Lough Kinale, then S to Lough Derravaragh, SW to Lough

Tron, and, after a winding course through Ballymahon, empties into Lough Ree, which is itself part of the course of the Shannon. There are no fewer than twenty-six loughs in Westmeath and twenty-one in Longford. Lough Ree, extending for 26 km from Athlone at its southern end to Lanesborough at the N, is much the largest; next in size is Lough Sheelin, where Cavan, Longford, Meath and Westmeath meet; then come three large loughs, all in Westmeath: Lough Derravaragh near Castlepollard, and Lough Owel and Lough Ennell, one above and one below the county town of Mullingar. From the passage graves at Sliabh na Cailighe – the Hill of the Witch – near Oldcastle, the visitor will have a similar view to that of St Patrick from the hill of Slane, only now, some forty kilometres further W, the folds in the hills are filled with glittering lakes. From such a vantage point this wetland country of reedy loughs and low hills has a beauty of its own. Often it is a bare, unpopulated landscape distilling in itself a sense of ancient Ireland, yet such romantic visions must carry with them the certainty that the architecture here will be of a modest kind. In comparison with Meath and Louth, Westmeath and Longford were never wealthy counties. In 1846, after more than a century of agricultural improvement, the *Parliamentary Gazetteer of Ireland* reported that almost thirteen per cent of the land of Westmeath was not capable of being cultivated, while in Longford the proportion of uncultivated land was almost a quarter. In both counties five per cent of the surface area is covered by water, but there are no mountains to create a picturesque effect, beyond some isolated hills that rise to a hundred or a hundred and fifty metres.

One small district of Co. Louth provides a complete contrast to the pattern of arable fields and lake-filled wetlands which prevails in most of North Leinster. This is Cooley, a dramatic granite peninsula, geologically part of the Mountains of Mourne but cut off from them by a strip of water that has preserved its Norse name – the curling fjord – as Carlingford Lough. This is a forgotten mountainous area, a neck of high land marking the break between Northern Ireland and the Republic with a range of individual summits that forms a magnificent backdrop to the northern shore of Dundalk Bay, rising to 592 metres in the dramatic peak of Slieve Foy directly above the medieval port of Carlingford.

In 1841, the last pre-famine year for which census figures are available, the population of the four counties stood at 552,598. Twenty years later, in 1861, death and emigration had reduced that figure to 363,659. By 1881 the population had fallen to 297,960, and by 1901 it had dropped again to 241,618, or less than half the total number of people before the impact of the famine. In 1986 the total population of 290,566 was still slightly less than it had been a hundred years before. A more significant feature of the present century is the drift away from the midland counties and the rising importance of the east-coast towns of Drogheda and Dundalk. A comparison of each county's census figures for 1841 and 1986 makes this clear: the population of

Louth was 111,979 in 1841 and 91,810 in 1986, representing a decline of 18 per cent; the figures for Meath are 183,828 and 103,881, a decline of 43 per cent; Westmeath falls from 141,300 to 63,379, a decline of 55 per cent, and Longford witnesses the most dramatic decline, falling from 115,491 to a mere 31,496, which represents a loss of population from 1841 to 1986 of 73 per cent. It is the midland counties that have suffered the worst depopulation. It is also worth noting that, while every county has now a growing population, the break in the downward trend came first in Louth, and as early as the 1930s, in Meath in 1946, in Westmeath in 1966 and in Longford only in 1979.

The four North Leinster counties add up to about 2,215 square miles (574,090 hectares), or just a little less than one fourteenth part of the whole country. Within this area the distribution of major towns is quite unbalanced. Louth, which is the smallest Irish county and takes its name from an almost non-existent village, contains the only two towns with populations over 20,000: Dundalk, the largest, with a population in 1986 of 26,669, and Drogheda, next in size at 24,086. Both towns have grown through industry and commercial activity and also because of their position on the railway link between Dublin and Belfast. Indeed for almost a century Dundalk possessed an important railway coach-building industry. It is perhaps an accident of geography that Drogheda has found itself mostly on the northern bank of the Boyne and therefore not in Meath, which it has always served as a port. Otherwise Meath, like Westmeath and Longford, lacks any substantial town. Hugh de Lacy's capital at Trim, the setting of several late medieval parliaments, is now quite small, and even Navan, the county town since early in the C 19, has a population of no more than 3,660. The midland towns of Longford, Mullingar and Athlone each grew up as reception and service centres for the agricultural produce of the areas they served. The radiating pattern of roads, extending like spiders' webs from each centre, makes their function clear: nine roads at Mullingar, seven at Longford and five at Athlone, which is strategically sited at the famous long ford across the Shannon. Each of these towns has some large buildings of note, yet as they are rural centres of an agricultural economy that saw decline for more than a century, it would be unreasonable to expect great architecture. The populations in 1986 were still quite small: Longford had 6,457 inhabitants, Athlone 8,815 and Mullingar 8,077. As is so often the case in Ireland, many of the best and most interesting buildings appear, not in an urban context, but singly as detached examples of their type – an abbey, a castle or a mansion house – alone in the countryside.

Early Christian Monuments

The form of Christianity established by St Patrick in Ireland flourished from the C 5 until the early C 12. North Leinster is rich in both the number and quality of the monuments that survive from this period, with evidence of monastic life at seventeen separate sites. Though modest in scale, early Irish monasteries were normally formed out of a combination of four distinctive architectural elements: a small single-cell, stone-built church or oratory; a detached round tower; a monumental high cross; and an enclosing wall or ditch of oval or circular form. In Ireland a large circular enclosure, a rath, cashel or ring fort, had provided the characteristic form for any settlement from the Bronze Age onwards, and the Celtic church simply appropriated this form for its own use. The enclosure also contained thatched huts for the monks of the community. An important monastery might include several individual churches and crosses, though only rarely, as at Glendalough in Co. Wicklow and Clonmacnoise in Co. Offaly, were extra belfries provided as additions to churches. The round tower was never duplicated.

Of the four architectural elements, the wall that marked the confines of the enclosure has, inevitably, proved the least durable. It survives today more often in the curve of a street, or as an undulation in the surface of a field, than as an architectural feature, and this is the case at the two monastic sites of real artistic significance, Kells in Co. Meath and Monasterboice in Co. Louth. The two provide a convenient illustration of the different destinies which might befall such sites, for the monastic monuments at Kells are now surrounded by a busy market town, standing partly within the main churchyard and partly without, while Monasterboice, which gave place in the C12 to the nearby Cistercian foundation of Mellifont, now occupies a gentle southern slope, alone in empty fields.

The ROUND TOWERS at Kells and Monasterboice, though 17
incomplete and lacking their conical roofs, are the best-preserved examples of their type in the four counties. These towers, which are unique to Irish monasticism, fulfilled a variety of functions. They served as belfries and, in an age without maps, which knew no roads beyond a track or bridlepath, they could also act as landmarks to indicate the location of the monastery. Silhouetted against a low horizon to the W of the main road from Drogheda to Dundalk, the dark pencil of grey stone that marks the site of Monasterboice performs just such a function today. At times of unrest or when a monastery was attacked by Viking raiders, the towers of Irish monasteries served both as look-out posts and as places of ultimate retreat in which the valuables of the community might be stored. It is this use that accounts for the inaccessible height of their doors and perhaps also for the quantity of windows at the belfry stage – four, set at the cardinal points, at Monasterboice and, unusually, five at Kells. The towers are often built in shallow courses of rubble stone, and it is a tribute to the technical skill of the masons of the C10 and C11 that the gently tapering profile they follow as they rise is executed with absolute precision, despite the roughness of the materials employed. At Monasterboice the upper stage has now acquired a distinct kink, but this distortion only serves to emphasize the quality of the original work. Reduced shafts of two further round towers survive at Donaghmore in Co. Meath and at Dromiskin in Co. Louth,

while the ghost of a third has left its imprint in the N wall of the belfry tower of Duleek priory in Co. Meath.

The intrinsic monumentality of an architecture of stone is well
expressed by the remains of CELTIC CHURCHES in the area.
22 Two survive intact: St Colmcille's House at Kells, dating perhaps
from the C 9, and St Mochta's House at Louth of the C 10 or C 11.
The substantial remains of St Fechin's Church at Fore should
also be mentioned here. Despite the simplicity of their form these
are structures of a serious architectural intention. Built entirely
of stone, they are constructed with high pitched roofs, supported
on semicircular barrel-vaults with miniature attic roof-spaces built
in stone above the vaults. The antae (extended side walls of
massive masonry) which are often a feature in such buildings are
missing at Kells and Louth but may be noted at Fore, and also at
the two ruined churches in Co. Longford, St Mel at Ardagh and
St Diarmaid on Inchcleraun Island. Fore and St Diarmaid's
Church preserve the flat-headed doorways typical of these buildings. An elaborately carved lintel, comparable to those preserved
at Raphoe in Co. Donegal and at Maghera in Co. Derry, survives
in the graveyard at Dunshaughlin, though all other traces of the
church it once adorned have vanished.

At Monasterboice the church ruins are late medieval, and no
detail now remains; the glory of this site is its HIGH CROSSES,
17–18, two of which, Muiredach's Cross and the West Cross, still stand
23 complete and are amongst the grandest sculptural monuments of
their date anywhere in Europe. If Irish monastic churches generally are small, the scale of these magnificent sculptural monuments is truly imperial. Muiredach's Cross is 18 ft (5.5 m) high,
and the West Cross rises still higher to 23 ft (6.9 m), a slender yet
substantial shaft supporting a wide nimbus in stone high up in
the air. Closely linked in style are the high crosses at Kells,
which, if less complete, are noteworthy for the intriguing evidence
supplied by the unfinished cross on the working methods of Celtic
20 sculptors. At Duleek is an elegant and much smaller high cross,
almost perfectly preserved, and parts of others survive at Bealin
Twyford (Moydrum Castle), Co. Westmeath, at Castlekeeran
(Crossakiel) and Killary (Lobinstown), Co. Meath, and at Dromiskin and Termonfeckin in Co. Louth.

Medieval Architecture

Towards the end of the C 12 the little church of St Fechin at Fore was extended by the addition of a chancel. This alteration marks an important development in the Irish church as the comparatively unstructured and even egalitarian patterns of Celtic Christianity were replaced by a more regular organization, based on the continental system of dioceses and parishes. The provision of a special area within a church – a presbytery or chancel – set aside for the use of a priest or bishop enhanced the authority of the clergy and reinforced the hierarchies of the new parochial system, first introduced to Ireland in 1111, as a result of the Synod of Rathbreasail. Though the ruling of the synod was not immediate in its effect, as the century advanced the church authorities increasingly made additions to earlier buildings to bring them into line with a pattern which had been in use for centuries in other parts of Europe.

In North Leinster, the remains of small Romanesque churches of the C12 or early C13, hardly differing in scale from their Celtic predecessors but now distinguished from them by the existence of a separate chancel, occur at Cannistown and Cruicetown (Nobber), Co. Meath, and at the Chancel Church on Inchcleraun Island in Co. Longford. These are modest examples of a major architectural trend which is marked most clearly by the historic site of Mellifont, the first Cistercian abbey in Ireland, founded by St Malachy in 1142. Malachy was the most significant bishop of the Irish C12. He was ordained *c.* 1119, when he was twenty-five, and acquired a good knowledge of religious organizations in England and on the Continent. His work in Ireland, a part of the general religious revival in Europe, was to reform Irish monasticism, principally by the introduction of the rule of particular continental orders and by bringing the Irish church generally into line with Roman and Western Christianity as he knew it. Mellifont Abbey was to play a central role in these developments. It is no accident therefore that its great church (now reduced to little more than its foundations) was built under the direction of a European architect, named *Robert*, sent from France by St Bernard of Clairvaux. Here the semicircular side chapels which opened off both transepts were clearly Romanesque in style and continental in their origin. The church was subsequently enlarged and rebuilt in an early Gothic style, but the abbey complex still preserves one of the most perfect and unusual monuments of Irish Romanesque architecture, the octagonal lavabo, a sophisticated
design of *c.* 1200 which was set prominently as a freestanding 24–5
two-storey structure at the southern end of the cloister.

Of the Cistercian houses founded from Mellifont in this part of Ireland little more than fragments remain. At Bective Abbey, begun after 1147, none of the original structure survives, though
there are substantial ruins of later buildings. Kilbeggan, founded 49
in 1150, and complete in 1570, has totally disappeared; Abbeyshrule of *c.* 1200 retains no more than a pair of round-headed lancets in the chancel gable, while at Abbeylaragh (Granard), founded in 1211, only the walls of the crossing survive. Though the Cistercians in Ireland began in this part of the country, the best examples of their architecture now lie outside North Leinster, at Baltinglass in Co. Wicklow, Boyle in Co. Roscommon, Dunbrody in Co. Wexford and at Jerpoint in Co. Kilkenny.

The second regular order introduced by St Malachy, the Augustinian Canons, was to become the most widely diffused religious order of medieval Ireland. In North Leinster no fewer than twenty-seven separate communities are recorded, of which eighteen were major monasteries with a continuous life and history until the suppression of religious houses in the C16. Augustinian monasteries at Clonard, Duleek, Inchcleraun, Kells, Knock (near Tallanstown), Louth and Trim all owed their foundation, or their

adoption of the Augustinian (Arroasian) rule, to Malachy. Of these foundations even less survives than of their Cistercian counterparts. The priory church at Louth, which was also a cathedral, is today no more than a long masonry shell of nave and choir, with some cutstone detail. More remains of the ruins of Ballyboggan Abbey near Clonard, where an inordinately long nave, almost without windows, opens directly into an elevated choir, once lit by a group of lancets in the E wall and in the sides at the altar end. Set dramatically above a curve in the Yellow River the tall rubble walls of the abbey provide, in their sheer bulk, an evocative monument of Irish C13 monasticism. The most substantial remains of an Augustinian site are found in the ruins
29 of St Mary's Priory at Duleek, a cell of Llanthony, founded by Hugh de Lacy in 1182, of which a later W tower and an arcaded S aisle survive. Mention should also be made of the small church
28 of All Saints Priory, founded *c.* 1244 on Saints Island, at Lough Ree in Co. Longford. These remote ruins are rewarding and, though of an almost miniature scale, preserve a range of mid-C13 windows, together with later work, an intact E window with intersecting tracery and stone fragments of an unusually rich cloister arcade.

Changes in the patterns of Irish life, begun by Cistercian and Augustinian example, were carried through by force of arms with the arrival of the Normans in 1169. A pretext for their coming to Ireland was provided when Dermot MacMurrough, King of Leinster, threatened by the High King, Rory O'Connor of Connaught, sought the support of the marcher lords of South Wales in regaining his kingdom. The more important of these auxiliaries, Maurice FitzGerald and Robert FitzStephen, established themselves in Wexford, while Richard de Clare, Earl of Pembroke, known to Irish history as 'Strongbow', married Dermot's daughter, Aoife, and, in defiance of Irish law, seized the kingdom of Leinster when Dermot died in 1171. In October the same year the English King, Henry II, arrived in Ireland with a large army, not to conquer the country but to ensure that these powerful barons did not establish independent Irish principalities which might later threaten his authority. Strongbow then received the grant of Leinster, FitzGerald and FitzStephen were confirmed in their Wexford lands, and Hugh de Lacy, who had travelled to Ireland with the King and was to remain behind as his 'Justiciar' or Viceroy, was granted the former kingdom of Meath. All held their lands as the King's tenants, while the principal ports of the country, as well as Co. Dublin and the town of Drogheda (from 1120), were retained as the property of the Crown.

The native Irish rulers, alarmed by the military strength of the Norman barons, saw in the English King a protector of their own positions and were thus prepared to recognize him as overlord of Ireland. Before coming to Ireland King Henry had procured the support of the papacy, so that the more progressive members of the Irish clergy, who had often found their reforms blocked by native family interests, also welcomed his intervention. Under the Archbishop of Dublin, Laurence O'Toole, a national synod was held at Cashel, Co. Tipperary, reinforcing the earlier reforms of the church and bringing its organization into line with the English Roman Catholicism. Thus the whole framework of feudal society, secular and ecclesiastical, was introduced to Ireland. King Henry spent six months here, leaving on Easter Monday 1172. In 1177 he transferred the lordship of the country to his younger son, John, then aged ten, no doubt with the intention of providing in time a permanently resident and separate royal line in Ireland. Meanwhile the proper government of the country rested in the hands of the Justiciar, Hugh de Lacy.

Nothing could better exemplify the new order of the Norman
lords than the ruins of the great de Lacy castle at Trim. The 43
vast bulk of the keep, set high on a mound and geometrically symmetrical, with four rectangular towers projecting from the centre of each side, was both a symbolic and a real expression of their power. The castle was intended to confirm the hold of Hugh de Lacy on his new territory and also, by its superior and impressive architecture, to overawe the local population. It stands today as a monument to the ambition and efficiency of this small, swarthy soldier whose ruthless conquest of the kingdom of Meath, in flagrant disregard for the hereditary rights of its last king, Murchadh O'Melaghlin, created an earldom of over half a million acres of rich farm land, parcelled out as eighteen separate baronies each with their dependent manors, and planted with monasteries and new towns. It was de Lacy who first introduced to Ireland the territorial division into baronies and, in granting these to his followers, brought a new nobility into being – Barnewall of Crickstown, Fitzthomas of Kells, Fleming of Slane, Misset of Lune, Nangle of Navan, Nugent of Delvin, Petit of Mullingar, Pheipo of Skreen, Tyrrell of Fertullagh and others – which was to survive almost until the battle of the Boyne. Once secure in his estate, de Lacy adopted a policy of co-existence with some of the old chiefs' families so that O'Carrols, O'Connors, O'Farrells and O'Melaghlins preserved the possession of some if not all of their lands.

Louth, the most northern county of Leinster, fell to Norman control only through the activities of another adventurer, John de Courcy, who in 1177, without royal authority, embarked on the conquest of Ulster, to which the O'Carrol kingdom of Oriel – the modern counties of Louth, Monaghan and Armagh – was added in 1183. Most of de Courcy's territory and the bulk of his building activities lay beyond Leinster, but the small medieval port of Carlingford, on the southern shore of the lough, probably owes its development to him. Two years later, in 1185, Prince John, as Lord of Ireland, confirmed this part of the country in Norman hands, annexing for himself the barony of Louth and granting Dundalk to Bertram de Verdun and Ardee to Gilbert Pipard. The
remains of Roche Castle at Kilcurry, begun in the 1230s, provide 47
a dramatic memorial of the de Verdun power in this area, while the strength of the Norman burghs and their need for protection are vividly characterized by the ring of fortifications which
developed round the town of Drogheda, particularly at St Lau- 45
rence's Gate, and by the later castles built at Ardee.

The confrontation of Gaelic Ireland with modern Europe which the Norman conquest represents is characterized powerfully in the account of Hugh de Lacy's death given in *The Annals of Ulster*. The Earl had built a strong castle at Durrow, Co. Offaly, and had demolished, as was the Norman custom, much of an Irish monastery founded by St Colmcille to provide stone for its construction. Such scant respect for the holy places of the country caused deep offence, and in July 1186 when de Lacy was inspecting the work he was attacked by a youth, Gilla O'Meyey, who hacked off his head. His body was later buried in the Cistercian abbey at Bective and his head was taken to St Thomas's Church in Dublin. It was said that Henry II was not displeased by the news of the murder, for de Lacy had recently married the daughter of Rory O'Connor and was thought likely to threaten royal authority in Ireland by establishing himself as an independent prince. Some twenty-four years later just such a threat from de Lacy's sons, Walter and Hugh, the Earls of Meath and Ulster, brought King John to Ireland for three months in the summer of 1210. John landed at Waterford, marched his army to Kilkenny and then swept through the country to Dublin, Trim and Carlingford before confronting the Earls at Carrickfergus in Co. Antrim. The
46 redoubtable stone enclosure known as King John's Castle at Carlingford remains as a memorial of this campaign.

It was under King John that Ireland was first divided, for administrative purposes, into separate counties, though the division was far from complete and the territories of the great Norman magnates were left intact as independent liberties. Thus in the Irish Parliament of 1297 the members came from the nine counties of Connaught, Cork, Dublin, Kerry, Kildare, Limerick, Louth, Tipperary and Waterford and from the five extensive liberties of Carlow, Kilkenny, Meath, Ulster and Wexford. The de Lacy territory of Meath was to survive as a single unit until 1543, when, under Henry VIII, Meath and Westmeath were created: twenty-six years later, in the reign of Queen Elizabeth, the more distant Annaly country was separated from Westmeath to create the county of Longford. Thus it was only in the later C16 that Louth, Meath, Westmeath and Longford came into being as the administrative units which have survived to the present day.

As Trim was the military and administrative capital of the region throughout the Middle Ages, so it became an important centre for MEDIEVAL RELIGIOUS ARCHITECTURE. In 1206 Simon de Rochfort, the first Norman Bishop of Meath, transferred the diocesan cathedral from Clonard to Newtown Trim, a new site on the banks of the Boyne, hardly one mile downstream from Trim itself. Though much reduced, the shell of his great church still survives with, close beside it, the church and friary buildings of the Hospital of St John, built in the same period. Trim itself was noted for its great Augustinian Abbey of St Mary,
32 of which only the refectory and the beautiful Yellow Steeple, a five-storey C14 tower, remain. A plain belfry tower from a late medieval church survives as part of the small Protestant cathedral.

The fate of the churches in Trim demonstrates the general point that the development of Ireland's medieval architecture can now be traced more often through ruined buildings than in complete structures. Indeed in the four counties covered by this volume there is only one medieval church still in use, the Franciscan friary church at Multyfarnham, now much restored and rebuilt. In the mid-C19 the late medieval fortified church of St Munna at Taghmon, near Portneshangan, was restored by *Joseph* 34
Welland as a Protestant parish church; today, though its vaulted roof remains in place, it has become an ancient monument in the care of the state and has lost its fittings and furniture. Substantial architectural details from the late medieval church at Castlelost were reused in 1831 at Meedin Chapel near Tyrrellspass, which remains in use.

The group of ecclesiastical ruins at Fore provides a second evocative complex of medieval architecture, perhaps the most 50
memorable after Trim. At this site, now hardly even a village, some early church ruins and the extensive remains of a fortified Benedictine abbey, founded by Hugh de Lacy, nestle in a narrow valley on the edge of the English Pale. Good belfry towers with crenellated parapets and full tracery survive as isolated incidents in the townscapes of Drogheda and Dundalk, and in country settings at Duleek, Multyfarnham and Slane; but much of the other medieval architecture of the area has been reduced to featureless walls. The impressive mass of the church at Skreen has today huge empty openings where traceried windows once were. The long nave and choir of Louth Abbey are almost as featureless; and there is now no detail left in the extensive Dominican friary at Carlingford, founded in 1305. 6

Since so much cut stone has been robbed from Irish church ruins it may be worth listing those sites where good WINDOW DETAILS remain. Of Romanesque work there are two windows at Cloondara Church ruin, Co. Longford, narrow slits which are widely splayed on the interior to form high round-headed openings of irregular ashlar blocks. Three perfect lights, similar, though larger and later, survive in the S wall of the church at Saints Island, and one small round-headed light remains from the old chapter 37
house at Mellifont. The pattern of three grouped lancets which was to become typical of early Gothic architecture first appears in round-headed (and therefore Romanesque) form in the grandly scaled E window of the chancel at Fore Abbey, while it may be seen in its C13 Gothic form in the restored E window at St John's Hospital at Newtown Trim. The second church at Mellifont and Trim Cathedral both had similar groups of lancets at their E ends, but of these only a vestige remains today. The pattern was to be relentlessly reproduced in the C19 in numerous Gothic Revival churches.

Saints Island church also provides an excellent example of a complete E window of intersecting tracery from the C15. The 28
side-lights of the choir of Louth Abbey are similar, though these are no longer complete and are now walled up. The three-light E window of the church ruins at Killucan provides the unique case

of plate tracery in North Leinster. Another pattern of a plain but elegant window appears, a little later in the century, in the group of three round-headed lancets, divided by slender octagonal mullions, which is used for the gable window of the S aisle of Duleek Priory and for the E end of Ballygarth Church nearby at
37 Julianstown. The chapter house at Mellifont has three paired cusped lights with Decorated tracery, while the S transept of the Franciscan friary at Multyfarnham retains an interesting window with unusual tracery, a sparse three-light design, with ogee-heads and sleek, oval-lobed upper lights, a type of austere late Gothic, characteristic of the W of Ireland, which also appears in the ruins of Rathreagh Church, Kilglass, but nowhere else in North Leinster.

The degree of elaboration which tracery could reach in Irish C15 work is well illustrated by the three Plunkett churches at Killeen, Dunsany and Rathmore, where a slender framework of mullions, arranged in two or three lights, is decorated at the top by a shallow infill of elliptical cusped arches surmounted by a complex arrangement of mouchettes (a dagger-shaped pattern) and irregular trefoil lights. This is showy work, intended to
38 impress. The E window at Killeen (which apparently served as model for the C19 E window at Dunsany) is in this style, but the other original work there, particularly the W window, suggests a flowing and less rectangular taste, and a similar, more elegant

Medieval Irish window openings and tracery. 1. Fore Abbey. 2. St John's Hospital, Newtown Trim. 3. Saints Island Church. 4. Rathmore Church. 5. Multyfarnham Abbey. 6. Trim Cathedral. 7. St Mary's Priory, Duleek

pattern of flowing lobes is also found in the E window of Rathmore. A late example of intersecting tracery – enlivened with cusps and an elliptical lower cusped arch – is at Mansfieldstown Church (Stabannan), reconstructed in 1691 but reusing a C15 E window. The late window added at the base of the tower of the church at Slane is an ambitious but awkward affair. These traceried 1
windows are regularly accommodated within a wide arch, which is often supported on the inner face by a separate chamfered rib. An outer elliptical arch of heavy masonry is used to support the upper floors of the two sides of the C15 cloister at Bective Abbey, and, as ellipses gained popularity in late medieval Ireland, the new window added to Duleek Priory in 1597 is an elegantly attenuated pattern of four slender shafts ending in elliptical heads within an elliptical arch.

A common arrangement found in Irish late Gothic work is a type of window where two cusped lights are grouped together under a flat heading with a label moulding on the exterior and a shallow flat arch supporting the masonry inside. This arrangement survives in the E windows of the small late church at Templecross (Ballynacarrigy), the parish church ruins at Dromiskin and Mellifont, and in the side windows at Rathmore Church and at other sites. A richer and more elaborate pattern, grouping three cusped lights together, with six inverted triangular panels filling the spandrels between the arch and the top of the lights, is found at Moymet Church, at Trim Cathedral and in the late window inserted into the S wall of the church at Bective Abbey. All are probably of the C16; at Trim and Moymet the spandrels are open lights, while at Bective they are treated as stone panels. These windows and the panelling on the fonts and altar tombs of the three Plunkett churches are the closest that architecture in North Leinster comes to a Perpendicular form of Gothic before the C19. In the age of the Gothic Revival two notable early examples are at Collon and St Patrick's, Dundalk. 100

A type of BELLCOTE which developed in Ireland in the late Middle Ages, sometimes known as a Fingall belfry, combines two or more open arches in a rectangular block of masonry on the W gable of a church. Examples of these occur at Abbeyshrule, Donaghmore, Mellifont Parish Church, Ballygarth (Julianstown) and Foyran (Finnea). At the last two the bellcotes are of three arches; at Foyran Church they are set in two tiers. The churches at Cannistown, Cruicetown (Nobber) and Clogher Head preserve the stumps of similar bellcotes.

LATE MEDIEVAL SCULPTURE, though not extensive in North Leinster, survives in sufficient quantity to give at least a flavour of what has been lost and to evoke, in the tomb-chest monuments and the recumbent effigies which they support, an image of the people who worshipped in these places. Pre-eminent among a number of examples are the Plunkett monuments in the three 39
churches of Dunsany, Killeen and Rathmore – the sides decorated with foliated ogee arcading filled with figures of angels, saints and bishops in delicate relief – and the Preston tombs at Duleek and Stamullen, all in Co. Meath. Stamullen also preserves a large 41

monumental slab of a cadaver – a macabre sculpted image of a decaying corpse; further examples may be found in St Peter's Churchyard in Drogheda and at Beaulieu in Co. Louth. Two
36 fonts from the C15 survive at Dunsany Church and at Trim Cathedral; a third, dating from the C16 and originally at Crickstown Church, is now at Curragha Church, Ratoath.

Examples of MEDIEVAL DOMESTIC ARCHITECTURE are widely spread throughout the area: in 1941 Harold Leask listed at least 227 castles in these four counties. There are the great defensive castles of the Normans, founded in the late C12 or C13 and surviving in various states of preservation, at Athlone, Castle Roche (Kilcurry), Carlingford, Delvin (Castletown-Delvin) and of course at Trim. Besides these Norman fortresses, two basic types of fortified house exist: the large baronial castles, built as the principal seats of important families, and the smaller tower houses which were put up all over the country, usually in a later period and by men of much less consequence than the baronial lords.

Scale, rather than any other feature, distinguishes the baronial castles. Though the dates of their foundation are rarely known the castles share a common approach to architectural design and are built usually as rectangular blocks of masonry with substantial extra accommodation provided by rectangular towers added at each angle. In the purest form, as for example at Ardee and
51 Dardistown (Julianstown), the aesthetic expression is powerfully geometrical, almost as if the designers had taken the rectangular
43 forms of Trim Castle, with its absolute symmetry and square towers, as the standard for a lordly residence. Although these baronial castles do not copy the design of Trim in detail – their towers are at the corners rather than in the centre of each side – nevertheless they seem to make a similar and deliberate statement of authority in the keep-like massing of their walls and the careful near-symmetry of many of their façades. The Plunkett castles of
90 Killeen and Dunsany, though both extended and altered in the C18 and C19, are good examples of this type, as are the extensive
48 ruins of Trimlestown, built by the Barnewalls in the C15, and the two castles at Liscarton, which all make use of a similar plan. Each has a long rectangular hall, built above barrel-vaulted basements and approached by a wide stairway, sometimes in straight flights and quite different in scale from the winding spiral stairs of smaller tower houses. Other large castles built between the C14 and the C16 are Athcarne (Duleek), Clongill, and Riverstown (Tara), all of which make use of square towers attached to some of the angles of the main block. This use of angle towers also appears in houses of a less impressive scale, such as the accommodation block added to Bective Abbey, the 'castle' at St John's
27 Hospital, Newtown Trim, and in the original C15 building at
55 Athlumney Castle (Navan).

In the C15 and C16, alternatives to the castle with corner towers are common in the W of the region. Here smooth sheer walls, sometimes of impressive bulk, seem to be the master mason's ideal. Portlick Castle near Glassan is the supreme example, a large and gaunt rectangular block, four storeys high and three windows wide, with only the box of a machicolated chute positioned above the door to break the severity of the walls. The corner towers are here contained entirely within the rectangular outline of the block of the castle's plan. Boherquill (Street) and Rattin (Kinnegad) exhibit the same restraint in their rectangular planning and an austere precision in the construction of their walls. Rathcline Castle near Lanesborough, now reduced to one long three-storey wall, seems, apart from a single corner tower, to have been essentially a long rectangle, and at Lynch's Castle at Summerhill, a large and plain rectangular castle forms the basis of what became a complex stepped plan.

The commonest type of dwelling for an Irish landowner in the later Middle Ages is clearly demonstrated by the quantity of TOWER HOUSES existing throughout the country. As these were erected for the most part by minor families who have left no records, few can be securely dated; in most cases even the name of the builders is now unknown. The tower houses themselves, however, survive in large numbers. In this *North Leinster* volume a total of forty-five are noticed: sixteen in Louth; two in Longford; thirteen in Meath, and fourteen in Westmeath. The recent government *Archaeological Survey of Co. Louth* (1991) records remnants of twenty-six tower houses in that county.

In its essentials the tower house was a vertical dwelling, often no larger than a single room, perhaps 25 ft by 18 ft (7.5 m by 5.5 m) in its internal plan, with one room built over the other and rising to a height of three or (less usually) four storeys. Security against attack by fire was provided by a barrel-vaulted ceiling of stone built over the ground floor, which was often subdivided horizontally to provide a timber loft for storage. A single spiral stair led to the upper floors, expressed in many cases as a separate turret, square or circular, placed at the corner of the tower. The stair was often protected by a separate internal door, with a lobby at ground-floor level which could be defended by a 'murder hole' or trap door in the ceiling above. As the upper floors were invariably supported on timber beams, they have now disappeared, except where a tower house has been incorporated into a later dwelling. The spiral stair usually leads to a wall-walk at roof level. The wall-head was defended by battlements, which typically follow the pattern of Irish crenellations, with a double-stepped profile and high-pitched triangular coping stones. Within the battlements was the gabled roof of the house, thatched or stone slated, with overlapping stone slabs laid in a saddle and trough pattern across the wall-walk to carry the water off the roof and out through a series of weep holes just below parapet level.

Considerable local variations, perhaps reflecting a difference in date or else the presence of different building teams, occur in the detailing of these houses: in Co. Louth a number of castles such as Heynestown (Blackrock), Kilincoole (Readypenny Crossroads), Milltown (Dromiskin), Richardstown (Stabannan) and Smarmore (Ardee) use rounded corners and round (or sometimes oval) corner turrets to create architecture of considerable plasticity.

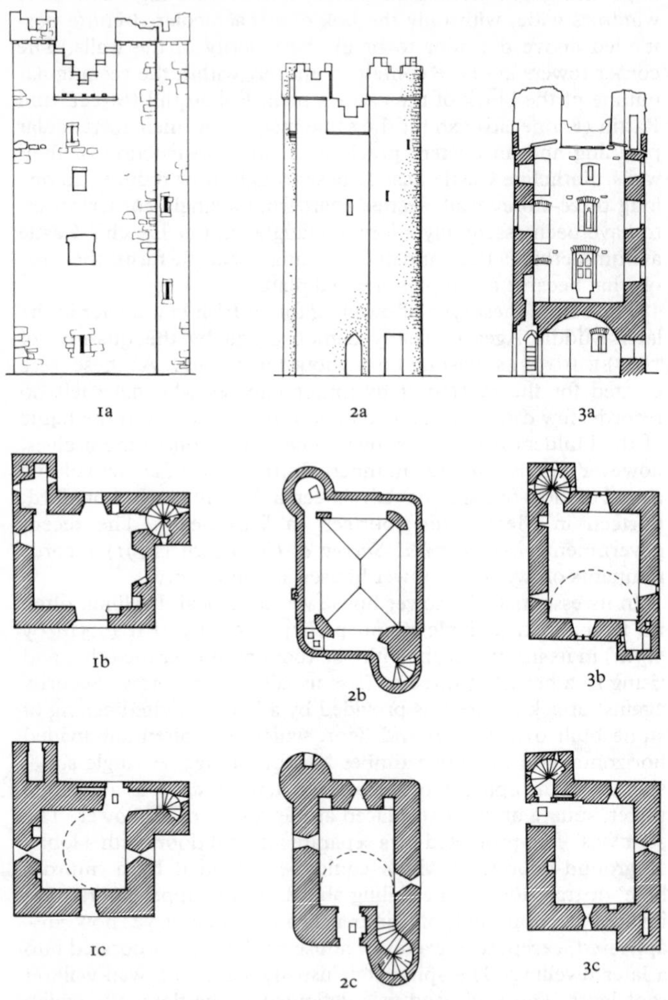

Tower houses. 1. Dunmahon Castle (Blackrock): (a) S elevation; (b) first-floor plan; (c) ground-floor plan. 2. Milltown Castle (Dromiskin): (a) SE elevation; (b) plan of wall-walk level; (c) plan of ground floor (restored). 3. Roodstown Castle (Stabannan): (a) section; (b) first-floor plan; (c) ground-floor plan

51 Donore (Ballivor) and Dardistown (Julianstown) in Co. Meath are also of this type, but in the western part of the region a sheer architecture with sharp rectangular surfaces, as exemplified by Tyrrellspass Castle of 1410, is more common. The earlier tower houses tend to have a less flamboyant skyline. The steps in their battlements are shallower and the elevated corner sections less pronounced. Castlerea (Ardagh), Elfeet (Inchcleraun) and

Mornin (Kenagh), all in Co. Longford, and Martinstown (Castletown-Delvin), Rattin (Kinnegad) and Syonan (Horseleap) in Co. Westmeath are good examples of a large and plain rectangular type, of impressive bulk, which is often without additional turrets. Donore Castle, built in 1598 near Horseleap in Co. Westmeath (not to be confused with Donore Castle in Co. Meath), is one of the largest and most perfectly preserved examples of this type.

One celebrated historical document relates to Irish tower houses as a group. This is the statute of 1429 from the minority of King Henry VI which, in a time of extreme difficulty in English politics, offered a subsidy of ten pounds 'to every liege-man of the King' who was prepared to build a castle within ten years in any of the four counties of the Pale: Dublin, Meath (that is Meath, Westmeath and Longford), Louth and Kildare. The statute sets down the minimum size for these small defensive structures as 20 ft in length, 16 ft in breadth and 40 ft in height (6 m, 4.8 m and 12 m). A subsequent statute reduced the size for tower houses in Meath to no more than 15 ft by 12 ft (4.5 m by 3.6 m), and in 1449 a limit was placed on the numbers to be built. The small tower house at Donore (Ballivor), Co. Meath, is usually cited as an example of these '£10 castles': Newcastle, near Castlepollard in Co. Westmeath, is another, and Roodstown (Stabannan) and 52
Dunmahon (Blackrock) castles in Co. Louth, which has many tower houses, are quite probably two more. Good examples of the small scale of some of the later castles are provided by the so-called 'Mint' at Carlingford, and by the diminutive castle of Moygaddy (Moyglare), Co. Meath, which preserves an unusual form of roof construction with huge flat slabs of stone laid horizontally and overlapping each other. This form of construction is also used in the NE corner tower of the larger castle at Liscarton.

Like other medieval architecture of Ireland the tower houses of North Leinster have suffered much from the robbery of their dressed stone. Often they seem to have been used as a quarry for later agricultural buildings, so that many survive today as little more than shapeless stumps, providing perhaps a barrel-vaulted shelter for cattle but little that is likely to be of interest to an architectural historian. In such a ruin the determined visitor may nonetheless derive some satisfaction by detecting the remnants of certain characteristic tower house elements. The ground-floor ceiling will frequently retain traces of the wattle matting used very widely throughout the later medieval period as shuttering for the construction of a vault. Many examples remain and an extensive use of the technique may still be seen in the otherwise unremarkable basement range which was once part of the castle at Balsoon, Co. Meath, across the river from Bective Abbey. In Co. Louth a common pattern of window opening at the base of a wall, and therefore frequently surviving, is an X-shape reveal recessed into the thickness of the wall, splayed both on the inside and on the outside, to provide a maximum field of cover from the loop while economizing on the need for any large lintel. Door openings are normally small in scale and are often built as simple two-centred Gothic arches framed by long shafts of single-chamfered stones. A recess in the surface of the wall into which the door can 'fold' is not uncommon. On the upper floors the window openings are regularly enlarged and these are often designed to provide seats, after the pattern of the larger Norman castles, on either side of the window itself.

As well as these features, late medieval masons developed a spiral stair in Ireland quite different from the rounded newel type which the Normans had introduced. The Irish spiral stair is economical in its use of material and can be built of small stones, with several pieces fitted together to form an individual step. As the stability of the stair depends on the cantilever principle, a stone newel is not necessary, and instead of a centre stalk of masonry the inside edge of each step is carried to a precise arris, which in the best examples is often of finely worked masonry. In this design the profile of the edge of the stair follows the pattern of an extended helix, which may sometimes be noticed in the rising line of steps where a stair can be viewed through a doorway and is therefore seen side on. It is also worth noting that this Irish pattern, even in spiral stairs of small dimensions, allows more space for figures to move up and down. An example of the Norman newel type may be seen in the section of a spiral stair surviving in the N transept of Mellifont Abbey, while all the tower house stairs which are not straight are of the Irish helix type. Particularly elegant examples may also be found in the stairs of the church towers at Duleek and Slane and at the Yellow Steeple at Trim.

Much of the special character in Irish architecture of the C 14 to the C 16 may be attributed to the comparative independence of Irish society in the later medieval period. The two historical events which mark the limits of this period both took place in Co. Louth. In 1315 Edward Bruce, brother of Robert the Bruce, King of Scots, invaded the country and was crowned High King of Ireland at a ceremony in Dundalk. Although he was to die within three years, on 14 October 1318, fighting against an Anglo-Norman force led by John de Bermingham, the effect of his invasion was to weaken the English hold on Ireland. It was not until the reign of Elizabeth that the royal authority was re-established throughout the country. The submission of Hugh O'Neill, Earl of Tyrone and the last of the great Irish lords to hold out against the Crown, which marks the culmination of the Queen's policy in Ireland, took place before the Lord Deputy Mountjoy, in the historic setting of Mellifont Abbey, on 30 March 1603, six days after Elizabeth herself had died.

Elizabethan and Jacobean Buildings

Neither the accession of Elizabeth in 1558 nor that of her kinsman James in 1603 had much effect on the architecture of North Leinster. As the leading families did not rise in revolt against the Crown, the confiscation and resettlement of land which marked the Jacobean plantation of Ulster had no sequel in this part of the

country. Occasionally a trace of the English and Scottish craftsmen who were brought to Ireland is found in the buildings of
this area, at Robertstown Castle, in the new range at Athlumney
Castle, outside Navan, and in the domestic additions to Bective 49
Abbey, converted into a mansion house by a variety of different
owners from the middle of the C16. Tall chimneys, square mullioned windows and high gables characterize much of this work,
but nowhere in these four counties, throughout the first half of
the century, was a piece of sustained regular architecture built to
a symmetrical plan.

Medieval churches continued in use and the majority of the
country's landowners were content to continue living in their
castles or tower houses. From the mid-C16 onwards the standard
way to increase the space provided by a tower house was to build
a wing, usually no more than one room thick, from one side of the
tower. Usually the wing was slightly lower than the battlemented
parapet of the tower itself. At Dardistown (Julianstown) a long
wing was added *c.* 1550 and further extended in 1589. Carstown 56
has a long two-storey range, with a dated chimney lintel of 1612;
later in the century a short gabled wing was built beside the tower
of Ballug, near Grange (both are now ruined). Boherquill (Street)
and Killeenbrack (Almorita) in Co. Westmeath, and Clongill and
Carrickdexter (Slane) in Co. Meath all had substantial ranges
added to their original towers. New freestanding houses are rare
before the end of the C17. Fennor Castle, on the S bank of the 57
Boyne at Slane, is the shell of one such building with thick walls
and one regular main façade, while Odder Castle, near Tara,
though remodelled, retains a regular front and balanced ranges
of early C17 chimneys with diagonal stacks. Castle Forbes in Co.
Longford, built by Sir Arthur Forbes *c.* 1628, had a similar façade
and the same diagonal chimneys, but that house was completely
rebuilt after a fire in the C19. A unique example of artillery
fortification is provided by the surviving salient bastion at Castlejordan, added in the early C17 to a house which had been rebuilt
in the reign of Henry VIII. None of these buildings preserves any
decorative detail, and it is only in the monuments to Sir Lucas
Dillon at Newtown Trim of 1586 and to Sir Nathaniel Fox at 59
Rathreagh Church (Kilglass) of 1634 that the contemporary 58
sophistication of classical decoration bursts momentarily into
life. The Dillon Monument carries coats of arms in elaborate
cartouches along the sides of its altar tomb; the larger wall memorial at Rathreagh makes a convincing use of the strapwork and
elongated obelisks characteristic of Jacobean taste. Despite such
a brave display, the angular nature of what remains of the effigies
here, and the rudimentary Doric columns and entablature of the
church door indicate clearly the limitations of a provincial mason's
understanding of classical forms.

Later Stuart Architecture

The storming of Drogheda by Cromwell on 11 September 1649
and the massacre of its garrison and such Roman Catholic clergy

as the troops discovered – one of the most notorious and best-remembered events in Irish history – dealt a fatal blow both to Catholic and to Royalist hopes at the mid-century. It was succeeded forty years later by the rout of the Irish Catholic army on 1 July 1690, when William of Orange defeated his father-in-law, James II, at the battle of the Boyne, three miles upstream from the town. Taken together Drogheda and the Boyne were to set the stage for more than two centuries of Protestant rule in Ireland. As a consequence of the Williamite wars, some 270 estates, comprising almost one million acres, were confiscated, leaving little more than one-seventh of the entire kingdom in the hands of its former Roman Catholic owners. Under the new regime architectural patronage was exercised almost exclusively by an elite minority of Protestant landowners and found its most characteristic expression in one structure, the country house, which, more than any other, came to symbolize the shift in power.

Beaulieu, at the mouth of the Boyne near Drogheda, is a
61–2 Caroline house – at least in its appearance – a symmetrical block with a heavy modillion cornice at eaves level, high hipped roof, paired chimneystacks and fine classical details executed in cut brickwork. It was built by the family of Sir Henry Tichbourne, who commanded the troops that captured the estate in 1642 on the collapse of Sir Phelim O'Neill's rebellion. O'Neill had made his headquarters at the house, which was previously a Plunkett property. At Slane, twelve miles upstream, the Flemings also forfeited their estates after 1641. From 1703 their castle was rebuilt by the Williamite General Henry Conyngham as a long rectangular block with forestanding corner towers and bell-cast roofs. Further inland again, the estate of Stackallen was granted to Gustavus Hamilton, later raised to the peerage as Viscount Boyne, who had commanded a regiment at the battle of the
60 Boyne. He rebuilt the house from *c.* 1710, as a tall U-shaped block with ample eaves pediments on its S and W fronts. At Lanesborough Sir George Lane obtained plans from England to rebuild Rathcline Castle *c.* 1666, and, though these came to little or nothing, an elaborate water garden was laid out, E from the house. (Traces still remain today.) At Barbavilla, William Smyth, a son of the Protestant Bishop of Kilmore and Ardagh, who had bought the Fitzwilliam estates in Westmeath, built another new house *c.* 1730 on a regular, if now old-fashioned, rectangular plan apparently prepared by *Sir Thomas Burgh*, Surveyor General of Fortifications and Buildings in Ireland.

Balrath-Bury, near Kells, is said to date from 1671 and was built by a Gilbert Nicholson on lands confiscated from Sir Nicholas Plunkett. It is described as 'a good substantial building, both spacious and convenient' in 1855, but no trace of the original fabric survived a colonial-style rebuilding in the 1930s. Platten Hall, near Duleek in Co. Meath, is another major loss. This house was built *c.* 1700 by Alderman John Graham on an estate forfeited by the D'Arcy family. Platten was one of the more sophisticated and most substantial houses of its period, a tall tripartite, brick-built façade, three storeys high and nine bays wide, with fine freestone detail. The house had the shallow segmental-headed windows and scrolled keystones typical of English Board of Works buildings at the end of the C17, and a magnificent two-storey entrance hall occupied the whole centre of the front. About 1830 the top floor was removed, and the house was demolished in the 1950s. Piedmont House (Gyles Quay), on the Cooley peninsula in Co. Louth, is a much more modest building, one room thick, with heavy chimney gables and a proper architrave of dressed granite round the door as its only refined feature. It dates from before 1697 and is the sole surviving example of a type of late C17 gentleman's house of which the two-storey ruins at Syddon House, Co. Meath, recently demolished, might have provided another.

In Longford town the Aungier family exercised their patronage in the construction of a markethouse which still stands as a robust example of commercial classicism dating from the late Stuart period. New churches do not appear to have been required at this time, though the little late Gothic church of St Mary at Mansfieldstown (Stabannan) had to be reconstructed after the Williamite wars.

Early Georgian Architecture

The success of the Protestant cause and the effective obliteration of political opposition brought to the country a century of peace. From 1691 until the Rebellion of 1798, Ireland saw few dramatic events. The succession of George I in 1714 might provoke the Scots to a full-scale rebellion within one year, and another in 1745, yet no equivalent revolt was to threaten the peace of Ireland. It was a century of consolidation, of a gradual improvement in the methods of agriculture and trade, and an era which witnessed the growth of large landed estates. While the old nobility was reduced to ingenious and often humiliating expedients to retain its land, the 'Protestant nation' prospered. Its Members of Parliament, the Lords and Commons in Dublin, found much of the province of Leinster a convenient location in which to establish their seats. A circuit of some thirty miles encompassed Drogheda, Slane, Navan, Trim and Enfield, while a little more than fifty miles brought Dundalk, Ardee, Kells, Castlepollard, Mullingar and Kilbeggan within the sphere of influence of the capital. In the context of Ireland as a whole these four counties contained agricultural land of high value, and it was only in the furthest parts of Westmeath and in Longford that an estate might seem to be inconveniently distant.

At first no great originality characterized the big houses of North Leinster. Many of them expressed the status of the proprietor in an orderly plan and in the convenient disposition of regularly proportioned rooms. A plain rectangular house, solidly built and on a substantial scale, was a sufficient novelty in itself, and throughout the century the rectangular or square block of a country house remained an Irish architectural norm. Seventeenth-century builders had tended to think in terms of houses that were one room thick, and their new buildings, like the additions they made to tower houses, were designed in single ranges. The layout for an C18 house was different, for its plan was devised to economize, as far as possible, on building materials and to conserve heat.

The classic model for an C18 country house in Ireland was the DOUBLE-PILE PLAN. In its simplest form the plan is an arrangement of six rooms, with two ranges (or piles), each of three rooms, placed back to back. The middle room at the front becomes the hall, opening into rooms on either side and leading through to the principal reception room at the centre of the back, which also has one room on each side of it. When the plan is extended slightly, as was usually the case, a corridor runs at the back of the hall between the two rows of rooms, and it is here that the main and the back stairs can conveniently be placed, lit

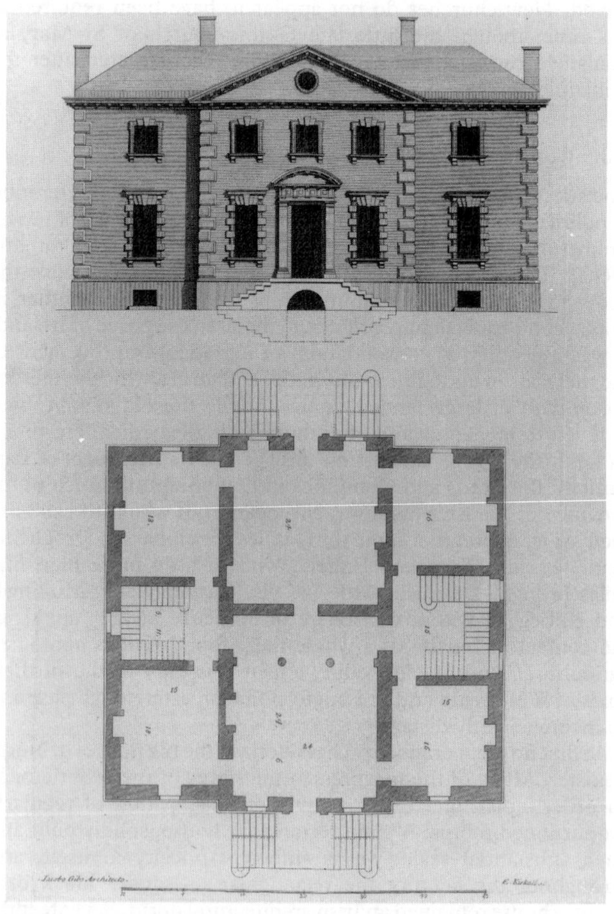

A double-pile plan from James Gibbs' *Book of Architecture* (1728)

by windows in the side walls which can be placed at the half level of the landings without any interruption of the fenestration of the fronts. The main elevation resulting from a double-pile plan is either three, five or seven windows wide and is always symmetrical. The sides will often show the double gables and chimneystacks which result from the double pile, or, if the architecture is more self-conscious, the roofs may slope back from the sides as well as from the front and the chimneystacks will be brought together to sit comfortably in the middle of the house. Stone House (Dunleer) and Ardronan, the former Dromiskin rectory, both in Co. Louth, are good examples of houses of some quality of finish which, like many a big farmhouse, expose their gable ends. Ledwithstown House (Ballymahon) in Co. Longford, 64
Drumcree (Collinstown) in Co. Westmeath and Whitewood Lodge in Co. Meath are more elaborate architectural designs, with hipped roofs and balanced chimneystacks, brought back and removed from the side walls.

The double-pile plan, already common in C17 Britain, was introduced to Irish architecture by *Sir Edward Lovett Pearce* – his Cashel Palace in Co. Tipperary of 1731 is a text-book example – and was given currency throughout Ireland by his assistant *Richard Castle*. Very many Irish Georgian houses – farms, villas, rectories and mansions – base their layout either exactly on this plan or on a variant. Even in a building where it does not seem to apply, the existence of a long cross-corridor at basement level or on the upper floors can represent the basic starting point of the double-pile plan, though subsequent alterations on the main floor have eradicated all traces of its use. The plan is widely employed throughout North Leinster; well-known examples are at Ballsgrove in Drogheda of 1734, Bellinter of 1750, Beauparc of 1755, Ardbraccan of 1773, Drumcar of 1777, and there are many more.

The only truly great country house to be built in North Leinster was Summerhill, designed *c.* 1730 by *Sir Edward Lovett Pearce* for Hercules Langford Rowley. The house was burnt during the Civil War of 1922 and its ruins were demolished in the 1950s. Only the avenue, two rusticated and pedimented gateways and a hollow filled with rubble now remain. By any standard Summerhill was a phenomenal house. The main front, facing N, extended over 300 ft (90 m) and was built throughout of ashlar limestone blocks. At its core lay a sophisticated two-storey block, built on a basement, with four giant-order Corinthian columns defining on the façade the position of the central hall. Unusually the centrepiece of the house eschewed the use of any pediment, and a continuous entablature and balustrade ran across the length of the main block. The front was extended by short square wings into quadrant walls, which curved forward to meet two flanking towers with square pavilion blocks beyond; on a line with these were the pedimented gates. Pearce adapted the double-pile plan as the starting point of this grand design, though at Summerhill it was greatly expanded to incorporate a superb two-storey hall, in the form of a pure cube, with a pair of monumental staircases opening in the

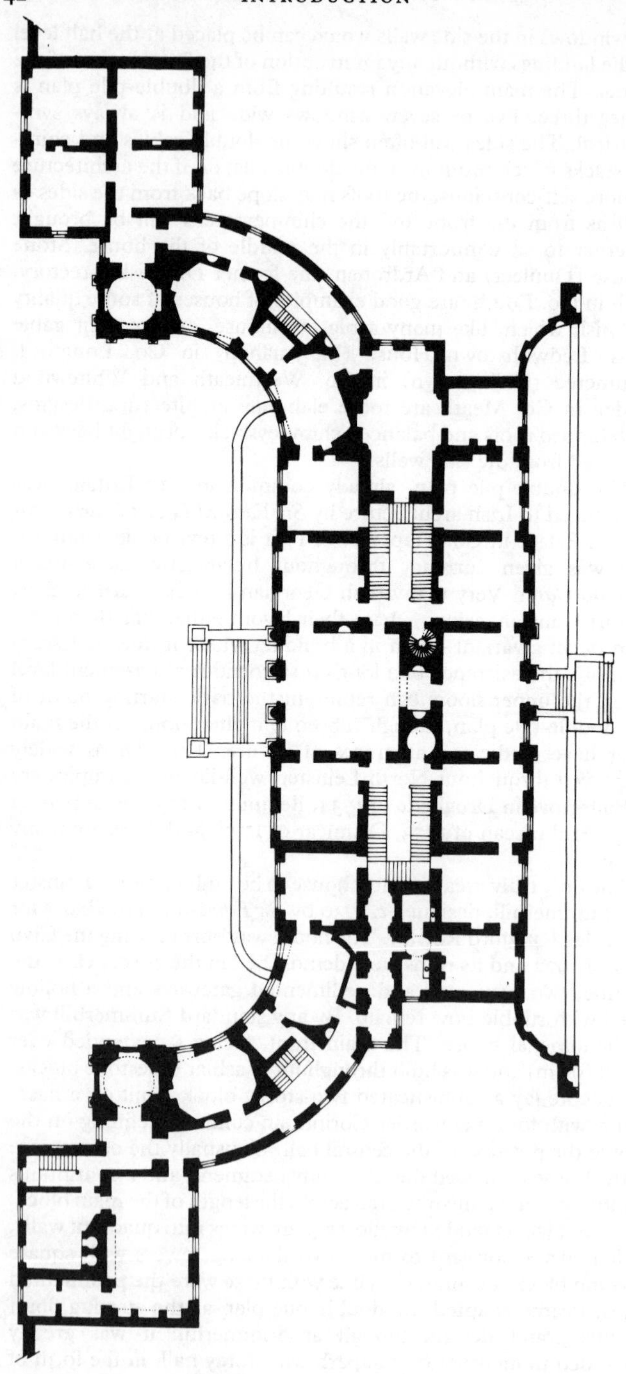

Summerhill, Co. Meath. Plan

centre of either side and rising at roof level to arcaded chimney towers in the manner of Vanbrugh and Hawksmoor.

The destruction of Summerhill has left many questions unanswered, and it is not clear to what extent the entrance front, with its corner towers and two-storey quadrants, received its final form at the end of the C 18. It is, however, evident that this remarkable building set the programme for later country houses within the Dublin Pale. No architect before the age of neoclassicism ever copied the grandeur of Pearce's attached giant order, but the austere rectangular proportions of the main block, the use of quadrants to create a forecourt and the plain pavilion blocks flanking the entrance front were soon to be absorbed into the common language of the builders of country houses, their architects and masons.

One figure more than any other achieved this result, the German draughtsman *Richard Castle*, whom Pearce had taken on to assist with the preparation of drawings for the Irish Houses of Parliament and on whom the responsibility for the whole design devolved after Pearce's death in 1733. Castle's architecture lacks the refinement of his master's and shows a tendency to use decorative motifs indiscriminately, almost for their own sake. It was Castle who added the quadrant colonnades and pavilion wings to Castletown in Co. Kildare and who made the plan in 1742 for Russborough in Co. Wicklow. Both designs have an elaborate, self-consciously architectural character. The house in North Leinster which comes closest to them in terms of its display
is a late work, Bellinter, built for John Preston M.P. and begun 65
in 1750, one year before Castle's death. Like Summerhill, Bellinter has a rectangular main block – with a continuous cornice and no main pediment – and builds to a climax with straight wings, forestanding pavilions and quadrant walls, broken by niches and pierced by high gate piers, flanking the central block. The proportions of the house are those of a villa rather than a great mansion, and the layout, with the progressive importance given to elements as they build towards the centre, clearly quotes Palladian precedents.

Castle is usually credited with the dissemination of Palladianism throughout Ireland, yet the full programme of centre and flanking pavilions, as seen in the layout of Bellinter, is little employed throughout the country and very rarely in North Leinster. Castle himself had proposed this layout in the 1730s at Ardbraccan for the Bishop of Meath, though only the quadrant walls and flanking pavilions – with a characteristic range of vaulted stables – were completed to his design. A system of wide quadrants and flanking wings was also adopted at Swainstown (Kilmessan), an unusual house which Castle seems to have altered for the brother of his client at Bellinter. At Beauparc, built above a bend in the river Boyne in 1755, the pattern is used for the last time.

Throughout the country the type of architecture which Castle's example encouraged is best represented by Whitewood Lodge of
1735 and Ledwithstown House (Ballymahon) of 1746. These 64
houses rely for their architectural idiom on Pearce's and Castle's

flanking pavilions rather than on their main blocks. The architecture which is here proposed is simple, astylar and economical. Both houses are attributed to Castle, and both are built as simple cubes of masonry, three windows wide on the front and sides, with dressed stone window surrounds, a cornice at roof level and parapet above. The roofs are hipped, with the chimneys brought together in big central stacks. Like the designs of Robert and Roger Morris in Britain, these houses depend for their effect on their simplicity and on the marked preponderance of wall surface over window openings.

Castle used the same sparse idiom for two larger houses in Co. Westmeath: Waterstown (Glassan), designed *c.* 1740, a massively plain rectangular house with a high parapet, three storeys over a
67 basement and seven windows wide, and Tudenham Park (Molyskar), *c.* 1743, a pure square block of finely worked ashlar masonry, also seven bays by three storeys, with a delicate eaves cornice and blocking course. Both houses were built for Irish M.P.s, and both are now no more than ruined shells. The square of Tudenham is broken in the centre of each side by deep bows – the full width of a room inside – which rise the whole height of the house, and the front is distinguished by an unusual succession of openings at the middle bay – a pedimented doorcase, blank niche and dished oculus. These elements recur elsewhere in Castle's architecture; the pattern of the central bay is used in his Dublin town houses and in another North Leinster house attributed to him, Dollardstown (Donaghmore), long a ruin and now demolished.

The type of high square block initiated by Richard Castle was to endure in Irish country-house architecture well into the next century. Examples from the middle of the C18 are Ballynahowen Court and Rosmead (Castletown-Delvin) in Co. Westmeath and Drewstown House, Co. Meath; later versions of the type are at Killua House, near Clonmellon (prior to its castellation), Rockview (Dysart) and South Hill (Castletown-Delvin), all in Co. Westmeath, at Mitchelstown House (Athboy), Co. Meath and at Ardagh Glebe in Co. Longford. In later examples the parapet at roof level is replaced by an exposed hipped roof rising from a gutter or thin eaves cornice, and often even the architrave surround to the windows is omitted. Such late houses impress largely by their bulk. Large, plain and bleak, their character made a distinctive impact well into the C19 and within the European architectural tradition seems unique to the Irish countryside.

In Co. Louth and the eastern parts of Co. Meath the monumental solidity of Castle's style seems to have had less influence. In Drogheda, the James Barlow House of 1734 in West Street and the Henry Singleton House of *c.* 1740 in St Laurence Street set precedents for brick-built façades which became standard for the merchants' houses in Drogheda and Dundalk. This street architecture also influenced the farms and gentlemen's houses of the coastal countryside. These buildings are less monumental than their inland counterparts; here when an attempt is made at architectural effect it is restricted to the façade, and the rest of

the building is left to be managed pragmatically. Ardee House of *c.* 1780 and the now reduced Lisrenny at Tallanstown are cases in point: both long, three-storey blocks, seven windows wide, and with little detail save a tripartite doorcase. Dunboyne Castle and Dowth Hall, country houses designed for noble proprietors, most probably by *George Darley*, in 1764 and *c.* 1765, have both quite smart façades, yet their architecture stops at the sides. Somerville, at Kentstown, Co. Meath, appears to have been the same in its original form. Stone House near Dunleer, Co. Louth, of *c.* 1760 and Moyglare House in Co. Meath, perhaps of *c.* 1780, both similarly ignore their sides. It is also worth noting that in a number of these front-only houses the position of the stairs is moved from the side of the house. In a building designed as part of a terrace, a side stair, at least as a main stair, is not easily lit. The Singleton House in Drogheda had its main stair at the back of the building, opening directly into the hall, a pattern which was adopted as a variation of the double pile at a number of country houses: Dollardstown (Donaghmore), Kingsfort (Moynalty) and Drews-town in Co. Meath, Barmeath in Co. Louth, and Ballinlough in 70
Co. Westmeath.

While the extent of decoration on a front can stop at the level of a fanlit doorcase in freestone, a rather more ambitious formula proved popular throughout the country from about the middle of the C18. Duleek House in Co. Meath, which gained a new front in ashlar limestone at about this time, provides a classic example of the type. The façade is a three-bay, three-storey design which breaks forward in the centre, with a heavy eaves cornice and blocking course. In the central bay a pedimented doorcase with side-lights is surmounted by a Venetian window on the first floor, with a low tripartite window on the top storey. The identical formula is used at Newpass, near Rathowen, in Co. Westmeath, and it reappears in essentially the same form, except that the top floor has a Diocletian window, in *Nathaniel Clements*' elegant façade at Beauparc, Co. Meath, in the large town house that closes the view down Market Street in Trim, at Meares Court near Almorita of *c.* 1760, at Hilltown near Castlepollard, and, just beyond Longford on the opposite shore of Lough Ree, at Scregg House, Co. Roscommon. Occasionally more modest houses also adopted some form of central emphasis: at Parkstown, the former Ballivor glebe-house in Co. Meath, two blank niches are set one above the other over the entrance to an otherwise plain five-bay, three-storey house. Johnsbrook House (Clonmellon) in Co. Meath places a Diocletian window in its pediment, while Tir-achorka, the shell of a ruined farmhouse in Co. Meath, had a Venetian window doorcase, a Diocletian window above and a lunette window in the central pediment.

A small number of VILLAS, built in the middle third of the C18, offer an architectural diet of more sophistication. Of these, Gaulstown, near Castlepollard, is the earliest: a diminutive classical house built on a cruciform plan, possibly *c.* 1730. Its stocky character, with a Palladian doorcase – like the Villa Poiana – and a rough-cast pediment supported on heavy dentils, seems worthy

of the little houses designed by Vanbrugh or the domestic doodles of Pearce. In villa design, as so often, it was *Castle* who in 1740
66 gave the lead, building a long, low classical house, Belvedere, as a retreat for Robert Rochfort, Lord Belvedere, overlooking Lough Ennell in Co. Westmeath. The building employs its architect's usual vocabulary of rusticated door and window surrounds, Venetian windows and an eaves parapet, but departs from the norm in its extended floor plan, which sets four rooms in a row, those at either end opening through semicircular bow windows to views N and S. The example of Belvedere seems to have inspired *George Pentland*, who in 1757 designed Dysart, a two-storey villa with three storeys at the back. This is something of a poor man's version of Belvedere, for it is rendered in cement with a plain gutter at eaves level. It makes use of Richard Castle's door–niche–oculus progression on the main front – replacing the oculus by a shallow Diocletian window which Castle also used – and its plan repeats the idea of deep bow windows, looking N and S, in the rooms at the back of the house. The pattern appears again at Mount Hanover (Bellewstown), Co. Meath, where the windows are set in angled bays rather than a semicircular bow, and in the early C19 at Glencara, near Ballymore in Co. Westmeath. Fancy plans reach their apogee at Castle Cor, Co. Longford, a whimsical hunting retreat designed around one huge octagonal room with four fireplaces set into one square pier in the middle of the room. Rectangular ante-rooms open on every second side, with tall windows in between.

A different sort of architecture which offered the Georgian age scope for an ideal plan is provided by the IMPROVED FARMHOUSE. Two pretty examples are Bridestream House, at Moyglare, Co. Meath, a charming classical box with a pedimented central villa, miniature quadrants and flanking blocks, dating from *c.* 1750, and Kilcarty, at Kilmessan, Co. Meath, a long and low façade, with short wings and a symmetrical office court behind, designed by *Thomas Ivory* in the 1770s. Conscious architectural improvements of an ideal character may also be noted at Hamwood, Co. Meath, a house of 1764 which in the 1780s gained a pair of quadrant wings that terminate in pretty octagonal pavilions like garden buildings attached to the house. Johnstown at Enfield, Co. Meath, is a larger three-storey house of *c.* 1750, also extended by low wings, and given neat terminal pavilions faced with blind Venetian windows and flanking an office court behind. Johnstown is perhaps not so much ideal architecture as a medium-sized ordinary house with careful architectural additions. As a five-bay, three-storey block with gables and big chimneys, it is typical of countless houses built throughout North Leinster from *c.* 1740 until the end of the century.

Throughout the C18 many CASTLES and tower houses in North Leinster continued to be inhabited and were enlarged by their owners. Often these houses had remained in the hands of Catholic families – Barnewall of Trimlestown, Taafe of Smarmore (near Ardee), Plunkett of Killeen, Dunsany and Louth Hall (Tallanstown) – and before the repeal of anti-Catholic legislation,

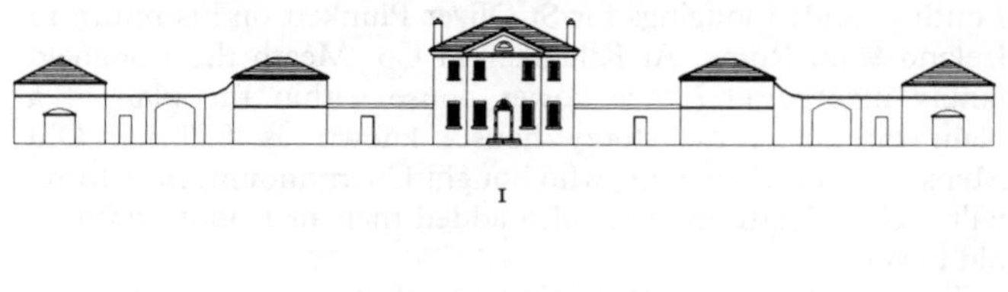

1

2

3

4

Model farms. 1. Bridestream House (Moyglare). 2. Johnstown (Enfield). 3. Kilcarty (Kilmessan). 4. Hamwood

which began in 1778, new building tended to be modest. The normal pattern, as in the C17, was to add a wing to one side of the tower. Thus the tower houses at Ballygarth (Julianstown), Skreen and Richardstown (Stabannan) each gained a low mid-Georgian three-bay, three-storey house on one side. Smarmore (Ardee) received a similar one-sided addition, and then its tower became a central feature by the addition of a further three-bay block on the other side. A larger seven-bay, three-storey house was added at Thomastown Castle (Tallanstown) and, largest of all, a nine-bay, three-storey wing – though only one room thick –

at Louth Hall (Tallanstown), itself an historic castle, where Lord Louth provided lodgings for St Oliver Plunkett on his return to Ireland from Rome. At Kildalkey in Co. Meath the Longfield family incorporated their tower house within the plan of a plain three-bay, two-storey house, known as Kilbride Old Mansion. The Chaloners, who bought Cherrymount, near Moynalty, Co. Meath, in 1704, also added their first house onto an old tower.

Though alteration, dereliction and destruction have taken a
heavy toll of Georgian architecture in Ireland, North Leinster has
still just enough buildings of quality to form an impression of
the interiors of this period. Nothing by *Pearce* survives, but the
substantial, straightforward classicism of *Castle*'s rooms, with six-
and eight-panelled doors and lugged architraves, is well rep-
68 resented by the interiors at Ledwithstown, Belvedere and Bellinter. The staircases in the last two houses have moulded timber
balusters which mimic the forms of stone architecture: a fat
baroque profile at Bellinter and a more slender pattern at Belvedere, derived from the balustrade invented by Bramante for
his Tempietto in Rome. Two houses of the mid-century whose
architects are unknown but whose craftsmanship is of a high
70 quality are Drewstown in Co. Meath and Ballinlough Castle, not
far distant in Co. Westmeath. Both have distinctive two-storey
entrance halls with galleries at first-floor level and handsome stairs
with turned banisters which open off their halls. A third staircase
of great quality may be seen at Barmeath Castle, which also
retains a fine rococo library with original bookcases and decorative
plasterwork. Free plasterwork of an almost sculpturesque quality
decorates the staircase and saloon at Dunboyne Castle, and there
75 is other remarkable work in the same taste in the chancel of St
74 Peter's Church, Drogheda. In the principal rooms at Dowth Hall,
the slender recessed panels, filled with palm branches and free
leaf forms, suggest the presence of the Dublin master plasterer
Robert West, who may also have worked in the saloon at Bellinter.
The main rooms at Belvedere also have pretty ceilings decorated
with light-hearted and charming rococo designs, and merchant
houses in Dundalk and Drogheda display similar work.

Comparatively few CHURCHES and PUBLIC BUILDINGS were
erected in this period. At Athlone, Dundalk, and Trim the medieval churches were adapted for Protestant worship, and it was
only at Longford and at Drogheda that large new churches were
required. St John's, Longford, founded in 1710, was largely rebuilt
71–2 in the 1780s and has since been altered and enlarged. St Peter's,
Drogheda, built to designs of *Hugh Darley* from 1748, remains
much as he left it, a large and very handsome example of a type
of galleried building that had been pioneered by Sir Christopher
Wren at St James's, Piccadilly, and which Irish people had first
encountered in the Dublin churches of St Ann's, St Mary's and
St Werburgh's. A small classical church, now abandoned, was
built by Bishop Maxwell at Ardbraccan, presumably in the 1770s;
two further plain churches with good classical doorcases were
built at Drumcondrath and at Kilcommick (Kenagh), now a ruin.

A delightful little chapel, with a miniature U-shaped gallery, 77
forms an integral part of Wilson's Hospital, Co. Westmeath. This 69
residential charitable school, founded in 1759, was built to designs of a local man, *John Pentland*, who provided a smart Palladian façade to screen a somewhat old-fashioned arcaded courtyard. Pentland's façade makes conspicuous use of a pair of Venetian windows at either end of the elevation, and this standard motif – used equally to suggest gentility in domestic work and civility in public architecture – appears prominently at the Drogheda Mayoralty House of 1769 and at Longford Courthouse, a routine design indistinguishable from a large town house and built, surprisingly for its style, as late as 1791. By contrast the Tholsel at 11
Drogheda, designed by *George Darley* in 1765, stands at a turning point not just in the town but in Irish classical architecture as a whole.

Mid-Georgian Architecture

The death of Richard Castle in 1751 corresponds closely with the end of the first phase of British Palladianism, and the deaths of its main protagonists – William Kent and William Adam in 1748, Roger Morris in 1749, Lord Pembroke in 1750 and Lord Burlington, the principal advocate of this severe taste, in 1753. The architecture that followed was of an altogether lighter sort: rustication became restrained, keystones were used sparingly, the profiles of mouldings became less ponderous and their projection was less pronounced. Within an interior, friezes were filled with fretwork or with fragile carving that was deeply undercut, while columns, which for the Palladians had been smooth-shafted cylinders, acquired the extra delicacy of fluting. In Ireland the taste for lightness spread gradually. It appears first in the shift of emphasis from an architectural interior to the more relaxed patterns of rococo decoration, and for some considerable time no corresponding change can be noticed on the exterior of buildings. In a sense a stylistic vacuum had followed Castle's death, for though a number of architects – Francis Bindon, Nathaniel Clements, Thomas Ivory, George Semple and Michael Wills – were active in the capital in the 1750s and 1760s, no single figure emerged to impose a particular style. It was only imperceptibly that exterior architecture became more refined.

George Darley's Tholsel at Drogheda fits neatly into this process. 11
It does not stand out as a radical departure from the architecture which preceded it, and yet in certain significant ways it seems to point towards the future. Its architecture is logical, and the effect is tidy rather than emphatic. Darley uses thin mouldings and shallow cornices, particularly on the cupola tower, where the pilasters and half-columns of the upper stages are delicately scaled. The ground floor of the building is also treated in a new way. It is not simply a rusticated wall interrupted by windows, which was the common solution of Irish Palladianism, but an elegant succession of tall arcades of a type which Sir William

Chambers had published in his *Treatise on Architecture* in 1757 and which would gain greater currency in Ireland after 1781 and their use by James Gandon at the Dublin Customs House. Chambers and Gandon are of course the two English architects who played a decisive role in establishing neoclassical architecture in Ireland, and Darley's Tholsel, for all its provincial setting, points in the same direction.

The event which proved crucial for the development of neoclassical architecture in Ireland was a competition held in 1769 for the design of the Royal Exchange in Dublin (now the City Hall). On this occasion the hopes of the Irish architectural profession were routed: Gandon won second place and the first prize went to an ex-student of the Royal Society of Arts in London, Thomas Cooley, who at the age of twenty-nine came to Dublin to superintend the building and was to spend the rest of his short career working in Ireland as an architect. It is of some significance that English architects took part in the competition. The men who commissioned public works in Dublin were now prepared to look beyond the Irish capital for their designs, reflecting perhaps a growing cosmopolitanism and an awareness, even a pride, in the strength of the national economy at this time. Even some of the best-established British architects might now consider that Ireland offered a real opportunity for their advancement: Isaac Ware, John Carr of York, Capability Brown, Robert Adam and James Stuart all either visited the country themselves or provided designs for Irish clients. This had not happened before and there is no doubt that the influx of such metropolitan practitioners had an invigorating effect on local design.

The elegant neoclassicism and refined plasterwork of *Robert Adam* made their first appearance in Dublin in 1765, at a town house in Mary Street, the property of Hercules Rowley. Rowley was the owner of Summerhill in Co. Meath, where Adam was also employed to make a survey with a view to the improvement and modification of that great mansion. Nothing remains of these jobs, but in 1772 an extensive scheme for the alteration and decoration of Headfort House in Co. Meath was begun to Adam's
78 designs. The magnificent two-storey dining hall or 'Great Room' there provides a unique example of the mature Adam manner in Ireland. *James Wyatt*, at the start of his career, was to establish an extensive Irish practice, and his example had considerable influence on Irish interior design, notable in the work of *Michael Stapleton*. In 1773 Wyatt provided designs for the completion of Ardbraccan, and later, from 1785, he was responsible for rebuilding Slane Castle, though at both these houses he was ultimately to give place to other designers.

When so much of Irish building in the Georgian period is the work of anonymous designers it is tempting to look for sources amongst contemporary architectural literature. The quality of much mid-century plasterwork in Ireland offers a clear demonstration of the artistic advantages which accrued to tradesmen who were able to base their work on continental patterns. Some of the European engravings which were collected by Robert West are now in the Irish Architectural Archive in Dublin, and the La Franchini brothers, the major stuccoists to work for Pearce and Castle, are known to have copied continental plates. In the same way a great many builders throughout the century clearly had access to architectural pattern books published either on the Continent, where Irish preference seems to have been for French authors, or else in England. The fashion for superimposing tripartite doors, Venetian and Diocletian windows, discussed above, may well have derived from such sources. In the second half of the century the works of the English carpenter William Pain proved particularly popular; his *Builder's Companion and Workman's Assistant* of 1758 was already on sale in Dublin in the year it came out, and it achieved wide currency in Ireland. Pain produced many architectural titles, and his straightforward designs for rectangular three-storey houses with plain façades offered patterns for many a family home in the country and many a merchant's house in town. A set of designs for front doors with Doric, Ionic and Corinthian columns supporting an open pediment and filled by a fanlight was copied in the streets of Dublin and in houses throughout the country. These designs had first appeared in the third edition of the *Builder's Companion* in 1769 and were to be reissued in Pain's *Practical House Carpenter* of 1788, a volume which proved particularly popular with mason architects and went through many editions. Towards the end of the C18 it was also Pain's plates which were to familiarize Irish tradesmen with the greater refinement and new motifs of Adam's and Wyatt's interiors.

Among professional designers the quiet genius of this period and the man who perhaps made the most distinguished contribution to Irish architecture in the 1770s was *Thomas Cooley*, winner of the Exchange competition. Cooley brought a sophisticated understanding to the practice of architecture and, though his individual patrons could not match the unique opportunity he enjoyed in Dublin, his employment on a number of their houses was to enrich the country with a series of fresh ideas and delicate interiors. The originality of Cooley's decorative detail, inventive, exacting in its craftsmanship and full of wit, is unmatched by any of his contemporaries, and far exceeds the understanding of pattern-book designers. Cooley elides architectural elements: friezes die into cornices; the dentils of the Ionic order shrink to the scale of little blocks set below the soffit of a moulding, while coffers lose their substance in polygonal patterns of the shallowest recession. It was Cooley who succeeded Wyatt as the architect of Ardbraccan, who provided the pretty spire, of slender silhouette, for the medieval belfry at Kells, and who, in 1784 –
the last year of his life – designed Rokeby Hall, Co. Louth, for 80
the Protestant Archbishop of Armagh, Richard Robinson. Had Cooley lived longer, he might well have performed a decisive role in the development of Irish neoclassical architecture. Death robbed him of that distinction, yet it was Cooley's last work at Rokeby, and the responsibility for its completion, that provided the vital opportunity for his successor, *Francis Johnston*, a native

of Armagh who, as a young man and *protégé* of the Archbishop, had first trained in Cooley's office. Johnston inherited to the full both the refinement of detail and the suave manipulation of classical elements that had informed his master's style. By the turn of the century he had become the dominant figure in the capital, and it is probably not too much to say that with Johnston the architectural profession in Ireland finally comes of age.

Johnston had an eclectic taste: while his predecessors had been content to work within the limits of a classical norm, his architecture drew on a variety of sources, so that beside the freely interpreted classicism of Cooley an austere Greek style, an early form of neo-Gothic and a picturesque neo-medievalism all take their place. Such stylistic pluralism is characteristic of the end of the C18, and Johnston's mature works in Dublin, St George's Church, Hardwicke Place, the General Post Office, the Chapel Royal and the picturesque additions he made to Dublin Castle – all important commissions, supported by substantial government funds – neatly demonstrate the range of styles which he had mastered and which his example served to promote.

81–2 It is Townley Hall, in Co. Louth, begun in 1794, which is Johnston's masterpiece. Here an informed patron and an artist of the most exacting standards combine to produce an austere structure which in its rigorous logic may bear comparison with *avant-garde* architecture anywhere in Europe. The basic concept of a domed cylindrical hall set centrally in a cube of masonry is patently antique, though in the context of Co. Louth the plan owes perhaps as much to Cooley's Exchange or to Gandon's Four Courts as it does to ancient Rome. Johnston's architecture depends for its effect on pure form, on the proportion of large rectangular spaces and on a rational use of simple detail, much more than on the parade of any particular style. His best buildings – and this is surely an index of his sophistication and his modernity – are astylar. The same severity of taste which Johnston developed at Townley Hall informs the additions he made to Corbalton Hall (Skreen), the interiors he completed at Slane Castle, both in Co. Meath, and the serenely proportioned Ballynegall, now a sad ruin near Portneshangan, in Co. Westmeath.

At the end of the century, the practice of architecture in Ireland remained the exclusive preserve of a small group of professional men, and Johnston was much employed in the design of churches and church buildings for the Catholic community. His plain T-plan churches at Drogheda and Kells have now been replaced by later buildings, and the best example of the type of straightforward Georgian architecture which he promoted for his Catholic clients is the large Siena Convent, set above the river at Drogheda and built from 1792. Smaller in scale and quite different in character are the little Gothic churches which Johnston designed for Primate Robinson, at Ballymakenny and Termonfeckin, and probably also at Baronstown (Kilcurry), all in Co. Louth. These are very much in the thin linear manner of his master Cooley, though at Ballymakenny he achieved a handsome spire which gave rise to many imitations in Protestant country churches in the next century. Kilmessan Glebe House, which is attributed to Johnston, and Galtrim, a *ferme ornée*, designed as a rectory *c.* 1800, for the Protestant clergyman who was the son-in-law of his patron at Townley Hall, are examples of his miniature villa style. Galtrim seems to have been designed to accommodate a deep thatched roof on its garden front, a reminder of the picturesque cult of vernacular elements in rural architecture which was to become a notable feature in Georgian design after 1800.

A further change in taste in which Johnston was to play a significant role was the establishment of the GEORGIAN GOTHIC CASTLE. Ireland had once two remarkable houses built in the manner of Sir John Vanbrugh's symmetrical castle designs: Wardtown in Co. Donegal, 1740, and Arch Hall in Co. Meath. Both were symmetrical designs in which the central hall was treated as a projecting bow, with round towers at the corners of the main front. Both were classically detailed, with round- and segmental-headed windows, and both had classical plasterwork in their interiors. Though now only their shells remain, Wardtown and Arch Hall should be mentioned in any survey of Georgian Gothic castles as early examples of the romantic response to the massiveness of castle architecture which was later to be evoked in a more picturesque way. Within North Leinster, the rebuilding from 1785 of Slane Castle, on its dramatic site above the Boyne, is the next castle-style house in this sequence.

What the C18 saw in Irish castles was, above all else, the attractive stepped profile of their late medieval battlements. These are quoted in the anonymous castellated additions made to Ballinlough Castle *c.* 1790, and at Louth Hall (Tallanstown), enlarged and castellated by *Richard Johnston c.* 1805. *Francis Johnston* employed the motif in the extensive additions he made to
Killeen Castle in 1802–3, on the round towers he added to Tul- 90
lynally Castle in 1806 and again in his proposals to gothicize 89
Headfort House in the same year. None of these houses uses neo-medieval detail in a convincing or archaeologically correct way: what their owners and their architects hoped to achieve was a style that would allude to the medieval past without quoting its forms in a literal way. As the mood of the new architecture was distinctly poetic, the mind was to be stimulated by visual references rather than by any exact replica. Aesthetic theory around 1800 laid much stress on the pleasures of allusion in architecture and on the desirability of developing a style that would be appropriate to the setting in which a building was placed. To Johnston and his contemporaries at the turn of the century the massing and romantic silhouette of a castle was soon to seem the most appropriate pattern for a modern Irish house.

Though FOLLIES and GARDEN BUILDINGS are not especially numerous in this part of Ireland, building of this type undoubtedly played a part in familiarizing patrons with the range of architectural styles which Johnston's career so aptly demonstrates; a number of estates in North Leinster contain attractive examples of the genre. Usually the mansions that gave rise to them have gone and these characterful oddities remain today as forlorn

survivors in empty fields. First in date, as in order of importance, is the octagonal baptistery-like tower, topped by a spire, which *Richard Castle* designed as a pigeon house for Waterstown (Glassan) *c.* 1749. The grounds also contain a grotto and a pedimented brick archway. At Dangan Castle an C 18 obelisk, recently restored, sits on top of a small hill supported on an arched pedestal and steps; in the C 18 the estate had many more such monuments. Another obelisk, at Killua Castle (Clonmellon), marks the spot where Sir Walter Raleigh planted the first potato in Ireland, and a third, of which only the base remains, records King William's victory at the battle of the Boyne (*see* Oldbridge). The arched obelisk as a feature is peculiar to Irish classicism and was reproduced over a century later, and on a grand scale, in the Brindley
96 Testimonial of 1880, a monument to a Master of Hounds, erected near Ashbourne. Bold classical archways of ashlar stone, with pediments and niches, are all that is left of Summerhill House. At Arch Hall a similar pedimented archway is set on the main axis opposite the ruins of the house. At Bloomsbury, near Donaghpatrick, a domed hexagonal fishing temple, built of warm red bricks, presides on a small promontory above the waters of the Moynalty. These are the classical garden monuments of the C 18.

Wayward illogicality is the essential element in the design of a really good folly, and at Larchhill House near Moyglare the remnants of a rococo garden contain a wonderful variety of structures: odd pebble-dashed towers, a wilfully clumsy rotunda on a mound above a grotto arch, a 'stonehenge' in the middle of a field, a five-sided fort with Irish crenellations, known as 'Gibraltar', and some wall alcoves with shell work. The gardens at Drewstown and Barmeath both preserve pretty rockwork bridges, while the
93 later gate lodge to Bracklyn House is a *tour de force* of rockwork design. More sedate, though in a similar idiom, is the battlemented lodge at Somerville (Kentstown).

The earliest stirrings of the Gothic Revival appear at the remark-
92 able Jealous Wall at Belvedere, apparently the shattered fragment of some feudal palace, though built only in 1760 and probably designed by *Thomas Wright* of Durham, who also contributed a Gothick gateway and octagon in the grounds. Wright was an astronomer, a free-thinker and an amateur Palladian architect of some note. He was also a friend of Lord Limerick, with whom he stayed at Dundalk and to whom he dedicated his *Louthiana* (1748), an enthusiastic survey of tower houses and other antiquities in Co. Louth. Gothic of a free-and-easy pattern similar to Wright's follies and drawings appears in the Winter family burial vault at Agher (Summerhill) – a pretty design with loopy pinnacles and blank quatrefoils – and in the gaunt shell of the Summerhill Gothic Mausoleum, N of the site of the house. *Henry Aaron*
95 *Baker*'s Pillar of Lloyd, 1791, is more seriously Gothic – a practical tower in stone, set on a hill-top W of Kells, and intended for use as a beacon.

In the C 19 the follies are either towers or gateways. Two picturesque gateways at Slane Castle, one set at the centre of an impressive run of crenellated wall, were designed by *Francis*

Johnston c. 1801. It was probably his assistant, *James Shiel*, who provided the memorable Gothic arch and lodge for Dunsany Castle *c.* 1840, and Shiel may also have been responsible for the pretty castle cottage in the grounds of Killua Castle. Other battlemented gateways with tall paired octagonal towers are at the entrance to Bellingham Castle (Castlebellingham) and at Rathaldron Castle near Navan. The entrance to Cruicetown House (Nobber), Co. Meath, is marked by a pair of toy towers with a segmental line of stone voussoirs stretching between them in a thin arch. This is pure folly architecture, whereas the tower of the ruined Protestant church at Castletown, Co. Meath, is not, though its architecture offers such a disarming mixture of Gothicism and classicism that it cannot be excluded. The Maiden Tower at Mornington is an exceptionally slender shaft of stone with a C19 crenellated parapet, and Drummond Tower, in the grounds of Monasterboice House (Tinure Cross), Co. Meath, is a miniature early Victorian tower house, with the hard stone detail more typical of a contemporary industrial building than of a pleasure house. The battlemented clocktower at Kenagh is, properly speaking, a florid Victorian public monument, and by the time it was built in 1876, Gothic architecture was already well established as the preferred stylistic option of any serious architect in Ireland.

Architecture after 1800

The conjunction of French revolutionary ideas and Irish nationalism which provoked the rebellion of 1798 saw confrontation between Irishmen and government forces at Ballinahinch, Naas, Carlow and Wexford and brought a force of 900 regular French troops, which had landed under General Humbert in Co. Mayo, to perhaps the most elegant piece of recent public architecture in
Westmeath, Wilson's Hospital at Multyfarnham, where the 69
United Irishmen had mustered on 5 September. Though the Franco-Irish army was defeated within two days, the consequences of the uprising were more enduring and, in the longer term, had an impact both on the morale of the ruling class and on architectural patronage well into the next century. The Act of Union, whereby the Irish Parliament voted away its own existence in the spring of 1800, was a direct response to the unsettled state in the country: it removed executive power to Westminster, and, in order to secure its passage, the government found it necessary to compensate the Irish House of Lords, the owners of borough seats and the holders of public offices for the loss of their privileges. New peerages were promised, jobs were offered and cash, at a rate of £7,000 per parliamentary seat, was made available. Catholic emancipation, keenly promoted as a goal which the Union could achieve but which George III subsequently refused to countenance, became an insistent political issue for the first three decades of the new century, and Catholic churches began to be built in large numbers. To the financial effects of the Act of Union should be added the stimulus which the wars with

Revolutionary, and later Napoleonic, France provided for the national economy. During the war years, Irish agricultural production increased steadily, and landed estates which had previously done little more than balance their books became profitable. The Union removed the fiscal disabilities under which Irish commerce had previously had to operate, and trade flourished. These factors, aided by the cash payments made as a consequence of the Act of Union, must go some way to explain the spate of architectural activity which lasted throughout the country from 1800 into the early 1830s.

The building of COUNTRY HOUSES, many of modest to moderate proportions, is most extensive in this period and, in terms of the range of styles that were adopted, more varied than previously. North Leinster is largely made up of good agricultural land and is as a result well provided with ample, sensible houses built as generous if unambitious rectangular blocks. These houses invariably have symmetrical façades and are usually of two or three storeys. Their fronts will be either three or five windows wide and may be built on a semi-basement. The Church of Ireland glebe-houses which were partly funded by government are a group whose date is often known, though their plans and appearance follow no particular pattern, as they were built to meet the requirements of individual and often strongly independent clergy. The contrast in the style of glebe-houses in North Leinster is neatly marked by a comparison of Ardagh Glebe, an astonishingly cubic block, three bays wide and three storeys high, with a massive chimney of no fewer than twenty-eight pots at the centre of its roof, and the glebes at Kilmessan and Clonmore (Tinure Cross), houses of great charm with modest and symmetrical central blocks set between lower flanking wings.

For the smaller houses in the country there is now often no information about the families who built them, their date or architect, and only stylistic features can provide a guide to their chronology. In the forty years between 1780 and 1820 domestic architecture in the country generally became more self-conscious. Before the end of the C18, gentlemen's houses were often finished in rough-cast lime mortar, had slate roofs which ended in gables at the sides and had a simple gutter at eaves level across the front. The windows were not large, and the front door, which was frequently the only decorative feature, was often arranged in a standard tripartite pattern with narrow windows – side-lights – on either side of the door. By *c.* 1790 a number of these elements had changed: fewer houses were to be left with a rough-cast finish; the size of windows and of window panes was increased and, on the ground floor at least, many ran down to floor level. Fanlights became fashionable, at first as semicircular designs, like those in the town houses built in Merrion Square, Dublin, in the 1780s, and later with depressed elliptical or segmental heads which permitted a wide arch, the same width as the hall inside, but did not impose a correspondingly high ceiling, which could be inconvenient in a smaller house. As families sought to give their homes more consequence, the plain gutter was replaced either by a shallow parapet or a stone cornice with a blocking course above, or else by carrying the roof forward on overhanging eaves, supported by timber brackets. By *c.* 1820 forestanding porches, either of four columns or of two columns held between projecting walls, had become common, as had the type of wide, flat-headed, tripartite window, divided by narrow mullions into three parts, which in Ireland was commonly called a Wyatt window. A Wyatt window was frequently used to mark the centre of a façade immediately above the porch. In the same period the ground-floor windows of a front may be placed within shallow relieving arches, with either semicircular or segmental heads.

By 1800 fashionable houses in North Leinster had ceased to be built in three storeys. The new look favoured a lower extended elevation, and the better houses tended to be designed to be read as blocks of building rather than as façades. Two patterns in the arrangement of floor levels were popular: many houses were built with the ground and first floor of equal height, following the example of Francis Johnston's mature work, while others, usually designed as square villas, made play of an emphatic difference between the windows of the ground floor and a low upper storey, which was often accommodated below wide overhanging eaves. Bective House, Kilineer House (near Drogheda) and Bracklyn House are good examples of the ample style of country-house architecture which resulted from the use of two equal storeys. Newhaggard (Trim), Stephenstown House (Knockbridge) and Glananea are further examples where the difference between the two floor levels is hardly marked. The villa type has many late C 18 precursors. Belview and Bobsville near Crossakiel, Stackallen Glebe House near Rathkenny, and Harristown near Charlestown are all pleasant three-bay, two-storey houses with hipped roofs, while the mature form, which seems to owe its origin in Ireland to the example of *Sir Richard Morrison*, is represented by Annagor (Bellewstown), Belvin Hall (Skreen), Brownstown (Kentstown) and Tullyard (Trim), a handsome house which might be by Morrison himself, and by the delightful Moyglare Glebe House, reminiscent of an illustration by J. M. Gandy.

Larger classical houses after Johnston's work are comparatively few. One which may be associated with Sir Richard Morrison is Somerville House (Kentstown), a mid-Georgian house which was turned back to front – as had happened earlier at Dunboyne Castle – by the introduction of an ingeniously planned hall, placed in the centre of the N front. Mountpleasant near Ballymascanlon is a long stuccoed design extended in the early Victorian period; the Red House, Ardee, is a tall brick building with shallow hipped roofs, almost too large for its astylar idiom, while Middleton Park (Castletown Geoghegan) by *George Papworth*, *c.* 1850, on the shore of Lough Ennell, is a virtual replica of Johnston's Ballynegall. One figure who contributed a distinctive type of country house to the area was the English architect *John Hargrave*, a pupil of Thomas Harrison of Chester, who settled in Ireland and carried out a number of important commissions for public buildings before his death in a yachting accident. Coolamber Manor near

Street, *c.* 1830, is his most ambitious design in the area, a wide low house with a central segmental bow window and façades faceted by pilaster-like strips between each window bay. Anonymous houses with good cutstone façades, pediments in the centre bay and plain classical details which may be associated with Hargrave, or perhaps *Thomas Duff*, are Pilltown (Julianstown), Aclare House (Drumcondrath) and Hayes (Donaghmore), which has a distinguished interior of fine late neoclassical plasterwork.

The antidote to rural domestic classicism is provided by the castle-style or CASTELLATED COUNTRY HOUSES which became a marked feature of Irish architecture after 1800. The origin of this type of architecture in Ireland lies in the prevalence of many late medieval tower houses which had been extended by the addition of a plain wing and which had remained in use as houses into the late Georgian period. The aesthetic of the Picturesque, which became widespread in cultured circles in the 1790s, meant that towers and battlements were now valued for the varied outline and broken silhouette they gave to the mass of a building, and many of the plain wings added to tower houses gained new battlements and extra neo-medieval detail in this period. Ballygarth Castle (Julianstown) and Louth Hall (Tallanstown) provide good examples of the trend, while at Trimlestown the castle was more than doubled in size by the addition of a long castellated wing and bay window. The extension of Rathaldron Castle near Navan and the neo-medieval details added to Skreen Castle are instances of this taste surviving into the early Victorian period.

Residence in a castle might also support claims to an ancient lineage and, in an age of romantic and nationalist sensibilities, could suggest a flattering connection with the earlier history of the country when Norman barons ruled the Dublin Pale. Moreover the architectural detail which characterized a castle – rubble walls, battlements, pointed arches and a mullioned window or two, usually built in timber – were less expensive than the architecture of a fully developed classical scheme, so that patrons with pretensions to an up-to-date taste but a limited budget found the castle style an attractive alternative form for a new house. Newcastle House, near Tyrrellspass, Tobertynan House, near Rathmoylon, and Drumcashel, near Stabannan, offer examples of the modest, indeed almost miniature, scale of some of these new castles – simple square houses with battlements – while Lisnabin near Killucan is one of the prettiest new castles of the period in Ireland, with a charmingly light-hearted Gothic interior.

The practices of two architects, *Francis Johnston* and *Sir Richard Morrison*, dominated the castle-building movement in this part of Ireland, and in both cases the idiom of the office seems to have resulted from the contribution of younger men with possibly more interest in the new language of Picturesque Gothic design. Johnston was influenced by his clerk *James Shiel*, while Sir Richard is said to have relied on the knowledge of his son, *William Vitruvius Morrison*, who made a tour through England to study Tudor architecture and was for a while his father's junior partner.

Country houses where they worked together are Killeen and Moydrum, possibly Gormanston, and certainly Tullynally (then called Pakenham Hall – where Johnston, Shiel and Sir Richard were each employed in succession). Shiel worked on his own account, and to good effect, at Dunsany and Killeen, and was probably responsible for the castellated alterations at Killua (Clonmellon) and the final design of Knockdrin.

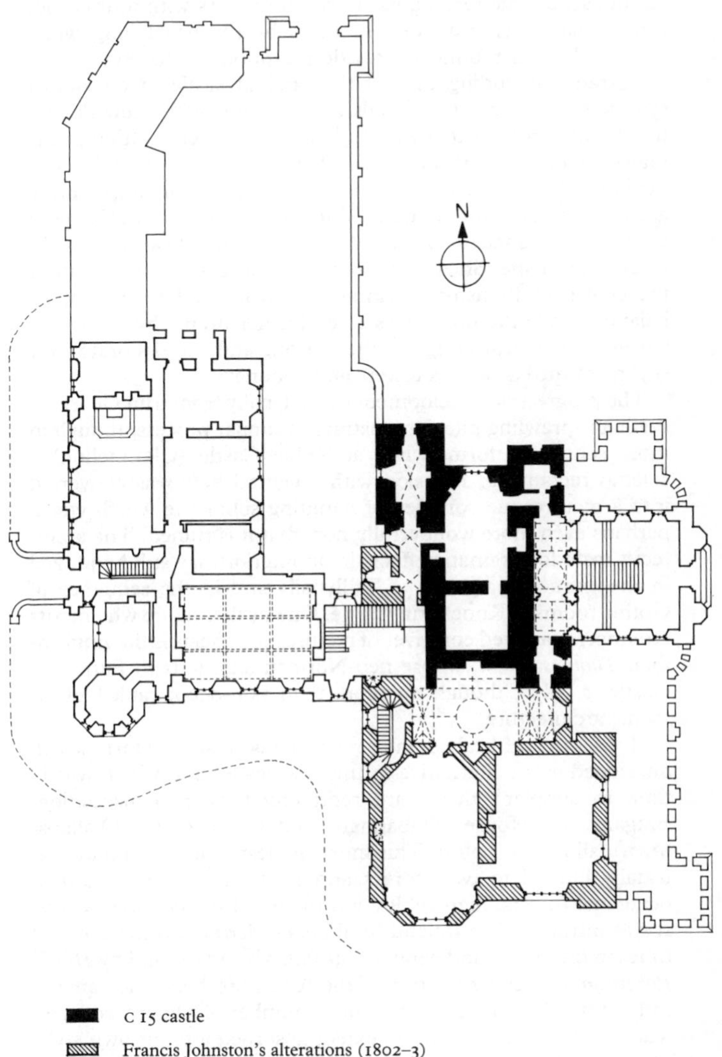

Killeen Castle, Co. Meath. Plan

The impact of the younger men was to move castle-style architecture away from its old loyalties to symmetry and to pretty but insubstantial Gothic details towards a more robust, irregular massing with vigorous neo-Gothic detailing which, in the hands of William Morrison, could have an almost archaeological charm. Johnston's recasting of Tullynally and the design of Gormanston are based on symmetrical concepts, whereas all the later buildings
90 are not. The development of Killeen Castle, though the house is now a gutted ruin, demonstrates these processes succinctly. The old house, a large rectangular tower of the C15 with four corner turrets, had been extended to the S by the usual long wing, which Johnston rebuilt to provide reception rooms and a new, W entrance including part of the original castle in an almost symmetrical façade. The details were delicate, with a few slender mouldings, Irish battlements and fanciful plaster vaulting in the interior hall. By 1840 taste had changed, so that the additions made by Shiel were intended to give Killeen, not simply more accommodation, but a quite different presence, much more evocative of ancient power than Johnston's neat and well-balanced scheme. Shiel's new wing was designed to break out of the centre of Johnston's symmetrical front and to disrupt its balance, while the house was given further drama by a turreted entrance hall projecting on the E front and an elaborate new skyline of turrets, access towers and chimneys.

The progressive development of Tullynally from trim Georgian castle to sprawling pile demonstrates a similar process, though in more schematic form, while at Killua Castle (Clonmellon) a solemn rectangular mansion with a central bow was converted into a picturesque complex of haunting silhouette which works perhaps even more wonderfully now that it is ruined. The architect's taste for dramatic effects in an interior may still be judged in the extraordinary hall of Tullynally and in the sequence of Gothic rooms at Knockdrin Castle. One further figure who merits attention as a noted contriver of picturesque effects is the English-
91 man *Thomas Smith*, whose neo-Norman additions to Barmeath Castle, *c.* 1835, though no more than skin-deep, rank high as scenic architecture.

Houses in an Elizabethan or revived Tudor style, a taste which developed as an alternative to the new castles and which was in time to supplant them, are represented by Ballymascanlon, Braganstown House (Stabannan) and Glyde Court (Tallanstown), all in Co. Louth. This more modest style of building was usually limited to two storeys and is characterized by narrow octagonal turrets, high gables and ranges of tall chimney shafts. It was introduced to Ireland by *William Morrison*, who used it at times in the courts and wings of his father's castles, and by *Daniel Robertson*, a younger relation of the Adam brothers who came to Ireland in 1829, after working on a number of Oxford colleges, whose details are to a certain extent absorbed into his own style. Morrison probably designed the delightful group of picturesque
94 Tudor cottages at Castlebellingham between 1826 and 1830, while Robertson was responsible for Carriglass Manor, 1838–45,

a finely articulated Elizabethan design built on a complex plan. *Thomas Duff*, noted for his early Perpendicular churches, prepared a grandiose scheme for an elaborate turreted mansion at Ravensdale but nothing other than a large model (which survives) came of this proposal.

One consequence of the Act of Union, probably unforeseen in 1800, was the fact that it tended to encourage a NEW CHURCH BUILDING programme within the established Church of Ireland. In its principal provisions the Act had appeared to threaten the status of the ruling class, a Protestant landed minority which even at its greatest extent made up little more than ten per cent of the entire population. It was, however, on these people that the government depended if post-Union Ireland were to be godly and quietly governed, and it was for this reason, and for the benefit of this small community, that Parliament voted substantial sums from 1801 to 1821 to support a programme of Irish church building. Throughout this period the provision of grants and loans was the responsibility of a committee of the Church of Ireland, the Board of First Fruits. This pre-dated the Act and had come into being to allocate a fund made up from a proportion of the stipends of all clergy presented to a living in the first year in which they held their benefice. Around 1800 the Board's own funds averaged no more than £400 each year, yet with government support it was enabled to meet an expenditure of over a million pounds by 1821. The Board continued to fund church buildings and to assist with the construction of rectories and glebe-houses until 1833, when its work was transferred to a new body, the Irish Ecclesiastical Commission.

The needs of rural congregations in the established Church of Ireland in the first half of the C19 were not complicated. What was required was a good plain hall, with a tower to make a bit of a show in the community and to establish the presence of the church. If the building were sufficiently self-conscious to adopt an identifiable style, that style would invariably be Gothic, though in the more modest examples it was Gothic of a most rudimentary kind. The new churches have rubble walls and pitched slate roofs, timber Y-tracery mullions filled with quarry glass, pointed-arch doorways framed in freestone, and flat plaster ceilings inside. The classic Board of First Fruits structure is a tower and hall church of this character. Well over fifty were built in the four counties of this volume in a period of perhaps twenty-five years. There is inevitably a good deal of repetition and much similarity in the designs. The central administration, combined with a preference on the part of most incumbents for good value, tended to ensure that this would be the case; yet within the limitations of the basic form, the Board of First Fruits churches can display an intriguing variety.

The most modest churches are quite plain rendered halls, to which a diminutive and rather narrow square tower, sometimes with shallow clasping buttresses, is attached: good examples of this type are at Ballymaglasson (Dunshaughlin), Clonmellon, Dunshaughlin, Horseleap, Killintown (Multyfarnham), Moate,

Omeath and Rathowen. Larger towers fill a greater proportion of the gable against which they are built and give a more substantial and less toy-like appearance to the church: examples here are Ballymacormick (Killashee), Beaulieu, Clonard, Drumcree (Collinstown), Mayne (Castlepollard) and Rochfortbridge, while a particularly robust design on a cruciform plan appears in three
103 churches at Clonbroney (Ballinalee), Killoe and Newtownforbes, all in Co. Longford. Though the tower is frequently no more than a block at the W end, a common variant in the plan of these churches (which appears to have been copied from C 18 buildings such as St John's Church at Longford) encloses its base in two narrow flanking rooms level with its front. The churches at Ballymakenny (Termonfeckin), Kilglass and Street offer examples of this, and some more elaborate designs with spires also adapt the plan to provide pinnacled extensions on either side of the belfry, as at Crossakiel and Tyrrellspass. The highly decorative Forgney Church (Ballymahon) makes a unique contribution by extending the flanking rooms into bold bow-fronted projections, all with battlements, which mask a very plain hall behind. A further variant – not particularly common – provides for a flat two-storey façade with the tower rising through the central bay; this occurs at Ardagh, Ardee and Rathowen.

In addition to providing a tower as a landmark, a number of churches were further embellished by building an octagonal spire within the pinnacles and battlements of the tower. Such spires added considerably to the expense of a church and appear to have been adopted very much as a symbol of parochial status. The churches at Ballivor, Ballymahon, Crossakiel, Dromiskin, Duleek, Killucan, Mullingar and Reynella (Dysart) are all of this type. St Sinian at Tyrrellspass is a particularly memorable example, as it occupies a commanding position above the broad expanse of the semicircular village green, laid out by the philanthropic and dynamic Countess of Belvedere. Inevitably where a local person of some standing was involved the quality of detail and degree of decoration could rise markedly. At Newtownforbes, not only the Board but Lord Granard contributed to the rebuild-
101 ing of the C 17 cruciform church in 1820, and the result is an interior remarkable for its ambitious display of Gothick details and for its pretty plasterwork vaults. At Portneshangan Parish Church, the joint patronage of James Gibbons of Ballynegall and Sir Richard Levinge of Knockdrin secured a design by *John Hargrave* for a large and thoroughly competent Perpendicular Gothic church (1824), complete with a fine spire, crenellated eaves and gables. Kilcommick Church at Kenagh (1832), built for the Dowager Countess of Ross to designs of *William Farrell*, employs a charming system of minute transept porches to accommodate the family's needs, while at Edgeworthstown Church (1811) Richard Lovell Edgeworth, a proprietor of almost manic ingenuity, devised a steel and copper spire which was to be winched up within the framework of the church tower and avoided
102 the expense of stone. It stood for many years. Kilbixy Church, built *c.* 1810 in fine dressed ashlar throughout and at the expense

of Lord Sunderlin of Baronstown, is one of the most elaborate and perhaps the most endearing of all these churches. It is a tall box of stone, divided by sharp clean shafts of pinnacled buttresses, has a pretty Decorated E window flanked by vaulted niches and a charmingly slender tower, enriched with blank arcading at the parapet.

A pioneer in the use of accurate Gothic detail whose churches are of more than passing interest is the amateur architect and designer, the *Rev. Daniel Augustus Beaufort*, rector of Navan in Co. Meath and of Collon in Co. Louth. Beaufort designed both churches himself, carrying out alterations and extensions at Navan, which has a pretty insubstantial Gothic vault in plaster and four-centred arched windows, and rebuilding Collon Church, 100
at least as far as the interior is concerned, on the model of King's College Chapel, Cambridge. The new church at Collon was first proposed in 1810 and begun in 1813, which makes it a remarkably early instance of accurately revived Gothic architecture, in advance of any comparable work in Scotland and hardly equalled in the practice of English architects beyond the Gothic work of James Wyatt.

Early CATHOLIC CHURCHES in North Leinster are few. The first is St James at Grange, at the end of the Cooley peninsula in 97
Co. Louth. It dates from 1762, is probably the work of the mason architect *Thaddeus Gallagher*, and is now the oldest surviving Catholic church in the Archdiocese of Armagh. Its structure is of two periods and neatly demonstrates in one building both the forms that were popular with Catholic builders following the relaxation on the Penal Laws which had begun in the 1770s. The oldest part is a narrow hall, entered from the front at either end, with the altar placed in the middle of the long wall and set, like the pulpit of a Presbyterian church, between a pair of high round-headed windows. The parallel with Presbyterian planning is no accident; both Catholic and Nonconformist congregations had to manage without resources and with little official support, so that a form which worked well for one community was frequently copied by the other. Presbyterian churches in C17 Scotland (and later in Ulster) had also developed a T-shaped plan, built of simple gabled ranges, with galleries accommodated in each of the arms of the T. The Catholic church at Grange was extended in the early C19 to copy this pattern, gaining a primitive rendered tower and sacristy behind the altar at the same time. There are deep galleries at the end of each wing, and in the original design 98
the church had an elaborate classical altar with Ionic columns, suggesting a more sophisticated taste than is indicated by its white-washed walls and graded slate roofs and tower.

An unbridled enthusiasm in the Catholic hierarchy either for renovation and enlargement or simply for change for its own sake has left little in North Leinster as pure or as appealing as Grange. There are of course many small to medium-sized rural chapels built between 1800 and 1850, and in these cases, where renovation rather than rebuilding has occurred, the layout of the earliest plan can often be detected in the structure. At Taghshinny (Kenagh),

Co. Longford, a long-plan church similar to Grange survives, with the same lateral porches and, in place of the tower, a short chancel, also added later, with a large Gothic window and off-set octagonal belfry tower. The little chapel at Emper (Ballynacarrigy), Co. Westmeath, also extended, in the centre of the long side preserves the lateral doors which are the classic feature of the long-plan church. This plan was also employed at Loughanvalley, near Castletown-Geoghegan in Co. Westmeath, a slated rectangular hall with four ample Y-traceried windows set parallel to the line of the road, and at the large church at Courtbane (Kilcurry), Co. Louth.

Throughout the Irish countryside the T-plan church is the ubiquitous Catholic type. In many cases these buildings were developed out of an earlier long-plan church (Tallanstown in Co. Louth is a particularly attractive example); others were erected as T-plan designs from the start. The architecture of these churches is rooted in a vernacular building tradition and is usually modest. The materials available to a poor people did not change between the later Georgian and the Victorian periods, and there is often little detail to indicate the date of a building. When the bulk of the population lived in single-storey thatched cottages, a large plain hall with a good slate roof was already an architectural event. Scale may offer some indication: small churches tend to be early; larger structures with prominent pitched roofs are usually of a later date – but size is not always a sure guide. The interior joinery may also suggest the period of a church, though it is often the internal finishes that have proven most vulnerable to change.

Where a T-plan church attempts some architectural display, it is usually the gable at the end of the leg of the T which is decorated and is sometimes brought into a formal relationship with a railed

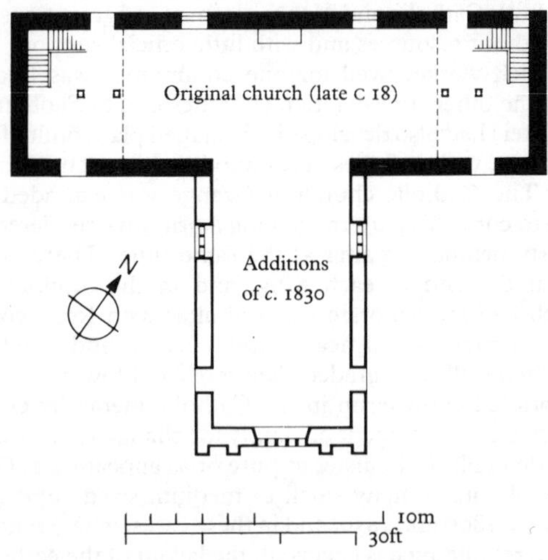

Tallanstown Church, Co. Louth. Plan

area before the church. The gable façade may be given battlements and finials, as at Ballypousta (Ardee), Co. Louth, or it may be built in ashlar when the rest of the church is of rendered rubble, as in the attractive and very modest little chapel at Newtown (Lobinstown). In churches of the 1840s this gable is often distinguished by a bellcote. By the middle of the century, as a result of the increased understanding of Gothic architecture, lancet windows – grouped in three in a gable – replaced the wider windows and Georgian proportions of earlier designs.

As the scale and size of the Catholic churches increased, the rectangular plan came back into favour, only now it was wider than the long-plan churches and the altar was placed in the traditional position for a medieval building, at the end of the longer axis. This plan provided ample space for a large congregation, and if there were a gallery it was placed at the back, facing the high altar. Two churches of this type, which at the time of visiting preserved original interiors with ambitious Gothic wooden detailing, are at Batterstown (Dunshaughlin) and Donore (Oldbridge) in Co. Meath.

A rare but significant kind of Catholic church is the type which seems to imitate the tower and hall pattern of the Church of Ireland. A few Catholic building projects received government support in the 1820s and early 1830s, and these buildings can sometimes look deceptively Protestant, although they are invariably distinguished from their Church of Ireland counterparts by the use of a cross on the gable or tower, which the Protestant buildings always lack. Churches at Kilcurley (Dundalk) in Co. Louth, Newtowncashel (Inchcleraun) in Co. Longford and Rathowen in Co. Westmeath are of this type, while the Protestant pattern of a two-storey front with central tower provided the starting point for the designers of two grand Catholic churches at Lanesborough, Co. Longford, and at Rosemount, near Horseleap, Co. Westmeath. The large rectangular block and hipped roof typical of many a Presbyterian church in Ulster is quoted unusually in the big church at Knockbridge, Co. Louth; another unique design is at Parsonstown (Portneshangan), Co. Westmeath, a long three-bay lancet hall which, like some of its medieval predecessors, incorporates a three-storey house under the same roof at the W end. In this big plain church the conjunction of chimneystacks and a gable cross is memorable.

The PUBLIC BUILDINGS of this period mirror the course of the British campaigns against the French. A state of war brought soldiers into Irish barracks, created full employment and made Irish agriculture profitable: the peace which followed in 1815 tended to depress agricultural prices, left the troops of disbanded regiments dependent on the country, and increased vagrancy. The buildings which mark the better state of Irish agriculture at the end of the century are the markethouses, erected by individuals and by the County Grand Juries to serve local commerce, while the government, alarmed by the events of 1798 and fearing the possibility of an enemy invasion, greatly extended the barracks at Drogheda, Dundalk and Athlone. Neither the markethouses

nor the barracks have any real architectural pretensions: they are sensible, workman-like buildings in stone with minimal details derived from a classical vernacular tradition. The barracks at Athlone impress by the sheer scale of the ranges of late Georgian
109 buildings, while the markethouses at Ballymahon and Killucan are handsome designs.

The government's response to lawlessness after 1815 is demonstrated by the extensive rebuilding of courthouses throughout the country. As a result Dundalk possesses one of the most finely detailed monuments of the Greek Revival movement in Europe
83 in the courthouse by *Edward Parke* and *John Bowden*, begun in 1813, which incorporates an archaeological replica of the portico of the Thesion in Athens between plain flanking walls. No other late neoclassical building in Ireland quite matches the monumental solemnity of this austere design. *Francis Johnston* provided a plain rectangular hall with a pedimental gable and enormous sash windows for the courthouse at Kells in 1802, and *Sir Richard Morrison* built an uninspired Palladian block, old-fashioned for its date, at Trim *c.* 1810. It was perhaps *John Hargrave* who gave the most individual designs; the small courthouse of 1828 at Moate, marked by a shallow segmental bay, is like a villa in a Regency spa town, while his Italianate Roman design of *c.* 1824
84 for Mullingar possesses real *gravitas*. So too does the massively rusticated retaining wall, a design that seems fully conscious of later neoclassical developments on the Continent, which is all that remains of Hargrave's gaol buildings of 1827 at Trim.

Victorian Architecture

Catholic Emancipation, a political decision which, more than any other event, was to encourage the creation of new buildings throughout the country in the C19, was granted by Parliament in 1829, just eight years before the accession of Queen Victoria in 1837. There can be no doubt that it was this legislation which provided the essential impetus for much of the most interesting architecture in Ireland in the Victorian age. Increasingly, as the century progresses, it is the Catholic church which acts as the significant patron in North Leinster and, while the tides of ascendancy taste ebb and flow between the restraint of Greek classicism, the neatness of neo-Tudor or the irregular picturesqueness of late Georgian castles, CATHOLIC CHURCH ARCHITECTURE moves consistently towards a purposeful and rational employment of architectural style, sometimes classical but more usually in a Gothic Revival taste. As the Victorian age matured in Ireland so did the architecture of the Catholic community, almost as if its builders had first to assimilate the greater opportunities that lay before them and then to enlarge their vision to memorialize a hard-won independence in stone.

In Dublin, and in many of the major Irish cities, both the self-conscious purpose and the distinctness of the Catholic church were to be expressed in a type of continental architecture, French or Italian in its origin, which was patently different from the

norms established in the C18 and made no reference to the conventional pattern of British buildings. English architecture could not offer a contemporary model for a modern Catholic church, and a clergy which had trained abroad looked inevitably to Europe for its inspiration. North Leinster has only one example of the type of architecture which resulted from these attitudes, but it is one of the most spectacular churches in the entire country, the Cathedral of St Mel in Longford, begun to designs of *John* 117–18
B. Keane in 1840 – just five years before the onset of the Irish famine. The building of this great church was an ambitious plan for any Irish community and an astonishing achievement for an impoverished rural diocese, where rubble-built thatched churches were the norm. Even without the Famine, it is unlikely that the cathedral could have been completed in a single building programme; in the event the façade was finished off after Keane's death and in a temporary manner to designs of *John Bourke* in 1861, and it was not until 1893 that the present massive portico of six Ionic columns – its pediment filled with narrative sculptures of the early Irish church – was erected, as a substitute for that intended by Keane, under the supervision of *George C. Ashlin*. Keane had trained as a clerk in the office of Sir Richard Morrison and knew well how to apply the stylistic range of his former master, but he had also been responsible for the design of two classical porticoes in Dublin, Greek Doric at the Pro-Cathedral and Ionic at the Church of St Francis Xavier, and there can be no question of his allegiance to continental standards in his masterpiece in Longford.

John Bourke, Keane's successor at St Mel's, was perhaps the only other Catholic architect, native to Victorian Ireland, systematically to employ an Italianate classical style. His obituary, when he died in middle age in 1871, speaks first of his practical qualities, the brevity and perspicuity of his specifications and the shrewd intelligence he brought to bear on all the more difficult questions of a building's construction: 'a man of sterling purpose and of unswerving integrity', who stood as 'justice personified between contractor and client'. This resolute moral character rather than any imaginative dash pervades Bourke's architecture. Building committees who employed him got reasonable, practical architecture for their cash: robust common sense characterizes his classical work. Bourke may be plain, yet somehow he is never dull. He had a liking, perhaps a little old-fashioned for his age, for an astylar Italianate manner, using square towers with shallow hipped roofs, which mark the centre of the Hevey Institute at Mullingar, built from 1854, and the long and barely articulated block of St Mel's Diocesan Seminary and schools at Longford, 128
begun in 1863.

In the design of GOTHIC REVIVAL CHURCHES the first and most notable figure after Dr Beaufort is *Thomas Duff*, who was a partner in a building business with Thomas Jackson of Belfast and who also practised as an architect from Newry in Co. Down. Duff was born *c.* 1805 and has the distinction of creating the first thoroughly understood Gothic Revival buildings in Ireland. An

early work, attributed to him, St Mary's at Ardee, begun in the year of Emancipation, gives no hint on its exterior of the stylistic command its architect was later to display; the façade is a flat, two-storeyed affair of a type which was widely employed in North Leinster in the 1830s and 1840s. Its three bays are divided by shallow buttresses, with wide two-centred arches at ground-floor level and pointed windows above, crowned by a battlemented parapet and bellcote. The Catholic churches at Lobinstown (1857) and Kentstown (1844), and the façade of the former church at Rathkenny (*c.* 1837), all in Co. Meath, conform to this model; a similarly elevational style survives in some timber reredoses at Tallanstown (1855) and at Haggardstown (Blackrock) in Co. Louth (1855) and Killallon (Clonmellon) in Co. Westmeath (1837). Though Duff's façade at Ardee is of a standard type, the interior of the church, an arcaded nave carried on quatrefoil timber shafts of Tudor Gothic character, with ribbed vaults in plaster, has a three-dimensional richness which is rare in the Catholic churches of this period and anticipates the achievement of his more ambitious designs. The shift in archaeological empha-
105 sis in Duff's next church, St Patrick's Pro-Cathedral in Dundalk, can be explained properly only as the effect of a study tour he is known to have made to the South-West of England, where his partner Thomas Jackson had relatives, at some time in the 1830s. St Patrick's was begun in 1837 and is a design in the purest style
106 of C16 Gothic, substantially built of stone, with a spacious nave flanked by arcades of four-centred arches with piers of a complex multi-shafted plan built in brownish granite. Bath Abbey as much as the often quoted source of King's College Chapel, Cambridge, seems to stand behind much of its design. For its date the command of Gothic detail, and even more of Gothic *spirit*, is unparalleled in Ireland, and St Patrick's remains the most perfect Gothic church of its period in the entire country. In 1839 Duff designed the Gothic Presbyterian church at Dundalk, less archaeological in spirit on account of the Presbyterian need for a galleried design; then in 1840, in complete contrast to Keane's huge classical scheme for Longford, he submitted a design in Perpendicular Gothic for St Patrick's Cathedral, Armagh. The building, which promised another delicate church in the manner of Bath Abbey, was begun in the same year, though the work had soon to be laid aside on account of the Famine, and by 1848 Duff had died.

The exceptional quality of Duff's Perpendicular work is neatly illustrated by a comparison with another ambitious Catholic design, the church at Sandpit (Termonfeckin) in Co. Louth, which was begun at the height of the Famine in 1848. This building, whose architect is unknown and which appears on the outside as nothing more than a large and plain hall, preserves a
104 remarkable arcaded interior in what seems to be a naively decorative form of Early English Gothic. Both the scale and the date make it impossible to question the intention of such a church, yet its essentially decorative style and wayward use of historical elements are in sharp contrast both with Duff's historicism and

with another new church in rural Co. Meath, the first authentic exercise in Ireland in a revived Early English style. This is the Church of St Alphonsus Liguori (and St Skyre) at Kilskyre, begun in 1847 to designs of *James Joseph McCarthy*, then just thirty and about to become the leading figure in Ireland of the Ecclesiological movement, which held authenticity and a strict regard for the principles of C13 architecture to be the very touchstones of success.

McCarthy's church at Kilskyre is informed by the aesthetic principle of the truthful exposure of structural elements which had been introduced to English – and Irish – architecture by the example of A. W. N. Pugin. It stood in the vanguard of Irish ecclesiastical taste and, as such, demonstrates the principal elements of a style which was to become the stock-in-trade of many church architects until the end of the century. The plan avoids the symmetry of earlier Gothic designs and consists of a chancel, nave and aisles with an off-set tower against the gable and a porch opening from the second bay on one side. Inside, the pointed nave arcade is supported on alternating octagonal and circular shafts of polished limestone, and the rafters of the roof are exposed. Hailed by *The Catholic Directory* as a building of the 'true and ancient Catholic type', Kilskyre launched McCarthy as the foremost exponent in Ireland of the 'pointed style'. In the 1850s it was McCarthy who, as artistic heir to Thomas Duff, was to receive the commissions to complete both Armagh and Dundalk Cathedrals, and there is thus a satisfying continuity in the fact that in 1864 it was he also who added the chancel to Duff's early church at Ardee. North Leinster was to offer few further opportunities to McCarthy. From 1859 he was employed by Lord Granard, to rebuild Castle Forbes itself (*see* p. 77) and to design a new Catholic church for the village of Newtownforbes (recently sadly mutilated). In the same years McCarthy virtually rebuilt the Carmelite church at Moate, Co. Westmeath, adding an arcade and side aisles to the old building and placing a monumental tower and spire across its gable end, in a manner reminiscent both of the work of Pugin and of Robert Pierce's twin churches in Wexford of 1851.

A lesser figure who displays an understanding of Gothic design almost equal to McCarthy's, and may either have trained in his office or worked as a superintending architect for his designs, is *John Murray* of Dundalk, a local architect whose career has emerged from the pages of provincial newspapers. Murray came to prominence in the 1860s, enjoying a thriving practice as the designer of several ambitious Catholic churches in mid-Victorian Co. Louth. Invariably Early English in design, they follow the example of McCarthy's work in their effective use of local masonry, in the crispness of their detailing and in the striking and distinctive juxtaposition of the separate elements of their plan. Murray began with minor works, church alterations and the addition of towers and spires to country churches; his first independent commissions were St Mary's at Lordship, near Gyles Quay, 1858 and St Nicholas's, Dundalk, 1859, quickly followed

by St Malachy's at the opposite end of the same town in 1862. St Columkille's Church of 1866 at Togher, Murray's most accomplished design, has a tall nave, chancel, aisles and tower, executed in crisp local rubble, with impeccable limestone trim. Like Duff, Murray suffered on several occasions from the disadvantages of an extended building contract and from the petering out of parochial funds. His churches at Lordship and Collon and the two town churches in Dundalk were never entirely finished:
120 St Mary Boharboy (Grange), a late design of 1877, is by contrast perfectly complete, with a slender spire which greatly enlivens the flat coastal landscape of its setting.

In the same period that Murray was setting up his provincial practice, the reliable *John Bourke* designed a number of solemn churches in an early Gothic idiom. First amongst these was his project of 1850 for a lancet-style church at Clonmore (Togher) in Co. Louth. This was to remain unbuilt, but three further
119 commissions followed: St Mary's, Athlone, an austere, spare church with a slender broach spire and graded lancet windows, built in 1857–61; Drumraney Church, Kilkenny West, a perfect country church on a cruciform plan of 1858; and St Mary's, Granard, of 1867, a finely detailed church, closely similar in style and worthy of its spectacular site, riding high above the roofs of the town at the foot of the great Norman motte. St Augustine's Church in Drogheda, designed in 1859 by an obscure architect, *M. B. Moran*, is another example of the popularity of the Early English lancet style in this period.

In 1861 Bourke made designs for the Church of St Peter and St Paul at Moate, but, finding his integrity compromised by disagreements with the parish priest, he resigned the commission, and in 1867 the job was transferred to *William Francis Caldbeck*, an architect better known for his commercial work and his country houses. As the pupil and successor of the Dublin architect William Deane Butler, Caldbeck had maintained the broad basis of Butler's practice and was to contribute a number of Gothic churches to this part of the country. Caldbeck's church designs demonstrate the extent to which a purposeful, serious style of revived C13 Gothic had been absorbed by Irish architectural offices in the 1850s and 1860s. There is in many of these buildings a sense of routine performance and an architectural intention which does not aspire to more than a fashionable competence. The churches at Moate and at Edgeworthstown, completed in 1872, the year of Caldbeck's death, are good examples of such thorough building, while the convents and convent chapels he built at Clondalkin, Co. Dublin, where his family came from, at Trim and at Kells – all designed *c.* 1858 and all on a smaller scale – strike a happier and more individual note. His Presentation Convent at Mullingar (1869) reverts to the dull style of many large Victorian Catholic institutions.

The wholesale rebuilding of CHURCH OF IRELAND CHURCHES after the Act of Union meant that in the Victorian period, especially in country parishes, there was not much work to be done. From 1833 the activities of the Board of First Fruits had been vested in the new Irish Ecclesiastical Commission which, for a period of ten years, continued the appointments of separate architects for the four Archdioceses – William Farrell for Armagh, James Paine for Cashel, Frederick Darley for Dublin and Joseph Welland for Tuam. In 1843 a reorganization of the Commission placed the responsibility for overseeing the buildings of the established church with *Joseph Welland* alone. Welland had been a pupil of John Bowden and as such must have been involved in the design of many of the later tower-and-hall-type churches erected with the support of the Board of First Fruits. After the Irish Church Act of 1833 he had charge of all the churches in the Tuam Division and, with the advantages of this position, seems to have developed the particular interest which secured him overall control in 1843. The Archdiocese of Tuam does not include any of the counties in North Leinster, yet even before Welland took over general control he had designed a number of small churches at Kilkenny West, at Loughcrew, and at Eglish in Co. Offaly. These little buildings, dating from *c.* 1838 onwards, were plain rectangular halls of the most simple character whose shallow gables, unbuttressed walls and narrow round-headed lancets, with ventilation boxes below, gave no hint of the vigorous massing or the proper understanding of Gothic design which Welland's later work would demonstrate. The jump in quality can only be attributed to the attention which Welland must have given to A. W. N. Pugin's polemical publications – *Contrasts* (1836), *The True Principles of Pointed or Christian Architecture* (1841), *An Apology for the Revival of Christian Architecture* (1843) and, significantly, the two articles in *The Dublin Review*, in 1843 on 'The present State of Ecclesiastical Architecture in England'. Welland's mature work offers a Protestant alternative to the large Gothic churches of the McCarthy school. His buildings benefit from a fine sense of picturesque composition, for Welland understood the advantages which deeply stepped buttresses, high gables and asymmetrical porches – all built in substantial masonry – can give to a design, and, while his Catholic counterparts had often to make a little money go a long way and could run out of funds in the process, the Protestant community had greater financial resources and much smaller congregations to accommodate. At the mid-century the Catholic Gothic churches sometimes ran the risk of appearing flimsy and too long, while Welland's work, which was no less up-to-date than McCarthy's in its application of Puginesque principles, is satisfyingly solid. The churches he designed at Bective, 1851, Castlebellingham, 1852, Kildalkey (now demolished), 1855, and at Julianstown, a rebuilding of 1860, offer attractive examples of the genre within North Leinster, while the parish church at Moyglare, built in 1866 to designs of *Edward McAllister*, an inspecting architect for the Commissioners, who was drowned while bathing at Clontarf at the age of twenty-eight, neatly demonstrates the dissemination of Welland's style in the work of later men.

The Church of Ireland, in the Victorian age, displayed little enthusiasm for the high-church tendencies of the Oxford Move-

ment and remained, for the most part, relentlessly low. The little parish church built at Drumcar in 1845 provides the one exception to this rule. This simple lancet hall depends on the design of John Henry Newman's church at Littlemore in Oxfordshire, which had been published in 1840 by the Society for Promoting Gothic Architecture; it was evidently the tractarian enthusiasm of John McClintock, later first Lord Rathdonnell, which was responsible for such a disturbing outbreak of High Anglicanism in Co. Louth! In 1868 *Slater & Carpenter*, an English firm with High Gothic Revival principles, were engaged to extend the choir of Drumcar Church and to design the dumpy octagonal McClintock Mausoleum opposite the N door of the church. This assertive style of Protestant High Victorian architecture also appears memorably, if only for a moment, in another mausoleum, the imposing Gothic
127 octagon of the Taylour family at Headfort House, erected for the second Marquess of Headfort to designs of *James Franklin Fuller* in 1869, the very year in which Gladstone disestablished the Irish Anglican church. Perhaps the massive assurance of both these sombre octagonal sepulchres makes a political point and derives more from the conscious confidence of aristocratic lineage than from any theological certainties.

While the Catholic and Protestant communities consolidated their respective positions with new churches, the business world was expanding rapidly, with a network of commercial institutions for the Irish banking companies and new communications provided by an expanding railway system. In the period before the Famine each depended on the other and their destinies are interlinked. The RAILWAY AGE in Ireland opens in 1834 with the construction of the line from Dublin to Dunlaoghaire (then recently renamed Kingstown) to facilitate communications between Great Britain and Ireland by linking the capital to its port and the English ferries. The second line to open, the Ulster Railway, began at Great Victoria Street, Belfast, and ran through the Lagan valley to connect the country's industrial capital with the linen mill towns of Lisburn in 1839, Lurgan in 1841 and Portadown in 1842. The third line, the Dublin and Drogheda Railway, opened in 1844 and brought the miracle of mechanical transport to North Leinster. Much the most ambitious project of the period, with long marine embankments in Dublin Bay, Malahide and to the N of Donabate, the line had run into financial difficulties by 1843 and was saved from failure only by the technical and parliamentary expertise of Sir John MacNeill, who had worked as an assistant engineer with Thomas Telford. MacNeill came from Co. Louth and had been appointed Professor of Civil Engineering at Trinity College, Dublin, in 1842. The line extended for over thirty-two miles to link the capital with the port of Drogheda and the Boyne navigation system. Handsome stone stations of an Italianate character mark its original termini at Amien Street, Dublin, and on the high shoulder immediately S of Drogheda.

By 1849 a further route, operated by the Dublin and Belfast Junction Railway Company and planned by MacNeill, linked

Drogheda with Dundalk, extending in 1850 beyond Sir John's own home at Mountpleasant, which became a temporary halt, to Jonesborough in Co. Armagh. By 1852 the line had been taken as far as the Belfast Junction station at Portadown, where it met the Ulster Railway system, and MacNeill could turn his attention to the Boyne estuary, then the only remaining impediment to a continuous connection between Dublin and Belfast. A temporary viaduct was erected over the river within a year, and by 1855 the majestic stone arcades of the N and S viaducts and the lofty masonry piers of the bridge itself, one of the most memorable achievements of Irish Victorian engineering, were in place.

This main line still forms an essential part of the modern railway system, but the branches which ran inland along the Boyne valley to Navan (1850), to Kells (1853) and to Oldcastle (1863), or from Dundalk to Castleblaney in Co. Monaghan (1849), have either closed entirely or operate only for freight traffic. At Navan, the line which crosses the Boyne required a second grand viaduct from MacNeill, in rough-faced blue limestone, which forms a notable feature just downstream from the town. Several of the former stations on these lines survive and are usually the work of MacNeill's successor, *N. A. Mills*, appointed chief engineer in 1877, one year after the different companies had amalgamated to form the Great Northern Railway. The former station at Navan (1885) and the present stations at Dunleer (1881) and Dundalk (1894) are good examples of his trim and workmanlike style, with long, low ranges of polychromatic brickwork, shielded by glazed timber canopies, where black brick courses interlace segmental-headed windows framed with yellow hoods.

While the Dublin and Drogheda Railway developed a route to the N, the Midland Great Western Railway carried its line westward. The company opened the first section of its line in 1847, starting at its grand terminus at Broadstone Station, Dublin, and following the line of the Royal Canal which for much of its length marks the southern boundary of Co. Meath. The first section ended at the Hill of Down, a little N of Clonard. In 1848 the line was extended to Killucan and Mullingar, and by 1851 it had been carried via Athlone – where the railway crosses the Shannon on a remarkable low-slung bridge of iron latticework – to Galway, on the western coastline, a distance of some 130 miles (over 200 km). In 1855 Multyfarnham, Edgeworthstown and Longford were added to the network, while in the early 1860s the Dublin and Meath Railway (absorbed by the M.G.W.R. in 1888) provided connections throughout the county to Trim and Athboy, Bective and Navan. As a major commercial centre of the midlands, Athlone was to witness one of the most celebrated battles of the railway age, when the directors of the Great Southern and Western Railway, whose principal routes were to Cork and Limerick, first built a branch line to Tullamore in Co. Offaly and then sought leave to extend the line from Tullamore into the heart of the M.G.W.R. territory at Athlone. Such flagrant commercial opportunism was bitterly resented and vociferously resisted by the M.G.W.R. board, both in Parliament and in the national

press, yet, despite the argument that the area was already adequately served and that government subsidies to the G.S.W.R. line could not be justified, the scheme was in the end approved. As a result Athlone has two railway stations: an unusual, extended block, bulky and uncompromising, on the W side of the Shannon, designed in 1851 by *J. S. Mulvany*, as architect to the original
110 company, and a suave Italianate terminus built seven years later for the invading rival to the design of *George Wilkinson*. Mulvany is also credited with a number of the smaller stations on the line, such as Moate and Killucan, which are functional brick buildings with stone dressings and short projecting wings surmounted by shallow pediments. Wilkinson seems subsequently to have worked for both companies, and the larger two-storey stations between Mullingar and Longford were built to his designs.

The predominant use of a moderate Italianate classicism in the architecture of the railway companies is broadly reflected in COMMERCIAL ARCHITECTURE and COUNTRY HOUSE DESIGN about the mid-century. Provincial taste remained conservative. During the famine years there was neither the patronage nor the will to strike out in a new direction, and even for some time afterwards the distinction was observed that church work was Gothic while secular work was not. The career of *William Caldbeck* makes this clear. From 1853 until his death in 1872 Caldbeck was employed as the architect to the National Bank, for whom he designed at least twenty-six branches, five of them in North Leinster. His first work as the bank's architect was for its premises at Kells, designed in 1852. Other branches, built at Moate in 1854–6, at Mullingar in 1858, and at Longford and Dundalk, both *c.* 1860, adopt essentially the same formula, a five-bay, three-storey front in which the outer bays, containing the entrances, are slightly advanced, with an arcade of three windows between to light the banking hall. The ground floor is built of freestone with stucco above; over the windows of the outer bays Caldbeck employs segmental relieving arches, a motif taken from his master W. D. Butler. There was no doubt a benefit for the banking company in possessing a corporate architectural image, and it was only in the minor details of the decoration – elaborated or reduced according to the status of the town where the branch was to be built – that Caldbeck's designs differed. In the matter of country-house architecture his approach was much the same. Williamstown House, a moderate-sized Italianate villa near Castlebellingham, was designed by Caldbeck in 1856: its plan is repeated
113 and its style replicated at Clonhugh Lodge (Multyfarnham) in Co. Westmeath and at Kilbride Old Mansion (Kildalkey) in Co. Meath. Each house has a five-bay, two-storey front, with an advanced central porch flanked by columns and surmounted by three narrow round-headed windows and a bracketed eaves pediment. It may well be that other versions of this pleasantly unassertive design at Bloomsbury (Donaghpatrick), Glen House near Drogheda, and Rosnaree (Slane) are also by Caldbeck.

In 1845 the architect chosen by the Bank of Ireland to design its premises throughout the provinces was *Sandham Symes*, a pupil of William Farrell, whose unexceptional, polite architecture he had fully absorbed. In the course of fifteen years Symes was to design or redesign over forty banks. He popularized the palazzo-style bank building, in which segmental-headed windows provide a definitive Victorian motif, and the degree of elaboration – the presence or lack of sculptural keystones, aedicules and pediments to first-floor windows – varies, as with Caldbeck's work, according to the importance of each branch. The contrast between the Bank of Ireland branches in Drogheda (1873) and Navan (1879) well illustrates the progress of stylistic gradation. Symes designed two Italianate villas in North Leinster, Hartlands near Clonmellon in 1861, an intriguing L-shaped house with a tall square tower in the re-entrant angle and widely overhanging eaves, and Rahinstown near Summerhill of *c.* 1870, an enormous and conventional Italianate block in the manner of the great stucco palaces which Charles Lanyon had designed for his Ulster clients a full generation before. Another bank worth note is the handsome Ulster Bank in Longford, 1863, by *James Bell, Junior*, the son of the County Surveyor.

Victorian HOSPITALS AND SCHOOLS offered a contrast to the classicism of commercial design and were often built in a gabled collegiate idiom. An early and unusually fine example is provided by the former Louth County Infirmary in Dundalk, designed by *Thomas Smith* of Hertfordshire in 1834, whose sophisticated Tudor Gothic scheme includes the remarkable detail of a set of cast-iron corbel heads which are used as label stops on the arcades of the main façades. Much more sinister are the UNION WORKHOUSES which were erected throughout the entire country to designs of *George Wilkinson*, who was first induced to come to Ireland as architect to the Poor Law Commissioners in 1838. Wilkinson produced a series of standard designs with long ranges of utilitarian buildings straddling an axial line and approached through a detached entrance block which served as the governor's house. It was the government's intention that the buildings should be erected swiftly, and the repetitive nature of Wilkinson's designs, coupled with their meagre use of architectural detail – some label mouldings, paired bargeboards or simplified Elizabethan gables – meant that the timescale was closely observed; the majority of these intimidating structures were completed between 1840 and 1846. In better times many have been converted to hospitals, and others have been demolished. The former workhouse at Mullingar, now a hospital, is a characteristic example;
on the outskirts of the same town, St Loman's Hospital, built as 129
a lunatic asylum in 1855 to designs of *J. S. Mulvany*, is a hardly less threatening complex. Three storeys high and no fewer than forty-one bays in length, it expands the early Victorian collegiate style almost to its limits. The design, with repeated ranks of paired windows, seems to owe something to Pugin's work at Maynooth, but it is sharper and more firmly handled; Mulvany's careful division of the façade into sections, with gabled chimneystacks and further projecting gabled blocks, saves the design from monotony and even gives it grandeur. A similar effect, though on a

126 more human scale, is achieved at the Mercy Convent, Ardee, of 1858, an impressive Gothic school designed by *John Neville*, who practised architecture in Dundalk and in 1840, at the age of twenty-seven, was appointed Louth County Surveyor, a position which he held for forty-six years.

The creation of the post of County Surveyor was one result of the Grand Jury Act of 1836, which was intended to regulate the expenditure of government loans and public moneys throughout the Irish counties. The excessive 'plunder of the public purse' and laissez-faire attitudes which had characterized the earlier administration of public business in the Irish countryside would now end and the county administration of C19 Ireland take a more responsible – and a more upright – course. In the execution of his duties John Neville was to become one of the most conscientious, efficient and ultimately most powerful surveyors in the whole country, and his career may serve as an epitome of a mid-Victorian regional practice at its best. During his term of office Neville supervised the construction of an extensive country road system, designed and built the many bridges which were necessary for it, planned public buildings, maintained an extensive private practice and still found the time to publish the results of the practical experience he had gained in hydraulic engineering in the *Transactions of the Institute of Civil Engineers in Ireland*. In 1847 the Dublin and Belfast Junction Railway Company came up against the new authority of the surveyor during the laying of their Co. Louth lines, for Neville had severely criticized a number of the company's bridges, which he believed to be unsafe; in the next year he obtained a court order to have two taken down and to alter many others. The only large-scale public building which
111 Neville designed in his official capacity was the Louth County Gaol at Dundalk, a towered Italianate composition, disconcertingly like an Irish railway terminus or marine villa, built between 1845 and 1853. His country-house practice is in a similar understated classical style, which seems to some extent to depend on the example of William Caldbeck; the villas of Shanlis, near Ardee, built in 1858, and Cardistown, near Charlestown, 1865, are good examples. A further aspect of Neville's practice is demonstrated by the number of convents for which he made designs, perhaps because his two daughters, Barbara and Mary, had both become nuns. All Neville's convents were designed for the Sisters of Mercy: at Limerick in 1851, at Ardee in 1858, additions at Dundalk, and the convents at Roscommon and Omagh in 1859. In a government report on county surveyors of 1857 a number of witnesses criticized the lack of any architectural knowledge or quality in the works then being produced. The commission found, however, that there were some four or five surveyors in Ireland who were skilled architects and had managed to combine private practice with their county duties: Charles Lanyon, the surveyor of Co. Antrim, and John Neville were cited as the prime examples. At a time when the fields of both the civil engineer and the architect were rapidly enlarged, Neville's ability to succeed in both seems rare. By comparison, little is known of *James Bell*, an

architect and builder in Trim whom Maria Edgeworth knew as 'a plain, practical, chubby, innocent-looking youngish man with hair roughed up anyhow', who helped her with her cottage designs. Bell was appointed superintendent in 1834 and later became County Surveyor for Longford, a post which he held until 1868.

Later Victorian Architecture

The pattern of Irish architecure changes pace with the work of
William G. Murray, who was often employed by the Provincial
Bank. In 1846 he had designed the Hibernian Savings Bank
building at Kells, one of the earliest examples in the region of an
Italianate building intended for commercial use. His Provincial
Bank at Athlone of *c.* 1855 is a more solid design, not unlike
Wilkinson's station in the same town, with a shallow hipped roof
and rich modillion eaves cornice; but his bank at Omagh in Co.
Tyrone, built in 1853, changes to a type of Ruskinian Gothic
which seems to reflect something of the impact of Deane and
Woodward's Natural History Museum in Trinity College,
Dublin, and it is this style, in an even more eclectic form, which
is employed on the façade of the Provincial Bank in Drogheda of
c. 1865, which Murray probably designed. The Drogheda bank
uses a heady mixture of elements, with coupled shafts of polished
granite columns dividing the windows of the banking hall, foliated
capitals, moulded reveals to the upper floor windows, a C16 type
of cornice with deep console brackets and spherical stone bosses
embedded in its masonry. In the same street the Whitworth Hall, 12
built in 1864 to designs of the Belfast architect *William Joseph
Barre*, experiments with an equally unorthodox architecture in
brick, using triple-chamfered reveals to the first-floor windows,
decorative stone paterae in the façade and another emphatically
bracketed cornice at eaves level.

This sort of architecture represents a radical shift in taste and
a move towards the more expressive use of materials which is also
found in some of the LATER COUNTRY HOUSES of the C19. Here
the rebuilding of Castle Forbes by *J. J. McCarthy* must have had 123
a significant influence. The date of McCarthy's scheme for the
house is not clear, and subsequent alterations have almost completely
removed its original Gothic interior; what little remains is
in a distinctly new taste, exposing the building materials – pine
doors, Caen stone chimneypieces and stained-glass roof lights –
in a new way which emphasizes the sense of the house, even in
its interior, as a succession of *built* spaces. The dark grey walls of
Clonyn Castle, built for Lord Greville to designs of *John McCurdy* 122
between 1867 and 1876, emphasize its solid structure, and though
the castellated model of the house is distinctly old-fashioned for
its date, the random rubble construction with expressive white
pointing is equally characteristic of the taste of the period. So
too is the interior, which treats a country house like a Gothic 121
department store, open at its centre, with arcaded galleries supported
on squat marble shafts surrounding the central stair.

Later romantic houses are less extreme in character. There are
125 two notable examples, both near Navan: Dowdstown House of *c.* 1870, attributed to *John Lanyon*, of *Lanyon, Lynn and Lanyon* (possibly with the assistance of *Samuel Pepys Close*), which employs many of the picturesque tricks of the Lanyon office, and
124 Ardmulchan Castle, an exotic import in at least two respects, for it was built to the designs of the Edinburgh architect *Sidney Mitchell* (from 1902) and is in a distinctly English Elizabethan manorial style, constructed of brick and imported red sandstone for a Scotsman whose principal estate was in Angus. Ardmulchan has a superbly confident barrel-vaulted two-storey hall, lit by enormous mullioned windows and decorated with exuberant revived Mannerist plasterwork of the type associated with the court of James I. It is a fine design by one of Scotland's last and most brilliant exponents of the Picturesque.

The course of CATHOLIC CHURCH BUILDING in the last third of the C19 is not easily described. While most architects around 1850 had been prepared to work in a C13 lancet style, and had believed – or at any rate were content to accept the notion – that this represented 'the purest taste', by 1870 a wider range of styles prevailed. The greater variety was in part a consequence of the almost universal acceptance that Gothic architecture then enjoyed and of the artistic need, after a generation of 'early pointed' buildings, for younger architects to develop an alternative idiom. Just as, in an earlier era, continental classicism had been espoused by the hierarchy of the Catholic Church, so now the profession sought a greater variety of motifs in French and northern European forms. As nothing had altered the needs of clergy or congregations in these years, the architectural changes tended to be cosmetic. Windows became wider and were filled with patterns of bar tracery; façades gained horizontal arcading; wheel windows appeared on W fronts, and spires were given gablets and lucarnes and took on prettier silhouettes. The big church of St
131 Peter in Drogheda, designed in 1884 by *O'Neill & Byrne* and begun just one year after the death of John O'Neill, is a clear example of this shift of emphasis and contrasts interestingly with the same firm's more orthodox work at Ashbourne Church of 1882 or even with *W. H. Byrne*'s church at Stabannan, a regular lancet design, begun in 1884. By the time the rebuilding in Drogheda was complete – for Byrne was employed first to extend and only later to replace a Francis Johnston church, which J. J. McCarthy had already reworked – the old square-ended choir, an obligatory feature of church design in the 1850s, had been replaced by a polygonal sanctuary, which owed its origin to French architecture and which became a standard element in the many later churches by this firm.

A similar emphasis on continental models marks the work of *Pugin & Ashlin*, a partnership formed between *Edward Welby Pugin* and *George Coppinger Ashlin*, under which Ashlin took over responsibility for Pugin's work in Ireland from 1862 until 1869 and which served to introduce to Irish church building the Francophile motifs adopted by E. W. Pugin. The Dominican Church

of St Mary Magdalen in Drogheda, designed by Ashlin in 1870, masses in an unorthodox, bulky way with a squat saddleback tower, tucked into the corner of a transept, which has no place in English Gothic. Ashlin's church at Castletown-Delvin (1873) is 132
perhaps more characteristic, similar to many of the medium-sized churches he was to design for the suburban areas of Dublin, with a tower and spire set beside the gable end of the nave, which is dominated by a wide and deeply recessed geometrical window.

Both Byrne and Ashlin enjoyed huge church practices which continued well into the C20 and often brought them to work within and to alter interiors designed by other men. A third figure of this period, who was to make a distinctive contribution before his early death in 1899, is the younger *William Hague*, who was the son of a successful builder in Co. Cavan and, early in his career, had the good fortune to win at least three competitions – a Presbyterian church in Londonderry, Sligo Town Hall and the Bishop's Residence and Chapel (Cathedral House) at Mullingar. The churches at Culmullin (Dunshaughlin), 1876, Termonfeckin, 1883, and Ballynahowen, *c.* 1895, are pleasant examples of Hague's work in North Leinster; one of his finest designs, with a spacious and well-ordered interior, is the rich and ambitiously detailed Church of St Patrick at Trim, begun in 1891 and completed in its interior fittings by W. H. Byrne after Hague's death. In his later work Hague had collaborated with *T. F. McNamara*, who, like Byrne, completed a number of his works. The Church of St Michael at Castletown Geoghegan, 1885, is an attractive 133
and early design by McNamara working on his own. Its plan makes use of an interesting and economical pattern where an aisle-less nave opens, towards the sanctuary end, through paired arches into short transepts. This pattern was widely adopted in suburban and rural churches throughout the whole country.

Twentieth-century Architecture

Towards the end of the C19 the stylistic variety of church building was to be enriched by a number of motifs taken from the early Irish church. From this process, almost of archaeological quotation, there developed a type of architecture best described perhaps as medieval free-style but often referred to as HIBERNO-ROMANESQUE or more directly as the CELTIC REVIVAL style. In Co. Meath an early monument to these developments is the round-tower belfry built beside Slane Church at the end of the C18, anticipating architectural events by some seventy years. This little tower, however, is something of an oddity, and North Leinster does not contain any other early instances of Celtic Revival work. In this region it is work from the two biggest Catholic architectural offices which provides examples of the movement: George Ashlin, who had taken his clerk John Coleman into partnership and in the later years of his practice was to operate as *Ashlin & Coleman*, and William Byrne, who had changed the title of his practice from O'Neill & Byrne to *W. H. Byrne & Son*. Ashlin's work in this manner is never quite stylistically defined or

clearly derived from a single Romanesque source. Contemporary journalism found it hard to characterize, and it is probably best to note simply that a significant number of the later churches from Ashlin's office revert to round-headed windows in place of Gothic pointed designs and to square towers with pyramid or ogee-domed roofs instead of spires. The large church built in
135 1890 for the Redemptorists at Dundalk is a case in point (though the monastery itself is still in Ashlin's institutional Gothic style), while a later and pleasant example of the firm's Hiberno-Romanesque manner, which continued after Ashlin's death at the age of eighty-four in 1922, is provided by the Church of SS Peter and Paul at Dromiskin, built in 1926 and closely based on the earlier Church of the Sacred Heart near Newry, Co. Down, of 1916.

The Romanesque work of W. H. Byrne & Son divides into two categories. There is first a type of minimalist Romanesque: churches built by the firm around the turn of the century have the tidy, neat appearance of architecture that is workmanly – and not without elegance – but seems cold and lacking in character. These buildings are as immediately identifiable as the convent blocks built by the same firm, where an office style and the use of standard office detail swamp originality. Mellifont Parish Church, Tullyallen (Tinure Cross), Co. Louth, of 1898 and the churches of the Nativity and of Our Lady of Lourdes near Summerhill, built in 1901 and 1911, are clear examples of the benefits and the dangers of standardization. All have round-headed lancet windows, and big geometrical wheels in their gables, framed by slender colonnettes at the reveals. The firm's later manner is much more particular, reflecting the personal interest of *Ralph Byrne*, an eclectic designer whose understanding of historical style
136 was unsurpassed; the little Church of St Oliver Plunkett built at Blackrock in 1923 makes confident and convincing use of Hiberno-Romanesque motifs and of an Irish round tower. Byrne's most elaborate statement in this manner must be the multi-gabled Church of the Four Masters, built for Donegal town in 1931; the Blackrock church is a more straightforward design but it gains over the later work by its careful detail, and it makes good use of the varied textures of different stones.

The large Franciscan church of 1930 at Athlone and St Columban's College, built near Navan in 1934–43, are the last examples of the Hiberno-Romanesque style within North Leinster; both are by *Alfred Jones* of Jones & Kelly. As a C 20 descendant of King Cormack's little church at Cashel, Co. Tipperary, the
140 chapel in the College works well. Though the choice of style might seem unpromising for a collegiate church, the proportions of its interior are spacious and the design is enhanced by a generous and intelligent use of carefully selected Irish marble. The one other enormous institution from the early years of the
130 C 20 is St Finian's College, Mullingar, built in 1902–8 to designs of *J. J. O'Callaghan*, a late Victorian Dublin architect who enjoyed a successful and extensive commercial practice. Approached by a monumental flight of steps and entered through a massively heavy arcaded loggia, the college is rather like a railway company's

seaside hotel stranded in the Irish countryside. Its extraordinary bulk distils something of the sense of satisfaction that the Catholic hierarchy took in this building, but it is hard to imagine that the students for whom it was intended ever learnt to feel affection for its daunting façades.

Following the partition of Ireland in 1922, the architectural style of churches in this region has been dominated by a conservative classicism established and reinforced in the monumental work of *Ralph Byrne* at Mullingar in 1932 and at Athlone in 1935. The 137–9
construction of these buildings coincided with the emphatic assertion of the symbolic value of the architectural orders by the governments of Germany, Italy and Spain and gave currency to the classical idiom up to the opening of the Second World War.

The predominant conservatism of Irish taste has meant that in these four counties there is little recent architecture which expresses the ideals of Modernism. St Laurence's Community 141
School in Drogheda by *Michael Scott* of 1934 represents the idiom of the new architecture with metal-framed windows and horizontal glazing patterns; the Boys Technical Schools in Dundalk of 1935, by *John F. McGahon & Son*, develops a similar style. Otherwise there are few new buildings of note from this period. Isolationist and nationalist policies in the 1940s reduced the Irish economy virtually to a stand-still. When limited development became possible in the countryside in the 1950s and early 1960s, such new buildings as could be built were forced to adopt utilitarian methods of construction providing the maximum space at a minimal cost. Too often in towns in Leinster, and indeed throughout the country, no thought was given to the impact of alien and ersatz materials, or of routine building methods, on the existing character of a place. As a result much of the building activity of the last forty years in Ireland has diminished rather than enhanced the environment: only the utilitarianism of Modernism took root, while its basic philosophy of design and complementary concepts of form went for the most part unnoticed. The result has been a lot of very dull building: lumpish rectangular blocks, dropped down into the countryside or tacked onto older structures with an absolute disregard for the requirements of their site and for the most rudimentary principles of design. School buildings, hotel extensions and commercial premises all offend, with repetitive and undifferentiated units of building, curtain walls divided by concrete mullions, blank end gables of rustic brick, concrete paths and concrete paving, cement coping stones and mean little gates with underscaled ironwork. Such is the depressing legacy of the 1950s and the 1960s in the towns and countryside.

The art of architecture cannot thrive without an informed clientele, and until the later 1960s or early 1970s local business, local building committees, the bank companies and, let it be said, even the official government building agency, the Office of Public Works, took the most prosaic view of their various responsibilities. In this situation the commission of 1964 given by the General Electric Company to *Michael Scott & Partners* for a new factory

in Dundalk acquires special significance. Their building, on the W of the town, is a model of logical design and lucid articulation. Moreover it set a standard for local industrial buildings, to be
143 followed in 1970 by a second commission, now from the Carroll Cigarette Company, for a new factory S of the town. The Carroll factory is in a lighter idiom, designed by one of Michael Scott's younger partners, *Ronald Tallon* of what had become *Scott, Tallon, Walker*. The building is elegant, modern and beautifully conceived within its setting. If its forms today seem to derive too clearly from the example of Mies van der Rohe, and to reflect an era in which climatic considerations were of little interest to an architect, it still stands as a monument to its age and as a worthy exemplar of good modern design.

In the 1970s and the 1980s architecture in Ireland, when it is not just dull building, tended to reflect either the concerns of post-modernism, with its irreverent and often superficial allusions to past styles, or – and this is an increasing tendency – the desire to rehabilitate and therefore to retain old buildings for some new form of use. The work of *Fergus Flynn Rodgers* in and around Dundalk provides some noted examples of quirky, if witty, domestic and commercial post-modernism, while *Patrick Shaffrey's* West End Arcade of 1984 in Drogheda is an attractive example of rehabilitation and rebuilding within an established urban setting.

Churches provide one category of building in which contemporary architects have found continuous employment, and here it must be said that the Irish clergy, both Catholic and Protestant, often display a total disregard for the architecture entrusted to their care. As the Protestant community shrinks – in the twenty-six counties of the Republic of Ireland it now represents no more than 3.8 per cent of the entire population – churches are closed, deconsecrated and unroofed, with little consideration of their relative architectural merit or of the value of the stained glass and monuments they contain. A minority community cannot preserve, without state aid, its entire architectural inheritance, and when churches of the quality of Portneshangan are lost without notice, support or prior discussion, the entire nation is left worse off. Some redundant Church of Ireland churches have found new uses as heritage centres, community buildings and even as holiday homes, but they are singularly few within North Leinster.

With the Catholic church it is not yet falling numbers, though these must cause concern, which threaten historic buildings: rather it is the clergy's taste for the new. In conservation circles, people who find the picturesque appealing rarely choose to live in the type of cramped and ill-lit period cottages whose preservation they promote, and there is, no doubt, a similar observation to be made in justification of the type of drastic renovation and even total rebuilding of many Irish C19 churches. A small T-plan chapel, whitewashed and set behind a wall of limestone rubble, may charm the visitor who sees it once, yet it is possible that the building gives less satisfaction to those who have to use it regularly, week in and week out. Architectural historians, and

those members of the public who are concerned for the history of their country, enjoy old buildings. They value the sense of place which their presence can reinforce, yet the clergy and the members of a congregation are often encouraged to look for something new. As a result too much that was of real quality has been lost in North Leinster, and too often, when the shell of a building has survived, an uncompromising enthusiasm for the requirements of the new liturgy – essentially metaphysical and inimical to built objects – has been adduced as a pretext for the removal of traditional altars and the destruction of sanctuary furnishings. The work of the Catholic church architects of the Victorian period in Ireland deserves more careful consideration and, indeed, a future in the next century. North Leinster provides some instances of proper conservation – notably at Grange Church of 1762 – but there are other instances where modern designs of quality, such as the church at Ardee by *Guy Moloney*, have been achieved only at the cost of abandoning a distinguished earlier building which took its place well within the fabric of the town. Other new churches which have added to the interest of the region are the Church of the Redeemer, Dundalk, of 1966 by *Frank Corr & Oonagh Madden*, an uncompromising fan-shaped structure with a wide and spacious interior, built on a green-field site; Our Lady Queen of Peace at Coosan, Athlone, of 1973 by *Noel Heavey*, with a ribbed ceiling which floats above the congregation; and the churches by *Liam McCormick* at Laytown, near Julianstown, of
1979 and in Julianstown of 1982, which develop respectively an 142
architecture of white rough-cast walls and the romantic potential of large and high slate roofs, pitched in the countryside almost like a tent.

A NOTE ON BUILDING MATERIALS

BY CHRISTINE CASEY

In contrast to the stupendous variety of rock formation in the area of North West Ulster, the flat central plain of Ireland which incorporates most of North Leinster is remarkably homogeneous in its geological formation. Here, instead of dramatic outcrops of granite, quartz, schist and basalt, are vast low-lying beds of limestone interspersed at intervals by veins of slate or sandstone. While for the geologist this may render the region a less lively subject for analysis, the case is different for architectural enthusiasts, whose pleasure will stem rather from the area's diverse and inventive use of available materials and from the many nuances of colour and texture to be found in the deposits of the various localities. As a more workable stone than the igneous rocks or the granites of northern Ireland, limestone provided a greater incentive to masons to perfect their craft, and some of the finest workmanship in the entire country is to be found along the river Boyne. The widespread deposits of limestone of good quality similarly ensured that crisp squared or coursed rubble masonry was as viable as the more common Ulster harled or rough-cast finishing. Dressed ashlar masonry, which first made its appearance in Ireland with the works of the Surveyor General, Sir William Robinson, in the later C17, did not make distinct progress in Ireland for a hundred years. In Louth and Meath, however, it came into use in the early C18, following the lead of Speaker Conolly's great house at Castletown in Co. Kildare. In Ulster the first proper ashlar house was not built until Downhill of 1784: here spectacular and colourful scenery might be said to have claimed its price, while the comparatively drab plains of the Pale yielded a wealth of first-rate building stone.

In the medieval period builders almost invariably used local materials for general work, procuring other, more distant, stone only for the decorative or finer parts of a building. Greywacke sandstones and mudstones of the Silurian period are plentiful in North Leinster and are the dominant rocks to be found in Co. Louth. The early medieval stone-roofed oratories at Louth and Kells are good instances of local Silurian whinstone, a volcanic stone which occurs in all clay-slate rocks. Difficult to work and used principally as rubble, it is employed here to produce ambitious roof structures, the thinly cleaved flags masterfully superimposed in a barely perceptible step-like construction. The round towers also at Kells and at Monasterboice were built of thin slate quarried locally. At Mellifont too most of the rubble walling was composed of slate, and evidence of quarrying still remains near the monastery gatehouse. The monastic settlement at Kells made particular use of this stone on account of its position on the narrow ridge of slate which divides the two principal limestone deposits of Meath. Local fields of green whinstone were similarly utilized in medieval building construction at Carlingford, Co. Louth. Other areas were more fortunate and settlements such as the borough of Trim and the Cistercian monastery at Bective had plentiful supplies of local grey limestone, which they used in rubble walling.

Most of these materials, though eminently suitable for general building purposes, were not pliable enough for the framing and adornment of apertures, and in any conscious architectural work of the early medieval period sandstone of some kind is employed for the surrounds and details of doors and windows. Though deposits are modest in comparison to the quantity of both slate and limestone, some sandstone is found in North Leinster: in Meath, along the S bank of the Boyne between Navan and the sea, and at Hayestown, NW of Kells, near Kingscourt. Longford's geological formation, though predominantly a continuation of the slate areas of S Ulster, also includes some beds of yellow sandstone and of sandstone conglomerates, particularly in the vicinity of Ardagh and Longford town. In Westmeath some patches of red sandstone can be found at Moate and Killucan, though these apparently have not been much exploited by builders. The nearest sandstone in the vicinity of Louth is a hard gritty variety found at Nobber in NE Meath.

Although the colour and quality of masonry often allow identification of the source quarry, particularly in the case of finer limestones, this is not always so with less pure formations. At Mellifont, for instance, the source for the hard quartzy sandstone of the dressed masonry is still unclear; did it come from the Kingscourt quarries, as claimed by George Wilkinson in his C19 survey, or from the more plausible source at Johnstown near Navan, from whence it might have been transported along the Boyne? At Kells, on the other hand, the sandstone used for the dressings of the round tower and for the monumental sculptural crosses is sure to have come from NW Meath. Throughout the entire area of North Leinster sandstone mouldings were used extensively from the C11 to the mid-C13. Examples abound: at Dunshaughlin a pre-Romanesque sandstone lintel; at Monasterboice the dressings of the round tower; at Newtown Trim an old red sandstone double sedilia and, at Trim Castle, arch frames and the springers of the great hall, again of the old red variety. Dressings were not entirely confined to sandstone, however, and in the case of wealthy foundations foreign stones were sometimes imported for polychromatic effect. At Mellifont during the C13, when Anglo-Norman authority was at its strongest, soft fine-grained limestone for sculptural work was imported from Caen in Normandy. Similarly at Drogheda and Monasterboice evidence survives of Dundry stone from Somersetshire, a soft oolitic limestone which was imported into Ireland during the C13. Fragments of colonnettes and black basalt capitals to the lancet windows of the cathedral at Newtown Trim – similar to contemporary work at Christ Church, Dublin – suggest the transportation of stone either from Ulster or from England or Wales.

When resources were more limited and fine materials for building were unobtainable, craftsmen improvised in order to produce an effect of opulence. Though paint fragments on medieval buildings are now few and hard to find, the piscina at Fore Abbey preserves an all-over pattern of white 'bricks', drawn with blue pointing and decorated with rosettes, which it is believed would originally have covered all the walls of the church – an imitation of the effect of smooth masonry drawn on walls of rough limestone rubble erected on the furthermost perimeter of the Norman Pale.

From *c.* 1260, thanks to more sophisticated quarrying and stone-cutting techniques, native limestone came into use for dressed masonry as well as for general building purposes, thereby achieving sharper and more durable carved work. Throughout the ensuing three centuries, crisply wrought window tracery, from the wilds of Saints Island in Co. Longford to the urbanity of Dunsany and Killeen, bears witness to the quality of this hard grey crystalline stone in achieving both clean lines and intricate profiles. Equally demonstrative of its calibre are the simpler carved and cusped lights of late medieval tower houses, as at Roodstown, near Stabannan, Co. Louth, or the carved ornament
54 of spandrels, as at Talbot's Castle, Trim, and the Mint at Carlingford, the inscriptions and ornaments on Donore Castle near Horseleap in Co. Westmeath, and the cloister arcades at Bective and Fore.

An exception to the habitual use of limestone for dressed work is seen in Co. Longford, where the tower house of Castlerea near Ardagh employs a local hybrid of red sandstone, quartz pebble and limestone quarried from Slieve Caldragh and appropriately called 'pudding stone'.

The Longford towers are in fact characterized by a looser masonry than their counterparts within the Pale. Perhaps nowhere more than in the tower houses of Meath and Louth is the quality of late medieval limestone masonry so forcefully manifest. The sharp arrised angularity of Roodstown Castle and the curvilinear silhouette of Kilincoole Castle (Readypenny Crossroads), both in Co. Louth, are consummate examples of the medieval mason's art. In Meath, arguably the most spectacular instance of early limestone masonry in the entire region is Lynch's Castle at Summerhill. In ecclesiastical building, undoubtedly the most memorable masonry achievement is the stupendous Yellow Steeple at Trim, with its virtually airborne spiral stair. The use of random, squared or rubble limestone continued throughout the post-medieval period, and despite an increasing preference for ashlar it remained a standard walling material for public and domestic architecture. In the C18 *Richard Castle* used rough limestone to good effect at houses such as Belvedere or Bellinter, and particularly so at Whitewood Lodge in Co. Meath, where the solid coarse masonry perfectly complements the plain stocky quality of the architect's design.

While rubble walling in slate or limestone continued to be used for general building purposes, the quarrying of fine limestone developed markedly, until by the C18 the employment of ashlar masonry for public and domestic uses was both possible and desirable. The great mansion of Summerhill, begun in 1731, was undoubtedly the region's most spectacular instance of smoothly dressed stone, though the mid-C18 public buildings of Drogheda and a number of smaller country houses demonstrate its more general usage.

There were throughout the region ten or more quarries of good-quality stone, the best of these along the Boyne in Louth and Meath. The northernmost limestone quarry of note was at Ross beside Lough Sheelin, the source of a pale, almost white limestone, seen in rough form at Ross Castle near Finnea and formerly in finely chiselled splendour at Loughcrew House (demolished in 1968). The columns of Longford Cathedral portico were also from Ross quarry. A darker, though still whitish-grey, strain was quarried near Loughcrew, at Crossdrum. More famous than either of these, however, is Ardbraccan stone, a fine very crystalline light grey stone, widely used throughout the entire county and nowhere better seen than in the impeccable droved ashlar of Ardbraccan House itself. A somewhat paler silvery limestone was quarried close to Drogheda at Sheep-Hill in Co. Louth, and this provided the stone for most of Drogheda's Georgian public buildings. The *Darley family* of stonecutters, masons and builders were closely associated with the Louth–Meath limestone quarries and with building activity throughout the area. The standard of workmanship which could be achieved in the dressing and assemblage of masonry is best seen in the exacting craftsmanship of *Francis Johnston*'s Townley Hall, begun in 1794. Sheep-Hill limestone continued to be used throughout the C19 and was extensively employed in G. E. Street's restoration of Christ Church Cathedral, Dublin.

In Westmeath and Longford limestone, though plentiful, was not as high in quality as that of the eastern counties, tending to be either darker or more blue in colour. Near Mullingar a black type of stone was quarried, similar to the dark blue-black strain found at Creeve, near Longford, and also at Granard and Rathcline. Of these the Creeve limestone, capable of producing blocks of 10 ft by 6 ft (3 m by 1.8 m), was the most coveted; it can be seen in the masonry of Carriglass Manor. Further afield, near Moate in Co. Westmeath, a pale watery-blue stone was found, a distinctive strain memorable particularly in *John Hargrave*'s façade of Moate Courthouse (1828). The early C20 County Buildings at Mullingar has too a particularly bluish hue to the stone. The darker calp limestones, though not coveted by Georgian builders, truly came into their own during the C19, when interest in polychromatic effects brought about the juxtaposition of dark, almost black limestone rubble with silver or white-grey freestone dressings. The church towers at Dunleer and Dromin

(Stabannan) in Co. Louth spring to mind, as do *John Murray*'s church at Togher and the Puginesque convent by *John Neville* at Ardee. The former Catholic church at Mullingar also used a black local stone, together with a fine silver limestone. Of surviving buildings, the sombre dark grey masonry of Clonyn Castle provides a prominent example. Development away from a finely chiselled finish to rougher textural effects similarly promoted the use of less genteel materials, in particular the rock-facing of masonry which found such popularity from the early C19 onward. *George Ashlin*'s work throughout the region affords plentiful examples of this manner.

Rough-cast, stuccoed and rendered buildings abound in North Leinster, as they do throughout Ireland. *Francis Johnston*'s cool stuccoed elegance at Cloncarneel (Kildalkey), *John MacNeill*'s colonial stucco at Mountpleasant (Ballymascanlon) or *George Papworth*'s Italianate at Middleton Park (*see* Castletown Geogheghan) are all as accomplished in their way as the Darleys' earlier ashlar. The baking of bricks was widespread throughout the region certainly from the mid-C18. Beaulieu, probably of 1710–20, is noteworthy in this context for its sparing employment of brick, suggesting a limited, perhaps foreign source of supply in the later Stuart period. The Markethouse at Longford, conceivably of late C17 date, is probably the earliest surviving instance of brick construction in North Leinster, while the mid-C18 town houses of Drogheda are the area's most eloquent expression of the craft. Later C19 interest in polychromy is reflected in the use of blue and yellow industrial brick, seen particularly in the buildings of the Great Northern Railway in Louth and Meath.

The homogeneous character of North Leinster's geological formation has the natural effect of highlighting the use of any vaguely uncommon building materials. The most memorable example of Portland stone masonry in the region is undoubtedly the very grand portico of Dundalk Courthouse (1813–19), a rare instance of this expensive material being imported for a provincial building project. Sandstone, used extensively for carved work in the early Middle Ages but eclipsed by limestone in the C13, underwent a modest renaissance in the Victorian period. The absence of any large sandstone beds in the region, however, made extensive use impossible, and the few memorable sandstone buildings of North Leinster are all constructed from imported stone. Two notable instances are *Thomas Turner*'s screen at St Patrick's Pro-Cathedral, Dundalk (1849), made from Glasgow sandstone and now sadly corroded, and Ardmulchan Castle (1902–4), the sandstone for which was brought from its builder's Scottish estate. While no granite is to be found in the flat lands of North Leinster, the proximity of Newry and Mourne granite ensured that the stone was employed in the NE of the region, principally at Dundalk and the surrounding area. St Patrick's Pro-Cathedral and the Courthouse at Dundalk are good crisp examples of this hard quartzy stone, which was also used extensively in Louth during the Victorian period for rusticated and vermiculated work.

If the essential architectural material of North Leinster is stone, timber and metal, as the nuts and bolts of building construction, also merit attention. With medieval buildings the problem is decay; while the bolt-holes, bar-holes, glass-grooves, portcullis grooves and door-checks survive in many a castle and tower house, the building elements that once occupied these places have long since departed. The last surviving timber-framed building in the region, the Bathe House in Drogheda, was demolished in the early C 19.

Original roof timbers, though more in evidence, are also of limited extent and often difficult of access. One notable exception, recently dated, is the massive one-foot-square oak beam which roofs the ground-floor chamber of Tyrrellspass Castle. The tree from which this was made began to grow in 1280 and was felled in the autumn of 1410, a neat *terminus ante quem* for the building of the castle and a vivid evocation of building activity in the late medieval period. A further reminder of early methods of construction is the widespread evidence of wickerwork centering, to be seen on many late medieval vaults throughout North Leinster: King John's Castle at Carlingford, Kilincoole Castle (Readypenny Crossroads) in Co. Louth and Moymet Castle in Co. Meath have clear examples. Similarly the innumerable putlock holes which chequer the walls of churches and abbeys throughout the region recall the scaffolding systems which made these buildings possible.

In the C 17 and C 18 the wainscotting of interiors as an insulation against cold and damp ensured that joinery played an increasing role in building practice. Sadly most of these rooms are now gone; the most conspicuous recent losses in North Leinster are the oak-panelled interiors of Platten Hall near Duleek in Co. Meath and the Henry Singleton House in Drogheda. Survivals include the early C 18 entrance halls at Ballinlough Castle and Drewstown House and individual rooms at Bellinter, Swainstown (Kilmessan) and Rathkenny House in Co. Meath. In the early part of the C 18 the bulk of ornamental joinery was executed in oak, whereas in the later Georgian period mahogany was increasingly used. The neoclassical taste for finely droved ashlar masonry found its parallel in a preference for smoothly finished joinery with thin applied mouldings, in contrast to the sturdy fielded panelling of the early Georgian period. At Ardbraccan in Co. 79
Meath, the curving of the inner edge of the mahogany doors used throughout the ground floor, all on a swivel rather than a hinge, offers a measure of the absolute refinement of late C 18 building.

Metalwork is a more valuable and reusable commodity than old timbers, so it is hardly surprising that no early example has survived in the buildings of North Leinster. The C 18 is somewhat better served, again by the instance of Drogheda, where many Georgian town house railings and lamp-posts still remain. The Victorian period is the richest in decorative metalwork, in particular at Dundalk, where Alexander Shekleton's iron works produced a wealth of first-rate cast-iron ornament, still visible in window grilles, balconies, railings and ridge-cresting throughout the town. A singular item produced by the firm and one of the oddities of the region is a series of cast-iron corbel heads which form the exterior label stops of the early C 19 Tudor-Gothic former Louth County Infirmary at Dundalk.

THE EARLIEST ARCHITECTURE IN NORTH LEINSTER

BY GEORGE EOGAN

Mesolithic people, the earliest inhabitants of the modern counties of North Leinster (*c.* 8000–4000 B.C.), have left only limited traces of their existence. These consist of impermanent camp sites on the sea coast or lake shore which were used by a people taking fish. No evidence for buildings has come to light, although hut sites are known from other parts of the country, such as Mount Sandel in Co. Derry. Their tool range was limited to flint blades that could have been used in fishing and scrapers for dressing wood or hides.

As soon as the earliest farming communities had been established (between 4000 and 3000 B.C.) major changes took place. These Neolithic people exploited the natural resources of their country to a far greater extent. They collected a special type of rock, from as far afield as North Antrim, for making stone axes and they utilized the land for growing crops and keeping domestic animals. That they lived in fairly substantial houses of up to 12 metres long is demonstrated by a wooden building excavated at Knowth, which measured 10.70 m by 9.10 m internally. This is one of the earliest examples of domestic architecture in North Leinster.

Perhaps the most remarkable activity of these people was the ritual practices which centred on their burials and involved the building of tombs. For these, single large stones – megaliths – were used, some of a truly spectacular size, and were manoeuvred into place by skilful building techniques which in themselves represent a remarkable achievement. Two types of Neolithic tomb are known: one is the long barrow tomb, of which there are two sub-forms, the court tomb and what appears to be a derivative of it, the portal tomb, commonly known in Ireland as a dolmen; the other is the passage tomb. In their original form both types were covered with stone or earthen mounds, though, as the material surrounding portal tombs is now almost always completely eroded, it may be that their cap-stones were intended to stand exposed. A third main type of megalithic tomb, the wedge-shaped tomb, comes at the end of the series.

Court tombs are represented in these four counties by a dozen examples, nearly all of them concentrated in the Cooley peninsula. These are part of a much wider distribution of up to 400 such tombs which are found N of a line from Dundalk Bay to Connemara. Within the overall family of court tombs there are variations, but in North Leinster the vast majority are single

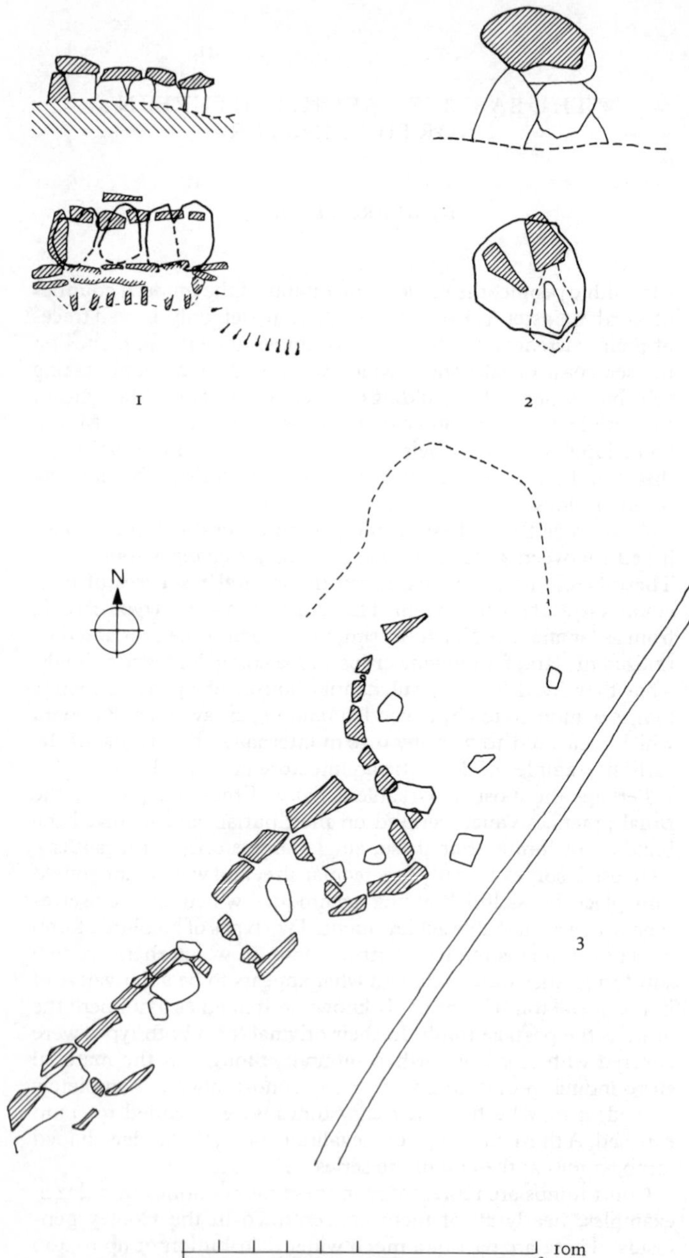

1. Paddock. Wedge-shaped tomb. 2. Proleek. Portal tomb.
3. Rockmarshall. Court tomb

tombs. None is intact, though in some cases a considerable amount of the structure survives. In a single court tomb the long stone mound, or cairn, is trapezoidal in shape. For an edging, upright stones could have been used. The court, at the broader eastern end, is generally semicircular in plan and is faced by large uprights. The entrance to the burial chamber is at the centre of the court, and the stones which flank the entrance are usually the tallest in the façade. The burial chamber is approximately parallel-sided and is formed by upright stones – orthostats – on the sides and roofed by lintels transversely placed. To increase the height, or to narrow the width, limited corbelling was sometimes used, but it is more normal for the lintels to rest directly on the orthostats. The chamber is always divided into two or more segments by the use of a jamb stone on either side and a sillstone across the floor in between. Sometimes there are small subsidiary chambers placed laterally within the cairn.

The burial rite was cremation, and there is evidence of communal burial. Grave goods include undecorated round-based shouldered pottery vessels, leaf- and lozenge-shaped flint arrowheads, hollow and rounded scrapers in flint, and polished stone axes. It is rare to find items of personal adornment such as beads. The single court tomb at Rockmarshall (near Ballymascanlon), Co. Louth, is a good example of the type.

Structurally and ritually the dual court tombs are similar, the main difference of course being that there is a semicircular, or approximately semicircular, court at each end of the cairn, which tends to be rectangular. Accordingly the burial chambers are back-to-back. The only definite example of a dual court tomb in North Leinster is at COMMONS, also in Co. Louth, near Carlingford, but its preservation is limited. Here the cairn is about 22 m long. One burial chamber is about 10 m long, averages 1.3 m in width and may have been divided into three segments of similar length. The other chamber is much shorter, 4.4 m long, and averages 1.2 m in width. It is divided into two segments.

There are four known portal tombs in the area under review. Visually these are spectacular monuments, as a visit to PROLEEK, in the grounds of Ballymascanlon House, just N of Dundalk, shows. Here, unencumbered by cairn or other covering mound, a massive cap-stone, nearly 4 m long and over 3 m wide, sits atop three uprights 2.3 m in height. Basically a portal tomb consists of a small rectangular chamber formed by upright stones, with a portal at the eastern end. This consists of the two tallest uprights and a sillstone between. Today portal tombs have a denuded appearance; nevertheless there is clear evidence for the presence of a cairn, either long, as at Ballykeel in South Armagh, or rounded, as at Aghnaskeagh near Proleek. There are about 180 known examples in Ireland, mainly in the northern two-thirds of the country, though there is also a group with an eastern distribution southwards to Waterford. The type is also found across the Irish Sea in Wales and Cornwall. Portal tombs appear to have originated in Ireland, and it is thought that their forerunners may have been the lateral chambers in court tombs already referred to. It is worth noting that in both the burial rite and grave goods are similar.

The other type of Neolithic megalithic tomb is altogether more spectacular and grand. This is the passage tomb, of which there are up to a hundred examples in North Leinster. They are concentrated in the valleys of the Boyne and the Blackwater, and it is also in that region that the most outstanding examples of this type of monument, not only by Irish but also by European standards, are found. The passage tomb is an international type which in Ireland began to be built *c.* 3000 B.C. On insular distribution it is represented by many hundreds of examples, with a continental distribution extending from southern Spain to southern Sweden and in Ireland and the W of Britain right up to the Shetland Islands. In Ireland there are perhaps three hundred examples. Again the main concentration is to the N of the central plain, but some tombs are also found as far S as Wicklow and Waterford and in Tipperary. There are variations in tomb plan, but, as the name implies, monuments of this class all have a passage leading into a chamber. The covering mound of stones or earth is circular and is delimited by large stone blocks – kerbstones – set round the edge. Passage tombs were usually built on elevations, sometimes on mountain-tops, and were concentrated in groups as cemeteries. Indeed it is in the area covered by this volume that two of Europe's most notable passage tomb cemeteries are found: one in that portion of the Boyne valley between Slane and Oldbridge called Brugh na Boínne, and the other not far from the source of the Blackwater, a tributary of the Boyne, at Sliabh na Caillighe or Loughcrew.

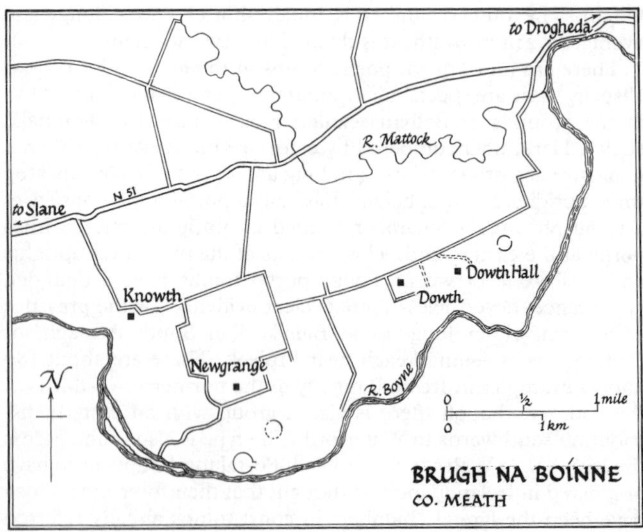

While Brugh na Boínne is a low-lying area, the three outstanding sites, Newgrange, Dowth and Knowth, are prominently situated on hill-tops. These, and indeed the other tombs in the cemetery, are remarkable sites whose building demanded major contributions from society, not only materially but also educationally, as such elaborate buildings could not have been constructed without the aid of trained experts in design and construction on the one hand and skilled builders and craftsmen on the other. At the time when any one of the three great sites was being constructed this was undoubtedly the largest building programme then under way in any part of Ireland, and even in contemporary western and northern Europe. This becomes clear when we examine these sites.

The building of NEWGRANGE involved the procuring of at least 170 large stones, each over a tonne in weight, which, since 16
most were of a distinctive type of palaeozoic rock, must have been derived from an area at least two miles away to the N, possibly farther. This meant large-scale transportation. The cairn, which covers just over an acre (two-fifths of a hectare) and is 11 m at its maximum height, could have consumed at least 200,000 tonnes of stones. These had to be collected over the surfaces of the fields or in the bed of the river Boyne. The edging is formed with ninety-seven kerbstones, of which the smallest is 1.7 m long; many are 2 m in length, and the largest is 4.5 m. The average is 1.2 m in height above the old ground surface. At present the front of the tomb, above the kerbstones, has a near-vertical face of quartz stones, almost 3 m high, which is secured and maintained in position by a reinforced concrete wall constructed behind it. Professor Michael O'Kelly, who excavated Newgrange, believed that this reproduced the original appearance of the edge of the cairn, but it would have been very difficult to build a unifaced vertical wall of this height using angular quartz stones, especially where the original backing was the loose cairn stones of the mound. It is more likely that the quartz stones were spread at ground level, where they were found, or else that they were used on the sloping side of the cairn.

The entrance to the tomb is on the SE side and is aligned so as to allow the rising sun briefly to penetrate right into the chamber at dawn on 21 December, the shortest day in each year. The tomb is 24 m in total length, and consists of a parallel-sided passage, virtually 19 m long and averaging 1 m wide, leading into a chamber. Forty-three orthostats, each around 2 m in height, were used in the construction of the passage. Extra slabs were placed on top of these to increase the height, and this is particularly the case in the inner half of the passage. The roof consisted of large transversely placed slabs above the orthostats, of which the two outer examples are up to 4 m long. In plan the central area of the tomb is not very pronounced; a recess branches off to both left and right, while at the end there is a third recess, making a 'cruciform' arrangement which is characteristic of passage tombs. A remarkable feature of the chamber is its roof, whose construction was an outstanding achievement. Above the orthostats

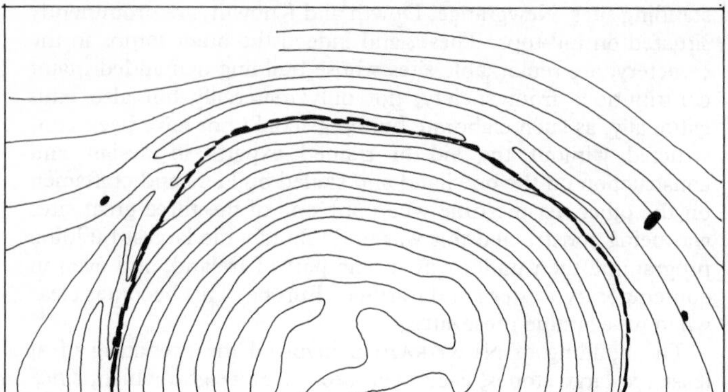

Newgrange. General plan

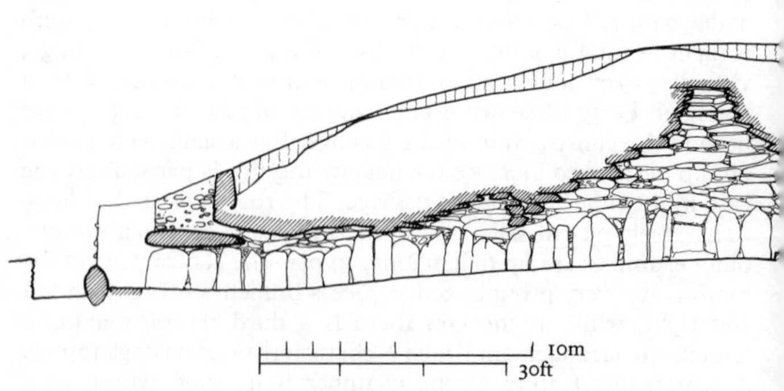

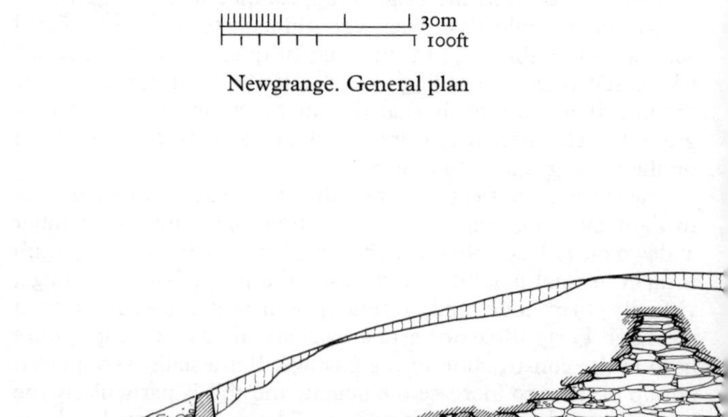

Newgrange. Sectional elevation

dry-stone work makes skilful use of the corbelling technique to create a beehive-shaped structure, some 6 m high, which is roofed by a single cap-stone.

Detailed information about DOWTH is less. Diggings in the earlier part of the C 19 have mutilated part of the principal mound, which now has a deep hollow in its crown, with the stone cover exposed. The mound is 85 m in diameter and 15 m in height and covers two-fifths of a hectare. It is delimited by a series of kerbstones; not all of these are visible, but the total appears to be about 115. The site has two tombs, both facing westwards, and it is possible that excavation might produce more.

Dowth North is a cruciform tomb with an annexe in the shape of a reverse L opening off the right-hand recess. The main tomb, almost 15 m in total length, consists of a parallel-sided passage slightly over 10 m long, though about 2.5 m is now missing owing to the digging of a souterrain – an underground storage chamber – during the early Christian period. The surviving portion is 8.2 m long and almost 1 m in average width and is formed by seventeen orthostats roofed by eight cap-stones. The chamber is 3.85 m long and is formed by nineteen orthostats. It appears to have had a corbelled roof but was in a ruinous state when discovered in 1847. Three sillstones divide the passage into three segments.

From the back of the kerbstone before the entrance to the inner face of the backstone of the chamber, Dowth South is 9 m long. The passage, 4.5 m long, widens from 75 cm at the entrance to 1.3 m at the inner end, where a sillstone marks it off from the chamber. It is constructed from three orthostats on either side and roofed with four cap-stones. The rounded chamber, about 5 m in diameter, was constructed from fifteen or possibly sixteen orthostats. It is likely that the roof was corbelled, but it had collapsed at the time of discovery. Leading off the chamber on the right-hand side there is a wedge-shaped recess, 2.9 m long, formed from three orthostats, one on each side and one at the back, and widening inwards. The roof, which consists of slabs placed in corbel fashion, is about 2 m in height.

The third site, KNOWTH, is at the western end of the cemetery. A remarkable feature here is the existence of a cemetery of about twenty individual tombs. The form of individual tombs varies between cruciform and undifferentiated, and amongst them there are some substantial structures, such as Sites 2 and 15, with mounds up to 20 m in diameter and passages that are 13.5 m and 9.2 m in length. The principal mound, which is circular in form, measures 80 m by 95 m and is about 10 m in height. The area covered is about an acre and a half, or three-fifths of a hectare. The central part of the mound consists exclusively of loose stones, but the outer part is of alternating layers of redeposited turfs, boulder clay, shale and small stones. This was probably intended to stabilize the edge, which at ground level was bordered by 127 kerbstones averaging over a metre in length. The mound covers two large tombs. The line of kerbs curves inwards on both the E and W sides to form a shallow recessed area before the entrance to each tomb. These were placed back-to-back. The Western

Tomb, discovered in 1967, is 34.2 m long. The digging of a ditch in late Iron Age times (the early centuries A.D.) destroyed about 4 m of the passage. If it extended to the kerb it must have been built from about ninety-four orthostats; today eighty survive. The lintels usually rested on the orthostats, but in some places, especially within the chamber, the heights of the sides were increased by the use of smaller stones on top of the orthostats. The parallel-sided passage, averaging about 1 m wide, is straight for over three-quarters of the way; it then bends slightly to the right, and immediately after the bend there is a sillstone. Shortly beyond this the passage widens into a sort of bottle-shaped chamber that is sub-divided by two sillstones. From the bend inwards the passage also increases in height and the inner cap-stones are larger than usual.

The Eastern Tomb at Knowth was discovered in 1968. It is slightly over 40 m long and is thus the longest megalithic passage tomb known. The digging of the late Iron Age ditch also destroyed part of the straight passage, which presumably extended out to the back of the kerbstone and was therefore very long, with eighty-seven orthostats, seventy-three of which survive. The passage is 85 cm in width. The orthostats average 1.5 m in height above the old surface. Fifty-two cap-stones survive, but originally there would have been another four or five. Sometimes they rested directly on the orthostats, but in some places flatstones, including large rectangular flags 1 m long, were placed on top. This is especially so in the inner portion of the passage, where a considerable amount of dry-stone walling was used to increase the height of the sides. There is a sillstone close to the junction with the chamber and another one a little further back. The chamber is cruciform and, as is usual, the right-hand recess is the largest. It was constructed from twenty-one orthostats and measures 8.16 m across and 5.6 m in length. The roof, 6 m in height, is beehive-shaped and was built by corbelling.

In addition to the three majestic monuments, up to forty mounds or the remains of mounds occur within the cemetery. Some of these are quite substantial structures and show that considerable care and planning went into their construction. Although passage tombs are spread throughout the Brugh na Boínne cemetery, there is a major concentration of up to twenty tombs at Knowth (as already mentioned), fewer at Newgrange and Ballincrad. Future excavations may reveal a concentration close to the large Dowth tomb.

14, 15 The other outstanding cemetery is at LOUGHCREW, Sliabh na Caillighe, close to Oldcastle. This has a more dramatic location in hill country and consists of around thirty tombs. They concentrate in three main clusters, Carnbane West, Carnbane East and Patrickstown. Visitors may gain access to the principal monuments at both Carnbane East and West. As at Brugh na Boínne each summit has a prominent site – two on Carnbane West – with smaller tombs close by. The larger of the two, Cairn D, is 55 m in diameter; its chamber has not yet been discovered. The other main site, Cairn L, is smaller, 41 m in diameter, and is surrounded by forty-three kerbstones, which are curved inwards before the entrance. Today there is a 6 m gap between the kerb and the start of the passage, and evidence is not available to indicate whether the passage originally extended to the kerb. The passage is 4.3 m long and about 1 m in average width. There is a substantial, elongated chamber, 5 m long, which, unusually, has eight internal recesses, although the cruciform tradition is maintained by the fact that the end recess and those about the middle on each side are more prominent. The chamber on the right is the largest, as is customary.

The central site, Cairn T, Carnbane East, is the finest site in the cemetery, and probably even the finest within Ireland outside the three great Brugh na Boínne tombs. The cairn is 35 m in diameter and is delimited by thirty-nine kerbstones. These curve inwards to form a recess before the entrance to the tomb on the eastern side. The tomb is a well-defined example of a cruciform tomb, with a prominent central octagonal-shaped area which is 2.5 m long. The passage, a little over 4 m long, averages 1.3 m in width and is constructed with ten orthostats, but a pair of stones, set jamb-like on either side, has the effect of dividing the passage into inner and outer segments. Surveys of the tomb prepared in the C19 also show a sillstone across the passage between these 'jambs'. The chamber is constructed of fifteen orthostats, and there is a sillstone across the entrance to each recess and to the passage. The chamber, including the recesses, is 5 m across and slightly over 3 m in height; the roof was apparently corbelled but has been damaged.

In the coastal lands of Meath SE of Duleek, and also in adjoining parts of Co. Dublin, there is a group of passage tombs, now poorly preserved, some of which have even been eroded by coastal action. A little way inland, on a prominent ridge overlooking the sea, there is a group of some half-dozen mounds at FOURKNOCKS. Three have been excavated; one seems to be of Early Bronze Age date, but the other two are passage tombs. One is an unusual structure with a short megalithic passage leading to an unroofed trench. The other has an orthostatically lined passage about 5 m long, which opens into a most impressive chamber, somewhat pear-shaped in form, with three side recesses. The recesses are relatively small in relation to the overall size of the chamber, which covers an area of almost 42 square metres and is by far the largest passage tomb in Ireland. The round covering mound is almost 20 m in diameter and is delimited by a kerb consisting of a low 'bank' of small stones. The remains of over sixty individuals were buried here.

The earliest building so far known at TARA is also a passage tomb, the 'Mound of the Hostages'. The tomb, 4 m long, consists of a rectangular area, with no clear-cut division between passage and chamber. The core of the round mound consists of loose stones, which are covered by a mantle of clay, making the whole structure almost 22 m in diameter. A kerb is not present. Despite its small size the tomb contained the remains of over one hundred individuals and a variety of grave goods associated with them.

The BURIAL RITE in passage tombs was normally cremation, and deposits of ashes were usually confined to the recesses, if present. The deposits can contain the remains of more than one person. There is also evidence for successive burials of unburnt bodies at Fourknocks and in the Mound of the Hostages at Tara. Grave goods occur but not in great quantity. These consist of the remains of pottery vessels, bone and antler pins, and beads and pendants, often made of unusual stone such as serpentine. A spectacular object came from the right-hand recess of the Eastern tomb in the large Knowth tomb. This is an ovoid mace-head, 79 mm long, fashioned from a block of flint. All six surfaces are ornamented with motifs, lozenges and spirals, in relief. The perforation is perfectly cylindrical.

A notable feature of passage tombs is the ART displayed on the structural stones both internally and externally. This was applied by incising or picking the surface. The motifs are non-representational and include curvilinear and angular designs, either of circles and spirals or of triangles, lozenges and zig-zags. It is obvious that this art had a significant ritual role, for not only were some of the decorated stones spectacular pieces in themselves – for instance the Newgrange entrance stone and those within the tomb at Fourknocks – but it is also clear that certain types of design were largely confined to certain parts of tombs. This is especially evident at Knowth, where the curvilinear art is largely reserved for the exterior while the angular motifs are mostly internal and are therefore to be more directly associated with the accompanying burials.

As was the case with the builders of the long-barrow tombs, the passage-tomb people were also successful farmers. They lived in circular wooden houses, as the evidence from Knowth demonstrates. They had a range of pottery vessels that served as household utensils and also stone artefacts such as flint knives, scrapers and stone axeheads.

Despite the fact that they are the most common tomb in Ireland, close to 500 examples being known, only four wedge-shaped tombs occur in North Leinster. They date from the centuries before 2000 B.C. Such tombs consist of an orthostatically constructed rectangular-shaped burial chamber, with a portico at the entrance end and occasionally a closed chamber at the rear, the division being effected by a transverse slab set on its narrow edge and also having jambs in some tombs. The roof consists of slabs resting directly on the side orthostats. Parallel to the chamber walls on the outside there are often one or more rows of walling formed of orthostats. The shape of the covering cairn varies, but a wedge shape is common. On the western side there is a straight front, and the entrance is situated at the mid-point. The burial rite appears to have been predominantly cremation but inhumation was also practised. Grave goods include sherds of flat-based coarse pottery, but there is also a new pottery type, the beaker, characterized by its fine ware and geometrical decoration. In North Leinster fairly well-preserved examples of wedge-shaped tombs occur at PROLEEK (beside the portal tomb) and at

PADDOCK (Monasterboice), both in Co. Louth. Examples at LICKBLA (Castlepollard), Co. Westmeath, and EDENAGORA (near Kingscourt in Co. Cavan), Co. Meath, are less well preserved. Wedge-shaped tombs are usually associated with good grazing lands. No definite evidence for home sites has come to light, although some of the house sites at Knockadoon, Lough Gur, Co. Limerick (for example Site L), may be contemporary.

A study of the megalithic tombs of North Leinster clearly demonstrates not only the architectural and engineering ability of their builders but also a comprehension of design and vision within the landscape. The passage tombs in particular clearly demonstrate the mastery of difficult building techniques in the raising of large orthostats and in the construction of the splendid corbelled roofs at Newgrange and Knowth East. Such features also indicate the presence of the Neolithic equivalent of a structural engineer, as a knowledge of stress and strain can be considered a necessity to ensure the stability of these monuments. Indeed one can say that in this area, more particularly in the Brugh na Boínne and Sliabh na Caillighe, a wealthy farming society existed, a society that had educated members who performed the role of professionals in bringing about the construction of some of Europe's most spectacular achievements in Neolithic architecture.

FURTHER READING

Since the publication of the first volume in the *Buildings of Ireland* series, the historiography of Irish architecture has expanded significantly. While major studies continue to address the country as a whole, attention is increasingly being focused upon particular local environments. Given this development, the standard classics retain their authority, and the architectural history of North Leinster relies upon these as firmly as that of North West Ulster. For the early Christian and medieval period the most useful sources are Harold G. Leask's *Irish Churches and Monastic Buildings* (3 vols., 1955–60) and *Irish Castles* (1941); Françoise Henry's *Irish Art* (3 vols., 1965–70); Aubrey Gwynn and R. Neville Hadcock's *Medieval Religious Houses Ireland* (1970); John Hunt's *Irish Medieval Figure Sculpture 1200–1600* (1974); Peter Harbison's *Guide to the National Monuments* (1970); and Roger A. Stalley's *Architecture and Sculpture in Ireland 1150–1350* (1971). Hilary Richardson and John Scarry's *Introduction to Irish High Crosses* (1990) provides a brief account of the stylistic development of the Irish crosses and a useful description and photographic record of the crosses at fifty-five sites. The extensive study by Peter Harbison, *The High Crosses of Ireland: an iconographical and photographic survey* (Bonn, 1992), which proposes different identifications for many of the major high crosses, including those at Kells and Monasterboice, appeared too recently for its arguments to be included in this volume. For medieval architecture the most significant additions to the literature on North Leinster are Roger Stalley's 'Mellifont Abbey: a study of its architectural history', in *The Proceedings of the Royal Irish Academy*, Vol. 80, C, No. 14, and his *Cistercian Architecture in Ireland* (1987). Victor M. Buckley and P. David Sweetman's *Archaeological Survey of Co. Louth*, published by the Office of Public Works in 1991, provides detailed factual accounts of the archaeology and medieval architecture of that county but was issued too recently to contribute substantially to these pages. *The Archaeological Inventory of Co. Meath* (O.P.W., 1991), the only other official account which treats of a county in North Leinster, is essentially a handlist: the survey volume remains in preparation. *The Irish Historic Towns Atlas*, planned as a series of fascicles to be published by the Royal Irish Academy, deals with the town of Kells in the Fourth Number (1990), by Anngret Simms, and with the town of Mullingar in the Fifth (1992), by J. H. Andrews and K. M. Davies. These include documentary accounts of the historical development of the respective towns. As yet unpublished, though of major importance, is the work carried out by John Bradley, Andrew Halpin and Heather King for the Urban Archaeological Survey. As a study of the principal medieval towns in each county, these urban surveys offer detailed illustrated accounts of surviving buildings and monuments accompanied by useful syntheses of the existing documentary evidence. They are available for consultation through the relevant council authorities. The most detailed study of this kind in North Leinster is the independently commissioned *Survey and Report on the Archaeology of the Town and District of Dundalk* carried out by Paul Gosling for Dundalk Urban District Council, which also awaits publication.

Documentation of post-medieval Irish architecture has advanced particularly well in the last decade. Maurice Craig's *The Architecture of Ireland from the Earliest Times to 1880* (1982) and *Classic Irish Houses of the Middle Size* (1976) provide a comprehensive over-view of Irish historic architecture. Though Gandon built very little within North Leinster, Edward McParland's monograph *James Gandon* (1985) provides a most valuable context for the buildings of Cooley and Johnston treated in this volume, while the catalogue raisonné of *The Architecture of Richard and William Vitruvius Morrison* (1989), edited by Ann Martha Rowan and published by the Irish Architectural Archive, enlarges on the careers of two significant later figures who both worked in North Leinster. Irish domestic architecture generally is well served by Mark Bence-Jones, *Burke's Guide to Irish Country Houses* (1978), which though brief and occasionally too condensed in its information is nevertheless the most valuable directory of Irish country houses in existence. The more recent *Vanishing Country Houses of Ireland* (1988), by the Knight of Glin, David Griffin and Nicholas Robinson, is a useful if depressing record of houses past or passing. A book of particular interest for North Leinster, which has so much fine C18 plasterwork, is Joseph McDonnell's *Irish Eighteenth-century Stuccowork and its European Sources* (1991), which deals with a number of buildings included in this volume.

A good general account of Irish building types is provided by Niall McCullough and Valerie Mulvin in *A Lost Tradition: the nature of architecture in Ireland* (1987). Bridges as a specific building type are addressed in the very useful *Irish Stone Bridges: history and heritage* by Peter O'Keefe and Tom Simington (1991). Though North Leinster is by no means rich in good C20 buildings, it is worth knowing that other parts of the country have been better served, and Sean Rothery's *Ireland and the New Architecture* (1991) is an excellent and illuminating study of modern Irish architecture.

Finally no account of recent Irish architectural historiography would be complete without reference to the very valuable *A Bibliography of Irish Architectural History* by Edward McParland, reprinted from *Irish Historical Studies* XXVI, No. 102 (November 1988).

NORTH LEINSTER

ABBEYSHRULE

LF *2050*

Today the most interesting feature of Abbeyshrule is its history; it was the fifth Cistercian monastery to be founded in Ireland, colonized from Mellifont *c.* 1200 and patronized by the O'Farrells of Annaly. What survives of the monastery, alongside the river Inny, is most disappointing, an overgrown shambles; what cut-stone detail there is is obscured by ivy and briar. Two buildings remain, the shell of the abbey church, N of a cloister garth, and a large residential tower which stood at the SE corner of the monastic complex. The church was a long and relatively narrow building, approximately 135 ft (40 m) in length. The most interesting feature of the structure is provided by three small vaulted compartments forming a deep screen or pulpitum between the nave and chancel and crowned by a double bellcote. The central compartment opens through a narrow pointed arch into the nave. Crudely executed, these compartments have no clearly datable features. The tower at the SE corner of the cloister is now entirely overgrown but had formerly a circular stair turret at the NE angle. This may have been built after Dissolution. In 1569 Elizabeth I granted Abbeyshrule to Sir Robert Dillon, Chief Justice of Common Pleas.

OUR LADY OF LOURDES, ABBEYSHRULE PARISH CHURCH. 1980 by *John Kernan*. A small post-modernist church that displays all the trademarks of that vaguely dubbed style. Foremost of these is undoubtedly variety: the desire to get beyond simplistic box shapes to something more varied in profile – hexagonal, pentagonal, octagonal ... Never immediately self-evident, the plans of such buildings are always ambiguous, often confusing. Gone too are flat, gabled and hipped roofs, replaced by unfamiliar sectioned slopes, often with fin-like clerestories. Abbeyshrule Parish Church, despite a measure of such post-modern contrivance, is attractive. A white rendered pentagonal block, with the chancel and the main entrance on a short central axis. A big slated roof covers the centre of the nave, sloping right down over the entrance and framed on each side by two tall fin-like side sections of the nave. The sanctuary is an attractive arrangement: a triangular space opening from the nave through a round-headed arch with big plate-glass windows overlooking the field behind the church. – SCULPTURE AND FITTINGS by *Ray Carroll*.

CLYNAN WATERMILL. 1 km SW. Handsome early C19 limestone mill at Tennelick on the Inny river W of Abbeyshrule village. Main block of five bays and four storeys, built of crisp limestone rubble with punched quoins, keystones and lintels.

2050 ALMORITA WM

Country parish in W Co. Westmeath, close to the Longford border.

ALMORITA PARISH CHURCH (C of I). Plain hall and tower church, rebuilt in 1816 on the site of a former building. Chancel and vestry of 1887 by *J. F. Fuller*. – MONUMENTS. Ludovic Meares †1704, John Meares †1776; two slate plaques with painted lettering and the armorial crest of the Meares family, patrons of the church. John Meares †1776; neoclassical plaque with a woman weeping on an urn.

MEARES COURT. 3.5 km NW. *c.* 1760. Large Palladian house built by the Meares family; the seat of John Meares in 1786. A rectangular block, three storeys over a semi-basement, with a hipped roof behind a parapet. Rough-cast, with limestone ashlar trim. The entrance front is of five bays, with a classic Irish Palladian centre bay: steps, a pedimented doorcase with side-lights, a Venetian window on the first floor and a Diocletian window above. The ground-floor windows have flat entablatures and moulded architraves. Plate glass replaces the original glazing. Although a sophisticated vocabulary is employed, the façade is awkward in its effect, perhaps because the relatively large windows are all cramped towards the centre of the block, leaving broad bands of plain wall at either end. Although this is a good deal less busy, there is a resemblance here to such amateur work as Drewstown House in Co. Meath.

In plan the house was originally L-shaped: one room deep on the E and two rooms deep on the W, with the principal stair projecting as the leg of the L immediately behind the hall. In the later C18 a second room was added on the E to make the plan approximately rectangular. Two of the main rooms retain pretty rococo plasterwork in room cornices and coves. The stair is handsome, with three banisters per tread and an arcade of two arches across the landing at first-floor level. As in a Dublin town house, the back stairs are set immediately beside the main stair on the W and connect the basement to the attic floor.

MOUNT DALTON. 2.5 km E. Built in 1784 by Richard Dalton, an émigré who had served in the Austrian army, risen to high rank and been ennobled as a Count of the Holy Roman Empire. Not long after, he returned to the Continent as governor of the Austrian Netherlands; eventually he became chamberlain and privy counsellor to the Emperor, and died in Brussels in 1790. In the early C19 Mount Dalton was the seat of Oliver Begg, patron of Milltown chapel. Two storeys over a basement, with a fine elevated site commanding extensive views of the countryside around. Somewhat stunted in stature: there may well be truth in the tradition that this was originally a three-storey building. An absolutely blank W wall recalls the former presence of a W wing. The removal of the original sash windows and major alterations to the first-floor layout also suggest a radical transformation of the original fabric. Mount Dalton is still a handsome house: five-bay front, with a certain horizontal emphasis in the string-course incorporating the first-floor sills, flat entablatures to the windows and, as the focal point, a good-quality Pain-style tripartite doorcase. The plan has the not so common arrangement of the principal and back stair set side by side off the hall. – A pyramidal garden MONUMENT erected by Dalton and dedicated diplomatically to Maria Theresa, the Emperor Joseph *and* George III has been removed and re-erected at Durrow Railway Station, Co. Laois.

ST MATTHEW, MILLTOWN PARISH CHURCH. 2.5 km NE. *c.* 1840. Simple T-plan Gothic chapel. Cement-rendered, with Y-tracery windows and a detached octagonal belfry, of dressed rubble with a conical slate roof, built near the W end. A plaque commemorates the builder, the Rev. John Coughlan, †1848 and the donor, Oliver Begg of Mount Dalton, †1848. The tower was erected in 1855. The interior is plain, with deal wall panelling and a pretty cast-iron rail to the gallery. Late C 19 altar furniture. – MONUMENT. The Rev. Peter Kellaghan †1894 by *J. Ryan.*

ST BRIGID'S CHURCH RUINS, KILLARE. 3 km SW, beside St Brigid's Well. Fragmentary remains of a small rectangular medieval church measuring approximately 40 ft by 18 ft (12 m by 5.5 m). Cutstone fragments built into the perimeter of the well include part of a round-headed doorway, a chamfered jamb tapering to a point and some stones with pocked tooling, all suggestive of a late medieval date.

HALSTON. 3 km SW. Originally a mid-C 18 house of two storeys on a basement, three bays wide, with a symmetrical plan and only one room thick. About 1820 this was altered and extended for the Boyd-Gamble family, turning it into a square block, with a shallow hipped roof and the classical appearance of a Richard Morrison villa. Still of three bays and two storeys, but now laid out on a deep plan with a wide entrance and stairhall running through the centre of the house with large rooms lit by generous sash windows on either side. Upstairs are tell-tale earlier features such as fielded panelling in the front of the house and floor-board joins. The front is quite flat with a recessed porch and a pair of Tuscan columns *in antis*. Two screens of Ionic columns in scagliola divide the entrance hall. The stair landing at the back is lit by a Venetian window, with a Diocletian window to light the lower level.

OUR LADY OF GOOD COUNSEL AND ST THERESE OF LISIEUX, BROTTONSTOWN. 6 km E. Harled and gabled hall erected by Fr John Cantwell P.P. in 1840 and renovated in 1955 and 1979. A plain building with lancet windows, unsympathetically modernized with pretentiously shaped quoins and a mean roof. Modern angular tapering belltower with a canopied belfry stage.

ST OLIVER, MOYVORE. 3.5 km NW. A nice little T-plan church of *c.* 1840. Plain Gothic and lancet windows, stone trim and hoodmouldings. Squat freestanding Gothic belfry with fishtail slating. Inside, three galleries, a mosaiced chancel with a triple-light geometric window, and pleasantly coloured C19 primitive-style glass.

CHURCH OF THE IMMACULATE CONCEPTION, FORGNEY. 7 km NW. Small mid-C19 T-plan chapel with Y-tracery sash windows. Inside, timber panelled ceiling and a harled semicircular sanctuary lit by paired cusped lights with quatrefoil tracery.

KILLEENBRACK CASTLE. 9 km S. The ruin of a late C16 or early C17 fortified house, with substantial remains of a bawn and outhouses. The castle is a large, four-storey structure, measuring roughly 14 ft by 22 ft (4.2 m by 6.6 m) internally, with high gables over the E and W walls, a tall stone chimney in the centre of the N wall and a ruined circular stair turret at the SE angle. The rooms were lit by large rectangular mullioned windows in the S and W walls, with smaller windows and musket loops to the stair and in the E wall. A chimneypiece with pocked tooling survives at first-floor level, as do the stone corbels for the ceiling timbers. Adjoining the tower on the E is a longer and lower wing, clearly a later addition, and on the W and S are the perimeter walls of the castle bawn.

ST BRIGID, BOHER. 5.5 km S. *c.* 1940 by *Ralph Byrne*. Small country church in Byrne's brand of Hiberno-Romanesque classicism. Horizontally channelled limestone entrance gable expressed as a tall round-headed relieving arch framing a round-headed window and a flat-lintelled entrance. The gable is flanked by a tall Italianate campanile with a domed Tuscan belfry stage.

GLENCARA HOUSE. 1.5 km SE. Substantial villa of 1824 set in open parkland. The original house was a square, two-storey block with three windows across the front and three tripartite windows on each of the side elevations. A bracketed eaves cornice supports a shallow hipped roof. On the front, the ground-floor windows are set in elliptical relieving arches with a continuous sill which fills the width of the arch, while the windows of the first floor are set on a continuous string-course which ends in strips of quoins at the corners of the façade. All the windows have moulded architraves. The doorcase, set in an elliptical arch, is an ambitious tripartite design with flanking Ionic columns and a wide fanlight. Its stonework is remarkable as the mason has made use of a wide variety of droved chisels, which gives the limestone a vigorous ribbed effect, in some places like tweed, elsewhere like corduroy or Genoa cloth. The volutes of the Ionic capitals spiral forward with matching but unorthodox vigour. Inside, the hall connects directly with a square stair rising under a domed skylight.

At some time, perhaps *c.* 1840, Glencara was made grander by the addition to the side elevations of a pair of large canted bay windows which are checked back slightly from the front of the house but considerably extend its width and weight. They rise the full height of the earlier house, whose eaves cornice continues round them, but are built of limestone ashlar, in contrast to the render of the main house. The window openings have no architraves. At this date the centre of the house was dignified by the addition of a four-columned Doric porch whose scale and orthodox character are in distinct contrast to the more wayward detail of the doorcase behind. Within the canted bay windows the two front rooms have, rather unexpectedly, curved bowed projections. Though its architects are unknown, Glencara rises well above the rural norm and it is clear that designers of some ability worked here.

More idiosyncratic masonry appears in the STABLE YARD behind the house, where chamfered doorways are surrounded by bulbous Michelin-like voussoirs. In the WALLED GARDEN is an avenue of hornbeam said to have been planted to celebrate Waterloo.

ARCH HALL

ME *8070*

The fragmentary shell of a large early Georgian house whose design has been attributed to *Sir Edward Lovett Pearce*. All that survives is a three-storey, nine-bay entrance front with cylindrical turret-like bows at each end and a broader three-bay semicircular bow at the centre of the façade. Thoroughly reworked in the C19, the façade, formerly of brick, is now drably rendered in cement. It has curious paired Romanesque windows and Italianate sills to the attic storey. Thus an early Georgian castle idiom was here transformed into a hybrid Victorian chateau; conical slated roofs added to the end bows completed the Chambord effect.

The destruction of Arch Hall is unfortunate as it was one of a small group of Irish buildings – Wardtown in Co. Donegal (also now in ruins) is another – which may be considered as descendants of Vanbrugh's castle style and his geometrical designs, making a rare use of bow windows and circular rooms at an early date. Behind the façade the house is only one room deep, built over a brick-vaulted basement. The hall, originally a large space with curved ends, was flanked by a reception room on each side. The room to the r. maintains its original dimensions of roughly 18 ft (5.5 m) square. Throughout the fabric, fragments of plaster panels cling to the brickwork, and in one of the corner towers a shallow saucer dome is ornamented with plaster coffering and egg-and-dart mouldings. – GRAND ARCH, in a field S of the house. A large folly-like rubble archway with a rustic, pinnacled attic storey and low flanking wings, all in an C18 romantic idiom. This stood across the original avenue to the house, now approached from the rear, and was presumably responsible for the estate's distinctive name. – E of the house, over a narrow stream, a tall grotto-type rubble BRIDGE crowned by a square chimney-like construction, possibly a plinth for a monument.

2060

ARDAGH

LF

ARDAGH VILLAGE. Steeply pitched roofs, pointed gables with wavy bargeboards, brick chimneys, mullioned windows and quarry glass – all the classic features of early Victorian estate architecture – are to be found in this comparatively rare example of improvement in a later C19 Irish estate. For thirty-four years the village had been in the care of Sir George Ralph Fetherston (1784–1853) and his English wife, Frances Solly from Essex. It was Sir George's nephew, however, Sir Thomas John Fetherston, who gave the place its present form, employing *J. Rawson Carroll*, a High Victorian Gothic architect based in Dublin, to improve the village in 1862–3 as a memorial to his uncle. It is planned round a triangular green, bounded on the N by the grounds of Ardagh House and on the E by the Protestant parish church, with detached estate cottages on the S and W. Those on the W form a very picturesque group, sited on a curving road which skirts the perimeter of the former Fetherston demesne. Single- and two-storey cottages, built of snecked limestone rubble, with advanced gabled bays, gabled porches and neat rubble boundary walls. The focal point of the group is the CLOCKTOWER, on an open site at the bend of the road. Built in 1863, this is a pretty Gothic design in limestone ashlar; octagonal buttressed base, with crocketed pinnacles to the buttresses, tapering to a gabled clock stage and crowned by a spirelet. An inscription commemorates Sir George Fetherston's 'life-long devotion to the moral and social improvement of his tenantry'.

ST MEL'S CATHEDRAL. The ruin of a limestone single-cell C8 building with one surviving anta, or side wall, projecting beyond the N gable. The walls of the church now stand to a height of no more than 6 ft (1.8 m). At roughly 28 ft by 20 ft (8.5 m by 6 m) internally, St Mel's Cathedral is no bigger than a spacious sitting room. The striking contrast of these humble dimensions with the C19 Church of St Brigid just across the road vividly illustrates the coenobitic character of the early Irish church. The building replaced the original cathedral, founded by St Patrick in the C5 and entrusted by him to St Mel, whom he consecrated first Bishop of Ardagh. Excavations in 1961 found traces of a former timber building, perhaps one of several which preceded the existing stone structure. Conjectural reconstructions of such timber buildings propose a rectangular single-cell structure, length and breadth in a proportion of 3:2 respectively, with a W doorway, an E window and a steeply pitched roof. Thus the proportions of the stone church do not differ greatly from its predecessor, and the antae which projected at its W end also have their origins in wooden buildings, in the supports for the roof timbers in advance of the gable. What is most striking about the cathedral is its stupendous cyclopean masonry, many stones 8 ft (2.5 m) long and 3 ft (0.9 m) deep, laid in regular courses – a vigorous primitivism of which any Mycenaean mason might be proud.

ST PATRICK, ARDAGH PARISH CHURCH (C of I). 1810. A substantial three-bay hall and tower church with the characteristic Longford feature of vestibules flanking the tower and projecting beyond the walls of the nave. Cardboard cut-out Gothic, with flush corner quoins, blank pointed windows and crossed loops to the vestibules, and a Doric-cum-Gothic frieze across the front at roof level. The nave was remodelled in the later C19. St Patrick's was for a while a cathedral church until the Dioceses of Ardagh and Kilmore were united. – LYCHGATE. A charming timber gate with a red tiled roof, by *J. Rawson Carroll*. NW of here is the ruin of the C18 parish church, now a featureless limestone rubble hall, containing monuments to the Fetherston family.

ST BRIGID, ARDAGH PARISH CHURCH. 1878–81 by *William Hague*. A well massed and richly ornamented church, nicely located on a broad open site E of the village. Horizontally rather than axially sited, so that the N flank effectively becomes the principal elevation. The conventional arrangement of nave, chancel, aisles and transepts is given further interest by placing the church tower in the angle of the chancel and the N transept and by adding to it a romantic turreted stair tower. This creates an extremely successful massing of transept, tower, turret and chancel and provides an effective focal point to the N elevation. Tower and spire are richly decorated with gargoyles, pinnacles, crockets and lucarnes. The W entrance gable is more conventional, with a big four-light geometric window, though its massing is also enriched by a lean-to porch across the front, with a projecting central gable. Six lancets, complete with carved hoodmouldings and label stops, light the aisles, with three triple-light windows to the clerestory, crowned by odd curly label stops. Inside, the nave is carried on a three-bay arcade of clustered polished granite shafts with bold Ruskinian capitals and is crowned by a rich timber panelled roof. The chancel is lit by five cusped lights with tracery of trefoils and quatrefoils. – STAINED GLASS. E window: Sacred Heart, 1919 by *Mayer & Co.* Aisles, W end: Baptism and Visitation, *J. Watson* of Youghal.

ARDAGH HOUSE. Large, rendered two-storey house, predominantly C19 in appearance, with extensive C20 additions built to facilitate its modern function as a domestic science college. Formerly the seat of the Fetherston family, the house was built by Thomas Fetherston in the first half of the C18, certainly before 1745, when it is said to have provided inspiration for the plot of Oliver Goldsmith's *She Stoops to Conquer*, as Goldsmith mistook Fetherston's house for an inn. That building is the principal eight-bay entrance block; originally of three storeys over a basement, it was reduced to two after a fire in 1948. Now much altered, it clearly followed a double-pile plan, with a large entrance hall, the principal stair in the centre of the E flank and the reception rooms opening off the hall. The decoration is now C19 and neoclassical in character. All that survives from the early Georgian house is fielded panels to the shuttering and door jambs. In the C19, the house was extended by adding a ballroom at the SE corner, a projecting three-bay block with ample sash windows and a hipped roof with oversailing bracketed eaves. A classical porch and arcaded conservatory were also added to the entrance front. Most of the C19 alterations were carried out either by Sir George Fetherston, who landscaped the demesne grounds, or by Sir Thomas, who built a large stable court and erected the picturesque estate buildings in Ardagh village. The STABLES of 1863 by *J. Rawson Carroll* are attractive redbrick ranges with slated half-hipped roofs in a vaguely Scandinavian idiom.

GLEBE HOUSE. 1823. A massively solid cubic block, three storeys high and three windows wide on each front, built over a sunk basement. Harled, with plain sash windows, a single-storey, single-bay pedimented porch, and a huge brick chimneystack at the centre of a shallow hipped roof. Plain and substantial like many a big country rectory.

NEIGHBOURHOOD

BALLYCLOGHAN PARISH CHURCH. 2 km S. 1860 by *John Bourke*. Small E.E. Gothic hall and chancel built of snecked and punched limestone rubble with ashlar trim. Seven-bay hall with a timber cross-braced roof. Single lancets to the nave and a graded triple-lancet window in the chancel.

BAWN HOUSE. 4.5 km W. The scanty ruins of a late C16 or early C17 castle or fortified house, consisting of a square, two-storey tower, with ruined mullioned windows and box-like musket loops, and fragments of a second building with a round angle tower pierced at the base by similar loops. The site has long been associated with a nunnery reputedly founded by St Patrick. In 1786 it formed part of the estate of a Mr C. Barnes.

CASTLEREA. 4 km W. Large rectangular tower on an open elevated location, W of Ardagh Hill. Like Mornin Castle (E of Kenagh), it is a bulky pile built of a loose rubble masonry. Here the stone is of particular interest – a local hybrid of red sandstone, quartz pebble and limestone, quarried from Slieve Caldragh and aptly dubbed ‘pudding stone’. (The Markethouse in Longford town employs it in the arcade rustication.) Castlerea is of three storeys over a once vaulted basement. The internal arrangement is not as straightforward as in the usual tower-house plan, and as at Mornin mural tunnelling is employed. Here a long vaulted passage runs the length of the S wall, giving access at each level to the spiral stair at one end and the principal chamber at the other. A murder hole is poised immediately above the ground-floor vestibule. On the upper floors the passage is matched by a second in the

N wall, and the principal chamber at each level has also large alcove-like recesses. Traces of wickerwork centering are still visible in the main vault, and pocked tooling to the doorcases suggests a C16 date. An O'Ferrall stronghold; two likely contenders as builder of Castlerea are William O'Ferrall and Richard O'Ferrall, both of whom were dynasts of the surrounding territory and bishops of Ardagh, the former at the close of the C15 and the latter between 1541 and 1553. In 1612 the 'castle and lands of Castlereagh with a watermill' were the property of 'Richard Brown and Mary his wife, lately wife of James Mc Irriel Farrall'.

ARDBRACCAN

ME *8060*

The history of this impressive C18 mansion, seat of the bishops of Meath, presents a classic case of putting the cart before the horse. The house was begun in the 1730s for Bishop Arthur Price, to designs by *Richard Castle*, who clearly envisaged a typical Palladian house with a large central block joined by curved links to kitchen and stable wings. When Price was raised to the Archbishopric of Cashel, building activity ceased at Ardbraccan; only the wings had been completed, and they served as accommodation for successive, and presumably less worldly, bishops until the 1770s. They survive today as rectangular four-bay, two-storey blocks with hipped roofs and central chimneystacks. The architecture is simple: sash windows, twelve-pane below and six- above, with a continuous string-course between. The S kitchen wing, now remodelled internally, had originally a two-storey kitchen with a gallery or walkway to facilitate efficient supervision. The N stable wing, similar to Castle's work at Strokestown in Co. Roscommon, and to other stable blocks by him, is groin-vaulted throughout, the vaults carried on Tuscan columns set on the deep round bases that are characteristic of Castle's architecture and derive ultimately from the bases of the minor order of Palladio's basilica at Vicenza.

The decision to complete the house was made by Henry Maxwell, a younger son of the first Lord Farnham and Bishop of Meath for thirty-two years from 1766 to 1798. In 1773 he obtained a preliminary design for the central block from *James Wyatt*. This shows a simple seven-bay, two-storey block above a basement, astylar and studiously understated, with regular sash windows, embellished only by architraves at ground-floor level, an Ionic doorcase and string-courses. The existing house, a reticent seven-bay, two-storey building of grey Ardbraccan limestone, although almost certainly not by Wyatt, differs little from his conception, and both *Thomas Cooley* and the *Rev. Daniel A. Beaufort*, the amateur architect who provided the later and more detailed designs for the house, were undoubtedly guided by it. Amongst many designs for Ardbraccan by Cooley and Beaufort respectively, only one unsigned drawing for the principal elevation departs radically from Wyatt's drawings. This consists of a two-storey, three-bay front in a thin Adamesque idiom, with paired giant Ionic pilasters and Ionic tripartite windows set in relieving arches on the ground floor. The rest stick to a seven-bay format, with or without a pedimented central emphasis and with minor variations in detail. Cooley's plans are restrained and nearer to Wyatt's than Beaufort's, which are often fussily grandiose and old-fashioned. As Wyatt left no model for the garden front, proposals for this elevation were less inhibited. What was built is a simple seven-bay façade – the three centre bays advanced and expressed as full-length windows on the ground floor, set in round-headed relieving arches, a design close to Cooley's drawings of 1775, though they lack the rather gauche arches of the design as built.

In one sense the plan of Ardbraccan follows the traditional double-pile layout: a hall flanked by public rooms, with the principal and service stairs in the middle on each side and three rooms at the rear. What is different is that the usual large square hall is here placed in the centre at the rear, behind a narrow vaulted vestibule, an arrangement which first appears in Cooley's plans of 1773 and 1774 and permits the rooms on either side to be large rectangular spaces, each with three windows, instead of the more common near square plan.

The ground plan for the unsigned and unexecuted Adamesque design was the most unusual and up-to-date of all the proposals: a rectangular hall, elliptical stairhall and circular saloon, all on a central axis, flanked on each side by dining and drawing rooms, parlour and library.

Internal features suggest the close involvement of Cooley: the square, ample proportions, the free yet restrained treatment of anthemion and foliate motifs to the joinery and plasterwork, particularly the bay-leaf garlands in the dining room and the simplified – and freely treated – mutule cornice in the stairhall. An elegant finishing touch is the curved inner edge of the
79 mahogany doors throughout the ground floor, all of which operate on a swivel rather than a hinge, a measure of the absolute refinement of late C18 building. Ardbraccan is a sophisticated house, cool and reticent rather than graceful, and more elegant than endearing.

ARDBRACCAN CHURCH. In woodland SE from the house. The spirit which produced the cool reticence of Bishop Maxwell's palace was also at work in Ardbraccan Churchyard. However, 'elegant' is not quite the term here, where a stripped astylar idiom has the effect of primitive sobriety rather than understated neoclassical *chic*. This is a building in the tradition of Inigo Jones' famous 'barn' at Covent Garden, a blunt primitivist essay that is handsome in a sombre, almost literary fashion. Simple four-bay gabled hall lit by round-headed windows, with a plain limestone ashlar entrance front relieved only by a modest Tuscan porch. Built by Maxwell, presumably also during the 1770s, it may reflect the renewed interest of neoclassical architects in Vitruvius and in the effects to be achieved by returning to a rustic idiom. The interior is a plain hall, not in use at the time of writing.

CHURCH TOWER. Freestanding late medieval tower near the E gable of the church. A church has stood at Ardbraccan since the C 7 foundation of Bishop Braccan, though the present tower probably dates to the C 15. It is crowned by a thinner, somewhat off-centre belfry stage and spire which appear to be C 18. Built of limestone rubble with remnants of plaster rendering on the exterior; inside, a wondrous cavern of crisply wrought masonry rising to a giddy assembly of trusses supporting the spire. The spiral stair at the NW angle is lit by loops, while at the centre of each of the four floors are more elaborate single or paired lights. Ogee-headed, with cusping and hoodmouldings, these suggest the C 15 or C 16.

MONTGOMERY MONUMENT. In the graveyard directly opposite the belfry. Large early C 17 monument to George Montgomery, Bishop of Meath, †1620. Formerly Dean of Norwich, Bishop of Derry, Raphoe and Clogher, and chaplain to James I, Montgomery was a high-flier who spent more of his time at Court than in any of his several benefices. Appointed to the Bishopric of Meath in 1610, he did not come to Ardbraccan until 1614 and appears to have done little in the way of diocesan development or reform. He died in London and was brought for burial to Ardbraccan. The monument was restored during the mid-C 18 by Bishop Henry Maule, which may explain its present odd configuration of plaques and sculpted panels. It has the appearance of a spartan Jacobean wall monument, more square than vertical in emphasis and freestanding, with the mere hint of a central pediment above the uppermost plaque and none of the usual superimposed orders. Its principal interest lies in the deeply recessed central panel, which contains three half-length figures of Montgomery, his wife and daughter. These are quaint rather than accomplished, unlike the charming half-diapered border of alternating leaves and flowers which frames the group and suggests that the sculptor here was more at home in a decorative idiom than with portraiture. On the back of the monument is a simple framed plaque to a now far more memorable man, Richard Pococke, traveller and bishop, interred here in 1765.

ARDEE

LO *9090*

The great Ulster saga *Táin Bó Cúailnge* tells of Cúchulainn's last combat with Queen Maeve's warrior Ferdia, which took place at a river ford. Ardee or Áth Fhirdia, on the river Dee, was reputedly the ford of Ferdia, and, in later and less heroic times, the place continued to be of strategic importance in Ulster's struggles with the south. The Normans were the first to establish a garrison here, when the barony of Ardee was granted to Gilbert Pipard, whose family had accompanied King John to Ireland in 1185. Pipard erected a castle, probably on the earthwork known as

Castleguard, E of the town, which as late as 1795 still contained the remains of two octagonal buildings. In 1207 Roger Pipard founded a monastery and hospital for the Crutched Friars or *Fratres Cruciferi*, under the rule of St Augustine, dedicated to St John. A century later, his descendant Ralph Pipard established a Carmelite monastery dedicated to the Virgin. The medieval parish church of St Mary, also an early Pipard foundation, was destroyed by the Scots during the invasion of Edward Bruce in 1315. The inhabitants of Ardee fled for refuge to the church, which was then burnt by Bruce's men.

Between 1376 and 1416 the town received five murage grants, but nothing now survives of its fortifications apart from a small fragment of Cappock's gate, W of the main street. In the C15 and C16, the role of Ardee, more often than not, was as a mustering place during government campaigns against the Ulster Irish. Several Lords Deputy stayed in the town, and two, Sir John Stanley and James Butler, the White Earl of Ormonde, died there as a result of their expeditions. Even today a view from the roofs of the two castles in the main street brings the town's historic role vividly alive: to the E lie the flat lands of Louth with the fortified tower houses of Roodstown and Richardstown; to the N and NW the mountains of Down and Armagh and between the gateway to Ulster.

In the modern period Ardee exchanged its military role for a commercial one. A market charter was granted to the town corporation in the C17 and since then it has been a thriving market centre. During the C18 it was dominated physically by its markethouse, sited absolutely in the middle of the main street. The building remained there until 1810, when the present markethouse square was laid out; the unpretentious classical market that was built then on the W side was demolished in 1987. Ardee is an attractive place, a nice broad-street town lined by some good houses with interesting shopfronts, while it is lent distinction by its two later medieval tower houses near the centre of the town. The area around the river at the S end of the town is more intimate, even quaint, with rubble walls and a wooded riverside walk.

ST LEGER'S CASTLE. At the S end of the main street, and reputedly the castle founded in 1207 by Roger Pipard, though this building is much later in date. Its predecessor was probably a temporary structure located at nearby Castleguard. There are several documentary references to St Leger's Castle during the C15. The largest fortified medieval town house to survive in Ireland, it is a large four-storey rectangular tower, with projecting towers at the N and S ends facing the main street and a battlemented roof-walk. The original entrance is in the NW angle, with a murder hole immediately inside the entrance and a machicolation posed high above it. Though the interior was much remodelled to convert the castle to a court house and gaol, the ground floor preserves its round barrel-vault, a spiral stair in the NW angle and some small corbelled rooms in the SW turret.

In the early C19 the wall-heads were lowered and the steep stone gables of the original building were replaced by a hipped roof. Crenellated parapets were also added and a diminutive two-storey, three-bay rubble and redbrick block was inserted between the projecting towers. Most of the windows are modern, apart from a twinlight cusped ogee-headed window in the NW turrets and single loops on the upper floors. In 1755, when Thomas Wright visited St Leger's Castle, he found there 'a poor grey-headed man, imprisoned for a debt of six shillings'. He released him, adding the comment 'There are many such objects of charity to be found in the Irish prisons which would require but a small sum of money to set them at liberty.' At the rear of the castle the grim C19 bridewell, erected in 1863, is by *John Neville*; a plain square block with tiny windows and massive jambs and lintels.

HATCH CASTLE. Rectangular, four-storey tower house with rounded corners and a façade only one window wide. C15 or C16 and for centuries a property of the Hatch family. Two semicircular turrets project at the rear. The castle is sandwiched between ordinary two- and three-storey houses on the main street. In 1837 it was described by Lewis as 'recently fitted up as a dwelling by Wm Hatch', which probably accounts for the new battlements, windows and hoodmouldings. Quaint interior, with timber panelling in the barrel-vaulted hall and a carpeted turret-stair.

ST MARY, ARDEE PARISH CHURCH (C of I). Large plain church with a picturesque façade and, inside, the fragmentary remains of a medieval church. Since the C18 these remains have been confused with Roger Pipard's Hospital of St John, but recent research has shown them to be part of Ardee's medieval parish church. The battlemented front is of *c.* 1810. Very much a romantic Gothic screen, not unlike the stable folly at nearby Red House, with a central three-stage belltower flanked by low battlemented walls ending in mock turrets. The pitched roofs of the church proper peep up behind: a broad, five-bay hall with a short chancel and a S aisle. The aisle is divided from the nave by a medieval arcade of four chamfered and moulded arches carried on massive octagonal piers with moulded capitals. Although now much plastered over, the three chamfered orders and moulded labels of the arcade are clearly of C15 character. A round-headed door in the easternmost pier leads to a spiral stair which gave access to the rood screen. The E wall, also heavily plastered, had originally a large pointed opening with intersecting tracery. In the SE corner of the aisle is a rectangular cupboard recess and a small holy-water stoup decorated with lines of beaded ornament. The church is lit by C19 Gothic windows with intersecting tracery and quarry glass. – FONT. Ancient baptismal font dug up from the graveyard at Mansfieldstown (*see* Stabannan); thick stone shaft and bowl, decorated below the rim with a scalloped floral moulding on a raised border which extends down over the corners. – CROSS. W of the church entrance, the head of a late medieval, perhaps mid-C16 cross. W face: Crucifixion beneath a triple arched canopy. E face: Virgin and Child beneath an ogee-headed canopy.

CHANTRY COLLEGE. E of St Mary's Church. The fragmentary ruin of a chantry college which was established before 1487 by Walter Verdon, chaplain of Ardee. In that year the college was described as 'lying near the east side of the parochial church with a garden attached, to the intent that certain chaplains employed in the church of St Mary's might be compelled to reside there in common in a hall and rooms fittingly laid out and constructed and support themselves on the fruits and emoluments of their services'. What survives of the college is the southern part of the building, which contained the residential apartments. The remainder of the college would have contained the commons room and kitchen. The surviving building is a rectangular three-storey structure with high pointed gables containing an attic storey, a garderobe cupboard in the first-floor apartment and evidence of a spiral stair at the NE corner of the upper floors. Though much more modest than the impressive remains of the Fleming foundation at Slane, the college at Ardee is considered an important addition to the small number of such colleges known in Ireland.

ST MARY, FORMER CATHOLIC CHURCH, John Street. 1829. Attributed to *Thomas Duff*. A singular instance of the thoughtless desecration of one of the most handsome church interiors of the late Georgian age. St Mary's was once a fine example of a type of design which Duff helped to popularize during the 1830s. A rectangular hall screened by a battlemented three-bay entrance front with projecting centre bay and bellcote. Buttress-like pilasters rising to finials frame pointed arches on the ground floor, with lancets above. The character of the façade lies in its masonry, coursed rubble of mixed colours with crisp limestone trim. The interior is remarkably sophisticated: a nine-bay arcade of moulded two-centred arches is carried on quatrefoil shafts and supports a plaster rib-vault. Open cinquefoils in the spandrels of the arcade served originally as ventilation ducts. Although building began in 1829, work was still being supervised by Duff as late as 1846. Galleries erected in 1832 run the length of each aisle; they have flat panelled roofs with decorative braces.

St Mary's is now in use as a church hall, with a makeshift stage at the N end screening the CHANCEL. This was an extension to the original church in a C15 Gothic idiom, added in 1864 by *J. J. McCarthy*. After complaints that those sitting in the aisles were unable to see the bingo board, the lower parts of the clustered shafts in the nave have recently been cut away, leaving only the rough core!

CHURCH OF THE NATIVITY OF OUR LADY. 1974 by *Guy Moloney & Associates*. On an open site opposite Duff's building. An octagonal steel-framed church with low walls and a very large slated roof, giving a marquee-like appearance. This effect is strengthened by the glazed exterior walls, articulated as vertical concrete posts. Brick masonry is confined to four sides of the octagon – porches, confessionals, sacristy and crying rooms. Inside, the octagonal structure is emphasized in a range of eight rough-cast I-beam piers that form an inner octagon around a central sanctuary. Here an octagonal pine baldacchino is suspended above the altar. The spacious octagonal truss and roof faced with slatted pine are the dominant element in the interior. – STATIONS OF THE CROSS in etched glass and enamel; TABERNACLE and CRUCIFIX; all by *George Walsh*. STAINED GLASS. C19 Saints, transferred here from old St Mary's.

CONVENT OF MERCY. 1858 by *John Neville*. Institutional 126
Gothic, well handled to create a picturesque composition at the S end of the town. Much of the effect is achieved by the masonry, good-quality coursed rubble with extensive limestone trim, set off with steep slated roofs and clustered cylindrical chimneys. Although the main front of the convent is almost symmetrical, Neville follows the contemporary doctrines of Pugin and Ruskin in providing an irregular mass and establishing a clear articulation of the individual parts. The main building is of three storeys, with an E entrance front. A recessed three-bay centre with a single-storey arcaded porch, Perp in detail, is flanked on each side by two-bay gabled blocks, one of which has a two-storey bay window. A small convent chapel of *c.* 1870 was added on the left, but the most effective element in the group is the school house, with a tall blank gable and a big central chimney, set well back beside one end of the convent block. A four-stage tapering belltower, with slated spire, covers the junction of the two parts. The interior is exceptionally rich, with elaborate plaster cornices bearing nuns' heads, pine doors and brass Gothic keyhole surrounds. The stalls in the convent chapel are by *Patrick and Brian Moonan* of Drakestown (also responsible for the carving at St Patrick's College Chapel, Maynooth).

ST BRIGID'S MENTAL HOSPITAL. 1933 by *H. T. Wright*. Extensive redbrick hospital complex. The plan, roughly H-shaped, consists of two long and narrow flat-roofed ranges of wards, with a central administrative block between. The administrative building is an odd blend of old and new, a five-bay, two-storey Wren-style house with cross-mullioned windows, crowned by a central two-stage clocktower in a blocky, stripped-down classical style.

BANK OF IRELAND. Attractive brick bank building of *c.* 1890. A four-bay, two-storey gabled block with small pavilion-like entrance blocks at each end and a carriage arch adjoining on the S. Redbrick, with blue-brick trim and cream rendered borders and cornices.

ULSTER BANK. A building which for all the world looks like a three-storey, four-bay late Georgian house remodelled in the early C20 as a bank. However, the regularity of the façade and the great difference in scale from the surrounding houses suggest a complete and deliberate C19 rebuild in a traditional style. Cement-rendered, with corner quoins. Sash windows to the upper floors. Pilastered three-bay shopfront to the cash office and a broad carriage arch flanking the entrance.

ARDEE HOUSE. W of the town, off Market Street. Big redbrick Georgian house built *c.* 1780 for the Ruxton family, whose ancestor, Captain John Ruxton, was granted part of the former property of the Flemings of Slane during the Cromwellian plantation. This is a very plain, large house, seven windows wide on each front, three storeys and a sunk basement, with big chimneystacks at the sides and a parapet hiding the roof. Stone quoins and a tripartite pedimented doorcase. Two rooms deep, with a central hall and staircase behind. Now a hospital for the elderly, with many messy additions.

TOWER HOUSE. Off Jervis Street on the W side of the town and now part of a farmyard. Rectangular stone castle, C15 in appearance, and of three storeys with the stair in the SE angle. Inside, barrel-vaulted ground-floor chamber with wall cupboards and an arched recess. On the first floor, a garderobe in the N wall; on the second and principal floor, window seats and press recesses. This tower house stood outside the medieval walls of Ardee.

NEIGHBOURHOOD

RED HOUSE. 1.5 km N on the Dundalk Road. An attractive miniature estate, sheltered from the road by a belt of woodland, with a large, three-storey house of Regency appearance attached to a tall thin wing. The wing, with small windows and broad areas of masonry, is said to be late C17 or early C18. The main block, with a shallow roof and wide projecting eaves, was built for William Parkinson Ruxton of Ardee House, who inherited the property in 1806. It is a substantial redbrick square, five bays on the front and four bays on the S side, with large tripartite windows and a square bay window added here at ground level. The entrance front has a polygonal porch after the manner of a *cottage orné*. The early C19 STABLES on the side are screened by a castellated wall and have a central battlemented section.

DOWDSTOWN HOUSE. 3.5 km NE. Small two-storey house of the late C18 adjoining a square Italianate house of *c.* 1860. Three bays by four, shallow hipped roof, bracketed eaves and brick chimneys. Vermiculated quoins and consoled architraves with the same dog and ram heads used by *John Neville* at Shanlis House (*see* below).

PEPPERSTOWN HOUSE. 3.5 km NE. Like Dowdstown but more modest; a small C18 house, gable-ended, originally of three bays with substantial additions in a weak Italianate style of *c.* 1870. The stables are dated 1752 and a millstump nearby is dated 1751. Pepperstown was the seat of the Shekleton family.

BALTRASNA. 1.5 km SE. Italianate of *c.* 1870. An accomplished if dull rectangular block. Two storeys on a semi-basement, with a broad hipped roof, central brick chimneys and bracketed eaves. Three-bay principal elevation and garden front, both with shallow bracketed central gable, performing the function of a pediment and framing an ornamental crest. Oriel bay windows flank an ornate and confused classical porch in the entrance. Segment-headed plate-glass windows throughout.

KILDEMOCK 'JUMPING CHURCH'. 2 km SSE, at Millockstown. Anciently the parish church of St Diomoc. Following the Norman settlement it was granted by Sir Ralph Pipard to the Knights Templars at nearby Kilsaran, who changed the dedication to St Catherine. When their order was suppressed in 1312 their properties, including Kildemock, passed to the Knights Hospitallers of St John. By 1622 both church and chancel were ruinous. What survives is a small rubble ruin, the low walls of a nave and chancel unremarkable but for the W gable, which stands, very curiously, within its own foundation. A well supported tradition attributes this oddity to a great wind in the year 1716 which severed the gable clean from its foundation and brought it to rest within the walls of the church. In 1738 one contemporary witness, a surgeon called Dobbs, wrote to the Bishop of Dromore that 'the affair of Molick's town church near Ardee in the County of Louth is well attested by my brother and all the neighbours hereabouts who saw it before and after the storm. I had the curiosity to go and see it myself and observed ye western gable-end broke off, in a straight line from its foundation just above the ground and placed perpendicular about two feet forward in the body of the church.'

KILDEMOCK HOUSE. 2 km SSE. *c.* 1790. Described in 1803 as the house of the Rev. Dr Disney. Reminiscent of Kilsaran Rectory (*see* Castlebellingham), a very tall double-pile gabled house. Three storeys over a basement, with a plain symmetrical entrance front of five bays. Regular sash windows and a pedimented doorcase framing a rectangular fanlight and a big eight-panel door.

SHANLIS HOUSE. 3 km SW. Built for Henry Milling in 1858 to designs of *John Neville*. A handsome Italianate house, two storeys over a basement, two rooms deep and tripartite in plan, with central stair and entrance hall. Rich architecture. The principal five-bay elevation is perhaps a little crowded, with a large Italianate porch held between quoined pilaster strips repeated again at the corners, with elaborate consoled architraves to the ground-floor windows between. Similar detailing to Dowdstown House (*see* above). Two-bay sides with very widely spaced windows.

ST CATHERINE, BALLYPOUSTA PARISH CHURCH. 3.5 km SSW, at Drakestown. 1831. Small T-plan church with a bellcote over a battlemented entrance, lancet windows and a clumsy new porch. – STAINED GLASS. Twinlight windows in altar wall: Annunciation and Nativity, 1896. Transepts: Annunciation and Immaculate Conception, 1920s, transferred here from old St Mary's, Ardee.

SMARMORE CASTLE. 4 km SSW. Until recently the seat of the Taafe family, who built the castle *c.* 1320. Sir William Taafe of

Smarmore was appointed last constable of Ardee Castle in 1597. A small three-storey tower house, today rather toy-like, with rounded corners and a round NW turret, flanked by two late C18 wings with shallow slated roofs. The setting is memorable for its tall fir trees and rookery. The earliest part of the modern house lies to the rear of the castle itself and is a gabled two-storey block of *c.* 1740, with very long sash windows on the upper floor. The two- and three-storey blocks that flank the tower, each of three bays, date to the later C18. In the early C19 the tower was given a battlemented parapet, pointed sash windows and hoodmouldings with helmeted figures as label stops.

9070

ARDMULCHAN CASTLE

ME

5 km NE of Navan

124 For architectural historians Ardmulchan is *the* Scottish experience in Ireland, a battlemented and gabled mansion rising in beautiful parkland and set dramatically at a steep point on the southern bank of the Boyne, so that the house may enjoy romantic views across the river to Dunmoe Castle. This is very much a Scotsman's house in Ireland, not a C17 plantation castle such as may be found in Ulster, or indeed at Robertstown Castle in Co. Meath, but a house for a wealthy Edwardian, Fitzroy Fletcher of Letham Grange near Forfar in Angus, who built Ardmulchan as a hunting lodge from 1902 to 1904. Fletcher's architect was a Scot, the accomplished late Victorian designer *Sidney Mitchell* of Edinburgh; his tradesmen were all Scottish too – joiners, slaters, plumbers, tilers from Edinburgh, Brechin or Arbroath – from firms known to Mitchell, and even the sandstone for the mullioned windows was brought from a quarry on Fletcher's Angus estate. Only the warm red brick of the house is of Irish origin, made by Portmarnock Brickworks at Baldoyle, and carried, like all the other materials, directly to the site by the barges of the Boyne Navigation Company.

Mitchell understood very well the principles of picturesque composition. Ardmulchan masses grandly, with a showy, asymmetrical entrance front dominated by an enormous mullioned and transomed window – more English Elizabethan than Scottish – set beside a grandiose classical doorway with paired flanking columns and neo-C17 detail. These elements are held between projecting blocks of a solid character, with tall gables at third-storey level, while a battlemented tower of five storeys, which contains the watertanks, rises from the back of the composition. The sides of the house are similarly asymmetrical, with a long, low range of kitchens and office buildings on the S end; but the front to the Boyne is quite symmetrical – three mullioned canted bay windows, with a narrow gabled section of wall between each bay – and then the watertank tower as an accent at one end. This layout is, once again, absolutely Scottish, for Mitchell has taken over a popular country house plan-type developed and perfected by his predecessor in Edinburgh,

David Bryce. The irregular entrance façade and symmetrical garden front broken by a range of evenly disposed bay windows is a classic Bryce model, and so too is the layout of the interior; Bryce regularly placed a long internal hall at right angles to the entrance door with a stair at one end. Mitchell uses this plan too: at Ardmulchan a vast vaulted hall fills the centre of the house with the principal rooms arranged in an L-shape along its side and across one end.

The hall, lavishly detailed like a Jacobean mansion, with high oak panelling, an arcaded screens passage, and a huge chimneybreast opposite the mullioned window, is the *raison d'être* of the house. A squint box in the NW corner and an arcaded gallery at bedroom-floor level provide close-up views of its superb plasterwork frieze, alternating shields with hunting trophies and supporting the high coffered ceiling, enriched with wreaths and strapwork. This plasterwork uses authentic C17 patterns and is the work of Messrs *G. Rome & Co.* who practised from Dublin and Glasgow. More of their strapwork and coffering decorates the main rooms, which mix Jacobean and mid-Georgian taste with dentil cornices, fielded panelling and lugged architraves. Two rooms employ the classic device of late Victorian domestic architecture, popularized by Norman Shaw – the angle nook – and all have elaborate chimneypieces with marble insets. Mr Fletcher can hardly have been popular in Co. Meath for importing such a quantity of tradesmen to build his house but there is no question that they built exceptionally well.

ARDMULCHAN CHURCH RUINS. In a field E of the house and occupying another fine site on a bend of the Boyne. Late medieval church tower of two storeys, with the remains of a third floor on the W side, where the wall has a large plain window opening. E of the tower are low, ivy-grown walls of a rectangular church some 78 ft (23.7 m) long. The tower, no more than 10 ft (3 m) square inside, is vaulted, with a straight stair on the S side. The room above, now roofless, was lit by narrow loops with deep embrasures and preserves the door check and bolt hole in the wall as well as the holes for ceiling joists. Three holes in the floor were presumably for bell ropes.

ASHBOURNE

ME *0050*

CHURCH OF THE IMMACULATE CONCEPTION. 1882–6 by *O'Neill & Byrne*. A standard but pleasant Victorian Gothic church. Gabled five-bay hall and apsidal chancel built of limestone rubble with ashlar trim. The front gable has a Gothic doorway, with twin lancets flanking a canopied statue above. Short buttresses at each corner and a bellcote. Inside, the roof has braced kingpost trusses with a pretty pierced quatrefoil border. Mosaiced apse lit by lancets.

In 1981 the church was converted by *Edward N. Smith and Associates* to form a T-plan with a big barn-like gabled addition at the centre of the N nave wall. The original altar was placed at the junction of the two buildings. The extension, which is larger than the original church, consists of a massive slated roof with a low limestone base, carried internally on a series of laminated timber portal frames with exposed purlins and rafters. Lighting is provided by three tall half-dormers cut into the slope of the roof on each side. These are treated unsympathetically in the exterior, with broad borders of copper flashing which look clumsy. Inside, the junction between old and new is resolved as a rectangular proscenium arch. The corbels formerly set into the original nave wall, now reinforced with concrete to support the trusses, are suspended somewhat uncomfortably above the sanctuary. Despite these details it is a successful adaptation of a small traditional church to meet modern requirements, far preferable to dereliction and decay, the path taken by nearby Dunshaughlin.

ST NICHOLAS CHURCH RUIN. 3 km E at Greenogue. Ruins of the nave and chancel of a narrow medieval church. The chancel was 36 ft (10.8 m) long. In the C13 Greenogue was closely associated with the ecclesiastical establishment in Dublin, and the chartuleries of St Mary's Abbey and St Thomas' Abbey in Dublin record that in the years 1226–8 the church and all its possessions were granted to the monastery of St Thomas. Fragments of Y-tracery found at the site may be of this date. A decorative floor tile of the C14 or C15 was also found here, suggesting that the place continued to prosper during this period. The tile is one of a recognizable four-tile design, forming a central pattern of quatrefoils and concave-sided rectangles surrounded by subsidiary patterns, all in a bright orange and yellow-green glaze. Tiled floors were generally found only in monasteries, cathedrals or wealthier churches, so the tile is an intriguing find in this small and seemingly modest rural church.

The church stands in a graveyard and is built of limestone rubble, with a punched stone surround to the entrance arch in the N wall of the nave. In modern times, probably during the C19, a small two-storey gabled building was built into the angle formed by the chancel arch and the nave. In the gable of this structure is the fragment of a single cusped ogee-headed light with dished spandrels of C14 or C15 date. This fragment, with the floor tile, suggests that St Nicholas was substantially renovated during this period.

DONAGHMORE CATHOLIC CHURCH. 2 km E. Built by the Rev. Pat Goff in 1840. Large four-bay lancet hall, rough-cast, with limestone pinnacles and a cross to the entrance gable. Modernized inside.

96 BRINDLEY TESTIMONIAL. 1.5 km N, in a field on the E side of the main road to Slane. There is a touch of self-conscious historicism in this monument of 1880 to a famous huntsman, for its form, an obelisk on a classical arch, is copied directly, or parodied, from Irish C18 prototypes (*see* Dangan Castle and Oldbridge in this volume). This memorial, set commandingly

on a motte or rath, bears the inscription: 'Erected as a lasting testimony to Charles Brindley as an affectionate remembrance of his faithful services as huntsman for thirty five years to the Ward Hounds. January 1880'. The form is fine: there is a railed enclosure; a podium of granite steps; a pedestal bearing the inscription and sculpted panels; four short Doric shafts of square columns supporting a heavy entablature, and then an ashlar stone obelisk rising to a height of over 30 ft (9 m). Nor is the monument without humour. The dumpiness of the Doric columns seems playfully absurd, while the ox skulls of an orthodox Doric frieze are here replaced by lively little heads of deer with soft ears and branching antlers. The sculpted panels show, on the S face, Mr Brindley, mounted, beside a gate; on the E, two hounds; on the N, the stag they are all supposed to be chasing.

ATHBOY

ME *7060*

The area around Athboy has a long history of settlement, due both to its location in the middle of a rich agricultural region and to its central position in the context of the county Meath as a whole. One mile E of here is the Hill of Ward, an ancient Celtic site where a great pagan gathering took place yearly at Samhain, the beginning of winter, in which all the men of Ireland took part. An important Norman manor and later one of the four walled towns of Meath. Athboy is mentioned in several medieval charters, most significantly a charter of Henry II, which absolved all the inhabitants from tolls and taxes, and one of 1407, which empowered the burgesses to levy tolls on all foreign merchants coming to the town. The place rapidly became a thriving market centre, a role it fulfilled until the C19, by which time both the town and its market rights had become the property of the Bligh family, Earls of Darnley.

ST JAMES, ATHBOY PARISH CHURCH (C of I). Nicely sited, well back from the main street, in a large graveyard whose rubble boundary walls wind in picturesque fashion round and behind the houses on its N side. The church tower is of the C15, a substantial, bulky structure of limestone rubble with hard edges, narrowing above the second storey and with only a few slit lights and a simple louvred belfry (early C19?) to break the wall surface. Rectangular in plan, of five storeys, with a stair turret in the NE angle and battlemented parapet. A crease line in the E wall indicated the position of the former nave roof. The tower has sometimes been described as surviving from the Norman Carmelite friary at Athboy; this is a confusion, as it was always part of the medieval parish church.

The present church is of two distinct periods. Adjoining the tower, a simple C18 hall with intersecting Y-tracery windows – now converted to a church hall – with a small cruciform church attached to it. This is of the early C19 Board of First Fruits type, though not apparently built until after 1846, when complaints were made of the 'incommodious' ancient structure. Contrary to tradition, the jambs and mullions of the E window are not medieval, though the exterior label stops of ivy-leaf design are C16 carvings reused.

Beside the belfry is a late medieval SCULPTED TOMB-CHEST with recumbent effigies of a knight and a lady, who may be of the Cruise or Cusack family. The effigies are badly worn and the male figure is broken in several places. He wears a suit of armour and grasps a sword, attached to a belt round his waist by a ring and straps. The lady has a double-peaked head-dress – rather like a bishop's mitre – and wears a mantle over a pleated gown. Both figures once had canopies above their heads. Sections of the tomb sides also survive, showing, on one panel, St Michael weighing souls, with Christ as a seated judge, swords issuing from his neck, and two of the Just below his arms, and, on a second panel in a crocketed frame, a resurrection scene, with Christ stepping out of his tomb across the body of a sleeping soldier. These panels are early C16.

ST LAURENCE. 1837–45. Big five-bay lancet hall, with a square tower flush with the façade and rising above the gabled entrance front. A plain building with simple Gothic details. Buttresses and pinnacles to the façade and, inside, three plaster arches to the altar wall. Nice panelled and painted ceiling. – STAINED GLASS. High Victorian pictorial glass, with one Clarke-like window in the tower. – MONUMENT. The Rev. James Rickard P.P. †1848.

OTHER BUILDINGS. The former MARKETHOUSE, near the middle of the main street, on the S side, is a modestly attractive building of squared rubble. Two storeys and three bays, with an arcaded ground floor and square-headed windows above. Gabled roof with decorative exposed rafters. Erected by the Earls of Darnley some time before 1828, when tolls were forcibly resisted in the town. TOWNHALL. Victorian municipal Gothic of *c.* 1860. Of coursed limestone with brick trim. Two-storey, six-bay entrance front, with a tall dormer roof and gabled end bays containing the entrances. Square-headed windows to the centre bays have carved tympana above. An asset to the town. Across the street, the ULSTER BANK is by *G. F. Beckett and C. A. Harrington*, 1925. Pleasant hybrid classicism. Two storeys, with a tall roof behind a parapet; three-bay redbrick first floor with cornice and tripartite windows. Seven-bay shopfront with Doric pilasters, a deep entablature and round-headed central doorcase.

NEIGHBOURHOOD

DANE'S COURT. 0.5 km S. Modest C18 house which appears to have been constructed in two stages. The main block is a two-storey, four-bay gabled range with some surviving fielded panelling and a handsome classical doorcase in dressed grey limestone. At a right angle to the S end of the main block is a two-bay, two-storey gabled range which also retains fragments of C18 joinery. Adjoining the house at its N gable end is a simple C19 addition. Formerly known as Dance's Court; in 1836 the property of H. Biddulph Warner Esquire.

MITCHELSTOWN HOUSE. 2 km SE. Handsome three-storey house of late Georgian character, probably built *c.* 1800. Harled three-bay entrance front with sash windows and an elegant limestone doorcase with a broad elliptical fanlight. Later Greek-revival porch and blocked surrounds to the windows. Standard plan, comprising a large central hall with reception rooms on each side and to the rear.

BALLYFALLON HOUSE. 2.5 km S. Modest country house of two storeys over a basement. Its early C19 appearance is modified by the addition of more recent classical trimmings. Attractive grey-blue limestone doorcase. The residence of a Mr Martley in 1836.

CLIFTON LODGE. 3.5 km SE. Simple three-bay, two-storey house built of snecked limestone rubble, principally grey, mixed with an attractive ochre-coloured stone. Pretty regency-style gate lodge with oversailing bracketed eaves and a bowed Wyatt window.

CAUSESTOWN CASTLE. 2.5 km SW. In a field alongside the main Athboy–Delvin road. The remains of a small late medieval tower house. A rectangular tower with curved NE and SW angles and circular towers at the NW and SE corners. The stair was located in the NW tower and garderobe closets in the SE tower, which still stands to third-floor level. The barrel-vaulted ground-floor chamber has also been preserved.

ATHLONE

WM *0040*

Situated at the heart of the Irish midlands, straddling the river Shannon, the town of Athlone stands in the provinces of Leinster and Connacht. Since the later Middle Ages this has been a place of enormous strategic significance, a major crossing point between E and W, and an important market centre. The town has a chequered history of confiscation and siege, of destruction and renewal. Vitally important to all this, as the name of the town – Ford of Luan – suggests, is the bridge or ford over the Shannon, and even today the key to the character of the place still lies in its command of the river.

From the C10 onward, references point to the existence of a bridge at Athlone. The earliest were wickerwork structures, including that constructed in 1120 by Turloch Mor O'Connor, High King of Ireland, followed nine years later by a castle built to protect the crossing from attack. This pattern of a bridge followed by a back-up fortification is repeated several times during Athlone's history. The Normans quickly recognized the town's strategic significance, and *c.* 1199 a motte was erected on the W bank of the Shannon, probably by Geoffrey de Costentin, the principal Norman grantee in the area.

After the visit of King John in 1210 even greater energies were expended in strengthening and fortifying the borough. John de Grey, the King's Justiciar of Ireland, held Athlone and Dublin as his joint seats of office, thus formally acknowledging the significance both of a provincial capital and more importantly of Athlone as a bulwark against the Connaught Irish. Thus from the early C13 onward a stone castle was built upon the existing motte. In 1216 a Cistercian abbey was established in the town, followed in 1241 by a Franciscan friary, though of these nothing survives.

By 1234 it is clear that the settlement at Athlone had spread to both sides of the river and in 1305 a reference to the 'bridge between the castle and the town' clearly establishes the more prolific growth on the Leinster bank of the river. A grant of murage was made in 1251, but there seems to have been no extensive fortification of the town itself until the later C16, though renewed repairs to the castle suggest more than passive resistance to Tudor rule on behalf of the Irish clans.

Work on walls and fortifications began in earnest in the last quarter of the C16, carried out by Sir Nicholas Malby in return for a grant of the abbeys of Athlone. In the early C17, following the accession of James I, more extensive building activity was carried out by Sir Charles Wilmot, which was completed by 1636. In 1682 Sir Henry Piers described the fortifications as 'very strong walls with large flankers of lime and stone according to the rules of modern fortification. The inside of these walls and bulwarks was lined with a large rampart of stone and earth; the outside was made not easily accessible by a large deep graff: round about on the flankers were several great guns. The town on the Connacht side was also fortified with great ramparts of earth, flankers and a large deep graff...' These walls, enclosing an area of 14 statute miles, had five bastions and two principal gates. Little remains today: on the W the walls were demolished to make way for the military barracks, while on the E fragments survive. The wall of St Mary's churchyard incorporates part of the town's N wall, and one complete bastion survives near Court Devenish.

Public building in the opening years of the C17 was accompanied by renewed domestic works. In 1619 James I's confirmation of grants to the 'protestant townsmen' of Athlone carried the condition that 'everyone build his house after the English manner'. The inhabitants obediently honoured their obligation, and Sir Henry Piers recorded that up until the mid-C17 the Leinster side of the town was 'fairly built as to outward appearance, most houses boasting ... newly hewn coins and arches'. However, this beauty, Piers concluded, 'was all without doors, for within they were ill-shaped and ill-contrived'. The wars of the 1640s did much damage to Athlone; it was taken by the confederate Catholics of Connacht in 1642 and was held by them until 1650, when it again fell, this time to Coote's Cromwellian army. In the ensuing decades much rebuilding and restoration was carried out by Cromwellian settlers but once again their work proved vain, as the town was destroyed during the Williamite wars and again in 1697, when a freak electric storm set the whole place on fire.

In 1833 the *Dublin Penny Journal* could remark that Athlone had 'no antique buildings' nor any 'marks of ancient power or splendour'. Given its tempestuous history this is not surprising. For Athlone the C18 and C19 was a period of renewal. Yet, though its architecture is now predominantly Victorian or modern, the town is still remarkable, particularly on the Leinster side, for its tortuous old street patterns and it is still the Shannon, now spanned by two C19 bridges, that gives Athlone its distinctive air.

ATHLONE CASTLE. Set on the W side of the Shannon Bridge, 86
the castle has since the C13 guarded the gateway to Connaught. Today its low bulk is somewhat outclassed by the showy façade of the parish church of St Peter and St Paul. Yet its strategic location must once have made it impressive. Earliest references to the castle of Athlone date to the beginning of the C13, when a building was erected on the motte constructed by Geoffrey de Costentin. Presumably too fresh and unstable a foundation for a stone structure, this earthwork may well have been the cause of an infamous accident at Athlone in 1211 when a tower collapsed killing Richard de Tuit and eight others. The castle was built not by de Costentin but by Sir John de Grey, Lord Justiciar of Ireland, who established a seat here in 1210. From then on it was used as a provincial headquarters. Throughout the C13 references abound to sporadic building work at the castle, and it was presumably at this time that the massive E curtain wall and angle bastions were erected. By the C15 certainly the castle would have assumed its present D-shaped plan, formed by a tall thick curtain wall protecting a freestanding polygonal keep inside. In the late C16 the castle sustained much damage, and in August 1601 Samuel Molyneux, Clerk of the Royal Works in Ireland, made a report of the extensive repairs needed at Athlone. Again in 1651, following the Cromwellian wars, *Miles Symner*, a military engineer, was ordered to carry out repairs to the building for its renewed use as a headquarters by the Lord Deputy. During the Williamite wars the castle suffered renewed hostilities and by the end of the C18 it was found to be in a ruinous state.

In 1793 *Charles Tarrant* made a detailed report on the building, stating that the S wall was largely collapsed, that large breaches were made on the E and N sides, and that the W wall stood to a maximum of 25 ft (7.5 m). Tarrant attributed the damage more to the townspeople of Athlone than to military assault, as the castle was used as a quarry for private buildings and had its base excavated for use as cellars by the market traders. The keep he described as 'a strong tower of about 40 ft [12 m] diameter ... now about 5 ft 10 inches [1.7 m] high'. A map made by Tarrant shows rows of dwelling houses built almost directly against the E, W and N sides of the enclosure. On Tarrant's recommendations extensive repairs to the building commenced *c.* 1800 and continued probably until 1827, the date of a plaque on the N face. Though preserving in outline the plan of the medieval castle, the existing building, a crisp pentangular curtain wall, with a freestanding keep and two large rounded bastions facing the river, owes most to the late Georgian reconstruction. Though the Irish midlands might seem an unlikely centre of revolutionary fervour, the government anxiety which led to the creation of the coast-line chain of martello towers also inspired the rebuilding at Athlone. Here the two main bastions and the central platform were designed for artillery fire and shelter. The keep, also rebuilt since Tarrant's description, is an irregular circle, expressively articulated with plain hard-edged openings on two storeys and around the top a series of blocky C19 machicolations. Today the castle museum houses many relics of Athlone's past, including a collection of plaques and inscriptions.

ST MARY, ATHLONE PARISH CHURCH (EAST) (C of I). Conspicuously situated right in the heart of Athlone. Simple Gothic hall of 1823, with a belfry of 1620 flanking the entrance gable. Built of limestone rubble, with three big pointed windows in each wall, the church is an unambitious structure, adjoined by an E.E. chancel of 1869 by *J. Rawson Carroll*. The tower, which has been much reworked since the C17, is a four-storey building with a slight base batter, a battlemented parapet, one large round-headed window and, inside, the usual barrel-vaulted basement. The bell in the tower was that used by General Ginkel to signal the final assault over the river ford in 1691. Inside the church, a sense of the traditions and history of Athlone is preserved in the many memorial tablets which adorn the walls. – MONUMENTS. Sir Matthew de Renzi, traveller and linguist, †1634. A small marble monument, more remarkable for its account of Renzi's eventful life than for itself. Captain Richard St George †1664 and his wife, Ann, †1643. A very large black-and-gold baroque aedicule, impressive for its scale if provincial in its detail. Mrs Abigail Handcock †1680. A handsome florid baroque aedicule with pilasters, scroll brackets and an hourglass. Gustavas Handcock, magistrate and M.P. of Waterstown, †1751. A handsome slate and marble plaque adorned with urns, shells, brackets and swags, by *Cornelius Sheehan*. William Handcock, M.P. and a commissioner of the Board of Works, †1794. By *Edward Smith*; an ambitious neoclassical monument depicting a matronly Mrs Susan Handcock leaning wistfully upon a large oval portrait relief of her husband. The pin-prick, dot-like eyes of Mr and Mrs Handcock make them almost seem caricatures. Laurence McDowall, Lieut-Col. of the Renfrewshire Militia, †1815.

ST PETER, ATHLONE PARISH CHURCH (WEST) (C of I). 1840 by *Joseph Welland*. Four-bay pointed Gothic hall and shallow chancel, with an unusually large and deep gabled porch surmounted by a diminutive belltower. Built of chequered rubble masonry with limestone ashlar trim. Diagonal corner buttresses with spiky pinnacles and a battlemented parapet to the porch and tower. Lancets to the nave and a triple-lancet window to the chancel, all with hoodmouldings. In 1985 the churchyard of St Peter's was donated by the Church of Ireland to the people of Athlone for use as a public park. The redevelopment makes an attractive public space, bounded on the N by a row of prettily painted new houses with slated canopies and brick chimneys. – MONUMENT. A limestone obelisk re-erected to the memory of the dead interred in St Peter's burial ground. The new railings are meagre and inappropriate.

ST MARY, ATHLONE PARISH CHURCH (EAST). 1857–61 by 119
John Bourke. The original post-Emancipation parish church of Athlone. A handsome, if routine, lancet design, built of coursed limestone rubble and standing on an elevated site N of the town centre. Memorable for its elegant four-storey tower and slender broach spire. With the exception of the tower, the church is remarkably similar in design to Bourke's church of St Mary at Granard. Nave, transepts and chancel, giving a tall cruciform building with E.E. and geometric detail. In both buildings the entrance gable has a group of five graded lancets, two of them blind and all framed by limestone colonnettes. Inside, a four-bay nave is carried on an arcade of moulded two-centred arches supported on cylindrical shafts, here of granite ashlar. The clerestory of twin cusped lights has paired arches on colonnettes set flush with the nave wall to give an authentic clerestory or triforium effect. As at Granard, the nave has an elaborate cross-braced timber roof with decorative openwork hammerbeams. The chancel in each case is lit by a big five-light window with a geometric tracery pattern of daggers and trefoils. Whereas at Granard the tower flanks the S transept, here it adjoins the W gable. It is clear that Bourke's Athlone design, begun in 1857, was the starting point for St Mary's at Granard. As early as 1846 Bourke had exhibited at the Royal Hibernian Academy a design for the proposed church of St Mary at Athlone, but the project had to be delayed for over a decade because of the Famine. – MONUMENT. The Very Rev. T. Kilroe † 1865. An aedicule with a relief carving of Father Kilroe presenting a model of the church to the Virgin and Child, executed in a Florentine Quattrocento idiom. Possibly by *Farrell* of Glasnevin, who in the same year made designs for an alternative monument.

ST PETER AND ST PAUL, ATHLONE PARISH CHURCH 139
(WEST). 1935–7 by *Ralph Byrne*. Like the same architect's Cathedral of Christ the King at Mullingar, this church gives an immediate impression of grandiose intentions. No one visiting Athlone can fail to register this showy late classical construction rising beside the Shannon, but a building of such patent pretension demands a more conscious integration with the city it seeks to serve than Byrne has been able to achive. The idiom is South European baroque, with a high pedimented façade, flanked by paired campanili open at the uppermost stage and ending in ogee domes. Byrne, an immensely well-read architect, meant no doubt to hint at memories of Melk, the Theatine Church in Munich or Vierzehnheiligen by quoting this formula.

Certainly in the 1930s he was building in a patently Catholic – even anti-British – style, but this late baroque scheme calls for a special setting and this is what is lacking at Athlone. As the central focus of a busy square, or withdrawn as a place of pilgrimage on a hill-top site, the church might generate real architectural energy; here it seems out of place and at odds with its surroundings, too grand for a site that is mean.

Despite the poor site, Byrne's architecture can give a good deal of pleasure, for the façades of his church are carefully designed and the architectural elements are always scrupulously defined. The main front begins with a tall Doric porch, of four columns with a projecting flat roof, sufficiently Irish to recall innumerable similar porches on Victorian country houses – the work of men like Lanyon and Caldbeck – throughout the country. Above the porch, and of exactly the same width, the W end of the church rises to a plain gable pediment with a gesticulating statue at its peak and one large round-headed window below. The window is also quite plain but it is recessed within a shallow vertical panel, after the fashion of Gandon's Customs House, and the imposts of its arch are continued as horizontal cornices across the whole façade. The features of this main window – its shallow recession and horizontal emphasis – offer a key to Byrne's whole process of design, for St Peter and St Paul is built up on patterns of planar recession and of sustained horizontal lines. Immediately after the porch the façade steps back slightly to a broad plain bay of stone work on each side supporting the twin campanili that rise high above the roofs of the church. The Doric order of the porch runs across these bays, dividing the ground from the first floor, and projects on the side elevations to create a blind side porch supported by two freestanding columns. As a result the columnar theme of the front is continued round the sides, and these blind porches are repeated at each end of the side elevations. The Doric frieze, now flush with the surface of the wall and now projected, may recall another famous classical site in Ireland, this time not Gandon's Customs House, but Sir William Chambers' Casino at Marino; so Byrne's classicism of the 1930s is rooted in the Irish classical tradition or, more properly, in Irish neoclassicism. There are even reverberations of Francis Johnston in the round-headed windows of the outer bays recessed within relieving arches, each with a big keystone. So there is much to admire here and much use of native forms. Where the design goes astray is in its lack of restraint. Byrne may be brilliantly eclectic but his borrowings are uncontrolled and range too far. The campanili on the front, with their broken silhouette, open arches and corner Corinthian columns, have nothing whatever to do with the rectangular severity of the façade below. They come from Baroque models, from Borromini and Wren. They do not combine with neo-neoclassicism nor with the church's unusual bowl-shaped dome, which derives from yet another source and seems to be Byrne's response to Lutyens at New Delhi!

The interior is grand, though perhaps it is primarily the scale which impresses. Essentially the church is three big vaulted cells, with the Lutyens dome placed over the central cell and an apse and semi-dome at the altar end. The nave has no aisles and is flanked instead by distinct side chapels corresponding to each of the vaulted units. Despite major differences in scale and plan, Byrne seems to have taken his inspiration from Palladio's great Church of San Giorgio Maggiore in Venice. As at San Giorgio, a giant Corinthian order is employed throughout the church – though here it is pilasters only, not half-columns, which support bold salient entablature blocks. The sanctuary has a baroque baldacchino carried on twisted columns of red-and-white marble, and the full scope of 1930s eclecticism is manifested in the adornment of the side chapels, with large Della Robbia-style roundels, Michelangelo's *Moses*, the Vatican *Pietà*, a Bolognese classicist Crucifixion and a Sienese Virgin and Child. The mosaic work is by the *Alinari* brothers.

ST ANTHONY, FRANCISCAN CHURCH. 1930 by *Jones and Kelly*. Standing in such close proximity to Clonmacnoise, it was perhaps inevitable that Athlone should have at least one monument to the Hiberno-Romanesque revival. It is this big church, set in a narrow side street in the E of the town and, though covered with round-arched motifs and a welter of zigzag decoration, too flat in its surfaces to be considered a success. The main façade is a tall gabled design with a large Romanesque wheel window – overlaid in a typical 1930s way by a raised Greek cross – set above a gabled doorway which derives from the church at Roscrea. A round-tower campanile with conical stone roof abuts the gable, and the façade is extended on either side by flat-topped walls with heavy Romanesque doorways that open into the aisles.

The interior, crudely and emphatically Romanesque, demonstrates the difficulty of inflating what is essentially a small-scale style of architecture to accommodate a large congregation. Round-headed arches abound – as triple lights with nook-shafting in the clerestory, and as six notched arches in each of the nave arcades. Quatrefoil shafts of unpolished granite support the nave arcade. The chancel arch is round-headed again, with three orders of arch rings and scalloped capitals. It opens into a semicircular apse. – STAINED GLASS. In the apse: St Francis; St Louis; St Anthony of Padua; St Elizabeth of Hungary and St Clare of Assisi, by *Harry Clarke*. – In the apse, a copy of the San Damiano CRUCIFIX by *Muriel Brandt*.

OUR LADY QUEEN OF PEACE, COOSAN. 2 km N. 1973 by *Noel Heavey*. The new brutalism in suburban Athlone. A large, low rectangle of concrete and grey brick, with a very deep concrete fascia and an oblique pyramidal roof pierced by many small skylights. At its apex a pointed, nozzle-like lantern not at the geometric centre of the roof. Framed by panels of concrete formwork with narrow slit-like windows between, the exterior of the church has a gross, unwelcoming monumentality and is certainly no preparation for the drama hidden within, for Heavey has devised an astonishing interior, a modern evocation of Herbert Read's Gothic masons lifting 'a dome over the heads of a wondering congregation'. Dominated by a spectacular ribbed ceiling pierced by triangular lights, the church must command the emotions of all who worship here. As the pyramid is oblique and the lantern is offset, the system of coffers tightens up in one corner of the building, giving a diaper pattern to the roof above the altar. A bold, modern and highly successful interior.

WESLEYAN METHODIST CHAPEL. 1865 by *Alfred G. Jones*. A small gabled hall of rock-faced limestone rubble with an octagonal sanctuary, lit by a small spire-like cupola. The entrance gable, on North Gate Street, is an attractively solid three-bay façade with a gabled porch and wheel window above, a pointed doorway on each side and large buttress-cum-spirelets flanking the gable at each end.

PRESBYTERIAN CHURCH. 1859 by *E. P. Gribbon*. On the SW quayside; now derelict. Small gabled hall with a triple-light Dec window to the entrance gable and a circular rose at the opposite gable end. Originally of limestone, now cement-rendered.

THE BOWER, CONVENT OF MERCY. 1889, probably by *W. H. Byrne*. A tall, dull two-storey building with a steep gabled roof and a seven-bay entrance front. This is expressed as a curious assortment of lancets, mullioned windows, dormer windows and, on the ground floor, straightforward plate-glass windows. The central bay is advanced and gabled, with a statue niche high up in the gable and a slated finial behind, set above the roof ridge of the main block. The building stretches out behind to give an extensive rectangular plan, with a central courtyard.

ATHLONE UNION WORKHOUSE. 1839–41 by *George Wilkinson*. Now a fire station and a branch of the Regional Technical College. The usual formula with a five-bay, two-storey governor's house in a picturesque gabled style set before a long three-storey, fifteen-bay range, terminating in double-gabled blocks at each end. In 1850 the inmates of Athlone workhouse rioted en masse by throwing tins of stir-about against the walls of the hall and demolishing the windows.

CUSTUME BARRACKS. Since the later Middle Ages Athlone has been an important garrison town, and a substantial barracks has served the castle here since the C17. The first reference to the modern barrack is a debt in 1691 which was due to Major Thomas Handcock for erecting stables and other buildings for the garrison. A century later, in 1793, the engineer Charles Tarrant reported to the Board of Ordnance that Athlone had a barracks for four troops 'with stables, a riding house, infirmary, barrack, master's storeroom and yard and house, a powder magazine arched with a storeroom over it and another building for artillery and stores'. Tarrant also commented on the low-lying position of the barracks, concluding that without some expenditure the complex was indefensible: 'merely a place for lodging and exercises'. About 1800 Tarrant's recommendations were acted upon and new buildings, including a hospital, were constructed by the Athlone contractor Robert Walker. In 1851 more buildings were added to the complex, including a grandiose rusticated and pedimented GATEWAY on the E side, and in 1860 the barracks was further enlarged. Some of this work was carried out at the expense of the Midland Great Western Railway to compensate for its interference with the barrack property in bringing the railway line W of the Shannon. The barrack wall which bounds Grace Road, the wharf alongside the Shannon and two grand cutstone entrance gates were all financed by the railway company. Inside the barracks, the oldest buildings are located on the S side of the enclosure in and around what was known as Pump Square. On the W edge of the barracks a six-bay, two-storey block with small sash windows and a very large, steeply pitched roof may date to the early C18. The long seventeen-bay, three-storey range which forms the southern boundary of the barracks appears to have been built *c.* 1800 in a conservative Georgian idiom and is similar to early C19 work at Mullingar Barracks; rough-cast, with limestone block surrounds to the doors and windows and an archway in the central bay. To the N is a collection of mid-C19 structures in a mixture of limestone and brick, including an excellent single-storey block of *c.* 1850 with ten round-headed sash windows and a shallow eaves pediment over the central pair. Drawings of 1851 by J. Constable, clerk of works, for the grand gateway facing the wharf are preserved at Cathal Brugha Military Barracks military archives, as are drawings of 1873 for new quarters for married soldiers.

POST OFFICE. 1935. C20 classicism in smooth limestone ashlar. A tall three-bay, single-storey limestone block, flat-roofed, with two-bay lower wings. The centre has two long, round-headed windows to one side of a tall square-headed doorcase.

ALLIED IRISH BANK. The former Provincial Bank, by *W. G. Murray*, *c.* 1855. Handsome Italianate building of fine limestone masonry, occupying a conspicuous site E of the Shannon Bridge. Set on what was the marketplace of Athlone it is appropriate that this design should emulate the traditional Georgian markethouse: a two-storey block with a shallow hipped roof, square-headed windows to the first floor and a rusticated and arcaded basement storey, here filled with a central door and windows. Nicely detailed, with raised corner quoins, a continuous first-floor string-course, rich modillion eaves cornice and architraves to the first-floor windows. A neat balustraded footbridge provides access to the Shannon Bridge.

COURT DEVENISH. When Sir Henry Piers remarked upon the quality of domestic building in Athlone during the early C17 he drew attention in particular to a house 'built backward from the street by one Devenish'; this 'exceeded all the rest for politeness of architecture'. Court Devenish, the only survivor of Athlone's C17 town houses, was built in 1620 by George

Devenish and stood immediately inside the N wall of the town. Today, much reduced, it occupies the grounds of a late Georgian house built in 1791 using stones from the older fabric. Only the S façade remains; three storeys built of coursed rubble masonry with cutstone corner quoins, a square-headed entrance and rectangular mullioned and transomed windows, with hoodmouldings, grooved jambs and glazing bar holes. A plaque dated 1737 was later inserted into the masonry, which is also inscribed in places with C 19 graffiti.

SHANNON BRIDGE. 1844 by *Rhodes and McMahon*, respectively the engineer and contractor. Low and elegant Italianate bridge of limestone ashlar, composed of three broad elliptical arches, each 60 ft (18 m) wide, with pilasters between, a deep parapet and blocking course. Built by the Shannon Navigation Commissioners; opened on Saturday, 9 November 1844. It is the immediate successor to Sir Henry Sidney's bridge of 1566, which was, by all accounts, an elaborate classical design, richly ornamented with sculptural monuments and tablets. After 250 years of service the Elizabethan bridge was in decay; in 1837 John O'Donovan described its state as 'scandalous' and expressed the hope that the Shannon would 'sweep it away to make the authorities build a decent one'.

SHANNON RAILWAY BRIDGE. 1850 by *G. W. Munans*, engineer, and *Fox, Hendersons*, contractors. Handsome iron bridge; six spans of wrought-iron girders carried on six pairs of massive Doric shafts, with the two widest spans bridged by latticework elliptical girders. Brightly painted and rusted at water level; there is something tremendously evocative about this bridge, redolent of mid-Victorian Ireland and crammed seaside trains to Galway.

110 GREAT SOUTHERN AND WESTERN RAILWAY COMPANY STATION. On the E side of the town. 1858 by *George Wilkinson*. Elegantly simple, Italianate block, with a wide-hipped roof and oversailing bracketed eaves; five-bay, two-storey, with the windows set widely apart, flanked on each side by single-storey, single-bay wings with shallow hipped roofs. Snecked limestone rubble. Square-headed plate-glass windows in moulded surrounds and with architraves on the ground floor. The entrance is in a charming recessed loggia of three arches. None of the original interior remains.

MIDLAND GREAT WESTERN RAILWAY STATION. 1851 by *J. S. Mulvany*. Larger and more elaborate than the rival station E of the river, though ultimately a less satisfactory design. The façade, a long, seventeen-bay, Italianate frontage, is of two storeys, curiously articulated with a projecting three-bay centre and four other projected bays. Square, single-storey porches in the second, seventh, eleventh and sixteenth bays – i.e. at each projection – give the station the air of some superior early Victorian residential terrace. Mulvany's detailing is quirky, with a superimposed pilastered order Doric (of a sort) on the ground floor and a broad bracket above. This is repeated, as a bracket to support the eaves, above the centre of each of the first-floor windows. Inside, the former N platform has cast-iron shafts with ornate foliate brackets supporting a timber canopy roof, while the S platform has clustered shafts and stylized acanthus capitals. Derelict at the time of writing.

BALLINALEE LF *2080*

Small village in the parish of Clonbroney in N Co. Longford. Situated on the river Camlin; the place-name Béal Átha na Lao denotes the mouth of the Ford of the Calves. A C17 plantation borough, the village was known throughout the C18 as St Johnstown after its founder, Oliver St John.

ST JOHN, CLONBRONEY PARISH CHURCH (C of I). At the S 103
end of the village. 1830. A neat little hall, tower and transept church in a cheerful Gothic idiom by *John Hargrave*. More highly finished than the usual First Fruits offering, with a facing of cut limestone to the tower and transepts, a continuous battlemented parapet and large triple-light Y-tracery windows with hoodmouldings and quarry glass. Simple interior, renovated in the later C19, with a deeply moulded chancel arch springing from clustered colonnettes.

CHURCH OF THE HOLY TRINITY, BALLINALEE. 1945 by *W. H. Byrne*. Tall, seven-bay, gabled hall, with a projecting and narrower gallery and entrance hall. All in a minimal Romanesque idiom. Harled with stone dressings; three tall round-headed lancets to the entrance gable. Broad lintelled and recessed entrances, with the inclined jambs of early Irish church buildings.

CLONBRONEY PARISH CHURCH. 3 km SE. 1912. A quirky and brilliantly original remodelling by *R. M. Butler* of a C19 T-plan chapel, prompted apparently by the parish priest's experience of Moorish architecture while a seminarian in Salamanca. The result is perhaps more evocative of Ludwig II's Bavaria. The transformation of the chapel was effected by adding two dumpy round towers with conical spires flanking the entrance gable, replacing the old gabled roof with a sprocketed hipped roof and masking the eaves with a deep moulded cornice which runs around the entire building. The outcome is curiously effective. Simple interior lit by pointed Y-tracery windows. – MONUMENTS. The Rev. Thomas Parkinson †1827. The Rev. Charles Gilchrest †1842. The Rev. Patrick Lee †1877.

BALLINAMUCK LF *1090*

The place where General Humbert and a small force of other Frenchmen made their final stand with the Longford rebels on 8 September 1798. A centenary monument of a pikeman in white marble recalls their bravery.

ST PATRICK, BALLINAMUCK PARISH CHURCH. A pleasant

church of *c.* 1930, modernized in 1961. Long hall with a short chancel and a square tower flanking the N side of the nave. Large round-headed windows and a roof structure like a portal frame.

ST MARY, DRUMLISH PARISH CHURCH. 5 km SW. 1907. Built for the Rev. Canon John Reville; renovated in 1969. A cruciform church, nave, chancel and transepts flanked by a three-stage tower and slated spire. Plain cement-rendered façade with round-headed lancets and a round entrance arch. Spacious clean-cut interior with a broad, cross-braced timber roof and a wide chancel arch supported on colonnettes.

6060 BALLINLOUGH CASTLE WM

All that anyone might hope for in an Irish country house is present at Ballinlough Castle. A wooded lakeside setting, a charming and eccentric house of several building periods and a family history of distinction. It is a tribute both to the capabilities of the C18 gentleman-architect and to the tenacity of the Catholic O'Reilly family, who remained in ownership of Ballinlough from the later Middle Ages. Having accepted a baronetcy in the late C18, Sir Hugh O'Reilly changed the family name to Nugent in 1812. During the C19 the pursuit of military careers in the Austrian army (as was common among the Irish Catholic ascendancy) caused a hiatus in the family's occupation of the estate. It was only in 1927, after the lands had been disposed of by the Land Commission and the house earmarked for demolition, that Sir Hugh Nugent returned to Ballinlough, recovered the castle and began the work of restoration. Today the house is among the most elegant in North Leinster.

Charm rather than sophistication is the keynote of Ballinlough. To begin with, it is very clearly a house of two distinct periods: first a seven-bay, two-storey early Georgian house with three advanced centre bays rising into an attic storey. Harled, with long, narrow sash windows and a rubble crenellated parapet. Adjoining this at a right angle on the N is a big four-bay Georgian Gothic wing. Boxy, with large sash windows, a crenellated parapet and two substantial round corner turrets like those at Malahide Castle, Co. Dublin. The only clear evidence of the C17 house is a big chimneystack at the S gable end of the old block and a closed-up window between the two first-floor rooms served by the chimney, suggesting that a narrower C17 house stood at the SW angle of the existing building. An achievement of arms dated 1617 is attached to the central attic storey. The second phase of the building is problematic in that while the windows have the long narrow proportions and exposed sash boxes of the late C17 or early C18, the interior joinery and plasterwork, which are very close to Drewstown House in Co. Meath, look to be of *c.* 1740. In the advanced centre bays the windows are particularly narrow, just two sash panes wide, giving the façade a quaint provincial appearance. The narrow central first-floor window is round-topped.

Behind this façade is a two-storey hall and stair with a bridge 70
gallery giving access to the bedrooms on each side. In contrast to the simplicity of the exterior, this is exuberantly decorated, with carved rococo ornament and plasterwork. Oak lugged surrounds to the windows and doors and fielded plaster panels to the walls. The latter are embellished by swags of foliage and flowers. The stair is particularly elaborate, with three round fluted balusters per tread, a foliated scroll to the tread ends and even carving on the baluster pedestals. The base of the gallery has foliate scrolls incorporating grimacing masks. Yet this riot of richness is not always well judged: at the entrance end of the hall, exuberance turns to clumsiness. Here the SW angle is badly miscalculated and the window is sandwiched against the wall with no room for its lugged surround on one side. Botched workmanship is one possible explanation, but this is refuted by the evidence of the hall at Drewstown House, where remarkably an identical miscalculation occurs. Drewstown has been attributed to the amateur *Francis Bindon* and there is certainly some reason to suppose that both interiors were designed by the same hand, though the exterior fabric of Ballinlough is less sophisticated and presumably of an earlier date.

On the first floor the narrow proportions of the windows are echoed by tall narrow doors. The SE corner room preserves a handsome early Georgian interior, wainscotted throughout, with a corner chimneybreast. Several of the chimneypieces are of black Kilkenny marble with basket grates. In the drawing room and the stair well is some reeded and scalloped neo-classical decoration.

The N castellated wing of Ballinlough has been attributed first to *Wyatt* and later, more convincingly, to the amateur *Thomas Wogan Browne*, to whom is also given Malahide Castle, the home of Sir Hugh O'Reilly's sister Margaret, who married Richard Talbot in 1765. The new wing at Ballinlough was probably added by Sir Hugh O'Reilly *c.* 1790 and is a very elegant Georgian Gothic design. The ground floor contains a large drawing room and dining room planned *en suite*, with four first-floor bedrooms approached by a vaulted corridor above. The dining room and drawing room are remarkable, first, in having rounded angles instead of sharp arrised corners (gib doors lead into each of the corner turrets) and, secondly, in the very odd plasterwork design. The cornices employ unusual Gothic pendant motifs, and the double doors dividing the two rooms have a curious arched frame incorporating Gothic and neoclassical motifs. Yet if these ornaments smack of pattern-book models, the assured elegance of the two rooms is far from derivative or amateurish. Large spacious interiors, lit by more than ample eighteen-pane sash windows overlooking the woods and lake. The chimneypieces are exceptionally fine: in the drawing room a white marble transom with a frieze of swags and urns is supported at each end by a Roman female term; this is identical to a Wyatt chimneypiece at Curraghmore, Co. Wexford. The dining-room chimneypiece, perhaps brought from the older house, seems earlier in date and close to one at Drewstown; it has a bold and simple entablature and cornice in polychrome marble carried on tall engaged Tuscan shafts.

6050 BALLIVOR ME

BALLIVOR PARISH CHURCH (C of I). 1821. Pretty hall and tower church. Stocky three-stage tower with diagonal buttresses, pinnacles and needle spire. Three-bay hall with the usual blank N wall and three decorated windows on the S side. Plain interior.

ST COLUMBANUS, BALLIVOR PARISH CHURCH. 1821 and 1921. Low, T-plan church with two big lancets and a door in the entrance gable, flanked by a buttressed belltower which lacks its upper floors. Three-bay nave and single-bay transepts, dominated inside by a high-pitched timber roof.

PARKSTOWN. 1 km E. *c.* 1770. Tall thin three-storey gable-ended house. Harled five-bay entrance front, with regular windows arranged towards the centre, leaving a broad band of masonry at each end. The central bay is emphasized by a Pain-type limestone doorcase with Tuscan pilasters and by two blank niches on the floors above.

DONORE CASTLE. 4 km SSE. Small and well-preserved C15 tower house with a pleasant situation on a bend of the Boyne. At 12 ft 9 in. by 19 ft 9 in. (3.8 m by 6 m) internally, the castle is very close to the specifications laid down for a tower house to qualify for the 1429 castle-building grant. A square, four-storey structure with rounded angles, a battered base and a circular stair turret projecting diagonally from the SW angle. Simple loop windows and a lintelled entrance protected by a machicolation high up in the roof-walk. The wall-head is intact, but battlements and gables are missing. A square opening in the roof just inside the entrance, now blocked by a large stone, was formerly a murder hole. The now ruinous stair is of the usual spiral type, the stair slabs tapering to a sharp central point. Pointed cutstone arches frame the entrances to the upper chambers. Now maintained by the Office of Public Works.

1050 BALLYMAHON LF

One long and very broad main street; neat, simple and so far preserved from the onslaught of plastic and neon which has destroyed so many traditional Irish streetscapes. Late Georgian two- and three-storey gabled houses, colour-washed, in rows of three and four. The town was developed in the early to mid-C19 by two principal parties, the Shuldham family of Moigh House and the King-Harmans of Newcastle, through their land agent

Ambrose Bole. The usual public buildings, two churches, a bank and a markethouse are sited on each side of the street.

BALLYMAHON PARISH CHURCH (C of I). 1824. Harled cruciform church consisting of a three-bay hall and single-bay transepts, with a three-stage tower and needle spire. Round-headed windows frame paired cusped lights with quatrefoil tracery and pretty Gothic glazing. Idiosyncratic corbelled pinnacles to the tower.

ST MATTHEW. 1902 by *Hague & McNamara*. Cruciform Gothic church with a pinnacled four-storey tower flanking the entrance front. Built of snecked grey limestone rubble with extensive pale limestone trim, giving an attractive if busy surface pattern. Five cusped lancets light the nave. The entrance gable has a pair of twinlight windows with odd reticulated tracery set above a gabled porch. Inside, a curious hybrid king-cum-queenpost roof and Ruskinian colonnettes to chancel and transept arches. A small nuns' choir is tucked in between the chancel and the W transept, to serve the Convent of Mercy behind the church. – STAINED GLASS. The most satisfying feature of the interior, all of 1905 by *Mayer of Munich*, a perfect illustration of the firm's rich colouring and eclectic pictorial style. Transepts: Resurrection; Assumption of the Virgin. Chancel: Christ, St Patrick and St Brigid. – The modern REREDOS is ugly.

MARKETHOUSE. 1819 by *S. Mullen*. The classic two-storey, three-bay market building, with segmental-headed arches throughout the ground floor, square-headed windows set in segmental-headed relieving arches on the upper storey and an eaves pediment to the central bay. The latter bears the arms of the Shuldham family, local landowners who erected the building. The original design among the Shuldham papers indicates that the roof was intended to support a central clock-house and a slated canopy ran around the building at first-floor level – hence the lighter colour of the protected stone on the ground floor. The upper storey was used in the C19 for petty sessions.

NATIONAL BANK. *c.* 1860. Freestanding three-storey, five-bay building with an Italianate limestone façade. The ground floor, which contains the banking hall, has a round-headed arcade, advanced in the outer entrance bays, which frame three round-headed windows between – all of ashlar. The upper floors are of punched limestone, more simply treated, with square- and segmental-headed windows all set in tight recessed frames. The façade ends in a crisp ashlar eaves cornice and is flanked at ground-floor level by a gate on one side and a low curtain wall on the other – the classic William Caldbeck formula.

TASHINNY PARISH CHURCH (C of I). 4.5 km NE. Founded in the C17 by the Annelly family of Tennelick, rebuilt in 1784 and again in the 1830s. Small, four-bay hall, harled except for its gable end, which is of limestone rubble with two twin lancets and a bellcote. Spoilt by an ugly modern porch. – MONUMENT. Judge Gore † 1753 by *John Van Nost the Younger*. A handsome and ambitious monument; Gore rises from his tomb to be greeted by cherubs bearing a medallion portrait of his wife Bridgit, who had died twenty-five years before: a design ultimately derived from Roubiliac's memorial to Mary Myddleton in Wrexham.

MOIGH (MOYGH) HOUSE. 1.5 km W. Two-storey Regency-style house built in the early C19 for the Shuldam family. The three-bay principal front is harled, with a low hipped roof, bracketed eaves and tripartite windows throughout. It is adjoined on one side by a projecting single-bay extension of 1851 by *James Bell.*

FORGNEY PARISH CHURCH (C of I). 3.5 km SE. Harled three-bay hall of 1810 with an attractive Gothic frontispiece added in 1813 at the expense of the Countess of Rosse. This is a three-stage rubble tower flanked by battlemented rendered vestibules with unusual rounded ends. Good raised corner quoins to the tower and hoodmouldings to the windows and door. – STAINED GLASS. Goldsmith Memorial Window, 1897. The Rev. Charles Goldsmith, father of the poet, was minister here from 1718 to 1730; Oliver Goldsmith was born in 1729 at nearby Pallas, and his rural idyll 'sweet Auburn' is the border country of Westmeath and E Co. Longford.

CREEVAGHMORE. 2.5 km SE. Substantial early Georgian farmhouse with an interesting plan and a charming vernacular-classical entrance front that relies for its effect on the management of proportion. Seven-bay, two-storey elevation with a gabled roof, end chimneystacks and an eaves pediment over the three centre bays. The windows are of a regular size in the four outer bays, but on each side of the central entrance bay they narrow to long thin openings, just two panes wide. There is a handsome Gibbs surround to the door. The house is harled, without an eaves cornice, and the windows have partially exposed sash boxes. The plan, which is symmetrical in the main gabled block, with rooms disposed on either side of a central stairhall, expands at the rear into a large U-shape with two gabled blocks projecting into a large farmyard. Although Creevaghmore probably pre-dates the Rev. John Payne's *Twelve Designs for Country Houses* (1753), its plan, as Maurice Craig suggests, bears a remarkable resemblance to Plate IX of that volume. Given its real practical value, with the kitchens and offices accommodated in the farmyard ranges, it was probably a popular contemporary farmhouse plan-type.

64 LEDWITHSTOWN HOUSE. 4.5 km NW. 1746. Although there is no contemporary evidence for the architect of this house, few can question its attribution by Maurice Craig to *Richard Castle.* Ledwithstown is the epitome of Castle's solid, stocky, masculine architecture. It is a modest double-pile house of two storeys over a basement; rough plastered with limestone trim, simply but vigorously expressed, and crowned by a hipped roof with two large and emphatic chimneystacks which together almost equal the width of the roof ridge. Just short of a perfect square, at 48 ft by 47 ft (14.6 m by 14.3 m), the house has four three-bay elevations, articulated with segmental-headed

windows in the basement and fifteen-pane sash windows on the principal storeys, each framed by stout limestone surrounds with central keystones. On the E and W elevations, centrally placed windows between storeys light the principal and side stairs. Raised corner quoins emphasize the angles of the building, and the roof is hidden behind a plain limestone cornice and a heavy parapet. The Palladian device of a tetrastyle Tuscan temple front, such as Pearce used at Bellamont Forest, Co. Cavan, or Castle at Russborough House, Co. Wicklow, is here scaled down and flattened into a pilaster form to create a tripartite main doorway, approached by a broad flight of steps. The interior is laid out as a classic double-pile plan – an ample entrance hall flanked by two rooms, with the principal and back stair opening to left and right off the back of the hall and two more substantial rooms filling the rear elevation, as a result of which the windows here are positioned for internal effect. The basement displays a similar spinal arrangement, with rooms set to the front and rear of a vaulted central passage. Although Ledwithstown almost became a ruin, extensive remnants of the original plasterwork and joinery bear witness to what must once have been a very fine interior. Lugged and round-topped fielded panels, egg-and-dart and dentil cornices, decoration with baskets and shells, in plasterwork on the principal floor and timber wainscotting in the upper storey. The house has recently been rescued from near dereliction and is being restored.

NEWCASTLE. 2.5 km E. The C17 estate of the Sheppard family, which passed through marriage to Wentworth Harman in 1619 and remained the seat of the Harman family throughout the C18. Between 1765 and 1784 it was the home of the Very Rev. Cutts Harman (1706–84), who had built the famous octagonal hunting lodge of Castle Cor (q.v.) W of Ballymahon. If anything of the Sheppard house survives at Newcastle it is not in evidence, and the present building is a large gabled three-storey mid-Georgian house, probably built *c.* 1750 by Dean Harman's elder brother. Later in the C18 it was enlarged and altered by the addition of a single-storey E wing and a two-storey W wing. A small curly Dutch gable over the centre bay is more likely to be a C19 addition than an original feature and is echoed in the small C19 porch projecting from the principal entrance. Plate glass replaces the original stout sash bars, and the double-gabled roof and neat brick chimneys are also entirely C19. The original seven-bay, three-storey block was two rooms deep, with a central entrance hall flanked by two large reception rooms, and the stairhall was located off centre at the rear of the building. Although now much altered, some six-panel doors and fielded shuttering survive. Upstairs, the first-floor bedroom corridor preserves a coved ceiling, a dentil cornice and six-panel doors. Some of the rooms also have dentil cornices and black fossilized marble chimneypieces. In one room at the rear are lugged window surrounds with a raised horizontal 'lug' to the top of the surround – an early Georgian feature found in the work of the Pearce–Castle school. The rest of the decoration is neoclassical in character, coeval with the single-storey E wing added *c.* 1790. This contains two large rooms back to back, with pretty Adamesque plaster ceilings: in the drawing room (to the front of the house), a large oval pattern set in a rectangular frame adorned with musical instruments and oak garlands; in the former dining room behind it, a diamond pattern with urn and foliage motifs. The main stair has similar plasterwork ornament with a frieze and foliage, urns and swags in place of the by then old-fashioned Vitruvian scroll. – MITCHELSTOWN CRESTS. Mounted on the E wall of a narrow C19 Gothic addition to this wing are a number of carved armorial crests brought here from Mitchelstown Castle in Co. Cork following its destruction by fire in 1922 (by which time the Harmans had become King-Harmans through intermarriage with the Kings of Mitchelstown).

0010 BALLYMASCANLON LO

An early C19 row of picturesque cottages, with a gabled centrepiece, a high-pitched roof, tall redbrick chimneys, pretty Gothic glazing and decorative bargeboards.

ST MARY (C of I). Built *c.* 1820, perhaps incorporating part of an earlier church. Cruciform, with a bulky W tower. Cusped Y-traceried windows and a triple-light E window. Inside, an elaborately painted sanctuary and timber cusped screens in the transepts. – MONUMENT. James McClelland † 1831 by *T. Kirk.* CHURCH RUINS. The remains of a small early medieval, perhaps C9, church, similar to that at nearby Faughart (*see* Kilcurry). Across the road is ST MARY'S PAROCHIAL HALL, a simple late C19 gabled three-bay building, redbrick with bluebrick trim.

BALLYMASCANLON HOUSE. Late C18 seven-bay, two-storey house converted *c.* 1840 into an irregular Tudor Gothic mansion, with high-pitched gables, mullioned windows and hoodmouldings. Now an hotel. The narrow double-gabled block on the W, with the main door of the house, is part of the early Victorian building added to the gable end of the older house, whose main elevation was the present garden front. Here the centre bay originally projected forward. This can still be discerned, but its focal position is now negated by the later addition on the W and by a gable, at eaves level, over the E end of the old front. Windows too have been changed. Inside and behind this now off-centre projection was the main hall of the original house, now a top-lit room with a circular first-floor landing ringed by a decorative cast-iron handrail. The interior is now altogether C19 in character; the only C18 feature is a large polychrome marble chimneypiece in the room N of the hall. Much extended with hotel bedrooms and functions suites.

MOUNTPLEASANT. 1.5 km W. Early Victorian home of the railway engineer Sir John MacNeill. A mid-Georgian and Regency house extended several times before 1850, when it was further enlarged and entirely remodelled in a relaxed classical vein. A grandiose stuccoed entrance front, with a two-storey central block and single-storey wings, is dominated by a giant, if somewhat attenuated, free Corinthian portico. The columns, of grey limestone, are rather too narrow for the job they perform and are too widely spaced. The garden front is more sober: a two-storey, pedimented centre with big tripartite windows, flanked by balustraded single-storey bows. The Ordnance Survey map of 1836 shows only a single bow, which MacNeill balanced in his additions of *c.* 1850. The interior is now mid-C19 in character, with a showy T-plan staircase in the entrance hall. Among the service buildings behind the house is a nice five-bay, two-storey range with a wide hipped roof. It is built of coursed rubble with brick and granite trim and is articulated as three large arches with a door and window at either end.

MOUNTPLEASANT FLAX MILL. Two-storey and extensive Victorian industrial complex, sheds, a tall chimney and wheel-house of redbrick and limestone rubble, designed by *John MacNeill* and completed in 1851. An ill-fated venture, the mill was burnt out in 1857 and the resulting loss ultimately forced MacNeill to sell up the estate in 1868.

BELLURGAN PARK. 1.5 km E. Handsome if simple late C18 two-storey house adjoining a humbler gabled house of *c.* 1740, both with S-facing entrance fronts and both built for members of the Tipping family, resident at Bellurgan since the C17. The earlier house, two-storey and now of three bays, with modern ground-floor windows, was originally a five-bay house with a central door and hallway. When the larger house was erected, probably during the 1790s, it overlapped the existing structure and incorporated two bays of the older building in its NE corner. Upstairs in the old house are some six-panel doors in lugged surrounds and the original coved ceilings. The largest ceiling, roughly 20 ft (6 m) square, has charming rococo plasterwork of birds, fruit, garlands and flower-baskets which looks *c.* 1760. The late C18 house is tripartite in plan: a central hall with stairs behind, flanked by very generously proportioned dining and drawing rooms which at 30 ft by 20 ft (9 m by 6 m) provide a striking contrast with the smaller, more intimate proportions of the early Georgian rooms next door. The entrance front is of seven bays, of which the centre three bays project forward slightly. Continuous stone eaves cornice, central classical doorcase and nicely proportioned sash windows that are particularly long and low on the ground floor.

ST MARY, BELLURGAN. 2 km E. Small T-plan church. Late C19, with three pointed-arch entrances and a big lancet above the central door. Cement-rendered with quoined surrounds. Quaint interior, with Gothic choir gallery, interior porches, timber panelled roof and two pretty quatrefoil windows in the sanctuary wall.

2040 ## BALLYMORE WM

'Ballymore, a market town, having two fairs per year is seated on the west side of Lough Seudy. Here was founded a strong garrison of the English forces toward the latter end of the war of 1641 ... This was the chief fortress of the county. Here is now a church ... and adjoining the town the old dissolved monastery of Plary.' Sir Henry Piers' description of 1682 will no doubt surprise the modern visitor to Ballymore, a village which now holds no visible reminders of its former significance. Today it offers no more than the usual public buildings, a derelict Protestant church at the E end of the village and a handsome mid-C19 Catholic church on the W side.

ST OWEN, BALLYMORE FORMER PARISH CHURCH (C of I). 1827. Roofless hall and tower church set in a charming walled churchyard in the midst of grazing lands. Three-bay hall and three-storey tower of coursed rubble with ashlar trim. The usual practical blank N wall here complete with chimneystack. The churchyard contains an earlier ruin: a tiny gabled church with a pointed entrance and a triple-light mullioned window. Some pocked tooling to the entrance suggests a C16 or C17 date. This simple little building is presumably the church recorded by Piers in 1682.

CHURCH OF THE MOST HOLY REDEEMER, BALLYMORE. *c.* 1850 and later. A curious hybrid, partly vernacular mid-C19 Tudor-Gothic, overlaid by a later taste for more authentic E.E. Gothic. The body of the church is a big, boxy hall, rough-cast and lit by six tall four-centred windows, with three pinnacled buttresses to each side. In contrast its front is of limestone rubble with extensive ashlar trim. A tall three-storey tower is set before the entrance gable, topped by a slated pyramidal roof. Here the style is more richly Gothic. The tower front is pierced by a great triple-light Dec window at first-floor level, with pointed lights above and below. Flanking the tower are tall, narrow gabled bays with geometric windows and wheel windows and entrances below. The interior is big and bright, with an unusual timber roof, made in the pattern of a series of rib-vaults, meeting in a flat central panel with six central pendant bosses stepping along the nave. The chancel, continuous with the nave, is lit by a four-light geometric window answering that in the tower. – MONUMENTS. Francis Magan †1841; an elegant white marble neoclassical monument by *G. Ryan* of Dublin. The Rev. Simon Clarke P.P. †1881, the Rev. Peter Molloy †1883 and the Rev. Christopher Keghan P.P. †1890; three Gothic niches.

BALLYMORE CASTLE. A ruined circular stone tower which was described in 1690 as a 'round stone castle' and in 1837 as a remnant of the Augustinian priory of St Mary, and which continues to baffle scholars. All that survives is the ground floor and part of the upper walls of a solid circular structure with walls over 6 ft (1.8 m) thick and an internal diameter of almost

12 ft (3.6 m). Inside, the ground-floor chamber has a pointed barrel-vault with arrow loops. There is a mural stair W of the entrance.

BALLYNACARRIGY

WM *3050*

ST BIGSEACH, BALLYNACARRIGY. Substantial early Victorian T-plan chapel. Harled with limestone trim and timber Y-tracery sash windows, some with intersecting tracery. Inside, each arm of the T has a Gothic panelled gallery with a cast-iron handrail. Four-centred chancel arch with reredos and Gothic statue niches. A polygonal holy-water stoup with vineleaf carrying on its underside, built into the exterior nave wall, is clearly medieval, perhaps from Templecross or Tristernagh. – MONUMENTS. Michael Mullen P.P. †1867 by *Farrell & Son.* P. Murtagh P.P. †1892.

TRISTERNAGH ABBEY. 4 km NE. An imposing fragment of the Augustinian abbey founded *c.* 1200 by Geoffrey de Costentin, incorporated in the late C18 into a modern Gothic residence. Early travellers describe Tristernagh as a substantial T-plan church with an octagonal tower and steeple over the crossing. Yet all that survives now is the heavily buttressed W gable, with a double-chamfered arched doorway and a wide lancet opening above. Two bays of the nave of the church are embedded in Georgian domestic work. The nave arcade has two pointed and chamfered arches springing from octagonal piers with Scotia-moulded capitals – classic E.E. C13 work. This must once have been a handsome aisled church (rebuilt in the C14 on the site of the original monastery). At the Dissolution, Tristernagh was granted to the Piers family, who remained here until the C19. In 1783 Sir William Pigot Piers dismantled the old abbey, incorporating as much of the arcade as survived in rebuilding his home. By the early C19 the place had apparently become so dilapidated as to provide the model for Maria Edgeworth's *Castle Rackrent.*

TEMPLECROSS CHURCH. 3.5 km NE. The ruins of this small and very charming late C15 chapel and tower are situated at the entrance to Tristernagh demesne. They have been left alone, unaltered, more complete and altogether more satisfying than the remains of the abbey. The church, a simple rectangular structure with an E gable, is short and built of coursed limestone rubble and punched limestone trim. The tower, of two storeys, has a barrel-vaulted basement, a door in the S wall and a straight mural stair rising in the W wall. Above the vault, the priest's room, now roofless and overgrown, has a fireplace, press recesses and an opening looking into the church proper. The church is entered either from the tower or directly through a N door. Single-light windows in the side walls and a two-light E window with cusped ogees, dished spandrels and a shallow segmental head to the arch of the reveal – all very similar to Derrybrusk Old Church in Co. Fermanagh, which is mid-C16. Piscina below the S wall window. In the C17 Templecross

Church was used as a chapel of ease to the then ruinous church of Kilbixy. – MONUMENT. Lord Henry Piers †1620; set into the S wall, a rectangular limestone tablet in a moulded classical frame with a raised Latin inscription, armorial crest and carved angels' heads.

SONNA CATHOLIC CHURCH. 5 km SE. 1838. Simple rough-cast Gothic church, T-plan, with Y-tracery sash windows and an apsidal chancel of 1859. Timber panelled roof and the original simple pews.

EMPER CHURCHYARD. 2 km W. An impressive early Victorian tabernacle monument stands in this churchyard. Four tapering piers, square in plan but with primitive Doric capitals, support a massive entablature with miniature pediments and antefixae. The monument is nameless but carries the date 1841.

EMPER CATHOLIC CHURCH. 3 km W. 1829. Simple lancet hall erected in Emancipation year by the Rev. C. Banon P.P., retaining the early C19 layout for Catholic and Nonconformist chapels with doors at either end of the long façade and the altar (or pulpit) at the middle. In the mid-C19 the church was converted to a T-plan design, and a sacristy was added as a low gabled room in the centre of the main front.

0030

BALLYNAHOWEN COURT WM

The largest and grandest Georgian house in S Co. Westmeath, built in 1746 by Edmond Malone and his wife, Ruth Judge of Gageborough, who were married in 1734. Malone was a lawyer, called to the English bar in 1730 and to the Irish bar in 1740; he was M.P. for Granard in 1760 and was appointed a Judge of the Court of Common Pleas in 1766. The sophistication of Ballynahowen Court suggests that he was a travelled and cultured patron. The house is tall and square – a big redbrick, three-storey block in the manner of Richard Castle, with a hipped roof rising behind a parapet and cornice and a large central chimneystack – solid handsome architecture that is made even more appealing by virtue of its rarity in this part of the country.

The long straight drive approaching the house from the E reveals all that is best in the building, a blocky geometric profile and a symmetrical three-bay entrance front of warm red brick and limestone trim. Broad expanses of brick masonry frame relatively narrow sash windows, set in moulded limestone surrounds. Raised corner quoins distinguish the ground floor; a deep string-course marks out the first-floor level, and the top floor ends in a crisply moulded limestone cornice. A fanlit doorcase and long side-lights, with pretty geometric-patterned glazing, are framed by four Tuscan pilasters supporting a broad limestone pediment. It has no entablature and is thus a little ungainly, yet the rest of this façade breathes sophistication. The four-bay rear elevation does not live up to the promise of the entrance front. Today it is much altered and cement-rendered. A single-storey, three-bay C19 wing adjoins the S flank of the house, but the N side is original: a handsome five-bay design, brick and limestone once again, with a pediment to the central ground-floor window and moulded frames to the windows on all floors.

After such architectural promise the interior is disappointing, as the house was thoroughly altered *c.* 1800. Only the plan of Edmond Malone's building survives: a deep front hall flanked by reception rooms with the principal and back stair set alongside each other in the centre of the S side. A large dining room runs along the W garden front, with a very substantial drawing room filling the NW corner of the building. The joinery throughout the principal floor is all of C19 date, and the fenestration has also been altered by the introduction of a large window at the W end of the drawing room. Adamesque plasterwork in the main rooms, the best being the ceiling of the drawing room, a series of ovals within rectangles filled with beaded garlands and scrolls, classical medallion busts and a pattern of leafy trails filling the borders and spandrels. This work has the delicate high relief of *James Talbot* more than the Stapleton manner.

BALLYNAHOWEN PARISH CHURCH. 1 km SE. 1902. Designed by *William Hague* and brought to completion after his death in 1899 by his partner, *T. F. McNamara*. A standard essay in E.E. Gothic, built of a yellow-coloured rubble with grey limestone trim. Hall, transepts and chancel with lancets, pointed arches and big five-light geometric windows to the two principal gables. A three-stage tower with spire flanks the entrance gable. The only jarring note in the design is the over-elaborate belfry stage to the tower, complete with pinnacles, broach spire and lucarnes, all in limestone ashlar and clearly McNamara's contribution to the design. Inside, a five-bay lancet hall opens into shallow transepts through paired pointed arches carried on columns of polished granite with limestone E.E. capitals. An unusual feature is the pointed statue niches with Caen stone figures of saints which fill the spaces between the windows in the nave. The sanctuary has recently been rearranged and the reredos removed. – STAINED GLASS. E window: the arrival of St Columcille at Tara, vividly coloured, Mayer-like pictorial glass.

BALRATH CROSSROADS

ME *0060*

Here, on the E side of the busy main road from Dublin to Slane and the North, is a late Victorian Tudor Gothic police barracks and post office with tall gables, finials and hoodmouldings. Nothing else beyond fields, hedges and a late Gothic memorial cross, let into a space in a field wall opposite.

BALRATH CROSS. Slab cross, 5 ft (1.5 m) high, with short arms that widen towards the ends. An awkward rendering of the Crucifixion on one face, a female saint on the other. A now incomplete inscription in raised Gothic lettering, 'orare pro anima B . . .', bore the name of the Bathe family, and the cross may be related to the C17 wayside monuments in the Duleek area erected by Jenet Dowdall in memory of her husband, William Bathe, †1599. Another inscription lower down, incised in Roman capitals, records that the cross was 'beautified' in 1727 by Sir Andrew Aylmer and his wife, Catherine.

CHURCH OF THE IMMACULATE CONCEPTION. 3 km S, at Rathfeigh. 1874 by *O'Neill and Byrne*. Small five-bay hall, chancel and lean-to porch, all with steeply pitched slated roofs and E.E. detail, looking outside just like a little chapel of ease of the Church of Ireland. The site, at the end of a broad cul-de-sac lined by some low thatched cottages, contributes to this effect. Inside is an open kingpost roof with pretty foiled braces and a painted wagon roof to the chancel.

BALRATH HOUSE. 0.5 km E. Erected in 1780 by the Walsh family, owners of the mill which now stands ruinous across the road. Charming three-storey, three-bay gabled house, rough-cast, with limestone quoins and Gibbs surrounds to the windows. The plan is just one room deep, with a hall in the middle and a dining room and drawing room on either side. Both have pretty neoclassical plasterwork, similar in style to that at Somerville nearby (*see* Kentstown). The drawing room has a frieze of fruit, flowers and musical instruments and a polychrome marble chimneypiece. The dining room, which has an elliptical niche in the back wall, has a border of feathers, swags, urns and rams' heads and a Kilkenny marble chimneypiece.

BALLYMAGARVEY HOUSE. 0.3 km SW. Two-storey gabled house of the mid- to late C18. The five-bay front has its windows arranged in an a–b–a pattern and a small eaves pediment over the centre bay. Moulded window surrounds and corner quoins. Later C19 square porch and, adjoining the S gable, a curved and battlemented addition that is windowless.

THE GROVE. 1 km NE. Pleasant Regency-style gabled house with a single-bay extension at each end. Oversailing bracketed eaves. Fifteen-pane sash windows on the ground floor, twelve-pane above. Tripartite windows in elliptical relieving arches are set in the outer bays. Pretty fanlit Doric doorcase.

MULLAGHFIN. 1.5 km NE. Handsome late C18 gabled farmhouse of two storeys over a basement, with a neat five-bay entrance front. Square-headed doorcase with console brackets, dentil frieze and narrow side-lights. Two small windows are set high up to light the attics in the gable ends.

WESTON. 2.5 km N. Gabled three-bay house of the later C19 with a neo-Georgian porch adjoining one end bay. Coursed rubble with stuccoed trim. Plate-glass windows set in relieving arches in the ground floor.

5060

BARBAVILLA WM

Probably the last Irish country house to be built in the C17 tradition of Beaulieu (q.v.), Eyrecourt in Co. Galway or Ballyburley in Co. Offaly, and as such decidedly old-fashioned for its date of 1730. This may be explained by the fact that William Smyth, the builder of Barbavilla, was a relative of Ireland's foremost late C17 architect and engineer, *Sir Thomas Burgh*, who may have advised on the planning of the house before his death in 1730. The commendable desire on the part of Irish husbands to compliment their wives has given rise to many a hybrid house name: Barbavilla, a gem amongst such oddities, immortalizes Mrs Smyth, née Barbara Ingoldsby. Although the place is greatly altered, so that only the house survives, *A Terrier of Barbavilla* of 1731 shows an extensive formal estate, with offices and outhouses providing flanking courts to each front; a bowed piece of water on the S front with radiating paths leading to temples; and a semicircular bowling green on the N with three radiating avenues cut as a *patte-d'oie* through wooded plantations beyond. In effect the grounds once presented the combination of Dutch and French taste which marks the work of Burgh as an architect.

Today it is principally the proportions and bulk of Barbavilla that proclaim its early date. The house has not come through its two and a half centuries unscathed, and the visitor must eradicate, in imagination, a lot of later detail before the big Georgian house will stand out clearly. It is worth the effort, for the design has a classic grandeur that sets Barbavilla well above the ordinary level of country-house building in Ireland. In the work of mental restoration the first thing to remove is the corrugated metal sheeting of the roof; next the two-storey porch in the centre of the N front, the lop-sided late Victorian oriel near the centre of the S front, and most of the window joinery, which mixes late Georgian and Victorian sash windows with Edwardian casement designs. What remains is a handsome C18 design, nine bays wide and two storeys high above a high basement. The house is built of dark brick with limestone string-courses and sills, all of which have the moulded profiles characteristic of early classical work in Ireland. The two outer bays and the middle three bays are slightly advanced and have pediments at eaves level which give the main façades, facing N and S, unusual grandeur. And in fact these outer pediments prove to be part of a late C18 enlargement in which the ends of the house were rebuilt and the building was extended sideways. The proof of this lies in the plan in the *Terrier* which shows the original house to have been no more than six bays wide. When the building was enlarged the dressed stone from the side elevations was reused across the new longer fronts, a fact which is evident today from the quite rough stonework of the eaves cornice along the W side of the house.

In its original plan Barbavilla offered a classic example of a double-pile house, with an ample corridor, 8 ft (2.5 m) wide, running between two ranges of rooms. The later additions, which date possibly from the 1790s, close the ends of this corridor on the main floor, and all the interior detail, save for a few fielded panel doors, is of this later date. The dining room at the W corner of the S front is especially pretty, with an elegant chimneypiece on the long wall flanked by shallow niches decorated with refined neoclassical plasterwork and small painted roundels.

0080 BARMEATH CASTLE LO

91 The builders of Barmeath, the Bellews, are amongst the earliest Anglo-Norman families to settle in Ireland, tracing their descent from Roger de Bellew, who came to Ireland with Henry II in the C12. It was no doubt the self-conscious awareness of this baronial lineage which encouraged Sir Patrick Bellew (1798–1866), the first Lord Bellew, to turn his sensible mid-Georgian home into a Norman pile of straggling plan and flamboyant silhouette. This sort of transformation was particularly fashionable with Irish landowners in the early C19. There are many instances in North Leinster of houses being altered into castles, yet few are as exuberant as Barmeath and no other castellated skin of brick and stucco disguises a more excellent interior. At Barmeath part of a genuine tower house remains embedded in the present castle. It is recorded in an C18 map of the estate, though its presence can now be discerned only in the unusual thickness of the window openings at the NE corner of the building. Otherwise the house is of two periods: the mid-C18 and the later 1830s.

A guide to the original appearance of Barmeath is given in a painting of 1783. At that time it was a straightforward house: a plain rectangular block, two rooms deep and three storeys high, with seven windows across the front and a central main door. The end elevations, like those of many an unpretentious Irish country house, had paired chimneystacks and gables rising over the side windows. The C19 alterations, carried out to the designs of *Thomas Smith*, an engineer from Hertfordshire who had also worked in Dundalk, replace rational good sense with wild baronial fantasy. Smith removed the end gables, replaced the eaves cornice of the house with battlements, and added, at each end of the original front, ample round towers which rise a storey higher and have bold machicolations and huge arrow loops. The yard at the back of the building was screened on the SW by a long two-storey wing with picturesque bartizans, diagonal buttresses, a central projecting section and tall mullioned lights. On the N, Smith provided a Norman gateway to the yard, with a pair of dumpy machicolated towers, and he also added, to the NW corner of the house itself, a new entrance tower, rectangular in plan, with a circular stair turret, which gives an asymmetrical accent to the entire composition. The whole building was cased in cement – lined to look like blocks of stone – and hoodmouldings were added above the windows.

Smith's new tower is symbolic of a number of changes taking place in country-house architecture in the 1830s. Its neo-Norman style had first appeared in Ireland at Killymoon Castle in Co. Tyrone, designed by John Nash in 1802. Later fully-fledged examples of the style are at Gosford Castle, Co. Armagh, by Thomas Hopper, 1818, and at Glenstall Castle, Co. Limerick, by William Barnwell, 1839. There is an overblown, operatic quality about Barmeath which accords well with these noted examples: the entrance tower has a portcullis in stone set into a chevron-decorated archway with neo-medieval heads as corbel stops for the main mouldings; so the house was certainly redesigned in an up-to-date taste. From the point of view of the early Victorian family it also worked better after Smith's alterations; the four-square Georgian plan, with a hall set in the middle of the front of a building, was, by the 1830s, considered to be inconvenient. By placing the entrance tower lop-sidedly on the NW corner of the old house, Smith could alter the line of the drive so that it no longer came up to and across the main front of the building. The principal rooms thus gained privacy, while all the activity of arrivals and departures, involving coachmen, stable boys and other servants, was removed to one end of the building. Built out as an extension of the house, the gate tower also acted as a *porte cochère* so that the family could dismount from their horses or get out of their carriages under cover and, as part of a very serviceable plan, the horses or vehicles could then go on into the yard behind.

A neo-medieval lobby off the *porte cochère*, with a heavy flat lierne vault and central octagonal boss, is the only part of the house which attempts to sustain the style of the exterior. The rest of Barmeath is finished in a fine taste, mostly with mid-C18 rococo classical details or, on the drawing-room floor, in light Tudor manner. The core of the house is the hall and staircase which occupy the centre of the main range and are linked by an arcaded screen. The room is square in plan, lit by an Ionic Palladian window with a boldly scaled modillion cornice. The staircase is particularly handsome, with fluted Ionic banisters, their lower sections filled with fillets, a swept rail and a generous spiral newel. At first-floor level the doors have egg-and-dart mouldings, lugged architraves and crossed palms in their pediments. The doorcase to the drawing room, placed centrally on the landing at the top of the stairs, is flanked by half Corinthian columns and has a finely carved frieze and a swan-necked pediment. All this work seems to date from *c.* 1750. The finest room, the library, set on the NE side of the house above the entrance lobby, is possibly a little later. Lined on its N and S walls with tall mahogany break-front bookcases, each framed by Ionic pilasters and surmounted by a broken pediment, it offers a remarkable example of Irish rococo taste. The fretwork borders and angular lattice carving of the bookcases are oriental in inspiration and must reflect the mid-C18 taste for chinoiserie, made popular by pattern books such as Thomas Chippendale's *Gentleman and Cabinet Maker's Director* (1754). The ceiling has a deep plasterwork cove filled with interlaced garland ropes, a free acanthus border, oval motifs and shells set diagonally in the corners. Free scrolls, flowers and birds occupy the flat area with, in the centre, a rather artless arrangement of Masonic symbols, including three set-squares, three pairs of dividers, clouds and the eye of God. The room was used by male members of the family for Masonic lodge meetings. The long first-floor drawing room and a second sitting room at the S end of the front were redesigned by Smith. They have pretty diaper reeded ceilings of a neo-Elizabethan pattern, with irregular octagonal centres.

An explanation for the quality of the interiors at Barmeath may lie in the remarkable propensity which Bellews displayed for marrying heiresses in the C18. In 1688 Patrick Bellew of Barmeath was created a Baronet of Ireland. His son Sir John Bellew, the second Baronet, married an heiress; so did the third Baronet, Sir Edward, who died in 1741, and the fifth Baronet, Sir Patrick, who inherited in 1750 and died in 1795. His successor, Sir Edward, the sixth Baronet, did the same, and it was no doubt his accumulated wealth and that of his bride, Anne, the sole heir of Richard Strange of Rockwell Castle in Co. Kilkenny, which enabled his son, Patrick, the first Lord Bellew, to recast the house in its elaborate castle style. Lord Bellew's wife was a Spanish noblewoman, Anna Fermina, daughter of Don José Maria de Mendoza y Rios of Seville.

Traces of the rococo garden of the C18 house survive in a pretty rockwork BRIDGE S of the house.

1070 BEAULIEU LO

61 An elegant two-storey country house with a hipped dormer roof, big brick chimneystacks symmetrically massed and an emphatic eaves cornice. Its style derives ultimately from the domestic works of Inigo Jones and offers a rigorous blend of Dutch and classical influence which became common in English architecture around the mid-C17 and lasted into the age of Queen Anne. Peter Mills, Hugh May, Sir Roger Pratt and masons like William Stanton and Edward Marshall are the main practitioners of this style in Great Britain – even Sir Christopher Wren could be included, but with Wren architecture is more sophisticated, and the essence of Beaulieu, and the style on which it is based, is one of comfortable relaxation and ease. The classical orders do not much matter, and indeed they are hardly present here. Cement-rendered with pale redbrick trim, Beaulieu has two show façades, the W front and a S garden façade. The entrance is of seven bays, with the two end bays brought forward. It has corner quoins and a moulded first-floor string-course. The windows (thin Georgian sash bars replace the original cross-framed timber mullions) are framed by flat brick surrounds, and the doorcase, of fine-gauged brick, consists of two Corinthian pilasters supporting a large segmental-headed pediment that bumps up to the sill of the window above. The arrangement of the dormer windows, three

over the centre three bays and one above each two-bay projection, is a classic mid-C17 practice and effectively balances the design. There can be little doubt that an architect of experience was employed here. The garden front is a simpler six-bay elevation with two doorcases, one in the centre of each principal room, both crowned by large pediments.

Inside, the contrast between a great central two-storey 62
hall and relatively small low rooms is a legacy of medieval architecture, classicized by Elizabethan and Stuart architects. The hall is a tall, two-storey space; there is an enormous chimneypiece with bolection mouldings on the N wall, bolection-moulded wainscotting and regular doorcases framed by large round-headed timber arches. These have carved baroque achievements of arms and weaponry in the spandrels.

Beaulieu has long been considered the finest example of Irish domestic architecture to survive from the Restoration period. Traditionally its builder was Sir Henry Tichbourne, a Londoner who played a prominent part in suppressing Sir Phelim O'Neill's rebellion in 1642 and, as a consequence, took possession at first as a custodian of the castle and lands of Beaulieu, which had until then belonged to a branch of the Plunkett family. Tichbourne became marshal of the Irish army on the restoration of Charles II in 1660; he died in 1667 and was succeeded by his son William, who is believed to have completed the building. Alterations to the interior have been attributed to William's son, another Henry Tichbourne, who was created Baron Ferrard of Beaulieu in 1718.

The claim that such a house could be built here, just four miles from Drogheda, less than fifteen years after Cromwell's sack of the town is an arresting though not entirely improbable assumption. While fashionable architectural taste was usually slow to arrive in Ireland, it is conceivable that a man of Henry Tichbourne's status might have constructed a sophisticated building such as Beaulieu in 1660. But one difficulty with this thesis is a complete absence of documentary evidence for any building activity at Beaulieu during this period, although there is a considerable corpus of contemporary archival material. Harold O'Sullivan, an historian of C17 Louth, believed instead that an existing manor house was appropriated by Henry Tichbourne and served as the family residence for the remainder of the century. Recent research by Dr Edward McParland corroborates this view.

The discovery of an early C18 correspondence between Lord Ferrard and Lord Molesworth suggests that the building work carried out at Beaulieu between 1710 and 1720 was much more extensive than hitherto imagined and that in fact the house may well date largely to this period. Now it appears that the younger Henry Tichbourne, rather than merely embellishing the entrance hall, thoroughly remodelled – even perhaps largely rebuilt – an existing house. Despite the initial jolt of such thorough-going revisionism, there is no great surprise in this altered view of Beaulieu's chronology. Similar houses had been built (*c.* 1710) by the future Lord Boyne at Stackallen and by Henry Bellingham at Castlebellingham (the latter now demolished). At Castle Coole in Co. Fermanagh the original house was of the same type and was built in 1702 to the designs of John Curle. Significantly the architect of Lord Ferrard's building works at Beaulieu was *John Curle*.

In the hall, the timber carvings of trophies and arms include those of William Tichbourne and his wife, Judith Bysse, and the arms of Ferrard conferred on Henry Tichbourne in 1718. These bear a striking resemblance to contemporary plasterwork at Stackallen House. S of the hall is the drawing room, wainscotted throughout with bolection-moulded panelling and a rich compartmental plasterwork ceiling in which dense garlands of foliage and flowers frame an oval central panel containing a classical *trompe-l'œil* scene in the manner of Verrio. The study and dining room have similar wainscotting throughout. Two staircases are located behind the hall at each end of the house. On the S side the principal C17 stair is comfortable but not large, made of oak with short classical balusters. This was given a subsidiary role when Henry Tichbourne installed the more elaborate and spacious stairhall to the N. Although not so grandiose as the stair at Stackallen, this has the same thin Italianate balusters and Corinthian newel posts and is almost certainly by the same craftsmen.

The house is adjoined on the N by a handsome STABLE RANGE, single-storey, with a tall hipped dormer roof, brick chimneys and a broad pedimented centrepiece.

BEAULIEU CHURCH. SW from the front of the house. Miniature hall and tower type. Square tower of two storeys, with Y-tracery belfry window, battlements and needle-like corner pinnacles. Two-bay nave. Windows with timber Y-tracery and quarry glass. – TOMB SLABS. Outside, set against the tower wall. Late medieval C15 or early C16. CADAVER MONUMENT. Embedded in the S exterior wall of the church. The tomb cover of a gruesome funerary monument, probably of the mid-C15. Carved on a coffin-shaped slab is the life-size skeletal effigy of a female figure in an advanced state of decomposition. Together with an effigy at Stamullen (q.v.), this is considered among the earliest representations of cadaver figures in Irish medieval sculpture. So close is the resemblance between the Beaulieu and Stamullen monuments that they are thought to be the work of the same craftsman. Both are unusual in depicting a female headdress worn over the funerary shroud. Both monuments display a remarkably lurid range of reptilian life. Worms, toads, lizards and newts slide in and around the shrouds of the respective figures, who may well have been the victims of a plague which swept the Irish Pale in 1447–50. As at Stamullen, no identifying inscription survives, and the dating of the figure by Helen Roe is based on stylistic evidence. CROSS SLAB. Flat slab decorated with a raised foliated cross, with fleur-de-lys head and arms.

BEAUPARC

ME *9070*

Handsome Palladian house built in 1755 for Gustavus Lambart, M.P. for Kilbeggan, who had succeeded to the estate two years earlier. The building, set on a curve of the S bank of the Boyne and high above the river, makes good use of its site: the bulk of the house entirely blocks any view of the water, so that it is only on entering the rooms at the back that the visitor is aware of its spectacular position and magnificent views along a steep and wooded stretch of the Boyne. The style of Beauparc's architecture, particularly its central window arrangement, is reminiscent of Richard Castle. It is too late to be by him, however, and, as it is more restrained and understated, is usually attributed to the amateur architect *Nathaniel Clements*.

The house is a large rectangular block facing E and W, two rooms deep and three storeys high above a full basement. Broad five-bay entrance front of dressed ashlar, with sash windows in architrave frames flanking a central tripartite Doric doorcase, a Venetian window above and a Diocletian window on the top floor. First-floor string-course and raised corner quoins. Continuous eaves cornice and blocking course below a hipped roof. Low convex quadrants, linking the house to two-storey wings, were added in 1778 by Charles Lambart to designs by another amateur, the *Rev. Daniel Augustus Beaufort*. The garden front, directly above the river, is also of five bays, with a deep semicircular bow in the centre which was probably an addition by Beaufort.

The interior is laid out as a variant of the standard mid-C18 double-pile plan. The hall, with a predictable large Doric cornice and six doors in lugged frames, opens directly to the drawing room, with a dining room and sitting room on either side. The latter retains its original modillion cornice and two stuccoed niches flanking the chimneybreast. The main stair is

Beauparc. Central block: elevation

located off the hall to one side and is lit by a big Venetian window at landing level. It has a good modillion room cornice and a C19 anthemion frieze, marking the change from the ground to the first floor, where an Irish Palladian house has usually a Vitruvian scroll. The staircase is in mahogany, of handsome proportions, with two Tuscan balusters per tread and side modillion motifs carved onto the tread ends. Neoclassical chimneypieces, plasterwork and some vaguely Gothick joinery in different rooms suggest minor alterations in the early C19, perhaps for Gustavus Lambart II, who married in 1810. The cross-corridor of the double-pile plan appears in the basement and at bedroom-floor level, where, unusually, it is vaulted. The large central bedroom at the rear has an internal apse backing onto this corridor which echoes its bowed window nicely. The service stair is also in an unusual position, opening off the hall at the front of the house.

8050

BECTIVE ABBEY

ME

49 On 14 January 1147 a small group of Cistercian monks walked to Bective from Mellifont Abbey in Co. Louth to begin the task of setting up the first daughter house in Mellifont's affiliation. Built on land granted by Murchadh O'Melaghlin, King of Meath, the new abbey was dedicated to the Virgin Mary and by the early C13 had become a thriving monastic community. Such was its prestige that in 1196 the body of Hugh de Lacy, the first Norman Lord of Meath, was brought here for burial before its transfer, nine years later, to St Mary's Abbey in Dublin. As at Mellifont, the community at Bective experienced some difficulty in the early C13, when relations with the Cistercian mother house at Clairvaux grew strained. The dispute was resolved more quickly here, however, and in 1228 Bective was affiliated to Clairvaux and the prior of Beaubec in Normandy was appointed abbot. As Anglo-Norman influence increased, Bective, no more than four miles from the centre of power at Trim, became an exclusive community, so that by 1386 men of Irish birth were effectively barred from entering the monastery. Generous lay patronage ensured its continued prosperity despite a fall in numbers in the C15, when the church was reduced in size. Thus, at the dissolution of the monasteries in 1537, the abbey was recorded as possessing a total of 4,400 acres (1,780 ha) of land throughout Meath. At that time its buildings and surrounding lands were transferred to an English administrator in Ireland, Thomas Agard, who adapted the abbey for use as a domestic residence. He was followed by a succession of wealthy and powerful occupants: in 1544 the Lord Chancellor, John Allen; in 1552 Andrew Wyse, the treasurer of Ireland; in 1559 Sir Bartholomew Dillon and in 1639 Sir Richard Bolton, Chief Baron of the Exchequer and later Lord Lieutenant of Ireland. That a lay grantee chose to settle on the Bective estate and to live in the refurbished abbey accounts

both for the building's present appearance and for its extensive preservation.

Seen from the S the abbey has been described as 'a sprawling Tudor manor house dominated by the great tower erected by the monks'. It does not look like an ecclesiastical complex. Two sides of its cloister survive as a courtyard within the domestic buildings, but the abbey church itself has all but disappeared. As originally planned, the site and layout of Bective conformed to C12 Cistercian conventions. It is set in broad fields on the N bank of the river Boyne, with a cloister garth at its centre, an aisled church with short transepts to the N, a refectory to the S and dormitories and other buildings in the E and W ranges. Of the first mid-C12 monastery nothing now survives; in contrast to Mellifont there is no Romanesque work at Bective. The earliest remains are represented by the chapter house, on the SE, a plain rectangular structure, and one wall of the abbey church, dating from *c.* 1274–1300. This now forms the N wall of the cloister garth, from where it appears as a confusing jumble of a blocked archway, an inserted C16 mullioned window and a ruined rubble wall. From the N side its original function as the S wall of the nave of the church becomes apparent. Here a series of five tall Gothic arches, two-centred and trimmed with red sandstone, once formed the S arcade of the nave, opening into a S aisle. Only the arch from the cloister passage is now open; the others were walled up when the church was reduced in size and lost its aisles some time in the C15. Though severe, the late C13 church was of much more impressive proportions than its successor: it extended for an extra bay beyond the present W wall, which is of the C15, and the nave was lit at clerestory level by elegant quatrefoil windows set within two-centred relieving arches and with steeply sloping sills to ensure that the light was equally distributed within the building. Three of these openings survive and in one the quatrefoil window is almost perfect. This type of clerestory light is very much a feature of Irish C13 architecture and can also be found at Hore Abbey, Co. Tipperary, Gowran collegiate church, Co. Kilkenny, and Kilkenny Cathedral. The arch which opened into the S transept still stands entire but it is narrower than the original and may be the result of a decision to add a tower over the crossing in the C15, as happened at Mellifont. Several low sections of stonework survive to indicate the position of the N wall of the nave, but the E end of the church has gone completely and the nave now opens to a view of trees, lush fields and the waters of the Boyne.

Of the monastic buildings, only the E range occupies its original position on line with the S transept. The CHAPTER HOUSE, located at the SE corner of the cloister, is a low rectangular chamber, modest in scale, with a ceiling of four groin vaults which spring from a central chamfered column; two windows in the E wall. The dormitory ran across the top of this building and was enlarged in the C16, when Thomas

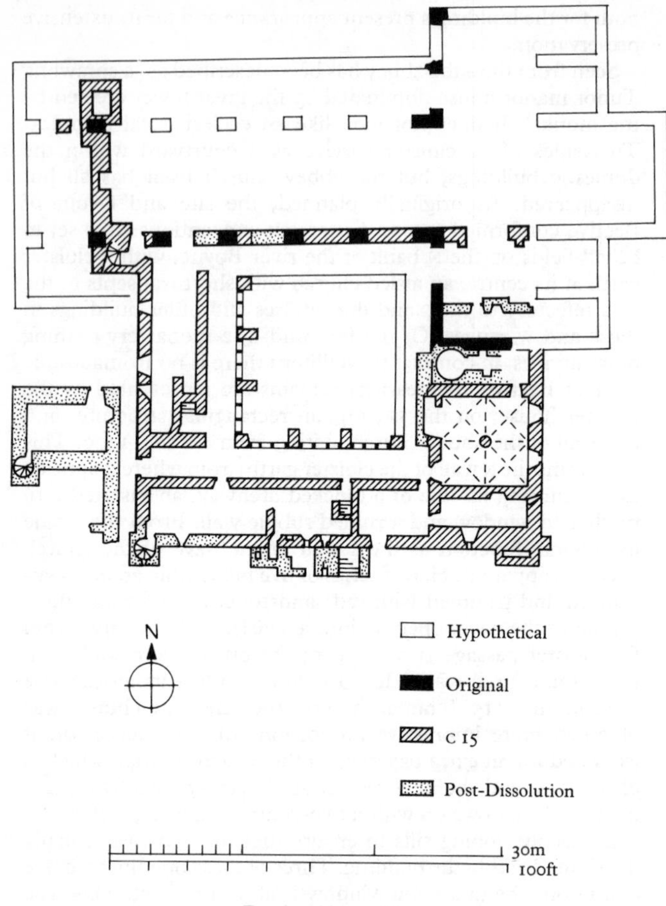

Bective Abbey. Plan

Agard converted the monastery buildings into a house, by the addition of an extra floor with a mullioned four-light window in a new gable overlooking the S front.

The other two ranges at Bective, on the S and W, are essentially a C15 rebuilding which was reworked when the abbey became a house. As the original church had extended further W it was perhaps inevitable that when it was reduced the W range of the monastery building was also cut back. As a
31 result, the monks' quarters were reduced and a new CLOISTER had to be built within the limits of a smaller space. It is intimate in scale, no more than 33 ft (9.9 m) square, and, though quite untypical of its order, is the best-preserved Cistercian cloister in Ireland. The sense of intimacy is greatly increased by the height of the surrounding walls, for the cloister passages were planned to be built not beyond the walls of the new S and W

ranges but within them; thus the upper floors rise directly above the cloister arcades, which, because of the weight of the masonry above them, are recessed within deep elliptical arches and reinforced by substantial square buttresses. This system of carrying the upper floors over the cloister passages is typical of Irish C15 friary architecture, particularly of the work of Franciscan builders, and gives a quite distinct character to the cloister garth.

Each arcade is formed of three miniature arches supported on a system of double column shafts. In accordance with common Irish practice the exterior and interior shafts are tied into the one structure by a solid stone panel which joins them, greatly increasing the sense of weight in what are quite slender piers. Worked in hard grey Ardbraccan limestone, each arcade is made up of three two-centred arches which spring from short piers of clustered shafts. Each group of three arches is contained within an elliptical relieving arch which is almost flat at the top. On the exterior the shafts of the arcades have bell capitals; their arches are simply chamfered and they have no ornament. On the inner face, however, the work is embellished with cusps, foot ornaments and hoodmouldings which spring from triple roll-moulded capitals. At the SW corner of the cloister a panel between the outer and the inner shaft is decorated with the figure of an ecclesiastic set into a crocketed, ogee-headed niche. His unidentified escutcheon carrys three fleur-de-lys. On the N and E walls crease lines and a series of plain corbel stones, which once supported a timber wall-plate, make it clear that the circuit of the cloister was completed as a covered space, with lean-to roofs on these two sides. Perhaps there was an intention to complete the building with stone arcades on all its sides, but the work was never put in hand.

At the SW corner of the building the monks erected a substantial square tower house of three storeys over a vaulted basement. With square corner turrets and a spiral stair in the SW corner, it is similar in form to many late medieval tower houses in North Leinster and to the tower house at Athlumney Castle nearby (*see* Navan). It may have been built to provide lodgings for the abbot, and it is certainly the most dramatic element in the mass of the abbey buildings today. The foundations of a further tower are W of this building.

The reduction of the monastery buildings and their reconstruction in the C15 undoubtedly determined the fate of the abbey after the Dissolution. Its manageable size and neat modern appearance clearly appealed to Thomas Agard and his successors, and the abbey was quite easily transformed into a fine country house. The monks' cloister became the loggia or courtyard of the household, the sacristy which adjoined the S transept was converted to a bakehouse, with a large bread oven, and the monks' dormitory above it was remodelled into two large rooms with big chimneypieces and new mullioned windows. The refectory which filled the upper floor of the S range was largely rebuilt as the GREAT HALL of the new mansion. Big rectangular windows were inserted into its S front and the house was approached by a flight of external stairs and entered by an archway in the SW corner. The crease line of a gabled roof appears on the wall of the tower house at the W end of the hall, which suggests that the room had an open timber roof like many a contemporary manor house in Tudor England. An opening above the front door gave access to a timber gallery at this end of the hall and there may also have been a screens passage. A dog-leg stair about the centre of the hall connects with the lower floor, where the kitchens and buttery were placed. Agard or one of his successors added the big chimneys on the E and S ranges.

BECTIVE BRIDGE. SE of Bective Abbey. A long and picturesque bridge of limestone rubble which spans the river Boyne close to the abbey. It comprises ten arches of segmental and semicircular profile and has long triangular cutwaters on its upriver face. A late C17 date has been suggested, but the earliest documentary evidence for a bridge at Bective is Grand Jury expenditure of 1821.

BECTIVE HOUSE. 3 km NE. Sophisticated stuccoed house set high above the Boyne and built *c.* 1800 by the Bolton family, then owners of Bective Abbey. Understated architecture in the spirit of Francis Johnston: a long, low rectangular house with two storeys of large sash windows on the principal fronts, the upper-floor window sills linked to form a continuous stringcourse, corner quoins treated as vertical strips, and a well-proportioned cornice and blocking course which completely hides the roof. The front is of seven bays, with moulded architraves to the windows and a square Doric porch with tripartite side windows. The side elevation is plainer, with five bays, and later C19 extensions beyond. The main house is two rooms deep on a tripartite plan, with a large and restrained central stairhall. The GATE LODGE is a pretty design inside an impressive ashlar gateway. T-plan, with a shallow hipped roof, overhanging eaves and a Doric loggia at the door. The drive winds picturesquely through magnificent beech woods.

ST MARY, BECTIVE PARISH CHURCH (C of I). 3 km NE, beside the main road in the demesne of Bective House. Picturesque hall and tower church erected to the design of *Joseph Welland*, architect to the Ecclesiastical Commissioners. Paid for by Richard Bolton between 1851 and 1854. The chancel was added in 1858. A nice clear-cut design, typical of its architect, with minimal surface decoration and good limestone masonry. Three-stage pinnacled tower, tall four-bay nave and single-bay chancel; each unit is defined by diagonal corner buttresses.

BALSOON HOUSE. 1 km N, on the S bank of the Boyne. A modest but interesting group of buildings in a pleasant setting on a bend of the river overlooking Bective Abbey and Bridge. Balsoon was occupied by the Norman family of Ussher from *c.* 1300 to 1713 and is the burial place of Archbishop Henry Ussher, one of the founders of Trinity College, Dublin. The present house is mid-Victorian, a two-storey Italianate block built over a basement with a three-bay front and two-bay sides. Wide hipped roof and bracketed eaves cornice. The front door is an elaborately moulded design incorporating foliated consoles with Greek key and guilloche motifs. Behind the house a flight of steps leads down to the flagged basement of a redbrick Georgian former house which measures some 44 ft by 50 ft (13.2 m by 15 m). Beyond this again is a long, low grassy mound with an C 18 grotto-like front. Inside is an extensive barrel-vaulted late medieval structure, 61 ft (18.6 m) long by 11 ft (3.3 m) wide, divided by cross-walls into five rectangular chambers. The vault is remarkable for its perfectly preserved wickerwork centering. This is the only surviving remnant of a castle erected in 1590 by Archbishop Ussher, then Rector of Assey and later Primate of Armagh. On the drive, the AGENT'S HOUSE is a pretty three-bay, two-storey design built of rubble and red brick, with pointed Gothick glazing to the ground floor.

BELLEWSTOWN

ME *0060*

A crossroads and racecourse on top of a hill, whose wooded N ascent is one of the loveliest slopes in Co. Meath.

BELLEWSTOWN CHAPEL. Plain T-plan church with the usual lancets and pointed entrances. Tenders for plastering the interior were requested by Nicholas Boylan of Hilltown in 1838, which may well be the date of the building.

COLLIERSTOWN HOUSE. 0.5 km S. Three-storey gabled house with a three-bay entrance front and a later square porch. Reputedly erected *c.* 1775; the interior joinery and plasterwork look more like 1790.

BEAUMONT. 2 km N. Built by J. McCann, who owned an extensive flour and oatmeal mill situated on the river Nanny beside the house. Described in 1837 as 'just recently erected'. Regency in flavour, the house is a narrow rectangular block with a bowed projection in the centre of the rear elevation. Two storeys crowned by the ubiquitous wide hipped roof with oversailing bracketed eaves. Elegant five-bay entrance front simply expressed as long sash windows of eighteen panes, with regular twelve-pane windows above. At the centre, a limestone porch carried on four freestanding Doric columns.

MOUNT HANOVER. 2.5 km NW. Very tall gabled Georgian house, three storeys over a basement, with canted bay windows on both side elevations rising through the full three storeys. An early to mid-C 18 date might be construed from the appearance of the entrance front. Long fifteen-pane sash windows with thick glazing bars diminishing abruptly to squat six-pane windows on the top floor, with large expanses of blank masonry between. Now ivy-covered. The architecture is hard to read. The doorcase is firmly of the mid-C 18 and is identical to the one at nearby Beybeg House, erected in 1758 (*see* Julianstown). Inside, the stair is located at a right angle to the hall. Behind are two larger rooms ending in bows which have decorative rococo plasterwork.

ANNAGOR. 2.5 km N. Rectangular Regency house. Two storeys over a basement, with a three-bay entrance front. Low wide hipped roof with oversailing bracketed eaves. A central Doric doorcase with a pretty elliptical fanlight is set above a low flight of steps. The outer windows are set in segment-headed relieving arches.

KILSHARVAN. 2.5 km NE. Large, two-storey Regency-revival house of *c.* 1880. Five-bay entrance front with two bows flanking a central Doric porch. Adjoining the house on the W is a smaller C18 house which retains its graded slating. At the rear are the remains of a watermill and a bleach green with a circular watchtower.

KILSHARVAN CHURCH RUINS. Near Kilsharvan house. Ivy-grown remains of a late medieval nave and chancel, with two round-headed doorways facing each other across the nave. Buried under creepers, a twinlight window of two double-cusped lights with simple tracery. – MONUMENT. Philip Tonge †1772; a classical aedicule.

ARDCATH CHURCH RUINS. 4 km SW. Long narrow medieval church comprising a nave and choir separated by a pointed chancel arch. Bellcote and blocked-up lancet to the W gable and a pointed E window with fragmentary stone mullions that suggest three pointed C13 lights. Brief documentary references to the church range from 1421 to *Usher's Visitation* of 1622.

ST MARY. 4 km SW, at Ardcath. 1859–73. Tall Gothic church, hard and handsome on an elevated site. Five-bay lancet hall with buttresses between each bay, diagonal at the corners, and shallow transepts now closed off with glass and timber screens. Four-light geometric windows to the entrance gable and a circular plate-tracery window above the altar. Ugly modern ceiling. In January 1875 a 'well-bred heifer, a sheep and a lamb, £3 and a silver watch' were raffled and the proceeds used to complete the church, which had been dedicated in 1863. ALTAR by *Barff*. – STAINED GLASS. Mater Dolorosa by *Mayer & Co.*

8060

BELLINTER

ME

65 Small yet very complete Irish Palladian house designed by *Richard Castle* and built from 1750 onwards for the brewer and M.P. John Preston, whose son became Lord Tara. As the architect died in February 1751, the extent to which the finish of the building represents his ideas must remain in doubt. Bellinter is a classic statement of the mid-C18 country-house ideal: a central two-storey block, linked by low, single-storey wings to flanking pavilions which project forward and form a court before the house. Beyond the pavilions, quadrant walls, decorated with niches, screen the stable yard on the E and the kitchen court on the W. High gate piers terminating in rococo urns mark the entry to both yards.

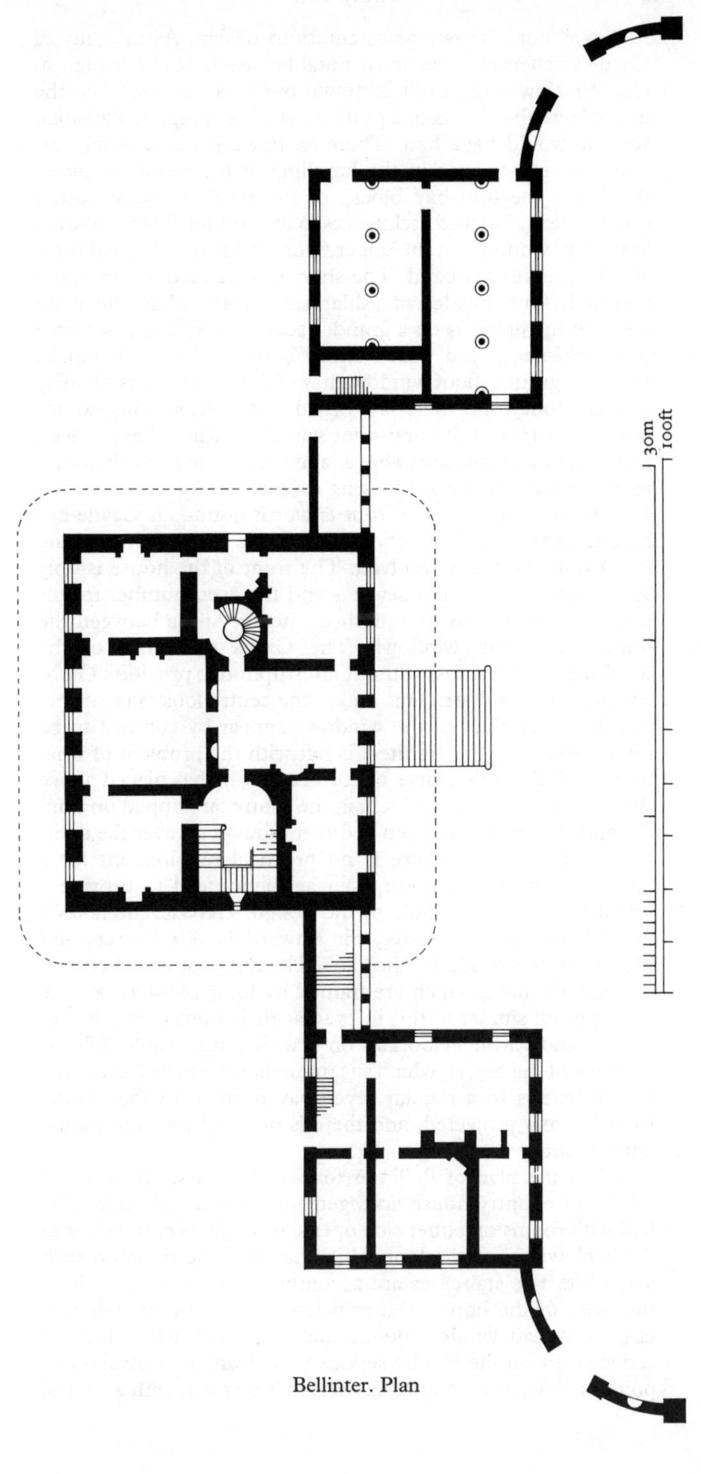

Bellinter. Plan

This is not a showy or ostentatious design. As in many of Castle's schemes – the most notable case is Russborough in Co. Wicklow – the front is drawn out to a long line and the house lacks the climax of a portico, which a complete Palladian scheme would have had. There is, however, a pleasant gradation of importance in the handling of the elements across the front: the four-bay blocks of the pavilions have corner quoins, heavy blocked architraves to the ground-floor windows, low plain windows on the upper floor, and simple hipped roofs above an eaves platband. The short linking sections are more polished, four arcades of ashlar stonework, while the main block of the house is on a grander scale, taller, as it is set on a semi-basement, and much more consciously architectural. Here the ground-floor windows have Gibbs surrounds of finely drafted stonework; there is a broad platband, a string-course linking the sills of the first-floor windows, which have lugged architraves with cornices above; and the façade is finished by a refined entablature and blocking course.

The centrepiece of the front is worth noting, as Castle has here attempted a conjunction of elements which is interesting if not quite perfectly resolved. The front of the house is only six windows wide – not seven – and the even number means that the door has to be squashed into the space between the third and fourth windows. The Gibbs surrounds of the windows are run across without interruption to provide a Gibbs surround to the door. This makes the centre look very strong, but the outer sides of the windows appear by contrast to be rather weak and the architect is left with the problem of what to do with the little ledges of cornice that he has placed above the outer windows and which, in the centre, are tipped up from the ends to suggest an open pediment drawn up over the door. On the upper floor there is no practical requirement for a central opening, but there is an aesthetic need to provide a visual focus in the middle of the design. Here Castle takes a motif from his old master, Sir Edward Lovett Pearce, and places a round-headed niche flanked by Ionic columns between the two windows, which are framed by Ionic pilasters. Pearce used a motif similar to this in 1729 at Bellamont Forest in Co. Cavan, and Castle elaborates on it with considerable skill. At the back of the house, which sits immediately above the Boyne, Castle reverts to a regular seven-bay front, with the middle room slightly projected, and there is no need for these subtle adjustments.

Inside, the plan of Bellinter follows the classic British and Irish C18 country-house arrangement – the double pile. The hall with rooms on either side opens, through a central door in the back wall, into a saloon which has also one room on each side of it. The staircases are accommodated in the middle of the sides of the house: the principal stair to the W, where a large Venetian window floods the space with light, and the service stair on the E. The service stair, from a constructional point of view, is a remarkable design. It is spiral, with a central circular well, and is built of self-supporting oak treads cantilevered out from the walls; it runs from the top to the bottom of the house, while the main stair only joins the two principal floors.

The interiors of the house today date from two periods: the mid-C 18, when Castle's design was completed, and *c.* 1820, when some modernizations were made. The principal contribution of the early C 19 was to convert the external arcades into glazed conservatories and lighten the effect of the interiors. Double doors were added to join the saloon with the drawing room at the back of the house and most of the earlier glazing bars were replaced by lighter sections. Fielded panelling survives in all the first-floor bedrooms and is particularly well seen in two unaltered rooms at the top of the stairs. The HALL is decorated with an emphatic Doric room cornice in plaster, with heavy mutules on the ceiling, and has plasterwork panels with trophies or arms on its walls. Niches flank the door to the saloon and there is an enormous grey stone chimneypiece characteristic of Castle's manner. The doorcases have heavy lugged surrounds with triangular guttae as decorations and then, somewhat unexpectedly, additional mutule cornices on a different scale, which are not part of the original scheme and may have been added in an attempt to lighten the effect of the house. The SALOON has a fine, flat rococo ceiling in the manner of *Robert West*.

The MAIN STAIRCASE is the architectural complement of the hall, with heavy Italianate balustrades, panelled side walls and an elaborated Vitruvian scroll marking the division between the ground and first floors. It has a high coved ceiling and opens through a Palladian arch with double Corinthian columns into a LOBBY in the centre of the first floor. This type 68
of circulation space at the level of the principal bedrooms is a characteristic feature of the grander houses designed by Pearce and Castle and originates, like the niche on the main façade, at Bellamont Forest. The Bellinter lobby is top-lit by a delightful oval lantern with four sash windows in its sides – the only part of the house to retain its robust mid-C 18 glazing bars – and is screened to the N by a colonnade of substantial Ionic columns. This is a busy space as no surface is left undecorated. The doors have lugged surrounds; the walls have fielded panelling; and on the ceiling some apprentice carpenters and plasterers seem to have been let loose to provide an uncontrolled display of every type of fret, fillet and cornice of which they are masters. The ceiling is an architectural riot, would-be symmetrical but not properly balanced, with odd skew beams whose elaborate decoration does nothing to disguise their clumsiness. Castle, one feels, must have been dead before this went up, and Lady Tara, who is credited with the alterations of the early C 19, must have longed to get rid of it!

Bellinter is now an adult education and retreat centre administered by the Sisters of Sion. In 1965, when the community took over the property, the kitchen and stable pavilions were ruinous. They have since been reconstructed, the kitchen pavilion as bedrooms and the stables as a house for the community, incorporating some of Castle's characteristic Doric stable columns.

4040 BELVEDERE WM

5, 66 The rustic Palladian house of Belvedere was designed by *Richard Castle* in 1740. It is a charming building set on the E shore of Lough Ennell where, for once, this most overworked of country house names is fully justified by a serene and beautiful location. 'Greater and more magnificent scenes are often met with,' wrote Arthur Young in 1777, 'but nowhere a more beautiful or singular one.' Here Richard Castle seems to have been inspired: the carelessness and routine character which can on occasion mar his work are entirely absent. Sturdy and handsome rather than gracefully elegant, this is nonetheless a sophisticated design which must rank among Castle's best. It is also innovative in providing the earliest example of the use of bow-ended rooms in any home in Ireland. Perhaps the impetus for creativity lies in the fact that this was not a regular commission for a complete house with all its attendant needs, but the presumably more attractive proposition of a lake-side lodge for the fishing parties of his patron, Robert Rochfort, Lord Belvedere. (Castle had also designed the Rochforts' long-demolished principal residence at Gaulston some five miles SE of here.)

Like its many European predecessors, Belvedere sits upon an elevated site, excavated in the mid-C19 as a series of terraces. It is not, however, a large or ornate house, but a simple two-storey block with semicircular bowed ends and a five-bay entrance front, articulated as a pair of advanced single-bay blocks flanking a recessed three-bay centre. A continuous cornice and blank parapet give the house a low-lying appearance, and two tall chimneystacks at each end of the central block emphasize its tripartite structure. The roof is completely invisible, which enhances the impression of the house as a casino. The materials are coursed limestone rubble with ashlar trim. The façades are expressed in a classic early Georgian idiom: sash windows to the central block, twelve panes below, set in Gibbs surrounds, and six panes above, in simple cutstone frames. Venetian windows occupy the ground floor of the advanced bays, with flat-headed tripartite windows above (originally designed by Castle as Diocletian windows). The bowed ends have a stark severity, with three sash windows on each floor and the curve of the bow emphasized by its high blank parapet. Raised corner quoins mark each break on the façade, while the main door is absolutely typical of its architect, displaying both his delight in boldly rusticated masonry blocks and – a feature he was to bequeath to Irish front-door design – a pair of Tuscan columns set within the arch of the doorway immediately in front of the jambs of the door. The overall effect of the design is quiet and urban.

The plan of Belvedere is now L-shaped, as a simple late Georgian wing was added behind the NW bow in the later C 18. The original design by Castle was one room deep and perfectly symmetrical, with four principal reception rooms on the ground floor and four bedrooms on the upper storey. Kitchens and servants' quarters are in the basement. The stair, which rises in a shallow U-shaped flight, is set in a separate block projecting slightly at the centre of the rear elevation. It communicated with a short corridor passing along the back of the main rooms on each floor. The largest and grandest rooms, the drawing room and dining room, were located at either end of the house in the rooms with bow windows, while the central three-bay block was divided into two smaller units. This plan was sadly destroyed in the later C 19, when the two centre rooms were made into one expansive hall with a timber internal porch and their rear walls were broken down and replaced by a wide and ungainly Ionic screen which opens directly into the stairhall. As a result the house is now open from front to rear. The stair is lit by a Venetian window and has turned balusters of a slender symmetrical design set on a continuous string with foliated decoration. It is not a grand design. The joinery throughout the house is of fine quality and in oak: panelled wainscotting and lugged door surrounds trimmed with beading, Vitruvian scroll and egg-and-dart borders. The drawing room and dining room use a fluted Scamozzian Ionic order within the Venetian windows. The chimneypieces are lavishly carved with masks, herms and garlands of flowers and fruit.

Belvedere's crowning glory is the rococo plasterwork of the main rooms, executed *c.* 1760. Bordered by rich modillion cornices and friezes embellished with garlands, egg-and-dart and shells, each ceiling is developed around a central figurative motif. In the hall, Jupiter astride an eagle hurling thunderbolts across the sky and (in what was once the small adjoining room) a group of sleeping cupids in a starry moonlit sky. The shape of the two large rooms with their bowed extensions gives scope for greater variety of form, and the ceiling designs here follow an elongated and stylized heart-shape profile. Exquisite examples of rococo decoration, with asymmetrical volutes, shells and garlands, encircle – in the drawing room – cupids among clouds and – in the dining room – medallions of Juno, Minerva and Venus. The stucco artist is not known, though the work has been attributed to *Barthelemij Cramillion* and is typical of the Wessobrun school.

Although Belvedere was designed as a lodge, upon its completion in 1743 Robert Rochfort abandoned his home at Gaulston and made this his principal residence. The cause of this move was not the charm of Lough Ennell but a sordid scandal in which Rochfort accused his young wife, Mary Molesworth, of adultery with his brother Arthur. In 1736 Rochfort, then a wealthy and self-indulgent widower in his mid-twenties, had chosen for his second wife Mary, the sixteen-year-old daughter of Viscount Molesworth. From the outset the union was not happy, nor was it improved by Rochfort's childish resentment when his wife's first child was a daughter. The birth of a son in the following year prompted some sort of rapprochement, but this was shortlived and Rochfort's absences from Gaulston became longer and more frequent. Lonely and isolated, Mary Rochfort depended increasingly upon the company of her neighbours and her in-laws, Arthur Rochfort, her husband's younger brother, and his wife, Sarah. Whether or not a liaison developed between Mary and Arthur Rochfort remains in doubt, though Robert Rochfort was convinced of the fact. Arthur made a hasty retreat to Europe where he remained until 1754; he was sued for damages by his brother and, failing to meet the bill of £25,000, was gaoled for sixteen years. Gaulston was Mary Rochfort's prison for thirty years. Meanwhile Lord Belvedere lived and entertained lavishly at Belvedere. In 1773 James Caldwell of Castle Caldwell in Co. Fermanagh recounted his experience of Rochfort's dining room, where a company of three were attended by 'four valets de chambre in laced clothes and seven or eight footmen'. On the Earl's death in 1779 Mary Rochfort, old and distraught, was released from her confinement and brought to join her daughter in England.

Though Castle's Diocletian windows were to be converted to a more ordinary tripartite design in early Victorian times, Belvedere escaped far more radical remodellings, as several schemes were prepared in 1857 by Sandham Symes and in 1859 by William Slater to convert the house, first in an Italianate
5 and then in a chateau style. Subsequently the set of terraces with rather tame and repetitive arcaded balustrades was added, possibly to designs of *Ninian Niven*, gardener to the Chief Secretary for Ireland and curator of the botanic gardens at Glasnevin, who had drawn up extensive plans for the grounds in 1857. The terraces provide an excellent platform from which to view the lough, but they seriously disrupt the delicate relationship of the villa with its setting, which remains one of the most charming planned landscapes in Ireland. Here the undulating contour of the land has been used to great advantage, helped now and then by a bank which has been enlarged or a valley whose sides have been made a little steeper. The ground, broken with small groups of trees and single specimens, has much of the fragile charm of a willow-pattern plate by Wedgwood and, like its porcelain counterpart, creates a series of contrived views, using little buildings to punctuate the design. Indeed the grounds of Belvedere are distinguished for a collection of ruined follies which epitomize the mid-C18 taste for melancholy speculation. The most spectacular of these is
92 the JEALOUS WALL, SW of the house, the largest 'sham ruin' in Ireland, which offers yet another testament, though prettier and more innocuous, to Robert Rochfort's resentment and implacable tyranny. The wall is the outcome of a quarrel between the Earl and his second brother, George, the ruin of whose home, Rochfort House or Tudenham Park, still stands

a short distance away (*see* Molyskar). Formerly the two houses were within sight of each other. Whether or not jealousy of the scale and opulence of Tudenham Park was the crux of the fraternal quarrel, Lord Belvedere decided to build a vast screen wall to block the view to his brother's house and put practical but unsightly farm buildings behind it. The Jealous Wall is, in fact, a spectacular partition. From the grounds of the house it appears like a shattered fragment from a medieval building of once enormous bulk. Two polygonal towers with craggy broken silhouettes flank broad, flat towers, with a giddy façade, some 40 ft (12 m) high, set in between. This rises from a base of three pointed-arched recesses to a row of 'broken' windows, one of which retains Y-tracery, with a range of little clerestory windows above. No one today would be deceived by this sort of imitation, yet, as a piece of theatre, the wall is memorable.

The Jealous Wall closes the view S from the house. On the N the landscape was calculated to provide a variety of views from the bow window of the dining room and, though these are now blocked by evergreens planted in the C20, the effect of the original design may still be imagined. Across a wide dell on the NW, and crowning a little hillock which is surrounded by trees, is the GOTHIC OCTAGON, a primitive structure in rubble stone lined with brick and apparently once used as a conservatory. Now open to the sky, it has wide ogee-headed Gothick arches surmounted by blocked pointed quatrefoils. The building is a little like an C18 Gothic parody of the lavabo at Mellifont, which may not be entirely accidental. On the side facing the house the octagon is set above two shallow bastions as mock fortifications. Behind, steps and a path lead down to a wooded walk along the edge of the lough. Further N, and presiding over a long vale which extends back to the house, is the SHAM RUIN GATEWAY. Here gigantic arrow loops flank an archway built of rustic rocks, with an upper storey of pointed arches and a grotesque oriel window in between. The battlements above have the exaggerated profiles of a row of stalagmites. Old accounts attribute the Jealous Wall to an otherwise unrecorded architect from Florence called *Barradotte*. However, the source for all three pieces of romantic folly is the astronomer, mathematician, antiquarian and amateur architect *Thomas Wright* of Durham, whose *Six Original Designs of Grottos* (1758) provides precise models for the gateway and whose grotto is the inspiration for the overall symmetrical layout of the Jealous Wall. Wright had already spent some time in Ireland in 1747 when, in the company of Lord Limerick, he prepared surveys of the antiquities of Co. Louth, published in the following year as *Louthiana*, a book which includes the first known illustration of the Mellifont Lavabo. It may be that Wright was known to Lord Belvedere and designed these follies specially for the estate in Westmeath, publishing them later in his book of grottos. Alternatively the Earl may have owned Wright's book and copied or concocted them from it.

0000 ## BLACKROCK LO

Seaside village with a view across to the Cooley peninsula and a good Catholic church.

136 ST OLIVER PLUNKETT. 1923 by *Ralph Byrne*. A bold Hiberno-Romanesque church impressively sited on an eminence overlooking Dundalk Bay. Built of coursed limestone rubble with granite dressings, the contrast of stone in dark grey and silver emphasizing its architectural elements. Simple hall plan, with a small apsidal sanctuary at the W end. The entrance gable is expressed as a giant round-headed arch with two orders of arch rings, framing a wheel window, a row of blind arcading and a round entrance arch. The gable front is buttressed on the S by a short polygonal tower, which contains the baptistery, and on the N by a complete Irish round tower, whose stair provides access to the choir gallery at the back of the church. There is nothing very novel in this Celtic Revival plan – Timothy Hevey had developed essentially the same scheme fifty years before at Raphoe and Dunleavey in Co. Donegal, and the side elevations go back even further, to the neo-Norman churches of Sir Robert Smirke – but Ralph Byrne's detailing is firm. As a whole the church masses well; nothing is skimped here, which may mean that the Catholic parishioners of Blackrock were conscious of a certain national significance in their decision to build a new church, in an Irish style and dedicated to an Irish patriot (not then canonized), in the year after Irish independence had been won.

The interior is lucid and orderly: a three-bay nave, articulated by a blind round arcade framing triple-lancet windows, also round-headed. The arches are 'carried' on broad pier-like pilasters with angle colonnettes, scalloped capitals and panels of Celtic interlacing. A round-headed chancel arch frames the smaller arch of the apse, which is flanked by more round-headed niches above the side altars.

ST NICHOLAS. 3 km SW, at Heynestown. Early hall and tower type church, built in 1803 and remodelled in 1827. Harled, with limestone trim. Three-bay hall, chancel and three-stage tower. In the churchyard are two tombs of the Fortesque family, Viscounts Clermont, of 1756 and 1759.

HEYNESTOWN CASTLE. Beside the church, probably of C16 date, a square three-storey tower built of boulders and rubble stone, with four round corner turrets. A large semicircular arch, spanning between the turrets on both E and W elevations, once carried the battlements forward from the face of the wall. The interior is vaulted, with a dividing wall running E and W. Fireplace and press recesses. Garderobes in the NW tower at second- and third-floor levels. The SE tower contains the stair well.

DUNMAHON CASTLE. 3 km W. The ruin of a late medieval tower house standing on the flat pasture land of N Louth and as such a very welcome vertical accent in the landscape. Like Roodstown Castle near Stabannan, Dunmahon is a crisp limestone and greywacke rubble tower of three storeys over a vaulted basement, with square corner turrets and octagonal angle towers to the battlemented parapet. Square in plan, with a square stair turret projecting at the NE angle and a smaller garderobe tower at the NW corner. A pointed entrance arch is located between the two towers on the N face at a right angle to the entrance of the spiral stair. The vestibule was protected by a murder hole. The windows are for the most part simple loops, with both internal and external splay to the basement storey. The S wall had more elaborate fenestration, with lintelled windows crowned by hoodmouldings. Inside is the classic vaulted basement and three upper rooms, each with a garderobe chamber.

Nothing is known of the castle's history before the mid-C17, when it was the scene of a famous massacre, long lamented in local folklore. Though documentary accounts differ in both date and detail, it appears that at some point during the 1640s the garrison at Dundalk murdered over 200 local inhabitants who had gathered in the castle to celebrate Mass. Apparently the evil deed was accomplished by the trickery of the local commander, Townley, who gained admission to the building by seducing Eva Walters, the daughter of Dunmahon's Roman Catholic proprietor.

HAGGARDSTOWN CHURCH RUIN. 1.5 km W. The ruin of a late medieval nave-and-chancel church with a double bellcote over the W gable and opposing doorways in the nave. The church was repaired in 1622 but was again ruinous in 1692.

HAGGARDSTOWN CHURCH. 2 km W. 1855. Simple barn-style rural chapel, with the altar at the centre of the long N wall and a short broad nave projecting to the S and forming a Gothic entrance front. Rendered, with pointed windows and simple E.E. detail. Inside is a charming timber Gothick reredos.

BRACKLYN HOUSE

WM *5050*

6 km NNE of Killucan

A fantastic neo-mannerist composition of rocks and arches – a grotto-cum-grand-gateway – provides a rather confusing intro- 93
duction to an understated, if exceptionally well-proportioned late C18 house. The grotto, built presumably as a pair of gate lodges, is of coarse limestone rubble and consists of a broad central archway surmounted by a pyramidal-shaped bellcote, with a rectangular cell-like chamber on each side. The whole building is designed to emphasize mass, with unhewn boulders as voussoirs and lumps of stone projecting below the pyramid – all authentically rustic in an overgrown, tangled state today.

The house, by comparison, is an essay in crisp precision, a neat rectangular block, with a five-bay, two-storey front – the windows set wide apart – and of a sheer, clean appearance, with the façade carried up to a thin blocking course which almost entirely conceals a low hipped roof and two symmetrical banks of chimneys. The building, like so many Irish houses, is rendered in smooth cement: had it been of brick it would be like an early work of the young John Soane in Norfolk. The house dates from *c.* 1790.

In the mid-C19 it gained a correctly detailed Tuscan porch, which projects as a limestone cube from the centre of the façade; single-storey, single-bay wings have been added in the C20. The plan is tripartite and two rooms deep, with a central entrance hall and top-lit staircase set axially behind. Reception rooms open either side off the hall. The dining room has pretty neoclassical decorations with semicircular niches ornamented with playing putti and a polychrome marble chimneypiece. The hall and stairhall were altered when the porch was added and now have a mid-C19 character, with heavy cornices supported by console brackets framing the openings and casts of the Elgin marbles set above the doors. In the late C18 Bracklyn was acquired from the Packenhams by the Fetherston Haugh family, who built the present house.

8060 CANNISTOWN ME

CHURCH OF ST BRIGID. The substantial remains of a rectangular medieval church, comprising a long nave and chancel. With the exception of the N side of the nave, all the walls stand almost to roof level, and the W gable is intact, with the base of a double bellcote rising from it. The site is an old one: a monastery called Eascair Brannan was reputedly founded here by St Finian of Clonard in the C6. Following the Norman invasion, the lands were granted to the Nangles, who built a castle and, at the end of the C12, a church which became the parish church of the area. What stands today was rebuilt and possibly enlarged in the late C15 or early C16. The principal feature of the church is the late C12 or C13 chancel arch, a round-headed opening with triple roll mouldings, the centre roll filleted. The arch springs from a clustered shaft with stiffleaf capitals and a carved impost on each side, one representing an otter hunt and the other identified as the arrest of Christ. In contrast to these enrichments, the windows are plain: in the nave, the remains of a double-cusped lancet; in the chancel, two single lancets. The E window is now a wide, and late, flat-headed opening. There is a simple piscina recess in the S wall and another in the W gable. In the chancel a nicely moulded string-course runs along the top of the window arches. Within the church are several fragments of carved and moulded stone, some inserted above to the l. and r. of the chancel arch, others on the walls.

1010 CARLINGFORD LO

A quaint town, nestling at the foot of the Cooley mountains on the S shore of Carlingford Lough, and one of the very few Irish towns to retain an authentic medieval character. The place was a

Norman foundation which grew up around the castle erected here *c.* 1210 to defend the coastal pass against the Ulster Irish. Carlingford's intimate atmosphere, although largely due to the number of surviving medieval buildings, owes much to the fact that it has hardly developed beyond its medieval boundary, still discernible when the town is viewed from the mountain slope above it. The present houses and shops still reflect the medieval street layout, with long narrow allotments behind. What has been described as Carlingford's 'medieval suggestiveness' derives therefore from the town's failure to expand commercially or otherwise since the C17, a direct result of the decline in coastal traffic and the growth of internal transport in the post-medieval period.

KING JOHN'S CASTLE. *c.* 1210. Large and imposing limestone 46
castle situated on a rocky outcrop above Carlingford Lough. Hardly erected by King John, who spent only three days in Carlingford in 1210; very probably built before his visit, by either de Courcy or de Lacy, and subsequently named in the King's honour. In 1261 the castle was extended eastward towards the Lough, but by 1388, owing to the frequent attacks by the Irish, the building was deemed unsafe and money was granted for extensive repairs. Just over a century later, in 1501, the whole of Carlingford had been so badly damaged by Scots and Irish attacks that certain tolls were granted to enclose the town with a stone wall. The castle was captured by Lord Inchiquin in 1649 but surrendered in the following year to Sir Charles Coote. Forty years later, in the campaigns of James II against William of Orange, it was slighted by retreating Jacobite forces and was later used as a hospital by General Schomberg. By 1778 the building was ruinous, though in the opinion of one concerned traveller it remained 'a place of great consequence' which 'ought to be repaired and preserved'. This task was begun by the Marquess of Anglesey in the later C19 and has been continued by the Office of Public Works.

A good instance of plain, strong military architecture, the existing castle is roughly D-shaped, the product of several building campaigns. The original and apparently oval-shaped fortress constitutes what is now the W curved part of the D. This was simply a large open courtyard, enclosed by thick curtain walls with very deep embrasures framing loopholes on two levels. The rough corbels which supported the first-floor wall-walk are still visible on the E side above the present entrance. Access to this castle was by a barbican – a narrow passage between two gates – in the centre of the wall; its foundations are still in evidence. At the SW corner is a tall square tower, again with loops and embrasures, and a similar tower probably stood on the NW side.

The second major building period is of 1261. This saw the construction of the massive wall, which runs N–S across the middle of the existing castle, and which formed the W wall of a range of new apartments, built in two storeys over a basement

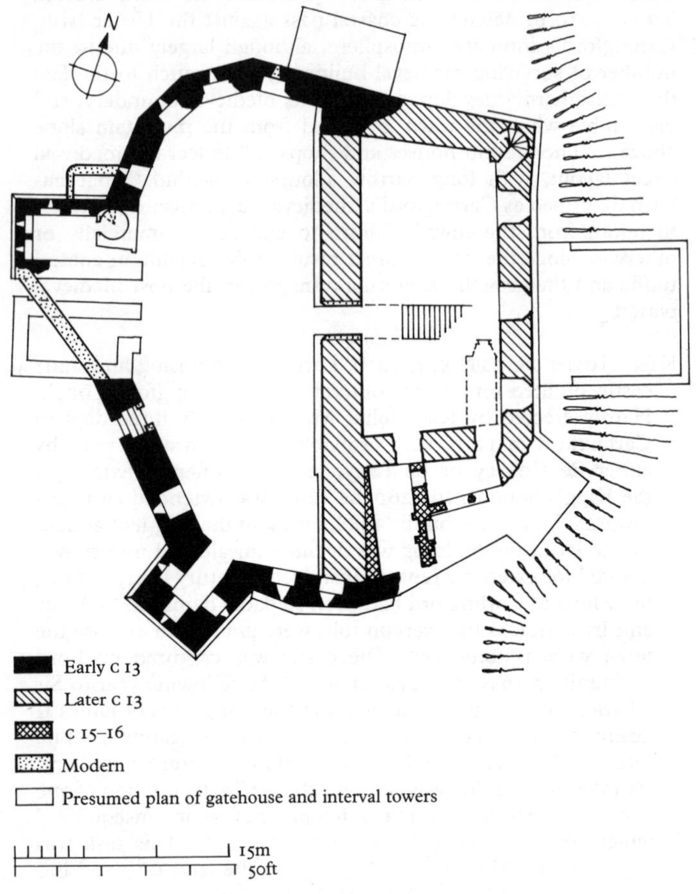

Carlingford, King John's Castle. Plan

with a great hall at first-floor level. Nothing remains of this today beyond the vaulted basement and the exterior walls with a spiral stair in the NE corner. In the basement, marks of the original wickerwork centering are clearly visible. An archway (now blocked) at the base of the steps led to a platform overlooking the centre pier.

The SE corner of the building contained the marshal's domestic quarters. This is the most sophisticated and probably the latest addition to the castle, dating perhaps to the C15. Here are the traces of several first-floor chambers with well-preserved chimneybreasts and a handsome double-arched screen that divided two apartments, both of which were still intact in 1748. The defensive position of King John's Castle above the coastal pass was dramatically exaggerated by the deep cutting made by G.N.R. engineers in 1872.

DOMINICAN ABBEY. The abbey was founded here in 1305 by 6
Richard de Burgh, Earl of Ulster, and by the time of its dissolution is recorded as possessing all the usual monastic buildings, church, belfry, chapter house, dormitory, kitchen etc. All that remains today is the gauntly impressive shell of the Friars' Church, a large and imposing structure 125 ft (37.5 m) in length and 22 ft (6.6 m) wide inside. Two deep pointed arches with chamfered jambs divide the church into nave and choir after the common pattern of Irish medieval friaries. Above is a narrow rectangular belfry, approached by a staircase in the S wall.

The vault, which is pierced by a rectangular hole for the bellrope, still bears the impression of the medieval wickerwork centering. Above it the tower is of two storeys; the ringing stage on the upper level was originally surmounted by a parapet. The windows in the N and S walls of the nave and chancel are now blocked and devoid of cutstone detail. Only the outline of the great E window, which would have contained a group of lancets, survives. The W end of the church has a fortified appearance, with two square towers and a machicolated turret positioned centrally above the main entrance. Defensive precautions were particularly necessary here as the abbey was sited outside the medieval town wall. The W entrance is a pointed arch with a moulded label of late C15 or early C16 character. Little survives of the claustral buildings, which formed a rectangular complex S of the church. An external string-course to the S wall of the nave marks the line of the cloister roof, while the gable line of the E range is preserved as a line of slates on the S wall of the chancel. The windows of the S wall are set unusually high up, above the former cloister roof-line. In the adjoining field are a fragmentary S wall of the E range and the portion of a rectangular building, perhaps the prior's castle. A short distance E of the church are the remains of the abbey's watermill and fishpond.

MINT. Although a mint was established at Carlingford in 1467, little other than tradition associates it with the small tower house that now bears its name. A typical example of a C16 fortified town house, greatly enhanced by its position in a narrow lane leading to the Tholsel gate. The Mint is of three storeys with a slight batter, a battlemented parapet and a large machicolation above the door. Originally the building will have had gables and a pitched roof behind the wall-walk at roof level. The materials are coursed rubble with granite corner stones and limestone dressings. Inside are stone window seats, cupboard recesses and a round-headed door leading to a garderobe at the rear. Above all, the Mint is remarkable for its 54
windows, ogee-headed lancets, single and paired, with one cross-mullioned window on the first floor; all have limestone surrounds carved with Celtic motifs of interlaced knots, animal and human heads. A medieval head, now very weathered, juts out above the entrance.

THOLSEL. A small rubble building consisting of a single-storey chamber arched over the narrow Tholsel Street. Narrow pointed windows in each elevation, with a plain entrance on the N side approached by a flight of stone steps. Probably one of the original town gates, the Tholsel for centuries accommodated meetings of the town council and on one occasion was the venue for a provincial parliament. The building was extensively repaired in the C19 by Lord Anglesey, and the archway with portcullis groove is probably the only early work to survive.

TAAFE'S CASTLE. According to tradition this castle was erected during the wars between Elizabeth I and the O'Neill of Ulster in the latter half of the C16. A taller and more massive tower house than the Mint, with little or no ornamentation. Overhanging battlemented parapet, SW turret and a machicolation over the original entrance. Expressed for the most part by simple loops, with a single ogee-headed window on the E face. Nothing is known of the castle's history beyond its presumed ownership by the Taafe family, Earls of Carlingford.

CHURCH OF THE HOLY TRINITY. Medieval and modern. Large limestone belltower with a pronounced batter, an advanced parapet and stepped battlements, adjoining a long plain hall. The tower is probably late medieval and was incorporated into a church founded here in the 1660s. The existing church, built in 1821, is of five bays, harled, with Y-traceried windows and a round-headed triple-light E window. Inside, a two-centred chancel arch with arched recesses on each side of the sanctuary. – MONUMENT. A flat funerary tablet with a draped urn to Ross S. Moore †1855; by *Thomas Farrell.*

ST MICHAEL. 1870. Five-bay lancet hall with a single-bay chancel, of coursed limestone rubble. Gabled and buttressed, with a bellcote over the entrance front. Triple-light Perp E and W windows. In 1959 *W. H. Byrne & Son* prepared designs for a new classical church with a giant order and a freestanding campanile. Fortunately for the medieval spirit of Carlingford this scheme was not carried through.

GHAN HOUSE. Early to mid-C18 house already begun by a Mr Stannus in 1726, when he is reported to have stolen the flagstones from the nave of the nearby abbey and used them as a pavement before his own front door. The building is L-shape in plan, comprising two long gabled blocks. The house proper is a two-storey double-pile of eight bays with an E entrance front and the stair in the NW corner. At a right angle to the stair well is a tall single-storey range, one room deep and of six bays, set above a brick-vaulted basement lit by semicircular windows at ground level. Although much altered, the interior retains some fielded wainscotting, coved ceilings and lugged surrounds framing six-panel doors. The windows have been lengthened in the principal rooms. On the first floor is a large drawing room, probably originally two rooms and half the length of the main front, which has a coved ceiling decorated with quaint provincial rococo plasterwork of flower garlands and medallion busts; it looks *c.* 1740.

OTHER BUILDINGS. Across the street from Ghan House is a fine two-storey, five-bay thatched house with regular sash windows and the entrance off-centre; probably late C18. NEWRY STREET, Carlingford's main street, is lined by an assortment of two- and three-storey houses painted in a variety of sea-side colours and with a number of modest yet nice C19 shop-fronts. The GARDA BARRACKS is the former COASTGUARD STATION of 1848 by *Jacob Owen*, a cottage-like seven-bay, two-storey block with projecting gabled ends. The PAROCHIAL HALL of 1925 is a two-bay rubble hall with a cement-rendered Italianate façade, two storeys over a deep basement and clearly too tall for this narrow street. Next door is the tiny PRESBYTERIAN CHURCH of 1869 by *Robert Young*, a four-bay lancet hall of squared limestone with granite trim. Diagonal buttresses, triple-light window and a pointed arch flanked by lancets. Next to this, the diminutive COURTHOUSE, an unassuming 1930s design in white cement; flat three-bay façade with blocky corner piers, parapet and porch. Polygonal gate piers flanking steps like an Edwardian garden and curved outer walls.

CARRIGLASS MANOR LF *1070*

Two highly distinctive periods of Irish architecture and two of its 115
most distinguished personalities are represented by the buildings at Carriglass. The stables, farmyard and triumphal arch entrance were designed by *James Gandon* between 1792 and 1804; the house was built to the designs of *Daniel Robertson* from 1838 to 1845. Gandon is Ireland's greatest classicist, Robertson the undisputed master of the picturesque manor house. The contrast in their manners is instructive and enjoyable. Two families employed the two architects. In the C18 the estate (which appears as both Carrickglass and Kerryglass) belonged to the Gleadowe-Newcomen family. Gandon's client in 1792 was Sir William Gleadowe-Newcomen, a banker whose business kept him principally in Dublin and who, with characteristic practicality, developed the stables, gardens and farm buildings of the estate before tackling the house. Gandon drew up plans for an unusual neoclassical villa, a condensed geometric exercise, with blank windows on its entrance front and a shallow oval saloon behind; but the design was never built. His STABLES and FARMYARD capture something of the severe excellence promised in this villa scheme. They are laid out axially as two large interconnecting courtyards, with arched gateways set across the longer central axis. The stableyard, at the N end, is of ashlar limestone, while the farmyard, to the S, uses a more rustic effect, with rendered, lime-washed walls, set off with dark limestone trim. This yard is surrounded by long low buildings, while the stableyard is of uniform two-storey blocks. The contrast probably means that the stables were built

on their own, *c.* 1792, and that the farmyard was added later, certainly by 1804. The stylistic difference has also been interpreted (by Maurice Craig and the Knight of Glin) as a metaphor for the superior status accorded to the horse over mere agricultural activity, a distinction which is carried through to the archways that give entry to the yards. The stable arch, nearest the house, is heroic: a cubic mass of stone pierced by a wide round-headed opening with a shallow pediment above. Typical of Gandon's manner are the shallow mutules below the pediment cornice and the blank tablet with guttae set above the arch. The entrance to the farmyard is consciously primitive, a wide masonry pier with uninterrupted horizontal channelling and two elliptical arches, set one inside the other, which seem to anticipate the functional aesthetic of railway engineering. It is assumed that this rugged wall was intended to support a superstructure, possibly a clocktower, that would have risen in picturesque composition above the whole group. No satisfactory explanation has ever been offered for the skew line of the farmyard arch which makes one of the rusticated sides doubly deep. Perhaps it is no more than a conscious mannerism, the spirit of Giulio Romano alive in the Age of Reason, for Gandon's farmyard façades, albeit in a rustic vein, play entertaining tricks on the visitor who looks for symmetry or arithmetical exactness in architectural design.

The TRIUMPHAL ARCH at the entry to the estate offers more unsettling architecture. It bears an obvious relationship to the two archways – also rather shallow – which mark the centres of the arcaded screens at the Four Courts in Dublin, but it may perhaps also be interpreted as a wilful neoclassical parody of the favourite motif of the earlier Palladians, the Venetian window. In such a reading the architect's blank niches in the piers become the side-lights of a window, and the unorthodox platband with dentils which finishes the composition might be considered as a severe room cornice. In the evolution of his designs Gandon has a capacity continually to reverse interior and exterior concepts, a process which is neatly demonstrated here. The CASTELLATED LODGE on the main drive, with pointed windows inside Gothic arches, is in the same heavy idiom as Gandon's Gothic scheme for Slane Castle. The GARDENER'S HOUSE, in the walled garden W of the demesne, is also Gandonian; a small three-bay, two-storey front, built in brick, with ground-floor relieving arches and a central lunette above the door.

Early in the C19 the Carriglass estate was purchased by Thomas Lefroy, one of the most distinguished lawyers of his day, who was called to the Irish bar in 1797 and two years later married an heiress, Mary Paul, of Silver Spring in Co. Wexford. Lefroy became a bencher of the King's Inn in 1819, a Baron of the Court of Exchequer in 1841 and Lord Chief Justice of Ireland eleven years later. The success of his professional career, coupled perhaps with Mrs Lefroy's own wealth, provided the funds to rebuild Carriglass. By 1837, when the project first began, Gandonian classicism was quite outmoded. Daniel Robertson, the Lefroys' architect, did sometimes work in a vigorous and rather busy Roman manner, but the house at Carriglass, which now added 'Manor' to its name, was rebuilt in a free Elizabethan style which Robertson had made peculiarly his own.

The new house occupies an elevated site and is designed to group effectively from a variety of angles. In contrast to the late Georgian ideal, which sought to minimize the impact of the servants' quarters, these rooms are now on a level with the rest of the house, not hidden underneath it, and are employed to add picturesque effects and incident to the design. The composition is clever, for though the principal façades are both intrinsically symmetrical, the silhouette of the house is constantly changing, with a variety of intriguing patterns.

The key to the entrance front is the pair of tall octagonal turrets, 10 ft (3 m) in diameter, at the corners of the façade. These would be common enough in many early C19 Tudor designs, but Robertson gives them dramatic impact by placing them, not at either end of a battlemented façade of much the same height, but as twin towers which rise a full storey above the slates of a low two-storey block. A gable containing the front door surmounted by an oriel window projects from the centre of the façade, with simple mullioned windows on either side and half-dormers above. One of these projects and the other is flush with the wall. The garden front uses dormers again, two on either side of a broad bay window, with large three-light mullioned windows below. Here absolute symmetry is avoided by projecting the mullioned window, which lights the dining room on the W, while its pair, which lights the drawing room on the E, is flush with the wall. The E, or end, elevation of the house is quite asymmetrical: two gables side by side, one projected and narrower than the other, with a square bay-window squashed against it and containing a large cusped Perp window to light the landing of the stairs. The kitchen wing and offices extend as low gabled additions at the far end of the house. A four-bay Tudor-arched conservatory screens the service yard on the garden front.

Robertson's architecture seems especially designed to take advantage of the sharp edges which Irish limestone takes and holds. Carriglass Manor is, above all else, a sharply detailed house, with English C16 mouldings (which Robertson had learnt from the collegiate buildings of Oxford) precisely disposed across its façades. There is too a certain practicality in his decision to employ stone corbel brackets below the eaves, carrying the edge of the slates well beyond the walls. This detail, despite the romantic style, gives the house a cleanly functional air – like the later Gothic architecture in Ireland of E. W. Godwin – and it also permits the sustained use of half-dormer windows on both main fronts without the need for unsightly guttering and down-pipes. This is skilful design of considerable quality.

The interiors have much of the charm of Regency Gothic
116 continuing in the early Victorian age. Wide four-centred archways in the inner hall or gallery spring from cluster shafts with C16 profiles. The doors have Perp panelling and are set in stilted square arches. The ceilings are flat, with plaster ribs, miniature bosses and cavetto cornices, filled appropriately with roses and lilac in the drawing room, oakleaf and holly in the library, and grapes and vineleaves in the dining room. Stained glass fills the smaller panels in the windows. The chimneypieces are Perp-panelled, shallow late Gothic designs in marble.

Robertson's working drawings for Carriglass allow the course of the building work to be plotted in some detail. The overall shape of the scheme seems to have been agreed by March 1837, with alterations made to the design of the kitchen offices in October the same year. The first proposal included a Gothic *porte cochère* which was omitted in the scheme as built. Work probably began in the spring of 1838 but progressed slowly, as the corbel brackets for the eaves of the main house were not detailed until April 1839, and more masonry work was still being drawn out to full size in August that year. Details for the few cast metal gutter heads for the bay windows are dated 1840, which no doubt marks the year of the completion of the shell of the house. Drawings for the joiners were still being made in May and July 1842. In 1837 Robertson had proposed a stair like the present one, which rises in three flights, but in January 1841 he produced an alternative, and grander, double-return design; it was not until May 1843 – five years after the house had been begun – that the design of the main staircase reached its final form. Drawings for the plasterwork of the main rooms date from the same time, but the details of the inner hall were not provided by Robertson until July 1845. For a house of this size the rate of progress seems incredibly slow, with workmen on the site for more than seven years. The contractor for the mason work, which is excellent, was *William Dennin*; the coats of arms were carved by *Andrew Coffey*, and the Clerk of Works appears to have been a Mr Simmons. The paving of the entrance hall is of Ballynamuck stone.

1080

CARSTOWN

LO

56 A unique and fascinating house, set in high, flat lands netted with country roads some 2.5 km W of Termonfeckin. Carstown demonstrates the development of Irish domestic architecture from the late Middle Ages to the modern period perhaps more succinctly than any other place in North Leinster. The building is a rare survival of the type of C17 Irish manor house, which followed the late medieval tower houses of the C15 and C16. Built as a long gabled range, it consists of a single storey over a tall basement, with an attic storey above, lit by dormers that are perhaps a later alteration to the original fabric and have

certainly been rebuilt. This grand if unsophisticated building has a substantial C17 chimneystack at its W end, five gabled dormer windows and a steeply pitched roof. The entrance is off-centre to the E between two of the dormer bays and is approached by an impressive limestone flight of steps projecting some 24 ft (7.2 m) in front of the main door. The fenestration, now much altered, is a mixture of C18 and C19 sash windows, though the small irregular basement windows preserve the impression of musket loops.

The date and the builders of Carstown are commemorated by two sculpted panels, one above the entrance and the other above the principal chimneypiece, both of which bear the date 1612, armorial crests and the initials OP and KH, which are identified as Oliver Plunkett and his wife, Katherine Hussey, daughter of James Hussey of Galtrim. Oliver Plunkett's father, Alexander, was the sixth son of Oliver, first Lord Louth.

While the elevation of Carstown might suggest a single date for the entire structure, irregularities in the plan and the survival of some medieval details demonstrate that an earlier Plunkett tower house has been absorbed into the later building. In elevational terms the tower constitutes the two bays to the right of the external stair. It was a substantial structure, some 25 ft (7.5 m) by 20 ft (6 m) internally, with a pointed-arch entrance which still survives at its NW corner in the basement of the house. This is a two-centred arch with pocked tooling and tapering chamfers to its jambs; both its size and its detail suggest a late C15 date. Immediately inside and to the N of the arch a curve in the wall records the profile of the original spiral stair.

If the evidence for the tower is unmistakable, it is still not clear at what stage it was joined to the manor house of 1612. The union might have been effected from the outset, but it is also possible that it occurred at a much later date; with the exception of a chimneypiece, the interior detail in this part of the house is Victorian, while the detailing of the western range of the house is predominantly mid-C18 in character. A survey of 1774 which records a three-bay, two-storey house, occupied by 'the widow Brabazon', and a second 'good slated house', occupied by Philip Brabazon, provides food for thought. Perhaps the tower house survived as a separate building at this time and was only taken down and absorbed into the rest of the house *c.* 1860, when the large Victorian room on its first floor was created.

Though it is now much altered internally, a fairly clear picture of the 1612 house can be discerned, largely thanks to the massive limestone chimneypiece which survives in the N wall of the principal floor and which must once have formed the centrepiece of a larger great hall. Almost 9 ft (3 m) wide and 5 ft (1.5 m) high, the chimneypiece lintel has five joggled joints and, on the central keystone, the sculpted plaque of 1612. Some pocked tooling to the jambs suggests the reuse of dressed stones from the tower house, perhaps from quoins at its SW angle (if indeed the two structures were joined together at this time). The two partition walls which now divide the range into three rooms date from the early to mid-C18, with lugged surrounds to the doorcases and fielded panelling to the joinery. A staircase adjoining the rear of the C17 range and leading from the principal floor to the basement is also mid-Georgian in character. This stair well was later extended to provide a long narrow corridor running along the back of the main house. Later again, in the early C19, a three-bay, three-storey residential wing was added at the back. This extends perpendicularly from the central stair to give the house an irregular T-shaped plan. Beyond on the W, a curved Gothick wall screens the stable offices, while the yard, E of the house, is entered through a pretty battlemented and gabled entrance arch: all evidence of the renewed investment in the estate in the C19. It is a tragedy of modern Ireland that, despite its rarity and fine state of preservation, the only features of this remarkable building deemed worthy of a preservation order are the two carved plaques which commemorate its erection.

1090

CASTLEBELLINGHAM LO

A pretty village, nicely situated on the banks of the river Glyde and grouped around a triangular green. Though marred by heavy traffic, Castlebellingham is still an architectural treat, with a charming group of estate buildings – a big house, church and cottages – which presents the visitor with a perfect microcosm of rural life in early Victorian Ireland. The village came into being in the C17 to serve the needs of the Bellingham estate and was later sustained by a brewery founded here in the C19. That the lives of the Bellingham family made their imprint on the village is nicely illustrated by a number of Della Robbia-revival plaques put up throughout the village and by the positively Austrian freestanding crucifix at the entrance to the castle, all the legacy of Henry Bellingham, a zealous C19 convert to Catholicism.

BELLINGHAM CASTLE. A long and rather weakly modelled castellated house in the style of Sir Jeffry Wyatville, now painted white. The setting, however, is highly picturesque, with an old avenue of lime trees focusing on the house, rubble-built terrace walls beside the river Glyde, and the courses of two mill races creating islets in an informal C19 water garden. Originally this place was the site of a castle which was burnt down by the army of James II in 1690. A new house in the style of Beaulieu was erected here by Henry Bellingham in 1712 and completely remodelled in 1798. This house survives as the core of the present castle, a six-bay block in the middle of the front elevation. Two storeys over a basement, with a shallow bowed projection at the rear. Larger and later rooms with a bow facing to the river were added at the S end. Inside, C18 features which survive are a small brick-vaulted wine cellar, six-panel doors upstairs and, on the main floor, a number of thin Gothic door frames, probably dating from 1798. Neat neoclassical cornices and a Bossi-type chimneypiece. The later rooms have heavier moulded plasterwork. The exterior features of the house – towers, turrets, buttresses and crenellations – date from several remodellings. The first, of 1834, was by *Thomas Smith*, who had done similar work at Barmeath Castle; further alterations were made in 1843, with later extensions in the second half of the C19. The towered and battlemented gateway on the Dublin–Belfast road, solidly Romantic, probably dates from *c.* 1860.

KILSARAN PARISH CHURCH (C of I). 1852 by *Welland & Gillespie*. A quaint little building of rubble and limestone, set on a hillock above the road at the entrance to Bellingham Castle. A straightforward plan of nave, chancel and shallow transepts is here given a picturesque effect by the use of several characteristic Welland motifs: very widely splayed diagonal buttresses, a certain squatness in the tower and broach spire, and nice extra details such as a gabled window lighting the choir gallery and a projecting staircase turret in the tower. The nave is lit by paired lancets in crisp limestone frames; triple lancet windows to transepts and chancel.

THE WIDOWS' HOUSES. 1826–30. A charming group of pic- 94
turesque almshouses built to house the widows of estate employees. The largest and simplest of the group, immediately below the church, contains two houses with projecting gables, stone plaques and pointed windows with quarry glass. Adjoining the side farthest from the road is a small gabled porch which leads through a covered half-timbered walkway to the churchyard, erected in 1864 to mark the weddings of two Bellingham daughters. Facing these across a broad gravel path which was once the main approach to the castle are three irregularly planned two-storey cottages of *c.* 1830 with steeply pitched gable roofs and more elaborate detailing, including half-timbering, oriel windows, exuberant bargeboards, diamond-paned glass and tall brick chimneys. These cottages are in the same tradition as the celebrated group designed by John Nash at Blaise Hamlet, Gloucestershire, in 1810 and similar to Nash's thatched Swiss Cottage at Cahir, Co. Tipperary. Here in Co. Louth the architect is almost certainly *William Vitruvius Morrison*, whose picturesque gabled cottages at Lough Bray in Co. Wicklow and Carpenham, Rostrevor, in Co. Down, make use of all the features found here, in particular the square box-bay window of the middle house. The ALPINE CRUCIFIX set in the centre of the driveway was fashioned for the Bellinghams out of a royal oak blown down in 1902.

OTHER BUILDINGS. The PRESBYTERIAN MEETING HOUSE is a four-bay lancet hall of 1840; on the E side of the village, on the banks of the Glyde, is the former BREWERY, a redbrick factory complex built during the 1860s and 1880s. NW of the village, on the road to Dromiskin, a curved gate entrance a little like a cross between James Gibbs, Lloyd Wright and a liquorice allsort boldly announces a quirky 1980s, post-modernist design by *F. F. Rodgers*.

NEIGHBOURHOOD

KILSARAN PARISH CHURCH. 1 km S. 1814. Tall plain T-plan church with a later and more sophisticated Gothic entrance front of 1854. The church is harled, with pointed twinlight windows and a circular window above the altar. The entrance front has a three-stage battlemented tower, with triple-light window and double-louvred belfry, flanked by low battlemented wings. Stucco, with limestone quoins and hoodmouldings. – STAINED GLASS. N transept: Christ giving the Keys to Peter, by *Mayer* of Munich. – MONUMENTS. The Rev. J. Dullaghan † 1837 by *M. P. Harris*. Memorial to the Chester family, 1838, by *G. Ryan*.

KILSARAN RECTORY. 1.5 km SW. *c.* 1790. Described in 1810 as having a glebe of 19 acres (7.7 ha). Very tall three-storey house over a shallow basement. Entrance front of five bays with parapet, first-floor string-course and a later limestone pedimented porch. Regular sash windows with moulded surrounds.

KILSARAN HOUSE. 1 km S. Built in 1780 by the Bellingham family. Plain five-bay, two-storey house which originally had a three-bay bowed projection at the N end. Near the entrance gate, KILSARAN COMMUNITY CENTRE, 1985, by *F. F. Rodgers*; S of the entrance the former schoolhouse, 1825 by *A. Nicholls*.

MILESTOWN HOUSE. 1 km SE. An early C18 house burnt out in 1920 and rebuilt within the old walls by W. S. Barber in 1925; thus at least the shape of the original building is preserved. A large, two-storey rectangle with a hipped roof and extended entrance front. This has a three-bay centre with a Georgian porch flanked by exceptionally wide canted bays like an English rectory.

WILLIAMSTOWN HOUSE. 2 km SW. 1856–60 by *William Caldbeck*. Large Italianate house of a type which became common in the 1860s and 70s. A rectangular plan, two rooms deep, with a large central hall and stair well behind. Two storeys on a semi-basement, with a long five-bay entrance front and two-bay sides. Typical mid-Victorian Italianate details include corner pilaster quoins, stucco vermiculation around the basement windows and a large tripartite window with console brackets as the central feature in the first floor of the entrance front. This is surmounted by a shallow bracketed gable – like a pediment – and has a regular four-columned Ionic porch.

1050

CASTLE COR LF

2 km W of Ballymahon

Ideal architecture is rare in Ireland in any age and centralized planning even rarer. There are some C16 and early C17 fortified houses built on a square plan with four identical corner towers, such as Rathfarnham Castle, Co. Dublin, and Raphoe Palace, Co. Donegal; there is the astonishing castle of Spur Royal, built *c.* 1610 at Augher, Co. Tyrone, in the shape of an eight-point star; and there is Lord Charlemont's Casino at Marino, Co. Dublin, where Sir William Chambers fitted an elegant neoclassical trianon into the plan of a Greek cross set with a ring of sixteen columns round its exterior. There are these and there is Castle Cor, perhaps the most unusual building of the C18 anywhere in Ireland.

In its original form Castle Cor was a trianon, or fantasy house, built as a hunting retreat by the Very Rev. Cutts Harman (1706–84), a younger son of a local landed family, the Harmans of Newcastle. Mr Harman's taste was distinctly odd, for his house, described disarmingly in 1846 as 'a miniature copy of Windsor Castle', was designed by himself and is contrived round one huge octagonal room, 42 ft (12.6 m) across, with tall round-headed windows on every second side and single rectangular rooms extending outwards from the other walls, entered by central doors. These rooms are a good size, 20 ft by 14 ft (6 m by 4.2 m); originally they had fitted wainscot panelling and, as the house is on two floors, one contains a staircase to connect the kitchens and service rooms on the ground floor with the great room above.

The plan is in the shape of a windmill's sails and first appears in pattern book sources in the seventh book of Sebastiano Serlio, the C16 Italian architect. If Mr Harman really was his own architect such a source would be just what might be expected of an educated man in Ireland in the C18, and Harman was educated: in 1759 he became Dean of Waterford Cathedral, which will have brought him in contact with two other architects who may in some sense have contributed to his ideas. The first of these is William Halfpenny, the publisher of a large number of English Palladian pattern books, who in 1739 had been employed to make designs for the Bishop's Palace and a new cathedral at Waterford. Though neither of these was to be built, Halfpenny's published designs, which were widely known, often make use of fanciful plans, including the windmill plan, and bold projections such as are used at Castle Cor. Dean Harman must have known the architect's proposals for Waterford, as it was in his own period as Dean (1759–84) that the cathedral was rebuilt, now to designs of the local architect Thomas Roberts. This work did not begin until 1774, when the Dean was sixty-eight, and of the two men it seems more likely that Halfpenny, if any professional man, stands behind Castle Cor's design.

There is no record of the date of the house; the architectural detail of the interior suggests the first half of the C18, while the uncompromisingly ideal plan seems more appropriate to the establishment of a bachelor than a family man. Harman married *c.* 1740, was left a widower in 1762 and three years later inherited his brother's estate at Newcastle, Ballymahon.

He might have built the house as a trianon for his old age, yet this seems unlikely as by then he owned another estate and had considerable responsibilities as Dean of a cathedral in a different part of Ireland – to which he presented the organ – so that a date in the late 1730s is the most probable. After Dean Harman's death the house was bought by the Hussey family, who, in the early C19, added a plain three-bay, two-storey block with hipped roofs between the two projecting rooms on the S side of the octagon. Then, at the beginning of this century, the house was extended once more, now by a slightly larger replica of the Husseys' building, which added a single range of rooms directly across the front of their house. One of Dean Harman's projecting diagonal rooms was enlarged about the same time, so that the precision of the ideal concept of Castle Cor can hardly be understood from the exterior any more. It is best seen from the W side. The octagon is covered by sloping slated roofs that rise to a flat platform, and the diagonal rooms have hipped roofs with one chimney rising from the ridge.

Inside the GREAT ROOM survives intact. It is approached axially through the hall of the C20 house, a straight stair and finally the lobby of the C19 house, top-lit and decorated with architectural plasterwork and laurel wreaths. The surprise of the interior is provided by Dean Harman's heating arrangements, for the great room is warmed by no fewer than four fireplaces, clustered together as an architectural assemblage in the central space and treated with panache. Each fireplace is directly opposite a window. It is framed by tall Corinthian columns which support a rich entablature, cutting in and out over the columns and again at the centre, where a block with a face of Apollo is supported on console brackets and crowned by a segmental pediment. Architecturally the effect is extraordinary, but it is also rich and must have been more so in Dean Harman's day, when four identical mirrors were set above the four chimneypieces to reflect different views of the countryside through the four windows. Above the entablatures the chimneybreast changes to an octagonal column with a boldly scaled, projecting dentil cornice and a high coved ceiling above. The windows, which have fielded panel shutters, are framed by fluted Corinthian pilasters, and the doors are a five-panel design. All looks right for *c.* 1735. The house is now a nursing home.

CASTLE COR CASTLE. A motte, planted with trees and with some ruined walls, stands W of the house.

1080

CASTLE FORBES

LF

123 As it appears today, Castle Forbes is a massive and somewhat forbidding great house, the very epitome of an Irish Victorian mansion, rising solid and hard-edged in the flat and well-wooded parkland of a large demesne. Irish limestone and Irish

granite, particularly when selected by experienced professional architects and taken from good-quality quarries, hardly seem to weather. Castle Forbes, if it is too dark to look new, is still crisp and sharp and, to a modern eye, looks rather larger in its individual elements than is usual in a country house. Both its scale and its well-built character were contributed by its architect, for the house, unusually, is a grand domestic design by the leading Catholic church architect of the day, *James Joseph McCarthy*. The window openings are McCarthy's familiar paired lancets. Above the front door is a four-light mullioned window, typical of many a church clerestory, while pointed windows on the principal tower are paired cusped lancets with a quatrefoil above, identical to those that appear in the side aisles of the architect's churches throughout Ireland. Even the label mouldings above the windows rest on square blocks of stone that have been left uncarved, as happened with many of McCarthy's churches. So the details of Castle Forbes come out of the office ecclesiastical drawer and are made to serve the purposes of domestic architecture.

The Victorian house is set at the corner of a complex series of offices and yards, running as a range of low, two-storey buildings, N to a turreted gateway and a separate round turret, and W, past a battlemented tower with flanking walls, to a small battlemented block and then a long garden wall, also with crenellations, which extends for over 295 ft (90 m). The house is thus part of a larger setting and was intended to compose picturesquely as the culmination of two long views. At their apex McCarthy set an ample round tower, rather too dominant in the composition, with a battered base, five storeys and, at the top, a machicolated parapet, fully corbelled out, so that a visitor can look up the curving surface of the tower to squares of sky appearing between the corbels and the battlements. A second, square tower in the middle of the entrance front is four storeys high (with a chapel on the top floor), and the rest of the building is of two storeys set on a high basement.

Round towers at the corners of a Gothic mansion were very much part of the standard repertoire of motifs in English and Irish picturesque buildings in the early C19. McCarthy uses the motif late in its history and to odd effect, as the tower has no answering element at the other end of either the E or the S front. It makes the principal elevations lop-sided, and the soft, circular form is at variance with the somewhat institutional square style of the rest of the house. Indeed it looks like something stuck on; but it is just possible that there was an influence from the client in the choice of this feature. Castle Forbes is the seat of the Irish branch of the Forbes family, which originally came from Scotland. There is a second Castle Forbes at Whitehouse in Aberdeenshire, and that house, which was designed by Archibald Simpson in 1815, at the height of the picturesque movement, has a similar though slightly larger round tower set at one corner. In Ireland the family may have wanted to include an allusion to its Scottish origins and could have asked McCarthy to incorporate a single corner tower in the new house.

Arthur Forbes, the sixth son of William Forbes of Corss, settled in Ireland in 1620. In 1628 he became a baronet of Nova Scotia when he obtained a grant of lands in Co. Longford, including a large late medieval Irish castle, whose barrel-vaulted basment and first-floor wall – clearly identified by the use of rubble and boulder stone – still forms part of the entrance front of the present Castle Forbes. On the S side of this castle and a little in front of it Sir Arthur built a new L-shaped house: two storeys on a basement, with high hipped roofs, and a big stepped-chimney lum, on the S side, supporting a range of tall diagonal-shaped chimneystacks, typical of early C17 houses in Ireland. All the windows were paired mullioned lights. Sir Arthur's house must have been finished by 1632, the year in which he was killed in a duel in Hamburg. It was defended successfully by his widow, Jane Lauder, in 1641 and remained the family home until 1825, when most of the building was destroyed by a fire. Its appearance in the late C18 is accurately recorded in two views: a sketch of the S side by Thomas Auchtermuchty and an anonymous view of the main front dated July 1799. All that survives today is a coat of arms coupling three muzzled bear heads for Sir Arthur Forbes and a rampant griffon for Jane Lauder, with the initials AF and IL. These are above the battlemented gateway W of the house, and McCarthy's new mansion has replaced everything else.

In 1684 Sir Arthur's eldest son, who had succeeded to the estates, was raised to the peerage as the Earl of Granard. When the C17 house caught fire in 1825 it belonged to George Forbes, the sixth Earl; the hero on that occasion was a springer spaniel called Pilot which according to the inscription on his portrait 'pulled Viscount Forbes out of his bed when the Castle Forbes was on fire'. By this date the C17 house had gained extensive additions in two long, two-storey wings running back from the main house; and it seems that these, which still exist, were extended and adapted for family use following the fire. The W end of the long extension to the house dates from this period, with pretty Gothic castle details, such as dummy arrow slits, stepped battlements and a mullioned window copied from Pugin's *Specimens of Gothic Architecture* with carved label stops of a male and female head. This work was apparently carried out to designs of *John Hargrave*, who possibly made part of the ruins of the C17 house habitable at the same time.

The first notice of McCarthy being employed at Castle Forbes comes from *The Dublin Builder* for September 1859, which reported that 'a new range of stabling of a very superior character' was to be built to his designs for a cost of £4,000. The builder was to be a Mr R. Farrell. Exactly one year before, the seventh Earl, who had succeeded his grandfather in 1837 as a child of not quite four, was married, now aged twenty-five, to a wealthy Catholic heiress, Jane Colclough from Johnstown

Castle, Co. Wicklow. The new Countess of Granard had both the funds and the taste to commission a new castle from a rising Catholic architect; as Johnstown Castle, a design by Daniel Robertson, was a Gothic house with many towers, bay windows and a romantic silhouette, the style she would expect to build in must have been something similar, only bolder and more modern. No doubt when Castle Forbes was completed its hard firm details and bold pitch-pine interiors must have seemed radically different from the more delicate plaster Gothic of the late Georgian period or the tame manorial style popular for early Victorian houses.

McCarthy's design for Castle Forbes was published in *The Irish Builder* only in November 1880, and it is not clear whether the notice of 1859 should be taken at its face-value as referring only to the stable courtyards – £4,000 would seem a lot for what was built – or whether this date also marks the beginning of work on the house. Nor is it known when the work was finished. The Countess died in 1872, and it seems unlikely that it would not have been finished before then.

In 1923, not long after the eighth Earl had been elected a member of the Senate of the Irish Free State, Castle Forbes was set on fire. The S half of McCarthy's main block was burnt and, though the extent of the damage is not clear – perhaps it was not very great – the fire provided an opportunity for another remodelling of the house, now of McCarthy's interior, to suit the taste of the eighth Lord Granard and his American wife, Beatrice Mills. This work was largely the concern of the Countess, who, with the assistance of the London architect *F. W. Foster*, extended sections of the castle to change the proportions of McCarthy's rooms, making space for a series of historicist interiors to replace the Victorian rooms. In these alterations the dining-room wall was brought forward almost to the level of the entrance tower and lost, in the process, the large bay window which McCarthy had provided to light the 'high-table' end of the room. On the S front two balconies, with Ruskinian pierced stone fronts, were removed as inappropriate, and two windows were blanked out when the rooms inside were combined to create one long drawing room. Behind the main house, the W extension, a gabled manorial range which probably predated McCarthy's work, was rebuilt as a heavy, rectangular two-storey block to contain a large library.

All that remains of the Victorian interior is the GALLERY connecting the hall to the library – a long, high corridor with assertive, single-chamfer ribbed vaulting, springing from sharp prismatic corbels, as in authentic late Gothic work in Ireland, and surrounding three hexagonal roof-lights, authentically C 19, and filled with orange and brown stained glass and Forbes bears. The windows in the gallery are long Y-traceried lights. Niches opposite flank a large and plain neo-Norman fireplace, whose arch is decorated with studs. The MAIN TOWER ROOM is also unaltered since McCarthy's day. It has exposed pine shutters and a doorway framed by timber colonnettes with leaf-carved lintel and a crenellated cornice. Old photographs show that this was the standard door for the main rooms of the house. The dining room had the same and also a Caen stone chimneypiece with paired marble colonnettes supporting an armorial achievement. The CRYPT, or lower hall, is much as McCarthy left it, with shoulder arches to the windows and Romanesque brass door furniture inspired by the designs of Pugin or Burges. The main staircase was of white stone with coloured marble bosses.

In her refurbishment of the house Lady Granard was assisted by two teams of decorators: *Fernand Allard* from Paris and *Lenygon and Morant* of 31 Old Burlington Street, London. Allard designed the HALL and STAIRCASE, lining the walls with elegant pale grey ashlar blocks with broad white pointing, round-headed arches and divided mirrored doors. The ceiling cornice is a reticent pattern of shallow modillions and the stair rails are light wrought-iron scrolls in the manner of François Blondel. The English decorators, who also fitted out the Cunard liners in this period, provided three contrasting rooms. The DINING ROOM is a formal square, lined in oak, with bolection-moulded panelling, and given a *trompe l'œil* ceiling of a late baroque open dome. Fluted Corinthian columns supporting large segmental pediments frame the principal doors, giving the impression of a Wren-school room of *c.* 1700. The DRAWING ROOM is an English Palladian interior in the manner of William Kent, with paired chimneypieces with pedimented overmantels, fish-scaled console brackets and continuously carved mouldings. The ceiling has an C18 allegorical canvas showing the Genius of Architecture. The LIBRARY, a large rectangular room, is lined with bookcases of exposed timber *boiserie* with an ambitious ceiling canvas, possibly late C17 and Dutch, depicting Faith, Hope and Charity, in a moulded central oval, with figures of the four seasons set in each corner. The CHAPEL contains a gilt and timber late baroque retable, *c.* 1730 and probably French.

McCarthy's stableyard, behind the house and to the N, is approached by a detached GATEHOUSE, a small two-storey building with hipped roof and angle bartizans with conical slate roofs at each corner. It carries an achievement of arms of the seventh Earl, carved in high relief, over the entrance arch. The wall to the N of this may be part of the bawn wall of the original castle. Within the courtyard McCarthy built a long W range of stable offices; two storeys of coursed snecked rubble with a central carriage arch surmounted by a clocktower and flanked by battlemented gables. The façade is rather flat. At its N end a small square turret carries a royal coat of arms, C16 and apparently of Queen Elizabeth I.

A small TOWER and dovecote, SE, may once have been a flanker for the C17 house. It is 16 ft (4.8 m) square, with C19 battlements and C17 stone roosts for pigeons inside. S of the house are several mature Lebanon cedars, Spanish chestnut trees and an enclosed ITALIAN GARDEN, laid out on one long axis with a central fountain, urns and yew hedges focusing on a statue of Perseus after Canova. At the entrance to the ROSE GARDEN, the large ARMORIAL EAGLES, carved in stone and flanking the gateway, were once the supporters of the arms of the Earl of Tylney (Viscount Castlemaine and Baron Newtown in the Irish Peerage), which were brought to Castle Forbes when Lord Tylney's home, Wanstead House in Essex, the earliest Palladian country house, designed by Colen Campbell, was demolished *c.* 1812. The gates also carry an inscribed stone of 1567 recording the capture by Sir Henry Sidney of 'the great rebel Shane O'Nele', brought 'in Subjection to the Crown of England to the Great Joyie of the Realm'. In the park the ruin of a rectangular later medieval CHURCH, rubble-built with gables, has been adapted at the chancel end to serve as the family mausoleum.

CASTLEJORDAN

ME *5030*

A small rural village which developed around a medieval castle alongside the river Boyne.

CASTLEJORDAN. The fragmentary and ivy-grown remains of what appears to have been once an extensive military stronghold. Situated beside the river Boyne on the borders of Meath, Kildare and the Kings County (Offaly), Castlejordan was throughout the medieval period a place of strategic importance to the English Pale. Founded by the Jordans during the early C13, the castle was rebuilt during the reign of Henry VIII following a government decree of 1540. By the C17, Castlejordan had become the property of the Gifford family, who remained here until the early C19.

Today all that survives is the remnant of an extensive rectangular enclosure, with part of a late medieval tower house at its SE angle and a C17 bastion at the N end of its W flank. The tower house is a rectangular three-storey structure, with a circular stair turret at its NW corner. Some pretty pocked tooling to a limestone quoin in the doorcase of the principal first-floor chamber suggests a C16 date, and this work may well have been executed in the rebuilding of 1540. The bastion which stands outside the W wall of the enclosure is a rare survival of C17 fortified architecture in rural Ireland and the only building of its type remaining in North Leinster. In plan it resembles a double-scoop ice-cream cornet; a long pointed triangular projection adjoined at the rear or base by two circular turrets. Though this building is now much overgrown, its *raison d'être* is still very much in evidence in the proliferation of loops throughout its fabric. A fireplace in the E wall provided warmth for the men stationed here. Located at the NW angle of the castle enclosure, the bastion could provide flanking fire to three directions. A contrast of the two buildings neatly illustrates the great shift in emphasis from medieval to early modern defences.

While the tower depended upon the height and thickness of its walls for security, the later fortification relied upon the quality of its plan, which was geometrically configured to provide the maximum flanking fire for the castle and its curtain wall.

CASTLEJORDAN BRIDGE. The river Boyne runs along the eastern side of the former castle lands and was crossed a little way N of the walled enclosure by a medieval triple-arched bridge. Though now much altered and reinforced with concrete, the bridge preserves two of the original arches with the corbels for supporting the centering and traces of the wattle centering itself.

CASTLEJORDAN CHURCH TOWER. 1823. All that survives of the former Church of Ireland parish church is the belltower. This is an attractive Gothic-style tower with more and richer detail than is usual. Square in plan and three storeys high with pinnacles, label mouldings and diagonal stepped buttresses.

CASTLEJORDAN CHURCH. A rough-cast three-bay lancet hall with two-bay transepts. Corner quoins and triple-light E window.

CHURCH OF THE ASSUMPTION, BALLYNABRACKEY. 2 km NW. 1872. Ugly T-plan brick hall with a freestanding belfry. The interior is better, bright and airy with modern coloured stained glass. ALTAR FURNISHINGS from the previous church, bequeathed by the Rev. Patrick Kealy in 1875.

4070

CASTLEPOLLARD — WM

Castlepollard ranks with Collon, Slane, Tyrrellspass and Ardagh as one of the prettiest villages in North Leinster. Its picturesque village green is bounded by neat ranges of two-storey houses and public buildings, with the parish church forming a focal point at the S end. Castlepollard's urbane late Georgian character reflects the presence of not one but two 'improving' local landowners, the Pollard family of Kinturk House immediately adjoining the town, and the Earls of Longford at Tullynally. The rebuilding of the parish church in 1820 and of William Pollard's home in 1821 suggest that the village too was rebuilt at that time. The buildings lining the village green are of Regency style, with single fanlit doorcases, tripartite sash windows and oversailing bracketed eaves. The green itself is earlier, already in existence in the C18 and noted as the site of a dilapidated markethouse. On the E side, the ULSTER BANK is a Regency-revival design and blends well with the older buildings; the BANK OF IRELAND, presumably by *Sandham Symes*, is not so successful, with a rather messy Italianate façade.

CASTLEPOLLARD PARISH CHURCH (C of I). 1827. Pretty hall and tower church, with a good site on the S side of the village green. Rough-cast and rendered, with a cut limestone spire, battlements and thin octagonal corner turrets. Pointed sash Y-tracery windows to the W front and a roll-moulded entrance arch with a tripartite tympanum. Inside, a bright, boxy hall lit by three triple-light Y-tracery windows on each side. Shallow chancel with decorative High Victorian stained glass. – MONUMENTS. Catherine Gunning † 1751 aged nineteen; a charming irregular rococo oval. William Dutton Pollard † 1839; neoclassical plaque with a girl weeping upon an urn.

CHURCH RUIN. N of the village stands the ruin of the former parish church. A simple rubble hall and four-storey tower with little to remark besides odd, deeply splayed embrasures to the tower.

ST MICHAEL, CASTLEPOLLARD PARISH CHURCH. 1859. Substantial cruciform chapel, with a thin buttressed tower and spire to the entrance gable. Rendered, with Y-tracery windows and diagonal buttresses. The interior is broad and low, with exposed, cross-braced rafters. The nave opens into the transepts through pairs of squat two-centred arches. Mid-Victorian E.E. detail. Triple lancets light the transepts; five graded lancets to the chancel. – Emphatic Victorian Gothic ALTAR FURNITURE happily still complete. – MONUMENT. The Rev. Michael Gogarty † 1886; large Gothic altar-like monument.

KINTURK HOUSE. The C18 seat of the Pollard family, remodelled and extended by William Pollard in 1821 to designs by *C. R. Cockerell*, who was then working for the Naper family at Loughcrew. The original house – still the entrance front of the building – was a three-storey block, one room deep and three rooms long, with a five-bay entrance front of plain sash windows in moulded surrounds. A freestanding, tetrastyle Ionic porch was added by Cockerell in 1821 together with single-storey wings decorated with round-headed niches. In the original part of the house two large rooms flank a central entrance hall. The room on the r. has a pretty rococo ceiling, with strapwork motifs, shells, flourishes and two cupids at the centre, probably of *c.* 1760.

Cockerell's main contribution to the house was the addition of a second and larger block of three rooms at the rear of the earlier building, with a large central stairhall and spinal corridor between. The stair is a grand half-turn with landings, the treads of Portland stone with elegant brass balusters. Dim lighting is provided by a large square-headed window with primitive-style stained glass of 1838. The three rooms on the garden front have large ample proportions, with simple neoclassical plasterwork, Greek key, egg-and-dart borders, swags and medallions. The joinery here is very fine, with thin applied mouldings and fluted fans to the angles of the shuttering. In one room the windows are crowned by superb neoclassical pelmets, with figures of veiled classical matrons. The central room has a marble chimneypiece with female terms supporting a floral frieze. The garden front is seven bays wide and extends beyond the additional wings of the entrance front. Here the central bay is advanced, with long French windows opening onto the garden and squat tripartite windows above them on the upper storey. Now used as a hospital.

NEIGHBOURHOOD

HILLTOWN. 5 km NE. Large and bulky house of uncertain date, perhaps *c.* 1780. In its general aspect, and particularly from a distance, Hilltown resembles a substantial Palladian house of the mid-C18. Large three-storey rectangular block, raised over a semi-basement, with a wide hipped roof and a stone eaves cornice and blocking course. Five-bay entrance front with sash windows of twelve and six panes. The central bay has a tripartite doorcase, a square tripartite window on the first floor and a semicircular window on the top storey – that is a neoclassical variation on the classic Irish Palladian arrangement. The plan is symmetrical, with a central stair and entrance hall and large reception rooms on each side, ornamented by neoclassical friezes and thin applied mouldings to the shuttering.

HILLTOWN CASTLE. In the yard behind Hilltown House, the ground floor of a rectangular tower house with rounded angles, measuring approximately 20 ft by 30 ft (6 m by 9 m) internally. Entrance at the SE corner communicating directly with a straight mural stair in the thickness of the E wall. Chimney in the N wall and a loop with external splay on the W wall.

GAULSTOWN. 3 km NW. Modest house of villa-like proportions, probably built *c.* 1730 by the Lill family, who lived here during the C18. There is a self-conscious quality about this little building which quite belies its scale. While its style is undeniably rustic it is an aristocratic or cultivated rusticity, like the small buildings and academic geometric exercises indulged in by Sir John Vanbrugh and by his cousin Edward Lovett Pearce. Everything about Gaulstown suggests that it descends from such a distinguished pedigree and is either by *Pearce* or else by his associate *William Halfpenny*, who was working at Hillsborough in Co. Down and at Waterford in the 1730s.

Gaulstown is small yet its style is emphatic and the few features it possesses are all well placed and properly executed. Mass and geometry are the key to its power as a design. The house is three rooms wide, with three openings across its front, a window, a door and a window. It is of only one storey but is set on a tall basement – brick-vaulted throughout – and has attics lit by windows in its gable ends set each side of massive chimneystacks. The centre bay projects on each front – a plain gable at the back and a doughty little pediment on the front – so that the plan is cruciform, with two rooms (the hall and a room behind it) in the centre, and one room flanking these on each side. A staircase is tucked in between the hall and the W room. Of architectural decoration there is very little: the central room at the back has a plain Venetian window; otherwise decoration is restricted to the front, with lugged surrounds to the outer windows and a Venetian window adapted as a door in the centre. It has broad undecorated jambs in freestone and an arch with exaggerated voussoirs, the outer two of which continue as a horizontal plat-band above the windows in the wings. A small Diocletian window is set over the door and the

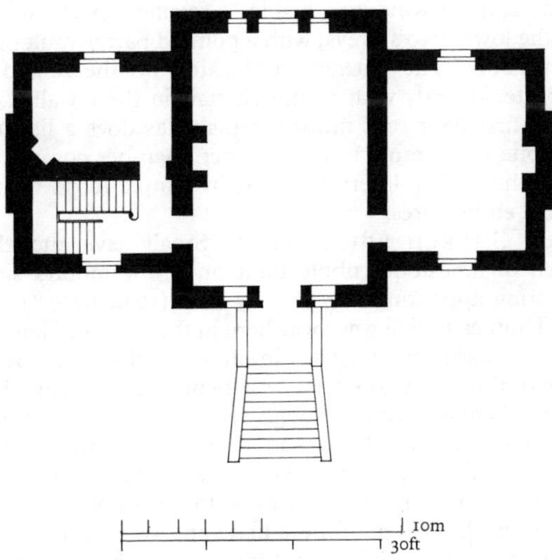

Castlepollard, Gaulstown. Plan and front elevation

pediment above it is emphasized with rustic mutules and heavy acroterion blocks.

CHURCH OF THE IMMACULATE CONCEPTION, MAYNE. 4 km NW. A traditional T-plan chapel built in 1841 on a site granted by the Dease family of Turbotstown. Thoroughly reconstructed in 1976 by the Rev. Patrick Fagan. Round- and segmental-headed windows in blocked surrounds are a welcome change from the ubiquitous lancet, for the church is a pleasant essay in C 19 vernacular classicism. A curious Victorian Romanesque E window is the only medieval concession. Though now bright, bare and pristine, there is nevertheless something appealingly direct about this crisp, clean-cut renovation.

TURBOTSTOWN HOUSE. 4.5 km NW. Substantial Greek-revival villa built *c.* 1830 by Gerald Dease to replace the C18 family house. A large, symmetrical house, two rooms deep, with a three-bay, two-storey entrance front of snecked and punched limestone rubble. The projecting central bay has a tetrastyle Greek Ionic porch and tripartite window above. Limestone eaves cornice, hipped roof and central chimneys. A lower two-storey extension to the S screens an extensive stablecourt.

NEWCASTLE. 6 km NW. Small and well-preserved tower house which, at approximately 20 ft by 18 ft (6 m by 5.5 m) internally, is close in scale to the specifications laid down by Parliament in 1429 for a castle to qualify for the £10 state grant. In the C19 du Noyer ascribed to Newcastle a C15 date. Four storeys built of limestone rubble, with a battered base, cutstone corner quoins and slit windows. Inside, a regular barrel-vault is set over the lower two storeys, with a pointed barrel-vault over the upper floors. The entrance is located on the N and communicates directly with a straight stair in the E wall. Corbels for the first-floor roof timbers remain, as does a flat-headed limestone door frame into the upper chamber complete with its bolt-hole. The interior was lit by simple loops with deep internal embrasures.

LICKBLA CHURCH RUIN. 3 km N. Small nave and chancel church of limestone rubble built on a low mound site and measuring approximately 56 ft by 19 ft (17 m by 5.7 m). The Rev. Thomas Rydell was vicar here in the reign of Henry VIII.

COOLURE. 3.5 km W. *c.* 1775. Simple and substantial Georgian house of three storeys over a basement, the home of a branch of the Pakenham family. Rough-cast, with a half-hipped roof. Three-bay entrance front and four bays to the rear. Sash windows with a segmental head to the ground- and first-floor windows. Classic later C18 plan, with a central entrance hall, the stair in the centre of the E flank and two reception rooms at the rear. Thin applied mouldings to the joinery and dull neoclassical cornices.

MAYNE PARISH CHURCH (C of I). 4.5 km W. Built in 1806 with a gift of £500 from the Board of First Fruits. Simple two-bay hall, cement-rendered, with timber Y-tracery windows, adjoined at the W end by a rubble three-stage tower and at the E by a shallow chancel. Curious big heart-like label stops to the entrance arch.

BENISON LODGE. 2.5 km S. A now derelict late C18 five-bay, two-storey house with a hipped roof, regular sash windows and a very good limestone Doric doorcase similar to that at Coolure (*see* above). Seat of the Rev. T. Smyth in 1836.

LOUGH PARK. 2.5 km E, on the shore of Lough Lene. Elegant two-storey late C18 house, unusual in being gabled and without a parapet. The W-facing entrance front has large and long sash windows on both floors set in moulded limestone surrounds and surmounted by alternating triangular and segmental pediments on the ground floor. A square porch projects from the centre bay, with a very good pedimented Doric doorcase in crisply wrought limestone and a big eleven-panel door. Seat of Nicholas Evans in 1836.

MILLTOWN CHAPEL. 3.5 km S. Small early C19 T-plan chapel. Rough-cast, with lancet windows and pointed arches with ugly mosaic tops. – MONUMENT. The Rev. Michael Lynch † 1845.

CASTLETOWN

ME *8080*

Rural parish in N Meath.

CASTLETOWN CHURCH RUINS (C of I). 1 km N of Castletown crossroads. A sad little church. Short two-bay hall with a three-stage pinnacled entrance tower, both roofless. Reconstructed in 1820 by *Robert Wiggins*, builder; the walls incorporate fragments of late medieval work. These are: two cusped ogee-headed lights on the second floor of the tower, a cusped niche on the first floor, a carved fragment attached to one of the pinnacles and a medieval stone head projecting from the nave wall. The pedimented limestone doorcase, framing a pointed arch, is presumably part of an C18 rebuilding. – MONUMENTS. Over the E window, a large fragment of a female effigy of late C15 date. – Interesting early Georgian wall monument to Philip Whittingham D.D. † 1743; a classical aedicule with an urn inside a broken pediment.

ST PATRICK. Early C19 cross-plan church, extended in 1877 into a longer nave, and enlarged again in the late C19 or early C20, when the chancel was rebuilt as an elaborate triple-bay Gothic sanctuary in the manner of Ashlin & Coleman. In the nave a timber classical aedicule now framing a Mayer-style Calvary was probably the original reredos. Polished stone shafts with foliated capitals support the sanctuary arcade, pinnacled reredos and side altars. STAINED GLASS. Sacred Heart; *Mayer & Co.* – MONUMENTS. The Rev. Hugh Carthy P.P. † 1848. The Rev. P. Gibney P.P. † 1873 by *Farrell & Son*. A HOLY-WATER STOUP is signed by the mason *Dennus McKenna*.

GRAVELMOUNT HOUSE. 1 km SE. Large three-storey, five-bay late Georgian house with a shallow hipped roof and no eaves cornice. Attractive ivy-grown façade, with very long sash windows diminishing abruptly on the top storey. Central fanlit doorcase flanked by freestanding Doric columns supporting an entablature.

DRAKERATH HOUSE. 3.5 km W. Victorian Italianate house near the site of a former medieval castle. A rectangular building with a wide-hipped roof and oversailing bracketed eaves. Projecting central porch with a triforium above and plate-glass windows in moulded surrounds on each side.

ST MICHAEL, STAHOLMOG. 4.5 km W. 1805. Tiny T-plan

chapel, recently refurbished. Behind the church the squat rubble tower is of 1885, erected by Fr P. J. Fagan P.P. – MONUMENT. The Rev. Laurence Ward P.P. †1852 by *Farrell & Son*. – In the E boundary wall of the churchyard is a carving of a semi-naked man which has been attributed to the late antique period. How did it get here?

6060 CASTLETOWN-DELVIN WM

Delvin or Castletown-Delvin was the centre of the lordship of Dealbhna, which was granted by Hugh de Lacy to his son-in-law Gilbert de Nugent. The ruined medieval castle of the Nugents still stands in the village, and nearby is their C19 residence, Clonyn Castle, one of the last great baronial mansions to be built in Ireland. A pleasant village in one street, Delvin is distinguished by the castle's twin-towered shell at the S end and by the very fine Catholic church on the N. Near the centre of the main street are some nice two-storey, three-bay late Georgian houses (the Post Office is one) with pretty curvilinear fanlights of *c.* 1830.

44 DELVIN CASTLE. The round-towered profile of modern Clonyn Castle was no doubt inspired by this, its late medieval predecessor – the seat of the Nugents until its destruction during the Cromwellian wars. Originally a large rectangular tower with four circular corner turrets, the castle is now reduced to an impressive twin-towered S wall, with substantial remnants of the E and W walls. Traditionally this is known as the castle built by Hugh de Lacy in 1181 and later given by him to his son-in-law Gilbert de Nugent as part of the sub-lordship of Dealbhna. That authorities now suggest either a C13 or a C15 date for the building highlights the problems of chronology which attend the study of late medieval architecture: keeps fortified with round corner towers are found in both periods. Here the windows, doors and press recesses are well-built, square-headed openings with few datable clues, despite their regularity and fine state of preservation.

132 CHURCH OF THE ASSUMPTION, DELVIN PARISH CHURCH. 1873 by *G. C. Ashlin*. Undoubtedly one of the most picturesque churches in the province; an accomplished small-scale essay in French Gothic with a charming garden setting beside the parochial house, which is also by Ashlin. A cruciform church of punched and snecked limestone rubble with ashlar trim. Nave, aisles, transepts and an apsidal chancel, with a large, well-scaled tower and spire flanking the entrance gable. The style, C13 French Gothic, is distinguished by pointed arches, lancets and large geometric windows. The entrance gable is expressed as a canopied pointed arch with a great four-light geometric window above it and pairs of very long thin lancets to the belltower. The spire, which rises over an open octagonal belfry, within the square of the tower, is unusually inventive, free and effective in its design. Triplets of cusped lancets light

the aisles of the church, with single lancets to the clerestory and three pointed twinlight windows to the apse. The interior is intimate in scale and brightly lit. The nave wall is carried on an arcade of four moulded two-centred arches supported on shafts of polished pink granite, with a variety of foliated capitals. The vividly coloured stained glass and pinnacled altar furniture are all of a piece. A pleasant church, satisfying both in the quality of its design and in the authenticity of its furnishings.

FORMER PARISH CHURCH (C of I). Deconsecrated and now roofless, the ruin of a late medieval belfry, a Board of First Fruits hall and a later C19 transept. The tower, at the W end of the church, is a square structure of limestone rubble with a long straight stair flanking the principal chamber and projecting on the E face. Adjoining it is a plain hall with traces of timber Y-tracery. The N transept was added by *Joseph Welland* with E.E. windows.

SESSIONS HOUSE. 1850 by *Florence Mahony*, County Surveyor. Plain gabled hall of coursed rubble with a rendered gabled façade.

BANK OF IRELAND. Formerly the Hibernian Bank; erected in 1920 to designs by *W. H. Byrne*. A two-storey, two-bay house, with a pyramidal hipped roof, square-headed windows and a projecting classical porch between the ground-floor windows. Simple but stylish.

ROSMEAD. 2.5 km NE. The gaunt yet impressive shell of a large stone box of a house, built *c.* 1780 by the Wood family. From the principal SE approach, Rosmead has the appearance of a vast three-storey, seven-bay cube. Crisp plain limestone masonry, with long windows diminishing in scale towards the top, a first-floor string-course, eaves cornice and blocking course. In the E elevation the three centre bays break forward; a single-storey tetrastyle porch formerly screened the principal entrance on the S front. Essentially two show façades; neither their proportions nor their detail is maintained in the undistinguished N and W elevations of the house. What survives of the interior is disappointing – round-headed arches and the traces of prim neoclassical cornices. The plan is irregular and much altered, with no two rooms of similar size and no fewer than three staircases. The position of the original stairhall, top-lit at the centre of the block, between the entrance hall and the central room of the E front, is a feature of early neoclassical designs in British country houses and is seen also at Markree Castle in Co. Sligo and Castle Blayney in Co. Monaghan. The columns from the S porch of Rosmead were removed and reused in the early C20 rebuilding of Balrath-Bury near Kells. – ENTRANCE GATEWAY. The very handsome limestone ashlar entrance arch to Rosmead was brought here from Glananea (q.v.). Classical round-headed arch, flanked by giant Corinthian pilasters 'supporting' a salient entablature and cornice with low walls on each side. These terminate in square piers topped by ornate urns. Keystones, masks, capitals and urns are executed in Portland stone.

CLONARNEY CHURCH. 2.5 km N. The fragment of a late medieval church tower, the barrel-vaulted basement chamber, with a spiral stair at the NW corner and a chimney in the E wall.

GILLISTOWN CASTLE. 1.5 km SW. The stump of a small late medieval tower house – a barrel-vaulted hall with press recesses and slit windows, entered through a round-headed arch on the W face. Built of limestone rubble, the tower has a battered base and had formerly two storeys above the basement. Only the E and part of the S walls survive from the upper storeys.

MARTINSTOWN CASTLE. 2.5 km S. Impressive four-storey tower house, larger than many and with an uncommon stair arrangement. The basement is the usual large single chamber roofed over by a long barrel-vault and retaining fine stone corbels with recesses for large timber beams. The entrance is on the longer S side, with a short spiral stair immediately beside it in the SW corner of the tower. This connects with a straight mural stair within the W wall, which leads, in turn, to a second spiral stair at the NW corner of the building. Access to the first floor was gained from the mural stair and to the second and third floors from the NW corner stair. The herringbone corbelled roof pattern over the mural stair is similar to C15 work at Talbot's Castle in Trim.

SOUTH HILL. 1.5 km E. Excessively large and exceedingly plain late Georgian block, three storeys high and five windows wide, all very widely spaced. A porch more like a garden pavilion, with a pilastered central block and three-bay conservatory-style wings, covers the central three bays at ground-floor level. The building, now a convent, is surrounded by utilitarian additions but can never have been more than a sturdy massive house astonishing in its expansive cold masonry. The style, noticeable particularly in the oddly overscaled square fanlight to the porch, is very characteristic of *William Farrell*, a neoclassicist who lacked the light touch!

Inside, the house is three rooms deep, with a central entrance hall and the staircase tucked in between front and rear on the N flank. The hall, however, is no conventional entrance area but rather an open-plan arrangement of two rooms: a small single-bay room on axis with the entrance, communicating through a Scamozzian Ionic screen with a large room on the right, which is lit by the 'conservatory' windows. This room, decorated with plaster roundels and panels after Thorvaldsen, is South Hill's best feature. In the vestibule, the fireplace has an engraved brass grate of *c.* 1800 signed by *Finney* of Duke Street. South Hill was a seat of the Chapman family, whose most famous offspring – if illegitimate – was Lawrence of Arabia.

3040

CASTLETOWN GEOGHEGAN WM

133 ST MICHAEL. 1885 by *T. F. McNamara*. An attractive church, pleasantly sited on a grassy, wooded site at one corner of the village. Cruciform plan; nave, chancel and transepts, with a

tall four-stage tower and broach spire flanking the gabled front. Built of limestone rubble with generous ashlar trim. Unusual in having the main entrance in a small gabled side porch rather than in the front gable, which here is expressed as two storeys with two cusped lancets below and two twinlight windows above. A tall plinth and canopied statue niche is set between. Inside, a five-bay nave opens through paired two-centred arches into shallow transepts and culminates in a broad apsed chancel the full width of the nave. Attractive Caen stone fittings. Sanctuary mosaic 1925–7.

MIDDLETON PARK. 1.5 km SE. *c.* 1850. Built for George Au- 112
gustus Boyd to designs by *George Papworth*. A handsome house in an Italianate, astylar idiom overlaid with Greek-revival detail and very clearly modelled on Francis Johnston's Ballynegall of 1808 (*see* Portneshangan). The same six-bay, two-storey rectangular block is here flanked on one side by a long, single-storey office range and on the other, just as at Ballynegall, by an elegant neoclassical conservatory with square Tuscan corner piers. The house is rendered, with a low hipped roof and, again like Johnston's design, an emphatic limestone cornice with pronounced mutules. In the entrance front the two centre bays break forward and are screened by a single-storey Greek Ionic porch. The major difference in expression between the two houses is the fenestration – here wide plate-glass windows, in contrast to Johnston's ample sash frames. The garden front also departs from its Georgian model in having one advanced centre bay with a tripartite window, in contrast to Ballynegall's three-bay bow. The internal arrangement is also quite different. Here the plan is centred around a grandiose limestone stairhall with a big double-return stair and balconied landings: a spartan megalomania worthy of ponderous Napoleonic portraits or the reveries of Citizen Kane.

JAMESTOWN. 3 km NW. Low, three-bay, two-storey late Georgian block. Superficially castellated on the front, with label mouldings and a Tudor doorway, much altered, flanked by long single-storey rubble wings. – CHAPEL RUINS. In the grounds, a plain, rubble lancet hall with a single lancet in the W gable.

DYSART CATHOLIC CHURCH. 3 km NE. Small C19 cruciform chapel, pebbledashed, with lancet windows and a freestanding mid-C20 belfry. – STAINED GLASS. E window, three lancets: in the centre, Christ in Majesty, which achieves a nice effect through black scumbling technique. It is flanked by a more vividly pictorial Joseph and The Virgin and Child (the latter of 1895).

CHURCH OF THE ASSUMPTION, LOUGHANVALLEY. 5 km NW. 1828. Late Georgian in style. Four-bay gabled hall, with wide Y-tracery lancets. Built by the Rev. A. W. McGuire and renovated in the later C19. – MONUMENTS. The Rev. Eugene Glynn †1841; the Rev. Christopher Lestrange †1874. – STAINED GLASS. E window: Boyhood of Christ, 1877, in an Italian primitive style.

CHURCHTOWN FORMER PROTESTANT CHURCH. 5 km N. Only the three-stage tower, with clasping buttresses and pinnacles, remains from the church built here in 1811. The glebe-house nearby is a three-bay, two-storey building of 1814.

9090

CHARLESTOWN

LO

A minor crossroads in open country N of Ardee.

CHARLESTOWN PARISH CHURCH (C of I). Hall and tower church erected to a standard design by *William Farrell* between 1825 and 1828. Three-storey tower with diagonal buttresses, pinnacles and a needle spire. The cost, excluding the spire, was £1,385. Y-traceried windows to the three-bay nave. Short chancel and vestry of 1869 by *William Fullerton*. – STAINED GLASS. N wall by *Harry Clarke*; Suffer the little children, by *Mayer & Co.*

Across the road, the ruins of the previous C18 church, now only ivy-grown walls and a pointed chancel arch. Also the SEXTON'S HOUSE of 1897. A nice five-bay, single-storey house with half-hipped gables. E of the church, CHARLESTOWN CEMETERY GATEWAY, 1919, neo-Jacobean in limestone ashlar.

RAHANNA. S of the church. Early to mid-C19. Plain rectangular house of simple Regency character. Two-storey, three-bay front, with shallow hipped roof and bracketed eaves. The centre bay is slightly recessed and filled with a tripartite window and a balustraded classical porch below. The side elevations are of four bays with an exposed basement.

HARRISTOWN HOUSE. 1 km SSE. Modest late Georgian block with a low hipped roof and a broad three-bay entrance front. Rough-cast, with regular sash windows and a delightful elliptical fanlight above a tripartite doorcase.

114 CARDISTOWN HOUSE. 2.5 km NW. 1865 by *John Neville*. Elegant two-storey Italianate house with a wide hipped roof, bracketed eaves and corner quoin pilasters. Of red brick with limestone trim. The three-bay entrance front has a central gable, a pedimented upper-floor window and a projecting Doric porch. Canted bay windows, with Doric pilasters at the corners, flank the porch. The four-bay sides are reticent but carefully detailed, with the windows set in panels of brick wall recessed between strips of rusticated quoins and limestone string-courses. A standard Irish country house and yet a subtle design, proving that the classical tradition was still very much alive for Neville in the 1860s.

CLONKEEN OLD CHURCH. 2.5 km W. Clonkeen has been the site of a religious foundation since the C6, and in the C9 is recorded as having two successive bishops. Little survives to tell of the place's former significance but a small barn-like church with a bellcote above the chancel and round-headed windows in deep embrasures. Now modernized and used as a community hall. Inside, an inscribed stone, dated 1573 and

1973, commemorates the earliest structure, part of which is incorporated in the present building. Of greater interest is the MONUMENT to John Chaubre †1718, a sophisticated baroque aedicule by *William Kidwell*. Grey and white marble, with Corinthian pilasters, broken segmental pediment, carved keystone and cupid's head bracket.

ST MALACHY. 3.5 km NW, at Reaghstown. Small, early C19 T-plan church, remodelled in 1867 and again by *W. H. Byrne* in 1922. Bellcote over the entrance gable and clasping corner buttresses rising to finials. Twinlight Y-traceried windows and a pointed-arch entrance. Inside, pointed chancel arch on angel corbels and an open kingpost roof. – STAINED GLASS. A good variety. Transepts: pictorial saints in Gothic niches of 1901. Vividly coloured Sacred Heart, the Virgin and Saints by *Miles Kearney & Son*, Dublin.

CLOGHER HEAD

LO *1080*

CLOGHERHEAD CHURCH RUINS. On an elevated site commanding a wonderful view southward along the coast. Probably C16. Nave and chancel with a well-preserved W gable and round-headed chancel arch. Flat-headed doors and loops in wide embrasures. One larger window survives in the S wall with fragments of dressed limestone mullions. The footing for a W bellcote survives.

ST MICHAEL'S CHURCH, HACKETTSCROSS. 1856 by *John Murray*. Six-bay, lancet hall of coursed rubble with limestone trim. W entrance gable with bellcote and corner buttresses. A large window without tracery is set rather blankly over the door. Lower chancel with a triple-light E window.

MAINE CHURCH RUINS. 1.5 km N. Ivy-grown rectangular church ruin. Probably C17 or early C18. N and S gables and most of the walls are intact with crudely built pointed entrance arches opposite each other in the side walls. No cutstone detail survives.

SS PETER AND PAUL. 4 km NW, at Walshestown. 1837. Immediately beside the road, a large and wide four-bay hall with a low square tower. A slender turret attached to one corner of the tower gives the church a distinctive silhouette of brownish stucco in imitation of sandstone. Minimal Perp, with diagonal buttresses, four-centred arches and hoodmouldings and cross-mullioned Y-tracery windows. Disappointing modern interior. The church was completed in 1837, possibly to designs by *Thomas Smith*, and was renovated in 1876 by *John Murray*, who added the tower turret and at the same time removed the battlements from the side walls. At the rear of the church, a nice echo of rural Ireland, is a stile to the masspath through the fields.

PARSONSTOWN CHURCH RUIN. 4 km NW. Well-preserved medieval parish church built *c.* 1528 of local greywacke and limestone rubble. A rectangular gabled structure with the remains of a double bellcote over the W gable and pointed arch entrances opposite each other at the W end of the nave. Twinlight ogee-headed window in the S wall and a single ogee light in the N wall. The cutstone detail is of punched-dressed limestone.

BARMEATH CHURCH RUIN. 6.5 km NW. Ruined church of local greywacke rubble. Over the W doorway an armorial slab carries an inscription stating that the church was built by Mary Dillon, relict of John Bellew, in 1697.

GLASPISTOL CASTLE. 1 km S. Late medieval tower house built on the coastline of S Louth by the Dowdall family, probably during the late C15. Though roofless, this is a well-preserved tower, complete with barrel-vaulted basement and spiral stair. The plan follows a familiar format; a rectangular four-storey tower, roughly 25 ft by 15 ft (7.5 m by 4.5 m) inside, with a square stair turret projecting from the north end of the E face. The entrance is on the N directly between the stair and a small rectangular guard room in the NW angle of the building. Beyond the vestibule is the usual vaulted basement, approximately 15 ft (4.5 m) square, with a pointed barrel-vault, traces of wickerwork centering, cupboard recesses and externally splayed arrow loops. On the upper floor is a grander chamber, 25 ft by 15 ft (7.5 m by 4.5 m), with the remnant of a large chimneypiece at its N end and a murder hole opening into the vestibule below. What is unusual here is a mural passage which runs almost the entire length of the W wall. It is entered from the main chamber through a narrow, centrally placed round-headed arch. The passage is lit from a loop at the S end and another in the W wall. A lintel just S of the entrance from the main chamber seems to distinguish the passage as two separate spaces, and a garderobe chute is located at the N end. Though now ruinous and difficult to read, a shorter passage appears to have existed on the second floor, but not on the uppermost storey. While mural tunnelling is a characteristic of Longford tower houses, it is an unusual feature in Co. Louth.

When the Dowdalls built Glaspistol is a matter for conjecture. In this the only reliable guide is the windows, whose cutstone detail would suggest a date in the late C15 or early C16. Those on the E side, facing the road and the Irish Sea, are the most ornate. On the first floor is a former twinlight mullioned window, with carved animal ornament in the spandrels and a square hoodmoulding. On the second storey is a simpler unadorned twinlight opening, on the top floor a single ogee-headed cusped light. Directly below the uppermost window is the armorial crest of the Dowdalls. The carving both here and in the windows is reminiscent of C15 work in Co. Meath (at Trim, Dunsany and Killeen). A crease line on the N face of the tower recalls the steeply pitched roof of an early residential addition to the tower, perhaps built by the Markey family, who acquired the property in the C17.

BLACK HALL. 3 km W. Early C19 house built for the Pentland family in a style greatly reminiscent of Francis Johnston. Rectangular two-storey block, cement-rendered, with a continuous cornice and blocking course. The entrance front is of three bays and is now dominated by a later C19 Ionic conservatory porch filling the ground floor of the central bay. This is unfortunate, as the façade was conceived as a planar composition relying for its effect on a subtle pattern of projection and recession. The two outer bays advance at both centre and ends to give a recessed central bay and the impression of corner pilasters at each end of the façade, while the ground-floor windows are set in tall shallow relieving arches restating the presence of the main block. The fenestration is the classic Regency repertoire: a Wyatt window above the entrance, with standard nine-pane sash windows on each side and long elegant sash windows stretching almost to floor level on the ground floor. Inside, a large rectangular entrance hall provides access to reception rooms on each side and a corridor and stairhall behind. The principal stair and back stairs flank each other at the centre of the rear elevation. The rooms are generously proportioned, with tall ceilings and Greek-revival decoration of *c.* 1830. – FOLLY TOWER. In the grounds, a three-stage C19 tower of coursed rubble, with a square corner stair tower lit by loops and a battlemented parapet.

PIPERSTOWN HOUSE. 6 km W. 1842. A curiously old-fashioned house for its date. Rectangular Georgian-style block of two storeys over a basement with a shallow hipped roof and a continuous cornice and blocking course. The five-bay entrance front is plainly articulated, with unadorned sash windows, corner quoins and a finely wrought blocked surround to the doorcase. Inside, mechanical Greek-revival plasterwork not dissimilar to that at Black Hall.

RATHDRUMMIN CHURCH TOWER. 5.5 km NW. The sole surviving fragment of Rathdrummin Parish Church, built in 1814 with a loan of £461 from the Board of First Fruits. Three-stage tower with the usual simple Gothic detail, adjoined by the W wall of the former church. Across the road is the former glebe-house, a three-bay, two-storey house with a big central chimneystack built in 1810.

CLONARD

ME *6040*

Little survives today to suggest that Clonard was once a place of significance. An abbey was founded here by St Finian in the C6, and from then until the early C13 Clonard was one of the principal bishoprics of Meath. On several occasions during the C9 its monastery was plundered and destroyed by the Danes. About 1145 two new abbeys were established, St Mary's for Augustinian canonesses and St Peter's for Augustinian canons. Then, *c.* 1185, Hugh de Lacy established a third Augustinian foundation, a priory dedicated to St John. He also built a castle, whose motte may still be seen across the road from the churchyard. When Simon de Rochfort became the first Anglo-Norman Bishop of Meath in

1192, he united the monasteries of St Peter and St John and, following an attack by the Irish, moved the episcopal see from Clonard to the new Victorine abbey at Newtown Trim. The ruins of a church and monastic complex stood at Clonard until the early C 19.

ST FINIAN, CLONARD PARISH CHURCH (C of I). 1810. Hall and tower type, with a three-stage belfry with battlements and corner pinnacles. Three-bay nave, all rough-cast. A carved medieval head is built into the belfry. Inside the church, the FONT is dated by Helen Roe to *c.* 1500. It is an octagonal bowl with a principal register of eight carved panels, and a second register of four on the tapering underside. On the principal register is a series of figure subjects including the Virgin and Child, Joseph leading an ass, a monk reading, the Baptism of Christ, a row of shield-bearing angels and several unidentified saints. The lower panels and base are carved with angels bearing shields, trees, leaves and flowers.

ST FINIAN, CLONARD PARISH CHURCH. 1807. Early T-plan church reroofed and renovated in 1870, when a three-storey Gothic belfry was built across the entrance gable. Cement-rendered, with raised corner quoins. Broad pointed windows with hoodmouldings. The belfry has a gabled roof. In 1984 the interior plaster was removed to expose limestone rubble walls with brick window trim. Holy-water stoups are dated 1807.

MOUNT HEVEY. 2 km NW. *c.* 1860. Square Italianate villa of a type popularized by *William Caldbeck* in the 1850s. Two storeys over a basement, with a wide hipped roof, bracketed eaves and central chimneystacks. Three-bay front and side elevations. The centre bay is advanced with a shallow eaves pediment on the entrance front and a triple-light window on the first floor with a projecting Ionic porch below. Cement-rendered, with corner quoin strips, a horizontally channelled ground floor and plate-glass windows.

KILLYON PARISH CHURCH. 4 km NE. By *J. A. Fehily*. An honest and clearcut C 20 modernist building, nicely located on a low hillside opposite the old church. Large rectangular hall, steel-framed, with a wide single-pitched roof. At the altar end an extension to one side converts the plan to an L-shape and provides space for a small gallery. The exterior, a little like a 1950s school, is finished in a mixture of brick and grey and white cement-rendering. S of the church is a freestanding bell-tower; tall square shaft built of honeycombed brickwork, with a flat concrete canopy to the belfry. The nicest feature of the design, and a very practical one, is a low canopy carried on concrete piloti which joins the tower to the entrance gable and continues along the S wall of the church to the gallery entrance. This unifies the design. The interior is bright and spacious if utilitarian. Lit from the S by five rectangular windows, each divided into five long narrow lights, and from the N by small windows set in cupboard-like recesses with opaque glass screens. The sanctuary, which is top-lit, has a plain brown brick wall with a centrally placed crucifix. The FORMER CATHOLIC CHURCH, across the road, is an early C19 T-plan building. Cement-rendered, with pointed arches, lancets and a free-standing three-storey belfry.

KILLYON MANOR. 4.5 km NE. It was not possible to visit this house, which has a most promising appearance suggestive of several building periods. Two substantial gabled blocks give a broadly T-shaped plan, with the entrance front in the base of the T. This is of five bays and three storeys, tall, with narrow sash windows and broad expanses of masonry indicative of an early date. C19 classical porch and curtain walls with blind arcading screening offices on each side. Gabled range to the rear with a steep roof, large chimneys and the upper windows set directly beneath the eaves.

BALLYBOGGAN ABBEY. 4 km S. The plain yet impressive ruin of the priory *De Laude Dei*, a foundation established in the C13 by Jordan Cumin for Canons Regular of St Augustine. All that survives is the ruined abbey church and traces of its cloister garth, but the remarkable dimensions of the church and the abbey's charming pastoral setting near the source of the river Boyne make any visit rewarding. This was a wealthy institution which at the Dissolution owned no less than 5,000 acres of rich arable and pasture land. The abbey was surrendered by its last prior, Thomas Bermingham, on 15 October 1537. A year later a sacred cross, much venerated in the later Middle Ages, was publicly burnt by zealous reformers.

Formerly a cruciform structure with transepts N and S, the church, which evidently has been rebuilt and altered at different periods, is now reduced to an extremely long and narrow nave and a high chancel. The dimensions, 193 ft (58.8 m) in length and 26 ft (7.8 m) in breadth, are truly remarkable for an Irish building of this period, even exceeding the C13 cathedral of the Victorine abbey at Newtown Trim, famous for its enormous scale, which at its fullest extent was still 7 ft (2.1 m) shorter, though its nave was 34 ft (10.2 m) wide. The longer, more contracted space at Ballyboggan, together with an apparent steep transition in floor levels between the nave and chancel, must have created dramatic spatial effects in the interior. Here, as at Trim, the nave is the largest element in the design, occupying 140 ft (42.5 m), which is almost three times the floor space of the chancel. The lighting of the interior, however, was not proportioned according to the size of each space: the nave appears always to have been dimly lit, with a mere three or four windows in each wall, while the chancel has tall groups of paired lancets on each side towards the E and a large E window.

If the spatial qualities of the church may still be envisaged from its ruin, ornamentation is another matter: little or no cutstone detail survives. A pair of lancets in the N wall of the chancel do preserve simple E.E. chamfered mouldings, probably reflecting the general character of the C13 interior. Given the wealth of the community and a building of such gigantic proportions it is fair to assume a generous degree of patronage, and there can be little doubt that the embellishment of the basic fabric continued until the end of the C15. In the chancel the fragment of a canopied tomb against the N wall is all that survives to tell this tale. Of the monastic buildings even less remains. A low linear mound preserves the line of the former cloister, while corbel brackets which supported the timbers and flashing of the cloister roof may be noted on the W wall of the fragmentary S transept and on the nave S wall. The abutment of the cloister roof against the side of the church must have dictated, as at Trim, the height of the windows which lit the nave.

8070

CLONGILL CROSSROADS ME

CLONGILL CASTLE. An ivy-grown tower house and adjoining it a long two-storey dwelling of C16 or C17 date, said to have been fired upon by Cromwell. The tower house retains its barrel-vaulted basement, a spiral stair in the SW tower, a small chamber in the NE tower and a chimneypiece on the second floor. The later dwelling is a long roofless shell with a chimneystack on the W gable. Both buildings are of limestone rubble intermixed with sandstone. The castle was for centuries the property of the Gerrard family, later occupants of Gibbstown house. Jonathan Swift addressed several letters to Samuel Gerrard of Clongill Castle, who was assisting him in purchasing lands for his projected hospital.

ST COLUMCILLE. 1.5 km N, at Fletcherstown. Late C18 T-plan barn church with a freestanding belfry, really just a pinnacled stone block with a bellcote on top. Inside the church a holy-water stoup bears the date 1785 and the name of the mason, *Francis Betagh*.

DOWDSTOWN HOUSE. 2 km NW. A gentleman farmer's house, erected in 1793 by Francis Crewe, whose initials are inscribed on the datestone. A simple gabled block, two storeys over a vaulted basement, three bays wide and two rooms deep. Rough-cast, with regular sash windows and a very fine doorcase with a large semicircular fanlight, side-lights and two limestone Doric columns. The door panels are of a type briefly in vogue at the turn of the century.

KILSHINE FORMER CHURCH (C of I). 2.5 km N. Early C19. Now a forgotten island in a sea of corn and barley. Straightforward hall and tower type church with a good spire. Two-bay nave and shallow chancel, near which is the Pollock family vault.

MOUNTAINSTOWN HOUSE. 2.5 km N. No mountain nor any town of that name stands anywhere even remotely near to Mountainstown House, which most probably derives its name from a mounting post or halt. Although exact details are not forthcoming the house appears to have been built *c.* 1720 by Richard Gibbons. In 1780 his only surviving child, Anne Gibbons, sold it to John Pollock, whose family had been renting the place for some time. Since then, Mountainstown has remained in the Pollock family.

Mountainstown has been described as 'naive' and 'bucolic'. Certainly it attempts a greater display of classicism than was usual for a house of this size in Ireland and in doing so it gets some features wrong. The original house is a rectangular block two storeys high, with six windows to the front and four at the sides. The central two bays of the front and side elevations are both slightly advanced and marked by shallow pediments at eaves level. Above the eaves is the usual high pitched roof with regular chimneys and lead flat associated with C17 domestic architecture. Two dormer windows of Wren or Queen Anne character flank the pediment on the main front. Though it is not unknown in Irish country houses, using two bays as a central focus under a pediment is always awkward, and here the awkwardness is emphasized by the addition of four giant-order pilasters, with Scamozzian Ionic capitals, flanking the central bays and at the ends of the façade, set about 2 ft (0.6 m) in from the corners. There is no frieze or architrave beneath the cornice, so these pilasters seem too big for the house and support a very imperfect entablature. The main door is also given a flamboyant touch and is treated as a Palladian window; this time the architecture is all complete, but the scale is too small for the windows that surround it, and despite the half urns placed at its apex and sides it is dwarfed in its setting. The house is set on a semi-basement and is approached by a fine perron with low railings.

In 1813 the main block of the house was extended by a long two-storey gabled wing built onto the SW corner and converting the house to an L-shaped plan. A wide canted bay masks the junction of the old and new work. The main rooms in this wing are lit by wide tripartite windows with regular sashes above. A single-storey kitchen wing extends to the right of the entrance front. N of the house is a good stableyard of low whitewashed ranges with small window openings and wide expanses of masonry.

ST CATHERINE. 2.5 km W, at Oristown. 1971 by *Fehily Associates*. A small modernist church with an irresolute exterior but an effective theatrical use of light inside. Rectangular in plan, with cut-out corners, the largest of which forms the main entrance, screened by concrete shafts with glass between. Otherwise the façade is windowless, whitewashed, with a low sloping roof. Lighting is provided by a clerestory like a shark-fin poised above the sanctuary. Long vertical windows in successive 'wings' stepping down the body of the church from the altar provide discreet side lighting.

GIBBSTOWN. 2 km S. Though it was demolished in 1965, Gibbstown house is still announced by a grandiose set of cast-iron gates at the junction of the Kells and Clongill road. This large Italianate house of the mid-C19 was burnt out in 1912 and rebuilt by *J. F. Fuller* in the same year. Demolition is perhaps the wrong description of Gibbstown's fate, as the building fabric was purchased by the monks at New Mellifont, who intended to reconstruct the entire building. It still lies in stacks of numbered blocks in the grounds of Oriel Temple (New Mellifont; *see* Collon). A cast-iron aviary from the house was recently removed from there to the West End Arcade in Drogheda.

6060 CLONMELLON WM

One long broad street lined by trees and rows of gabled houses, with two modest Gothic Revival churches. The village was much improved in the C 19 by the Chapman family, whose ruined Killua Castle lies to the E.

SS PETER AND PAUL, CLONMELLON PARISH CHURCH. Simple early Victorian T-plan chapel probably erected by the Rev. James Murray (†1844), extended and renovated in the late C 19 by the addition of a Perp-style chancel, porches and a freestanding belltower. Church and chancel have an attractive facing of limestone rubble; the tower is cement-rendered. Simple interior, with an open kingpost roof, lancets in the nave and transepts, and a triple-light Perp window in the chancel. – MONUMENTS. The Rev. John Murray †1809 and the Rev. James Murray †1844; a nice Gothic aedicule framing two inscribed black tablets. The Rev. James Dowling †1884 by *Pearse & Sharp*. – STAINED GLASS. High-Victorian pictorial windows donated by the Reilly family of Clonhugh.

ST LUCY, CLONMELLON PARISH CHURCH (C of I). Simple Board of First Fruits hall and tower church, cement-rendered, with three thin lancets to the nave and a triple-light E window. Reputedly built *c.* 1787 and remodelled. The tower has very thin clasping buttresses and tiny battlements. Long tree-lined approach from the village street.

KILLUA CASTLE. 1.5 km E. Now a picturesque castellated ruin rising gauntly on a hillside, Killua began life as a regular three-storey classical house, built by Sir Benjamin Chapman *c.* 1780, when it was called St Lucy. It was always a big house, but at some stage in the early C 19, perhaps *c.* 1830, it was enlarged and given a thorough Gothic overhaul, very probably to designs of *James Shiel*, whose coarse but not ineffective Gothic castle manner is documented in the additions of 1840 at Killeen (q.v.), which Killua resembles. Here one has the feeling that Sir Thomas Chapman and his wife, the new proprietors of St Lucy, indulged in architectural additions not so much from any real need for extra accommodation as because they wished to display a fine romantic taste. With a big classical block to start with, Shiel's gothicization is inevitably compromised. Had he been able to demolish a chunk of the old house to create a truly asymmetrical plan he might have achieved that type of evocative silhouette and loose grouping of masses that John Nash and the Pain brothers had made so fashionable in Ireland; but Shiel could not do anything so dramatic. Few late Georgian proprietors ever conceded that additions should begin with anything as radical as a partial demolition, so Sir Benjamin Chapman's classical mansion still peeps through the disguise of his son's Gothic pile.

St Lucy was a regular three-storey block, with a bow-fronted saloon – a common feature in a late C18 house – in the middle of the garden front, and a broad canted bay marking the centre of the entrance façade, with an octagonal hall inside. All survive in Shiel's remodelling, which did little more than add an emphatic course of battlements to the parapets and a variety of tower rooms tacked onto the corners of the old house. On the garden front the bowed saloon became a round tower, with a second, narrower and taller four-storey tower beside it at the SE corner of the house. Shiel added most on the entrance front, where two gloomy flat-fronted blocks, with an arrangement of tripartite windows in the upper storeys, project from the corners of the façade to create a shallow yet massive forecourt. The house is built of limestone rubble, with hoodmouldings over the windows, while the entrance is marked by a plastic and rather loose interpretation of a Tudor arch. The round-arched entrances of the octagonal entrance hall still have pretty neo-classical medallions and garlands in their lunettes, and the frieze is a composition of urns and palmettes.

The DEMESNE of Killua, now muddy pasture land, was once famous for its romantic landscape, its lake and garden buildings. Of these, the GOTHIC FOLLY RUIN is the sham fragment of an irregular range, very much in the manner of Thomas Wright, with a polygonal tower pierced by large quatrefoils on its upper storey and fragments of a window above, all contrived to provide a ghostly silhouette. More useful were the two gate lodges. The TEMPLE LODGE is a tetrastyle Ionic portico of *c.* 1770, unsophisticated in character, with a very high gabled pediment, acroterion blocks, Scamozzian Ionic capitals and plain niches to the interior wall. The CASTLE GATE LODGE is a pretty toy castle, three bays long and one storey high, with square turrets at each end and a forestanding square tower in the centre. String-courses, pointed niches, label mouldings and heavy battlements swamp this little house with architectural significance. It dates presumably from the same period as Shiel's alterations. Most conspicuous, on a mound SW of the garden front, is the OBELISK, erected to commemorate Sir Walter Raleigh's introduction of the potato into Ireland, a memorial which was to take on ironic significance in view of events in Ireland in the later 1840s.

HARTLANDS. 1.5 km N. 1861 by *S. Symes*. An asymmetrical L-shaped Italianate house, evidently reflecting Symes' interest in the Clydeside villas of Alexander 'Greek' Thomson; built for Captain Richard Donaldson. Two storeys, cement-rendered, with plate-glass windows, wide oversailing eaves and a three-storey Italianate campanile in an angle above the door at the centre of the entrance front. Each successive bay of the front steps backward to increase the asymmetry of the design. Inside, opulent gilded pelmets and moulded plasterwork detail.

St Bartholomew, Killallon Parish Church. 2.5 km w. Built in 1837 by the Rev. James Murray. Big T-plan chapel with, for this scale, too small a tower projecting from the centre of the entrance gable. Nicely located on a hill. Cement-rendered, with tall triple-light, Y-tracery windows and hood-mouldings. Inside, a big lofty hall with bare floorboards, a flat timber panelled ceiling and the simplest of wooden pews. The timber reredos against the altar wall is a charming mid-Victorian survival – a huge affair with three tall ogee-headed niches supported by four giant panelled pilasters in a mixture of classical and Gothic detail. Beneath the outer niches are pointed doors opening into the sacristy. Built in pre-Famine years for a congregation of 600, the church now caters for no more than 150 people.

Church of the Assumption, Ballinlough. 3.5 km s. 1829. T-plan church with a twin-towered battlemented front, attractive but now coated in an ugly pebbledash. Plain interior lit by lancet windows, with galleries carried on clustered timber shafts. Two original limestone holy-water stoups in the transepts. Late c 19 polychrome marble altar fittings and a very handsome altar rail. Built as a chapel of ease to Kilskyre.

Ballinlough National Schools. 3.5 km s. Two pointed-gabled blocks, with traceried windows, house girls' and boys' schoolrooms. They are linked by a short entrance block. Rendered, with corner quoins. Cheerful vernacular Gothic.

Heathstown House. 3.5 km se. 1831. Harled three-bay, two-storey house with a deeply projected central bay, canted and with a freestanding Tuscan porch. Sash windows and a low hipped roof, with a weathervane over the projecting bay. Two rooms deep, with a long, five-bay side elevation, a central entrance and stairhall. The ground falls away from the front to give a basement at the rear. Reputedly built with stones from Dervotstown Castle; in 1837 the home of Mr W. Dwyer.

Johnsbrook House. 4 km e. Handsome gentleman farmer's house of *c.* 1770, formerly derelict but recently thoroughly refurbished. Two storeys over a basement, with a wide-hipped roof and central chimneystacks; rough-cast, with crisp limestone dressings. Simple yet elegant five-bay entrance front: three narrow central bays, advanced and pedimented, with a Pain-style Doric doorcase flanked by small sash windows, three squat sash windows on the upper floor and a Diocletian window in the pediment. This is flanked on each side by a wide single bay with generous sash windows in blocked surrounds. Corner quoins frame the centre and ends of the façade. Much altered and extended at the rear.

5060

CLONYN CASTLE

WM

122 Contemporary with Ashford in Co. Mayo and Glenveagh in Co. Donegal, Clonyn is one of the last Victorian baronial castles to

be built in Ireland. The house rises as an imposing block of dark grey limestone, flanked at each corner by a tall round tower, complete with a battlemented parapet, 'peg' corbelling and a walled dry moat. The format is not essentially different from Roger Morris's Inveraray Castle of 1744, but the atmosphere has changed. The walls are heavy, battered towards the base, and the overall effect is one of sombre strength. A turreted porch and oriel window provide a centrepiece to the entrance front, and a square tower-like oratory projects on the S elevation, facing the Delvin–Mullingar road. The windows, which at once proclaim Clonyn's late C19 date, are ample round-headed lancets filled with plate glass.

Clonyn was the seat of the Nugents, later Earls of Westmeath, who received the lands of Delvin in the late C12 from Hugh de Lacy. In 1871, on the death of the eighth and last Earl, Clonyn passed to his only surviving child, Rosa, wife of the first Lord Greville. Designs for Clonyn had been commissioned from *John McCurdy* as early as 1867, but surviving drawings chart a series of alternative *McCurdy–Mitchell* proposals of the early 1870s, the last, for a *porte cochère*, dating to 1876, by which time presumably the house was well underway. The later designs were commissioned by Lord Greville. Given its protracted history and the presentation of several successive design proposals, one might expect significant changes to have occurred in the projected building between 1867 and 1876. However, this is not the case, and with the exception of additional storeys, slight alterations in room arrangements, and the addition or subtraction of elements such as oriel windows or a *porte cochère*, Clonyn was from outset to completion essentially the same heavy turreted pile.

Though cast in a grand idiom, Clonyn is not a large house. It has a symmetrical compact plan, with the rooms arranged in
two storeys around a grandiose hall. This is a big two-storey 121
space, top-lit, with a double-return stair in Caen stone, rising to an arcaded gallery whose shafts are of green marble with foliated Caen stone capitals. A varnished timber lantern springs from stone corbels above the arcade. The detail throughout is Romanesque in inspiration, though its revival here in a domestic context is more evocative of Thomas Hopper's enormous Norman castles at Gosford in Co. Armagh and Penrhyn in North Wales. The stair rail, for instance, is a miniature round-headed arcade, and the capitals of the gallery arcades are carved with foliage and intertwined dragons. The space in the circular towers, in characteristic Victorian fashion, is not treated as a separate room but forms part of the large rooms at each corner of the building. All are emphatically medieval, with exposed timber ceilings and beams resting on foliated corbels. The arms of Nugent and Greville adorn both the fireplace of the entrance hall and the door to the garden front.

In the grounds of the existing castle are the ruins of the last Nugent residence, a C17 house which was greatly enlarged and remodelled in a late Georgian Gothic idiom. A semicircular limestone plaque from this building is set into the staircase of the modern castle: it bears the Nugent arms and the date 1639. Otherwise, all that survives from the C17 is a long range of narrow rooms with corner fireplaces, one surviving diagonally set chimneystack, brick vaulting to one room and pocked tooling to the door jamb of another. At its E end is a small Gothick tower house, adjoined on the N by the shell of a large two-storey house with bay windows and simple Gothic detailing. Further W is a stone-flagged circular building, reputedly built for the training of horses.

0070

CLOONDARA LF

A pretty village with a unique waterside location straddling the Royal Canal, the river Camlin and a navigation cut from the canal to the Shannon – a picture postcard of weirs, locks and water. Cloondara is the terminal of the now disused Royal Canal; known otherwise as Richmond Harbour, it was completed in 1817, almost thirty years after the canal's inception at Dublin in 1789. The village was purpose-built to cater for the canal traffic – a row of one-, two- and three-storey gabled Georgian blocks to house the harbour master, the lock-keeper, the inn, storage and office facilities. Although the expected trade from the N Shannon did not materialize, Cloondara and the canal still thrived throughout the 1820s and 1830s. The great four-storey rubble-built mill on the W side of the canal was originally a distillery, which at its peak in the 1830s produced 10,000 gallons of whiskey each year. Decline began in the 1840s and was accelerated in 1845 by the sale of the Royal Canal to the Great Western Railway Company. Since 1972, however, work has been in progress to restore Cloondara and today it is a popular mooring place for summer cruisers.

CLOONDARA CHURCH RUIN. Small and satisfyingly solid ruin of a medieval church incorporating residential accommodation at its W end. Roofless gabled building of limestone rubble with large clearly defined corner quoins and a complete pointed arch and doorway in the N wall. The church is simply a nave, with a two-storey apartment at the W end made up of a vaulted ground-floor chamber, with a fireplace in the N wall, from which a straight stair leads to an upper chamber. Built of coarse and hammered limestone rubble but devoid of any distinctive cutstone or architectural features. The date of this miniature residence is impossible to discern, and it may or may not be coeval with the nave. The punched masonry and straight stair, however, are similar to much C15 work. A C13 date may be ascribed to the church proper on the strength of its two surviving windows in the S and E wall. Single round-headed lancets set in round deeply splayed embrasures of the type found in the C12 and C13 at Clonmacnoise, Co. Offaly, Ballintubber, Co. Mayo, and Banaher, Co. Derry. In the C19, Cloondara

Church was likened to the now derelict site of Abbeyderg, some five miles S of Longford, which was founded *c.* 1205 by Gormgal O'Quinn, Lord of Rathcline. A sole documentary reference to Cloondara records the death in 1323 of Giolla Airnin O'Casey, Archdeacon of Cluan-da-rath.

CLOONDARA CHURCH. Built by the Rev. R. Farrel in 1830. Three-bay gabled hall. Harled, with pointed sash windows and intersecting tracery.

COLLINSTOWN

WM *5060*

A large rectangular marketplace lined by low two-storey houses and formerly dominated by the village markethouse, which stood at its centre until *c.* 1950. During the C18 and C19 the village was patronized by the Smyths of Glananea.

ST MARY. T-plan chapel of late C19 appearance. Cement-rendered entrance gable with clasping buttresses, a pointed arch flanked by two lancets and above it three graded lights. – STAINED GLASS. Vividly coloured pictorial glass of the 1880s. – MONUMENT. The Rev. Luke Farrelly P.P. † 1884.

COLLINSTOWN FORMER CHAPEL OF EASE (C of I). A sad little derelict church. Board of First Fruits hall with a later C19 N transept by *Joseph Welland.* Timber Y-tracery windows, quarry glass and stencilled patterning to the walls. One pew complete with fireplace. – MONUMENTS. To the Smyth family; to the Monck sisters.

DRUMCREE PARISH CHURCH (C of I). 2.5 km E. 1811. Harled, three-bay hall and three-stage tower. Timber Y-tracery windows with quarry glass. Battlemented parapet to the nave and single-stepped buttresses between each bay, crowned by dunce's-hat-like pinnacles with ball finials.

DRUMCREE HOUSE. 2 km E. Like Barbavilla and Glananea, Drumcree House was a seat of the Smyth family. Chronologically it comes second in the group, built probably *c.* 1750; architecturally, because of its advanced state of dereliction it must now sadly rank last. Drumcree was a handsome building which could once hold its own with its neighbours. A two-storey rectangular house, two rooms deep, of symmetrical plan with a seven-bay limestone entrance front. Three advanced and pedimented centre bays with the customary Palladian combination of a pedimented doorcase and a Venetian motif on the upper storey. Limestone ashlar cornice, string-course, raised corner quoins and moulded window surrounds in the outer bays.

COLLON

LO *9080*

A charming village which, like Slane, is situated on a steep hill, around a crossroads. Although Collon was well established when Arthur Young stayed here *c.* 1775, its present appearance has a

Regency character. Rows of two-storey houses with slated roofs, overhanging eaves and redbrick chimneys; squat tripartite windows, wavy bargeboards, and a handful of *cottage orné*-style porches. A nice grassy marketplace provides a focus for the upper end of the village. The only major early C18 survival is the large three-storey house on the NE corner of the crossroads. This was built *c.* 1740 by Anthony Foster, Lord Chief Baron of the Exchequer, who had left the family home at Dunleer (q.v.) in order to develop the Collon estate. Thereafter the fortunes of the Foster family and of Collon are closely interlinked. Anthony's son, John Foster, became Speaker of the Irish House of Commons in 1785; his younger brother, William, became Chaplain to the House of Commons and Bishop of Cork, later acceding to the see of Kilmore and finally of Clogher. Thus by 1790 the Fosters were well established as one of the leading Commoner families in Ireland. John Foster died in 1828 and the family's political standing was maintained by his nephew, John Leslie Foster, M.P. for Louth and a leading Louth Grand Juror.

COLLON PARISH CHURCH (C of I). The situation of this church, conspicuous on a hillside beside the Dublin–Derry road, makes it almost an Irish architectural landmark. It is not the best church of its kind but it is absolutely characteristic of what Irishmen thought of as Tudor-Gothic taste in the late Georgian period. Tudor-Gothic as practised by architects like Francis Johnston or Thomas Duff is more sophisticated; there is something slightly naive, even clumsy, here, a certain bareness, an overt regularity and a lumpy quality in the detailing. Yet this naivety is also part of the building's charm and may be explained by the fact that its author was an amateur, the *Rev. Daniel Augustus Beaufort*, rector of Collon from 1789 to 1821.

Plans for the new church were mooted first in 1810, even though the then existing building was only of 1763 and had been enlarged in 1797 and 1809. One suggestion as to why a new church was considered necessary so soon was that John Foster needed a new family vault when the old one at Dunleer had become full! The Board of First Fruits made a grant of £800 and a loan of £1,700, and in July 1811 the foundation stone was laid. For his model Beaufort chose the Chapel of King's College, Cambridge, perhaps the supreme example of English Perp architecture, begun by Henry VI in 1446 and completed by Henry VIII 69 years later. The architecture of this great building, clear, rectangular and absolutely lucid in its development, was calculated to appeal to late Georgian taste; it represented Gothic at its most rational, and in the early C19 was destined to be the standard reference point for many a Gothic Revival design. Indeed after 1816, when its details were engraved and published by Augustus Pugin, it became an almost hackneyed design. What is remarkable about Daniel Beaufort's church at Collon is first its date – 1810 – and the extent to which he adheres to King's College Chapel in his own much smaller church.

The building in essence is a rectangular five-bay hall, with a projecting chancel flanked by a lean-to porch and vestry suggestive of the side chapels of King's. A large fourteen-light Perp window fills the E gable, which is flanked by thin octagonal turrets. That the turrets are located at the W end only is perhaps more reminiscent of St George's Chapel, Windsor, another popular Perp model considered by Beaufort, which also inspired the Perp panelling of the chancel. Smaller Perp windows, with buttresses between, fill the S wall, while the N wall, usually blank in Protestant churches of this date, is articulated as five blind windows.

If the Perp references are strongest on the front, the bareness of the sides appearing in consequence a little awkward, the
simplicity of the interior has absolute charm. A lovely blend of 100
spare elegance with delicate Tudor-Gothic ornament. Each bay is framed by slender clustered shafts rising to support a delicate plaster fan-vault with a major transverse rib, once again on the King's model, crossing the ceiling of the church. The chancel has a deep four-centred arch decorated with Perp panelling. The seating follows the collegiate arrangement, with a central aisle flanked by tiered choir stalls decorated with thin Gothic mouldings. Daniel Beaufort had close family connections with the Edgeworths of County Longford and both the fan-vault and the original hot-cockle heating system are said to have been devised by *William Edgeworth*. – STAINED GLASS. Designed by the rector's daughter, *Louisa Beaufort*, in bold clear-coloured abstract patterns, with the spacious firmament of sun, moon and stars in the intersections of the tracery in the E window. The glass was made and installed by *Edward Lowe* of Dublin. – MONUMENT. Catherine Letitia Foster †1814, erected by her daughter Harriet, Countess de Salis.* Elegant stele-like neoclassical monument in white marble with relief carving of a female profile in classical garb weeping upon an urn.

CHURCH OF MARY IMMACULATE. 1860–77 by *John Murray*. Victorian Gothic church with geometric tracery and E.E. detail. Dark squared limestone with light grey limestone trim. Nave, aisles and an unfinished tower flanking the entrance gable, lacking its belfry and spire, a fate shared by most of Murray's churches. Main door in an arched recess flanked by lancets with a big geometric window above. The interior is a lofty five-bay arcade of moulded two-centred arches carried on round limestone shafts. – STAINED GLASS. In the manner of the Clarke studios. – MONUMENT. Dorcas, wife of Percy Fitzgerald, author and artist, and eldest child of John, tenth Viscount Masserene and Ferrard, †1876; an elegant white marble effigy of a sleeping woman by the Belgian sculptor *Malempre*.

COLLON HOUSE. That practicality and sound common sense

*A charming anecdote is told of the young Harriet Foster who while at school in Rome in the early 1800s was proposed to by Count Mastai Ferretti, a young officer in the Papal Guard. On being refused, Count Ferretti joined the priesthood and in 1846 he was elected to the papacy as Pius IX.

were hallmarks of the Foster family is evident from the plainness and modesty of this their principal family home. Anthony Foster, founder of the family fortunes, built up an estate here *c.* 1740, buying most of his land from the Moore family, the Earls of Drogheda, whose profligate lifestyle had forced a succession of sales. Foster clearly learnt from their misfortunes, for his house reflects no desire for architectural display.

Collon House is a big, plain building on the corner of the crossroads, in fact two buildings joined together: the early Georgian residence built by Anthony Foster and a later addition, probably erected *c.* 1770. The house is L-shaped, made up of two two-storey gabled blocks, the earlier forming a seven-bay side elevation and the more modern providing an entrance front facing W. Within, there is notable change in scale from the intimate proportions of Anthony Foster's original dwelling to the much larger dimensions of the principal drawing room, entrance hall and stairhall. The former has fielded panelling, six-panel doors, simple marble chimneypieces and crisp plain cornices, whereas the later part of the house has more elaborate Corinthian cornices and a handsome half-turn stair with landings. The windows of the stairhall retain their early Georgian glazing bars, but the joinery in the hall and drawing room is late C18.

ORIEL TEMPLE. 0.5 km NE. The origins of these buildings, which now accommodate the Cistercian community of New Mellifont, lie in the embellishment of the Foster estates at Collon. Despite the importance of the family and John Leslie Foster's personal interest in architecture (demonstrated by his involvement in the building of Dundalk Courthouse), Oriel Temple never became a great family mansion. The house in Collon, though some sixty years old and in the centre of the village, seems always to have been adequate for Speaker Foster's needs. Oriel Temple was thus a trianon, or place for sylvan retreat, a garden house placed in the demesne of Anthony Foster *c.* 1776. In the following decade John Foster enlarged the temple to form a small villa, of which the drawing room resembled a Doric temple and was decorated with grisaille paintings of allegorical subjects by *Peter De Gree*. In 1787 Daniel Beaufort recorded in his journal that he visited De Gree at work in the temple. The sanctuary of the present chapel is the drawing room of Oriel Temple, the original steps of the Doric portico, now cased in wood, while the De Gree paintings were removed to Luttrellstown Castle, Co. Dublin.

Although modernized and adapted for liturgical purposes, the sanctuary preserves a charming neoclassical plasterwork ceiling in the manner of Michael Stapleton. Shallow elliptical vault rising from a crisp Ionic cornice decorated with a circular pattern within a rectangular frame. The circular motif focuses on a central foliated boss with successive fluted borders, encircled by a delicate flower-shaped pattern, where the 'petals' are garlands of ribbon tied in bows. Beyond the circle at each end of the rectangle and in the spandrels of the vault are stylized lutes, urns, garlands and shells like feathery grotesques. The quality of this ceiling lends some support to family tradition that *James Wyatt* gave designs for Oriel Temple. Foster's brother-in-law, Henry Maxwell, Bishop of Meath, did manage to obtain from Wyatt in 1773 preliminary sketches for his palace at Ardbraccan, and Foster may well have followed suit. Perhaps, as happened at Ardbraccan, Wyatt's plans were taken over and adapted by a local architect; the temple bears a marked resemblance to Primate Robinson's Chapel at Armagh, which makes the involvement of Thomas Cooley also seem likely. Whoever may claim the credit, it is certain that the miniature Doric temple, with its neoclassical interior and grisaille paintings, was one of the most elegant pleasure buildings of its date in Ireland.

Oriel Temple as it exists today is hard to read and, apart from the sanctuary, of little architectural value; the Foster villa has been rebuilt, enlarged and adapted with many routine utility buildings. A robust, if rustic, distyle Doric portico, in a primitive Greek idiom, survives as a single-storey porch in part of the old villa. Of more interest is the small rubble and brick HERMITAGE at the S end of the lake, a primitive and unusually substantial rustic structure which, looking more like the stump of some tower house, now sprouts bushes and trees from its roof. This is a romantic garden building of the later C18, housing two rooms, one square and the other apse-ended, with pointed windows, roughly formed niches, a fireplace in the first room and a corbelled vault. Here John Foster's wife, Margaret, and their daughter, later Lady Dufferin, played at being cottagers: cows have taken up residence today! A square SHELL HOUSE or grotto, also built by John Foster for his wife, is in a dell in woodlands to the W of the house. Its roof has been reconstructed and the shells have gone. N of the house, the former FARMYARD by *Edward Parke*, a courtyard of rubble farm offices, not unlike Drogheda Cornmarket, with colonnaded ranges and elliptical arched gateways in limestone ashlar. In the grounds, forlornly awaiting reconstruction, lie the numbered stones of Gibbstown (*see* Clongill Crossroads).

CROSSAKIEL

ME *6070*

Small C19 village built around a triangular green.

CROSSAKIEL OLD PARISH CHURCH (C of I). *c.* 1820. A spiky Board of First Fruits hall and tower church; more ambitious than usual, with battlemented vestibules flanking the tower, pinnacled buttresses to every angle and a good sharp profile to the spire. Three-bay nave with battlements and pinnacled E gable. Cement-rendered, with punched limestone dressings. Roofless and derelict in 1985.

HIGH CROSSES, Castlekeeran Churchyard, 10 km NE. Three plain high crosses, carved in sandstone, with the base of a fourth. They follow the form of the crosses at Kells and Monasterboice, with roll mouldings at the corners and a smaller rib moulding inside. The arms and rings employ interlace and abstract patterns to a limited extent. The South Cross is the tallest at 12 ft 8 in. (3.87 m) in height, and has an interlace boss at the centre of the S face. Decorative cylinders are set at the intersection of the shaft within the ring rather than on the ring itself. The North Cross is very similar but lacks the head of the cross shaft. The West Cross is lacking its S arm and has no carved decoration.

ARDGLASSON. 1 km W. A charming group of early C19 labourers' cottages, absolutely plain and absolutely regular, set back on either side of the road. Two long, low single-storey terraces. Each house has a door with a window either side, is built of random rubble, whitewashed and slated with brick chimneys, tiny windowpanes and plain timber doors – several with horseshoes hung above them. Sadly a number have already been spoiled by smooth modern plaster and unsympathetic glazing. A short distance W from here is a more self-consciously picturesque two-storey cottage of red and yellow diaper brickwork, with tall gables, decorative bargeboards and quarry glass.

CLONABREANY. 2.5 km W. *The Post Chaise Companion* noted a house belonging to a Mr Wade here in 1786. The house has long gone, though there remains a large rubble and limestone stable-court with a pedimented classical archway flanked by doors and circular *œils de bœuf*. E of this there is also the fragment of an early C19 gabled limestone block with tripartite window and segmental relieving arches.

BELVIEW. 3 km NW. *c.* 1765. A pleasant example of provincial Georgian classicism, sometimes attributed to *Nathaniel Clements*. A trim three-bay house of two storeys over a basement, linked to its offices and outhouses by curving curtain walls. Rough-cast, with corner quoins, moulded limestone keystones and window surrounds and a pedimented Pain-type Tuscan doorcase. The windows, twelve panes below and six above, are quite small, leaving the broad areas of masonry which characterize mid-Georgian work. The eaves course is unusually high, with a shallow hipped roof above. Inside, the house is two rooms deep, with a central hall giving access to two large reception rooms at the rear and flanked by a reception room on the E and the stair well on the W. This projects from the side elevation as a semicircular bow. Original six-panel doors in lugged surrounds and plain plaster cornices.

BOBSVILLE. 3 km W. *c.* 1765. The Irish taste for irony and self-mockery is surely caught in the hybrid name of Bob's ville. The house is contemporary with Belview (described above) and similar in being a two-storey, three-bay house with a basement and a hipped roof. Although here the sash windows have been replaced by plate glass, the arrangement of the openings close to the centre, leaving a broad band of masonry at each end, is again typical of mid-C18 building practice. The doorcase here, two rusticated pilasters with consoles supporting an open pediment, is a standard motif of the 1760s, seen in Parnell Square, Dublin, and at St Laurence Street in Drogheda. Like Belview, the house is also two rooms deep but in this case the central hall communicates directly with a handsome dog-leg stair, lit from a round-headed window in the rear elevation. The stair rail and joinery appear to be mid-C 19.

LAKEFIELD HOUSE. 5 km SW. A deceptive house which, except for the preponderance of wall over window, appears outside to be a standard two-storey, three-bay house of mid-C 19 date. Inside, lugged door surrounds and fossilized black marble chimneypieces establish its origins in the 1750s or 60s. Originally two rooms deep, with four principal rooms on the ground floor flanking a central entrance and stairhall. An early date is supported by the surrounding plantations, clumps and belts of trees interspersed with great oaks and, S of the house, the artificial lake which gave the place its name.

DANGAN CASTLE

ME *8050*

The ruined C 18 seat of the Wellesley family, celebrated by contemporaries for its stupendous demesne with canals, lakes, bowers and battleships; the birthplace in 1769 of the Duke of Wellington (at least according to his nurse, though his mother said he was born in Mornington House in Dublin). The most vivid surviving accounts of the house come from Mary Granville, later Mrs Delany, who visited here on two occasions as Mrs Pendarves and again twice following her second marriage. In 1732 she described the house as 'large, handsome and convenient', containing a 'charming large hall with an organ and harpsichord ... where music, dancing, shuttlecock, draughts and prayers take their turn.' Richard Wesley, first Baron Mornington, was then in the process of spending vast sums of money on improving the estate, and when Mrs Pendarves returned in the following year she commented that he had 'three canals in his gardens; in one of them ... the model of the king's yacht, the *Carolina* ... with much exactness to the original.' There was also a fir grove dedicated to Vesta and temples to Apollo and Fame. On her third visit to Dangan, in 1748, the new Mrs Delany found that the old house had been burnt down and was then rebuilding. The gardens too had altered from the more formal layout of French-inspired groves and Dutch canals to 'a great lake fifty feet broad and six hundred yards long', of irregular shape, with a fort, islands and ships in it, including a complete man-of-war. The demesne was landscaped to form hills and dales, with each vista closed by a 'tuft of trees, a statue, a seat, an obelisk or a pillar'. Four years later Dangan was no longer to Mrs Delany's taste, which now inclined towards the picturesque. The demesne she found 'grand but not pleasing ... no shade ... no retirement ... not like a gentle, soothing friend that leads you through flowery paths and delights every sense.' By 1776, when Arthur Young visited the estate, the picturesque had come to Dangan, with an extensive lake and plantations in the Brownian manner.

Of all this splendour only two brick obelisks at points N and S of the demesne survive. The house is now a mere shell, nothing more than the external walls of a large rectangular Georgian block, five bays long and two storeys high, built over a vaulted basement. Brick and rubble rough-cast, with a moulded limestone eaves cornice and a parapet. Despite its dilapidated state it is clear that this building can never have been elegant. Big and awkwardly proportioned, it well suits Mrs Delany's conclusion, 'grand but not pleasing'. Wellington's infamous retort concerning his Irish birthright comes to mind when describing this house, which truly has hardly more architectural pretension than a common stable. In plan the house consisted of a long rectangular block, two rooms deep, adjoined at the SE angle by a square four-storey block with a battered base and a brick-vaulted basement. Although now of C18 appearance, this tower-like block may incorporate part of the original Dangan Castle burnt in 1748. In 1793 the house and lands were sold to Captain Thomas Burrowes, who added two wings containing a chapel and a library. Nothing of these survives, but the chapel window was installed in Agher Church nearby (*see* Summerhill). Dangan Castle was gutted by fire in 1809 and has remained a romantic ruin ever since. What survives of the STABLEYARD is much more handsome than the remains of the house. A sturdy pedimented block with quoins, string-course and a central cutstone archway, surmounted by a square brick tower with a round-headed window to each face. Grand C18 vernacular classicism.

DELVIN *see* CASTLETOWN-DELVIN

8070 DONAGHMORE ME

An important early Irish monastic site 1.5 km NE of Navan on the Slane road. Situated on high ground above the Boyne this monastery was founded by St Patrick for Cruimthir Cassan – St Cassanus – whose relics were later preserved in the church. The monastery was plundered in 854. After the establishment of Norman power in Ireland, Donaghmore became a parish church. The only early monument is the ROUND TOWER, which is probably C12. Built of local limestone with sandstone trim, it has a two-tiered base and stands complete apart from a section of the conical roof. The doorway, some 12 ft (3.6 m) from the ground, has the very distinctive feature of a carving of the Crucifixion above it with a human head on either side. Only the round tower at Brechin, Angus, in Scotland repeats this feature of relief sculpture on the stone frame of a door.

The ruined parish church, rectangular and with a double bellcote on the W gable, is C15 or early C16. Fragments of stone cusped lights from the building lie in the graveyard.

Donaghmore, round tower. Doorway, from G. Petrie's *Ecclesiastical Architecture of Ireland* (1845)

DUNMOE CASTLE. 1.5 km E. An impressive ruin, magnificently sited high up above a bend in the Boyne. Like Roche Castle (*see* Kilcurry), Dunmoe is best seen from below or, in this case, from the opposite riverbank. From there it appears as a massive wall of limestone masonry flanked by circular corner towers which rise from a steeply battered base. On closer inspection the castle is disappointing in that there is simply no more of it. It was formerly a large square enclosure with four corner towers; now only the S wall survives. Dunmoe is said to have been one of the first castles erected in Meath by Hugh de Lacy, but what remains today may not have been built until the C15. Taken by Irish forces in 1641, and later attacked by Cromwell, the castle was restored in the reign of James II, when it was converted from a fortress into a castellated house. It was largely destroyed by fire in 1799. Within the castle enclosure is a small chapel and mausoleum. – MONUMENT. Thomas Casserly †1722.

HAYES. 4 km E. Attractive smaller country house erected *c.* 1770 by the Legge-Bourke family. Soundly built of coursed limestone rubble, at one time cement-rendered. Two storeys over a basement, with a low hipped roof, continuous eaves cornice and blocking course. The entrance front is of seven bays with a broad central section, slightly advanced and marked by a porch, with a tripartite window above and an eaves pediment. The porch, which is C 19, screens the original Tuscan doorcase. The garden front, with a central two-storey bow, flanked by three windows on each side, is reminiscent of nearby Beauparc, though on a much smaller scale. Both the main elevations have long twelve-pane sash windows on the ground floor, with squat, originally six-pane windows above. All are set in stone frames.

The plan is symmetrical: a central entrance hall, incorporating a large half-turn stair, with an elegant bowed drawing room behind. Most of the interior detail looks early C 19, with pretty neoclassical ceilings in the hall and drawing room and delicate beaded borders to the drawing-room joinery. The tripartite window lighting the stair must also date to this period. A more substantial modillion cornice in the former dining room is the only original decoration to survive. A large white marble chimneypiece was brought here from Somerville (*see* Kentstown).

DOLLARDSTOWN. 6.5 km NE. A large and impressive stone and redbrick house, designed in 1734 for Arthur Meredyth by *Richard Castle*, which stood as a derelict, ivy-grown shell until 1986, when it was completely demolished. Long seven-bay, three-storey block, flanked grandiosely by two tall freestanding pavilions, one of which remains today. The house employed the common Castle progression of door with aedicule, niche and oculus in the central bay and had an unusual side elevation of paired Venetian windows on the two main floors, with tripartite windows above. The hall and staircase had plaster panelling throughout, with pedimented door frames and the distinctive lugged panels and guttae so characteristic of Castle's work. All the ground-floor rooms had bold Ionic entablatures with pulvinated bay-leaf friezes; the upper floors had plain dentil cornices.

8070

DONAGHPATRICK

ME

A church, parochial hall and sexton's house that form a nice group at a country crossroads. Like Duleek, Domhnach Pádraig, or Church of St Patrick, is reputedly the site of one of the earliest *damhliags* or stone churches erected in Ireland. The tripartite *Life of Saint Patrick* states that this place was the site of a royal palace, granted to Patrick by Conaill, brother of the High King Laoghaire, following his baptism. Near here is Telltown, anciently Tailte, famous for the annual Telltown games at which all the princes and chieftains gathered and where Patrick was rejected by Conaill's brother Cairbre. A church survived at Domhnach Patrick throughout the Middle Ages, although burned in 745 and twice plundered, in 949 and 1156. By 1682 the medieval church is described as 'ruinous'.

ST PATRICK, DONAGHPATRICK PARISH CHURCH (C of I). 1866 by *J. F. Fuller*. A Victorian rebuilding incorporating a bulky medieval tower of coursed limestone rubble. The tower was residential, not a simple belltower, and like a tower house contained a single large room on each of its four storeys, complete with fireplaces, press recesses and a stair in the thickness of the N wall. Fuller's church has a three-bay nave of rock-faced limestone with an apsidal chancel, a vestry, and a lean-to gabled porch adjoining the S wall of the tower. Inside, panelled ceiling, Caen stone chancel arch and tiled chancel. – STAINED GLASS. E window: three cusped lights, The Ascension; in the nave: military themes; all by *Heaton, Butler & Bayne*. N wall: Fides et Spes; charming colouring, by *Sarah Purser*, 1930. – MONUMENTS. In the chancel, a C16 marble slab to the memory of Patrick Plunkett †1575 and his wife, Elizabeth Barnewell. In the tower are a number of inscribed date stones brought here from Randalstown (an important house begun in 1710 by Lieut-Col. Matthias Everard and demolished in the 1970s). Col. Matthias Everard †1714, a tall slab with shallow-relief carving of the Everard arms, skull and crossbones. This is flanked by small half-length military figures wearing helmets and sashes. – PARISH HALL. Gabled three-bay lancet hall of rock-faced limestone, erected in 1890 to designs by *R. S. Barnes*.

BLOOMSBURY. 3 km NW. Originally a simple two-storey Georgian house. Five bays wide and two bays deep, probably of early C19 date, and certainly existing before 1812. Originally rough-cast, the whole house is now cement-rendered to imitate ashlar work, with giant corner pilasters, a Greek Ionic porch and a small eaves pediment above the centre bay. All this refacing dates from 1858, when the house was extended and remodelled for Richard Barnewell by the Kells builder *Francis Nulty*. The enlargement consisted of building a second and larger rectangular block at the rear of the existing house, thus making the plan two ranges deep. The new garden front, at the back of the house, is a long low façade, two storeys over a semi-basement, and seven bays wide. The three centre bays break forward, with four giant pilasters supporting an entablature; round-headed french windows at ground-floor level. The end elevations of this wing have pediments, canted bay windows and giant corner pilasters. An attractive early Victorian classical design, reminiscent of *William Caldbeck*, who was working in Kells around the time of these alterations and who used Nulty on a number of other domestic commissions throughout Meath and Westmeath.

FISHING TEMPLE. At the meeting of the Blackwater and the Moynalty River, SW of the house, an octagonal brick-built later C18 temple. Some 14 ft (4 m) in diameter, with a boat house below and temple above. The walls of the temple have alternating sash windows and hollow roundels and are roofed by a brick dome. Ionic room cornice inside, and niches with a delicate fluted frieze detail at the impost level. A pretty building made useless by the lowering of the level of the Blackwater, so that even the boat house is now above water level.

BACHELORS LODGE. 1.5 km SE. A mid-C18 house of modest proportions, now ivy-grown. Built, presumably as a hunting lodge, by the Earl of Essex. Two-storey, three-bay entrance front with hipped roof. A tiny eaves pediment above the centre bay is pierced by a semicircular window. Dull Victorian porch with heavy balustrade. Inside, a handsome Tuscan stair, six-panel doors in lugged surrounds and in one room an Ionic plaster cornice that looks *c.* 1760.

CHURCH OF ST JOHN THE BAPTIST, KILBERRY. 4.5 km E, at Kilberry. Built in 1839 by the Rev. Matthew Kelsh and refurbished in 1959. Broad T-plan chapel, cement-rendered, with limestone corner quoins, timber Y-tracery lancets and four-centred arches. Two groups of modern lancets flank the entrance. – STAINED GLASS. Baptism of Christ, with other emblems and scenes from the life of Christ, by *J. Murphy & J. A. Devitt*, Monkstown, Dublin.

WOODVIEW HOUSE (formerly KILBERRY GLEBE). 3 km E. 1840. Simple late Georgian in style. Two storeys over a basement, with a low hipped roof. Three-bay entrance front. The main-floor windows are set in shallow relieving arches. Central fanlit doorcase, now screened by a 1930s Mendelsohn-style porch, nice in itself but not successful here. Clumsy timber bay windows of the late C19 project from the upper floor.

MARTRY MILL. 2 km W. This group of three two-storey rubble buildings, neatly and intelligently refurbished, is one of the few working watermills in Ireland. Built on shale rock on the S bank of the Blackwater, Martry Mill, though architecturally humble, marks a significant survival of old ways. The *Civil Survey* of 1641 indicates a mill on this site, and throughout the next three centuries this was the mill of the Tisdall estate at Charlesfort. Though once used for a flax mill, by the early C19 Martry operated exclusively as a corn mill. In the 1950s three sets of millstones were employed on grinding pinhead oatmeal. However, since 1986, owing to changes in the river level caused by land reclamation, only one set of stones is in use, and this with the frequent aid of electricity. While wholefood fashion ensures sustained demand for stone-ground produce, an imported power source does not compensate for the mill's lifeblood, water.

0070

DOWTH HALL

ME

In point of interior decoration this tall plain building is one of the more ambitious smaller country houses of North Leinster. The house, built for John, sixth Viscount Netterville, was described by Isaac Butler as 'rebuilding' in 1744, but the work appears to have begun somewhat later. It is a plain rectangular block with one show front, set on a low hill in rolling countryside above the banks of the Boyne. Clumps and belts of C 18 planting provide an appropriate setting. The main façade, two storeys by five bays, looks very much like a town house come down to the country, with a ground floor of V-jointed rustication, nicely chiselled in even textured limestone, and a plain central door framed by an enormous and rather gauche Doric aedicule with plain windows on each side. Above, the first floor is a proper *piano nobile*: built of ashlar and inordinately tall, with long sash windows decorated by alternately triangular and segmental pediments. A trim eaves cornice and blocking course complete the elevation. Turn the corner and all this architecture is abandoned in completely plain sides, four bays wide and neatly incorporating an extra upper floor not seen on the front or on the plain rear elevation, which overlooks a yard. The quality of the stonework and the urban, not to say street-like, character of the design suggest that Dowth Hall may well be the work of *George Darley*, the mason architect who in 1767 built the Nettervilles' town house in Dublin, between Findlater Place and Great Britain Street.

The glory of Dowth Hall lies in the vigorous late rococo plasterwork which decorates all the principal rooms of the ground floor. The hall opens directly to include a dog-leg main stair with a handsome and emphatic Doric frieze and fielded-panelled doors with robust lugged door surrounds. On the l. (S) is a small sitting room beside the secondary stairs; two main rooms, of two and three windows each, fill up the back of the building. The saloon or drawing room (originally the dining 74
room) is particularly fine, with a series of large, shallowly recessed panels which run from the chair rail to immediately below the room cornice. The panels alternate in size between tall narrow strips, filled with cusped rococo scrolls and tendrils, to wider areas with palm branches surrounding oval medallions above the doors; a broad area over the chimneypiece has naturalistic oak and ivy garlands hanging from a reeded moulding at the top. The whole scheme of the room and many of the individual mouldings are directly comparable to the dining room of Newman House, No. 86 St Stephen's Green, Dublin, decorated in the same years and attributed to Robert West. The shallowly coved room cornices with gadrooned lower mouldings are also characteristic of West's style. Bold architectural chimneypieces in the drawing room – grey and yellow marble with console brackets – and in the hall, which preserves its original Georgian basket grate. The doorways too are worth note: they use a standard six-panel door, but the moulding of the panels is of an unusual rounded form. The detail is very close to the joinery at Dunboyne Castle, built in 1764 to designs of George Darley. Other similarities in the two buildings reinforce the attribution of Dowth Hall to Darley. The palazzo-like aspect of the entrance fronts and the opulent rococo plasterwork interiors of both houses point to a single author. *Oliver*

Beahon, Darley's carpenter at Dunboyne, may well have also been responsible for the joinery at Dowth Hall.

NETTERVILLE CHARITIES ALMSHOUSES. 1877 by *George C. Ashlin*. Standing W of the house, and somewhat surprising in this rural setting, a slick essay in late Victorian institutional polychromy. Seven-bay, two-storey block, projecting to a T-plan at the rear, built of red brick with limestone and blue brick trim. The principal elevation has broad advanced and gabled end bays, with miniature gables over the five central bays. The windows are single or paired pointed lights with attractive chamfered reveals. A plaque records the building's erection with a surplus resulting from the 'provident management' of the Netterville charities by the trustees, Arthur James, Earl of Fingall, Richard Gradwell Esq of Dowth Hall and Malachy Stronghussey of Westtown, Co. Dublin. W of the almshouses is a small medieval tower house reworked in a romantic C18 idiom to give a two-bay, three-storey block with a thin battered and battlemented turret at the NE corner, dummy roundels and square-headed windows. On the W face of the turret is a late medieval ventilator wheel with three lobes. W of the tower, a small Gothick chapel, now roofless, had three bays of pointed windows and a small porch. Other romantic walls with simple Gothic arches create a precinct.

DOWTH PARISH CHURCH RUINS. The remains of a long nave and chancel church built of rubble stone, with a double bellcote on the W gable and a narrow Gothic lancet below with widely chamfered splayed reveals. Two round-headed doors give access to the nave on N and S walls. – MONUMENT. John Boyle O'Reilly, Irish-American patriot, b. at Dowth, 1844, d. at Hull near Boston, Massachusetts, 1890, by *T. H. Dennany*, Glasnevin; bust on a corbel bracket with interlace, flanked by allegorical figures of Ireland and America. Ireland has a wolfhound, sword and flag with harps and shamrocks; America has the stars and stripes and a Bill of Freedom.

6060 DREWSTOWN HOUSE ME

4 km E of Clonmellon

Drewstown House is an eccentric mid-C18 house of some pretension: an ambitious provincial design which produced rather curious results. Little is known of its reputed builder, Barry Barry, who was evidently a man of some sophistication. Arthur Young visited Drewstown in 1776, when the house was occupied by the Maxwell family. Drewstown is quite near to Ballinlough Castle, which stands across the county boundary in Westmeath, and there are strong similarities between the two houses. The name of *Francis Bindon*, painter and amateur architect, has been associated with both buildings.

Drewstown is a large three-storey block-like house with a deep bowed projection to the eastern garden front. Entrance front of seven bays, the centre three advanced, with ill-contrived classical decoration in the central entrance bay. Square Ionic porch with a scrolled round-headed window above and a squat pedimented window to the top floor. The house is rough-cast with limestone trim, and while the quality of the cutstone detail is very good, the detailing is ungainly and ill-proportioned, characteristics which are even more in evidence in the interior.

The plan is particularly noteworthy. Remarkably old-fashioned for its date, the house follows the tradition of Inigo Jones' Queen's House at Greenwich in having a large square two-storeyed entrance hall with the stair at the rear and a gallery around four sides at first-floor level. The hall is flanked on each side by reception rooms, which project beyond the stair in the rear elevation. Perhaps even more remarkable than the unusual plan is the almost complete survival of the entrance hall's early Georgian joinery. Fielded wainscotting over 5 ft (1.5 m) in height lines the hall, with moulded plaster panels above. The stairhall and gallery are also wainscotted, and the stair is richly carved, with three fluted balusters to each tread and Corinthian newel posts. The gallery balustrade is also original. The ceilings of the stairhall and gallery have simple rococo plasterwork decoration.

Despite its impressive plan and its solid C18 joinery, there are oddities in this interior which suggest that its designer lacked experience in large-scale domestic design. On the ground floor the segmental-headed pediments of the doors collide with the room cornice and with the underside of the gallery. Miscalculation is also clearly in evidence in the off-centre position of the entrance on the interior elevation, and the quite bizarre arrangement of the windows on the W side of the entrance bay, which are partially concealed by the internal wall of the adjoining room. Diagonally opposite, at the NE angle of the gallery, a pedimented doorcase collides with the corner of the room. Similar problems at Ballinlough point to a single designer for these interiors.

After the hall, the grandest interior at Drewstown is the bowed drawing room, which commands a view across the lake to the E of the house. The ceiling level here is significantly higher than that of the low rooms to the front of the house, and the room was evidently refurbished in the C19. Robust polychrome marble chimneypiece and a rich Corinthian ceiling cornice.

At the rear of the house is a long C18 stable and office range of coursed rubble with cutstone dressings; handsome Diocletian window in a blocked surround to the S gable. Opening from the yard through a pair of segmental-headed arches are two carriage bays roofed by four brick groin vaults springing from a central Tuscan column. To the E of the house is the lake, with a pretty rockwork bridge, and the remnants of C18 planting which must once have made a charming picturesque garden.

0070 DROGHEDA LO

13 Situated as it is on Ireland's most historic river, it is not surprising that Drogheda's origins and entire history are linked to the influence of the Boyne. The very name Drogheda, Droichead Átha, Bridge of the Ford, tells of the town's beginnings as a major crossing point on the Boyne, and its position only three miles from the mouth of the river made it one of the major ports on the NE coast. St Patrick landed here *c.* 432, and later the Vikings colonized the area, establishing a fort and harbour at Drogheda. But as in many towns on the E coast of Ireland real urban growth began only with the Anglo-Norman invasion in the C12, when Hugh de Lacy established a borough S of the Boyne, building upon the Viking fort a motte-and-bailey earthwork, the present Millmount, which remains one of the focal points of the town. At the same time the lands to the N, or Louth, side of the Boyne were granted to Bertram de Verdun. Thus for more than two centuries two rival boroughs existed; eventually they were united under one corporation in 1412. A legacy of the medieval boroughs is the existence of two distinct parishes within Drogheda, St Peter's on the N side of the river and St Mary's to the S.

Sure evidence of the town's growing prosperity following the Norman settlement was the establishment of no fewer than six separate religious foundations. The first of these, the Priory of St John the Baptist, was probably established in the later C12 by Hugh de Lacy. It was followed in 1203 by the hospital priory of St Laurence for Crouched Friars, founded by the mayor and citizens of Drogheda for the care of lepers. Three years later another hospital priory, for the care of the poor and dedicated to St Mary de Urso, was founded by Urso de Swemele. In 1224 a Dominican friary was founded by Lucas de Netterville, Archbishop of Armagh, and in 1240 a Franciscan friary was established. All that survives of these foundations is the fragmentary remains of two belfry towers. The tower of St Mary's Hospital Priory graces the centre of Drogheda, with its picturesque ruin near the N bank of the Boyne. The Dominican friary survives in the charming Magdalene Tower high up on the northern side of the town.

Throughout the C13 and C14 Drogheda was a prosperous urban centre enjoying a busy maritime trade. Its success was envied in the North, leading to raids by the Scots and the Ulster Irish, so that the town was soon compelled to strengthen its fortifications. The network of town walls, gateways and barbicans erected during the C14 survived for the most part until the C18. The walls, some 20 ft (6 m) high, had a circumference (which included the breadth of the river) of over one and a half miles and enclosed an area of 64 acres (26 ha). In present-day terms, the medieval town was bounded on the N by Patrick Street and

on the W by Trinity Street, by St Laurence's Gate to the E and to 12, 45
the S by St Mary's Protestant Church. Seventeen gates and nineteen towers were situated on the Louth side of the river, five gates and eleven towers on the Meath side. Considerable remains of the old wall are still discernible from the foot of Millmount to St Mary's Churchyard, and also near St Laurence's Gate. Although Georgian regularity and uniformity have left their mark on Drogheda, the basic street plan within the medieval walls has remained largely unaltered since the early C14. In 1791 the city was still surrounded by high walls and had four gates which were regularly closed at midnight.

Such was the prosperity of Drogheda during the medieval period that the Anglo-Norman archbishops of Armagh, rejected by the Dean and Chapter in Armagh itself, chose to make their residence here, comfortably within the boundaries of the Pale. That six parliaments were convened in Drogheda between 1441 and 1494 is a further measure of its importance at the end of the Middle Ages. But if Drogheda's success was of benefit in these ways, equally it attracted the attention of less benevolent parties. In the rebellion of 1641 the town was besieged by the army of Sir Phelim O'Neill, and only eight years later, in 1649, it was captured and the inhabitants savagely slaughtered by the soldiers of Oliver Cromwell. Recovery was speedy, however, and in 1699 the town was described by one English traveller as 'a handsome clean English-like town and the best I have seen in Ireland'. Throughout the Georgian period Drogheda's prosperity continued and made it for C18 architecture one of the best Irish towns. The Darley family of builder-architects was responsible for some handsome early Georgian building here, while the later C18 is dominated by Francis Johnston, brought to the town through the patronage of Richard Robinson, Archbishop of Armagh. The many Georgian survivals in St Laurence Street and Fair Street, together with
public buildings like St Peter's, the Tholsel and the Mayoralty 11, 71
House, help to recapture, despite modern wires, signs and general mess, something of Drogheda's C18 charm.

The text of this volume when first written included two very significant C18 buildings which in 1989 were summarily destroyed and therefore cannot be properly included in the description of Drogheda. However, such was their importance that some account of their history forms a necessary prelude to any modern survey of the town.

Henry Singleton's house, of *c.* 1740, and Mr Clarke's Free School, of 1728, stood side by side on the N side of St Laurence Street. Henry Singleton was Lord Chief Justice of Ireland, and his Drogheda house was an impressive seven-bay, three-storey redbrick building which boasted one of the finest oak-panelled interiors in the country. Next door to Singleton's house was a smaller Palladian building, also of red brick, begun in 1728 for Mr Clarke, schoolmaster of Drogheda Free School. An original drawing for the building survives and has been attributed to the architect *Michael Wills*, who worked as an assistant to Thomas Burgh in the 1720s.

These important C18 buildings were both in an advanced state of dereliction when first recorded for this volume in the mid-1980s, despite a long rehabilitation campaign by local conservationists and the existence of a High Court protection order. Early one Sunday morning in July 1989, a demolition crew moved onto the site and the buildings were pulled down. Since then, legal action taken by conservationists against the proprietors has resulted in several unprecedented court orders which augur well for the future of conservation in Ireland. However, at the time of writing the final outcome of these proceedings is still awaited, and hopes of a thorough reconstruction and restoration may or may not be realized.

Although the C19 saw a relative decline in Drogheda's prosperity, building continued apace in the shape of banks, warehouses, railways, commercial premises and ambitious High Victorian Catholic churches. The most prominent C19 legacy is the great viaduct over the Boyne, erected between 1851 and 1855 to designs by *Sir John MacNeill*, linking the railway systems of Belfast to those of Dublin. (The central span was replaced in steel by the *Motherwell Bridge and Engineering Company* (*G. B. Howden* Engineer) in 1932.) As is too often the case, the C20 has not been kind to Drogheda. However, the problems of the town lie not so much in the lack of quality in its new architecture as in the neglect and lack of concern for its historic buildings. In no other European city of this quality would buildings like the Drogheda Grammar School and Singleton House have been allowed to go to ruin. One glimmer of hope for the historic fabric is the West End Arcade of 1984, located in the former walled gardens between West Street and Fair Street: an instance of courageous planning and enlightened design.

MEDIEVAL BUILDINGS

30 ABBEY AND HOSPITAL OF ST MARY D'URSO. A rare and most picturesque ruin, comprising parts of the nave and chancel and the central tower of a C13 abbey, now forming a small thoroughfare called Abbeylane. Very aptly described as 'Ireland's only drive-in Friary', and as such a perfect expression of the State's lackadaisical attitude towards its historic buildings.

The abbey was founded *c.* 1206 by Urso de Swemele as a hospital for the poor. It was sited outside the medieval West Gate of the town. The shell of the friary church is all that survives. This comprises most of the E gable, with the line of a great pointed window and a well-preserved two-stage crossing tower carried on a pair of tall pointed arches. The tower is probably a later insertion. The belfry windows are paired lights of a late C15 or C16 type, transomed, with cusped ogee heads. Only patched fragments of the N and S nave walls survive and these are now built into the small cottages and outhouses which line Abbeylane. The gable of one cottage on the N side preserves a sandstone two-centred arch, complete with a weathered grotesque head.

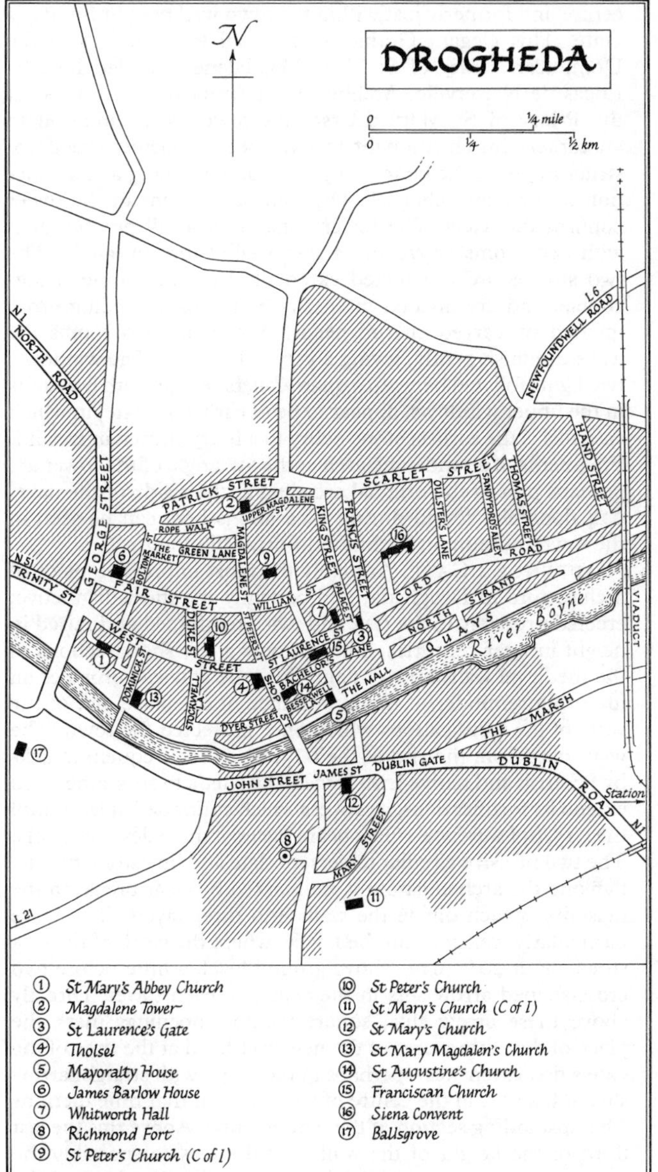

① St Mary's Abbey Church
② Magdalene Tower
③ St Laurence's Gate
④ Tholsel
⑤ Mayoralty House
⑥ James Barlow House
⑦ Whitworth Hall
⑧ Richmond Fort
⑨ St Peter's Church (C of I)
⑩ St Peter's Church
⑪ St Mary's Church (C of I)
⑫ St Mary's Church
⑬ St Mary Magdalen's Church
⑭ St Augustine's Church
⑮ Franciscan Church
⑯ Siena Convent
⑰ Ballsgrove

MAGDALENE TOWER. One of Drogheda's major landmarks, situated high on the N slope of the Boyne behind the town centre and formerly just within the town wall near St Sunday's Gate. This elegant Gothic tower is all that survives of the Dominican Friary of St Mary Magdalene, founded here by Lucas de Netterville, Archbishop of Armagh, in 1224. As at the Priory of St Mary d'Urso, the tower is an addition to an earlier church, thought to have been a narrow cruciform structure, with the belfry supported on corbelling at the junction of nave and chancel. The thin proportions of the tower confirm this view. The tower consists of a tall pointed arch with two rooms above and a stair well at the NW angle. The two storeys are articulated externally by a limestone string-course, and are divided internally by a groined ceiling ornamented by carved cherub heads. Above the two rooms the walls diminish gently, giving a very light effect. The windows, two lights foliated beneath a quatrefoil, taller and with transoms in the upper windows, appear to be of early C14 date, in which case this is the earliest stone belfry to a friary church in Ireland. Fragments of a sandstone arch at the SW angle of the tower are perhaps part of the original arcading at the S side of the nave. C14 floor tiles found during excavations here can be seen in the town museum in Richmond Fort, Millmount.

12, 45 ST LAURENCE'S GATE. Arguably the most impressive piece of architecture in Drogheda, and certainly the most distinctive; erected probably in the C13 and twice reinforced and raised in height in later centuries. Though only a few short sections of the medieval walls now remain, this lone gateway provides an imposing reminder of the importance of the place and of the scale of the fortifications which once protected the town. The walls date from the end of the C13, when too frequent attacks by Scottish and native Irish forced Drogheda to strengthen and extend its fortifications, a process which continued at least until the C15. St Laurence's Gate bears traces of these developments. The two massive circular towers, of slate and limestone rubble, flanking the arched gateway are marked by clear breaks in the masonry, which divide the walls into three layers. These are particularly well seen on the E face, where the work of the C13 stops about 20 ft (6 m) above ground level, a little before two cross-shaped arrow slits in the centre of each tower. Directly above these arrow slits, square window openings mark the place of the embrasures of the new wall-head at the time of the gate's first extension – perhaps in the C14 – with straight arrow slits to l. and r. in the centre of what were at that time merlons (the upstanding section of the battlements). Above this the last third of the height of the wall is of the C15 (or possibly the C16), with heavy stepped Irish battlements in place of the square merlons of the earlier builds.

On the W face the towers flank a portcullis gate and retaining wall. Each is supplied with garderobe shafts. One central round-headed window in the wall between the towers, at the level of the second build, is complete. Corbel and beam holes at this level are evidence of a timber platform which originally joined the two towers and from which the portcullis was operated. What remains today was not the actual gate into the town but a forework or barbican – like the barbican at Trim Castle – which was separated from the gate itself by a wet fosse and crossed by a drawbridge. The width of the barbican passage is marked on the W face by the short section of battlemented wall (given decorative battlements in the later Georgian period) which abuts the back of the towers. Both the barbican and the gate which stood behind it derive their name from the hospital friary of St Laurence, founded outside the town walls in 1203, probably on the site of the present Cord graveyard. St Laurence's Gate was one of the principal toll gates to the town. Set at the top of elegant mid-C18 St Laurence Street, the barbican is certainly imposing, but a better sense of its massive medieval scale is gained by approaching it from the smaller, less regular streets on the E side.

BUTTER GATE. A fragment of the medieval defences of Drogheda, on the S side of the Boyne W of Millmount. All that now survives is the ground floor of a hexagonal rubble gate-tower with a large entrance archway running from E to W and a portcullis groove. A fragment of the town wall projects from the S side of the tower.

CHURCHES ETC.

ST PETER, DROGHEDA PARISH CHURCH (C of I). 1748 by *Hugh Darley*. 'Strong' and 'masculine' are perhaps the best adjectives to describe this most impressive building, whose stocky classical tower and spire preside over the NE quarter of the town. Certainly among the best provincial churches erected in Ireland during the C18 and also one of the most richly endowed, patronized by, among others, the Marquis of Drogheda and the archbishops of Armagh. The site is an old one. Here stood the medieval church of St Peter, built between 1172 and 1206 and demolished only in 1748. From all accounts it was a monumental building, with no fewer than three chancels, or E chapels, an arcaded W aisle and a tall central steeple. Cutstone fragments of this church survive in and around the present building. In January 1748 Darley was called in to demolish old St Peter's, and the new church was well under way when Mrs Delany visited Drogheda in 1752. 71

The façade of St Peter's is a handsome Palladian design. Three bays and two storeys, of limestone ashlar, horizontally channelled, with a broad eaves pediment broken by the great central tower rising above it through two storeys. The tower is expressed as a giant round-headed entrance, a terse Diocletian window on the first floor and in the belfry stage corner pilasters, a round-headed opening, and above a Gibbsian bracketed oculus. But here the classicism ends. The original pyramidal stone steeple was replaced during the 1780s by a pinnacled clock-stage and Gothic needle spire to designs by *Francis Johnston*. It is a little thin for Darley's work but not incongruous. On walking around the exterior of St Peter's the initial sense of grandeur gives way to a second and perhaps more enduring impression. Darley the Palladian architect becomes Darley the sound provincial builder: this is a lumbering two-storey hall of rough limestone ashlar crowned by a big hipped roof.

Enter the church and elegance surges back; through the
72 tower vestibule into a big classical hall, galleries around three sides carried on octagonal oak piers and at gallery level a handsome Scamozzian Ionic order, also of oak, rising to support a long coved ceiling. The crowning glory of St Peter's is the chancel, a shallow recess flanked by two fine wall monuments and ornamented with wonderful late baroque plasterwork akin to that in the stairhall and drawing room at Russborough House, Co. Wicklow. Domestic more than religious in character, with blank lugged and mandorla-like frames surrounded by garlands of fruit and flowers, cornucopias, cloud-like whorls and a great bird on each side of the E window. Upon the basis of this plasterwork Joseph Mc Donnell has traced the *œuvre* of 'the St Peter's stuccodore'. One interesting feature of the church is the fenestration. One would expect the usual square- or round-headed windows, with perhaps a Palladian motif in the E wall. Here instead are the first inklings of C18 Gothic, a pointed E window with double Y-tracery, segmental- or round-headed windows to the aisles and galleries with simplistic stone tracery. The windows are framed in flush blocked architraves on the exterior, which combine oddly with the Gothic idiom but are apparently Darley's work. A painting of 1813 in the vestibule shows the church complete with box-pews, stove and chandeliers. – STAINED GLASS. Much High Victorian pictorial glass. Centre window S wall by *J. B. Capronnier*, Brussels, 1874. – MONUMENTS.
75 Henry Singleton, Recorder of Drogheda, later Lord Chief Justice of Ireland and, lastly, Master of the Rolls, †1780: an elaborate neoclassical wall monument, woman weeping on an urn, putti supporting an inscribed plaque and a portrait bust of Singleton; 1786, by the Irish sculptor *Thomas Hickey* but sculpted in London. John Ball †1813; simpler, with sarcophagus, urn and portrait bust. – Two classical aedicules in marble and slate, taken from old St Peter's and re-erected on the E wall of the N and S galleries: Ellish Walke †1701, Tobias Pullen †1712. – FONT. Medieval octagonal font. Two registers of panels framed by vine-stem: lower register, angels in niches; upper register, apostles and Baptism of Christ. – Embedded in the wall in the NE corner of the CHURCHYARD, a chilling funerary monument of *c.* 1520 depicting two decomposing skeletal bodies; to the memory of Sir Edmund Golding and his wife Elizabeth Flemying, daughter of the Baron of Slane.

131 ST PETER, WEST STREET. 1884 by *J. O'Neill and W. H. Byrne*. An ambitious exercise in florid French Gothic, of tall slender proportions and with a very nice spire, the tallest in Drogheda.

This church replaces an earlier building erected in 1791 to designs by *Francis Johnston* in that simple blend of classical and Gothic characteristic of the late C 18. In 1864 Johnston's church was largely extended and remodelled by *J. J. McCarthy*, who added a chancel and side chapels and planned a tower and spire for the entrance front. McCarthy's spire was never built, and O'Neill was first commissioned to add a tower, porch, baptistery and two bays onto the existing nave in 1884. Then in 1891 Byrne completed the rebuilding by the removal of all of Johnston's and McCarthy's work, adding the crossing, transepts and sanctuary. The new church, although dedicated to St Peter, was intended to commemorate the martyr-primate St Oliver Plunkett.

A big showy entrance front, perhaps a little flat, rises on two broad flights of steps above the main street. There is a large rose window in the entrance gable above a row of blind arcading, and a double entrance with tympanum and gabled hood. On the E, a slender turret and aisle; on the W an elegant C 13 tower and spire. The interior is unusually wide and spacious. A five-bay arcade of moulded two-centred arches is carried on tall polished granite shafts with big Caen stone bases and capitals. The plan is cruciform: the nave opening through paired arches into transepts and side chapels, the W chapel housing the reliquary of St Oliver Plunkett. At the crossing an unusual arrangement of a freestanding (polished granite) colonnette whose capital adjoins those of the principal shafts. The chancel is a five-sided apse which happily still frames the original pinnacled reredos. – STAINED GLASS by *Mayer*.

ST MARY (C of I). Simple hall and tower church of 1810, situated on the S side of Drogheda high up near the base of Richmond Fort. Of coursed rubble with limestone dressings; three-bay hall and a three-stage tower with pinnacles and needle spire. Built on the site of a C 13 Carmelite priory dedicated to the Virgin. The priory derived most of its revenue from tolls levied on butter entering the town by St John's Gate, popularly known as Butter Gate, situated at the foot of Millmount. When Cromwell advanced on Drogheda in 1649 attack was first directed on the churchyard of St Mary's, through which the Cromwellian army entered the town, having first demolished the church. All that remained in 1833 was the foundations of the old tower and the walls of a small vestry. – MONUMENT. The Duff effigial slab dated 1610, a broken limestone slab which has been reassembled and fixed to the S wall of the church. Figures of Henry Duff and his wife flanked by columns, with a heraldic device above.

ST MARY'S PARISH CHURCH. 1881–9 by *P. J. Dodd*. At first sight almost a carbon copy of St Peter's, West Street: a tall French Gothic church with a gabled entrance front. Rose window, hooded entrances and a tall thin C 13 tower and spire. But as St Mary's was begun almost two years before St Peter's, Dodd cannot have copied that design. The generic similarity is a symptom of the state of Irish church building in the High

Victorian period, and indeed on closer inspection differences between the buildings come to the fore. St Mary's is much smaller and altogether less accomplished; it is also built of dark rock-faced limestone, while St Peter's is of fine grey limestone ashlar. The plan here is a five-bay aisled hall with apsidal sanctuary. As at St Peter's, the shafts are of polished pink granite, with Caen stone capitals and bases. – STAINED GLASS. S aisle: life of the Virgin by *Mayer*. The saints in the apse and the St Joseph window in the Lady Chapel are by *Lobin* of Tours in Belgium.

ST MARY MAGDALEN'S DOMINICAN CHURCH. 1870–8. A nice C13 Gothic design by *George Ashlin*, well located on an open site beside the N bank of the Boyne. Gothic of a distinctly continental character from Northern France or Flanders. A small but tall cruciform church with a blockish apsidal sanctuary. An attractive saddleback tower, tucked in between the nave and the transept, contributes to a very positive sense of architectural mass. This effect is enhanced by the varying textures of the limestone masonry, coursed rubble walls to sill level and rock-faced stone above, set off by ashlar dressings. Four-bay nave and two-bay transepts, lit by triple-light geometric windows. The entrance gable front has a pointed arch flanked by thin pinnacled buttresses, with a big geometric window above. The interior of St Magdalen's is an anticlimax: a dull hall of rather mean proportions opening through paired arches into transepts. Ugly mosaics in the sanctuary.

ST AUGUSTINE'S, SHOP STREET. 1859–66 by *M. B. Moran*. Victorian Gothic, but with a bareness that looks almost modern. E.E., the windows in big pointed limestone plates cut through by double- and triple-lancet windows and by a great seven-lancet window in the entrance gable. An aisle on one side and, S, an unfinished belltower. Good bold treatment of offsets and buttresses. Inside, the church is more typical of provincial E.E. Gothic. A tall aisled hall, the nave carried on a five-bay arcade of chamfered two-centred arches. Shafts of smooth grey limestone with moulded capitals. Five-bay pinnacled reredos. – STAINED GLASS. The best feature of the interior is the E window by *Harry Clarke*. From l. to r.: St Augustine and St Monica, Augustine as the sledgehammer of heresy, Augustine and St Alypius on their conversion, Augustine alone, Baptism of Augustine, Augustine preaching to Augustinian friars, and finally, perhaps the best, the presentation of the cincture to St Monica by the Virgin. All wonderfully coloured, with the slender figures, elegantly falling draperies and hieratic poses characteristic of Clarke's decadent sensuous idiom.

FRANCISCAN CHURCH. 1829. Late Georgian Tudoresque Gothic, built into the steep slope that rises from the quay towards St Laurence Street; the church has the uncommon feature of entrances at ground and gallery level. The exterior is very cramped, so that the upper, Laurence Street, entrance is all that really shows – the upper part of a gabled hall with two pointed windows and a projecting Gothic porch, all of chequered slate and limestone masonry. This awkward site, hemmed in among surrounding buildings, is not a legacy of the penal days, but stems from the fact that the church occupies the ancient site of a Franciscan friary founded here in 1240. A white neo-baroque calvary in the courtyard before the church makes an evocative picture. Inside the porch a tiny stair leads to a deep choir gallery, while steps, in an area, lead down to the main floor level. The church is built on a T-plan, with galleries in each arm. The one at the back is exceptionally deep, supported on cluster shafts and extending to a third storey. Timber Y-traceried windows and Tudor, four-centred arches. The reredos is a happy survival, a three-bay Tudor-Gothic affair with big mouldings and colonnettes rising to pinnacles.

PRESBYTERIAN CHURCH, PALACE STREET. 1827 by *Austin Nicholls*. A diminutive descendant of King's College Chapel, Cambridge, recessed from the street front and set between a pair of modest, three-storey late Georgian houses, also recessed. The church is a simple two-bay hall of brick and limestone; the limestone ashlar entrance front is flanked by dinky octagonal turrets with battlemented tops and a large four-centred arch and elaborately cusped Perp window between. Charming carpenter's Gothic in stone!

FORMER METHODIST CHURCH. 1811; restored in 1911 and now a furniture store. A hall with a gallery around three sides carried on timber quatrefoil shafts. The handsome façade of limestone ashlar is set back from Laurence Street. Two storeys and three bays, with a cornice and blocking course, the centre bay projecting slightly. Gothic windows now filled with geometric sandstone tracery, dating most likely to 1911.

SIENA CONVENT. 1792–6 by *Francis Johnston*. A good example of institutional Georgian architecture on an elevated site E of St Laurence's Gate. The Siena Convent takes its origin from the Dominican community founded in 1722 by Mother Catherine Plunkett, grand-niece of St Oliver, whose reliquary was housed in the convent chapel throughout the C19. Plain seven-bay, four-storey block, with low gables, a stone cornice, quoins and regular sash windows diminishing to the top. Simple fanlit tripartite doorcase. Matching three-bay, three-storey wings were added in the 1840s. The convent chapel, which projects at the W end of the convent front, is by *G. C. Ashlin*, 1876. Big pedimented hall: the façade is of limestone and yellow brick, with three strings of blank panels between shallow Tuscan pilasters and a statue niche in the centre. The interior is grander: a large classical hall of six bays divided into two parts by a grandiose Venetian opening carried on Corinthian columns of polished pink granite, one part for the community, the other for the congregation. The altar now at the N wall was originally at the S end, and this part of the church is consequently more elaborate. Four giant Corinthian pilasters frame round-headed windows and blank panels in the E and W walls.

The altar reredos is a timber Palladian arch, flanked by niches bearing statues.

CHRISTIAN BROTHERS SCHOOL, Upper Magdalene Street. 1867 by *Pugin & Ashlin*. Crisp minimal institutional Gothic which relies for its effect on polychrome building materials. Originally a U-plan two-storeyed building, with advanced two-bay gabled ends; two-bay extensions were later added on each side. Segmental-headed plate-glass windows with side-lights on the ground floor of the gabled bays. Tall narrow central entrance with a circular traceried fanlight and attenuated shafts supporting a gabled canopy. Of red brick with black string-courses and limestone bands. Pierced bargeboards and pretty cresting to the roof ridge.

CONVENT OF THE SISTERS OF CHARITY. *See* p. 245.

PUBLIC BUILDINGS AND HOUSES

MAYORALTY HOUSE. On North Quay. 1769. Robust, mid-Georgian classicism, a characteristic market-cum-town hall building, traditional in Ireland, with an arcaded ground floor, assembly rooms above and a broad hipped roof. A modest rectangular block, three bays to the quay and one bay deep, with originally one unified floor space top and bottom. Built of squared limestone with fine ashlar detail; the façade is given central emphasis by a projecting centre bay with a Venetian window on the first floor and a pediment above. Upstairs, the ballroom, though now subdivided, retains its coved ceiling, with rococo garlands and flower baskets in the border and a big Corinthian cornice.

11 THOLSEL. At the junction of Shop Street and West Street. 1765–70 by *George Darley*. An assembly of Drogheda Corporation in January 1765 ordered the demolition of the old wooden tholsel and immediately embarked on an ambitious new building project. In August of the same year two plans for a new tholsel were submitted by M. Hamilton Bury and *George Darley*. These were then referred to the Dublin architect Christopher Myers, who recommended Darley's plan. The Corporation made a good decision, for Darley's design, which plays a crucial role in the townscape of Drogheda, is worthy of its site. It has two façades: a plain four-bay front to Shop Street and a three-bay entrance front to West Street, crowned by a slender tower. The architecture is in an early neoclassical idiom, with a tall ground floor – not the low basement beloved by the Palladians – expressed as a rusticated arcade, with round-headed windows set in relieving arches. Darley's detailing is delicate. The upper floor has plain sash windows with architraves set in an ashlar wall; in the entrance front these windows have shallow pediments, and the centre bay, which supports the cupola, breaks forward and has an eaves pediment. The cupola tower is in three stages, ending in an octagonal belfry and dome. The Tholsel was completed in 1770, when the Corporation acquired a new clock for the tower.

CORNMARKET. 1796 by *Francis Johnston*. In June 1786 the Corporation decided to spend £2,000 on a new cornmarket, and Johnston submitted appropriate designs in the following year. However, nine years were to elapse before anything was done, and building began only in June 1796. The result is a large enclosed marketplace, composed of two parallel ranges of sheds joined by a formal main façade. The sheds were supported throughout on elegant Doric columns, and their ends formed terminal pavilions to a long low entrance front. But the most interesting feature of the market yard is the entablature, which, as it is of bare timber, is an instance of that architectural primitivism which swept Europe during the 1780s and 1790s. If the designs Johnston submitted in 1787 were what was built, the Cornmarket provides a very early expression of this taste in his work. The façade is more traditional, a two-storey, three-bay central block, arcaded in the ground floor, with a timber lantern and weathervane on top, flanked by now infilled gate entrances, and balanced by the shed gables at each end.

WHITWORTH HALL. 1864 by *W. J. Barre*. A lively Victorian 12
façade in brick, terracotta and stone erupting between two plain Georgian houses on St Laurence Street. Two-storey, five-bay façade, the centre three bays projecting forward and expressed as a triforium on each floor, with round-headed windows in the outer bays. The style is hard to determine – Barre's most rigorous manner, vaguely Italian Gothic but with a tall Frenchified roof above the centre bays. The hall, now a darkened snooker room, has a gallery carried on cast-iron colonnettes, and the walls are adorned with plaster colonnettes and a big foliated cornice. Whitworth Hall was built by a Manchester businessman and native of Drogheda, Benjamin Whitworth, and Barre won the commission in a competition which drew entries from Lanyon and Lynn, William Caldbeck, Deane and Son, and John McCurdy.

RICHMOND FORT. 1808. The highest landmark in Drogheda, 87
the martello tower set upon the top of Millmount. Immediately below it are groups of plain late Georgian barrack buildings surrounded by a high boundary wall.

JAMES BARLOW HOUSE. Fair Street. Now the Garda Barracks. 76
1734. A substantial and sophisticated early Georgian house whose brick façade is adapted from Pearce's No. 9 Henrietta Street in Dublin. Double-pile plan of three storeys over a basement and five bays wide, with a stone eaves cornice supporting a shallow brick parapet, which is also segmented into five bays. Very strong central emphasis to the façade: a pedimented doorcase with a crisp blocked surround and above it an emphatic first-floor window flanked by scrolled volutes and crowned by a segmental pediment. A deep string-course runs across the façade on a level with the ground-floor pediment, and a second, thinner course incorporates the first-floor sills. As at the schoolmaster's house (*see* p. 233), both courses neatly incorporate the stone quoins at the corners of the building. The design has been attributed to Pearce's follower *Richard*

Castle, and the building does have that gracelessness found in Castle's lesser buildings. This is not helped by the modern grilled fenestration.

BALLSGROVE. Built in 1734 for the High Sheriff of Co. Louth, George Ball. Ballsgrove differs from Drogheda's other large Georgian houses in that it is not a proper town house but a villa or small country house, situated above the S bank of the Boyne and set in grounds which originally boasted charming terraced gardens sloping down to the river's edge. On the S bank of the river, alongside the modern ring road, stands the former entrance to the house, erected in 1804. Handsome limestone pedimented archway with Greek-key impost courses. Circular niches flanking the arch, and the Ball family arms in the tympanum. Ballsgrove has the usual double-pile plan, five bays wide, with a central entrance hall, but here, instead of a vertical three-storey façade, no more than two storeys over a basement, flanked by curved curtain walls ending in square piers. Fine brick façade with stone quoins, cornice and string-course, and a segmented brick parapet divided by short ped-estals between each bay. Regular sash windows on the upper floors; segmental-headed windows in the basement.

ST LAURENCE'S COMMUNITY SCHOOL etc. *See* Tour, below.

TOUR

To the traveller passing round Drogheda on the modern ring road, the town presents a dilapidated picture: neglected or broken-down grey rubble buildings set off here and there by the odd neon-sign. This is a far cry from the view which greeted Mrs Delany in 1752: 'little neat gardens, old walls covered with ivy, a ruined castle and a variety of objects, that makes a better and more pleasing show' than could easily be described. Drogheda, formerly one of the foremost towns in the country, has been reduced in the C 20 to shoddiness and decay. But to view it from the new road is to see the town at its worst; inside, it is still one of the most satisfying architectural ensembles in North Leinster.

Any tour of Drogheda should best begin at the Tholsel (*see* above), since medieval times the site of a public building and before that of a market cross. To the W lies WEST STREET, the principal shopping street of Drogheda, dominated by the Catholic Church of St Peter but with little else of quality. The FIRST NATIONAL BUILDING SOCIETY (No. 13), formerly the Munster and Leinster Bank, by *Walter Doolin*, 1894, is a tall, three-storey building, with a ground-floor arcade of limestone ashlar, redbrick above, with limestone trim. Two doors along is another limestone shopfront, rusticated and of three bays. WHITE HORSE INN, although the most ambitious C 19 façade on the street, is undistinguished. The POST OFFICE AND TELEPHONE EXCHANGE, small and blocky, with a glazed stair tower to one side, is by *A. Seymour Rice* and

Ronald Tallon, Office of Public Works, 1951. Behind No. 82 West Street is the WEST END ARCADE, a shopping development designed for Malachy Mc Closkey by *Patrick Shaffrey*, 1984, making imaginative use of the old back gardens of the Georgian houses in Fair Street. Tall rubble ivy- and wisteria-grown walls, with cutstone arches, timber beams from an old warehouse, a second-hand pedimented doorcase and a re-erected aviary from Gibbstown house (*see* Clongill Crossroads). Quarry-tiled walkways interspersed with plant beds and pieces of sculpture.

Leave by the centre's W gateway, and take the laneway uphill to FAIR STREET, which together with St Laurence Street boasts the finest Georgian houses in Drogheda. Although a good regular Georgian streetscape, the houses here are of particular interest for the variety they offer both in proportion and detail; some are built together in small blocks, others singly. Immediately l. of the laneway is a row of three early C19 redbrick houses, two bays and three storeys, with timber Doric doorframes and elliptical fanlights. Immediately r., Nos. 21–26 are a row of six three-storey houses over basements, four of red brick and two now cement-rendered. All have good blocked door-surrounds and some have original sash windows and six- or eleven-panel doors. Many retain fine mid-C18 interiors. The doorcases at Nos. 25 and 26 are simplest, perhaps earlier or just cheaper than the Gibbsian surrounds of the others. Nos. 19 and 20 are also of red brick but of different proportions and with later pedimented doorcases of the type popularized by William Pain during the 1770s. No. 18 is an individual, with a broader frontage, three bays widely spaced, a tripartite door and a carriage arch. Nos. 15 and 16 are similar to Nos. 21–24. Across the street are the late C19 buildings of the PRESENTATION CONVENT SCHOOLS: freestanding gabled blocks of red brick, with blue brick and limestone trim. No. 14 is much the largest house on the S side of the street, six bays and three storeys over a basement with a big ten-panel door and a blocked door-surround with a pediment carried on console brackets – a door type seen also in Laurence Street and probably of *c.* 1760.

The grandest house on Fair Street is the CONVENT OF THE SISTERS OF CHARITY on the N side of the street. A big palazzo-style house of five bays and three storeys over a basement faced entirely with fine grey ashlar limestone. The façade has a rusticated ground floor, moulded window surrounds and an eaves cornice and low parapet. The entrance is in a porch adjoining the E side of the building. Ravell's map of 1749 illustrates this house as the residence of Mr Shepard, which then had its entrance in the centre of the principal elevation. The interior is largely remodelled, with only some fielded panelling and a plain rococo ceiling surviving from the early C18. Continuing E from here, ST PETER'S CLOSE and ST JOHN'S HOME were built in 1816. Two redbrick ranges of charitable buildings with gabled ends formed into the pedimented wings in a simple formal façade, set off with limestone trim.

From St Peter's back to the Tholsel, and now l. into the once elegant ST LAURENCE STREET, recently desecrated by the demolition of Henry Singleton's house and Mr Clarke's Free School (*see* p. 233). All is not lost, however, and the street retains a substantial number of three- and four-storey C18 houses and is closed at its E end by St Laurence's Gate, Drogheda's principal fortified gateway (*see* Medieval Buildings, above), to the r. of which can be seen part of the original TOWN WALL. Beginning at the Tholsel end of the street, No. 46 on the r., the former PROVINCIAL BANK, *c.* 1865, is attributed to *W. G. Murray* and has a bold Ruskinian façade of four bays and three storeys. Two segmental-headed doorcases flank segmental-headed plate-glass windows with paired polished granite colonnettes between. Polished granite bosses to the first floor and a big cornice with fluted console brackets. Further along on the l., beside the former Methodist Church (*see* Churches, above), is the BANK OF IRELAND, a grand five-bay, two-storey palazzo of 1876, built in granite ashlar to designs of the bank's architect, *Sandham Symes*.

The houses on Laurence Street are more substantial and earlier in date than most of those in Fair Street. These are of *c.* 1760, three-storey houses over basements, with a lot more bare masonry than the later Georgian work, roofs peeping over low parapets and the windows not so regularly aligned as in the later C18 houses. Big blocked surrounds to six-panel doors, with curled brackets supporting open pediments and Y-traceried fanlights. The same meeting of classicism and Gothick as in St Peter's Church (*see* above). Inside, six-panel doors in lugged surrounds.

On the S side of the street are two interesting remodellings. One, near the Franciscan Church (*see* above) and surely built at the same time, is not unlike the timber reredos inside the church. Three bays and two storeys expressed as three giant blind pointed arches framing square-headed windows, with a giant panelled pilaster between each bay. Two doors along on the same side is the former BELFAST BANK, a grandiose late C19 Italianate remodelling of three large four-storey houses, now stuccoed and expressed as three broad bays. A vermiculated basement provides notional support for an elaborate *piano nobile*, expressed as a large pedimented triforium. Elaborate window surrounds and corner quoins.

At St Laurence's Gate, Laurence Street joins PALACE STREET,
141 at the top of which is ST LAURENCE'S COMMUNITY SCHOOL, 1934 by *Michael Scott*, a white three-storey Modern Movement building with a parapet, a blocky central tower, big metal windows and typical 30s geometric detail. Continuing E along WILLIAM STREET, past a small close with three large Georgian houses, to arrive at the charming ST PETERS PLACE ALMSHOUSES, popularly known as THE ALLEYS. Four picturesque terraces of narrow two-storey gabled houses of two

and three bays over basements. Five-panel doors and sash windows. These were erected between 1730 and 1750 by Primates Boulter and Marsh as housing for the widows of Church of Ireland clergy.

Some distance NE of the Alleys and somewhat off the tour trail on Scarlet Street is a remnant of the FORMER GAOL erected in 1818. Only the formal entrance and part of the curtain wall survive, now screening a bus depot, a three-bay frontispiece of punched limestone in the chaste institutional idiom of Johnston and his circle. Blank masonry walls with two shallow relieving arches flank the entrance arch, with two sunken classical panels set into the wall above.

Back to the Tholsel, S of which is the narrow SHOP STREET, leading to the quay, with two- and three-storey buildings of C19 character. Along the N quay, and between it and Laurence Street, is a series of narrow streets and lanes lined by small two-storey terraces of labourers' houses and fine big limestone rubble sheds and warehouses with redbrick trim and cutstone arches.

Enthusiasts of Irish C20 architecture may care to extend this tour to the HOSPITAL OF OUR LADY OF LOURDES, on the western edge of the town, whose diminutive chapel was designed by *Joseph Vincent Downes* in the mid-1930s. Downes considered this chapel among his favourite designs.

NEIGHBOURHOOD

KILINEER HOUSE. 2.5 km NW. Elegant early C19 house. Regency-style in cream stucco. Large, two-storey rectangular block, with a shallow roof, deep cornice and blocking course. Principal elevation of six bays, with a Doric porch projecting from the centre. Long sash windows on both floors and a double continuous string-course between the two floors. Three-bay side elevation, with architrave cornices over the ground-floor windows. Lovely garden with a colonnaded rose bower, lake and cast-iron footbridge.

BELTICHBOURNE HOUSE. 4 km NE. Later C19 redbrick house. Of irregular plan, with pronounced bracketed eaves, a projecting side entrance and bay windows to side and rear. The principal elevation has a tall gabled centrepiece expressed as three small segmental-headed windows on the ground floor, with three long narrow lancet-type windows above. An odd design.

NEWTOWN-STALABAN. 2.5 km NE. *c.* 1810. Two-storey house with a central fanlit doorcase and window above flanked by later canted bay windows. Nice Greek-revival detail to interior joinery.

GREENHILLS (PRESENTATION CONVENT). 1.5 km E, on the N bank of the Boyne. Late C18 house, Italianized *c.* 1870. Three-bay, two-storey front. Rectangular plan, with Regency bows at each end. Terrace overlooking the Boyne.

COLP CHURCH (C of I). 3.5 km ESE. Small three-bay hall with

a more than usually stocky square tower. Colp has long been the site of a religious foundation. In 1182 Hugh de Lacy founded an Augustinian abbey here, dependent on the abbey of Llanthony in Monmouthshire, but Colp had already been a place of worship before the Normans: one remnant of an earlier church lies in the porch, a small high cross of C10 date.

STAMEEN HOUSE. 2 km SE. Italianate house of *c.* 1870. Rectangular plan, such as William Caldbeck often used, with a large central entrance and stairhall with a columnar screen. Long principal elevation, with projecting centre bays, an Ionic porch and a bracketed gable framing a blank shield.

GLEN HOUSE. 3 km E. 1852. The dower house of nearby Stameen (*see* above) and of similar Italianate design. Gabled two-storey building of rectangular plan, with a large central entrance and stairhall. Cement-rendered, with the usual projecting centre bay, bracketed eaves and corner quoin pilasters.

STAMEEN VILLA. 2.5 km E. Large and rather dull Italianate two-storey house, with a low roof hidden by a cornice and parapet which forms a shallow stone pediment above the centre bay. Seven-bay principal elevation, with a projecting square Tuscan porch. Cement-rendered, with corner quoin pilasters.

141

DROMISKIN LO

ST RONAN, FORMER DROMISKIN PARISH CHURCH (C of I). The site of a monastery founded by St Lughaidh († 515) and later placed under the patronage of St Ronan († 664). All that remains of the early foundation is part of a large CELTIC CROSS, which was re-erected as a gravestone to the Lawless family in 1918. This has a raised boss at the centre of each side, and unidentified scenes, possibly of war and hunting, carved on the arms. The ROUND TOWER, now a mere stump, with conical roof and windows of 1880, was probably erected in the late C9 by Colman Mac Aillil, Abbot of Clonmacnoise and a native of Dromiskin. The recessed sandstone doorway on its E face was originally flanked by columns supporting a round-headed arch. The date of the pre-Reformation CHURCH RUIN is uncertain, as only the E gable and the base of the external walls survive. The twinlight double-cusped window probably dates to the C15, but it replaced an earlier pointed triple-light window. The First Fruits hall and tower church, now ivy-grown and derelict, was erected in 1821 to a standard design by *John Bowden*.

SS PETER AND PAUL. 1926 by *Ashlin & Coleman*. A straightforward basilican design, built on a plan first used by this firm at the Church of the Sacred Heart near Newry, Co. Down, in 1916. Nave, side aisles and short sanctuary, with a NW belltower and a small circular baptistery off the E aisle, all in an Italianate Romanesque style. Of rock-faced granite, with ashlar trim. The entrance gable contains a big wheel window, with a round-headed door below. Machicolated eaves motif to nave, aisles and tower. The belfry is consciously Italianate, with a triforium crowned by a slated ogee dome. The interior is bright and airy, with paired round-headed lancets and a triple lancet E window. The nave arcades are round-headed and supported on columns of polished grey granite with octagonal capitals. Round-headed niches to side altars and classical high altar flanked by free-standing angels. – MOSAIC by *Oppenheimer*.

ARDRONAN. The former rectory, of 1766. Handsome redbrick house, two storeys over a basement, with a three-bay frontage and a granite tripartite doorcase. Typical symmetrical plan, with two rooms at front and rear and the stair well set at right angles to the hall. Original C18 interior. The staircase has three Tuscan balusters to each tread. Six-panel doors in lugged surrounds. Several large neoclassical marble chimneypieces were installed in the C20.

MILLTOWN CASTLE. 2 km NW, in a farmyard. Traditionally one of the earliest fortified tower houses on the northern borders of the Pale. Milltown Castle differs from the usual square or rectangular Irish tower house in having rounded corners and round corner towers. The walls are slightly battered at the base. Rounded corners and semicircular towers are found in both C13 and C15 Irish buildings, and Milltown might well date from either period; perhaps it was built with the aid of the £10 castle-building grant of 1429. The tower is of three storeys over a barrel-vaulted basement, with slightly projecting towers for the stair and garderobe, and a corner chimney. Battlemented roof-walk and a murder hole above the E entrance. One apparently original timber beam supports the floor of the top storey. The castle was inhabited until the mid-C19. Its lower floors are much altered and the stair for the first two flights is late Georgian.

DRUMCAR

LO *0090*

DRUMCAR PARISH CHURCH (C of I). Small four-bay lancet hall, buttressed, with a bellcote over the W gable and a S porch. Of coursed rubble with limestone dressings. Erected by John McClintock, later first Lord Rathdonnell, on the model of John Henry Newman's church at Littlemore near Oxford. Plans and elevations of the Littlemore church were published in 1840 by the Society for Promoting Gothic Architecture. McClintock acquired a copy in 1841 and the church at Drumcar was completed in 1845: a neat illustration of the rapid spread of architectural styles in the C19. The chancel, with triple-light E window, is an addition of 1868 by *Slater & Carpenter*. – STAINED GLASS. E window: the Ascension, by *J. Clarke & Sons*, 1924. – LYCHGATE of 1895.

In the churchyard are the now featureless ruins of the previous church and, N of the chancel, the MCCLINTOCK MAUSOLEUM, also by *Slater & Carpenter* and of 1868. This superbly solid architectural monument is built to satisfy the dictates of a taste formed by Ruskin's *Seven Lamps of Archi-*

tecture and *The Stones of Venice*. An octagon of stone, with broad and squat stepped diagonal buttresses at each corner and a slated pyramid roof surmounted by a wrought-iron finial cross. An Early Gothic triforium, with heavy arches, robust colonnettes and stiffleaf capitals, frames a slit window, with pairs of sculpted shields in stone on either side.

DRUMCAR HOUSE. 1777. Formerly the seat of the McClintock family, Barons Rathdonnell; now St Mary's Hospital. Originally a large rectangular mansion, enjoying a clear view across country to Dundalk Bay. Three storeys over a basement; two rooms deep with a large central hall. Shallow hipped roof hidden behind a cornice and blocking course with central chimneystacks. The entrance front is of five bays with the windows arranged as a pair, a single central window and a pair, an elegant a–b–a rhythm. The proportions of the central block are now the most enduring aspect of the C18 house, which originally had a simple tripartite doorcase set in a shallow relieving arch and single-storey walls with niches and sunken panels joining the main block to a pedimented carriage arch on each side. The four-columned Doric porch with balcony is early to mid-C19, as are the moulded window surrounds and segmental-headed pediments to the ground-floor windows. Later two-storey, three-bay wings with recessed links; yet later ugly mansard roofs. Inside, the house was entirely renovated and remodelled by *Kelly and Jones* when it became a hospital in 1948.

ST FINIAN. 2 km E, at Dillonstown Cross. 1862–75 by *John Murray*, set to terminate a long vista from the Drumcar road. Small six-bay lancet hall, cement-rendered, with a gabled entrance front in coursed rubble. Triple lancet above a pointed door flanked by short lancets with diagonal corner buttresses. Dull interior with a modernized sanctuary.

8080

DRUMCONDRATH ME

Small country village set around a crossroads.

DRUMCONDRATH PARISH CHURCH (C of I). Simple two-bay hall and single-bay chancel, with a bellcote over the W entrance gable and a handsome pedimented Gibbs surround to the doorcase, suggesting a mid-C18 date. The interior was Gothicized in the C19, and the only Georgian features to survive are two horizontal panels of rococo plasterwork flanking the E window. The windows now have double Y-tracery and quarry glass. – STAINED GLASS. E window: beefy if attractive *art nouveau* figures of Fortitude, Faith, Truth and Justice, 1912. – MONUMENTS. Henry Corbet Singleton †1872; a pretentious Greek-revival plaque. The Rev. Robert Samuel Law †1892 by *Coates*, Dublin. Major Loftus Corbet Singleton †1881 by *J. Forsyth*, London.

SS PETER AND PAUL. Erected by Fr Patrick Sheridan in 1833.

Gutted by fire in 1974 and extensively renovated. Big plain T-plan church, lit by large lancet windows, with limestone buttresses and dressings to the entrance gable.

ACLARE HOUSE. 1.5 km S. Handsome neoclassical villa, reminiscent of the bare academic classicism of John B. Keane, John Hargrave or Thomas Duff. Built in 1840 for Henry Corbet Singleton, magistrate and Deputy Lieutenant of Co. Meath. A rectangular two-storey building, faced with unusually crisp Scottish sandstone – the only evidence of corrosion is on the inner E side of the portico. Three-bay entrance front, the central bay projecting and crowned by a shallow eaves pediment. Freestanding Greek Doric porch, with a tripartite window above; otherwise regular sash windows to front and side elevations. First-floor string-course and eaves cornice. After this chaste façade the interior seems routine. A rectangular plan, the central top-lit stairhall divided from the first-floor landing by a columnar screen. Large reception rooms, with neoclassical chimney-pieces and moulded plasterwork, flank the hall. Substantial rubble and redbrick stable range at the rear of the house, also of 1840.

NEWSTONE CASTLE. 2 km N. The ground floor of a medieval tower house with a high barrel-vault and a door in the SW wall. A tower at the SW angle survives to second-floor level. S of the tower house are the fragmentary ruins of a stone-built house, probably of C17 date. One large stone chimneypiece survives, with a wide segmental arch.

DRUMBRIDE CHURCH RUIN. 3 km N. A ruined rectangular structure worthy of note for the survival of a complete round-headed window in the E gable, suggestive of a C12 date. Motte and bailey S of the church.

SS PATRICK AND BRIGID, ARDAGH. 5.5 km NW. A big gabled rectangular hall built in 1843 and reconstructed in 1982. Simple exterior, rough-cast and whitewashed, with a slated roof. A lean-to extension at the centre of one long wall provided an entrance porch flanked by a vestry and crying room. On each side of this projection the wall has been opened up as a large full-length window.

DULEEK

ME *0060*

Small village beside the river Nanny, with a nice wooded green at the centre. The place-name is said to be derived from the *damhliag* (the house of stone or church of St Ciaran) which according to tradition was, like Donaghpatrick, one of the earliest stone churches to be built in Ireland. Duleek Cross, the ruins of St Mary's Priory and the spire of the derelict Protestant church provide a focus of architectural interest.

DULEEK CROSS. On the N side of the former Protestant church. 20
Small cross, about 5 ft (1.5 m) high, carved from a single piece of stone. Its form is of the classic C9 'high cross' type, with the circle or nimbus pierced (to isolate the arms from the shaft and

head) and slightly recessed. It is decorated with geometrical bosses. The cross lacks any decorative base, rising directly from the ground, and the cap-stone is missing, so that the tenon joint is exposed at the head of the shaft. A double roll moulding defines the edges of the cross with, on the W face, three sculptural scenes, which have been interpreted as – from top to bottom – the Annunciation, the Visitation and the Holy Family, set below the Crucifixion. Two ecclesiastics with croziers are in the arms of the cross, and the scene at its head shows St Paul and St Anthony fed by the raven in the wilderness. The sides and the E face are decorated with abstract motifs of whorls and interlace patterns. Winged beasts are carved on the ends of the arms.

29 ST MARY'S PRIORY. A priory for Augustinian canons was founded here by Hugh de Lacy in 1182, though the visible remains date mainly from the C14 and C15. The Norman church was built on the site of an earlier foundation, said to have been established in 488 by St Ciaran, a disciple of St Patrick who studied at the abbey of St Martin of Tours and whom Patrick consecrated Bishop of Duleek. A significant religious centre, the monastery survived successive raids between the C9 and the C12. After the battle of Clontarf and the death of Brian Boru in 1014, the wake of the great Irish chieftain was held here before his body was buried at Louth Abbey. The existing limestone cell-like building lying in a field N of the church was traditionally thought to be Ciaran's *damhliag*. It is probably only of late medieval date and is now so altered as to be of little significance. In 1835 John O'Donovan remarked that recent repairs to it had completely 'obliterated every appearance of its supposed antiquity' – an experience that is sadly all too common in Ireland even to this day!

What survives from the Augustinian foundation is the belfry tower of the main church, with the walls and E gable of the S aisle. Most of the foundations of the church itself have now disappeared or have been absorbed into the ground of the graveyard. The crease line of its roof – a tall and slightly lop-sided gable – can be seen clearly on the E face of the tower, from which it would appear that the medieval church – in its last form – was wide for an Irish church building, and certainly wider than the belfry tower at its W end, which opened into the body of the church through a high double-chamfered archway. The S wall of the church remains, with an arcade of three plain Gothic arches built on square piers of rubble stonework without any mouldings. This arcade connected the church with its S aisle. Here the E window is of three round-headed lights separated by slender octagonal mullions. It dates from 1597 and is a replacement by Sir John Bellew, whose arms, with those of his wife, Dame Ismay Nugent, appear below it. The voussoirs for a much wider opening appear high up in the present gable, suggesting the proportions for an earlier and more elaborate traceried form of E window.

The tower is an impressive ruin. Built of finely dressed ashlar, it makes a telling use of the slender string-courses typical of much late medieval architecture in Ireland, to sharpen the architectural effect and to mark a delicate set-back at each of its three storeys. At the top, where high Irish battlements mark each corner, the string-courses drop in precise vertical lines and then run horizontally to pick up the line of weep holes that drained the roof. The belfry windows, immediately below, are a four-light cross-mullioned type with pointed heads, common to church buildings and tower houses. At the SW corner a projecting turret contains a spiral stair which is an excellent example of Irish masonry and of the type of stair which omits any reference to a stone newel and carries the wedge shape of each step to a sharp point which rises as an extended helix. The line of the stair can be appreciated particularly well from the belfry stage, which also exposes the elliptical stone arches within the window openings and the system of stone shafts as struts at the corners of the battlements.

On the N wall of the belfry tower, the tapering concave 'excavation' in rubble stone is the trace of an earlier ROUND TOWER incorporated into the later structure and now demolished. A similar instance of a round tower being absorbed into a later medieval building occurs at Lusk Church, Co. Dublin, where the round tower forms one of four turrets at each corner of the belfry tower.

Fragments of CARVED STONEWORK are preserved in the belfry: these include sections of Gothic tracery and a Romanesque capital, either from the original W door or from the chancel arch, with a bearded head whose moustache is extended into a pattern of Celtic interlace. In the S aisle the TOMB-CHEST is of the second half of the C15. Erected for the Preston and Plunkett families, it is similar in workmanship to the Plunkett tomb-chests in the churches at Dunsany and Rathmore (qq.v.) and the St Lawrence tomb-chest at Howth in Co. Dublin. Shallow ogee niches carved on each side are decorated with leaves of stylized foliage which have coats of arms above on the N and S sides, figures within the niches on the other faces. These show, on the E, the Crucifixion, flanked by figures of angels with censers and St Michael thrusting a spear into the mouth of a dragon; on the W, a bishop, St Catherine with a down-turned sword and a spiral wheel in her left hand, an archbishop, and St Peter holding two huge keys in his right hand, a book in his left. The top of the tomb is not original and was put up in memory of John, Lord Bellew, †1692. The upper slab of a second TOMB is now built into the last arch of the S aisle arcade. This is an effigy of James Cusack, Bishop of Meath, †1688, showing the bishop holding a decorated crozier with his coat of arms in the top l. corner; the underside of the slab, now facing S, preserves a figure of presumably the same bishop, partially executed, with the crozier lying diagonally across the body. This uncompleted carving preserves an interesting record of the practice of C17 Irish sculptors; the figure is in the process of being excavated from a smooth block and has been 'roughed out' but left unfinished, with the chisel marks of the basic carving remaining. As such it is better preserved than the 'finished' figure on the other side.

ST CIARAN, FORMER DULEEK PARISH CHURCH (C of I). 1816. Hall and tower type. Large gabled hall, with a three-stage tower with pinnacles and spire. All typical Board of First Fruits architecture. Three triple-light Perp windows to the S wall with monuments formerly arranged along a blank wall opposite. Victorian E window. Open kingpost roof inside. Now derelict. – MONUMENT. Until recently, the building's saving grace – a confident freestanding statue in the porch of an equally assured Judge Stephen Trotter †*c.* 1765, attributed to *Peter Scheemakers*. Happily, this has been restored by the National Heritage Council and removed for safe keeping to the Incorporated Law Society of Ireland at Blackhall Place in Dublin.

ST CIARAN. 1812. Big five-bay gabled hall of coursed limestone rubble, with a three-bay cutstone entrance gable. Enlarged and remodelled in 1840 and again by *W. H. Byrne* in 1870. Gabled façade, with lancets above and flanking the door; coupled lancets with cinquefoils and quarry glass to the nave. Inside, a large dull hall, with sanctuary apse of 1870.

DULEEK WAYSIDE CROSS. Charming monument erected in 1601 to the memory of William Bathe of Athcarne †1599 by his wife, Jenet Dowdall, and thus related to the wayside cross at Annesbrook (*see* below). More a pillar than a cross, having instead of a cross-bar a deep band or belt of stone near the top of the shaft. This is carved with angels bearing religious emblems and armorial crests. The shaft, which is oblong in plan, has three moulded ogee-headed niches sculpted on each face bearing figures of saints: on the E, St Peter, St Patrick and St Ciaran; S, St Andrew, St Catherine, St Stephen; N, Mary Magdalene, St James, St Thomas. Carved on the W side of the projecting band is a small heart encircled by a ring which might be taken to represent the Sacred Heart; but, as that devotion was not instituted until the end of the C17, it more probably represents conjugal love. The scale of the cross gives it its charm, for the figures are stiff and rigidly conventional in contrast to the naturalism found in the late C17 cross at Athcarne (*see* below).

COURTHOUSE. Meath Grand Jury presentments for 1838 record the payment of £853 to John Trotter for building a sessions house at Duleek. The result was a modest T-shaped building of squared rubble with limestone trim. The only conscious architecture is on the entrance elevation: a gable end with Doric doorcase, fanlight, a simplified eaves pediment and corner quoins – all quite similar to Dunshaughlin Courthouse by Francis Johnston, from which it presumably derives.

DULEEK HOUSE. Substantial early Georgian house of two periods. The original big harled three-bay house, with a hipped roof, sash windows and broad expanses of bare masonry, now constitutes the rear of the building, which was enlarged *c.* 1750 for Thomas Trotter M.P., who added a brand-new house across the front of the old one, doubling its size and gaining, at least, a front of up-to-date Palladian appearance. The new house, also three storeys high, is one room deep and of tripartite plan. The staircase is placed centrally at the rear, in the older part of the house. The new façade is handsome if routine. A broad three-bay block of crisp limestone ashlar, the centre bay projecting and crowned by an eaves pediment with a continuous cornice and balustrade on each side. The central bay is given a classic Irish Palladian treatment: a tripartite Doric doorcase with a pediment over the door, a Venetian window above and, on the top floor, a flat-headed tripartite window. The masonry is of great quality. Smooth and precise, with monolithic mullions to the tripartite window and raised corner quoins to centre and ends. Inside, a large entrance hall with an emphatic Doric frieze and two freestanding Doric columns. On the back wall are three timber arches, the central arch framing the staircase, which has the ample balusters with deep curves also found at Bellinter. Indeed the whole of the 1750 addition is very much in the *Richard Castle* idiom and may be attributed to his office. The rooms flanking the hall both have neoclassical plasterwork and late C18 joinery. Those to the S end in shallow alcoves, expressed outside as three-bay, three-storey bows.

ANNESBROOK. 2 km S. Modest country house, low in its proportions and rough-cast with limestone trim. Two-storey, three-bay block with a shallow hipped roof erupting unexpectedly at the centre into a giant freestanding Ionic portico with curiously ornate capitals. Both the portico and a low N wing with a pretty Gothic dining room inside were added in 1821 by Henry Smith in anticipation of a call from George IV while on his way to visit Lady Conyngham at Slane; but the King is said never to have gone inside. The house cannot have been built much before the royal visit, perhaps between 1800 and 1810, as it bears a marked resemblance to several smaller country houses designed by *Francis Johnston* in that decade; the details of its gate lodge chimneys, curiously gadrooned, are identical to those of other Johnston lodges. Annesbrook is of rectangular tripartite plan. A bowed central projection at the rear houses the stairwell, an arrangement similar to Johnston's Corbalton Hall (1801; *see* Skreen), while the treatment of the ground-floor windows, which are set in relieving arches with Greek-key impost courses, is another echo of Corbalton and of Galtrim House, also by Johnston. The doorway, which has similar Greek-key detailing, is set within a relieving arch boldly framed by quoins, which the addition of the portico renders unnecessarily emphatic. If Johnston was involved in the design, as seems probable, it is unlikely that he was physically present. Here there is charm but none of the refinement of either Galtrim or Corbalton.

The N wing is equally plausible as a Johnston design. It is a single-storey, four-bay extension with a deep cornice entablature and blocking course. Narrow advanced end bays are expressed as blank niches with windows in two relieving arches lighting the dining room. Inside, this large rectangular room has a coved ceiling, a marble Gothic fireplace and three foiled ogee-headed niches at each end. The ceiling is covered in whimsical pattern-bookish plasterwork that combines rococo, classical and Gothic motifs.

ANNESBROOK CROSS. Outside the demesne, a wayside pillar cross with a carved capital and triangular finial to the top of the shaft. The Crucifixion is depicted as a sunken panel at the top of the cross; beneath it, the arms of Bathe and Dowdall and an inscription recording its erection by Jenet Dowdall in 1600, the year after the death of her husband, William Bathe of Athcarne. On the back of the shaft is a prayer to the Virgin. The monument is similar to, though less elaborate than, the Duleek Wayside Cross (*see* above), erected by Jenet Dowdall in the following year.

ATHCARNE CASTLE. 3.5 km SW. Tower house erected in 1590 by William Bathe, Crown Justice to the Court of Common Pleas, and his wife, Jenet Dowdall. Bathe died only nine years later, whereupon Jenet erected several wayside monuments to his memory throughout the surrounding countryside (*see* above). She was William Bathe's second wife and he her third husband. The Bathes were a prominent Anglo-Norman family to whom a grant of the lands of Athcarne was made in 1172 and who held higher positions in Irish society until the C17. During the C14 and C16 three Bathes became Lord Chief Justices of Ireland, while John de Bathe, father of the builder of Athcarne, was Attorney General in 1564 and later Chancellor of the Exchequer.

The castle, greatly altered and extended since the C16, is now ruinous and forms a large rectangular castellated house with an enclosed courtyard at the rear. William Bathe's tower house, with barrel-vaulted basement and two diagonally opposite corner towers, is incorporated at the E end, its upper storeys largely remodelled, including the early addition of tall Jacobean chimneys which give a nice silhouette. The later castellated house is prosaic: a dull rectangular block, two rooms deep and three storeys high, built probably *c.* 1830 and mostly of cement-rendered brick. A thin turret at the W end of the façade, whose battlements echo the chimneys of the tower house, is of coursed rubble-stone. The arms of Bathe and Dowdall were removed from the original castle and affixed here. In 1786 the old castle was let to one Henry Garrett; the additions were made for Sir William Plunkett de Bathe, owner in 1832.

THE WHITE CROSS. Near the entrance to Athcarne Castle. Tall slab-like cross, 8 ft (2.5 m) high, with short arms, bearing, on its S face, a large-scale high-relief carving of the Crucifixion and, on the N face, a smaller rendering of the Virgin and Child, with the arms of Bathe and Dowdall above. Erected in the late C17 by Cecilia Dowdall, most probably to mark the occasion of her marriage to Sir Luke Bathe of Athcarne in 1665. A comparison with the late medieval decoration of the Duleek and Annesbrook crosses, erected *c.* 1600, shows the remarkable transformation which had occurred in Irish sculpture in the space of sixty years. The White Cross, although still naive, lies firmly within the naturalist Renaissance tradition, the work of a sculptor who had clearly imbibed the influence of European classicism.

DUNBOYNE ME *0040*

Small village with a pleasant wooded green at its centre, bounded on the S by a neat row of C19 estate houses and taller slated houses, with two well-preserved late Victorian shopfronts.

DUNBOYNE OLD CASTLE. In the churchyard, W of the present church. The ruins of a C15 tower house, swathed in ivy and rising like some rectangular block of topiary. This is one of the few tower houses in Co. Meath for which a precise date can be given. The Statute Roles of Edward IV for 1475/76 state that 'Esmond (Botiller alias Persson) proposes by the Grace of God to commence to erect and complete a castle anew at Dunboyne'. Esmond was granted 12d. for every ploughland in Meath and given one year in which to complete his castle.

Three sides of the tower stand to the height of the wall-head. It measures some 13 ft by 12 ft (3.9 m by 3.6 m) internally and stands on a vaulted basement, now largely filled by fallen rubble. Details which remain are part of a canopied fireplace at first-floor level, the door check and bolt-hole to the entrance to this room, and sections of the stair, which was laid out in an unusual plan, a straight stair connecting the basement to the main hall and a spiral stair for the tower which was located in the thickness of the S wall behind the chimneybreast. Botiller's tower house stood to the W of the medieval church of St Peter and St Paul, which became ruinous in 1641. The chancel continued in use throughout the C18, though no trace remains today. In the porch of the modern church are fragments of sandstone tracery and limestone cross-mullions with raised roll mouldings. These must date from 1476 and presumably once formed part of the tower house.

ST PETER, DUNBOYNE PARISH CHURCH (C of I). 1866 by *S. Rollinson* of Chesterfield. Simple rectangular hall of snecked rubble with pale yellow brick trim. Semicircular chancel, continuous with the body of the church – a popular fashion for mid-Victorian Gothic churches in England – and the whole is covered by a tall slated roof. Paired lancets, W bellcote and S gabled porch. Nice.

HAMILTON MAUSOLEUM. In the churchyard, a large ivy-covered granite cube, with raised corner quoins, inscribed plaques, a Tuscan doorcase in limestone and a flaming urn as a central finial on the roof. Erected to the memory of Charles Hamilton, Lord Dunboyne, †1799. Nearby is a giant free-standing Tuscan aedicule erected to John McMiller †1756.

SS PETER AND PAUL. 1955 by *W. H. Byrne*. Set back from the village green, immediately S of the old and now derelict C 19 T-plan chapel. The contrast is familiar, modest vernacular Gothic versus inflated Hiberno-Romanesque. Tall gabled hall, of plain rough-cast exterior and a detached campanile flanking the entrance front. In the gable front Byrne employs a common device, a giant round-headed relieving arch, with three round-headed lancets inside it, a porch below and single lancets each side. Inside, a five-bay nave; base, bare and bleak, with a shallow barrel-vault over the nave and flat ceilings.

DUNBOYNE CASTLE. 1764 by *George Darley*. In a wooded park S from the village and visible from the old churchyard, a house which belies its plain façade, with an unorthodox plan and spectacular rococo plasterwork inside. The main front, facing N, is tall and flat. Seven bays and three storeys, with a rusticated ground floor and two tall floors above. The effect is like the front of a townhouse dropped in the country, especially at the W end, where the room at the front extends beyond the line of the whole block by one extra bay to provide a symmetrical front. On the rear elevation the house is six windows wide – not seven. A robust tripartite doorcase with Tuscan columns and open pediment frames the main door. The main façade is in composition stone, with odd aedicules to the upper windows.

Inside, the oddities and the charm of the plan appear at once. The hall is a deep rectangle, bow-ended, with a graceful if substantial arcade of alternating semicircular and elliptical arches on Doric pilasters round the walls. Full Doric cornice with mutules and guttae. The doors have lugged architraves: two at the end of the hall are deeply curved to fit the plan. These open l. to a passage between the front and back rooms and r. to the main stair, a giddy space, square in plan, with a substantial, heavily detailed timber staircase rising in broken flights to a high coved ceiling. The ceiling breaks into a riot of rococo plasterwork, with trophies dedicated to the hunt, martial achievements, the theatre and the arts. Lively stucco birds occupy the corner of each cove, and a massive Greek-key band marks out the central square of the ceiling. The rooms on either side of the hall are modest in scale and rectangular in plan. They have bold plain cornices and are unexceptional as mid-Georgian rooms.

The great surprise of Dunboyne Castle lies in the arrangement of the rooms at the back of the house. Here one very large room occupies half the rear elevation, with a long narrow closet, one bay wide, at its E end, and a shallow two-bay parlour on the W beyond the main staircase. The great room, originally a dining room and now a chapel, rises higher than any of the other rooms on the ground floor. It displaces vertically the saloon above it, a room of identical proportions which is approached by an extra flight and separate landing on the main stairs. Both rooms are bedecked with elaborate rococo plasterwork. The chapel has a Corinthian cornice and frieze with French horns and violins to decorate the ceiling. It is entered both from the stairhall, opening into one corner of the room, and centrally, though a very grand aediculed doorcase that quite dwarfs the narrow passage, between the front and the back, in which it is placed.

What accounts for this very odd plan? The answer appears to be the building programme and desire for improvements, not of a young heir but of an energetic widow. In 1759 the house belonged to Charles Hamilton and his young bride, Sarah. Within four years of their marriage Charles died, and it was Sarah Hamilton who in 1764 embarked on improvements. Fragmentary building accounts for the years 1764 to 1766 bear witness to an extensive remodelling by the Drogheda architect George Darley, who presumably gave the house most of its present appearance. What he and Sarah Hamilton had to work on was probably a straightforward house of a standard double-pile plan: five bays at the front, with a hall in the middle, a room each side and two rooms behind, with the back stairs to the l. between the front and back and the main stairs to the r. In the rebuilding the back stairs were removed to an extra bay, at the E end of the entrance front, creating the present passage where they had once been, and the front was extended by an extra bay to the W for symmetry. Darley, we may assume, redesigned the main stair and altered the floor levels on the S front at the same time, but he did not alter the principal structural walls of the house, hence the thin closet room beside the chapel.

The accounts also record the name of the carpenter responsible for the splendid carved doors in the hall and the carved pediment and columns of the principal doorcase to the chapel. He is *Oliver Beahon*, who in 1766 was engaged on flooring the closet on the ground floor, and repairing and replacing old windows, wainscotting and architraves. Beahon is a figure of some interest, as his doors at Dunboyne employ a particular type of fielded panel with, instead of the usual flat or bevelled edge, a distinctive rounded moulding which also appears at Dowth Hall, building in the same period as Dunboyne Castle. The design of the two houses is indeed very close. Both have the appearance of a town house in the country with a front façade where the ground floor is treated as a channelled basement with a *piano nobile* above. Opulent rococo plasterwork distinguishes both interiors, and the overall impression given by each building is of a vigorous splendour which just stops short of the ultimate in finesse.

COURTHILL. N of the church. Substantial square villa built for a Mr H. Greene *c.* 1835. The entrance front, as at many similar houses in the environs of Dublin, is three-bay and originally of two storeys, but is entered at first-floor level, up steps and through a recessed porch framed by Greek Doric columns. Inside, an elegant classical hall leads to a corridor running down the middle of the house, three rooms each side, and a modest side stair leading to the lower floor. The plasterwork cornices and central motifs are classical, to a large scale and date from 1838. About 1900 Courthill was enlarged by the addition of an extra storey within a tall mansard roof. The principal-floor windows were replaced by cross-shaped casements, and the front area was paved over and given a classical balustrade of cast-iron circles. The result is a curious hybrid, not easily disentangled. Is the pedimented gable over the entrance porch of the 1830s or seventy years later?

NORMANS GROVE. 2 km NE. This estate appears as Old Bracetown in the Down survey, and traces of what may be C 17 walls are used in the yard buildings and possibly in the kitchen wing. The property changed hands in 1748, when it was bought by the Lee Norman family, who gave the house a new name. Normans Grove is of two dates: the mid-C 18 and *c.* 1800. It is a long low house, one room deep, with a wide passage running the length of the house at the back and a central staircase projecting at the back in a direct line with the hall. The passage connects at the W end to a square kitchen block set back from the front and containing on the first floor a handsome large room with angle fireplace, lugged window and door surrounds and chair rail. All good standard work of *c.* 1750. Upstairs in the main house are more rooms of this character, four in a sequence across the front, each of two windows, except in the centre, where there are three. These rooms have shallow coombed ceilings. The façade is thus a wide nine-bay front with the upper-floor windows immediately below the eaves cornice and a projecting single bay in the centre, where the hall door has a robust cutstone Gibbs surround. At ground-floor level a late Georgian remodelling replaced the plain sash windows on either side of the door by large tripartite designs with moulded shafts of a *cottage orné* character. Inside, the two principal rooms and the hall were redecorated with shallow plasterwork cornices and finely panelled shutters in place of the fielded panels of the earlier parts of the house. The drawing room has a brass basket grate by *George Binns* of *c.* 1800. The staircase is now late C 19, as is the shallow hipped roof of the house. It may once have been thatched.

Substantial office court mostly in brick with eight sequential brick arcades and a two-acre walled garden. More C 18 brick walls, a ha-ha and a plain folly tower in the park S of the house.

SUMMERSEAT. 1.5 km SE. A 'gentleman's box' of *c.* 1750. Originally a rough-cast square house, three bays wide and two storeys high, with a parapet and high slate roof. A provincial Gibbs surround to the door. To this, single-storey, single-bay wings were added *c.* 1800, with pretty tripartite windows in stuccoed relieving arches on the S front.

DUNDALK

LO *0000*

Dundalk, the northernmost town in the province of Leinster, owes its historical significance to its command of the ancient and modern routes N to Ulster. Although originally part of the territory of the Conaille Muirthemhne, the town is a Norman foundation which grew up around the surviving motte and bailey of Castletown. Traditionally known as Dún Dealga or Fort of Dealga, and associated with the legendary hero Cúchulainn, the settlement was possibly initiated by John de Courcy, who early in 1178 passed through Meath and Louth on the way to his successful conquest of eastern Ulster. In 1185 King John granted the lands to his retainer Bertram de Verdun, whose family held them until the C14, when the property passed to the Bellew family. About 1475 Richard Bellew erected Castletown Castle inland and to the N of the present town. By then, however, strategic and commercial considerations had begun to affect Dundalk, bringing about the decline of the original settlement at Castletown and the establishment of a port and a new town further to the E.

As the new town of Dundalk was built on a narrow ridge of gravel the town developed on a strong linear emphasis, which is still notable today. One early name, 'Stratbaly', means simply street town. The present Bridge Street, Church Street and the northern end of Clanbrassil Street preserve the character of this original plan. The southern end of the town was a later C14 development growing round two earlier friaries, the Grey Friary and the Friary of St Leonard, to the E in Seatown, and both mid-C13 de Verdun foundations.

No sooner had the new town been established than it was plundered and burnt during the invasion of Edward Bruce in 1315. Indeed, the weakness of Anglo-Norman power in the C14 and C15 led to its continual harassment by the northern Irish, so that by the C16 Dundalk stood alone as the northern bastion of the Pale. Its strategic importance was fully realized by Hugh O'Neill, Earl of Tyrone, on the eve of his rebellion against Elizabeth I in 1595. According to Henry Duke, the governor of Dundalk, O'Neill had told his troops:

> that of any cities they must burn and destroy the town of Dundalk, lest the garrison should be laid there. Only Art McBarron was altogether against it, alleging that their ancestors and especially themselves for the most part had been bred and brought up there. The Earl confessed it to be true and said that he loved it best of any town in Ireland but nevertheless he would destroy it.

In the event Dundalk survived O'Neill's rebellion, but during the insurrection of 1641 it fell to the advancing army of Phelim O'Neill, and in 1648, after the bloody example of Drogheda, it promptly yielded to Jones, the Cromwellian commander. Forty-one years later, before the battle of the Boyne, the Williamite General Schomberg halted for a time at Dundalk. In 1695, following the confiscations, the lands of Dundalk were sold to a leading Williamite, James Hamilton of Tollymore, Co. Down, who died soon after in 1701. His son, also James Hamilton, became M.P. for Dundalk in 1715, was created Viscount Limerick in 1719 and finally in 1758 was raised to the earldom of Clanbrassil. During the 1740s, with the aid of the amateur architect *Thomas Wright* of Durham, James laid out his estate as an extensive ornamental demesne to the W of the existing town. He was also responsible for levelling the remains of the medieval town and moving the administrative centre from the northern end of the town, near his own residence, to the present market square, which he had created in the 1740s. A large linen manufactory established in 1743 at Parliament Square on the eastern borders of Dundalk resulted in a major new E–W axis. James Hamilton, second Earl of Clanbrassil, died childless in 1798, and his estates passed to his sister Anne and through her to Robert Jocelyn, Earl of Roden.

In the later C18 and C19 Dundalk became a thriving commercial centre, aided by the arrival of the railway in 1849. Although the layout and fabric of the town centre are essentially Georgian, the numerous flamboyant Italianate façades and Gothic Revival churches bear witness to substantial Victorian improvements. Significantly the most notable recent buildings in the town are factories (*see* pp. 275–6). Otherwise, modern architects have not been kind to Dundalk: the major new buildings – the Bank of Ireland, the Ulster Bank and the Imperial Hotel – are all works of little merit, intrusive, insensitive and disruptive of their environments.

CHURCHES

ST NICHOLAS, DUNDALK PARISH CHURCH (C of I). A most interesting church, intriguing more than beautiful, like a jigsaw puzzle of medieval, post-medieval and modern building pieces. Founded in the C13; extended in the C16 by the addition of several chantry chapels, and then largely remodelled following extensive damage sustained during the rebellion of 1641 and the Boyne campaign of William III in 1689. An inscribed slab of 1707 inset in the chancel wall states that the church, having suffered injury from time and wear, was then restored 'in a new and more elegant form'.

In its present state St Nicholas is a substantial cruciform structure, nave, transepts, polygonal chancel and SW tower. The most obvious medieval survival is the tall three-stage rubble tower with an awkward buttress-like projection at its SW corner, which houses a spiral stair. The green copper spire is modern and replaces a steeple designed by *Francis Johnston* in 1786. The nave, also of coursed rubble, incorporates masonry from as early as the C13, but was largely reconstructed in 1707. Two blocked-up arches evident in the S wall indicate

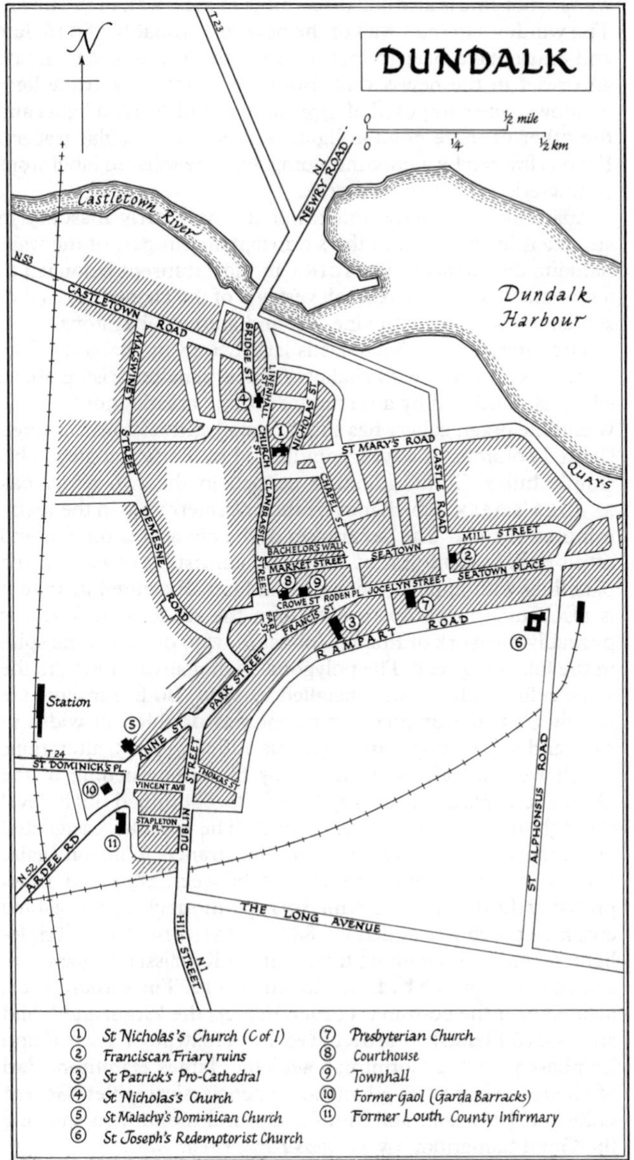
DUNDALK
N
0 ½ mile
0 ¼ ½ km
Castletown River
Dundalk Harbour
NEWRY ROAD
N1
T23
N53
CASTLETOWN ROAD
MACSWINEY STREET
BRIDGE ST
LINENHALL ST
CHURCH ST
NICHOLAS ST
ST MARY'S ROAD
CASTLE ROAD
QUAYS
CLANBRASSIL STREET
CHAPEL ST
DEMESNE ROAD
MILL STREET
BACHELOR'S WALK
SEATOWN
MARKET STREET
SEATOWN PLACE
CROWE ST
RODEN PL.
JOCELYN STREET
EARL ST
FRANCIS ST
RAMPART ROAD
PARK STREET
Station
T 24
ST DOMINICK'S PL.
ANNE ST
VINCENT AVE
THOMAS ST
STAPLETON PL.
DUBLIN STREET
ST ALPHONSUS ROAD
N 52
ARDEE RD
THE LONG AVENUE
HILL STREET
N1
① St Nicholas's Church (C of I)
② Franciscan Friary ruins
③ St Patrick's Pro-Cathedral
④ St Nicholas's Church
⑤ St Malachy's Dominican Church
⑥ St Joseph's Redemptorist Church
⑦ Presbyterian Church
⑧ Courthouse
⑨ Townhall
⑩ Former Gaol (Garda Barracks)
⑪ Former Louth County Infirmary

that the original church had an arcade opening into a S aisle whose roof-line is also still discernible in the E wall of the tower. The windows in the S wall of the nave are probably of C16 date and must have been removed from the ruinous C17 fabric and reset in the new S wall. Both are rectangular triple-light windows, one composed of three long round-headed lights and the other of three pointed lights with simple circular tracery. Each is framed by a hoodmoulding with the foliated label stops characteristic of Irish C15 work.

Apart from the nave and tower the only early masonry to survive is in the E half of the S transept and in part of the walls flanking the chancel. A PISCINA in the S transept belonged to a C16 chantry chapel. A small vestry N of the chancel has a C16 sandstone window with vine-leaf and animal label stops.

The interior of St Nicholas is largely C18 in character. The nave looks *c.* 1760, with shallow fielded panelling rising above sill level, bordered by a miniature Gothic arcade motif. At the W end the organ gallery has similar detail and rests on clustered shafted columns of a type popularized by Batty Langley. This simple bulky Gothic idiom is echoed in the two-seater oak READER'S DESK, which may be the one referred to in the vestry minutes of 1784. The decoration of the chancel is thinner and more elegant than that of the nave, consisting of flat stained panelling with applied Gothic mouldings. Executed in 1786 it is also much more up to date than the reader's desk and is probably the work of Francis Johnston, who designed the spire in the following year. The polygonal mahogany PULPIT, in the same refined idiom, was installed in 1799. Both transepts are largely C19; the original S transept was doubled in width in 1815 and a matching N transept was added in 1825, alterations which were largely necessitated by the strengthening of the Dundalk garrison after 1798 and its continued high level throughout the Napoleonic period. The chunky castellated appearance of the N transept looks like Francis Johnston again. Most of the windows were altered between 1801 and 1806, probably the date of the distinctive rope-motif glazing. A gabled entrance porch was added in 1888. – STAINED GLASS. Triple-light E window containing fragments of Renaissance glass presented to the church by Lord Roden in 1812. The earliest piece, located near the bottom r. corner, depicts the Virgin and Child and is C16 Flemish. – MONUMENTS. The wife of Vicar Ralph Lambart †1707; a Corinthian aedicule. James Hamilton, Earl of Clanbrassil, †1798; a handsome neoclassical tablet. George Gillichan †1817; an ambitious sculptural monument showing the Good Samaritan, by *Thomas Kirk*, 1819.

105 ST PATRICK'S PRO-CATHEDRAL. An ambitious post-Emancipation church begun in 1837 to designs of *Thomas Duff* and completed twelve years later. Duff died in 1848 and in the following year *Thomas Turner* won an open competition for the design of the Tudor screen, built across the forecourt of the church. In 1852 *J. J. McCarthy* was called in to furnish altar fittings, which were sculpted by *Thomas Kirk*. The church was

extensively redecorated in 1894, when its tall belfry was added by *Ashlin & Coleman.*

St Patrick's is an exceptionally fine late Georgian Gothic church, inspired by the most admired of Perp Gothic models, King's College Chapel, Cambridge, and Bath Abbey, which Duff had studied. Once a perfectly symmetrical design of gabled nave and lean-to aisles, it is now a more picturesque composition following the addition of the belfry at its NW corner, this too in a Perp style. The church is a long nine-bay hall of coursed brownish granite, with crenellated parapet and octagonal corner turrets, which are in fact the only feature derived from King's. Pinnacled buttresses divide each side bay. A single large Perp window fills each gable, and elaborately cusped windows light aisles and clerestory.

Seen on a summer evening the interior is breathtaking in its 106 elegance, a triumph of simplicity. Diamond-shaped cluster-shafted piers, with the thinnest of profiles, support the aisle arcades, whose chamfered reveals are incised with many light mouldings. The ceiling is a simple quadripartite vault with foliated bosses and angel corbel stops, all in plaster. The nave runs without interruption into a shallow two-bay chancel which opens through arches into side chapels. Here the very ornate mosaic, glass and polychrome marble fittings reflect later C 19 taste. Duff's original altar – donated by the Carroll family – is in the E side chapel. – STAINED GLASS. Altar and entrance gables: tiers of brightly coloured saints, by *Mayer of Munich.* Last two windows on E side: Christ and St Malachy, *Early & Son.* – MOSAIC. By *Oppenheimer*, 1909. – MONUMENTS. Gothic niche with portrait bust of Dr Cloyne †1850; *J. J. McCarthy & T. Kirk.*

ST MALACHY'S DOMINICAN CHURCH. 1862–6 by *John Murray.* A tall cruciform church with a steeply pitched roof contains a large five-bay nave opening through paired two-centred arches into shallow transepts and terminating in a polygonal apse. Built of coursed limestone rubble with a cut-stone façade and limestone dressings. The site is restricted, so that the exterior shows no more than an entrance gable with a large five-light Dec window flanked by an incomplete SE tower. Lancets light the nave, transepts and apse. – STAINED GLASS. Centre of apse: St Dominic Receiving the Rosary, by *Michael Healy*, 1913. – ALTAR FITTINGS. *Ashlin & Coleman.*

The adjoining MONASTERY, also by *John Murray*, is of 1867, tucked in between the W transept and nave; irregular vaguely Italian Gothic. ST MALACHY'S NATIONAL SCHOOLS behind consist of a six-bay rubble block with hoodmouldings of 1836 and a low redbrick, Tudoresque range of 1901 by *George Ashlin.*

ST JOSEPH'S REDEMPTORIST CHURCH. 1890 by *George* 135 *Ashlin.* A Hiberno-Romanesque church built on a basilican plan, with Byzantine overtones inside. Rock-faced Newry granite, with granite and Portland stone dressings. Gabled entrance front with a round-headed arch, carved tympanum and, above, two round-headed lancets flanking a canopied statue of St Joseph. Lombardic machicolated motif to the eaves of the gable, aisles and tower. Inside, the nave arcade is of five round-headed arches with polished pink granite shafts and white foliated capitals. Above, mini timber Ionic pilasters between the paired clerestory windows and a panelled barrel-vault. The sanctuary is top-lit, an apse decorated with a blind Ionic arcade and mosaics depicting the childhood of Jesus. – HIGH ALTAR by *Thomas Earley*.

The MONASTERY buildings, also by *Ashlin*, date from 1879 and 1881. L-shaped, with a connecting corridor to the church, forming a quadrangle. Rock-faced granite with yellow brick dressings, high pitched roof, pilaster strips along the front and a square stair tower at the rear.

ST NICHOLAS. 1859 by *John Murray*. Mid-Victorian Gothic squashed onto an island site at the N end of Dundalk's main street. Of coursed granite with limestone dressings. Inside, a five-bay limestone arcade of two-centred chamfered arches carried on columns with bulging E.E. capitals. *W. H. Byrne* added a double-gabled S transept in 1904 and a large N transept, complete with four-bay arcade and side aisles, and a polygonal mortuary chapel in 1937. In these extensions Byrne used a slightly later style of Gothic with delicate clustered shafts, thereby emulating the composite character of real medieval churches. His work is attractive. The rather stunted belltower, a miniature version of Magdalen Tower, Oxford, was completed in 1904.

CHURCH OF THE REDEEMER. 1966–7 by *Frank Corr & Oonagh Madden*. A handsome clear-cut modern design, based on a series of interlocking oval forms. The largest of these constitutes the main body of the church, sloping down to meet a much smaller oval sanctuary which rises above it as a 60-ft (18-m) tower. The plan is completed by a low segmental block which forms the entrance front of the church. This accommodates a central baptistery lit by a shallow saucer dome. The two main entrances located on either side of the baptistery have handsome COPPER DOORS, lettered by *Frank Morris* with early Christian prayers. The church is faced with slabs of smooth granite and crowned by a curved copper roof. A porch of low segmental-headed arches carried on granite piloti screens the entire entrance front. Above it, and lighting the nave, is a large rectangular window comprising a series of tall Dalles-de-Verre glass by *Gabriel Loire*.

Inside, the church is dominated by a wide ceiling of slatted pine carried on tall white shafts which create the sense of an ambulatory around the walls. At each end of the long axis, rising from floor to ceiling, are centred narrow windows, again by Loire. As in Corr & McCormick's Church of St Peter at Milford, Co. Donegal, there is in this interior a strong hint of Basil Spence. The SANCTUARY by *Ray Carroll* is a sheer granite wall with low-relief carving of the Last Supper at its base flanking a large enamelled Tabernacle. – CALVARY on top of the tower, a graphic metal sculpture by *Oisin Kelly*. The

STATIONS OF THE CROSS in cast iron along the entrance front are by *Imogen Stuart*.

PRESBYTERIAN CHURCH. 1839 by *Thomas Duff*. Small four-bay gabled hall in a Tudor-Gothic idiom whose site and proportions blend nicely with the little classical Methodist church across the street. Like Duff's nearby St Patrick's, this small building has a Perp window in each gable, four-centred arched entrances and pinnacled buttresses defining each bay. It is also of coursed brownish granite with granite dressings. Inside, a single-bay vestibule leads through two Tudor arches into the three-bay rectangular hall which is the church proper. A very pretty interior, with a curved U-shape pine gallery carried on cast-iron quatrefoil columns. Plaster panelled ceiling with decorative hammerbeams and rosettes. – STAINED GLASS. Central light of S window: Christ the Good Shepherd, by *Clokey* of Belfast, 1944.

METHODIST CHURCH. 1834. An attractive little classical façade which wraps around at each end to shield a simple two-storey, three-bay rubble hall. Nicely set back from the street. Three-bay, two-storey façade, with a horizontally channelled ground floor and Greek Ionic pilasters above supporting an eaves pediment and shallow attic. Perhaps by *Thomas Duff*, who practised this type of scholarly classicism as well as his more noted Gothic exercises. Renovated in 1916 by *G. F. Beckett*.

MONASTERIES. *See* Medieval Buildings and Tour, below.

MEDIEVAL BUILDINGS

The development of Dundalk has, with the exception of the fragmentary remains at St Nicholas Parish Church (*see* above), removed all medieval buildings from the town centre. What survives is now very much on the outskirts: a friary tower in Castle Road at the E side of the town and Castletown Mount and Castle – properly speaking, old Dundalk – 2 km NW.

FRANCISCAN FRIARY, 'SEATOWN CASTLE'. A three-stage buttressed and battlemented tower, probably C15. Formerly the belfry of a monastery founded here in the C13 by John de Verdun. Sacked and burned by Edward Bruce's soldiers in 1315; rebuilt and then destroyed by Lord Deputy Leonard Grey *c.* 1539. The tower is of coursed limestone rubble and sandstone trim. It stood at the SW corner of the church, evidence for which remains in the corbels on the N face which would have supported the nave roof. The ground floor, a barrel-vaulted room 11 ft (3.3 m) square, is entered through an arch on its E face. The windows are small and pointed in the lower stages, with large two-light windows on the top storey. The W window, now badly weathered, was clearly the most sophisticated, two cusped lights with simple geometric tracery and a carved grotesque head projecting above it.

DUN DEALGAN. A Norman motte of *c.* 1180, traditionally associated with the legendary hero Cúchulainn. Although there was perhaps some symbolic intuition in the choice of this site for a Norman fortification, its strategic location above the river ford at Toberona, controlling the ancient routeway to Ulster through the Moyry Pass, must have been of primary importance. What survives today is a high and wide earthen motte planted with trees. The present spiral ascent around the mound dates from the C18, as does the ruined castellated house within the enclosure. This is of two periods: a three-storey, hexagonal gazebo with adjoining entrance and stair tower in a primitive Gothic style, built in 1780 by Patrick Byrne of Seatown as a gift to his grand-nephew, with a set of additional two-storey rooms on the S and a yard to the N built *c.* 1840 to convert the tower into a country retreat. Burnt out in the 1920s and now a brick and stone ruin.

CASTLETOWN BELLEW. Erected *c.* 1475 by Richard Bellew, who received a parliamentary castle-building grant in 1474 and 1479. Large ivy-clad four-stage tower with distinct batter and four corner turrets crowned by modern crenellated parapets. The NE and SW towers are square, whereas the SE and NW are larger and of rectangular plan; the SW tower houses a spiral stair and the NW a garderobe chute. The interior originally had the characteristic barrel-vaulted hall, with three shorter storeys above. A renovation of the 1950s divided this hall into two storeys and installed new floors, windows and panelled walls throughout the castle, replacing or covering the mullioned windows and fireplaces which had been inserted in the late C16 by Sir John Bellew. The small tower rooms were and are accessible from the central block, with the exception of two SE and NW rooms on the third floor, which could be reached only by small communicating stairs from the second-floor chambers. Of these, the SE second-floor room was a chapel and the stairs led to the priest's room above. These uppermost tower rooms, now rubble-filled, were the only part of the original fabric to remain unaltered in the modern renovation.

CASTLETOWN CHURCH RUINS. Near the castle to the S, a small church dedicated to St John the Baptist. A long, rectangular gabled structure of uncoursed rubble, 60 ft by 20 ft (18 m by 6 m). Records indicate a church here in the C13, though the present remains are probably C15 or later. Primitive windows in the N are probably decadent rather than early, and the cutstone lancet in the S elevation gives a better indication of the church's period. Under the E window is an altar, now baldly mutilated, bearing the inscription: 'Sir Walter Bellew priest, erected this altar in honour of St John the Baptist, the first of Janvarie, Anno Domini 1631'. By 1758 the church was ivy-clad and in ruins.

PUBLIC BUILDINGS

8, 83 DUNDALK COURTHOUSE. 1813–19 by *Edward Parke* and *John Bowden*. An austere and impressive Greek-revival building, situated on a wooded square at the centre of the town and consisting of a severe neoclassical block with a hexastyle Doric portico screening an open entrance hall. Comparable in its striking sculptural impact to Schinkel's contemporary work in Berlin or Smirke's in London. The main structure is of crisp granite ashlar, the portico of Portland stone. The plan follows a popular model, James Gandon's Waterford Courthouse of 1784: a wide entrance hall occupying the full length of one side, two courtrooms opening in parallel off it, with the passage and stairs to the grand jury rooms in between. The entire entrance area is a tall single-storey structure, with the two-storey courtrooms just visible above the principal elevation. These accent the overall geometry of the design.

The finest feature of this building is undoubtedly its portico, nominally derived from Stuart and Revett's *Antiquities of Athens* and a replica of the Thesion. This is, however, no straightforward pattern-book job: the design is far more accomplished and departs dramatically from contemporary portico norms. This sophistication is seen particularly in the decision to set two massive columnar screens *within* the portico; their effect is to lend movement to the façade and to draw the onlooker deep into the hall, where the central staircase is set.

The name most closely linked with the history of Dundalk Courthouse is that of John Leslie Foster, a prominent Irish politician and Louth grand juror whose personal enthusiasm for the Greek revival was responsible for the 1813 contract stipulation that 'the patterns and true proportions of the rules of Grecian architecture as they are to be collected from the ruins of the city of Athens' were strictly to be followed. Such was Foster's involvement with the project that one mid-C19 source attributed the design to him. In fact designs for the building were commissioned from Parke, though Bowden, also of Dublin, was appointed supervising architect. Some time after 1813 Parke quarrelled with Foster, and Bowden assumed full control of the design. Substantial alterations were carried out some time between 1813 and 1819, when the contractor William Moore sued the courthouse overseers for £12,000 on account of alleged additions to the original plan. Among these alterations was the addition of the third and vital columnar screen. The quality of the finished building far exceeds anything in the respective *œuvres* of Parke or Bowden and the input of a third designer – Foster himself – or perhaps the assistance of a London architect, offered during the parliamentary session, is certainly worthy of consideration.

TOWNHALL. 1859–64 by *John Murray*. Originally designed as a 8
corn exchange but sold on completion in 1864 to the Town Commissioners. Two competitions were held for the proposed exchange: the first, in 1857, was won by Murray; the second followed when it was discovered that Murray's building could not be erected for £4,000. It was won by Bellamy & Hardy of Lincoln, but the commission returned to Murray when that scheme also proved too expensive. The result is a substantial two-storey building with an elaborate and now brightly painted

Italianate façade. Brick, with quoined pilasters at the ends and centre and extensive granite trim. Seven-bay frontage of 3:1:3 rhythm. Central porch with two Ionic columns *in antis* and a large pedimented window above. Rusticated ground floor.

111 FORMER GAOL (GARDA BARRACKS). 1845–53 by *John Neville*. An Italianate building of severe grandeur. Grey granite ashlar in the main block flanked by rubble walls with cutstone arches; well sited above a sloping semicircular green. The walls screen two long rubble-built gaol buildings (radiating from the central block), whose quoined chimneys are visible from the street below. The main building is of square shape with projecting corner blocks. Two storeys over a concealed basement. The principal elevation is of five bays, the centre three recessed, screened by a tall single-storey loggia and crowned by a square two-storey tower with a pyramidal roof. Square-headed windows to the ground floor; round-headed above. A deep band of vermiculated rustication provides a base for the building.

MILITARY BARRACKS. Originally Parliament Square, the site of a large linen manufactory erected here by Huguenots in 1737. This was described in 1781 as a 'large square with houses on three sides of it . . . the apartments of which are for the various branches of the business . . . the looms are in the cellars which have large windows even with the ground which occasions light to strike the looms; more buildings are going on about the fourth side and will when finished make it very considerable.' The buildings were occupied by the militia in 1798 and were demolished or remodelled in 1825 to accommodate a full-scale cavalry barracks.

All that survives from the C18 is a plain ten-bay, three-storey terrace with a low hipped roof, situated on the N side of the present barracks complex. This building has been completely remodelled, and the only early detail to survive is a massive Gibbs surround inside the archway at the W end. Six two-storey blocks of rubble and red brick date to the 1825 rebuilding. The barracks was further developed in 1865, when a new church and married quarters were built. Probably also of this date is the handsome clocktower, and the refurbished horse-lines at the S end of the complex.

FORMER LOUTH COUNTY INFIRMARY (MOTOR TAXATION OFFICE). 1834 by *Thomas Smith* of Hertfordshire. An attractive Tudor-Gothic building which closes a short vista from Dublin Street along Stapleton Place. Long two-storey redbrick block with tall sandstone chimneys and projecting gabled end-bays at front and rear. The principal elevation has a single-storey sandstone arcade and a projecting gabled centrepiece with four-centred arch and three-light window. Sandstone hoodmouldings to the windows and arches terminate in unusual cast-iron corbel heads. This uncommon use of metal rather than stone may be explained by the fact that Alexander Shekleton, Chairman of the Board of Governors, was also the owner of Dundalk Iron Works, founded in 1826, eight years before the hospital was built.

At the Dublin Street end of Stapleton Place are three houses in the same Tudor-Gothic idiom, tendered for by Shekleton in 1836 and clearly designed by *Smith*.

SCHOOLS, STATION etc. *See* Tour, below.

TOUR

The first thing the visitor will know about Dundalk is its location, on the main road half-way between Belfast and Dublin. With as yet no more than a ring road, the sheer volume of traffic is the town's greatest disadvantage, making it a dusty and noisy thoroughfare. This is unfortunate, as Dundalk has much to offer those with a taste for architecture and certainly merits a tour on foot. One pleasant feature is the leafy green oases which dispel the monotony usual in Irish street towns.

Bearing in mind the traffic and the historical fact that the town grew from N to S, the best place to begin is at the N, behind St Nicholas (C of I; *see* Churches, above) in ST MARY'S ROAD, a relatively secluded tree-lined street. Immediately behind St Nicholas is ST MARY'S CHURCH AND SCHOOLS, the former a plain eight-bay, lancet hall of rock-faced granite with a high pitched roof and polygonal chancel of 1937 by *Vincent J. O'Connell*; beside it a hodge-podge of C19 and C20 school buildings of which the INFIRMARY has an *opus sectile* window by *Richard King*, also of 1937.

Around the corner, N of the church in NICHOLAS STREET, is the MARIST BROTHERS MONASTERY, formerly CHURCH-HILL HOUSE and one of the very few C18 Georgian houses to survive in Dundalk. This is a three-storey, double-pile block with a five-bay front of red brick and granite trim, refaced *c.* 1940, and a central Doric doorcase of *c.* 1780 taken from William Pain's well-known *Practical House Carpenter* (first published 1758). In a parlour at the rear is a pretty ceiling with 73
rococo birds, squirrels and garlands of flowers. Past more school buildings, tall and warehouse-like, the centre, of 1874, by *John Murray*.

Left to WOLFE-TONE TERRACE, and on l. to LINENHALL STREET, to arrive before St Nicholas Catholic Church (*see* Churches, above) at the N end of Dundalk's main street. This, the long central artery of the town, begins life as CHURCH STREET around the medieval church of St Nicholas, and later expands into CLANBRASSIL STREET, now its greater part. Both streets are largely composed of big three-storey C18 and C19 houses with modern and C19 shopfronts. No. 17 CHURCH STREET makes a good start, the only C18 pedimented doorcase on the entire main street, beside a nice well-preserved C19 shopfront. Opposite St Nicholas is CARROLL'S CIGARETTE FACTORY, a redbrick factory building of 1895 by *S. Stephenson* which occupies the site of Dundalk House, Lord Clanbrassil's and later Lord Roden's residence. The entire W side of CLANBRASSIL STREET marks the E boundary of the C18 demesne which stretched from here westward to Castletown. Next comes CARROLL'S WHOLESALE OFFICES adjoining the factory – a fine Edwardian shopfront, *c.* 1910. Six bays, with a central entrance crowned by a big segmental pediment and flanked by segment-headed windows with pretty neo-rococo cast-iron grilles. Inside, the offices boast a panelled shop with original fittings, including gleaming brass weights and scales.

Church Street now becomes CLANBRASSIL STREET, longer and wider and containing most of Dundalk's commercial premises. As is characteristic of Irish streets, none of the buildings is freestanding, and architectural display is concentrated on the façades. In Dundalk these are particularly bold and ornate and clearly reflect the pretensions of a thriving business community. The upper storeys of No. 63 wear a stuccoed Italianate front of *c.* 1870, with panelled pilasters, bracketed cornice and elaborate window surrounds; consoles, volutes, rosettes and keystones bearing bearded heads abound in this façade. A little further along, No. 70, a High Victorian extravaganza of 1868, is by the County Surveyor, *John Neville*. Five giant arches frame the upper floors of the façade, with balustrade, more keystones and big diamond-shaped reliefs between each storey. Now a hardware shop, No. 70 was designed as a wine store and originally had a rusticated ground-floor arcade. Across the street, Nos. 32–33, Dearys, formerly Pattesons, was the largest and grandest store in C19 Dundalk. Divided into ladies' and gentlemen's departments, with very fine curved glass display windows, plinths, corner quoin pilasters and ball finials of pink and grey polished granite. No. 15, on the same side, is flamboyant, with lugged surrounds, vermiculated quoins, devil-like heads and shell keystones. Facing this is one of the few good recent designs, of 1983 by *F. F. Rodgers*: more than a hint of eastern promise in a row of paired blue-mosaic columns on deep boxy black bases, screening a recessed shopfront. On the same side is the POST OFFICE of 1899 by *Robert Cochrane*, Office of Public Works, stepped slightly back from the building line. An eclectic Tudor-cum-Queen Anne two-storey block, with projecting bay window, shaped parapet and side carriage arch. Next door, the ALLIED IRISH BANK, formerly the MUNSTER AND LEINSTER BANK, of 1930, is an instance of ambitious last-gasp classicism, in brown-red brick with extensive limestone trim. Rusticated basement and, above, a freely treated giant Doric and Ionic order; nice cast-iron grilles.

At this point Clanbrassil Street opens out into the MARKET SQUARE, a welcome break in the street line, laid out by *William Elgee* in the 1740s and the centre of the town ever since. The square focuses to the E on the solemn portico of the Courthouse (*see* Public Buildings, above), answered now by the town TOURIST OFFICE, a small building in the international style, 1984 by *John F. McGahon & Son*, which occupies the site of the C18 markethouse. On the NW corner of the square is the ULSTER BANK of 1898 by *Vincent Craig*, an Italianate building, red brick with granite basement. Diagonally opposite this is the

QUEEN'S HOTEL, originally of 1772, then a plain three-storey block with a low wide hipped roof, remodelled in 1885 to a big four-storey affair with a mansard roof, dormer windows and nice fish-scale slates.

Now S into EARL STREET. No. 3, the DUNDALK DEMOCRAT OFFICES of 1875, is by *Robert McArdle*, a handsome and scrupulously academic Greek Ionic façade. KING BRUCE'S TAVERN, at the junction of Earl Street and Park Street, is also Greek. PARK STREET is modest, with little of individual note but much to recommend it in terms of scale and character. It has one big ambitious façade, like an Italianate town house, the BANK OF IRELAND of *c.* 1845, by *George Halpin* and built very much as a major regional office. It was remodelled by *Millar & Symes c.* 1930. Next door, the PHOENIX BAR is an elaborate late Victorian pub with timber pilasters, stained-glass window screen and wayward quasi-classical detail. Across the street is the ugly five-storey IMPERIAL HOTEL, *c.* 1970, intrusive in scale and detail. A framed photograph in the foyer records the handsome block of late Georgian houses it has replaced.

Returning E through FRANCIS STREET to Roden Place, notice on the l. the fine row of big three-storey houses that is the E side of EARL STREET.

RODEN PLACE, which is dominated by St Patrick's Cathedral (*see* Churches, above), is a veritable enclave of late Georgian Dundalk. On the W is DOUGLAS PLACE, a row of three town houses screened by a small semicircular garden; the centre house, of late C18 date, retains a big pattern-book Doric doorcase and graded roof slates. On the NW corner of Roden Place and CROWE STREET is the former NATIONAL BANK of 1860 by *William Caldbeck*, a pleasant Italianate building whose scale and style blend well with its neighbour, the Townhall in Crowe Street (*see* Public Buildings, above); the banking floor is expressed as a rusticated three-bay arcade, decorated with keystones and vermiculated panels. Doorcases in the outer bays with heavy pediments supported on console brackets. Further E, on the N side of Roden Place, is a good group of town houses, built in 1851 and old-fashioned for their date, with Georgian sash windows, fanlit doorcases and handsome cast-iron balconies. Opposite these are two houses of two storeys over a basement, with C19 shaped gables, a rare survival of early Georgian Dundalk, dating to the 1740s. Behind these stands a very handsome later C19 distillery building of slate and limestone rubble, with redbrick quoins and window surrounds. Dominant central breakfront. At present roof-less, but happily being remodelled by the National Building Agency as a library and cultural centre.

The long vista E from RODEN PLACE, closed by a glimpse of the Cooley mountains, was created in the 1740s and laid out to connect with the former Huguenot Linen Works at the E end of the town. Here are JOCELYN STREET and SEATOWN PLACE, wide and handsome, flanked by rows of C18 and C19 Georgian houses. On Jocelyn Street is a seven-bay, five-storey range in an industrial classical idiom, similar to the distillery behind Roden Place and also being refurbished as a museum. The CONVENT OF MERCY is a large C18 house, of five bays and three storeys, with a Pain-style doorcase. In the front parlour there is a polychrome marble chimneypiece, with mahogany cupboards flanking the chimney breast. The Gothic convent chapel and adjoining five-bay Gothic range were built in 1859 by Thomas Regan, contractor, very probably to the designs of *John Neville*, County Surveyor. Mr Regan and his wife are buried beneath the chapel altar. Jocelyn Street and Seatown Place were further developed after the establishment of the garrison on the factory site during the 1790s (*see* Public Buildings: Military Barracks).

Following the establishment of the garrison on the factory site during the 1790s, the street was further developed.

Turn l. from Roden Place into CHAPEL STREET, passing on the corner the CENTURY BAR, *c.* 1900, with a chateau-style corner turret. The former VISCOUNT LIMERICK GRAMMAR SCHOOL (founded in 1725) was remodelled as a library by *Sir Thomas Manly Deane* in 1902. A rectangular block, with a hipped roof, five-bay front and central eaves pediment, it closes the view from Clanbrassil Street quite well. Across the street on a corner site is the former BOYS TECHNICAL SCHOOLS by *John F. McGahon & Son*, 1935, a stylish modern design in red brick with a high parapet and two blocky shafts flanking a canopied entrance, typical 30s rectangular details. The Christian Brothers Schools, in a more traditional idiom, are also by *John F. McGahon & Son*, *c.* 1950. On the opposite side of Chapel Street, Nos. 58–74, two-storey C19 houses with elliptical fanlit doorcases flanking arched entrances and pretty iron grilles to the windows. Further along is the CHRISTIAN BROTHERS MONASTERY, severe institutional Gothic of 1868, a tall narrow block with a high pitched roof and a central clocktower crowned by a slated spire. The new wing dates from 1908. On the corner with ST MARY'S ROAD, the WELLINGTON SCHOOL is a simple classical two-storey building with a pedimented centrepiece and a nice Regency Gothic house at the rear; *c.* 1810.

Lord Clanbrassil's demesne, filling the whole of the W of the town, kept railway engineers well away from the centre of Dundalk. The STATION is at the SW end, on CARRICK ROAD, and was built to designs of the G.N.R. chief engineer, *N. A. Mills*, in 1894. Further S from here, below the ARDEE ROAD, is the former G.N.R. RAILWAY AND COACH WORKS, a late Victorian complex of long gabled sheds with eaves pediments and blank oculi, managers' houses, a railway hall and terraces of two-storey workers' houses. All typical redbrick railway architecture with extensive yellow brick dressings. In ORIEL TERRACE, near Ice-house Hill in the old Clanbrassil demesne, is a group of interesting houses in the New International style, built in the 1930s by *John F. McGahon & Son* for members of the McGahon family.

FACTORIES

P. J. CARROLL FACTORY. 2 km s. 1970 by *Scott, Tallon, Walker.* 143
One of the best modern buildings in North Leinster and a rare instance of enlightened corporate patronage in provincial Ireland. Firmly within the Modernist tradition of Mies van der Rohe, this is an elegant utilitarian structure which relies for its effect upon harmonious proportions and good-quality building materials. Situated on an open grassy site at the edge of Dundalk's industrial estate, the factory is a low spreading structure of glass, concrete, brick and steel. It is built up by the repetition of a single modular unit, a 67 ft 6 in. (20.6 m) square steel bay legible throughout as a six-bay steel grid, with brick or glass infill and a clerestory floor containing the building's essential services. The entrance front to the Dublin Road reads as a long, tall, single-storey elevation in which the two principal functions of the building, administration and manufacture, are clearly defined. Five modular units, cage-like in glass and bronzed steel, comprise the administrative offices, and, stepped back significantly from the building line, five further modular units, faced with grey brick, screen the factory proper. The latter stretches to the rear considerably further than the glazed office block. In front is a steel sculpture, 'Three mobile shapes', by the German sculptor *Gerda Froemmel.* Inside is a fine collection of modern Irish art. This is a clever and sophisticated building which fits well in its setting and is impeccably maintained.

GEC FACTORY. 1964 by *Michael Scott & Partners.* A nicely conceived design by *Ronald Tallon* which received the RIAI gold medal for design for 1962–4. It is a large rectangular factory block with brick end walls and a long partially glazed entrance front to the Ard Easmuin road. A peristyle of tapered concrete piers runs around the exterior, supporting the roof, which reads as a projecting attic storey. This elegant modern post-and-lintel articulation is echoed in the treatment of the front wall, with concrete uprights and lintels providing the framework for a basement storey of brick and glass and the foundation for a glazed upper storey. This elevation expresses the two-storey administrative area to the front of the factory, while the processing areas to the rear and sides of the building are of double height. The white sheeting panels of the attic register are now tawdry and worn.

ESB TECHNICAL SERVICES CENTRE. 1990 by *Scott, Tallon, Walker.* A recent essay in high-tech modernism, clean, bright and streamlined, which clearly expresses the concerns of the Electricity Supply Board. The administrative offices consist of a long rectangular two-storey block with a cream-coloured grc-and-glass skin and a glazed and recessed double-height reception area. At the rear of the administrative offices are attractive top-lit yard buildings with textured concrete detailing.

NEIGHBOURHOOD

KILCURLEY PARISH CHURCH. 4 km W. Substantial early C19 T-plan church, modelled and extended in 1960 by *W. H. Byrne & Son*. The three-stage battlemented belltower with lancets and quarry glass is of 1876 by *John Murray*. The church is roughcast and the tower is of coursed rubble with limestone dressings.

0080 DUNLEER LO

During the 1830s and 40s Richard Bellew of Barmeath commissioned from *William Deane Butler* plans for ambitious improvements to the village of Dunleer. These proposals envisaged a symmetrical village layout comprising two semicircular crescents, one within the other, on the W side of the main street, whose central axis was a 'proposed' church and road on a line with the existing road to Barmeath. Sadly, nothing seems to have come of the plan: rather than a northern Tyrrellspass, Dunleer today is an ordinary street village that forms part of the busy Dublin–Belfast road.

DUNLEER PARISH CHURCH (C of I). Reputedly built on the site of the ancient abbey of Lann Leire; the present church is a plain four-bay hall of 1830 by *William Farrell*, with a later C19 chancel. The tower adjoining the W end is of more interest and probably dates to the C13, judging from the transitional mouldings of the entrance arch and of the small round-headed window on the first floor. Adjoining the N wall of the nave is a gabled two-bay hall, with pointed intersecting Y-tracery to the window. – MONUMENTS. Inside the tower are fragments of three early medieval incised slabs, each bearing a representation of a ringed cross. – In the nave: Alexander John Henry † 1866 by *Coates*; Catherine Henry † 1822. – S exterior wall of tower: early C18 inscribed shield to the Darly family. – FONT. A small black marble font supported on a single shaft inscribed 'John Singleton Rect^{r} of Dunleer 1732'. – TENISON MAUSOLEUM. E of the chancel, a small rectangular building of C18 date with a fine limestone ashlar façade, bold corner quoins and blocked surround.

ST BRIDGET. Tall early C19 T-plan chapel, with the altar in the long W wall and a three-stage tower and broach spire of 1859 at the E entrance end. The church is harled, with short pointed lancets in pairs; the tower is of rubble with limestone trim. Rich interior, with three galleries supported on wooden cluster-shafted columns and a splendid timber roof boasting an elaborate pattern of individually braced trusses, Caen stone Gothic reredos and side altars, mosaiced chancel and brightly coloured stained glass in the W window. All this dates to a renovation of 1884. – BAPTISTERY, in the leg of the T, enlivened by a font and a carved timber relief, mid-C19, of the Baptism of Christ, after Raphael, signed *Hugh Brown*.

DUNLEER RAILWAY STATION. 1881 by *N. A. Mills*. A modest single-storey, seven-bay gabled block of red brick, with blue and yellow brick trim. Segmental-headed windows and doorcase. Timber canopy to the three central bays.

RATHESCAR LODGE. 3.5 km W. Built as a hunting lodge in the mid-C18 by Anthony Foster, M.P. for Louth and later Lord Chief Baron of the Exchequer, whose main residence was at Collon (q.v.). On his death, his estate was divided between his two sons, John and William, the former Speaker of the House of Commons, the latter Chaplain to the House and successively Bishop of Cork, Kilmore and Clogher. John inherited Collon House and William received Rathescar Lodge, which he proceeded to expand into a more substantial and permanent dwelling. The present house is thus a conglomeration of late C18 and early C19 extensions. The central block, reworked inside, was the original house. It has a two-storey, three-bay front with a shallow attic and is articulated with three blind arches which frame the ground- and first-floor windows; central freestanding Doric porch. Single-bay Regency wings, with tripartite windows in relieving arches, flank the main block. The long S garden front is largely C19, the two central bays projecting forward and fronted by a cast-iron lattice porch.

PHILIPSTOWN CATHOLIC CHURCH. 4.5 km W. Plain little T-plan chapel. Harled, with Y-traceried lancets and a triple lancet window to the N entrance gable.

ATHCLARE CASTLE. 1.5 km S. Stocky four-storey tower house built in the C16 by the Barnewell family, with an adjoining C17 wing, tall and gabled. A plain building, whose only exterior ornament is its limestone corner quoins, in striking contrast to the fine cutstone detail at nearby Roodstown (*see* Stabannan). In the tower house the external stone entrance to the N probably replaces an original entrance on the E side. The spiral stair was located in the SE angle, with garderobe chambers at the SW. Inside, crisp cutstone doors survive, corbels, original timber beams and, the *pièce de résistance*, a large limestone chimneypiece with a pretty border of small flowers set in a hollow moulding and some tree vine-leaf decoration on the base.

STONE HOUSE. 3 km SE. A very handsome gabled three-storey house of *c.* 1760. Five-bay entrance front, with regular sash windows, a finely chiselled limestone pattern-book doorcase and corner quoins. Inside, a symmetrical double-pile plan, with the stair well at right angles to the central hall. Six-panel doors in lugged surrounds. Reputedly built by the Fosters of Collon; described in 1786 as the seat of Mr Owens.

DUNSANY

ME *9050*

ST NICHOLAS CHURCH RUINS. Ireland offers few examples of 35
buildings in the late Middle Ages as close in design and ancestry

as the Plunkett churches at Dunsany and Killeen. They are in fact twin churches, almost as similar in design as the famous twin churches of mid-C 19 Wexford; a third Plunkett church, at Rathmore, makes Dunsany almost one of a set of triplets.

When Sir Christopher Plunkett, Lord of Dunsany and Killeen and builder of St Mary's Church, Killeen, died, in 1445, the manor of Dunsany passed to his second son, Christopher Plunkett, who, together with his first wife, Anna Fitzgerald, built this church soon after. The building is modelled on his father's earlier church; indeed the plans are almost identical, and the same masons appear to have been employed at both buildings. But St Mary's, Killeen, a taller and longer building, is the more elegant and accomplished of the two, while sturdiness is the characteristic of Dunsany.

Though shorter and wider than its prototype, St Nicholas is still an impressive design: a nave and chancel, with a pair of tall, square towers at the W end and a large three-storey residential tower built against the N wall of the chancel. Both the tower house and the W front of the church, with its severe square turrets and machicolated wall-head, give a doughty, formidable character to this monument of later medieval Irish life.

The church is set on a slight rise in beautiful parkland and is surrounded by mature woods: its setting today seems perfect for a romantic monument, but it is quite different from the medieval reality. Something of the robust utility of St Nicholas's Church may be captured if we imagine the long uninterrupted line of its roof – most probably thatched – and indeed, for those who have an eye to details, there is evidence on the long N and S walls of the ingenious, if basic, gutter system of the church. The tops of the walls here dispense with the battlements common in late medieval Irish architecture and are protected instead by a curious system where pairs of flat stone slabs are laid along the top of the wall and incline towards a central gully which connects to projecting rain spouts. This can be seen from ground level as a wavy line at the top of the walls; a bird's-eye view of the gutters can be obtained from the wall-walk on the W gable, which is reached by a spiral stair in the SW turret. Like Killeen the church retains a number of complete and richly traceried windows and some fine monumental sculpture. It is entered by pointed doorways in the N and S walls, that on the S with fragments of moulded colonnettes on its exterior.

The interior is a long rectangular space divided by one heavy chancel arch, here round-headed rather than pointed as at Killeen, but sharing the same oddity of being not placed exactly on the axis between the centre of the nave and the E window. Was this a deliberate oddity, perhaps associated with the position of a rood screen, or simply a piece of botched workmanship replicated in one church on the basis of the other? In St Nicholas the jambs actually project beyond the springing of the chancel arch, as if intended to support a beam or part of a rood screen. Immediately W of this arch the side walls are hollowed out to accommodate lateral chapels – very shallow on the S but quite deep on the N side, where the nave wall is projected on the exterior to provide space. As at Killeen, a mural stair is located within the masonry of the N jamb of the chancel arch and rises, dog-leg fashion, to a gallery above the N side chapel. Though now mostly ruined, the windows of the church have Dec cusped tracery, made of daggers and foiled figures with, on the nave N wall, traces of the beginning of a Perp taste. The tracery of the E window, unlike all the other windows, is formed of a fine-grained yellow sandstone and is evidently a C19 insertion adapted from a pattern similar to the E window at Killeen, though not identical to it. The side mullions of this window are not tied back into the stonework, as are the others and those at Killeen, though the location of the tie stones for the original tracery can be identified clearly on the outside face of the gable wall. When and how this very proficient design was installed is not clear. The SEDILIA of three stalls recessed into the chancel S wall are original: three cusped ogee arches rising from shafts carved with thin moulded colonnettes, with traces of panelling in the spandrels, crocketed finials and, above, a square hoodmoulding ending with carved label stops of a vine-leaf and a human face.

Dunsany scores over Killeen in the higher quality and better preservation of its sculptural monuments. These are the APOSTLE FONT and the PLUNKETT ALTAR TOMB, both in the nave of the church. The font is an octagonal limestone 36
basin supported on a shaft and three-tiered plinth. Each face of the basin is decorated with two carved panels, one large panel to each side and a second smaller panel arranged below on the sloping underside. The octagonal shaft is also carved. On the principal register, the Apostles are arranged two to a panel, each bearing his appropriate emblem and set within ogee niches. The two remaining panels carry the Crucifixion and the *arma Christi*, the elements of Christ's Passion. On the lower tapering register are abstract and interlace designs, together with the pelican as a symbol of the church and a hound and hare. One panel is carved with a diagrammatic network, very similar to the rib-vault of the sedilia at Rathmore. The shaft is decorated with fretwork and with angels bearing armorial shields. It is assumed that the arms aligned with the Plunkett coat of arms are those of Christopher Plunkett's second wife, Joan FitzEustace, and on this basis the font is ascribed to the period 1460–80. The style of the carving is typical of the C15 in its mixture of naturalism and stylization, with ribbing applied indiscriminately to hair, robes and wings.

The Plunkett Altar Tomb, in the N side chapel, carries the recumbent effigies of a knight in full armour and a lady wearing 39
a twin-peaked wimple and a long woollen dress, fluted like a column shaft. Both figures are effectively solid in their modelling. They are presumed to be of Christopher Plunkett, the builder of the church, and Joan FitzEustace, his second wife.

The sides of the tomb are decorated, characteristically for the C15, with a series of crocketed ogee niches in shallow relief, with foliated cusps and armorial carvings in the spandrels. On the E face of the tomb the niches are filled with three unidentified figures, comparable in style to the carvings on the font; the W face carries a scene of the Flagellation, with angels with censers.

DUNSANY CASTLE. As with Killeen Castle, family tradition and old histories place the building of Dunsany Castle in the late C12 and name the builder as Hugh de Lacy. Christopher Plunkett was created Lord Dunsany in 1461, and the plan and proportions of the present castle seem more characteristic of the C15 than the earlier date. Dunsany is a long straggling castle, with, to judge from the thickness of its walls (for all medieval details have long disappeared in C18 and C19 refacings), two fortified towers set parallel to each other, at the E and W ends, and joined by a long straight range. The plan is not dissimilar in layout and extent to Liscarton Castle near Navan, another late medieval fortress, abandoned in the C18 and now a ruin. The larger of these 'castle' blocks extends from the present front door of the house to its extreme W end, which is fortified by two substantial square towers, projecting from the SW and NW corners. Precisely the same arrangement is found at Liscarton. The second 'castle' is marked on the exterior of the present house by a large early Victorian mullioned window, which projects at first-floor level, and by a tall flat turret beside it. At the main-floor level this castle contains the library. A three-storey, three-bay range links the two blocks.

Dunsany Castle has been extended and improved at least four times since the later C18. The start of this work probably dates from the succession of Randall, thirteenth Lord Dunsany, in 1781. His father had become a Protestant, enabling the family to develop their estates and take part in public life. To C18 tastes, old castles were inconvenient, especially in their narrow winding staircases. Lord Dunsany built a new block, behind the linking range, to take an elegant principal staircase and a secondary stair beside it. He also improved the romantic appeal of the house by raising the turrets and decorating their extra height with shallow panels of blind Gothic arcading. As in Johnston's additions to Killeen, the walls were rendered and the window openings were converted to Georgian sashes with pointed tops and pretty intersecting glazing bars. On the entrance front all this detail, except for the tops of the turrets, has disappeared, but the new stair wall and N elevation, which rises over later, low additions, still looks much as it must have done when the work was finished in the later 1780s.

The next agent of change in the history of the house was Elizabeth Kinnaird, whom the fourteenth Lord married as his second wife in 1823. Her brother, the Scottish peer Lord Kinnaird, had recently completed a spectacular neo-Gothic house, Rossie Priory in Perthshire, to the designs of William Atkinson. To Lady Dunsany's taste the delicate later C18

Gothic introduced by her father-in-law must have seemed flimsy and rather tame. Certainly it was in her lifetime that the S and W fronts of the castle took on their present form, with rather solid timber-mullioned windows decorated with cusps and set inside cutstone frames in a taste popularized in the countless Protestant churches erected by the Board of First Fruits in the first thirty years of the C19. This work has been attributed, on stylistic grounds, to *James Shiel*, who was working at Killeen in 1840. The flat projecting oriels and heavy Gothic labels are certainly characteristic of his manner, and it seems likely that it was he who designed the extra lower block, which steps forward slightly at the E end of the house, as well as the boldly detailed castellated gateway and yard wall further E. The single-storey additions at the back of the house, which include an Edwardian billiard room, were built in 1910.

The interiors of the castle seem predominantly of the late C18. The ENTRANCE HALL which connects with the new stair is a delicate mixture of Gothick and neoclassicism, with slender cluster-shafted columns on the walls supporting Gothic arches and pocket vaults, while the flat of the ceiling is decorated with shallow arabesques of plasterwork in a geometrical pattern. The MAIN STAIR offers a similar mixture of styles, with a marble floor paved in squares with the characteristic C18 black marble diamonds at each intersection. The stair itself is spacious, rising in parallel cantilevered flights with broad landings and a wide well in the middle. The tread ends are decorated with slender neoclassical modillion motifs and the banisters have slender, fluted shafts. By contrast the cornice below the landings has a diminutive corbelled pattern, while the ceiling, which is a shallow pointed vault, is decorated with a slender pattern of intersecting arches with a wiggly inner moulding to hint vaguely at cusps. The DRAWING ROOM on the first floor is a regular rectangular space in the link between the two 'castle' blocks. It is decorated with refined neoclassical plasterwork; a deep room cornice of swags, paterae and tripods, and a flat geometrical ceiling, divided after the fashion of Robert Adam into a central symmetrical square with separate rectangular patterns at either end. The C18 plasterwork is attributed to the Dublin stuccoist *Michael Stapleton*.

The DINING ROOM, below the drawing room, is in a heavier taste, with a flat Gothic ceiling divided into panels and heavy six-panel mahogany doors. This is presumably the work of James Shiel and prepares the visitor for more weight in the massively detailed LIBRARY, where the ceiling is decorated in a pattern of octagons and diamonds springing from thirty-six pendant ribbed brackets that run like cresting round the top of the room. The chimneypiece here is framed by three shafts of clustered columns (like beefed-up Batty Langley); the large Perp windows at either end of the room have the heavy shutters that Shiel liked to use, and there is more Perp panelling, faced with the large roll moulding that he and Johnston seem to have copied from Slane Abbey.

It was presumably Shiel who designed the MAIN GATE LODGE on the road between Dunshaughlin and Kilmessan, a miniature square castle with massive Irish battlements, and two heavily battered turrets flanking a four-centred archway with dummy portcullis. This is a strong design with satisfyingly prismatic stonework. Opposite, a WAYSIDE CROSS, erected on a stepped podium, hints at the manorial character of this location in medieval times.

CHURCH OF THE ASSUMPTION. By *William Hague*, 1893–4. A nice unpretentious country church. Low buttressed walls with a tall slated roof, a thin slated belfry perched on the vestry at the E end of the nave, and lancet windows, two to the entrance gable flanking a pointed arch and a statue niche. Inside, a broad hall and shallow chancel, the nave dominated by an open kingpost roof. Three lancets to the chancel. – FURNISHINGS. Pretty polychrome marble altar and reredos, the tabernacle rather like a fanciful Quattrocento church; formerly the altar to a private oratory at Killeen Castle.

9050 DUNSHAUGHLIN ME

One dull long street with a bad bend and a terrible road surface.

ST SEACHNAILL, DUNSHAUGHLIN PARISH CHURCH (C of I). A lone arch from a pointed medieval arcade, an assortment of cutstone fragments and an early C19 church now occupy the site of the early Christian church of St Seachnaill. Abbots are recorded here in the C8 and C9, as are attacks on the place throughout the C12. The large SANDSTONE SLAB mounted onto a low wall beneath the arcade fragment and bearing a carved representation of the Crucifixion is probably a lintel from the entrance to a C10 or C11 single-cell church. The surviving arch is the fragment of a late medieval church which, judging from the remains of several cusped ogee-headed windows, was still a thriving place of worship in the C15 and C16. The modern church was built in 1813 and, as proclaimed by the plaque over the door, was 'rebuilt and ornamented in AD 1847'. It is a plain three-bay hall, with a shallow chancel, Y-tracery windows and, at the W end, a three-stage battlemented tower. – FONT. Inside the church, an octagonal limestone font which in 1740 had a carved and painted canopy, sadly now gone. Five panels of the bowl's upper register are carved with animal and human heads.

CHURCH OF SS PATRICK AND SEACHNAILL. 1982. Large square gabled hall with a wide gabled porch, lit from the side elevations by tall triple-light windows with monolithic mullions. Rough-cast, with asbestos slated roof. The former parish church in the village is an early C19 T-plan church, given a Victorian Gothic remodelling between 1878 and 1882 with the addition of a new front and belfry. Triple-light geometric window to the entrance gable, with cusped lancets to transepts and nave. Renovated *c.* 1940 by *Ralph Byrne*. Unused in 1986.

FORMER UNION WORKHOUSE. 2 km S. 1839–41 by *George Wilkinson*. A large picturesque rubble building situated on the Dublin to Navan road. Originally designed as a five-bay, two-storey governor's house and two long seventeen-bay ranges behind with double-gabled blocks at each end. The masonry is a mixture of limestone and sandstone rubble; the windows have cross-mullions and wavy bargeboards to the upper floor and the gabled roof is punctuated by Tudor redbrick chimneys. In all this it is a routine Wilkinson design. What lends a certain distinction is the enlargement of the governor's block from a five-bay gabled house to a seven-bay range with a tall gabled projection at the W end. This has large mullioned windows with four-centred arches and windows to the ground floor. The resulting asymmetrical effect is a refreshing change from Wilkinson's usually balanced designs. Built to accommodate 400 people. Fever sheds were erected in 1847.

COURTHOUSE. 1799–1802 by *Francis Johnston*. A plain little gabled building situated on the village main street, its only conscious architectural feature a pedimented doorcase flanked by two Doric columns. T-shape plan, with jury rooms at the back and a single courtroom in the main block. It seems almost an insult for the Grand Jury to have asked Johnston for such a cheap piece of work!

DRUMREE CHURCH RUIN. 3 km W. A First Fruits three-stage tower and spire with diagonal corner buttresses and pinnacles. Across the road, DRUMREE RECTORY is of 1879 by *J. F. Fuller*; picturesque manorial style, with tall gables, mullioned and canted bay windows.

ST MARTIN, CULMULLIN. 5 km SW. 1876 by *William Hague*. On a busy street corner in a large town or city, St Martin's might be inconspicuous; located here at a quiet country crossroads it is quite startling. Stylish polychrome Gothic, achieved by a mixture of boulder-faced snecked rubble with red, yellow and blue engineering brick. Also unusual is the alignment of the church; the N wall of the nave serves as the entrance front, with a gabled porch at the W end and a romantic round turret belfry at the E crowned by a conical slated spire. Inside the novelty ends and the typical country chapel reappears: a whitewashed nave and chancel, lit by lancet windows, with a kingpost roof and decorative Victorian glass. – MONUMENT. The Rev. Robert O'Reilly † 1857.

BATTERSTOWN CHAPEL. 4.5 km S. Plain Gothic of *c.* 1830. Long three-bay hall with Y-traceried windows, rough-cast, with rendered corner quoins, bellcote and intersecting Y-traceried windows in the gable ends. Plain, common-sense interior. High altar added by *W. H. Byrne & Son*, 1946. MONUMENTS. J. J. Lynch P.P. † 1842; marble tablet surmounted by a slate obelisk. Elias Corbally † 1837; white marble tablet with a draped urn.

PARSONSTOWN MANOR. 5.5 km S. Small mid-C 18 lodge. Five-bay by two storeys; narrow windows, grouped in the centre, high hipped roof and dormers. Early C19 irregular wings on each side. Simple mid-C18 stair inside.

BALLYMAGLASSON HOUSE. 6 km S. Georgian revival in a mature setting. Long, seven-bay, two-storey house, with a shallow hipped roof and a canted bay for the central three windows on the garden front. Lugged surround and keystone to the front door. Early C19 stables, built of squared rubble, with an elliptical central archway and pediment. An octagon of columns stands N of the house.

BALLYMAGLASSON FORMER CHURCH (C of I). Beside the drive to Ballymaglasson House. 1800. Built with a gift of £600 from the Board of First Fruits. A diminutive church: the hall two bays long, with Y-traceried windows; the tower two storeys high, with blank upper windows and miniature pinnacles. Derelict at the time of writing.

5060

DYSART

WM

5 km SW of Castletown-Delvin

DYSART. A modest country house, but one of considerable architectural quality, built for Nicholas Ogle to designs of *George Pentland* in 1757. Like Richard Castle's Belvedere House, also in Westmeath, Dysart experiments with long, bow-ended reception rooms, only here the plan is more practical, as the house is two rooms deep and the bow-ended rooms are at the back. The house is built into a slope in the ground, which provides a further element of surprise, as what seems on the entrance front to be a fairly straightforward two-storey, three-bay house has lop-sided bows on its end elevations and appears as an impressively tall and elegantly narrow pile at the rear. The entrance front is conventional, with a hipped roof, slightly advanced centre bay and small eaves pediment. From the size of the house there is more than room for four windows across the front instead of three, but Pentland seems to have preferred a preponderance of wall over window, which gives the house much of its quality. Architecture, as self-conscious decoration, is reserved for the central bay, where a Doric doorcase – taken from William Pain's *Builder's Companion* (first published 1758) – is flanked by narrow side-lights, with a Venetian window above and rather too large a Diocletian window squashed into the pediment. This is something of a compromise, and indeed the Venetian window proves to be no more than a niche with side-lights, a device developed by Pearce and Castle and taken over by Pentland. There are many more windows on the narrow end elevations, and then an austere rear façade, with a pedimented two-bay central section flanked by broad blank walls. Such truly three-dimensional design is rarely encountered in rural Ireland.

ROCKVIEW. 1 km S. Tall, three-storey rectangular house with a shallow hipped roof and one massive central chimneystack, looking like a large, early C19 glebe-house, though built as a seat of the Fetherston-Haugh family. The reticent neoclassical style of Francis Johnston and his school comes to mind here. The proportions are Johnstonian, with a very shallow top storey. On the three-bay entrance front, the ground-floor windows are set in shallow arched recesses that have an air of Johnston, and on the N wall the stairhall projects in a semicircular bow. The plan is like that of Rokeby Hall: two rooms deep, with a large rectangular entrance hall opening at its farther end into a drawing room and dining room, with the principal and service stair set alongside each other on the N and a library on the W. Because it has two rooms across the back, the rear elevation has four windows (rather than an uneven number) – once again a Johnston trait.

Within, the decoration is delicate and demonstrates a characteristic Regency mixture of classical and Gothic motifs, with clustered colonnettes and classical entablatures to the doorcases, plaster flower-baskets, arabesques and vine-leaves on the ceilings and handsome mahogany doors with rope-moulded panel frames. Like several of Johnston's smaller houses in Co. Meath, Rockview was extended soon after it was built; a three-bay, two-storey block with a semicircular single-storey bow was added to the S. This is entered through mahogany double doors from the drawing room and is decorated with fluted joinery and neat neoclassical plasterwork. The white marble classical chimneypiece was brought here from Rosmead (*see* Castletown-Delvin). The square stepped porch at the front of the house, with pilasters with incised decoration and marginal glazing bars, was presumably added at the same time.

ST PATRICK, DYSART CATHOLIC CHURCH. 1 km SW. Later C19. Attractive little country church, pleasantly sited on a low rise and vigorously detailed. Cruciform plan, built of textured and snecked limestone rubble with generous ashlar trim and horizontal bands linking its lancet windows. A pinnacled spirelet erupts between two lancets at the centre of the entrance gable, with clasping buttresses flanking the main door below. Inside, the transepts are screened by two arches which continue the nave wall and are supported on E.E. columns. Open timber cross-braced roof; triple-lancet plate-tracery E window.

REYNELLA HOUSE. 4 km SW. Described in 1786 as an 'elegant seat with fine improvements belonging to Richard Reynell', the existing house is said to date from 1793. It is a long, plain, seven-bay, two-storey block, T-plan at the back, with a shallow roof supported on paired corbelled brackets in the manner of Sir Robert Taylor and a wide canted bay in the centre of the entrance front. The doorcase is a refined design in stone, with shallow console brackets. An ample octagonal entrance hall decorated with neoclassical niches is the house's best feature. It is flanked by large drawing and dining rooms, each with a late C18 engraved brass grate signed by a *Mr Clarke*.

REYNELLA PARISH CHURCH RUINS. 4 km SW. 1798. Derelict hall and tower church. Three-bay lancet hall and three-stage tower with a spire pierced by slit windows. Blank N wall and an apsidal limestone rubble chancel. – MONUMENT. Stone igloo-like monument to 'Old Cooke'. Early C19?

ST JOSEPH, TURIN. 6 km SW. 1972. Small and ugly octagonal building, tent-like, with walls of glass and brick and a deep timber fascia. Too metropolitan and unsympathetic in these surroundings. S of this church is the old early C19 chapel, a modest harled T-plan building with tall thin lancets and quoined surrounds.

EDGEWORTHSTOWN

2070 LF

A small country town, laid out in the late C17 by Sir John Edgeworth and famous since the C19 as the home of Richard Lovell Edgeworth, the educationalist and inventor, and of his most accomplished daughter, Maria Edgeworth, the novelist. The S end of the village, towards Edgeworthstown House, still bears the imprint of C18 improvement, while the remainder is late C19 and C20 in character. The curving main street is bounded at the SW corner by a charming row of three two-storey houses with elliptical relieving arches on the principal ground floor and tiny casement windows to the squat upper storey. Closing the street at its S end is the MARKETHOUSE, designed in 1829 by *James Bell*, a local builder and architect much patronized by the Edgeworths, who later became County Surveyor for Longford. It is a two-storey, five-bay block with a hipped roof, harled, with a limestone pedimented centrepiece bearing the Edgeworth arms. Simple and modest in scale, these buildings reflect the Edgeworths' well-intentioned if unambitious patronage of the village. Like the Fosters at Collon, with whom they were friendly, the Edgeworths were not wealthy. Richard Lovell Edgeworth, who described himself as a middling country gentleman, had on his death in 1817 an income of £4,000 per annum. A member of the Irish Committee on Education, he also involved himself in local and national politics, transport engineering, agriculture and architecture. From her father Maria Edgeworth inherited an absorbing interest in the Irish and their way of life, and her novels immortalize the vicissitudes of life on such small rural Irish estates in the early C19.

EDGEWORTHSTOWN HOUSE. Altered and extended beyond recognition, the former home of Maria Edgeworth is now Our Lady's Nursing Home. Architecturally it must always have been a confusing house. Richard Lovell Edgeworth inherited 'a tolerably good old-fashioned mansion' in 1782 and began to remodel it piecemeal almost as soon as he came into his estate. According to his daughter, the old house had been built on an inconvenient plan 'for the sake of preserving one old chimney that had remained from the former edifice'; all its rooms were laid out in a row as a suite of apartments, which she disliked as they lacked the advantage of any passages; and all were small and gloomy, with heavy cornices, little windows and corner fireplaces. The remodelling was ingenious if externally a little incoherent. Most of the new building was complete by 1787, when the Rev. Dr D. A. Beaufort visited the house and noted its unusual plan, but certain alterations, including a pair of flat-roofed extensions to the ground-floor rooms on the S, built to provide an extra space for the library, and a matching conservatory which opened off Mrs Edgeworth's dressing room, were not contrived until 1807, and it was only in 1812 that an oriel window was added to Maria's bedroom in the NW corner of the house. This gave 'a few feet in space with great additional light and cheerfulness', but was badly built and fell off well before the end of the century!

Edgeworthstown House, from J. N. Brewer's *Beauties of Ireland* (1825)

The Edgeworths' entrance faced E. A five-bay, two-storey front with a central recessed porch of Ionic columns *in antis*, and light single-storey canted bay windows on either side. A shallow dentil cornice with a low blocking course was set before a hipped roof, rather too high to be fashionable at its later C18 date. On the S side, the house is longer, of seven bays, with widely spaced windows except at the centre, where three bays are set close together and rise by an extra storey to an eaves pediment. On the W side the rectangular architectural idiom is changed, for here the centre of the front is broken by a slightly projecting and shallow-curved central bay, which adopts the classic mid-Georgian, Irish country-house pattern of superimposed tripartite openings, a Venetian window, a tripartite window and a Diocletian window, set one above the other.

Rising from an undulating parkland, with specimen trees, shrub roses and winding paths about the house, Edgeworthstown was once perhaps the perfect embodiment in

Ireland of the taste of Humphry Repton. Dr Beaufort noted its 'unusual style of large windows with small piers', which made it 'very cheerful'. Today, with no protective belt of trees, no gardens, but concrete kerbstones and a tarmac drive, its charm has vanished almost beyond recall. The house is joined on the N by a succession of plain gabled ranges ending in a small irregular-shaped chapel of 1982 by *Robinson, Keefe and Devane*. Nothing except the general aspect of the entrance front now even suggests an early date.

The novelties of Richard Lovell Edgeworth's interiors included some rooms with curved walls, particularly in the dining room in the centre of the S front, where a curved row of Scamozzian Ionic columns screened the N end of the room, and in the hall, which was originally oval. All of the new rooms have delicate understated cornices reminiscent of the taste of Thomas Cooley, though a room known as 'the Cabinet' and Mrs Edgeworth's dressing room kept their old-fashioned heavy cornices and high keyhole grates of the 1750s. The buoyant sense of the adventure in life and the delight in clever contrivance make Edgeworth comparable to another architectural amateur and inventor at the turn of the century, Thomas Jefferson, whose home at Monticello, Virginia, is hardly less ingenious. Edgeworth's many inventions included leather straps to prevent the spring doors from slamming; a central heating system whereby warm air was admitted into the room from above the chimneypieces; and a pump in the farmyard which carried water to the cisterns in the house and at the same time dispensed coins to beggars in return for a given time at the handle.

EDGEWORTHSTOWN PARISH CHURCH. 1811; renovated 1889. Like Edgeworthstown House, a rather dull building, given interest only by its association with the Edgeworths. Plain harled gabled hall, with the usual blank N wall and a limestone rubble belltower at the W end, crowned by a squat slated roof. A former spire, designed in 1811 with much to-do by *Richard Lovell Edgeworth*, collapsed in the late C19. Several articles by him on the spire survive to tell the tale (*see* p. 62). Inside, Edgeworth family MONUMENTS.

CHURCH OF THE ASSUMPTION. 1869–72 by *William Caldbeck*. Large cruciform Gothic church of limestone rubble, with a tall gable end facing the street, flanked on the W by a tower and spire with pinnacles and lucarnes. The belfry stage and spire are too small for the scale of the rest of the church and look like a parochial economy! E.E. detail, with tall cusped lancets lighting the nave and a four-light geometric window in the entrance gable with paired two-centred arches below. Inside, rich timber cross-braced roof, choir gallery and charming painted organ neatly framing the S window. Apsidal chancel with paired cusped lights filled with vividly coloured High Victorian glass and marble panelling to the walls. The new and modern timber lectern, altar table and chair blend well with the old.

1. *Scenery:* The hill of Slane, Co. Meath, with the old Parish Church of 1513 and the Franciscan College of 1512

2. *Scenery:* Fore Valley, Co. Westmeath
3. *Scenery:* Lough Derravaragh and the river Inny, Co. Westmeath
4. *Scenery:* The river Boyne at Slane, Co. Meath
5. *Scenery:* Lough Ennell from Belvedere, Co. Westmeath

2 | 4
3 | 5

6. *Medieval town:* Carlingford, ruins of the Dominican Abbey, with Slieve Foy, Co. Louth
7. *Villagescape:* Tyrrellspass, Co. Westmeath
8. *Townscape:* Dundalk, Roden Place; from left to right: Courthouse by Edward Parke and John Bowden, 1813–19; Townhall by John Murray, 1859–64; former National Bank by William Caldbeck, 1860
9. *Townscape:* Kells, Headfort Place, with the former National Bank by William Caldbeck, 1852
10. *Townscape:* Moate, Main Street, late Georgian

6	8
7	9
	10

HOTEL

11. *Townscape:* Drogheda, West Street and the Tholsel by George Darley, 1765–70
12. *Townscape:* Drogheda, St Laurence Street: Whitworth Hall by W. J. Barre, 1864, and St Laurence's Gate, probably thirteenth century
13. *Townscape:* Drogheda, air view looking towards the mouth of the Boyne: in the distance the railway viaduct by Sir John MacNeill, 1851–5; left, St Peter by Hugh Darley, 1748, and St Peter, West Street, by J. O'Neill and W. H. Byrne, 1884; in the foreground by the river, St Mary Magdalen's Dominican Church by George Ashlin, 1870–8

14. *Prehistory:* Loughcrew, passage tomb
15. *Prehistory:* Loughcrew, part of passage tomb, viewed from below
16. *Prehistory:* Newgrange, passage tomb

17. Monasterboice, round tower, and West Cross, probably early tenth century, east face
18. Monasterboice, Muiredach's Cross, early ninth century or *c.* 923, west face
19. Kells, South Cross (Cross of Patrick and Columba), eighth century, west face
20. Duleek Cross, tenth century, west face
21. Kells, Market Cross, ninth century, north face

17 | 18 19
20 21

22. Kells, St Colmcille's House, probably early ninth century
23. Monasterboice, Muiredach's Cross, detail of east face showing the Fall of Man and Cain killing Abel, early ninth century or *c.* 923
24. Mellifont Abbey, early thirteenth century, the lavabo
25. Mellifont Abbey, the lavabo, interior of north-east arch

22 | 24
23 | 25

26. Newtown Trim, refectory of the Victorine Abbey and choir of the Cathedral, early thirteenth century
27. Newtown Trim, Hospital Priory of St John the Baptist, early thirteenth century
28. Saints Island, Augustinian Priory, *c.* 1244, east window fifteenth century
29. Duleek, St Mary's Augustinian Priory, late twelfth to fourteenth century

26 | 28
27 | 29

30. Drogheda, St Mary's Hospital Priory, thirteenth century
31. Bective Cistercian Abbey, cloisters, fifteenth century
32. Trim, Augustinian Abbey of St Mary, Yellow Steeple, early fifteenth century

30 | 32
31 |

33. Killeen, St Mary's Church, early fifteenth century
34. Portneshangan, St Munna, Taghmon, fifteenth century
35. Dunsany, St Nicholas's Church, mid-fifteenth century
36. Dunsany, St Nicholas's Church, font, *c.* 1460

33 | 35
34 | 36

37. Mellifont Abbey, chapter house window, fourteenth century
38. Killeen, St Mary's Church, east window, early fifteenth century
39. Dunsany, St Nicholas's Church, Plunkett altar tomb, *c.* 1470
40. Skreen, St Columba's Church ruins, late fifteenth century
41. Stamullen Church, Preston Chantry Chapel, tombs, *c.* 1540
42. Nobber, Cruicetown Church, cross, late seventeenth century

37 38 | 40
39 | 41 42

43. Trim Castle, keep *c.* 1220, walls later thirteenth century
44. Castletown-Delvin, Delvin Castle, thirteenth century or later
45. Drogheda, St Laurence's Gate, probably thirteenth century and later
46. Carlingford, King John's Castle, *c.* 1210
47. Kilcurry, Roche Castle, begun in the 1230s
48. Trimlestown Castle, vaulted hall, probably fifteenth century

43	46
44 45	47
	48

49. Bective Abbey, fifteenth and sixteenth centuries
50. Fore, Benedictine Abbey, church late twelfth century, towers fifteenth century
51. Julianstown, Dardistown Castle, fifteenth and sixteenth centuries
52. Stabannan, Roodstown Castle, fifteenth century
53. Slane, Franciscan College, window, sixteenth century
54. Carlingford, the Mint, window, sixteenth century

49 | 51 52
50 | 53 54

55. Navan, Athlumney Castle, fifteenth and early seventeenth centuries
56. Carstown, 1612 and later
57. Slane, Fennor Castle, early seventeenth century
58. Kilglass, Rathreagh Church, Fox Monument, 1634
59. Newtown Trim, Parish Church, Dillon Monument, 1586

55 | 58
56 | 59
57

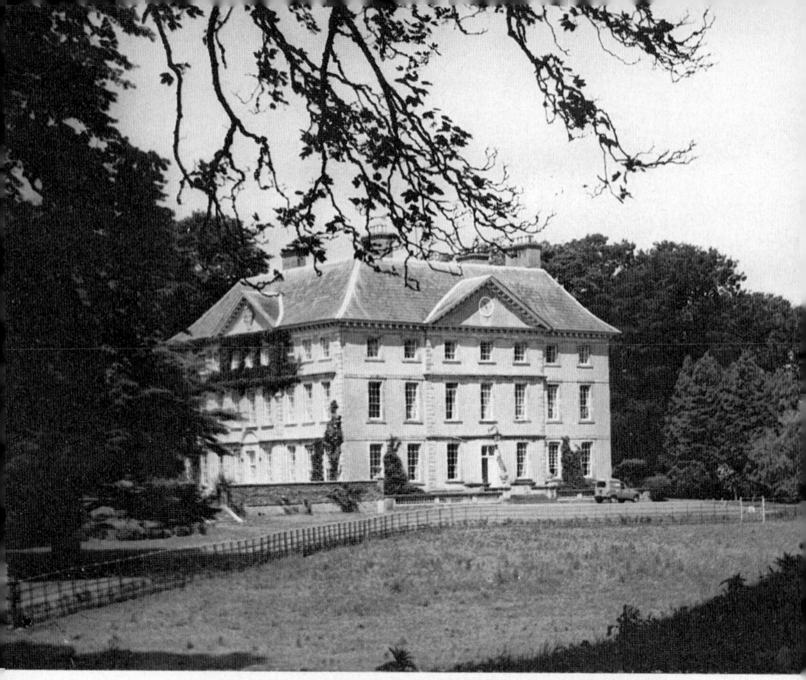

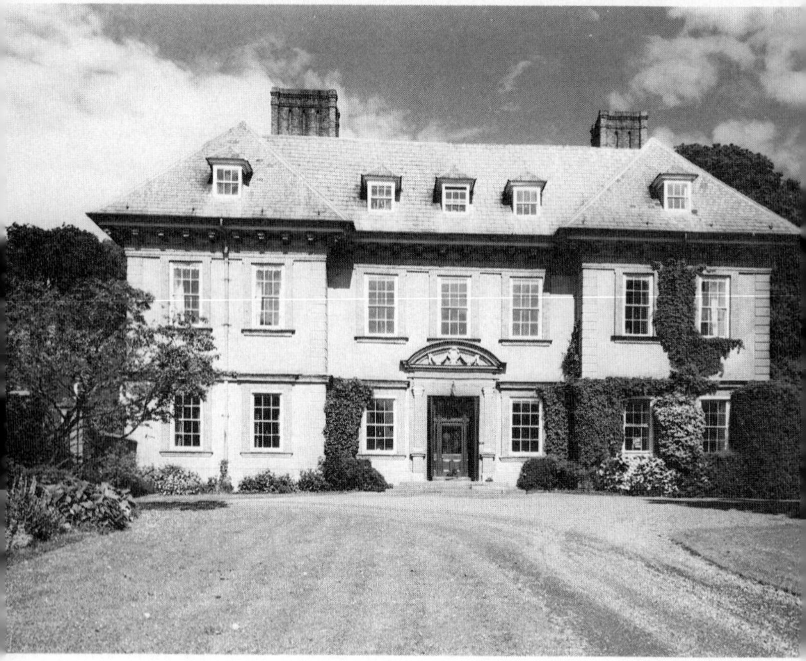

60. Stackallen House, south and west fronts, *c.* 1710–12
61. Beaulieu, west front, possibly 1710–20
62. Beaulieu, front hall, possibly 1710–20
63. Stackallen House, Boyne coat of arms on stairhall ceiling, *c.* 1712

60 | 62
61 | 63

64. Ballymahon, Ledwithstown House, attributed to Richard Castle, 1746
65. Bellinter by Richard Castle, 1750
66. Belvedere by Richard Castle, 1740
67. Molyskar, Tudenham Park, centre of main front, possibly by Richard Castle, *c.* 1743
68. Bellinter, the upper lobby, by Richard Castle, *c.* 1752

64 65 66	67 68

69. Wilson's Hospital, probably by John Pentland, 1759–61
70. Ballinlough Castle, hall, *c.* 1740
71. Drogheda, St Peter, by Hugh Darley, 1748, spire by Francis Johnston, 1780s
72. Drogheda, St Peter, by Hugh Darley, 1748, interior

69 | 71
70 | 72

73. Dundalk, Marist Brothers Monastery, plasterwork, *c.* 1750
74. Dowth Hall, plasterwork in saloon, possibly by Robert West, *c.* 1765
75. Drogheda, St Peter, Henry Singleton monument, by Thomas Hickey, *c.* 1780, and plasterwork of *c.* 1752
76. Drogheda, James Barlow House (Garda Barracks), staircase, 1734
77. Wilson's Hospital, probably by John Pentland, chapel, 1759–61

73 | 76
74 | 77
75 |

78. Headfort House, Great Room, by Robert Adam, 1775
79. Ardbraccan, hall doorcase, by Thomas Cooley, 1774
80. Rokeby Hall, columnar screen in hall, by Thomas Cooley and Francis Johnston, from *c.* 1785
81. Townley Hall, upper stairhall, by Francis Johnston, *c.* 1794–8
82. Townley Hall, entrance hall, looking into stairhall

78 | 81
79 80 | 82

83. Dundalk, Courthouse, by Edward Parke and John Bowden, 1813–19
84. Mullingar, Courthouse, by John Hargrave, *c.* 1824
85. Oldcastle, Gilson Endowed School, by C. R. Cockerell, 1823
86. Athlone Castle, medieval keep, reconstructed *c.* 1800
87. Drogheda, Richmond Fort, martello tower, 1808

83 | 85
84 | 86
 | 87

SCHOOL

88. Slane Castle, Gothic Saloon, probably by Thomas Hopper, 1813
89. Tullynally Castle, seventeenth century, castellated by Francis Johnston *c.* 1806, extended by James Shiel *c.* 1825 and by Sir Richard Morrison 1842–5
90. Killeen Castle, fifteenth century, extended by Francis Johnston from 1802 and recast by James Shiel 1840 (photo of 1962)
91. Barmeath Castle, early eighteenth century, Norman remodelling and additions by Thomas Smith *c.* 1835

88	90
89	91

92. Belvedere, Jealous Wall, probably by Thomas Wright, *c.* 1760
93. Bracklyn House, rockwork gateway, late eighteenth century
94. Castlebellingham, Widows' Houses, probably by William Vitruvius Morrison, 1826–30
95. Kells, Pillar of Lloyd, by Henry Aaron Baker, 1791
96. Ashbourne, Brindley Testimonial, 1880

92
93 | 95 96
94

In Loving Memory
of
CATHERINE CRAIG MacLARNON
AND OF HER HUSBAND
REV. JAMES ERNEST MacLARNON
HE WAS MINISTER OF THIS CHURCH
THEN EMERITUS MINISTER
ALLEN

97. Grange, St James, probably by Thaddeus Gallagher, 1762
98. Grange, St James, interior
99. Edgeworthstown, Corboy Presbyterian Church, mid-eighteenth century
100. Collon Parish Church, interior, by the Rev. D. A. Beaufort, 1810
101. Newtownforbes, St Paul, Clonguish Parish Church, interior, by John Hargrave, 1820

97 | 100
98 | 101
99

102. Kilbixy Parish Church, *c.* 1810
103. Ballinalee, St John, Clonbroney, by John Hargrave, 1830
104. Termonfeckin, Sandpit Church, interior, 1846
105. Dundalk, St Patrick's Pro-Cathedral, by Thomas Duff, 1837, belfry tower by Ashlin & Coleman, 1894
106. Dundalk, St Patrick's Pro-Cathedral, interior

102 103 104	105 106

107. Kilbeggan, Coola Mill, late eighteenth century to *c.* 1840
108. Slane Mill, 1766
109. Killucan, Markethouse, *c.* 1840
110. Athlone, former Great Southern and Western Railway Company Station, by George Wilkinson, 1858
111. Dundalk, former Gaol (Garda Barracks), by John Neville, 1845–53

107 108 109	110 111

112. Castletown Geoghegan, Middleton Park, by George Papworth, *c.* 1850
113. Multyfarnham, Clonhugh Lodge, by William Caldbeck, 1867
114. Charlestown, Cardistown House, by John Neville, 1865
115. Carriglass Manor, by Daniel Robertson, 1838–45
116. Carriglass Manor, staircase, 1843

112	115
113	116
114	

117. Longford, St Mel's Cathedral, by John B. Keane, from 1840, campanile by John Bourke, 1863, and portico by George C. Ashlin, 1889–93
118. Longford, St Mel's Cathedral, interior, by John B. Keane
119. Athlone, St Mary, Athlone Parish Church (East), by John Bourke, 1857–61
120. Grange, St Mary, Boharboy, by John Murray, 1877

117 | 119
118 | 120

121. Clonyn Castle, main stair well, by McCurdy and Mitchell, *c.* 1867–76
122. Clonyn Castle, exterior
123. Castle Forbes, perspective view of the house by J. J. McCarthy from *The Irish Builder* (15 November 1880)
124. Ardmulchan Castle, by Sidney Mitchell, 1902–4
125. Navan, Dowdstown House, possibly by John Lanyon, *c.* 1870

121 | 124
122 | 125
123 |

126. Ardee, Convent of Mercy, by John Neville, 1858
127. Headfort House, Taylour Family Mausoleum, by James Franklin Fuller, 1869
128. Longford, St Mel's Diocesan Seminary, by John Bourke, 1863
129. Mullingar, St Loman's Hospital, by J. S. Mulvany, 1855
130. Mullingar, St Finian's College, by J. J. O'Callaghan, 1902–8

126 | 128
127 | 129
| 130

131. Drogheda, St Peter, West Street, by O'Neill and Byrne, 1884
132. Castletown-Delvin, Church of the Assumption, by G. C. Ashlin, 1873
133. Castletown Geoghegan, St Michael, by T. F. McNamara, 1885

134. Trim, St Patrick, by William Hague, 1891–1902
135. Dundalk, St Joseph's Redemptorist Church, 1890, and Monastery, 1879 and 1881, by George Ashlin
136. Blackrock, St Oliver Plunkett, by Ralph Byrne, 1923

134 | 136
135

137. Mullingar, Cathedral of Christ the King, by Ralph Byrne, 1932–6
138. Mullingar, Cathedral of Christ the King, interior
139. Athlone, Church of St Peter and St Paul, by Ralph Byrne, 1935–7
140. Navan, St Columban's College, chapel by Jones and Kelly, 1934–43

137 | 139
138 | 140

141. Drogheda, St Laurence's Community School, by Michael Scott, 1934
142. Julianstown, Catholic Church, by Liam McCormick, 1982
143. Dundalk, Carroll Factory, by Scott, Tallon, Walker, 1970

ULSTER BANK. Early C20 Queen Anne Revival. Two-storey, five-bay redbrick block with a high hipped roof, dormers, eaves cornice and tall end chimneystacks. Limestone corner quoin strips, sash windows with architraves and a forestanding Doric porch.

NEIGHBOURHOOD

CORBOY PRESBYTERIAN CHURCH. 4 km NW. The typical mid- 99
C18 Ulster meeting house: a big plain harled hall, large high hipped roof and a six-bay entrance front with two round-headed doorcases in simple blocked stone surrounds, each flanked by two large round-headed windows. *c.* 1760 intersecting tracery to the fanlights and to the round top of the sash windows. Founded in 1675, Corboy had a thriving congregation throughout the C18. In 1740 John Wesley addressed 500 people here. Although the present church may incorporate some of the fabric of the C17 building it has clearly been thoroughly reworked in the mid-Georgian period.

CARTRONCAR HOUSE. 4.5 km NE. Ivy-grown two-storey, three-bay house built by the Bond family in 1832, when a joiner deposited a copy of the *Dublin Evening Post* behind the new shuttering.

TULLY PRESBYTERIAN CHURCH RUINS. 5.5 km NE. 1849. The roofless shell of a C19 Gothic church built by the Wilson-Sleators of Whitehill House. Gabled five-bay hall of snecked limestone rubble, with lancet windows, single and paired, and buttresses between each bay. In 1975 the mullions of the E window were donated by Tully Presbyterian Assembly to Multyfarnham Abbey, where they now form the structure of the E window in the Sacred Heart Chapel.

ENFIELD

ME *7040*

Post town on the main road to Kinnegad, Mullingar and the West. The proximity of the Royal Canal gave Enfield some consequence in the early C19, when it had 50 houses and a police station. It has not grown since then and is no more than a line of houses along a crooked street. A substantial group of late Georgian buildings marks its SE end.

JOHNSTOWN. 1.5 km S. Large, handsome house (*see* pp. 46–7), set in flat land with the remnants of C18 planting; the estate is recorded as belonging to a Mr J. H. Rorke, the proprietor of Enfield, in 1837. Johnstown is a square blockish house of *c.* 1750, flanked by a pair of low recessed wings whose ends are advanced to create pavilions decorated with blind Venetian windows. The pavilions have hipped roofs and run back as low, two-storey wings, creating a shallow court at the back of the building. The house, which is double-pile in plan, with the stair in the centre at the back, has a formal five-bay, three-storey front with eaves cornice and high parapet. Two pairs of large chimneystacks give solidity to each gable. The windows are of narrow proportions and the doorcase and fanlight have an unusual moulded and pedimented frame in finely worked freestone.

Though altered in the mid-C19, the interior preserves some six-panel doors and windows with fielded shutters. The rear elevation is irregular and not easily understood today; it appears to have had lunette windows on the upper floor as at Turvey House in Co. Dublin. One room, to the l. of the stair at the back of the house, has a good ceiling of fine rococo plasterwork, with putti, flower-baskets, shells and cartouches. Extensive ranges of stone-built stabling and farm buildings extend to the S.

4080 FINNEA WM

A small and pleasant village situated on a stream running between Lough Sheelin and Lough Inny, which is the boundary between Westmeath and Cavan. Finnea comprises one broad street running gently uphill to a nice two-storey, three-bay house which closes the vista at the top. The street has small trees along its length and a bridge over the county border at the lower end. In stark contrast to this urbane and picturesque atmosphere, Finnea's history, owing to its northerly border location, is a bloody one. In 1331 it was the site of Sir Anthony Lucy's defeat of the Ulster Irish. In 1644 General Monroe routed Lord Castlehaven's army here, and in 1651 Jones and Hewson with the Cromwellian army were victorious over a royalist contingent led by Pheagh Mac Hugh O'Byrne.

OUR LADY OF THE ANGELS, FINNEA PARISH CHURCH. 1 km S. 1904 by *Hague & McNamara*. Small five-bay lancet hall, cement-rendered, with three graded lancets above the entrance arch and pinnacled angle buttresses. Bright interior, with a pointed chancel arch. Ruskinian colonnettes and three lancets to the chancel.

TOGHER CASTLE. 2.5 km E. A luxuriant growth of ivy covers this fragment of a tower house, approximately 22 ft by 25 ft (6.6 m by 7.5 m) externally and built of limestone rubble. All that survives is the high S wall, with windows and window-seats, and traces of the other three sides.

ROSS CASTLE. 6 km ENE. Large tower house with a wonderful location high up on a pine-clad hill overlooking Lough Sheelin. Built probably in the late C15 by John O'Reilly, son of Phelim O'Reilly, heir presumptive to the Lordship of Breffni who had died imprisoned at Trim Castle in 1447. Ross Castle was the O'Reillys' isolated northern retreat, and remained the family seat until the C17. In 1644 Miles O'Reilly was killed during the defeat of the Confederate forces at the battle of Finnea. Having fallen into ruin, the tower was restored in 1864 by Anna Maria Dease, a lineal descendant of the O'Reillys. More recently, in

1970, the castle was thoroughly reconstructed and extended for modern use.

It is now an imposing four-storey tower, built of limestone rubble, with a pronounced base batter and a Victorian (and rather tame) battlemented parapet. The reconstruction is made plain by the regular surface and the pointing of the new masonry, particularly on the W face, where a good deal of the original limestone rubble stands in relief alongside the new walling. Also in 1970 a short flat-roofed, single-storey wing was added to the N side of the tower, connecting it to a second long E wing built into the curved profile of the high perimeter wall. The latter is perhaps the most effective element in the reconstruction, forming a defensive bawn-like enclosure around the tower. Most of the modern masonry is of rock-faced limestone rubble. In the tower proper, windows are few, no more than four to each face. At the base of the SW face is a splayed round-headed loop with pocked tooling to the lintel and jambs. Because of the extensive reconstruction Ross Castle's most impressive qualities are its massive battered profile and its spectacular embattled site. A touch of romance is added in the row of neat whitewashed thatched cottages standing immediately outside the bawn wall.

ROSS HOUSE. 5 km NE. Late Georgian classicism gone C20 rustic. A rectangular two-storey villa, now of bare limestone rubble but probably originally rendered, and probably built *c.* 1820. Principal entrance front of three bays, with big Wyatt windows flanking a tetrastyle Greek Ionic porch and now with large and very curious half-dormer windows on the first floor. These add the rustic touch, as they have been raised to break through the gutter line with segmental or triangular roofs. Originally they were presumably much lower and contained within the space below the eaves. Symmetrical plan, with large drawing and dining rooms flanking the central entrance hall. Simple neoclassical plasterwork. At the rear are extensive rubbled stable ranges, punched limestone with redbrick surrounds.

ST MICHAEL, CASTLETOWN. 3.5 km SE. Substantial T-plan Gothic chapel, built in 1840 and renovated *c.* 1950. Rendered, with corner quoins and Y-tracery sash windows. Limestone Tudor-Gothic entrance arch and a triple-light geometric window above. An awkward and inappropriate modern roof projects over the top of the entrance gable and slices through the transepts, which are rendered at their ends to walls of little more than 6 ft (1.8 m) high. A radical way to treat an old church with roof problems, but the mixture of styles is unsatisfactory. Big, bare, quiet interior, with a later Victorian chancel, pinnacled reredos and matching fittings. – STAINED GLASS. E window: Sacred Heart, Virgin and St Joseph, *Mayer of Munich*, 1902.

CARLANSTOWN CASTLE. 4.5 km SE. The scanty remains of what appears to have been a large C17 fortified bawn, roughly 200 ft (60 m) square, with circular towers at each angle. Like the circular keep of Low's Castle near Tyrrellspass, reputedly built during the Cromwellian Plantation, the towers at Carlanstown, though smaller, had a mural stair rising around a central chamber of three storeys. The only tower to survive stands at the SW corner of the enclosure. Built of limestone rubble, with pronounced base batter, this has a musket loop at ground-floor level and a narrow round-headed window on the first floor. Nothing survives to suggest the presence of a more substantial building within the bawn. In 1702 Robert Nugent, poet and politician, was born at Carlanstown. He was a leading figure in the Irish administration, but his fame rests more upon Horace Walpole's coining of the term 'Nugentize' in reference to Nugent's three successive marriages to wealthy widows.

FOYRAN CHURCH. 6.5 km SE. This hillside churchyard on the lower slopes at Mullaghreen has been the site of a church since the C6, when St Aidan established a community here. The early Christian church, destroyed in the C11, was rebuilt by the Normans when Foyran was granted to the Abbey of Fore. What survives today is the bare bones of a later medieval nave and chancel, with the very distinctive feature of a triple-arched bellcote over the W gable. The arches for the bells are set in a broad rectangular stack of masonry, with two arches surmounted by a third in triangular pattern. They are round-headed and presumably date from the C16. The masonry incorporates some quite massive limestone rubble, perhaps reused from an earlier building. The length of the church, both nave and chancel, is approximately 55 ft (16.5 m); there is some evidence that the chancel may have been barrel-vaulted. – MONUMENT. A wayside cross with a crude incised rendering of the Crucifixion, formerly mounted on the fence beside the road, was at the time of writing lying among long grass, shamefully forgotten.

7060

FORDSTOWN CROSSROADS ME

Crossroads at the centre of an extensive rural area between Kells and Athboy.

GIRLEY CATHOLIC CHURCH. 1 km W. A recently remodelled T-plan chapel whose origins go back to the late Georgian period, to judge from two holy-water stoups inscribed 1797 and 1813. The present walls are perhaps mid-C19, with twinlight Gothic windows to nave and transepts. The new gabled porch has an unsatisfactory modern mullioned window in hardwood, and the church has been given the overhanging eaves and heavy gable boards appropriate to a modern bungalow.

CHURCH OF CHRIST THE KING. 3 km NE, at Cortown. Minimal Romanesque. A seven-bay gabled hall, built to replace an early Victorian T-plan chapel. Gabled entrance front, with five-light window, gabled porch below, and offset belltower with a triple-arched belfry like a campanile. Faced with brown sandstone and limestone trim. Round-headed lancets throughout; inside, a coffered barrel-vault and a round chancel arch.

CORTOWN FORMER CHURCH (C of I). 3.5 km NE. 1847. Originally a small gabled hall of limestone rubble, with a steeply pitched roof and three lancets with quarry glass. Standard Ecclesiastical Commissioners' work. Remodelled *c.* 1960 as a two-storey house.

CHARLESFORT. 4 km NE. 1812. A low rectangular house built by the Tisdall family. Two storeys, over a basement at the back, with a shallow hipped roof. Cement-rendered, with corner quoins and a mid-C19 porch. In July 1813 Richard Chaloner of Kingsfort arrived here only to find the Tisdalls in Dublin and workmen of all sorts merrily employed building, to his mind, 'a very bad house'.

CHAMBERLAINSTOWN HOUSE. 2 km NW. 1907 by *W. H. Byrne & Son*. Neo-Georgian house built for Major Chamberlain. Of two storeys, with large bay windows flanking the front door, a round-headed doorcase and a tripartite window above. Symmetrical plan. The house is built of rock-faced limestone, with redbrick and limestone ashlar trim. In 1918 *Ralph Byrne* made plans to add a baroque porch and a small double-apsed billiard room to the r. of the main façade. The porch has since been removed; the billiard room was never built.

FORE

WM *5070*

Fore is a lovely and evocative place situated at the NW tip of the 2
Pale. A broad marshy valley that lies between two long narrow ridges of high land, on the N the Ben of Fore and on the S a rocky limestone outcrop known as Carraig Bhaile Fhobhar – a northern low-rise counterpart of the hills above Glendalough. 'The town of the spring' is so named because of an underwater stream which runs to Fore from Lough Lene. The monastic ruins here are among the finest in North Leinster, and as at Bective Abbey the evidence for several distinct building periods gives a satisfying sense of continuity. The town grew up around the monastery which was founded here *c.* 610 by St Fechin and which by 630 had a settlement of 300 monks. From the C8 to the C11 both abbey and town were constantly being attacked and were burnt so frequently it seems remarkable that any early building survives. The Church of St Fechin on the S hill-slope dates to the C10. About 1180 Fore found itself a part of Hugh de Lacy's lordship of Meath and the chosen site for a large new Benedictine foundation established by de Lacy as a dependency of the Abbey of St Taurin at Evreux in Normandy. The abbey, which was dedicated to St Taurin and St Fechin, was endowed by de Lacy's son Walter and was probably complete by 1210.

Throughout the C14, as a result of Anglo-French hostilities during the Hundred Years War, the Abbey of Fore, technically an alien property, became a pawn in a confusing struggle of conflicting lay and clerical interests. Greater stability of tenure was established in the C15; in 1449 Parliament proclaimed Fore an independent priory, no longer subject to Evreux. By that time, however, the place had become a vulnerable frontier town, open to constant attack from the Annaly Irish (of modern Co. Longford). In recognition of its exposed position parliamentary grants of murage were made in 1436 and again in 1463. The two surviving town gates probably date to this period. The abbey's aggressive fortifications also came into being at this time, when two successive priors, William England and William Croys, rebuilt the cloister and added two large battlemented residential towers to the complex. For all its former significance the ancient borough, now simple village, of Fore is architecturally unsophisticated. With the exception of the old gaol, which may pre-date 1700, all its buildings are modest C19 structures dotted about a small triangular marketplace and a village green.

CHURCH OF ST FECHIN. Situated high up on the S slope of the valley above the medieval town, the ruins of this C10 church are a remarkable survival in view of Fore's turbulent past. Now a nave and chancel church, it was originally a gabled single-cell building, 38 ft by 24 ft (11.5 m by 7.2 m), to which a chancel, 19 ft by 16½ ft (5.7 m by 5 m), was added in the C12. Of that first church, the W entrance gable, with its antae and trabeated door, is the most impressive feature; antae (prolongations of the side walls beyond the entrance front) are a classic feature of pre-C12 Irish churches, as are massive trabeated doorways. Precise dating is not possible. At Fore the W entrance is particularly strong, surmounted by a massive cyclopean lintel supported on inclined jambs. Carved on the lintel and jambs is a plain broad architrave and in the centre of the lintel a Greek cross with serifs enclosed within a circle. Inside, the much restored chancel arch is a pointed two-centred opening, with a bow-bell moulding of the early C13 terminating on the N side, in the carved figure of a seated monk: an amusing character with large bulging eyes, dressed in a belted knee-length tunic, his feet crossed and his hands resting on his knees. No windows survive either from the C10 or from the C12, and the E window, a single ogee-headed light (formerly twinlight), set beneath a square-headed hoodmoulding with dished or carved-out spandrels, is clearly a C15 insertion. – FONT. C13. At the W end of the nave, an irregular hemispherical limestone bowl, with four projecting bosses around the rim, perhaps originally carved masks or heads. Four half-round ribs run down the sides of the bowl, corresponding to the corner rolls of the shaft on which the font stands.

ANCHORITE CELL. Situated high up on Carraig Bhaile Fhobhar above St Fechin's Church, this building appears at first sight as a picturesque C19 addition to Fore's medieval heritage. A rectangular two-storey battlemented tower adjoined by a low four-bay chapel with a steeply pitched roof, the two enclosed by a regular battlemented boundary wall. Although much indeed is C19 embellishment, the squat rectangular tower is a late medieval structure, probably built in the C15 to replace an earlier cell. Of one storey, over a vaulted basement, the tower has a rounded SW angle and a buttress at the NW corner. A limestone gargoyle projects from the first floor of the S wall. Inside, the vault preserves the imprint of wickerwork centering and the chamber is lit by cusped ogee-headed windows in the E and S wall. The W wall is now a pointed chancel arch opening into the GREVILLE/NUGENT MAUSOLEUM, by *Pugin & Ashlin* and *Sibthorpe & Son*, built in 1867 by the Nugents, who had used the tower for that purpose since 1680. – MONUMENTS. N wall of the mausoleum: a handsome pink sandstone memorial bearing the armorial crest and motto of the Nugents, erected in 1680 by Richard Nugent, Earl of Westmeath, 'for the interrings of himselfe and his successors and also in special memory of Mary Countess of Westmeath, his wife and of Christopher Lord Baron of Delvin, his eldest son'. E wall: the side panel of a grey sandstone table tomb decorated in relief with the Crucifixion, figures and angels. The later inscription, not altogether clear, commemorates Patrick Beglan or Begley †1616, the last hermit of Fore.

TOWN GATES. Situated at the N and S extremities of the village, nestling at the foot of Carraig Bhaile Fhobhar, are two low limestone gate towers, erected probably during the fortification of the town in the mid-C15. A bank roughly 3 ft (0.9 m) high and 3 ft wide runs SW from the S gate up the side of the hill to join a second bank that continues to the N gate. The gates were plain rectangular two-storey structures, each framing an ample round-headed arch. In each case the upper storey has now gone. The S arch preserves the base of a spiral stair in one flank and the N gate has a murder hole and two large internal recesses.

Fore Abbey, from R. O'C. Newenham's *Picturesque Views of Ireland* (1830)

Evidence of C 16 or C 17 repairs is provided by moulded fragments of the original abbey cloister incorporated in the quoins of the S gate.

50 ABBEY OF SS TAURIN AND FECHIN. At the dissolution of the monasteries the Benedictine Abbey of Fore was described as having 'certain castles or towers and other houses or buildings

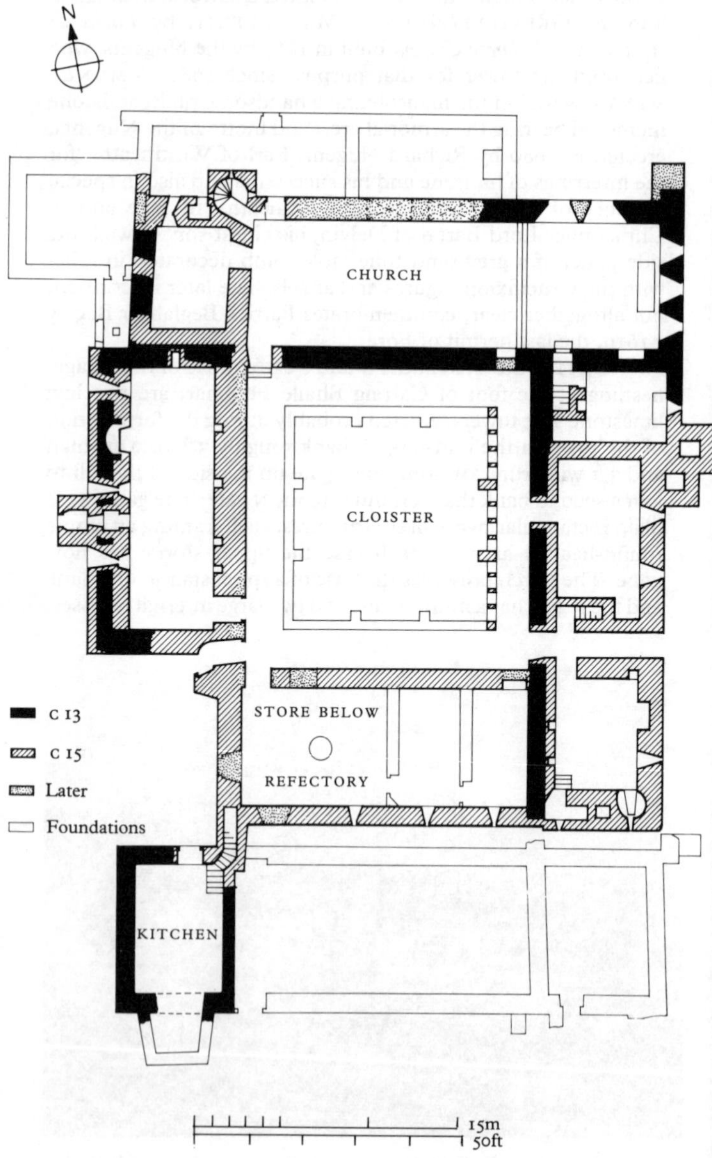

Fore Abbey. Plan

of stone at present in sufficient repair . . . very necessary for the defence of the country against the attacks of the wild Irish on the King's subjects'. Today Fore still wears a strongly fortified C15 appearance. With five staircases formerly providing access to the wall-walk of the abbey complex, and almost half of the monastic buildings built for occupants other than the regular monks, the strategic significance of the place as the NW outpost of the Pale is thrown into sharp relief. When *c.* 1185 Hugh de Lacy established the abbey as a dependency of Evreux, fortification, although significant, was not such a primary concern, and although the abbey was a Benedictine foundation, its buildings followed contemporary Cistercian norms. A large rectangular cloister, bounded on the N by the monks' church, on the S by the refectory, on the E and W by dormitories, offices and the chapter house. Most of the building was carried out by de Lacy's son Walter, probably before 1210. Of those buildings, however, all that survives is the church and part of the W range. In the church the windows of the E gable provide the earliest example in North Leinster of a type of tripartite pattern which was to become common in the later C13. Here are three round-headed, graded lancets, widely splayed to the interior, with a stepped moulded face to the inside wall. On the N wall of the choir are two ruined window openings with similar broad internal splay, and opposite them in the S wall is an aumbry-piscina, a niche framed by two chamfered round-headed arches. The plaster inside the niche is of unique interest, as it appears to preserve the pattern of the painted decoration of the interior of the church. This was once painted in an all-over pattern of white 'bricks', depicted in double bands of a rich blue and with red-brown rosettes in the centre of each brick. As at Bective, the abbey was reduced in scale in the C15: the ranges were remodelled around a new and contracted cloister garth, which was reduced from some 60 ft by 85 ft (18 m by 25.5 m) to the square proportions of 53 ft by 54 ft (15.9 m by 16.2 m); at the same time some 20 ft (6 m) was taken off the W end of the monks' church to provide for the insertion of a new W residential tower. A northern chapel which opened through two arches off the nave was blocked off when the N wall was patched up in 1870; its foundations are still visible from outside the abbey enclosure. Of the other three ranges, only the W wall of the W range occupies its original C13 position, although structurally it too was much remodelled in the C15. The foundations of the former E range survive outside the C15 wall; those of the original refectory lie S of the cloister and E of the kitchen at the SW corner of the abbey.

The principal reason for the reduction of the monastic community was the erratic fortune of the abbey itself, which throughout the C14 when England and France were at war had vacillated in ownership between lay and clerical hands. In 1340, for instance, upon the outbreak of hostilities, the abbey was confiscated by the crown, and part of the revenues were granted to the prior, William Tessone, to support himself and a mere five monks. Only in the C15, and especially after Parliament granted independence from Evreux in 1449, was there any sustained development of the abbey. The responsibility for the remodelling can be attributed to two men, William England, prior from 1418, and William Croys, his successor from 1441. Raids by the Annaly Irish are recorded in 1423 and 1428, and the town's murage grant in the 1430s may well coincide with the start of new building work within the abbey precinct.

The C15 cloister which visitors see today is a reconstruction from fragments unearthed during excavations in 1912. As rebuilt in the angle of the nave and the E range it is an essentially delicate, small-scale late Gothic design. Like many Irish cloisters it was buttressed in the middle, so that the cloister arcade of eight small arches is subdivided into two balanced sets of four, with a thick central pier. Each arch rises from a shafted pier with bell capitals and, as at Bective, cinque-cusping to the inner face of the arcade and random niche and foliage carvings to the spandrels and shafts. The C13 E range, behind the cloister arcade, would once have accommodated the chapter house and monks' dormitories but has been altered for domestic purposes in the C15, and the rooms on both levels have garderobes, chimneypieces and window seats. On the opposite side of the cloister, the W range preserves a section of its barrel-vaulted basement and a good C15 fireplace and garderobe tower in the W wall. At the SW corner of the cloister stand the ruins of the abbey kitchen and beyond it the remains of a small mill and an arched gateway. Outside the enclosure to the NE are the remains of the dovecote, a semicircular structure with three tiers of square recesses providing roosts for almost fifty birds.

The most dramatic features of Fore Abbey are also a legacy of the C15 remodelling: the two bulky towers added as fortification at the E and W end of the church. The E tower consists of three storeys built over a tall barrel-vaulted sacristy with a square garderobe turret at the SE angle, a battlemented parapet and, inside, on the E side of the sacristy, a remarkably steep straight stair leading to the upper storey. The W tower, whose W wall incorporates part of the gable of the C13 church, is a four-storey rectangular structure with a stair turret at the NE corner, a latrine at the NW corner and, inside, fireplaces, cupboards and window seats. The masonry here and throughout the abbey is of limestone rubble, and, although the sacristy stairs seem rough and crudely made, it is generally of good quality, particularly in the W tower stair turret. Here the limestone spiral stair comes to a perfect central point and the window openings are unusual and crisply wrought crossed loops. Although the abbey is patched up and deprived of much of its cutstone detail, its gaunt shell and extensive buildings still communicate some sense of the quality of life in a late medieval monastery built at what its inhabitants understood to be the very limits of the civilized world.

St Fechin, Fore Parish Church. A pretty little church of rock-faced limestone rubble, with a tower and spire flanking the entrance gable. The tower was completed in 1912 by *W. H. Byrne & Son*, who may well have been responsible for the entire design. The nave is a four-bay hall lit by cusped lancets, with a triple lancet window in the w gable. Inside, the chancel has a geometric window filled with Mayer-like stained glass, now partially obscured by modern infill of the pointed chancel arch. Despite this the new screen, articulated as a central chamfered opening with three lancets above, is an effective design which well expresses the special significance of the chancel.

GALTRIM HOUSE

ME *8050*

A delightful miniature country house, designed by *Francis Johnston*, and a formal stablecourt together form a diminutive Regency estate that is both simple and sophisticated: a meeting of vernacular farmhouse classicism with the suave neo-classicism associated with James Gandon. Maurice Craig suggests a twin ancestry for Galtrim in Ivory's Kilcarty (*see* Kilmessan) and Gandon's Emsworth, Co. Dublin. It was built between 1794 and 1809 by the Rev. Vesey Dawson, rector of Galtrim, whose wife was the daughter of Blayney Townley of Townley Hall. Doubtless Mr Dawson's intention was to house his wife in a proper manner, and allowing for the great reduction in grandeur and scale she can hardly have been disappointed. The house is a modest two-storey block, with a hipped roof, a deep limestone cornice and low single-storey wings. Rough-cast and washed in an attractive ochre colour. Four-bay entrance front, the two centre bays stepping forward slightly, with a wide tripartite Doric frame uniting the door and hall windows in a single group. A wide paved area extends before the door. The ground-floor windows in the outer bays introduce a familiar Johnston motif, set in shallow relieving arches with fluted impost courses. The sense of this building being a country house in miniature is confirmed by the garden front, where the usual semicircular bow with three windows – here sash windows extending to the ground – is flanked by large tripartite windows in single outer bays. One curious feature of Johnston's design on this front is the way in which the eaves of the bow are lower than those of the main block and have only a Victorian cast-iron gutter and no stone cornice. This, and the cut-off ends of the cornice over the outer bays, suggests that the bow was originally intended to be thatched, to give the house the picturesque *cottage orné* effect in vogue during the Regency period.

Inside, Johnston makes very effective use of semicircular and elliptical curves. The bow theme is resumed in the entrance hall and the stairhall, both of which have one curved inner wall, and on the first-floor landing, where two doorcases are incorporated beneath a curving segmental-headed archway and again in two semicircular niches in the dining room. Ornamentation is reticent yet pretty; shallow, barely recessed panels, crisply outlined, with scalloped patterning and leopard masks to the dining-room niches. The fireplaces retain some handsome engraved brass grates by *George Binns* of Dublin.

The STABLECOURT immediately to the E has the style and charm of a village markethouse; three long ranges built around a courtyard, with a two-storey, three-bay centre block, arcaded in the ground floor and crowned by a central clocktower.

GATE LODGE. *Johnston*'s original three-bay, single-storey cottage, an object to view across the miniature park, has been enlarged, congruously, into a modern house.

GLANANEA

5060 WM

A sophisticated house, known formerly as Ralphsdale after its builder, Ralph Smyth. The Smyth family, builders of Barbavilla (q.v.) and Drumcree House (*see* Collinstown) early in the C18, had a good record as patrons of quality architecture, and Ralph Smyth continues the family tradition here. The house dates from *c.* 1795 and the architect was *Samuel Wooley*. Ralphsdale has everything one might expect in a late C18 Irish villa: rectangular ample proportions, reticent neoclassical plasterwork and absolute refinement in the joinery and masonry detail. Like Ardbraccan in Co. Meath and Rokeby Hall in Co. Louth, Glananea, though in no way innovative, is a handsome building in a cool neoclassical idiom.

The house is of two storeys over a low basement, with a short concealed attic storey on the E, lit from the side. A parapet hiding the roof enhances the boxy effect. The principal E-facing elevation is perhaps a little old-fashioned, five bays on the ground-floor level, with a wide tripartite doorcase, and six bays above. The centre is slightly advanced, with quoins marking the break and at the corners of the façade. Tall fifteen-pane sash windows light the ground-floor rooms, with twelve-pane windows above. All are set in moulded limestone frames, with the elegant and unusual feature of a segmental shelf-like window sill with bracketed supports. The doorcase is a regular pattern-book affair, a bold Doric aedicule complete with triglyph frieze, entablature and central pediment, flanked by sidelights with pilasters and a full Doric entablature. Formerly harled, the façade was marble-dashed in 1980. The seven-bay, W-facing garden front looks more up-to-date, with the central three bays of the ground floor arched as at Ardbraccan.

The plan of Glananea follows contemporary norms: a large central entrance hall, with a spacious stairhall behind, reception rooms on each side at front and rear, and the service stair accommodated between two rooms on the S side. Symmetry is observed by placing the largest rooms in the house, the drawing and dining rooms, diagonally opposite each other at the SW and NE angles. The ceilings, mostly flat, are decorated in shallow relief with plaster garlands, ovals and medallions, while the joinery has delicate urns, swags and anthemion motifs. A small parlour at the NW angle of the house is unusual in having a shallow vaulted ceiling decorated with fans, scallops and figurative roundels. In the present drawing room, 25 ft by 30 ft (7.5 m by 9 m), N of the hall, the ceiling is prettily ornamented, with a central oval of Aurora encircled by a series of roundels with dancing figures bearing food and drink – no doubt the room was planned as a dining room.

Through the house are mahogany six-panel doors, some inlaid with scallop decoration and framed by jambs and architraves carved with urns and anthemions. Of the chimneypieces, the best are those in the hall and the NW parlour. The former has a yellow and white marble surround framing a lovely limestone ashlar basket grate with a fluted rim; the latter is a polychrome Adamesque design, with a carved central panel depicting the goddess Diana. The first-floor chimneypieces are of timber with applied cast-lead mouldings of sphinxes, garlands and beading.

Though much of Glananea's appeal lies in the quality and completeness of its decoration, the house now lacks its most famous C18 feature, Ralph Smyth's Grand Gate, which according to tradition earned its owner the title of 'Smyth with the gates'. If we are to believe the evidence of a perspective view made by Samuel Wooley in 1796, the title was not unwarranted. Here a tall Corinthian arch, decorated with urns, masks and swags and crowned by a unicorn, forms the centre of a grandiose semicircular sweep. Low Ionic colonnades flanked the arch, ending in tall square piers with carved roundels, statue niches and urns. These in turn are joined to curved quadrants which terminate in Gandonesque pavilions. The gateway was dismantled and moved in the C19 to Rosmead outside Castletown-Delvin, where it still stands. Now simply flanked by low walls ending in urn-topped piers, it is seemingly but a shadow of its former self.

GLASSAN

WM *0040*

Small neat village near the shores of Lough Ree, which serviced the Waterstown estate until its demise in the early C20.

WATERSTOWN. 0.5 km S. Enough survives of this once extensive demesne to give some impression of its former grandeur. One of the largest estates in S Westmeath, Waterstown was the property of the Handcock family: former Dillon lands which had been granted during the Cromwellian settlement to William Handcock of Twyford. About 1700 Handcock's son, also William, moved to Waterstown and began to develop the area. The creation of the Waterstown estate, however, was largely the work of William's son, Gustavas Handcock (1693–1751), and his wife, Elizabeth Temple. About 1740 he enlisted the services of *Richard Castle*, who designed Waterstown House, together with various buildings to ornament the estate's ten acres of pleasure gardens.

The house is now reduced to five bays of its original seven-bay frontage and a short overgrown section of the central spinal wall. Brick-built and faced with cut limestone, it stood three storeys on a basement, with unusually slender window openings. Rectangular, with a roof cornice and parapet. Thinly detailed Gibbsian surrounds to the ground-floor windows look weak and ill-proportioned. Thin lugged surrounds above. What survives of the interior dividing wall displays the classic early Georgian wall treatment: square- and segmental-headed lugged plaster panels and remnants of fielded wainscotting. Traces of a corner chimney can be seen at the NW angle, with a later cross-wall chimney at the E gable end.

The remains of once extensive walled GARDENS stand NE of the house. The entrance has a big ornamental arch topped by a pediment and flanked by single-storey pavilions with quoins, keystones and cornices. All is masterfully executed in red and yellow brick – an early C18 precursor of Victorian polychromy – and a worthy place of pilgrimage for post-modernists. Within the walled garden are a series of round-backed recesses for training vines. – On the hill N of the garden is a small rustic GROTTO, a single-storey, three-bay structure, with a façade of rude rubble stones. Inside is a fireplace in the W wall and three round niches on the N facing the entrance. – MONUMENT. Near the grotto stands an inscribed plaque commemorating the night of 'The Big Wind' and inscribed 'On the 6th January 1839 Ireland was visited with a tremendous hurricane which destroyed much of the fine old timber of this demesne'. – PIGEON HOUSE. *c.* 1749. One of the many monuments associated with the Pearce–Castle school that place an obelisk above an arch. At Waterstown the type is distinctly rustic – most like Mount Mapas on Killiney Hill, Co. Dublin – with a cubic block of rubble stone pierced by four round-headed arches – like the arch of Janus in Rome – with an octagonal tower, blunt spire and weathervane above. The arches are now walled up to make a lofty groin-vaulted room, lit by a door and open oculus on one side. There is a fireplace on the E side. If the building warrants its traditional title the birds must have been housed in the tower on top, which is now blocked up.

EASTHILL HOUSE. 1.5 km SW. Built in 1803 by the Temple family. Modest, single-storey Regency villa adjoined at the rear by a low, two-storey range. The principal block has a hipped roof with bracketed eaves and is rough-cast, with two large Wyatt windows flanking a central door with fanlight. Two large and elegant reception rooms are set on either side of the hall. Simple neoclassical plasterwork. Unusually for this date, the shutters have fielded panels, possibly reused from an earlier building.

HARMONY HALL. 1.5 km NW. Medium-sized country house built *c.* 1800 by a younger son of the Handcocks at Waterstown.

A low oblong block of two storeys over a basement, with a parapet screening a shallow hipped roof. Rough-cast, with limestone trim. Five-bay front, with a tripartite central doorcase surmounted by a segmental fanlight and with a small Wyatt window above. The sash bars have been replaced with plate glass.

LADYWELL. 1.5 km W. 1845 by *Sandham Symes*. Simple but sophisticated Italianate house in the manner of John Nash. Asymmetrical two-storey, six-bay entrance front. L-shaped, with a cast-iron conservatory in the angle, a low hipped roof and oversailing eaves. Composite cement-like facing, channelled to look like cutstone. The windows have flat entablatures with consoles on the ground floor. String-course incorporating the first-floor sills.

PORTLICK CASTLE. 3.5 km NW. Late medieval tower house, built by the Dillons and occupied by them until 1696, when Garret Dillon was attainted under the articles of Limerick. Portlick was then granted to Thomas Keightly, a member of King William's privy council of Ireland, who sold his interest to William Palmer of Dublin. Subsequently Keightly's grant was repudiated and the property, which reverted to the Crown, was sold to Robert Smyth, a descendant of the Smyths of Barbavilla and Drumcree. The family remained here throughout the C 18 and C 19, during which time Portlick has undergone much alternation and gained several additions.

The back of the building perhaps gives the best picture of its evolution. Here the Dillon tower house, a severe, rectangular block, is adjoined by a plain Georgian range, two storeys by seven bays. The tower, probably C 15, is of impressive bulk. Four storeys high, it incorporates within a regular plan four unprojected corner towers. As at Donore Castle, Horseleap, these appear on the exterior only as the thinnest of loops with small first- and second-floor mullioned windows in the central block, giving a harsh defensive character to the castle. The Georgian wing added by the Smyths is gabled and rough-cast, with sash windows on both floors and a centrally placed staircase. About 1860 further changes were made to the castle by Robert Ralph Smyth, who added a large castellated block across the front of the Georgian wing. Portlick's entrance front now reads as two towers joined by a low two-bay Georgian link. The new 'tower' is a two-storey rubble block with stepped battlements and large mullioned windows divided into the traditional late Georgian proportions of a Wyatt window. The original tower has a machicolation chute projecting above the original entrance and many small mullioned windows which appear to have been added during the Victorian rebuild.

CHURCH OF THE IMMACULATE CONCEPTION, TUBBERCLAIR PARISH CHURCH. 2.5 km N. Small, mid-Victorian Catholic church. T-plan and cement-rendered, with lancet windows, hoodmouldings, porches and corner buttresses. A rubble tower adjoins the entrance gable, topped by an octagonal belfry and slated spire. Nice interior, with a panelled ceiling and cross-braced roof truss. Simple early C 20 *art-nouveau*-style decoration. – MONUMENT. The Rev. John Kearney †1861, a large pinnacled niche by *Farrell & Son*.

BALLYNAKILL CASTLE. 2.5 km N. Two walls of a tower house basement storey, with traces of a barrel-vault and fragments of limestone window surrounds.

BENOWN PARISH CHURCH (C of I). 3 km NW. 1822. Simple, two-bay hall adjoined by a three-stage, rubble-built tower with pinnacles. Shallow chancel. Y-tracery windows, triple-light E window and a blank N wall. The interior has box pews.

AUBURN HOUSE. 3 km N. Long, low, two-storey house with a shallow hipped roof, brick chimneys and large sash windows. In the principal five-bay front the windows are set unusually wide apart and the three central bays break forward almost imperceptibly. Conflicting dates are given for the house, 1805 and 1836 (the earlier seems more likely), but sources agree on the builder, John Hogan, a solicitor who acquired the estate from the Napier family in settlement of legal costs!

1060

GORMANSTON CASTLE ME

The Gothic tale of a nobly born child who is banished, left in ignorance of his inheritance and finally restored to honour and his estates became the real experience of Jenico Preston, the builder of Gormanston Castle. The Prestons were one of the ancient Norman families of Ireland; they descended from Philip de Preston, who settled in Ireland in the C 13. His great-grandson became Lord High Chancellor of Ireland and was created Baron Gormanston *c.* 1370. In 1478 the fourth Lord was advanced to the title of Viscount. The Prestons' feudal castle

Gormanston Castle, from J. P. Neale's *Views of Seats* (1823)

and principal seat was at Carberry in Co. Kildare, which survives today as an evocative ruin. In the C17 the Lords Gormanston fell on evil times; the sixth Viscount was outlawed by Cromwell in 1653; he was restored to the title by Charles II, but his son forfeited the honours for adhering to James II in 1691. For a century the Gormanston title lay dormant, until the time of Jenico, the only child of the eleventh Lord, who in 1786, at the age of eleven, instead of inheriting his property, was spirited secretly to France, not to be restored to his family until government action secured his release, shortly before his marriage at the age of nineteen. The abduction of the heir to a forfeited Irish title so excited public opinion that George III not only restored the boy to his lands but in 1800 revived the title as well, recognizing Jenico as Lord Gormanston and premier Viscount in the Irish peerage.

With such a history it is understandable that the earliest account of the castle, published in J. P. Neale's *Views of Seats* (1823), should stress the great antiquity of the house, which it was claimed dated back to 1363. Its appearance now is that of a large Georgian castle, for Lord Gormanston, following the restoration of his peerage, built a grand new entrance front facing S across the end of the old house, which he rebuilt as a five-bay, three-storey castellated elevation. The house was intended to be a massive rectangular block with the tall round towers used in so many late Georgian castles – Ballinlough, Malahide in Co. Dublin, Clongowes in Co. Kildare and Tullynally – marking each corner. A towered Tudor gatehouse of four storeys provides the central focus of the entrance front, with a wide four-centred archway opening into a great hall with an equally wide mullioned window above. The front is nine bays wide, with pointed sash windows in the towers, square-headed elsewhere, all under label mouldings. The parapets are carried forward on a continuous corbel course and have stepped Irish battlements. The architect is not recorded; it is possible that the amateur castle-builder Thomas Wogan Brown had a hand in the design, or it may be an early neo-medieval work by Sir Richard Morrison. In 1820, when Lady Gormanston died, her husband lost his enthusiasm for building, and the W range, which would have completed the rectangle, was never built.

Within, the scale of the castle is impressive if a little bleak. The entrance hall is a huge two-storey room, 40 ft (12 m) deep, with a ceiling of three quadripartite vaults, 29 ft (8.7 m) high, which spring from tapering moulded corbels. It has late C19 oak panelling and a massive chimneypiece decorated with a series of Preston shields carved by *Georgina, Lady Gormanston*, in 1932. The dining room and library, either side of the hall, are spare, rectangular rooms, each 36 ft by 24 ft (10.8 m by 7.2 m), with neoclassical cornices and joinery with the thin applied mouldings that were in vogue *c.* 1800. The dining room has a fine white marble chimneypiece, with two freestanding caryatid figures supporting the transom, and a plaque of the cupid-seller in the centre. The drawing room, on the E front, is a full 40 ft (12 m) long. The stairs are simple and something of an anticlimax after the hall. The house is now a Franciscan college, with large modern extensions on the E side.

GORMANSTON CHAPEL AND YEW CLOISTER. Demolished in the late 1940s. This small rectangular chapel, NE from the house, was all that survived the Georgian rebuilding. It was approached through a 'cloister' of intertwined yew trees which was achieved by training the yews over a wooden frame to form a covered walkway, as in C17 gardens. Some cut-stone fragments of the church survive; chunky mouldings and mullions which suggest the early C17. The lintel of the door bore a 'Jansenist' crucifix, in which the arms of Christ are only partly extended, and a plaque above the door carried the Preston arms and the date 1687.

3080

GRANARD

LF

The most memorable feature of Granard is the great Norman earthwork, the largest in Ireland, which rises up at the W end of the main street, the site of a castle erected here in 1199 by Richard Tuite, who was granted the lands of Granard by Hugh de Lacy. Held by the de Gennevilles and de Mortimers during the C13, Granard was reclaimed in the C15 by the O'Fearghaills and soon became a significant Irish market centre. In 1419 Parliament enacted a statute forbidding English merchants from trading there because of the damage it had caused to the markets of Meath. By the late C16 the town had reverted to the Crown, and in 1618 it was granted with the surrounding lands to Sir Francis Aungier.

Neither castle nor any medieval building survives, and Granard today is a regular Georgian street town which was laid out during the late C18 and early C19. In 1787, when the Rev. Daniel Beaufort visited the place, it was a 'small town with a few neat looking houses and a footbarrack', whose proprietors, the McCartneys, had just recently erected a 'neat markethouse'. Building continued during the ensuing decades, and two wall plaques record the building of Moxhams Street in 1809 and Water Street, erected by Thomas Tuite in 1813. The houses are of the characteristic large-gabled type, two and three storeys high, with sash windows diminishing towards the eaves, fanlit doorcases and the occasional blocked door surround. By the mid-C19 the town had begun to decline and, with the notable exception of St Mary's Church, the townscape has changed little since then.

ST COLUMBKILLE, GRANARD PARISH CHURCH (C of I). Simple gabled hall and chancel, harled, with a four-stage rubble tower at the W end. Originally a C19 Gothic hall; remodelled and extended in 1930 by *Ralph Byrne* to give an C18 rustic classical look, with round-headed openings and a classical doorcase to the tower and round-headed windows to the nave.

ST MARY. 1867 by *John Bourke*. A good building that is made better by its splendid setting at the top of the town's main street, with the great Norman motte behind it. A prime instance both of skilful Victorian stage management and of the great confidence of the Irish Catholic Church in the mid-C 19. The effect is deceptive, accentuating the height of the church and thus exaggerating its overall size. St Mary's, though tall, is in fact quite a small building, a short four-bay nave with two-bay transepts and a short chancel. The tower which flanks the S transept is four storeys high, with tapering corner buttresses, a double-louvred belfry and a broach spire with lucarnes. Built of snecked limestone rubble with punched and ashlar trim. The detail is largely E.E. and exceptionally fine. A group of graded lancets and niches fills the entrance gable, framed by thin stone colonnettes. Cusped lancets in threes and pairs light the aisles and transept, and the E window consists of five cusped lights with geometric tracery. Nice clerestory with paired cusped lancets set in deep embrasures, framed by twin pointed arches on stone colonnettes, giving the effect of the classic E.E. galleried clerestory. The roof, a dominant feature of the interior, is an elaborate structure of hammerbeams and cross-braces, with decorative carved openwork. – STAINED GLASS. N transept: Christ in Majesty. Traditional figure in jewel-like colours; Clarke studios type. – MONUMENT. Ed. Canon McCaver P.P., who built the church, † 1877 aged 82.

MARKETHOUSE. *c.* 1785. Oddly located on a gently sloping site at a right angle to the main street, indicating perhaps that the single-street town plan is a product of the late Georgian period. The classic Georgian market building, two storeys with a low hipped roof, arcaded throughout the ground floor, with regular sash windows on the upper storey. Rendered, with corner quoins and C 19 drip-mouldings to the arches and windows. Built by the McCartneys; by the mid-C 19 it was the property of the Greville family. Described in 1889 as 'a disgraceful old building'; it was refurbished *c.* 1980 and now functions as a branch library.

CONVENT OF MERCY. 1892. Set back from the street at the E end of the town on the site of a workhouse erected in 1842. Conventional institutional Gothic. Long nine-bay front, with gabled projections, quoins, decorative bargeboards, statue niches and pointed windows.

BANK OF IRELAND (former HIBERNIAN BANK). Built in 1933 to designs by *Ralph Byrne*. Irish Georgian Revival. Rendered three-storey, three-bay front, with oversailing eaves. Horizontally channelled ground floor with a large round-headed fanlit door and two round-headed windows lighting the Banking Hall.

ULSTER BANK. 1870 by *Thomas Jackson & Son*. Two-storey, five-bay, gable-ended house, closing the view down a small side street. Typical of Jackson's provincial work, with Italianate bracketed eaves cornice, a first-floor string-course and a deep round-headed doorcase with flanking Doric columns.

NEIGHBOURHOOD

ABBEYLARAGH. 3 km SE. Fragment of an abbey founded here by Richard Tuite in 1211 and colonized in 1214 with monks from St Mary's Abbey, Dublin. Founded as a Benedictine abbey in 1147, St Mary's had adopted the Cistercian rule. In 1540, most of the church at Abbeylaragh was already demolished, and all that survives today is the ruined crossing tower, which was built up after Dissolution using materials from the rest of the building. From this it is clear that the church was a cruciform building and that the tower was supported on four great two-centred arches, of which only one, on the W side, survives complete. The outline of the arch into the S transept is still discernible in the built-up wall, as are the crease-lines of the building's gabled roof. Built into the S wall is a weathered sandstone carving, the subject of which is unclear; it has been identified alternately as a crude representation of the Virgin and Child or a variant of the *Sheila-na-Gig*. The abbey's early demise was no doubt accelerated by its location at the very northernmost tip of the Pale. At the Dissolution the commissioners would not consider visiting the place, for fear of the Irish. The monastic community had apparently been made of stern stuff, as in the year 1318 Pope John XXII received a remonstrance from the northern Irish princes, who complained that the monks at Abbeylaragh hunted the Irish during the day and sang vespers in the evenings.

ST BERNARD, ABBEYLARAGH. 3 km SE. 1958. Tall seven-bay gabled hall, built of rock-faced limestone rubble and ashlar trim. Angular modern lancets in pairs to the nave, with five to the entrance gable, which is narrower and projects forward from the front of the church. Canopied porch carried on four limestone monoliths. At the side of the church a detailed square belltower is crowned by a canopied belfry.

1000 GRANGE LO

97 ST JAMES. 1762, and, as such, one of the oldest surviving pre-Emancipation Catholic churches in the country. All trim and neat and brightly whitewashed. The church today is a long and low T-shaped building with gable ends and slated roofs, though it seems likely that in 1762 it was no more than a very long thin hall with a doorway at either end and the altar in the middle of the long wall. This is the old Catholic plan. Early in the C19 a battlemented sacristy and a plain belfry tower were added to the centre of this long front; about the same time an extra wing was added opposite the altar to convert the church to the
98 common T-plan form. Inside, there are timber galleries in each arm of the building, with fielded Georgian panelling across the front. The two galleries on each side of the altar are identical; that in the leg of the T has taller panels and a different frieze, which suggests a later date. Grange Church is probably the

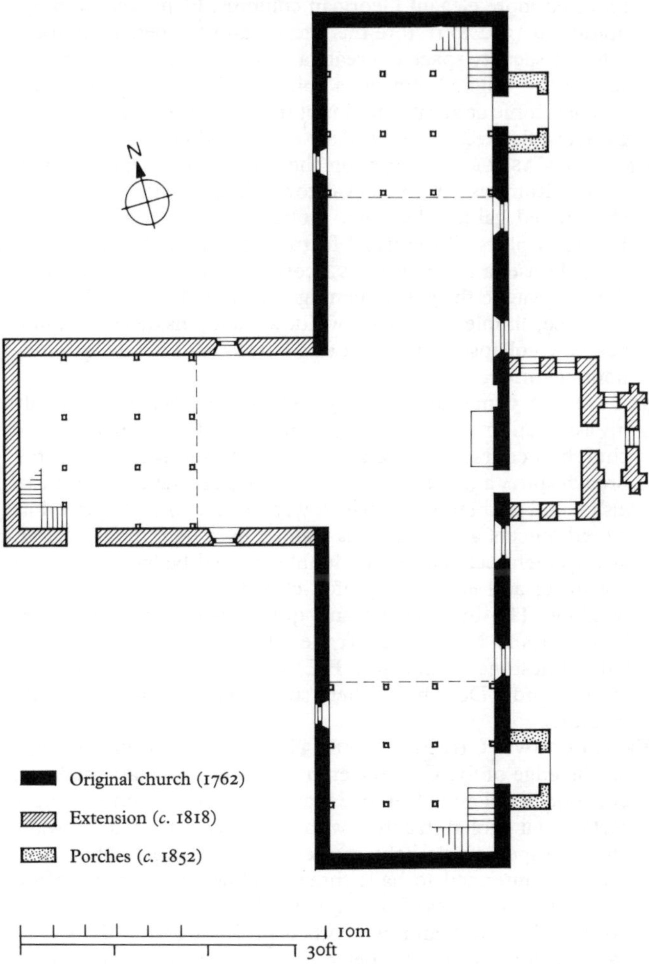

Grange, St James. Plan

work of *Thaddeus Gallagher*, a local builder and architect who is known to have worked at Tullymore Park in Co. Down. His son *James*, who changed his name to *Gallier*, emigrated to America and practised as an architect in New Orleans. In his *Autobiography* James Gallier claims to have reroofed the chapel *c.* 1818, which may be the date of this extra arm, the sacristy and belfry. The church has round-headed windows throughout, with Georgian glazing and pretty fanlights in gabled porches at either end of the long front. The porches themselves have exposed chamfered rafters inside and were added in the mid-Victorian restoration after 1852. The galleries inside are now supported on similar chamfered posts which must have replaced more elegant Georgian columns. Plans were in preparation in 1992 to restore the interior and to open an archway into the sacristy space to create a new sanctuary. Photographs record the original altar as a substantial aedicule with finely detailed Ionic columns, no doubt matching the columns of the galleries, flanked by a pair of six-panelled doors.

BALLUG CASTLE. 1.5 km S, on the E edge of the Cooley peninsula. Ruinous late medieval tower house, with a later and also ruined gabled dwelling, probably late C17, adjoining it. Ballug displays all the usual features of a modest C14 or C15 tower house: a turret at the SE corner housing the spiral stair, the doorway to the stairs opening immediately inside the main entrance, simple slit or loop windows, and, inside (although it has now collapsed), remains of a barrel-vault for the ground-floor chamber.

ST MARY. 2.5 km E, at Boharboy. 1877 by *John Murray*, probably in association with *J. J. McCarthy*. Mid-Victorian Gothic church of coursed local granite, hard and sharp-edged. Its tall broach spire, a C13 type, is visible for miles. Nave with lean-to aisles and a three-stage NW tower. The entrance gable has paired lancets and an oculus framed by a hoodmoulding, an arrangement echoed by the double-louvred belfry. Lancets to the tower and aisles, cinquefoil clerestory and triple lancet E
120 window. The interior tall and quite narrow, with a timber braced roof. Nave and arcade of six two-centred arches with limestone shafts and E.E. capitals. Elaborate Gothic reredos and a Dec choir gallery supported on polished granite columns.

TEMPLETOWN CHURCH RUIN. 3 km SE. Small ruined church on the edge of the Cooley peninsula, with some late medieval cutstone detail and clear evidence of a wooden rood screen. A rectangular gabled structure with entrances in the N and S walls and a cusped single-light window in the E gable, which was evidently intended to have three window embrasures. Inside the church, about 15 ft (4.5 m) from the E gable are two beam-holes in the N wall and two corbels projecting from the S wall, clear evidence of the timber rood screen which once divided the church into a nave and chancel.

2010 GREENORE LO

A small village, distinguished for its plantation of mature pine trees, developed in the late C19 to service the needs of the new Greenore harbour (completed in 1873) and of the Great Northern Railway. The largest building in the village is the former RAILWAY STATION and HOTEL, a monotonous fourteen-bay, two-storey block with the domed mansard roof and dormers beloved of railway kings, a later addition to the original hip-roofed building. Redbrick, with limestone and sandstone dressings. The former station entrance is a single-bay limestone ashlar porch at its W end. S of the hotel there is a street of attractive RAILWAY HOUSES, all of dark rock-faced limestone with brick dressings and completed in 1872. On the E side, a modest two-storey terrace with yellow-brick window and door surrounds; opposite these, more picturesque management houses, all classic railway company architecture, no doubt by *N. A. Mills*, the G.N.R.'s resident engineer; gables, redbrick quoins, string-courses and terracotta dressings. The former schoolhouse, now a bar, is a three-bay gabled hall with an entrance porch at each end. Beside this is the former GREENORE COOPERATION SOCIETY, a two-storey, five-bay house with a lean-to S wing and gabled three-storey N wing; redbrick, with terracotta detail.

GYLES QUAY

LO *1000*

This seaside resort, half-way along the southern shore of the Cooley peninsula between Ballymascanlon and Cooley Point, provides a convenient reference for a scattering of three rural churches and an interesting early classical house. The peninsula itself, one of the most evocative and picturesque regions in Leinster, with dramatic views across Carlingford Lough to the Mountains of Mourne in Co. Down, provides the setting for the culmination of Ireland's most famous Gaelic saga, the legendary *Táin Bó Cúailnge* (*Cattle Raid of Cooley*).

ST MARY, LORDSHIP. 1.5 km NW. 1858–74 by *John Murray*. A tidy plan, like Murray's Dominican Church at Dundalk, but lacking its tower and apse, and on a tiny scale. A high nave opens through paired two-centred arches into shallow transepts and ends in a short chancel. Gothic entrance front with diagonal corner buttresses, triple lancet window and a pointed doorway flanked by lancets. Tenders for carpentry work were advertised in 1858; but in 1874 the Rev. Fr Hughes proposed 'making another effort to complete the unfinished portion of the building' – presumably the transepts and chancel, which are cement-faced in contrast to the coursed yellow granite of the nave. Pretty interior, with modern stained glass. Timber lectern and chair recently designed by *Fr J. Keelan, P.P.*, to match the older altar.

MULLABOY CATHOLIC CHURCH. 3.5 km NE. Lovely situation on a mountain slope overlooking Dundalk Bay. *c.* 1880. Six-bay buttressed hall and two-bay chancel with a bellcote over the entrance gable. All of squared local granite. Tall slender lancets and steeply pitched roof. Bright interior with cross-braced timber roof. STATIONS OF THE CROSS carved by *John Haugh*.

BUSH CHAPEL OF EASE, CARLINGFORD PARISH (C of I). 3 km NE. 1844. Erected by the Upton family of Glyde Court. A tiny church in a heavy idiom reminiscent of *J. J. Lyons*, with very distinctive stepped pinnacles set above a corbel course of big square blocks. Four-bay hall with lower chancel; W porch and bellcote above. Very thin lancets with quarry glass. E window, a triple lancet. Interior with a cross-braced roof and pointed chancel arch. Beside the church is BUSH NATIONAL SCHOOL, probably of similar date. Three-bay schoolroom with a single-bay gabled break-front at one end. Lancets, quarry glass, quoins and tall chimneys.

PIEDMONT. 1.5 km N. Substantial early C18 house erected by Captain Blayney Townley following his marriage in 1692. Later in the C18 it became the property of the Fortesque family. A curious building which, as Maurice Craig has pointed out, displays a combination of primitive planning and construction with several quite accomplished features. Although there is symmetry in the single-pile tripartite plan, the central hall is a room with a corner fireplace and the distinctive triple-gabled rear elevation is a hangover from early C17 building methods. The entrance front, facing S, reveals its early date in the grouping of the five windows in an a–b–a rhythm towards the centre of the façade, leaving a broad mass of masonry at each corner. On the other hand, the stone cornice and door architrave are relatively sophisticated. But Piedmont was certainly an old-fashioned building for its date, with massive chimneystacks; it is later than Beaulieu and other such fashionable houses around Dublin yet quite unconscious of their architecture. Its isolated location among the foothills of the Cooley mountains must largely account for this ignorance.

9040

HAMWOOD

ME

A mid-Georgian house of considerable charm (*see* pp. 46–7), built for Charles Hamilton, agent for the Dukes of Leinster, who lived not three miles distant, though across the county border, at Carton in Co. Kildare. Hamwood, as first inhabited in 1764, was a tall square house of three storeys on a basement, with a high band of uninterrupted wall above the first-floor windows. The entrance was originally at the W end of the house, where a porch opened directly into the staircase. Not long after this square house was completed a pair of quadrant wings – simply curved passages – terminating in small octagonal pavilions was added. These stylish extensions may date from 1783 and add greatly to the quality of the house. Each quadrant has round-headed windows with tall keystones set within a relieving arch and tall finials between. The doors in the pavilions are framed by stone architraves with decorated blocks on the lintels; pine-apple finials decorate their octagonal roofs. The contrast of stone detail and rough-cast walls enhances the architectural character of the house.

In the C19 Hamwood was improved. The Duke of Leinster presented his agent with two pairs of granite steps like miniature *perrons* in front of the octagons, and, when this was done, the W corridor was lined in pine and gained a new tiled floor in a pretty pattern of coffee, pale yellow and cobalt blue. Where the old porch was, an extra wing was added, and all the windows in the house were replaced with plate glass. Substantial Georgian joinery survives inside, and there are three pretty chimneypieces with engraved brass grates made in Dublin *c.* 1800. Office buildings on the W, with a sunk farm road to the N and a garden bridge over it. Pretty gate lodge in an elaborate late C 19 picturesque style.

HEADFORT HOUSE

ME *7070*

A succession of handsome gate piers, surmounted by large ball finials which are blocked in the centre with a band of Greek-key pattern, marks the approaches to Headfort demesne. This is a great house which, in its relationship to the nearby town of Kells (q.v.), recalls the topography of many an English estate, for though Headfort is set at a little distance within its own landscaped park, the big house registers its presence in the ample street that links it with the town, in the spire which the Taylour family added to the Protestant church, and in the neat Courthouse built on a triangular lawn where the road forks to lead to Dublin or to the estate.

Headfort provides a classic and historically interesting example of an English family which profited from the reversal of Irish fortunes in the Cromwellian period. In 1660 the estate was purchased by Thomas Taylour of Ringmere in Sussex, who had come to Ireland in 1653 as an assistant of Sir William Petty, the author and originator of the *Down Survey*, the earliest accurate map of the country, drawn up for the Cromwellian government to facilitate the division and distribution of confiscated lands in Ireland. Petty was paid for much of this work by the grant of land, and it would appear that Taylour was equally fortunate. In 1704 his son Thomas became an Irish baronet, and in 1760 his great-grandson, Sir Thomas Taylour, who had played an active part in Irish politics as M.P. for Kells, was raised to the peerage as Baron Headfort. Within two years he was Viscount Headfort, and in 1766 he became Earl of Bective. In 1800 the second Earl, profiting from the distribution of honours at the time of the Act of Union, was created Marquess of Headfort.

Though the demesne of Headfort has always been celebrated as a landscape of considerable charm, the great house at its centre is plain in its appearance and old-fashioned in its plan. What gives the place a special quality is its setting and the series of suave neoclassical interiors for which *Robert Adam* gave designs between 1771 and 1775. The shell of the house is earlier and provides a good example of the type of enlarged double-pile plan common in English architecture from the later C 17, here rendered in its blandest form as a rectangular block of ashlar stonework, virtually unrelieved by any architectural incident, with two long façades, each eleven bays by three storeys over a sunk basement. On the entrance front the outer pair of bays and the centre three break forward slightly (as at Belan House, Co. Kildare); on the garden side only the centre part of the house is advanced. There are no pediments, only an eaves cornice and blocking course which partly hides hipped roofs and a regular range of chimneystacks. The doorways on each front are marked by plain Tuscan aedicules with half columns, and every window is framed by an architrave, lugged at ground-floor level. The fourth Duke of Rutland, Viceroy of Ireland, described Headfort as 'a long range of tasteless building', while George Hardinge in 1792 aptly characterized its design as 'more like a college or an infirmary'. Long straight ranges of office buildings, rendered, with round-headed windows and slated roofs, extend on a line with either front. Only its size – the main block is 142 ft (43.3 m) long – and the quality of its masonry give the exterior of Headfort some distinction.

The house was built for the first Earl, who succeeded to the estate in 1757 and began gathering material – bricks, slates and stone – for his intended building from 1758. The work went slowly. Though *Joseph Briggs*, the contractor for the masonry, was preparing stone in May 1761, the shell of the house was not completed before 1769, when the scaffolding was taken down. The joists were bought in 1767 and Adam was approached for designs for the interior only in 1771.

If the project was long in gestation, it came into being only after a variety of schemes had been considered. The Earl's father had commissioned designs from Richard Castle, whose plan for a seven-bay, two-storey house on a semi-basement represented a fusion of ideas explored at Summerhill and Bellinter. The scheme would have provided a main block, with a Palladian temple front, set in a deep square courtyard and linked by right-angled corridors to stable and kitchen wings. Castle's draughtsman John Ensor provided a reduced version of this design, eliminating the square courtyard, adding a balustrade at roof level and placing a pilastered order across the whole front. Then in 1765, presumably before work on the present house was far advanced, a sophisticated plan was procured from Sir William Chambers, who proposed a more complex building, with a wide, thirteen-bay garden front, reducing to more villa-like proportions on the entrance façade, where a seven-bay central block, with a high pedimented centre, was to be linked by colonnaded quadrants to stable and kitchen wings. Only after these designs had been considered and rejected – Castle's plan is rather unreasonably noted as 'a damn bad one' – was the present house begun. The Earl had perhaps a more prosaic view of what was needed than any of these architects, for the design that was built, based on a scheme by the Dublin architect *George Semple*, is straightforward to the point of monotony, with five rectangular rooms set in a row across each front and linked by a transverse corridor. The lack of sophistication in the planning is clearly illustrated by the principal staircase; though a handsome design, in mahogany, with Tuscan columns as its balusters, it occupies the front room, immediately to the l. of the entrance hall, and runs awkwardly across four of the windows of the façade. The basement rooms are groin-vaulted and the upper floors have robust joinery, with six-panel doors in lugged surrounds. 'From the thickness of the walls,' commented Arthur Young in 1776, 'I suppose it is the custom to build very substantially here'! It is unlikely that Semple finished Headfort, and the progress of the work was possibly overseen by *Thomas Cooley*, who certainly built the ornamental bridge in the park, added the spire to the church and was probably responsible for the series of architectural gates in the demesne wall.

The *Adam* contribution to Headfort is limited to the entrance hall, the saloon (in the centre of the garden front, immediately behind the hall), the drawing room (a small square room to the W of the saloon), the staircase ceiling, and the Great Room or 'Eating Parlour', E of the saloon. With the exception of the Eating Parlour, none is finished as completely as Adam intended. In the HALL, a room of handsome proportions, 30 ft by 24 ft (9 m by 7.2 m), the ceiling is as Adam designed it: a large oval patera, surrounded by garlands in swags set in an oval border with a repeated anthemion motif and square panels formed out of the border in the middle of each side. Decorated panels in the shape of harpsichord lids with tendrils and the bodies of half putti fill the corners. The stone chimneypiece, with side consoles, is presumably an Adam design but does not match the original drawings of 1771, while mahogany door-cases, used throughout the ground floor, with five fielded panels in each half door, are of a type quite unknown in the Adam office, and must be an alteration introduced by Lord Bective's joiner. The walls of the hall lack the panels of rich neoclassical plasterwork relief which Adam intended. In the MAIN STAIRCASE Adam planned to replace the mahogany stair by a flight of stone steps, with an iron balustrade, and to stop the stair at first-floor level, so that no more than a gallery landing would cross the upper space. This scheme would have provided a clear view of the ceiling, designed in January 1772, a shallow rosette, set in a border with garlanded swags and pendant roundels in the corners, which is the only part of Adam's design to be carried out. Here once again the architect's elaborate decorative wall panels were omitted, though they could never have been made to fit easily with the stair in its present form. The ceiling of the SALOON dates from November 1772 and provides a characteristic example of the architect's solution to the problem of decorating a rectangular space by reducing the area to a pure square and filling it with a symmetrical circular design. A painted roundel fills the centre. It is framed by a wide double border, filled with a delicate open pattern of alternating urn motifs and medallions of antique heads. Long panels of arabesque tendrils complete the ceiling at either end of the room. The DRAWING ROOM has a more open pattern of small roundels, similar to the style adopted in many of the rooms in the Adam brothers' Adelphi development in London.

78 The GREAT ROOM, one of Adam's most lofty interiors, was formed out of four smaller rooms on the garden front, two on the ground floor and two taken out of the bedroom floor above, where blocked windows appear on the exterior. The increase in height creates a remarkable space, which, to judge from the evidence of the Adam drawings, Lord Bective was not at first prepared to build. In 1771 Adam had proposed a room of this character, with one continuous segmental vault rising to a height of some 26 ft (7.8 m). The vault was to be decorated with alternating compartments of oval and rectangular plasterwork and ended in flat wall segments with tripods, arabesques and a circular sculptural plaque. Two chimneypieces on the N wall supported full Corinthian aedicules containing large circular panels of classical figures over the fireplaces. The room was to be hung with pictures, with gilt mirrors on the window wall. For four years this scheme lay in abeyance and it was not until December 1775 that the drawings for the present arrangement were prepared. What is different is that the long vault has been replaced by a high coved ceiling with a rectangular platform at its centre decorated in three square patterns. The original colours were pale ochre, cream and several shades of green. The effect is comparable to the drawing room Adam designed in 1768 for Admiral Parker at Saltram in Devon, and rather more delicate than the first proposal. The paired chimneypieces recur in the room as executed – and are sculpted in very fine white marble – though the aedicules are now without pediments, and painted neoclassical roundels replace the sculpted circular panels of the first design. Adam's drawings envisage large pictures of classical ruins in the style of Panini above the doors and between the chimneypieces but these were never installed, though elaborate plaster frames were formed on the walls. In a house where so many panels of wall plasterwork were omitted it is fortunate that the two long drops of vases, foliage and urns, which Adam set between the chimneypieces and the doors, were completed. Their craftsmanship is exquisite and is apparently the work of the plasterer *John McCullough*.

Arthur Young was appreciative of the improvements made to Headfort by Lord Bective: 'his Lordship's idea is not that of farming, but improving the lands about the house for beauty; for if let, they would be destroyed and ploughed. The grounds fall agreeable in front of the house to a winding narrow vale which is filled with wood where also is a river [the Blackwater] which Lord Bective intends to enlarge; and, on the other side, the lawn spreads over a large extent and is everywhere bounded by very fine plantations'.

Some thirty years after the completion of Headfort, Francis Johnston made a rather tame design for the gothicization of the house, adding stepped battlements above the blocking course and some four-centred Gothic window openings. Nothing came of these proposals, and today *George Semple*'s prosaic façade overlooks a formal terrace with a topiary garden and, beyond, the Earl's enlarged river with two islands formed in it. The garden and much of the planting is the work of the fourth Marquess, dating from the early C20. The BRIDGE to the E is by *Thomas Cooley*, *c.* 1770. The large FARMYARD, a court of two-storey buildings, 280 ft (85.3 m) square and built on a gentle slope, with a walled central area and two stone drinking troughs, was built by the Earl as part of his general scheme of improvements.

TAYLOUR FAMILY MAUSOLEUM. NW of the house. A massively austere octagonal shrine, built to designs of *James Franklin Fuller* in 1869, just one year before the death of the second Marquess of Headfort. Fuller had trained in England in the office of Alfred Waterhouse, whom he had assisted in the design of Manchester Assize Courts, before returning to Ireland in 1862. This solid family mausoleum has the chiselled edges and uncompromised mass of much of Waterhouse's work. Its form recalls the Temple Church, London, or the Round Church in Cambridge – converted to an octagonal form – with a steeply sloped stone roof rising to a buttressed octagonal lantern which supports a high octagonal spire. The openings are short two-light designs with chamfered cusped heads. Every detail is contrived to accentuate the weight of the design: the stone roofs are stepped in horizontal ribs, like the buttresses; the walls are of squared and snecked rubble, rock-faced, and the door, unexpectedly round-headed, is set within a heavy E.E. arch of two registers with paired colonnettes in polished marble. Above, an elongated gable bears a marquess's coronet and the Taylour coat of arms in patterns of blind tracery. The interior is centrally planned, with radiating arched recesses. A gloomy and memorable temple to aristocratic death, set in woodlands and now surrounded by yew trees, briars and ivy. 127

HORSELEAP

WM *2030*

A place memorable for its wonderful name, which is said to commemorate Hugh de Lacy's leap with his horse over the drawbridge of the now vanished Ardnurcher Castle when pursued by his enemies.

HORSELEAP/ARDNURCHER PARISH CHURCH (C of I). Described in 1836 as 'an ancient building in good repair', with a tower and spire which were added in 1822. The account must be mistaken, as the existing building looks nothing more than an early C19 hall and tower church, not unlike those at Coole (*see* Summerhill) and Mayne (*see* Castlepollard). Harled, with a blank N wall, Y-tracery window and a four-centred entrance arch. E of the buildings stands the stump of a ruined limestone gable which may well be the 'ancient' parish church of Horseleap. In 1682 Sir Henry Piers described 'a latebuilt church ... the roof whereof is a most curious frame and according to the new model of architecture'. Owing to particularly sandy soil in this area, the churchyard is a rabbit warren.

SS PETER AND PAUL. 1970 by *Noel Heavey*. Dull modern church in a mixture of cement and brownish brick. Broad gabled hall with an angular three-sided entrance gable, broad single-storey porches and confessionals and long narrow windows to the side elevation. In the central porch is a nice inscribed limestone slab commemorating the building of a former church in 1865.

MEELDRUM HOUSE. 2.5 km E. Tall three-storey late Georgian house with handsome elongated proportions. Gabled and brick-built, rendered over. In 1836 the property of a Mrs Clark. Thoroughly reworked in 1886.

DONORE CASTLE. 2 km E. A very rare instance of an Irish tower house which continued in use as a domestic dwelling from the late medieval period to the mid-C 20. Unfortunately recent neglect has taken its toll and what was for centuries a perfectly habitable building is rapidly becoming a ruin. This is tragic, as Donore Castle is undoubtedly one of the most interesting tower houses in North Leinster. To begin with it is one of the very few towers to have a recorded building date; and the quality and quantity of its dressed stone are unmatched in the Northern Pale. On the S wall a Latin inscription records the building of the castle by Brian Mc Geoghegan and his wife, Catherine O'Connor, in 1598. Brian was the son and heir of Conly Mc Geoghegan, Lord of the Territory of Kinel Fiacha, and Catherine was the daughter of Brian O'Connor, Lord of Offaly, and his wife, Mary Fitzgerald, daughter of the ninth Earl of Kildare. Donore was therefore a stronghold of the old Irish aristocracy.

Despite the dereliction of the interior the tower remains a very substantial structure with part of its pitched roof still peeping over the battlemented parapet. Approximately 30 ft by 40 ft (9 m by 12 m) in plan, it is unusually large, rendered the more massive in effect by the concentration of narrow lancet windows towards the centre of each face, with broad expanses of bare masonry on either of them. The entrance is on the E face. A chimney flue is located in the centre of the S wall; garderobe chute in the W wall. Inside, there were originally four floors above the ground-floor basement. A remarkable iron outer gate, or yett, protects the timber door of the tower. It is set into the outer jambs of the entrance arch and is laid out as a grid of flat iron bars, converting to a simple intersecting tracery pattern at the top.

The cutstone detail at Donore is of the greatest interest. Both the dressing and the carving of the limestone in the doors and windows of the tower demonstrate consummate craftsmanship. The delicate geometrical patterning on the jambs and soffit of the entrance arch is masterly. The stone is punched in a pocked pattern to impost level and then alternatively chiselled and polished in tiers of squares or triangles to give a chequered decorative effect. Above the entrance arch on each side are the carved heads of a king and a bishop; between them, above the apex of the arch, is a circular ornament in shallow relief, like a blind ventilator wheel. Carved spandrels to the windows on the E and N front of the tower employ interlaced motifs which are not dissimilar to the C16 carvings on the Mint in Carlingford. Further details worthy of note are a rope-moulded ventilator wheel and a musket loop with pocked tooling on the E face of the building. On the S face, the inscribed plaque which records the history of the castle was erected in 1809 by Richard Nagle (a seventh-generation descendant of its builder Brian Mc Geoghegan), who in that year had the castle 'restored' and 'cleaned of encumbrances', presumably thus demolishing its bawn and any other outbuildings.

SYONAN CASTLE. 1.5 km N. Substantial four-storey tower house built in the C16 by a branch of the Mc Geoghegan family and thus related to the nearby Donore Castle. Whereas the latter preserves its cement-rendering and cutstone detail, Syonan Castle has long been stripped of these. It is now a plain limestone bulk with base-batter to the walls and large corner stones with pocked tooling. Most of the window openings are now ruined, though a number of plain loops survive. In the reconstruction of the castle of Tyrrellspass two ogee-headed lancets with pocked tooling were procured from Syonan Castle.

The plan of the tower incorporates within its rectangular shape the usual large barrel-vaulted chamber, opening on the E into a N–S vaulted vestibule with a spiral stair at the SE corner. In both chambers traces of wickerwork centering survive. Originally there were two entrances to the tower, the existing opening on the S face, protected by a murder hole in the barrel-vaulted chamber, and a second entrance, now blocked, on the E face, also protected by a murder hole in the entrance vestibule. A garderobe chamber was located at the NW corner of the building. The castle was provided with running water from a stream on its E side.

ST THOMAS, ROSEMOUNT. 4 km NW. *c.* 1850. An attractive Gothic church, nicely located on a low hill site. Like Ballymore Church, this is essentially a big, boxy hall with an elaborate tower in the centre of a showy entrance front. Here, however, the façade is coeval with the church. A pinnacled four-stage tower, with thin octagonal corner turrets, a Tudor-arched entrance and simple pointed lights, is flanked by two short battlemented wings with corner pinnacles and single-light windows at first-floor level. This façade is returned for one bay and then steps back to the body of the church, a six-bay hall lit by tall lancets. Inside, once more like Ballymore, there is an unusual timber ceiling of flat panels with decorative Gothic brackets supporting transverse ribs and three ribbed timber vaults carried as Gothic decoration across the chancel end.

ROSEMOUNT HOUSE. 5 km NW. Diminutive Georgian country house erected by Brian Mc Geoghegan in 1773. Neat rectangular block of two storeys over a basement, with a parapet and blocking course and a more recent dormer roof. Built of coursed limestone rubble with droved ashlar trim. Whoever designed Rosemount was acquainted with the vocabulary of mid-C18 Palladianism. The three-bay, two-storey entrance front displays the familiar arrangement of a pedimented tripartite doorcase with a Venetian window above and sash windows in lugged surrounds to the outer bays.

GROUSE LODGE. 6 km NW. Attractive Regency-style house. Three bays and two storeys, gabled with overhanging eaves. Broad expanses of rendered masonry set off large sash windows, four panes wide by four panes deep. Central fanlit doorcase with side-lights. Symmetrical plan, with two large rooms flanking an entrance and stairhall.

9050

INCHCLERAUN LF

The Longford shore of Lough Ree is a quiet rural area with a wealth of evocative nomenclature: Elfeet Bay, Cow Island, Barley Harbour.

ELFEET CASTLE. 2.5 km E, near the shore of Lough Ree. The ruined and ivy-covered remains of a late medieval tower house. What survives is like a cross-section, showing two storeys over a vaulted basement, with a well-preserved fireplace at first-floor level. Legend has it that this was the home of Forbey, son of Conor Mac Neasa of Ulster, who killed Queen Maeve of Connaught while she was living at 'Grianan Maeve' on Inchcleraun Island. This deed he performed by catapulting a great stone from Elfeet two miles across Lough Ree to where Maeve was seated on the island shore. The story reflects the castle's strategic location as a defensive outpost on the border of Midhe and Connaught.

NEWTOWNCASHEL PARISH CHURCH. 4 km E. Sited on the top of a low hill, with an extensive view over the flat lands of W Co. Longford. Erected in 1833 by the Rev. E. McGaver. Tall plain T-plan chapel of snecked limestone rubble, with a three-storey battlemented tower projecting from the centre of the entrance gable. Raised corner quoins and large lancet windows.

NEWTOWNCASHEL VILLAGE GREEN, the focal point of a small neat village. – SCULPTURE. Abstract bogwood piece by *Michael Casey* of Barley Harbour, 1981.

9050

INCHCLERAUN ISLAND LF

Inchcleraun or Inis Clothrann is an island in Lough Ree due W of Elfeet Castle on the Longford shore. It is about one mile long and at its widest half a mile in breadth. The island is uninhabited and not easy to reach, though boats are available in fine weather from Barley Harbour. Travellers sailing by cruiser down the Shannon are probably the best placed to see the island, and a visit to Inchcleraun will provide a concise prologue to the more spectacular remains of early Christian buildings down the river at Clonmacnoise. Caught in isolation between Connaught and Leinster, it is hardly surprising that Inchcleraun's history and folklore is linked closely with the saga of Queen Maeve and the Ulster campaigns. The place derives its name from Maeve's sister Clothra, and according to tradition the island was the scene of Maeve's death caused by a rock catapulted across the lough from Elfeet Castle (*see* Inchcleraun).

The architectural interest of the island lies in the remains of its early Christian and later medieval churches. A monastery was founded here in the C6 by St Diarmaid, teacher of St Ciaran of Clonmacnoise. Throughout the Middle Ages the monastery received the patronage and protection of the Connaught nobility, but because of its vulnerable island site it was plundered repeatedly by ships from the Shannon. During the C12 Inchcleraun adopted the Augustinian rule and became a notable centre of learning.

The church ruins chart the history of the monastery from the early Middle Ages to the C15. Four churches are located at the E end of the island, with two separate structures to the S, some distance away. The former were enclosed within a protective stone cashel which later gained a Romanesque gateway, fragments of which are preserved inside Teampall Dhiarmada. The building stone appears to have been brought to the island from Longford.

TEAMPALL DHIARMADA. The earliest building on the island, within the cashel, is the church of Diarmaid and has been attributed to the very foundation of the monastery in the C6. Like St Mel's Cathedral at Ardagh, this more probably dates from the C8 and is the structure which replaced an earlier timber church. It follows the classic early arrangement of a rectangular single cell with projecting antae at the gable-ends and a trabeated doorway. This is, however, a tiny building, much smaller than the Ardagh church, measuring no more than 8 ft by 7 ft (2.5 m by 2.1 m) inside: a diminutive structure which must rank among the smallest churches in Ireland.

TEAMPALL MOR. This 'Great Church', the largest of the churches on the island, is certainly the most interesting from an architectural point of view. Directly N of Diarmaid's Church, it consists of a substantial single-cell church, some 47 ft by 22 ft (14.1 m by 6.6 m), adjoined on the NE by a sacristy and chapter house which constituted the E range of a former cloister garth. Of the church the most intriguing feature is the E gable, which has at its centre two thin pointed lancets set in deeply splayed internal embrasures. Though very similar in appearance from within the church, the exterior treatment of these windows is quite different; that on the N is bordered by a broad roll-moulded frame characteristic of the C12, while its neighbour has a much simpler unmoulded surround. A former double-arched piscina, set low down to the r. of the windows in the altar wall, had to be halved in size to accommodate the jambs of the plainer lancet on the S when it was added to the earlier window. Evidence for this change is supplied by the surviving fragment of the central octagonal shaft of the piscina. Adjoining the chancel to the N is the sacristy, a small vaulted room roughly 10 ft (3 m) square, lit by a single ogee-headed cusped light, with dished spandrels and a square hoodmoulding. All typical of the C15. The rectangular room adjoining the sacristy has been identified as the monastic chapter house, while the large first-floor chamber, which incorporates the combined floor-space of both lower rooms, has been described as a refectory. This room is noteworthy for a fine twinlight traceried window at the N end, once again of a C15 character.

The two remaining churches in the group have little architectural impact. The CHANCEL CHURCH is so named because of its division into a distinct nave and chancel; however, like the CHURCH OF THE DEAD it has no clearly datable features. A short distance S of this group is the WOMEN'S CHURCH, also of little architectural interest.

The CLOGAR, or belltower, is situated S of the churches on the highest point of the island. A rectangular structure, with a square tower at its W end and a primitive Hiberno-Romanesque E window, it is considered remarkable for its sharp arrised belfry, built at a time when round towers were the prevailing fashion. The tower's elevated site is a reminder of the constant attacks which threatened the community here throughout the medieval period.

1070 JULIANSTOWN ME

Small village situated on the banks of the Nannywater, with a group of late C19 estate buildings erected by the Peppers of Ballygarth Castle between 1890 and 1903. These begin with a row of picturesque two-storey houses with dormer windows, exposed rafters and red-tiled overhanging porches. Across the street is a small dispensary in similar vein and a large castellated constabulary barracks of 1903.

ST MARY, JULIANSTOWN PARISH CHURCH (C of I). For centuries this church has been remarkable for its exceptional state of repair. Bishop Dopping's visitation of 1685 records that while most other churches in the area were in ruins since 1641 Julianstown was in good repair and although unroofed had seats, a reading desk, a font and a pulpit: clearly the reflection of a zealous local congregation and generous patronage. This still appears to be the case, and the modern St Mary's maintains a polished High Victorian atmosphere. Erected first in 1770, the church has since been restored, rebuilt and enlarged, so that it now appears as a neat Tractarian design of 1861–3 by *Welland and Gillespie*. A low four-bay nave and short chancel, crowned by a steeply pitched roof, with a tower and spire flanking the W gable. Gabled porch adjoining the S wall. The church has lancets, plate-tracery windows and is built of rock-faced limestone with ashlar trim. The present rather bulky tower and spire, replacing Welland and Gillespie's thinner and more elegant design, is of 1910. Inside, fine timber roof with exposed rafters and purlins. Deeply moulded chancel arch with clustered colonnettes of limestone, Caen stone and polychrome marble, 1915. – STAINED GLASS. Opulent pictorial glass commemorating seven officers of the Royal Meath Regiment killed 1914–18. N wall: Christ and Mary Magdalene, 1899 by *Heaton, Butler & Bayne*. – MONUMENT. Maryana Jones † 1830; a slate plaque with marble draped urn.

In the churchyard, set into a low wall, is an intriguing carved frieze of the twelve Apostles, primitive chess-like figures set in a miniature round-headed arcade. Reputedly brought here from a private chapel in the castle of Ballylehane, Co. Laois, seat of the Hovenden family from 1549 to 1820.

FORMER CATHOLIC CHURCH. W of the village, beside the Nannywater. Erected between 1835 and 1837 on a site donated by the Osbornes of Dardistown Castle. Simple, three-bay gabled hall, rough-cast, with Y-tracery windows in limestone surrounds. Four-centred doorway and window to the W entrance gable.

CATHOLIC CHURCH. 1982 by *Liam McCormick*. A handsome 142
church in this architect's big slate roof idiom. Simply a large gabled roof sitting on the ground, with a pointed triangular tower and transept projecting from the S slope and a second, smaller roof intersecting the opposite slope to form confessionals and crying rooms. Completely covered with black asbestos tile, which looks equally well in brilliant sunshine and pouring rain. The interior, which is lit by triangular windows in the N roof slope and a low continuous window at floor level, feels Scandinavian, with exposed timber lining the roof and whitewashed altar wall.

BALLYGARTH CASTLE. 1.5 km E. During the medieval period, Ballygarth and the surrounding lands, as far as Mosney, were the property of the Barnewells, who built here a substantial three-storey tower house and near it a manorial church. Centuries later, following the Restoration, the castle and lands became the property of the Peppers, a family of Jacobite sympathies which received the estate from Charles II and remained here until 1979. Like so many Irish 'castles' Ballygarth reflects its evolution from a medieval stronghold to a modern country seat. Although the house was castellated in 1861 by *William and Thomas Louch*, its several building periods are still easily discerned. The entrance front faces S, with the Barnewell tower house at the W end, adjoining an early C19 entrance tower and then a simple three-bay Georgian block of 1782, barely disguised by its battlemented parapet. The tower house has two square corner towers, set diagonally, each containing spiral stairs. The large rooms on each of its floors are early Georgian rather than medieval in character, particularly the second-floor chamber, which is completely wainscotted, with a crisp dentil cornice and a Kilkenny marble chimneypiece. In the NW tower, shellwork on the underside of the spiral stair is probably the leisurely achievement of some C18 Pepper ladies. Although a link must have existed between the castle and the later Georgian house, the existing three-storey entrance tower is early C19, Gothic in feeling and perhaps enlarged and remodelled around an earlier building. The Georgian house was clearly not designed as an independent entity: rectangular in plan, it comprises on the ground floor a study and drawing room, with a dining room and stairhall at the rear. These rooms have pretty neoclassical friezes with Adamesque urns, swags and roundels. Behind is a large Victorian billiard room added to drawings of *R. J. Stirling* in 1889, with opulent neoclassical decorations and a charming view over the winding river.

BALLYGARTH OLD CHURCH RUINS. In the grounds of the castle. Substantial remains of what must have been the Barnewell manorial chapel. Although a ruin since 1641, large portions of the church remain, with some crisp cutstone detail. Today the whole fabric is endangered by enormous trees which surround the ruins and on occasion fall onto the building. Best-preserved are the tall E and W gables, whose details suggest two dates: the core is perhaps early C14 – see the piscina with nailhead decoration and the single lancet with cusped head in the W gable – while the E gable has evidently been restored in the late C15 or early C16, with a new window of three plain round-headed lights with chamfered limestone mullions set in a pointed window embrasure. This window opening has evidently been reduced in size by building up the lower part as a wall behind the altar. Perhaps the original E window had three tall lancets coming down to the level of the piscina in the SE corner or the windows in the S wall.

Adjoining the E gable are the remains of a lean-to N aisle with a twinlight W window – round-headed again – and near it a carved head projecting from the wall. The W gable is crowned by a massive triple-arched bellcote of a type common in late medieval churches in the Pale.

CORBALLIS. 2.5 km E. Late Georgian house of square proportions; the seat of J. Smith Taylor in 1837. Three bays and two storeys over a basement; rendered, with raised corner quoins and regular sash windows with limestone keystones. Italianate porch with pilasters and round-headed windows. Inside, Victorian plasterwork and elaborate gilded pelmets of *c.* 1870.

51 DARDISTOWN CASTLE. 2 km SW. An intriguing amalgam of medieval and modern buildings. Dardistown begins as a square C15 castle, extended in the later C16 by a wing from one side, which is crossed by a later range at one end – making the plan an elongated T – and culminates in a Victorian remodelling of these mid-Georgian buildings. The castle, erected in 1465 by John Walshe, is a large rectangular tower of four storeys, with four square corner towers that house two spiral stairs, small corbelled chambers and a garderobe on each floor – a plan similar to Sir Thomas Plunkett's castle at Dunsoghly, Co. Dublin. Most windows have been replaced, though two originals survive on the E face, paired double-cusped lights set in

square frames with hoodmouldings and in one case a cross-mullion. Inside, the principal rooms have shallow recesses in the masonry to accommodate open doors. On the W, adjoining the castle, is a plain Georgian range, five-bay, three-storey, lit by long sash windows. Its appearance is deceptive, as the ground floor represents the second major building period at Dardistown, a low single-storey extension added *c.* 1550 and further extended in 1589 by Dame Janet Sarsfield, Lady Dunsany. A plaque above the fine C16 doorway records this work. This door is round-headed and set within a moulded stone frame with a large and elegant hoodmoulding ending in horn-shaped scrolls.

The work above this extension looks late C18. One long staircase window – round-headed – runs through two storeys just before the junction of the wing with the third phase of the building, represented by a long seven-bay range lying at a right angle to the C16 house. This new front was built by the Osborne family, proprietors of Dardistown from *c.* 1600. Formerly it was a handsome Georgian house of *c.* 1760, with one tall storey set over a basement as the land rises to the S, away from the castle. The seven-bay entrance front had a gabled three-bay centrepiece and an Adamesque fanlit door. In the mid-C19 this front was altered by the addition of an extra storey, plate-glass windows and a shallow hipped roof.

CHURCH OF THE SACRED HEART, LAYTOWN. 3 km E. 1979 by *Liam McCormick*. A tall yellow brick gable, with a three-light lancet window and a two-centred arch, is all that remains of the mid-Victorian church. The architect has kept this historical frontispiece as the entrance to a short glass-covered tunnel leading to the new church, which is a low, white roughcast building of an irregular circular shape. The plan of the interior is like a fish – plaice-shaped – neatly arranged as a central nave with the confessionals, crying rooms and vestry unobtrusively located in the crescents of accommodation at each side. Ronchamps-style punch-out doors and windows to the curving nave walls. Dramatic shafted lighting around the side walls is provided by a hidden slatted clerestory in the roof. The focus of the church lies in the altar and E window located directly opposite the entrance. Here glass runs from floor to ceiling, with a rude cross placed centrally *outside* the building, and beyond is the sea and the sky. There is here a sense of quietude and spirituality that is sadly rare in modern Irish churches.

PILLTOWN HOUSE. 2.5 km N. Handsome neoclassical house in the bare academic idiom favoured in the late Georgian period in Ireland. Erected in 1838 for Thomas Brodigan, not dissimilar in style to Aclare House near Drumcondrath. Hargrave, Duff or Keane might all have designed these façades, but the plan of Pilltown is odd: a large rectangular two-storey block, symmetrically arranged but entered at its NW angle by a single-storey vestibule tacked on at the back. Is this picturesque asymmetry intentional or the result of alterations? At the NE corner the house sprouts another two-storey wing, and an untidy N elevation facing farm offices makes no attempt to hide irregularities. Set on a terraced bank, the S front is Pilltown's principal façade, a very proper five-bay, two-storey classical elevation. The central bay has a shallow eaves pediment and breaks forward as a semicircular bow at ground-floor level. Regular sash windows throughout, with pairs of narrow windows in the E wing, which is perhaps a later addition. Immaculate limestone ashlar masonry; pilaster strips, flat string-courses and a moulded eaves cornice. The entrance front consists of the three side bays of the main block, adjoined by a square single-storey domed vestibule with a square projected porch and two Ionic columns *in antis*. Inside, a circular top-lit hall with statue niches and, formerly, Dufour trompe-l'œil panels.

BEYBEG HOUSE. 3 km NW. A modest double-pile gabled house of two storeys over a basement, built in 1758 by the Smith family of Maine, Co. Louth. Five-bay entrance front with a good cutstone doorcase and plate-glass windows which now replace the original sash panes. Inside, a central entrance hall with reception rooms on each side and the stair off the hall to the r. Six-panel doors in lugged surrounds.

MOORE CHURCH RUINS. 1.5 km S. The overgrown chancel arch of a late medieval church which measured 83 ft by 27 ft (25.3 m by 8.2 m). The earliest reference to a church here is in 1302. In 1693 Bishop Dopping reported 'church and chancel ruind since 1641'. – MONUMENT. A lettered limestone slab embedded in the E side of the chancel arch; finely wrought limestone inscription: 'Here under lieth the body of Dame Jenet Sarsfield – Lady Dowager of Donsany who dyed the XXII of February AN DNI 1597'.

KELLS

ME *7070*

For centuries Kells has been one of the major thoroughfares of North Leinster, a routeway from Dublin and the E coast to the northern and western counties. The shape of the town naturally reflects this location, for, unlike the ubiquitous street towns in the S of Ireland, Kells has a cross-shaped or star plan which appears to have developed around the major routes converging here. According to certain theories the windows of Irish round towers were designed to command views of the roads leading to other principal monasteries, hence the uncommonly high number of five windows in the Kells tower. In the later medieval period there were five gates on the town's walled defences. An early tradition associated with the town is the statement written by C9 annalists that 'Ceannus was given to Colmcille the musical without battle'. If Colmcille did found a church here in the C6, nothing survives from it. The existing medieval monuments were built in the C9 by a group of Columban monks led by the abbot Ceallach, who had fled here from Iona following successive plunderings of the island by the Vikings. During the C10 and C11 Kells suffered a similar fate: the annals record successive sackings and burnings.

Through all this period the monastery's most prized possession was miraculously preserved – the great gospel of Colmcille or Book of Kells. In 1007 the book with its *cumhdach* was stolen from the sacristy of the church, and although the book was recovered two months later, the precious cover was not. The book is now in Trinity College, Dublin.

In 1152 Kells was the venue for a great all-Ireland church synod, presided over by the papal legate, Cardinal Paparo, part of a widespread C12 movement to strengthen papal power and prestige. At the synod Paparo constituted several new dioceses, one of which was Kells itself – probably by way of compensation for its then diminishing status as a monastic centre. In the Norman period the town saw the foundation of two new monasteries patronized by Hugh de Lacy, and at the same time a castle was built and the town was fortified. By then the distinctive circular street pattern was clearly established, with the old monastic settlement at its centre. The survey of 1655 describes Kells as 'a walled town with five gates, a castle, a high watchtower, the house called St Columcille's Cell, several houses and cabins in repair and two abbeys'. At that time the town was a thriving market centre administered by its own corporation, but by the next century it had become very much an estate town, the property of the Earl of Bective (later Marquess of Headfort), who built Headfort House outside the town and exercised an extensive patronage in the surrounding countryside.

If Kells' role as a major routeway is reflected in its physical layout, the town's greater significance as a medieval religious centre is neatly illustrated by the siting of the church and monastic buildings on an eminence at the very top of the town. The character of Kells is modest yet elegant, rows of two-storey late Georgian houses with some nice doorcases and C19 shopfronts.
9 Headfort Place is particularly handsome, a broad, roughly triangular clearing, bounded by most of the town's major public buildings and by rows of two- and three-storey houses with good doorcases and some carriage arches in blocked surrounds.

EARLY CHRISTIAN MONUMENTS

22 ST COLMCILLE'S HOUSE. Uphill, NW of St Colmcille's Churchyard, stands the earliest of Kells' ecclesiastical buildings, built probably in the early C9 by the newly established Columban community. Of rough coursed rubble, this is a tall gabled structure with the steeply pitched stone roof characteristic of Irish early Christian oratories at Devenish Island, Co. Fermanagh, Glendalough, Co. Wicklow, St MacDara's Island, Co. Galway, and on the Dingle Peninsula, Co Kerry. Here the site, sandwiched between modern bungalows, is less evocative, yet despite these and the modern doorway and steel ladder which gives access to the roof chamber, the building remains a remarkable structure, well worth the bother of locating the key and viewing the interior. The title 'house' is not entirely misleading in that the building was apparently used both as a church and as accommodation for the community. While romantic association with the Book of Kells once caused it to be interpreted as a scriptorium, a residential oratory seems the more likely proposition. At 19 ft by 15 ft 6in (5.7 m by 4.7 m) internally, it is clearly designed for the use of a small community rather than anything approaching a modern congregation. Similarly, the original position of the entrance, at first-floor level in the W wall, indicates both a defensive and a domestic aspect to the design. The building had three storeys, the ground floor (probably the chapel) divided from the upper storey by a wooden ceiling, and above the barrel-vault a tripartite roof-croft. The first floor probably served as living accommodation, with the roof-croft used as a dormitory. Access to the roof was gained through a trap doorway in the vault.

The most impressive aspect of the building is its wonderful roof profile and internal propping vault. Built of flat-bedded local whinstone, the steep roof pitch is a masterful accomplishment, belying its construction as a succession of tiny steps. The roof rests upon walls almost 4 ft (1.2 m) deep and an internal barrel-vault built on wickerwork centering. The pitch was further strengthened by the partition walls of the roof-croft. These tiny attic appartments, the largest measuring 5 ft by 4 ft (1.5 m by 1.2 m), are lit by small windows in the apex of each gable. Upon visiting Kells in 1836 John O'Donovan found that the building had recently been occupied by a poor family, found guilty of sheep-stealing. The dead sheep were discovered by the police in the darkened roof-croft apartments.

ROUND TOWER. At the SW corner of St Colmcille's Churchyard stands the least documented of Kells' religious monuments. It is to the early antiquarian George Petrie that we owe the measurement of the tower, which in 1795 he calculated as 99 ft (30.2 m) in height, with walls a little over 3 ft (0.9 m) thick at the door level. The tower is built of coursed rubble masonry and now lacks its conical masonry roof. It is entered by a N-facing doorway, characteristically located at first-floor level. The door is framed by large ashlar blocks and has inclined jambs, giving it the 'keyhole' profile which is a common feature in Irish early Christian architecture. An unusually high number of windows – five, instead of four at the cardinal points – lights the top section, with four other window openings set at various levels. Upon the premise that the windows of Irish round towers were designed to command views of principal routeways, it is assumed that Kells' central crossroads location dictated increased fenestration. No exact date is known. The Annals of the Four Masters record a murder in the Round Tower in 1076; it is usually dated to the early C11.

HIGH CROSSES. The four high crosses of Kells occupy a position that is somewhat distinct from contemporary sculptural activity in other parts of the country. At Kells a distinctive cross-fertilization of subjects and motifs with clear stylistic and iconographical affinities to each of the Northern, Midland and Nore Valley groups suggests either the use of drawn patterns or the presence of craftsmen who had travelled more than usual. None of the other regional groups displays such a diversely eclectic repertoire.

Though the exact dating of the groups of high crosses remains conjectural, it is clear that the Kells crosses represent several different stages of stylistic development, while one cross, left largely unfinished, raises significant questions about the actual sculpting and construction of these monuments. Three of the crosses still stand in St Colmcille's Churchyard; one is more conspicuously and picturesquely sited at the former market-place, at a junction of narrow streets in the centre of the town.

The SOUTH CROSS, which from a Latin inscription on its E side is also known as the CROSS OF PATRICK AND COLUMBA, stands near the Round Tower in the churchyard. It is the most complete and most legible of the four crosses at Kells. A ringed cross, about 11 ft (3.3 m) high, it is attributed to the later C8. Two particular features of the decoration are cited to support this dating: the abstract two-dimensional quality of much of its ornament, which flows continuously rather than being confined to framed panels (and which is related to contemporary manuscript illumination and to the C8 South Cross at Clonmacnoise), and secondly the unusual position of the Crucifixion scene on the upper shaft of the W face, a peculiarity also found at Killannery, Co. Leix, which has also been dated to the late C8.

The cross is extremely ornate, decorated with a profusion of flowing abstract ornament which leaves hardly any part of the surface uncarved. This profusion has led Helen Roe to compare it with the characteristic expression of manuscript art and to call it the 'manuscript' cross. In transferring flat patterns to three-dimensional forms obvious adjustments have taken place; nevertheless there remains a delicacy of surface and shallowness of relief which make the effect of the monument radically different from the clearly structured forms of the Market Cross (*see* below) or the two high crosses at Monasterboice (q.v.). The scenes here are contained *within* the abstract patterns rather than set out from their surroundings as independent sculptural elements.

Though not without problems as to the exact identifications,* the scenes are usually described as follows: E face, reading from the bottom: the base, possibly Noah drawing the animals into the Ark; an abstract motif of nine interlace wheels; The Fall of Man and Cain killing Abel, where Adam and Eve stand on either side of the tree of knowledge, their hands held towards the groin, while Cain hits Abel on the head; the three Israelites in the furnace – a scene of deliverance much favoured by the Ulster cross-makers – depicting a central angel spreading its wings to protect the men while soldiers on either side stoke the blaze; Daniel in the lions' den – another deliverance story – with two lions either side of a standing figure of Daniel. A boss of seven knots fills the centre of the cross; above it is a complicated double scene with, on the r., Christ blessing the five loaves and two fishes. The l. arm shows Abraham about to sacrifice Isaac – a redemption subject – and the arm has the two figures of St Paul and St Anthony in the desert.

19 Though largely abstract, the W face is celebrated for two scenes: the Crucifixion and Christ in Majesty. From the base to the top, the subjects have been identified as follows: the base, a procession of horsemen and a chariot, possibly representing the transfer of relics; a series of abstract motifs; the Crucifixion, awkwardly accommodated as a sculptural panel on the shaft of the cross, which leaves no space for Christ's extended arms; above, Christ in Majesty. Here Christ carries, over his r. shoulder, a flowering rod which indicates his eternal priesthood and, over his l., the slender cross of the Resurrection. On either side and above and below are the symbols of the four Evangelists: above Christ's head the angel of St Matthew holds aloft a roundel with the image of the Paschal Lamb; r. is the winged bull of St Luke, l. the winged lion of St Mark, each holding the book of his gospel, and beneath Christ's feet is the eagle of St John; abstract patterning to arms and top. The sides have mostly abstract patterns, with stories from the

*Dr Peter Harbison's recent three volumes, *The High Crosses of Ireland: an iconographical and photographic survey* (Bonn, 1992), appeared while this book was printing. His detailed and innovative discussion, with alternative identifications of a number of the scenes in Irish high crosses, could not be included in the accounts of Kells and Monasterboice given here.

life of David at the end of each arm: David killing a lion on the S side; David killing a bear – a large nude figure with a leaping animal – on the N side. St Peter and St Paul enthroned are on the N side, at the top of the shaft.

The EAST or UNFINISHED CROSS stands on the S side of the church towards the chancel end. This is the tallest of the Kells crosses, though work on it was stopped soon after the carving began and it is only partly completed. On a massive two-tiered base, the shaft and lower half of the ring stand 14 ft (4.2 m) high, so this was clearly intended to be a monument on a grand scale. If art historians lament the incompletion of the iconographical scheme, we are more than compensated by the evidence which the unfinished cross supplies on the mode of construction and practice of carving a high cross. The sides of the cross have, marked out on them, the outlines of the carved mouldings to frame the sculptural panels, while the principal faces are left with blank rectangular panels, projecting beyond the face of the moulded frames, ready for sculpting. The only scene in which the carving was substantially completed is the Crucifixion on the centre of the W face. Here the figure of Christ, tended by two angels, who float on either side of the head, is complete. So too are the two soldiers with the spear and the sponge held up to Christ on a pole, but the areas round his hands remain as rectangular blocks of uncarved stone. Here it was perhaps intended to add extra details, possibly, as in the West Cross at Monasterboice, figures of sheep as a commentary on the Passion.

In contrast to these areas the surviving sections of the ring are ornamented with finely finished interlace net patterns. Other partially completed scenes in the arm have been abandoned at different levels of cutting. The scene of four figures looking towards Christ on the r. was already almost fully modelled, while that on the l. has only a few initial strokes cut in the stone. It has been argued that, as this cross stands incomplete, the high crosses must have been erected in a rough state and finished *in situ*. For the fine carved work common sense might dictate such a finishing process, rather than the more obvious-seeming hypothesis that the carving was executed prior to the erection of a cross. The evidence is, however, inconclusive, in that this cross may have been erected only in a modern period. It is presumed that work on it was stopped because of a raid on the monastery. After the subsequent dispersal of the community, those who returned were presumably occupied with more pressing concerns.

The WEST CROSS, some 60 ft (18 m) W from the nave door, must once have been an impressive sculptural monument; even as a fragment, consisting now only of the base and shaft, it stands well over 12 ft (3.6 m) high. It is a later development than the South Cross, and the sculpted scenes here are contained within clearly defined rectangular panels. An inscription on the base (now illegible) is said to have requested prayers for Artgal the maker of the cross. An increase in the range and importance of the figure subjects, together with a bolder technical execution, provide the basis for an attribution to a later period, possibly the mid-C9.

For scriptural illustration the E side is clearly the finest, with six full figure scenes filling the shaft. The first five scenes, which are contained within a tall rectangular roll moulding, are linked by an inner and finer moulding which surrounds each scene and then divides and doubles back in the centre to form the bottom border of the scene above. The sixth (top) scene is marked off from the others by a double or second roll moulding which continues round the sides and suggests that the ring of the cross started immediately above this level.

From the base upwards the scenes shown are as follows. (1) The Baptism of Christ in the Jordan. In this scene the Irish sculptor has followed the tradition that Christ was baptized at the meeting of two rivers, the Jor and the Dan, which are shown flowing out of two separate circular pools, whose streams meet where the small figure of Christ stands. The dove of the Holy Spirit is shown above the upper pool, with two onlookers on the l. and St John the Baptist on the r. (2) The Miracle at Cana. Here Christ enters l.; before him the governor of the feast sits on a low stool with a row of four pots behind him and two more above. A servant standing top r. pours water down towards the pots; kneeling servants and the heads of three wedding guests make up the scene. (3) King David, with a harp, and three other figures. (4) The Presentation in the Temple. Here the figures, reading l. to r., are St Joseph with his staff, the Virgin carrying Jesus, Simeon standing behind a draped altar, and a figure entering on the r. carrying two doves (the traditional sacrifice offered by the poor). (5) An unidentified scene of five figures. (6) Christ's Entry into Jerusalem, now badly damaged.

On the W side is the former Artgal inscription, then the following scenes. (1) The Fall. Adam and Eve are shown according to the traditional iconography, standing on either side of a flourishing tree round which the serpent is twined. (2) Noah's Ark, a boat with high-built sides and square portholes, out of which four people look; the dove is perched on the roof. The remaining scenes are very weathered and have not been identified. The sides of the cross are decorated in varied abstract rectangular panels of diapers, spirals, knots and interlace. They are linked by the same doubling-back border that surrounds the sculptural scenes. Some are now very badly weathered.

The MARKET CROSS, like the West Cross, is dated to the C9. Somewhat heavy in its proportions, it stands almost complete, as a ringed cross 11 ft (3.3 m) high, with only the upper block of the top of the cross broken out from the nimbus. The cross is very richly carved, with bold, though now much weathered, figurative sculpture set within regular horizontal panels contained in a double roll moulding. The arcs of the ring have delicate interlaced Celtic ornament and are slightly recessed behind the face of the shaft and arms. The cross, which had fallen down, was re-erected here in 1688 by Robert Balfe, Sovereign of the Kells Corporation. It now faces approximately N and S. On the S, much of the side of the shaft has been cut away, perhaps as a result of its reputed one-time use as gallows.

The scenes are as follows. On the N – originally the W – side: 21
on the base block, Noah drawing the animals into the Ark. On the shaft: (1) An inscription of 1688, which obliterated one scene. (2) The Adoration of the Magi. The Virgin is sitting on the l. with the Christ Child held high in her arms; the three kings kneel before her, with St Joseph on the r. (3) The Miracle at Cana, with four servants kneeling and facing each other at the front, each holding a small square jar. Christ is top l., with three little pots between him and the governor of the feast, who is in the centre. The hand of God and an extra figure appear top r. (4) The Miracle of the Loaves and Fishes. Christ is here the central figure, with an assisting angel on either side. He extends his hands to bless the five loaves, bottom l., and the two fishes, bottom r. (5) The Crucifixion, in the centre of the cross. The scene in the r. arm shows St Peter and St Paul with the false prophet Simon Magus, who attempted to fly and is shown tumbling and upside down. The scene of two figures on the other arm has not been identified.

On the S – originally the E – side. Base: four armed horsemen. (1) An abstract panel of spirals. (2) Christ laid in the Sepulchre – and now headless – with two sleeping guards above his tomb and a slender cross (the symbol of the Resurrection). (3) Christ as an armed man appearing at the second coming. (4) The Fall and the death of Abel. Essentially the same scenes as on the South Cross, with Adam and Eve on either side of the tree of knowledge and Cain hitting Abel on the head. Within the head of the cross, a small scene shows the anointing of David; at the centre is Daniel in the lions' den, surrounded by four lions; on the l. arm is the Sacrifice of Isaac (in which Abraham and his sword are clearly seen), and on the r. arm a scene either of the Temptation of St Anthony or a representation of the deadly sin of Avarice.

Ten further scenes are shown on the sides of the cross shaft and on the arm ends; these are badly broken and most identifications are inconclusive. The two ends of the arms show David killing a lion and the meeting of St Paul and St Anthony in the desert. This last is a particularly handsome panel; the two saints hold their croziers to make a diagonal cross, and the raven sent by God to feed them flies down between them with a round loaf of bread in its beak. Beneath it a chalice emphasizes the eucharistic significance of the subject.

CHURCHES AND PUBLIC BUILDINGS

MEDIEVAL BELFRY TOWER. As a result of the synod of Kells, the early Christian monastic church became a parish church from 1152, and bishops were appointed here until the diocese was annexed to the Bishopric of Meath by Simon Rochfort in the later C12. Of the medieval church, which must have been enlarged to meet this new status, the only surviving link is the bulky late church tower, erected in 1578. An inscription states that the body of the church had fallen in 'ruin and decay' and was 're-edified' in 1578 through the 'diligence and care' of Hugh Brady, Bishop of Meath, Sir Thomas Garvie, Archdeacon of Meath and Dean of Christchurch, Dublin, and Nicholas D (Daly?), Sovereign of the Corporation of Kells, who personally oversaw the work. All three men are immortalized in carved portrait heads which project from the S wall.

The tower is a large square three-storey structure, built of limestone rubble, tapering very gradually upwards and well buttressed at each corner on the lower storey. A simple building, with a barrel-vaulted ground-floor chamber, plainly expressed by single and twinlight openings on the lower stages, with more elaborate windows on the top floor. Paired cusped lights with drop-like centre tracery, mullions and hood-mouldings. A plaque on the N wall records the donation of a window in 1578 by one of the town merchants. The crease-lines of a pitched roof are still visible on the tower's face, so that if the church was properly orientated the tower would have adjoined the N wall of the nave or N transept. The spire, perhaps a little too slender for such a substantial base, was erected in 1783 by Thomas, first Earl of Bective, to designs by *Thomas Cooley* executed by *John Walsh*, stonecutter.

The handsome churchyard GATE PIERS, rusticated, with ball finials and Greek key borders, like those at Headfort House, were also built for the first Earl.

ST COLMCILLE, KELLS PARISH CHURCH (C of I). 1811. A gabled, four-bay hall and single-bay chancel, built on a stepped plinth set into the steeply sloping site. Thin late C18 Johnston-type Gothic. Plain gable front, with a pointed doorway flanked by narrow sash lancets with hoodmouldings. Inside, a small square entrance hall, the doors framed by plaster arches with the attenuated colonnettes often found in Board of First Fruits churches. The church interior is a large, handsome hall, broader than the exterior suggests and roofed with a series of emphatic kingpost trusses. In contrast to the thin Gothic of the façade, the interior is of a rich Victorian Gothic, largely achieved through the amount of Gothic joinery: the roof, the main gallery, the reredos and a smaller gallery set in an arched recess in the blank N wall, which presumably contained the Headfort pews. Four cusped twinlight windows light the nave, with a group of cusped lancets in the chancel. This work dates from a refurbishment begun in 1858 with the addition of the chancel and completed in 1868. – MONUMENTS. Sir Thomas Taylour † 1736 and his wife, Lady Ann Taylour, † 1710. Grandiose wall monument beside the chancel arch; limestone and fossilized Kilkenny marble. Elaborate casket, plinth and Corinthian aedicule, adorned with swags, egg-and-dart, dolphins and rams' heads. The Taylour crest of an arrow-brandishing arm springs somewhat awkwardly from the pediment. – The Rev. James Smyth, Archdeacon of Meath, † 1759 and Catherine Vesey, his wife, † 1733, on the S wall. Simple but attractive; flat plinth and pylon of slate and marble. – Charles Woodward (grandfather of Benjamin Woodward, the architect) † 1793 and his wife, Esther Wade, † 1776; shallow neoclassical relief slate and marble aedicule.

KELLS CATHOLIC CHURCH. In 1798 a T-plan Gothic chapel designed by Francis Johnston was erected in Kells. The site was donated by Lord Headfort, who also presented the church with an oil painting of the Assumption claimed variously to be by Raphael or Guido Reni. Both church and painting have vanished, and what replaces them leaves much to be desired. The altarpiece was damaged in 1836, when vandals tore a large hole in it, and Johnston's church was also ripped apart throughout the C19. A new stone front was added in 1857, then in 1890 the apse and sanctuary were rebuilt by *William Hague*. By the time the building was demolished in 1958 little of Johnston's original design remained.

The present church, by *W. H. Byrne & Son*, 1958, dominates an open forecourt and is a nasty piece of architecture: a broad, angular hall flanked by a narrow tower. Front of rock-faced limestone and ashlar trim. Three square entrances with a large flat canopy and, above, a big triangular-headed window divided into five long lights by mullion strips. Inside, a long bare hall with a barrel-vaulted coffered nave and flat-roofed aisles. Triangular-headed windows to the clerestory. The materials are cork, aerobord, concrete and paint.

SACRED HEART ORPHANAGE AND SCHOOLS. A handsome classical design, built by Miss Catherine Dempsey of Kells in 1840 as a female school. A pair of two-storey, six-bay gabled blocks set parallel to each other, with their N gables joined by a long, single-storey wall with a central carriage arch. Each gable has a three-bay façade, stuccoed and elegantly treated, with rather tall gable pediments, sash windows, corner quoins and console brackets to the entrances. Two long horizontal plaques at first-floor level bear identical inscriptions commemorating the school's foundation. The carriage arch is round-headed, with a small pediment above; the link walls have three narrow blind arches. The marked similarity of the pedimented blocks to Francis Johnston's Courthouse and the proximity of William Murray's savings bank make it tempting to suggest Murray's involvement, using a conscious quotation from his former master.

Immediately E of the school is the diminutive MERCY CONVENT CHAPEL, a three-bay, Gothic nave and chancel of coursed rubble crowned by a steep slated roof, erected in 1858 to designs by *William Caldbeck*. In 1943 the chapel was extended by the addition of a new arm or transept N of the chancel. This is in fact a disused Presbyterian church brought to Kells in numbered blocks from a parish in rural Meath. A five-bay hall of rock-faced limestone rubble lined with red brick and expressed as thin lancets with quarry glass, a triple-graded lancet window in the gable and a low gabled porch. Taken together, these two tiny churches set in the small garden of the convent make quite a pretty group.

COURTHOUSE. 1802 by *Francis Johnston*. A small and elegant building of cubic proportions, nicely situated on a grassy island at the edge of the town. Two-storey, three-bay ashlar façade, articulated in the lower storey as a blind arcade, the central arch framing a fanlit doorcase and the outer arches containing large round-headed windows, each arch surmounted by a fluted keystone. The upper storey is simply three square-headed windows set on a continuous string-course formed by the window sills, with a pedimental gable above. Three-bay side elevations of coursed rubble, square-headed windows below and round-headed windows above. The rear elevation corresponds to a drawing by Francis Johnston dated February 1802. The interior was greatly altered during a renovation in 1948 by *W. H. Byrne & Son* which must account for the remarkable glazing, sixty-two panes per window!

RAILWAY STATION. W of the town. Erected in 1853 to designs by *George Papworth*. Low brick building. Advanced gable ends framed by broad limestone quoin strips, with round-headed windows set in relieving arches. Similar to Balbriggan Station in Co. Dublin.

OTHER BUILDINGS

The former HIBERNIAN SAVINGS BANK of 1846 by *William Murray* (now REYNOLDS COOPER AND MC CARRON) stands, to good effect, on an island site at the narrow N end of HEADFORT PLACE. It is a neat classical box with a distinct Regency flavour, despite its date. Five-bay, two-storey entrance front with a low roof concealed by the eaves cornice and a slightly projected Tuscan porch in limestone. Corner quoin strips and a large tripartite window above the porch. Opposite
9 the Catholic church (see above), the former NATIONAL BANK of 1852 is by *William Caldbeck*. A tall, three-storey Italianate building, five bays wide, with advanced end bays and a low curved curtain wall and carriage arch on each side. Limestone ashlar ground floor, horizontally channelled, with three round-headed windows lighting the banking hall and a doorcase at each end crowned by a consoled architrave. The upper storeys are stuccoed, with a limestone string-course and cornice. Square-headed windows, those in the outer bays set in relieving arches. Caldbeck used this design on several occasions; here it is particularly successful because he had space to add the curtain walls. Perhaps an odd mixture of town palace and country villa, but attractive nevertheless.

A second BANK on HEADFORT PLACE, of *c.* 1870, is either by Caldbeck or a direct crib from his banking *œuvre*. Again a three-storey block, this time of four bays, flanked by low curved walls. Stuccoed banking floor, expressed as a large segmental-headed window with a doorcase each side, all framed by Ruskinian nook-shafts with foliated capitals. The upper floors, of red brick with an emphatic limestone cornice, have segmental-headed windows.

In JOHN STREET, FITZSIMON'S BAKERY has a nice modernist façade, whitewashed and parapeted, with a square carriage arch flanked on one side by two rows of small windows set in long narrow vertical panels with typical 1930s geometric detail. In MARKET STREET is a small early C20 two-storey building with a pleasant late classical façade, formerly a PUBLIC HALL, now a shop.

NEIGHBOURHOOD

DULANE CHURCH RUINS. 2.5 km N. Small and very early ruined church on a site founded by St Cairnech in the C6. Remarkable for its W gable, which has projecting antae and a massive cyclopean doorway. Single-cell buildings with antae may be dated between C8 and C12; Dulane might well be of the early period, and is recorded as being burnt in 920, on the same day as the church at Kells.

WILLIAMSTOWN. 2.5 km N. Large late Georgian mansion, three storeys over a basement, with an unwieldly nine-bay entrance front, unified in appearance but of two dates. The house was probably erected during the last decades of the C18 and as such is an old-fashioned Palladian design. The front, of limestone ashlar, is rusticated over the entire ground floor. A continuous string-course connects the first-floor window sills with square windows above and the usual eaves cornice. Stone architraves surround the windows on the upper storeys, and there is a pediment over the central first-floor window. The pedimented porch, carried on two freestanding columns and complete with Doric frieze, is the most up-to-date element in the design. When first built, the house was only five bays wide. The two last bays on each side were added in 1858 by the then proprietor, George Garnett. As a result, the design has become monotonous and dull: it must have worked much better when only five bays long. When Garnett made his additions he altered the interior, which is now almost entirely C19 in character, with a screen of Ionic columns in the hall and plenty of moulded plasterwork.

WILLIAMSTOWN LODGE. 2.5 km N. *c.* 1860. A dower or agent's house of the Garnett family. Two-storey, three-bay block with a curved hipped roof and an arcaded timber veranda, flanked by a broad advanced and gabled bay with a similar curved roof profile. *John Skipton Mulvany* has been convincingly suggested as architect of this design.

ST CAIRNECH. 2 km NE, at Mullaghea. Early to mid-C19. A low T-plan lancet church made higgledy-piggledy by several small additions. Inside, simple panelling to sill level and two timber Ionic pilasters framing the altar wall.

ARCHDEACONRY HOUSE. 1 km N. Large harled house erected *c.* 1790 for the Archdeacon of Co. Meath. A plain cube of masonry, three storeys over a basement, with a low hipped roof and long sash windows, markedly diminishing on the upper storeys. Typical large rectory plan, with the entrance at the side, four bays with a projecting porch, and a flat, and featureless, five-bay front.

WILMOUNT. 2.5 km NW. A gentleman farmer's house of *c.* 1770. Two storeys, gable-ended, with a five-bay entrance front. Ample twelve-pane sash windows on the ground floor and six-pane windows above. Good limestone pedimented doorcase.

ROCKFIELD. 2 km S. Large late C18 mansion, consisting of a three-storey rectangular house, long and deep, and, behind it, a courtyard flanked on three sides by outhouses and extensions to the main building. The principal elevation is of nine bays, the windows widely spaced, with the central three projecting forward. Cement-rendered, and originally horizontally channelled on the ground floor. Low hipped roof and thin eaves cornice. Square-headed windows throughout, with entablatures on the first floor; pediment on console brackets to the centre first-floor window. Lugged surrounds on the top storey. Quoined corner strips on the ground floor become panelled pilasters on the upper storeys. Central freestanding Doric porch. Inside, the hall has a Doric frieze and a columnar screen; behind it a handsome cantilevered staircase with wrought-iron stair-rail. Clearly gone over in the Victorian period, probably in 1841, when *William Murray* exhibited designs for alterations at the R.H.A.

BALRATH-BURY. 3.5 km SW. A colonial-villa revival of *c.* 1930, built on the site of a two-storey C18 house, the former seat of the Nicholson family (*see* p. 38). A handsome rubble stableyard, with freestone cornices and eaves pediments, W of the house, is the only survival from the Georgian period. The architecture of the present house, mostly in white stucco, is careful yet too quirky to be a real success. In essence it is a nine-bay, two-storey Georgian-revival block, with a central portico *in antis* crowned by a pediment. The scale is too small, however, and the design is confused by a colonnaded veranda set across the front at ground-floor level and blocked by huge mullioned bay windows on either side of the door. This also interrupts the portico, which exists only at first-floor level supported on diminutive columns. A large Venetian window in the centre of the rear elevation lights the stairhall. Inside, reproduction C18 panelling and neoclassical chimneypieces.

DRUMBARAGH HOUSE. 3.5 km W. A four-square three-storey house with a large central chimneystack, built *c.* 1800, possibly to designs of *Francis Johnston*, and remodelled in the late 1860s by *William Caldbeck*. Italianate dressings on the exterior almost belie the house's early origin. Inside, Caldbeck's alterations were less extensive. The original dining room on the r. of the hall was given a large bay window at one end, thin neoclassical plasterwork and a new marble chimneypiece. Otherwise the interior of *c.* 1800 survives relatively intact: a central entrance hall with a large stairhall at the rear and reception rooms on each side. Particularly elegant mahogany doors and cleverly detailed door frames. The finest feature of the interior is the back wall of the entrance hall, which is treated as a shallow neoclassical niche containing a pair of doorcases with pretty plasterwork above and between. The house was extended at the rear by L. A. McDonnell *c.* 1900. Drumbaragh was the seat of the Woodward family. The *cottage-orné* gate lodge of 1839 is attributed to *Benjamin Woodward.*

PILLAR OF LLOYD. 1.5 km W. This serviceable tower, 100 ft 95
(30 m) high, with an octagonal lantern at its top, was designed in 1791 by *Henry Aaron Baker* and erected by the first Earl of Bective, who had been M.P. for Kells in 1747–60. Superficially the style is late Georgian Gothick; thin label mouldings above the round-headed door, a blank tablet – which was never inscribed – and three window openings, pointed, square and circular, which light the shaft of the tower, up to a deeply bracketed cornice supporting the parapet and railings that surround the lantern at the top. Patterns of Irish language prefer 'pillar' to 'column', but either description will do for this smooth cylindrical shaft, whose proportions and silhouette, despite the Gothick detail, forceably recall the authority of the Doric order and the functional character of a lighthouse. Nor was the pillar without use: a context for its design is provided by the French wars and the government's continual fear of invasion. In building his tower on the Hill of Lloyd, 'an elevation of 422 ft [128.6 m]', the Earl provided a convenient signalling station which could communicate at once with the whole of the Irish midlands. The entrance to the tower is now walled up: old gazetteers speak with enthusiasm of the view from the lantern, over all the country around Kells, and, in clear weather, the outlines of the vast fertile plain which extends to the Dublin mountains and to the bay of Donegal.

FAMINE GRAVEYARD. N of the Pillar. A rectangular enclosure, bordered by a hawthorn hedge, marks the burialground of victims of the Irish Famine who died in Kells workhouse between 1845 and 1849.

KENAGH

LF *1060*

Small street village, in the parish of Kilcommick, lined by simple single- and two-storey houses, with a handful of small thatched cottages.

HARMAN MEMORIAL CLOCKTOWER. A piece of whimsical toytown Gothic set at the centre of the village's main street. The tower of limestone rubble is turret-like, with a thin battered profile, supporting a corbelled and battlemented clock stage and a pyramidal slate roof. Mounted at the base of the tower is a classical aedicule framing a portrait roundel of Laurence King Harman † 1875, 'a good landlord and an upright man'.

KILCOMMICK PARISH CHURCH (C of I). 0.5 km S. 1832 by *William Farrell*. Charming hall and tower church with a good spiky profile. Erected at the expense of Jane, Dowager Countess of Ross. Three-bay hall and three-stage tower, with a small projecting chancel and shallow N and S transepts. Built of snecked limestone rubble, with punched stone buttresses and limestone ashlar dressings. The windows are pointed and of three lights, with an early Perp form of reticulated tracery, cross-mullions, quarry glass and hoodmouldings. The transepts are nicely articulated as three bays with a gable over the central window, a diminutive lancet on each side and pinnacled buttresses at centre and ends. – PULPIT by *R. Langrishe*, 1895.

KILCOMMICK OLD CHURCH. 2 km S. The ivygrown ruin of an C18 hall and tower church. Three bays to the hall, and the ground stage of the tower with a nicely tooled limestone blocked surround. Inset in the entrance arch of the churchyard are two inscribed plaques dating to 1649.

ST DOMINIC, KILCOMMOC PARISH CHURCH. 0.5 km N. 1981 by *John & Nuala Kernan*, Limerick. Pentagonal post-modernist church with the sanctuary and entrance aligned on the short longitudinal axis. White rendered walls are carried up in a parapet to mask the roof, which is higher at the rear than in the entrance front, with a small lantern tower perched above the sanctuary and a massive pediment projecting over the entrance. – ALTAR FURNITURE. By *Ray Carroll*.

The FORMER PARISH CHURCH, 3 km S, is an early C19 barn-style church, renovated in 1856 by the Rev. P. Egan.

MOSSTOWN DOVECOTE. 1 km NW. A handsome mid-C18 octagonal dovecote is all that survives of the once impressive Mosstown House, a C17 mansion built by Viscount Newcomen and from 1791 the seat of Alexander Kingston.

LISGLASSICK HOUSE. 3 km SE. Two-storey, five-bay Regency house, with a low hipped roof, sash windows and a squat Wyatt window above a fanlit doorcase.

GLENMORE HOUSE. 1.5 km E. Simple and attractive gabled farmhouse of *c.* 1780. Two storeys over a basement, with a five-bay entrance front, the centre three slightly advanced. Original sash windows replaced by plate glass.

MORNIN CASTLE. 4.5 km E. The N, W and E walls of a substantial late medieval tower house, not dissimilar in its bulky rectangular profile and loose, rather crude rubble masonry to Castlerea (a few miles N of here). Mornin originally comprised two storeys over a barrel-vaulted basement, with a spiral stair at the SW corner and a first-floor mural passage running around the W and N walls. The passage terminates in a small lancet-lit garderobe chamber, immediately behind the chimneypiece of the castle's principal vaulted chamber. Mornin was the seat of the most prominent branch of the O'Farrells; in 1612 the 'castle, town and lands of Mornyn' were confirmed to Roger Farrell, son of James Mac Irrel Farrall.

TAGHSHINNY PARISH CHURCH, CARRICKEDMOND. 6 km E. Early C19 chapel with high gabled roof, lancet windows and gabled porches at either end of the long front façade. Built out from the centre of the back to convert the church to a T-plan, and enlarged again in 1891 by the addition of a short chancel and an off-set polygonal belltower at the centre of the E front.

MOYDOW PARISH CHURCH (C of I). 5 km NE. Built in the mid-C18 and refurbished in 1831. Dull harled three-bay hall, with Y-tracery windows and a large porch.

MOYDOW CATHOLIC CHURCH. 4 km NE. Tall plain C19 T-plan chapel, harled, with a projecting rendered bellcote to the central gable.

KENTSTOWN

ME *9060*

The former estate village of the Somerville demesne is a modest collection of buildings loosely grouped around two country cross-roads.

KENTSTOWN PARISH CHURCH (C of I). Small hall and tower church with an apsidal chancel, begun in the later C18 and remodelled in the mid-C19. The tower is of three stages, harled and pinnacled, with an oval plaque above the door recording its erection in 1797 by Sir James Quayle Somerville. In 1810 the church was described as 'undergoing a thorough repair'. Inside, it is difficult to determine whether the early plasterwork and joinery date to the 1790s or the early C19. The elliptical chancel arch and triple-bay arcaded gallery are of thin neo-classical character, with slender applied mouldings to the joinery and a tightly bound reeded border to the arch. In contrast, the windows are paired round-headed lights with sharply wrought C19 mullions. In the sanctuary two paired lights with simple circular tracery flank a larger rose window above the altar table.

In the porch is a primitive FONT made in 1597 at the behest of Robert Hollywood, thought to have been brought here from the old church of Timoole. – MONUMENTS. Lady Catherine Somerville † 1775 by *Robert Mack*. Lady Mary Somerville † 1843 and Sir Marcus Somerville † 1831; sent from Rome by *William Theed the Younger*.

GLEBE-HOUSE. Across the road from the church, a handsome five-bay, two-storey house over a basement, with a hipped roof and central chimneystacks. Ample sash windows and a central fanlit doorcase are set off by wonderful rubble masonry with hints of brown and orange.

KENTSTOWN CATHOLIC CHURCH. Built by the Rev. J. Sheridan P.P. in 1844. Big five-bay gabled hall with a handsome limestone Gothick frontispiece of the type made popular by Thomas Duff during the 1830s. Built of good-quality squared limestone, the façade is of three bays and two storeys, with three Tudor-Gothic entrance arches below and three pointed twinlight windows above, complete with pinnacled buttresses, hoodmouldings and string-courses. Inside, the church is a big plain country hall, with an open timber-framed roof and a large four-centred arch to the altar wall. – MONUMENT. Eliza Jane, wife of Richard Walsh of Balrath, † 1847, aged twenty-six, in the fifth year of her marriage. ALTARPIECE. At the rear of the chapel, a Veronese-esque Mystic Marriage of St Catherine.

SOMERVILLE HOUSE. This large, and for the most part late Georgian, house is the big house which gave rise to Kentstown village. It has had an intriguing history, as its present architectural arrangement is the result of turning an earlier house back to front. Somerville was built by Sir James Somerville, who was Lord Mayor of Dublin in 1736 and also served as M.P. for the city. The plan of his house can be traced today only at basement level, where a series of vaulted rooms survive with joinery details that suggest a date of *c.* 1730. The back of Somerville was at that time four windows wide, while the front had five. Very deep window reveals in the dining room on the N suggest that this part of the house may incorporate the walls of an earlier building, and if this were the case it may explain the odd arrangement of the floor levels (also found at Dunboyne Castle), where the rear elevation is of three storeys while the front is only two. Some time about the end of the C18, when the house was lived in by Sir James's grandson, another Sir James, the rooms on the S front were modernized, with delicate plasterwork and inlaid six-panel doors with reeded architraves. The drawing room in the SE corner of the house gained a shallow saucer ceiling with eight rosettes round a floral centre, while the entrance hall – a high deep room, some 24 ft by 18 ft (7.2 m by 5.5 m) – was decorated with neoclassical wall panels, a room cornice of floral garlands and pocket vaults, and arabesque plasterwork in the cove of the ceiling. This is an impressive room with decoration of great quality, which may be by *Michael Stapleton*.

The plasterwork of the late C18 is curiously at odds with a heavier screen of double columns with pilaster responds which now fills the space before a semicircular bow window where the front door once stood. This work is part of the process of turning the front of the house to the back, when the hall became the principal drawing room and needed a sunny bow end. The alteration seems almost certainly to have been carried out by *Sir Richard Morrison*, and may date to *c.* 1831, when the property passed to the fifth Baronet, Sir William Meredyth Somerville, Chief Secretary for Ireland from 1847 to 1852, who was raised to the peerage as Baron Athlumney in 1866. A gate lodge to Somerville (now demolished) on the main road to Slane was exactly of a type often built by Morrison; and the style of a the new entrance hall – added on the N front, W of the dining room – closely resembles the entrance hall introduced by Morrison at Fota House, Co. Cork, in 1825, and uses the same *giallo antico* scagliola Ionic columns. The new hall is skilfully contrived within the old plan to provide a dashing neoclassical space, with double elliptical apses screened by paired columns set between pilaster responds. Three curved mahogany doors greet the visitor on entering the hall and the need for adaptation in an old shell appears only when the most important in the centre is discovered to be a dummy. Morrison's planning is ingenious, but the dislocation of axes between the front and the back of the house will always be uncomfortable to some tastes.

The treatment of the exterior of the house is bland. It now appears as a long tall block, stuccoed all over, with a plain stone cornice and balustraded parapet, raised by the addition of three extra quoins, so as to completely conceal the roof. Morrison's semicircular, single-storey bow projects in the middle of the S front, while a four-columned Ionic porch in ashlar limestone, which projects just far enough to incorporate the elliptical apse, marks the centre of the entrance front. The position of the chimneystacks on this façade makes it clear that the architect added an extra bay at the W end of the house. On the side elevations a row of shallow third-storey windows provides light to the attics.

A two-storey, stone-built STABLE YARD stands N of the house. At the centre is a pedimented archway surmounted by an octagonal castellated tower. A pair of houses flanks the archway, with tripartite windows looking into the courtyard: a pleasant design. On the W drive, ARCHWAY LODGE is a high rusticated arch flanked by pilasters, with substantial square rooms on either side. These have rustic Gibbs surrounds to the windows, formed of rubble and rock-faced stones, and have similar oculi above. A piece of romantically 'primitive' architecture which might date from the 1750s or, more probably, the 1790s.

BROWNSTOWN HOUSE. 1.5 km NW. A Regency-cum-neo-classical villa built by the Somervilles, probably *c.* 1801, and refurbished by new proprietors in 1837. Originally a simple stuccoed house of two storeys over a basement, with a three-bay front, a wide hipped roof with oversailing eaves, sash windows and a central fanlight doorcase. In 1837 the severe limestone porch was added to the façade and the ground-floor Wyatt windows gained their limestone pedimented frames – all very reminiscent of *John B. Keane*.

ASHFIELD HOUSE. 3.5 km N. By *William G. Murray*. A simple rendered three-storey, three-bay house which might well have slipped through the net were it not for its family associations. This was the home of Arthur George Murray, younger brother of the architect William Murray. While Ashfield has charm and a distinct ambience of the Victorian period, it is a modest building, with a standard symmetrical plan, a rear central stairhall, conservatory adjoining the W wall and a porch with two Tuscan columns *in antis*. A sense of humour is evident in four charming stone creatures which surmount the garden steps, parodies of the traditional lion couchant.

STAFFORDSTOWN HOUSE. 2.5 km W. Mid-C19 house built by the Butler family, adjoining a lower C18 range. Of two storeys over a basement, the modern house is one room deep and tripartite in plan. Rough-cast over brick and rubble masonry, with sash windows, corner quoins and a projecting porch with two Tuscan columns *in antis*. Wide hipped roof, with central chimneystacks and a stone eaves cornice. Not greatly dissimilar from Ashfield and given its proximity quite possibly also by *W. G. Murray*. At the rear the older range has a deep pitched roof, very substantial chimneys and sash windows. Prior to its acquisition by the Butler family, Staffordstown was the property of the Cusacks.

WALTERSTOWN CASTLE. 2 km SW. Fragment of a tower house, which gives a neat cross-section of the classic vaulted basement and superstructure. Here four storeys sat on a wide barrel-vaulted chamber. Two press recesses survive in the remains of the vaulted chamber, as do some sandstone mullions in the upper-floor windows.

WALTERSTOWN CATHOLIC CHURCH. 2 km SW. A small T-plan chapel, whose date in the C18 places it with Grange (q.v.) among the earliest pre-Emancipation churches in North Leinster. Neither as picturesque nor as authentically preserved as Grange, but a simple unpretentious structure of limestone rubble masonry with plain pointed windows. Improvements were made to the building in 1866; in 1984 further (hopefully conservative) reconstruction was in progress.

3030 KILBEGGAN WM

A small and neatly built late Georgian town which was patronized by the Lambart family from the C16 to the C19. A Cistercian abbey founded here in 1150 was granted at the Dissolution to Oliver Lambart, who demolished the monastic buildings and built a house on the site. In 1606 Sir Oliver Lambart obtained a market grant for the town, and six years later it received a royal charter of incorporation. Throughout the C18 Kilbeggan returned two members to Parliament but it was disenfranchised after the Union, when Gustavus Lambart received £15,000 in compensation. In 1787 the Rev. Daniel Beaufort described Kilbeggan as 'small, but . . . not ill built', and in 1836 the place had one hundred houses 'neatly built and slated'. A branch of the Royal Canal was extended here *c.* 1830.

Today Kilbeggan's one long main street is still lined by neat late Georgian houses: two- and three-storey houses of three, four and five bays with sash windows, fanlit doorcases and stone eaves cornices. The GARDA BARRACKS (former R.I.C.) is a pretty seven-bay gabled block, with round-headed doors and windows to the ground floor and regular sash windows above, the sills forming a first-floor string-course. At the E end of the town, towards the now derelict canal harbour, is a big HOTEL building forming an E-facing crescent: late C19 Tudor-Gothic, with tall gables, mullioned windows and hoodmouldings.

KILBEGGAN OLD PARISH CHURCH (C of I). Ruined three-stage tower of a church built in 1818 with a loan from the Board of First Fruits and renovated in 1832 with a loan granted by the Board of Works to Gustavus Lambart and Bernard Maguire. Nice Gothic detail in crisply wrought limestone.

CHURCH OF ST JAMES. 1976. Big, ugly rectangular hall, with overhanging slated roof pierced by horizontal clerestory windows and crowned at the centre by a curious slated spire and cross. The FORMER PARISH CHURCH stands immediately to the S, with the sanctuary end effectively forming the entrance front. Here a late Victorian Gothic chancel, projecting gabled side chapels and lean-to porches to the transepts group well to give quite a nicely massed building. Built *c.* 1805, the church was gothicized in 1889.

CONVENT OF MERCY. 1898 by *W. H. Byrne*. The standard design by this architect; nine-bay, two-storey building with three gabled projections on the entrance front and minimal Tudor-Gothic detail. The plan returns at each end to give a U-shaped building, of which the convent chapel constitutes the S limb.

LOCKE'S DISTILLERY. To the lover of architecture Locke's Distillery might best be described as picturesque; to the enthusiast of industrial archaeology this is a building which demands much more consideration than that afforded by the meandering eye. The buildings of Locke's Distillery, grouped together on the S bank of the river Brosna, are of various dates ranging from the late C 18 to the end of the C 19. In 1782 there were three small distilleries in Kilbeggan, one of which – that of William and John Codd – continued into the C 19. In 1833 Kilbeggan's distillers were Patrick Brett and Company: only in 1846 does John Locke's name appear. He probably took over Patrick Brett's premises, and Brett in turn had quite likely purchased the buildings of an existing distillery. Of the present complex the long gabled white-washed range along the street front, together with the adjoining mill building, would seem to be the earliest buildings, perhaps late C 18, with a group of later C 19 structures behind Locke's tall redbrick chimney. Inside the mill, brick floors, timber beams and whitewashed walls provide the framework for underbacks, damsels, mash-tuns and immense wooden vats. The great mill-wheel can generate up to 200 horsepower at full flood of the Brosna. About 1880 Lockes added a steam engine to their energy resources, made for them by Thornbull, Jack and Grant of Glasgow. Today the most remarkable thing here is the revitalization by the Kilbeggan Development Association of an historic industry which had lain dormant for over thirty years. In September 1984 the mill-wheel was made to turn again. The architect for the project is *Philip Ginell*.

LOCKE'S BOND WAREHOUSE. Opposite the distillery on the N bank of the Brosna stands a building that would be startling in any context but is especially so in the heart of rural Westmeath: a black ribbed tent-like warehouse, or perhaps half a giant concertina, laid along the earth – from planet Michelin! Attributed by local sources to the engineering firm of *Delap and*

Waller, *c.* 1930; the curious spanning was reputedly modelled upon the arch construction of the palace of Ctesiphon, which had been meticulously studied by Major Waller during contract work in Syria. Other sources suggest that it is a post-World War II Quonset structure.

MARKETHOUSE. 1828. The most attractive building in Kilbeggan and the focal point of the town's finest asset, the charming market square, which is bounded by ranges of two-storey late Georgian houses with steep slated roofs, sash windows and fanlit doorcases. The markethouse is a rectangular two-storey building, built of squared limestone rubble, with an ashlar facing to the ground floor. Five-bay principal entrance front, arcaded throughout the ground floor, with sash windows in lugged surrounds above. The end bays are gently advanced by two successive shallow projections with flat-headed doorcases set into the ground-floor arches. Recent cleaning of a shop at the NW corner of the building has spoiled its unity but revealed a plaque inscribed with the date 1828 and the name of the builder, *Patrick Phylan*. In 1824 the Board of Works received a loan application from Kilbeggan Corporation requesting £400 towards the building of a 'Tholsel, Market-house, yarn and linenhall'. However, the bulk of the building costs were defrayed by Gustavus Lambart.

COOLA MILL. Late C18 to *c.* 1840. The shell of an impressive four-storey mill building. L-shaped and rubble-built. A classic of the Irish countryside in its bulk and astylar functionalism.

BANK OF IRELAND. 1890 by *Millar & Symes*. Neat low-budget bank building. Two storeys, gabled with four windows to the first floor and a pair of generous segmental-headed windows lighting the cash office below. Minimal classical dressings.

3050

KILBIXY WM

Little survives to suggest that this was the site of an important early Christian church, founded by St Bigseach, and later of a large Norman borough. Clearly a coveted prize, the Church of St Bigseach was granted to Ralph de Petit, Archdeacon of Meath, by Geoffrey de Costentin in 1192. Later, in the early C13, it was regranted to the recently established Augustinian Abbey at Tristernagh. In the C15, references point to the existence of a leper house here. The town or borough of Kilbixy grew up around the Church of St Bigseach and a castle which had been built here *c.* 1190. In 1682 Sir Henry Piers recorded the tradition that this was once 'a town of great note, having ... twelve burgesses, in their scarlet gowns, a mayor or sovereign with other officers'. All that survives of that thriving medieval settlement is a small wooded motte N of Kilbixy Church and, to the SE, three ivy-clad walls of a large late medieval tower. This latter, a three-storey rectangular building, originally with two barrel-vaulted chambers, has been variously interpreted but is most likely to have been the C15 leper house.

KILBIXY PARISH CHURCH (C of I). *c.* 1810. Richly ornamented 102
hall and tower church built by the Malones of Baronstown House. Five-bay hall with a shallow projecting chancel and pretty three-stage tower. An expensive church, built of squared droved ashlar with polished ashlar trim. Y-tracery lancets to the nave, with hoodmouldings and quarry glass and a triple-light geometric E window. Pinnacled flat buttresses – like pilasters – define each bay; continuous battlemented parapet at eaves level, and a string-course used like a classical cornice. Idiosyncratic detailing continues on the tower, which is on the W wall of the church and has a deep panelled border of Gothic arches like a frieze below its parapet and pretty Gothic niches, thinly detailed, with quatrefoils above. The building, which had become derelict, has been reduced in a most curious way; like a bombed Hawksmoor church it is now entered as a roofless shell, with only the two bays at the E end consolidated to give a tiny church.

MALONE FAMILY MAUSOLEUM. An austere and impressive Greek-revival monument, redolent both of the Mausoleum at Halicarnassus and of the Lion Tomb at Cnidos. A single-storey limestone cube, approximately 18 ft (5.5 m) square, with corner pilasters and sheer ashlar masonry between. On the N front the wall is recessed beneath the entablature to give two Doric columns *in antis*, flanking a square-headed entrance. On the S face are the arms of the Malone family and the motto *Fidelis ad Veram*. Like both of its antique models, the square tomb chamber is crowned by a pyramidal stepped roof.

BARONSTOWN HOUSE. 1 km NE. Large late C18 house with the classic Palladian formula of a big three-storey central block linked by curved quadrants to long two-storey wings. Built by Richard Malone, the first and last Lord Sunderlin, the house was burnt twice and finally was replaced in 1904 by a large Tudor villa by *J. F. Fuller*. This too has been demolished, and all that survives is the ruined grand gates into the estate. The avenue is now one great loop road lined by small farm cottages, a classic illustration of Land Commission carvery in the 1920s.

EMPER CASTLE. 4 km NW. The NW corner of a large tower house. Built of limestone rubble, with large lumps of other walls still standing and the grass-grown foundations of a longer, lower structure (a hall?) adjoining it on the E. An X-loop with external splay remains in the W wall.

KILCURRY

LO *0010*

Rural parish in flat lands NW of Dundalk where the Castletown and Kilcurry rivers meet. The oldest building is the C17 BELLEWS BRIDGE, with the inscription 'This bridge was built by Sir John Bellewe of Roche, Knight and Dame Mary Birminghame of Dunfirth, his wife, anno 1674'. Several small churches and two castle ruins are in the area. Distances here are given as from Bellews Bridge.

ST BRIGID, FAUGHART PARISH CHURCH. 2 km NE. 1896–1900 by *W. H. Byrne*. A perfect illustration of energetic Celtic revivalism in a small country parish. Small cruciform church; nave, shallow transepts and apse, with a three-stage tower tucked in between the E transept and the nave. Built of rock-faced Newry granite in a Hiberno-Romanesque idiom. Extensive limestone trim. Round-headed arches, lancets and a simple wheel window in the entrance gable. Inside, a nice timber panelled roof and some interesting STAINED GLASS, mostly High Victorian *Mayer* glass, but with three Irish-made windows bearing scenes from Irish hagiography. The window in the E transept nearest the altar has scenes from the lives of St Colmcille, St Sechnell, St Patrick, St Brigid and St Dara. In the apse, the window on the extreme l. St Fanchea and St Enda, executed by *Sarah Purser* and an *Túr Gloine*. – CARVED PANEL on the baptistery press: The Baptism of Christ by *Oisin Kelly*, 1963. – PULPIT of Riga oak, 1907; again scenes from Irish hagiography, designed by local historian *W. G. Tempest* and executed by *J. & H. O'Hare*, Dundalk. – In the church is preserved a RELIC of St Brigid, a fragment of the saint's scull, housed beneath the high altar.

FAUGHART CHURCH RUIN. 4 km NE. The ruin of a nave-and-chancel church whose construction of rough granite boulders suggests a C12 date. Evidence of a double-ditched enclosure around the site suggests that the church was associated with a large settlement. The site is one of the most beautiful in North Leinster, with extensive views N and W to the hills of South Armagh, E to Dundalk Bay and the Mourne Mountains, and S across the flat plain of Co. Louth. Edward Bruce was killed in battle at Faughart in 1318.

BRIDGE-A-CRIN CHURCH. 0.75 km NW. Erected by the Rev. John Keanney P.P. and consecrated in 1853. Gabled and buttressed four-bay lancet hall, with a bellcote over the entrance gable, a late C19 chancel and modern porches. Coursed rubble, with limestone dressings. Timber cross-braced roof; tiled modern sanctuary. – STAINED GLASS. Nave: John the Baptist by *A. E. Childe*, 1899. Judith and St Thomas by *Michael Healy*, 1923. Altar wall: good High Victorian Adoration of the Magi.

BARONSTOWN FORMER PARISH CHURCH (C of I). 2.5 km W. Handsome little tower and hall church, now sadly derelict, situated on an eminence above the Dundalk–Castleblaney road. A standard design by *Thomas Cooley*, though probably carried out by *Francis Johnston* in 1783. The church was built by Primate Robinson, whose coat of arms is attached to the W wall of the tower. Three-bay harled hall, with a semicircular E end, lit by two Y-traceried windows, all with quarry glass and timber mouldings. Three-stage battlemented tower with flat clasping granite buttresses rising to finials. The interior has panelling to sill level and three horizontal recessed panels with egg-and-dart frames, high up on the N wall.

CHURCH OF THE SACRED HEART, COURTBANE. 8 km W. Simple mid-C19 rectangular gabled church, with a boldly grouped porch and bellcote added to the centre of the long E side *c.* 1870. Inside, a plain hall lit by large Gothic windows, originally with timber Y-tracery. Inside, the ceiling has been lowered and cuts across the top of the altar window awkwardly. – STAINED GLASS. St John the Baptist by *A. W. Lyons & Co.*, Dublin, 1963. Altar wall: Crucifix, in a vivid purple, blue and red, 1892.

BALREGAN CASTLE. 0.5 km N. Now a ruined stump in the middle of pasture, Balregan was formerly a significant outpost on the N border of the Pale, probably of C15 date. During the C17 the castle was owned by Sir John White, but it was in the possession of Viscount Limerick by the mid-C18, when it was illustrated by Thomas Wright as a four-stage tower house with three corner turrets, set within a large walled court.

WATER LODGE. Near the castle. Handsome C19 neo-Georgian house in a charming wooded setting. Square three-bay redbrick block, with limestone corner quoins, wide hipped roof, oversailing bracketed eaves and a fanlit Doric doorcase.

PHILIPSTOWN HOUSE AND MILL. 2 km W, near Baronstown Church. Extensive corn mill, millhouse and stores built by the Dundalk merchant James Kieran during the first two decades of the C19. The house is a large three-bay, two-storey building, rubble-built, with a wide hipped roof, central chimneys and a Doric door and fanlight. The mill consists of two four-storey gabled blocks with a tall redbrick chimney. Destroyed by fire in 1868, these are now leafy fairytale caverns.

FARNDREG HOUSE. 2 km NW. Small mid-C19 villa, formerly known as Woodlawn. Cement-rendered, with Italianate and Greek-revival detailing. The type of modest domestic design being produced during the 1870s by John Neville and Robert McArdle of Dundalk.

ROCHE CASTLE. 3.5 km NW. One of the first and greatest frontier 47
castles of the Pale, begun in the 1230s by Lady Rohesia de Verdun and completed by her son John de Verdun. Few buildings so vividly evoke the establishment of Anglo-Norman military power in Ireland. Raised high on a limestone outcrop, cliff-like on three sides, the bulk of the castle is truly impressive and, when seen from close quarters on a dull or stormy day, the height and scale of the S face can even now seem threatening. Access to the castle is from the road on the N side, where the prospect is less menacing though still impressive. A battlemented curtain wall with two massive circular bastions flanks the entrance on the E face. Like the earliest part of King John's Castle at Carlingford, Roche Castle is essentially one great walled enclosure; roughly triangular in shape, as dictated by the irregular form of the hill, and bounded by high curtain walls with battlemented wall-walks. The only covered buildings were the gatehouse, which had rooms on three levels, the round bastions and, immediately S of the gatehouse, forming part of the perimeter, a great two-storey hall, whose pointed first-floor windows were the only large window openings in the entire structure. In the centre of the castle stand the remains of a

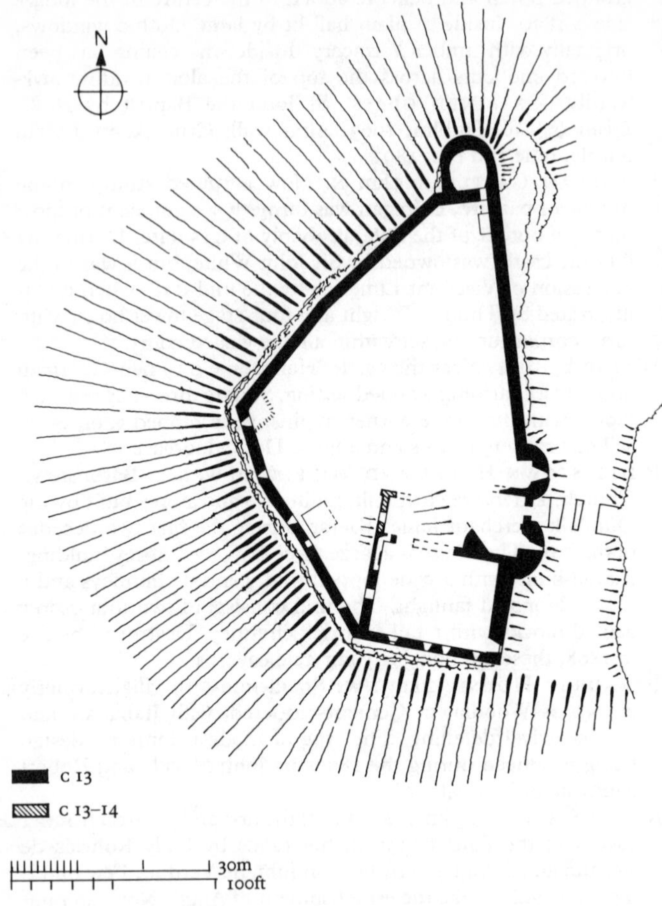

Kilcurry, Roche Castle. Plan

small square building; at the NW corner are the remains of a tower. Externally the building is stark, plain limestone rubble walls relieved only by slits of arrow loops. The castle had formerly a large walled bailey on the plateau to the S, separated from it by a rock-cut fosse. A hosting of all the English forces in Ireland was held here in 1561. In 1649 the building was slighted by Cromwell.

7050 KILDALKEY ME

KILDALKEY CHURCH RUIN. Fragmentary ruin of a small medieval church, consisting of a rubble gable with a very narrow chancel arch, and the N wall and basement storey of a W belltower. An abbey was reputedly founded here in the C5 by St Trena, a friend of St Mochta of Louth. Abbots are recorded throughout the C8 and C9, but the place seems to have been destroyed by the Danes. Rebuilt in the later medieval period, the abbey of Kildalkey and its possessions were granted in 1542 to Sir Anthony St Leger.

ST BRIGID. 1890–8 by *W. H. Byrne*. Neat little Gothic hall, chancel and N porch. All E.E.-style, like Welland's architecture of the 1850s. Bellcote over the W end, two lancets to the entrance gable and three graded lancets in the chancel. Inside, attractive timber cross-braced roof.

RATHCORMICK HOUSE. 2.5 km W. *c.* 1770. Large three-storey, gable-ended house, with a projecting stair well in the centre of the rear elevation. Since the C18 the seat of the Potterton family. Five-bay limestone entrance front, with regular sash windows diminishing abruptly to six panes on the upper floor. Continuous string-courses to the first and second floors. Projecting pedimented porch. Much altered internally.

KILBRIDE OLD MANSION. 5 km NE. The ruins of a medieval tower house, remodelled in the C18 by the Longfield family and enlarged in the mid-Victorian period by the addition of a substantial Italianate house. A microcosm on one site of landed-family building for over 400 years. The tower house is of three storeys over a vaulted basement, with a square stair turret at the NW corner and a second garderobe tower at the SE angle. In the C18 the Longfields decided to make a formal three-bay entrance front on the E side, with an entrance into the first floor. This was done by raising a mound of earth on the E of the tower to provide access to a new hall door, opening regular Georgian windows on either side, and adding a pedimented limestone doorcase. To create a regular façade the S wall of the castle had to be removed and the building extended to the S by about half of its original size. The result was a three-bay, two-storey elevation with an eaves pediment and attic window in the central bay. Inside the C18 house, a large semicircular recess in the E wall of the entrance hall – which continues into the adjoining room – marks the site of the second turret of the tower house, indicating its original square-type plan.

The shell of the Victorian mansion which adjoins the C18 façade at its SE corner is a substantial two-storey house in the Italianate idiom of *William Caldbeck*. It is closely similar to Caldbeck's Clonhugh Lodge in Co. Westmeath of 1867 (*see* Multyfarnham Abbey) and must also be by him: the same five-bay entrance front, with a projecting gabled centre bay, marked by an Ionic porch with an arcade of three windows above; the same rounded corners to the windows and brackets to the eaves. Canted bay window to the S-facing garden front, and long five-bay range behind.

WOODTOWN HOUSE. 4.5 km NW. Modest mid-Georgian country gentleman's house. Two storeys over a basement, with a five-bay entrance front, a semicircular bow rising through two storeys to the garden front, and a hipped roof with central chimneystacks. The front door has a handsome Gibbs surround, with an open pediment and a keystone in the centre of the lintel carved with a dove bearing an olive branch. Much altered in the C19, the house is now cement-rendered, with corner quoin strips, plate-glass windows and Victorian plasterwork and tiling.

CLONCARNEEL. 3.5 km S. The C18 home of the Dowdall family, formerly known as Clown. This is a tall gabled house, built as a single range, with a projecting stair well in the centre of the rear elevation and the usual fielded joinery to the interior. In 1801 Walter Dowdall decided to enlarge the house and commissioned designs for an extension from *Francis Johnston*, who was then working for Meath Grand Jury at Kells Courthouse. The result is a charming two-storey, five-bay block with a formal entrance front, facing W, and built across the main elevation of the earlier house. The new entrance front is a cool Regency design, with a projecting centre bay, unmarked by any pediment, and the whole crowned by a hipped roof so low as to be invisible. A measure of Johnston's attention to detail is the windows: long twelve-pane sash windows on the ground floor and smaller, almost square openings of sixteen panes instead of the usual six on the first floor. The doorcase is also unusual, as it does not quite follow the common early C19 tripartite arrangement under a wide fanlight; Johnston provides instead a broad limestone recess with a pretty leaded fanlight and splayed and fluted limestone panels on each side of the door. A delicate wrought-iron balcony adorns the centre first-floor window. Inside, the ground floor consists of a central entrance hall, flanked by a large drawing room and dining room. The hall is flagged and simply ornamented by a mutule cornice. The reception rooms, also reticent, have elegant neo-classical chimneypieces and engraved brass grates signed by *J & J*^{o} *Clarke*. In the dining room is a triple-arched timber press recess, carved with fluted shafts and lion masks.

MOYRATH CASTLE. 1 km S. A squat square medieval tower with rounded corners, reduced in height and given C19 battlements. Much remodelled and adjoined by a modern two-storey house with gables and plate-glass windows. According to tradition, the castle was built in 1219 by Lord Geoffrey de Montemarisio, though this was probably an earlier building. The castle was subsequently acquired by the Nugents and in 1836 it was the property of the absentee Henry Grattan, occupied by the Potterton family.

2060

KILGLASS LF

Parish S of Edgeworthstown on the border of Longford and Westmeath.

RATHREAGH (or LEGAN) CHURCH. Rural Ireland offers few

examples of early C17 architecture in a classical taste and none better than the elegant and astonishingly correct Doric doorcase and Ionic wall monument in this roofless parish church. The ruin is all that remains of the architectural activity of Sir Nathaniel Fox, who was granted the lands of Rathreagh in 1620, built a great house here, Foxhall, and, with his wife, Elizabeth Hussey, founded the Protestant church. It is a small rectangular building, of rubble limestone, with windows in the S and E walls and a W-facing entrance gable. The Doric doorcase is here. Two slightly tapered pilasters – too tall for a regular Doric order – support a complete entablature with triglyph frieze and cornice, which although correct have a certain naivety, a charming lack of finesse which characterizes youthful academic classicism. The proportions seem Netherlandish, as do the odd irregularities – fine stone strings two-thirds of the way up the shafts of the columns, and the central keystone of the arch of the doorway with an incised patera and moulded boss. Above the door an inscription records the renovation and extension of the church in 1772. At this stage the C18 masons clearly jumbled some of the mouldings when reassembling the doorcase, which has added further to its inconsequential charm. The interior is dominated by the Fox Monument of 58
1634, set against the blank N wall. A canopied structure, like a classical wall tomb, forms the backdrop to a limestone altar tomb, surmounted by the reclining effigy of Sir Nathaniel Fox. The statue, now reduced to a reclining torso and thigh, is depicted in C17 armour; from what remains it must always have been stiff and conventionalized, with the head awkwardly propped on the right arm. The architecture behind the figure is much more sophisticated, with coupled Ionic half-columns, supporting salient entablature blocks (of the correct proportion) from which an elliptical arch springs like a canopy, supporting a second frieze and cornice, with a strapwork gable decorated with a pediment, urns and obelisks above. Jacobean scrolls link the upper cornice to the entablature blocks, and cupid heads decorate the spandrels of the arch. A square recessed panel bears the Fox coat of arms, beneath which are two other shields and a Latin inscription commemorating Sir Nathaniel Fox † 1634.

KILGLASS PARISH CHURCH (C of I). *c.* 1810. Built on the site of an ancient nunnery; a hall and tower church with side vestibules flanking the tower and an apsidal chancel. Timber Y-tracery windows and a pointed entrance framed by a finely chiselled limestone surround. Renovated in 1860. The RECTORY, also of *c.* 1810, is of three bays and two storeys over a basement, with sash windows to the first floor, Wyatt windows on the ground floor and an enclosed central porch.

LENAMORE CATHOLIC CHURCH. *c.* 1840. Long, low gabled T-plan church, with gabled porches to nave and transepts, lancet windows and a bellcote on the nave gable. – MONUMENT. The Rev. Edward Duff P.P., of Legan and Ballycloghan, † 1864; by *Farrell & Son.*

1040 KILKENNY WEST WM

In the 1180s the De Lions or Dillons established themselves in the barony of Kilkenny West, where they built a castle and endowed a monastery for crutched friars dedicated to St John the Baptist. At the Dissolution the monastic buildings and lands were granted back to the then head of the family, Robert Dillon. Described as 'in ruins' in 1786; nothing now survives of the abbey, and the present parish church stands on the site. In a field across the road the SE corner of a late medieval tower house, with holes for roof-timbers and the embrasure of a large window, stands four storeys high.

KILKENNY WEST FORMER PARISH CHURCH (C of I). *c.* 1840, by *Joseph Welland*. Now roofless, a three-bay hall with a bellcote over the W end and round-headed lancets.

MORTUARY CHAPEL. 1680. A small barrel-vaulted structure, with a round-headed E window and a round-headed entrance arch with a hoodmoulding – showing the tenacity of late medieval detail. Buried in the churchyard is the Rev. Charles Goldsmith, father of the poet; he was curate here in 1730–47.

DRUMRANEY PARISH CHURCH. 4 km E. 1858 by *John Bourke*. Pretty country chapel in the distinctive C13 lancet Gothic idiom preferred at this time. Gabled hall with transepts and chancel, built of snecked rubble masonry in lovely shades of grey, with pale limestone ashlar trim. The nave gable has diagonal corner buttresses, a pointed statue niche at its apex and three graded lancets with hoodmouldings and quarry glass; the main entrance is through a porch on the side wall of the nave. The interior is all that a small country church should be: modest, neat and old-fashioned. Little has changed here since the C19. Lit by single lancets, the nave has traditional deal panelling to sill level and a panelled ceiling supported on an open cross-braced truss. The chancel is lit by three graded lancets and is decorated with late C19 mosaic. Pointed statue niches flank the chancel arch. – ALTAR RAIL. A Gothic arcade of 1950; the REREDOS and ALTAR, probably of similar date, are similarly old-fashioned. Gleaming brass candlesticks and an ornate sanctuary lamp complete the Victorian ambience.

DRUMRANEY NATIONAL SCHOOL. 4 km E. Later C19. Tall two-storey, five-bay block with advanced gabled end bays. Cement-rendered, with limestone corner quoins; square-headed multi-paned windows.

0070 KILLASHEE LF

Neat crossroads village built around an irregular square bounded on one side by a nice three-storey, six-bay Georgian block and on the other by low two-storey C19 dwellings.

KILLASHEE PARISH CHURCH (C of I). 1837. Tall thin hall

and tower church, built of limestone rubble with limestone dressings. Five-bay hall; two-storey tower which tapers above the first-floor string-course. Triple lancet E window; single lancets with quarry glass to the nave. Diagonal buttresses, battlements and pinnacles to the belfry.

ST PATRICK, KILLASHEE AND CLUANDONALD PARISH CHURCH. 1 km NE. 1829. Plain gabled T-plan chapel, built by Fr Richard O'Ferrall on a site obtained from the canal company. Inside, open kingpost roof and pretty cast-iron Gothic gallery.

CURRY CHURCH. 3 km E. Small late C 19 country church. Three-bay hall and chancel, cement-rendered; limestone rubble entrance tower and low ashlar broach spire.

KILLASHEE GLEBE HOUSE. Harled two-storey gabled house with big end chimneystacks. Three-bay entrance front, with narrow sash windows and broad expanses of masonry between. Nine fielded panels to the front door, crowned by a semicircular fanlight which has intersecting tracery of the type made popular by the Pain publications of the 1760s and 1770s. The union of the vicarages of Killashee and Cluandonald in 1781 may have been the occasion for building this new if somewhat old-fashioned glebe-house.

BALLYMACORMICK PARISH CHURCH (C of I). 3.5 km E. 1826. Stocky hall and tower church of coarse punched limestone. Twinlight Y-tracery windows, hoodmouldings and octagonal pinnacles to the tower. The church cost a total of £1,080 to build, £185 of which was donated by the local landowner, Mr W. Bond.

At Ballymacormick crossroads, 1 km N, is the remnant of a medieval nave and chancel CHURCH founded in the C 12 by the O'Fearghaills of Longford. Some pocked tooling and a single ogee-headed window suggest a C 15 or C 16 date for the present building.

DANESFORT. 3.5 km E, beside Ballymacormick Church and looking very much like a glebe-house. Two-storey, three-bay Regency-style house with a low hipped roof. Wyatt windows and an Ionic pedimented doorcase.

BALLINAMORE CASTLE. 3 km SE. Two large ivy-grown walls of what must have once been a large fortified house, with a line of square musket holes still visible in one wall. More remarkable than the castle today is its extensive boundary wall. The castle was built by Sir Richard Browne †1642 and his wife, Lady May Plunkett, both of whom were buried in a former church a short distance W from here.

KILLEEN

ME *9050*

A late medieval castle, enlarged on two occasions to make a romantic country house, and an ambitious medieval parish church – all now ruined – make up most of the architectural interest of this once famous estate. Two families have owned the lands of Killeen since the Norman invasion of Ireland: the Cusacks, descended from Geoffrey de Cusack, who held the land under Hugh de Lacy in the late C 12, and the Plunketts, descended from Sir Christopher Plunkett, who was Sheriff of Meath and Deputy to the Lord Lieutenant of Ireland, Sir Thomas Stanley, and in 1403 married Joan, the only daughter and heir of Sir Lucas Cusack. In 1628 Lucas Plunkett, the tenth Lord Killeen, was created Earl of Fingall; the estate remained a property of this title until the mid-C 20.

90 KILLEEN CASTLE. Plunkett family histories claim that the Killeen castle was originally built about the year 1180 by Sir Hugh de Lacy; and Elizabeth, Countess of Fingall, a celebrated Dublin hostess in the 1930s, made much in her memoirs, *Eighty Years Young*, of the privilege of possessing the oldest inhabited house in Ireland. She had feared in the 1920s that the I.R.A. would burn the building; it did, but not until 1981, and what remains does not suggest a date as venerable as family legend supposed.

Set on rising ground in mature parkland the bulk of the great house makes an impressive romantic ruin. The earliest part of the building is a tall rectangular castle, four storeys high, with square corner towers rising one storey higher. The silhouette has been improved by lines of battlements, machicolations and slender round turrets that are in reality disguised chimney-stacks. All the windows are sharply cut C 19 openings, but these alterations do not entirely mask the medieval origins of the castle or the original uncoursed masonry, which contrasts clearly with all the later work. The plan and layout cannot be C 12, and Killeen should rather be compared with the larger castles of the Irish C 15, Bunratty Castle in Co. Clare or, more importantly, Dunsoghly in Co. Dublin, built in the first half of the C 15 by Thomas Plunkett of Rathmore, the third son of Sir Christopher, Lord Killeen. Given the tendency of the Plunkett family to copy each other's buildings, as happened twice with Killeen Church, it seems probable that this castle provided the model for the son's building, so that Dunsoghly, in its unaltered form, would give a clear idea of the original appearance of Killeen. Both buildings have four corner towers of slightly different sizes, all tapering gracefully towards the top, though the C 19 battlements which project at Killeen make the taper harder to see. Sir Thomas Plunkett, as a recompense for his services to Henry VI in the Irish Wars, received a grant of money in 1426 and, having inherited an estate through his wife, it seems not improbable that his money should be spent on a modern house. This would place Killeen in the second quarter of the C 15 and not, as Lady Fingall fancied, 250 years before.

The recorded extensions to the castle (*see* pp. 59–60) both date from after 1800 and were carried out for the eighth and ninth Earls of Fingall. It is clear, however, that the original castle had already been enlarged by the addition of a wing on the S side. For most of the C 18 the house had been occupied by tenants; the seventh Earl had moved back only in 1779. Payments to a mason, Ian Quinn, for repairs to the castle are recorded from June 1780 to November 1781, but the first major enlargement of the building was made to designs of *Francis Johnston*, who between January 1802 and February 1803 put forward a variety of proposals for the house which were submitted to the gentleman architect *Thomas Wogan Browne* for criticism and correction. In the first place Johnston proposed only modest alterations, with a linking round tower, capped by an ogee dome; what was built was a substantial three-storey block with a basement, added to the S side of the castle, which almost doubled the E and W fronts and provided a new drawing room and dining room, with a Gothick lobby, hall and staircase. Johnston's rooms had large three- and four-light mullioned windows under long label mouldings, and the castle was given voguish irregularity by projecting the end of the dining room as a wide canted bay. This was carried up the façade as a corner polygonal tower, decorated with the stepped Irish battlements that are almost a hallmark of the architect's castle style. The entrance, in Johnston's castle, was in the middle of the W front.

Some thirty-eight years later the castle was enlarged again, this time to designs of *James Shiel*, whose proposals are dated May 1840. Where Johnston's work had been rough-cast, with a fine buff plaster, Shiel's additions are in ashlar limestone, so that, even in its ruined state, the different parts of the C19 house are clearly distinguished. Shiel had a fine sense of picturesque massing, and undoubtedly his work gives Killeen more presence, as a feudal pile, than it had before. Across one half of the W front he built a new dining-room wing, converting what had been one long range of building into an L-shaped block. Like the rest of the castle the wing is of three storeys over a basement, and it ends in a narrow square tower, with an octagonal corner turret, that nicely balances the mass of Johnston's bay window. The new wing blocked Johnston's front door, so Shiel contrived a dramatic new entrance, at the basement level on the E side, which projects boldly as a single-storey turreted block with crenellations, machicolations and much C16 English detail in finely cut stone. The interior was memorable as a generous rectangular hall, with pendant fan-vaulting in plasterwork and a central flight of steps rising to a recessed Gothic arcade. Above the porch Shiel added two stone oriels projecting from the face of the towers of the old castle, and the battlements and chimney turrets here are also his, as are the kitchen courtyard and sham chapel on the N.

ST MARY'S CHURCH RUINS. In trees immediately NW of the 33
castle. The ruins of a large late Gothic parish church, now a National Monument and maintained by the Office of Public Works. Where Killeen Castle has passed through many phases, the church is of one build and, apart from the loss of its roof, remains remarkably intact, a tall, gauntly elegant shell which must once have been a splendid building. Although the finest of its group, Killeen Church is best seen with the other Plunkett

foundations at Rathmore and Dunsany; the repeating pattern, which becomes apparent on visiting all three buildings, is immensely satisfying. The Church of St Mary at Killeen was built *c.* 1425 by Sir Christopher Plunkett, the first of his family to own Killeen and Dunsany (q.v.); it served both as a parish church and as a manorial chapel to Killeen Castle.

The church is a tall narrow building of limestone rubble, with two square turrets rising above its height at the W end and a large three-storey residential tower adjoining the NE corner. The turrets, which lend a defensive aspect to the building, accommodated a stair well and a belfry. The walls were formerly crowned by a now fragmentary battlemented wall-walk, supported on a course of slab stones for drainage. The NE tower, a feature seen also at Dunsany and Rathmore, has a vaulted basement and a straight mural stair leading to the upper storeys, which have the usual fireplaces and press recesses and are lit by narrow cusped windows.

Internally the church consists of a long nave and chancel, divided by a tall two-centre chancel arch, the S jamb of which is set curiously askew. Inserted within the N jamb of the arch is a narrow mural stair, framed by a sandstone moulding, which led formerly to the rood-loft. In the angles formed by the nave and the chancel are two wide segment-headed recesses which served as small side chapels. The church was entered through two pointed arches located opposite each other in the N and S walls, towards the W end of the nave.

In contrast to the usual dearth of cutstone detail in Irish medieval buildings, this interior has a wealth of carved ornament, both architectural and sculptural. The windows, three lights to each gable and paired lights to the sides, have flat ogee arches with cusps, daggers and quatrefoils making two patterns
38 of pretty Dec tracery. The E window (which apparently served as model for the C19 E window at Dunsany) exemplifies the elaborate tracery that is typical of the Plunkett churches (*see* pp. 30–1); the W window is especially charming, three double-cusped lights with a curvilinear butterfly-like pattern at the top. In the chancel, fine triple SEDILIA: three double-cusped ogee arches, with crocketed hoodmouldings, finials and pinnacles above the shafts, and a flat label moulding on top, decorated with a miniature dog-tooth motif. Inside, the seats are roofed with miniature ribbed vaults springing from filleted shafts. All of this Dec work is comparable to English late C14 models and, although therefore a little retarded, its character is fresh and youthful rather than decadent or conventionalized.

The SCULPTED MONUMENTS of Killeen are more vigorous and idiosyncratic. First, the FONT at the W end of the nave. An octagonal bowl whose armorial carvings are now largely obliterated. The surviving panels include a representation of the head of St John the Baptist. Now the much damaged PLUNKETT BOX-TOMB, a large limestone monument, located in the N side chapel, with the remains of figures of a Plunkett knight and a lady carved in sunken relief and set under elaborate canopies. Of the knight the only parts remaining are the head, l. shoulder and hands joined in prayer. The lady wears a turret head-dress, divided in the centre as two lobes. Sockets for iron fixings on the shaft between the knight and his lady have been interpreted by John Hunt as evidence that the tomb had a herse, that is an iron frame to support a hanging or tent and candles, which would be placed over the tomb on the anniversary of the deaths of the couple and other ceremonial occasions. Three of the carved sides of the tomb remain, bearing cusped and crocketed ogee niches, with angels in the spandrels supporting shields in their hands. On the S side these are Butler of de la Poer, and Plunkett impaling Cusack and Tuite. The shields on the E side refer to Christ: a heart pierced with swords, and the Instruments of the Passion, with the cross, spear, crown of thorns, nails and scourges. – An EFFIGY in the S side chapel opposite, carved in half-relief and set in a cusped ogee niche, is of a Plunkett knight. He is fully armed, with a sword hanging from his belt, and his l. foot lies on a small dog. Mid-C15. – In the chancel on the N side lies a MEMORIAL SLAB of a knight carved in very flat relief. He is fully armed and stands on a dragon, whose head appears between his feet. The slab is unusual in that the figure carries a large shield which comes down as far as the knees. The inscription round the border refers to a Cusack, one-time Lord of Killeen, and as the date cannot be earlier than the mid-C15, this is presumably an historicizing monument put up by the Plunketts to celebrate their lineage through Joan de Cusack. An EFFIGY of a bishop on the N side of the chancel is carved in half-relief and set in a cusped and crocketed ogee arch with panelling above it, as in the Plunkett tomb. The bishop wears a mitre and a complete set of vestments, and carries a thin crozier. At his r. cheek is a small figure of an angel, its hands raised in prayer. A long Gothic inscription round the sides of the slab refers to Richard Tuite, his wife Joan, Simon Cusack, son of Lord (Killeen), and identifies the bishop as Brother Galfrid Cusack, former bishop of Meath. Later C15.

In the centre of the chancel is the TOMB SLAB of the founders of the church, Sir Christopher Plunkett †1445 and his first wife, Joan Cusack. It is carved in flat relief, with effigies of Sir Christopher and his wife beneath cusped and crocketed niches. The figures are very worn. The knight is in full armour with his hands flat on his chest and stands on a little dog. The lady, whose figure is partly restored in cement, wears a turreted head-dress, and a gown with full sleeves and a skirt that falls in many tubular folds. Set into a window in the S chancel wall is the PLUNKETT-DILLON MEMORIAL. Two coats of arms are framed in a lugged limestone aedicule with a skull and cross-bones in the open pediment. Erected in 1681 to the memory of Nicholas Plunkett and his wife, Lady Jane Dillon, by their son-in-law, Valentine Browne of Ross, Co. Kerry.

Now fused with the grey masonry of the walls, these carved stone ornaments would originally have been resplendent, with bright primary colours in contrast to the white walls. As the church was a wealthy manorial foundation, the windows would have been filled with coloured glass and the floor of the chancel decorated with patterned tiles. Today, thinly elegant in a uniform grey, the church, if no more than a shadow of its former self, remains one of the most romantic medieval buildings in the country, with an evocative power that would have caught the imagination of Caspar David Friedrich.

1070

KILLOE

LO

7 km NE of Longford

Rural parish in flat lands on the river Crumlin.

CULLYFAD CHURCH. 1.5 km NE. 1826. Built for the Rev. John O'Reilly. Small whitewashed T-plan chapel, with round-headed windows and doors and nice colourful stained glass. An ugly modern confessional fills one end of the T.

ST CATHERINE, KILLOE PARISH CHURCH (C of I). 0.5 km S. 1824. Small and attractive church of unusual proportions and built of good-quality masonry. Gabled rectangular hall, with a chancel projecting from the centre of one long wall and a large, square, three-stage tower projecting from the other. What is odd is the large size of the tower in relation to the church. The interior is lit by ample three-light windows with intersecting tracery and quarry glass. The detailing is confident and crisp: diagonal buttresses, string-courses and pinnacles to the tower, and hoodmouldings to all the windows.

AGHABOYS CATHOLIC CHAPEL. 2 km NNW. Built in the year of Emancipation by the Rev. John O'Reilly P. P. Simple white-washed T-plan chapel, with buttresses, hoodmouldings, and a round-headed window to the entrance gable. Renovated in 1957, when a square tower with a canopied belfry was added to the W side of the entrance gable.

5050

KILLUCAN

WM

What is most striking about Killucan is its proximity to the village of Rathwire: two small villages sitting almost on top of one another, giving the effect of one large and irregular settlement, in contrast to the usual single-street country village. To complicate things further, the Catholic parish church of Killucan stands in Rathwire, while that of the Church of Ireland is located in Killucan. Both settlements are of medieval origin and were always closely linked; the manor of Rathwire with its motte-and-bailey castle afforded protection to the monastic and parish church of Killucan. Established in the reign of Edward I, the manor of Rathwire was granted in 1336 to John D'Arcy of Platten, Co. Meath, a statesman who was three times appointed Viceroy of Ireland. The manor flourished in the ensuing centuries and in

1598 was named as one of the seven market towns of Westmeath. After the Williamite wars the D'Arcy estates were granted to the family of Robert Pakenham, who died in 1703.

ST ETCHEN, KILLUCAN PARISH CHURCH (C of I). Killucan's medieval religious pedigree is a complex one: a metamorphosis of the parishes of Fearabile and Rathguaire, though ultimately rooted in a monastery founded here in the C6 by St Etchen, Bishop of Clonfad. By the late medieval period a substantial monastic church and several small adjoining chapels flourished here, protected by the nearby manor of Rathwire. Killucan in the late C17 is described by Sir Henry Piers as having 'a fair large chancel raised almost to the height of the body of the church: the whole well roofed and shingled'. On the N wall of the chancel at the E end stood 'a fair and handsome castle without roof', the mansion house he supposed of the vicar or curate. The ruined square tower and chancel of the old church still survive E from the present building, with a complete gable and triple-light mullioned window decorated with cusps, probably of the early C15. Fragments of the medieval fabric remain built into the present church: traces of blocked arches and heads of windows with C15-type dished spandrels in the S wall and, on the N side of the vestry, a moulded arch with a cavetto chamfer and carved roundels in the spandrels, perhaps of the C17.

The church itself, rebuilt between 1803 and 1815, is a classic hall and tower type, with diagonal buttresses, pinnacles and a spire. Three-bay nave with wide Y-traceried windows. The chancel end is cluttered by mid-Victorian extensions. – FONT. The earliest surviving fragment from the medieval period; square bowl supported on a pedestal with four engaged shafts and decorated with nailhead, trefoil and fleur-de-lys motifs characteristic of C12 and C13 work. Assigned to a mid-C13 date, it is one of the earliest datable fonts in the medieval kingdom of Midhe. – MONUMENT. Robert Pakenham † 1703. A handsome early C18 wall monument with volute-like scrolls to the top and sides; an urn above is flanked by memento mori of an hourglass and a skull and cross-bones.

ST JOSEPH, KILLUCAN PARISH CHURCH. 0.5 km S. Tall, plain cruciform church built in 1840 by the Rev. Eugene O'Rourke. Rendered, with stone trim; Gothic sash windows, and three cusped lancets to the chancel. In 1866 the Rev. O'Rourke decided upon repairs and three years later he added an incongruous Italianate campanile to the entrance gable. Built of squared limestone with ashlar trim and crowned by an arcaded triforium at belfry level, the tower looks like the work of *John Bourke*, who perhaps intended to recast the whole church.

METHODIST CHURCH. 1844. Four-bay gabled hall of snecked limestone rubble, lit by tall, round-headed sash windows.

KILLUCAN WAYSIDE CROSSES. Between Killucan and Rathwire, in a charming little grove evocative of the romantic past, stand three C16 and C17 wayside crosses with chamfered mouldings and raised inscriptions. The first is inscribed 'This stone was for Tir: McKin: and Alson Plunket his wife in the year 1531'. This formerly stood beside the Dublin–Athlone road and commemorates Tirlogh McKenny and his wife, who died in a road accident. The second cross, removed here from the centre of Killucan, is inscribed 'Arthur Darcy et K Fitzgerald me Feci na Dni 1604'. The third cross stands in its original position and was erected to commemorate 'John O Laghlin and his wife Jovan Hughes', both killed by a runaway horse.

109 MARKETHOUSE. Substantial three-storey, five-bay block of *c.* 1840, dominating a large open square. Good vernacular building rather than self-conscious 'architecture', with wide elliptical-headed arches on the ground floor and a slightly projected centre bay marked by a gable and clock. Built of coursed limestone rubble.

KILLUCAN RAILWAY STATION. 2 km S. Pretty brick-built station in a classical villa idiom. Two gabled pavilions, with sash windows in relieving arches, linked by a flat block behind a slated cast-iron canopy, attributed to *J. S. Mulvany*.

RATHWIRE HOUSE. 1 km S. Small and ornately decorated mid-C19 classical villa, following a popular late Georgian pattern. A tall single-storey block screens a plain two-storey range behind. Here, however, a two-storey, three-bay range added to the W spoils the symmetry and the illusion. The front, designed to appear as a long low villa, has a shallow hipped roof and a central Doric porch, flanked by two sash windows on each side. These have elaborate moulded architraves which almost fill the wall space from plinth to eaves. Raised quoins mark the corners of the building, which originally had canted bays round the corner at each end of the front. The interior is richly architectural in a showy, Victorian way. Two large rooms flank the entrance hall, each with high, coved ceilings, divided into compartments with strips of classical mouldings, and decorated with pendant bosses at the intersections. All *c.* 1860 in appearance. The stair, to the W behind the entrance vestibule, is top-lit and Jacobean in inspiration, with weighty classical balusters and strapwork overdoors.

LISNABIN. 2 km NW. An attractive, if boxy, two-storey castellated house built in 1824 for Edward Purdon. Very much a symmetrical Georgian castle with a three-bay entrance front and three-bay side elevations, each with regular sash windows with hoodmouldings and a battlemented parapet to hide the roof. Thin octagonal turrets mark each corner, with slightly larger towers flanking the principal entrance and a square battlemented tower rising in the centre of the house. The building materials are limestone rubble with ashlar trim. The nicest feature of the design is a low curved and battlemented curtain wall, running out from the house on the S to join a castellated gateway, and screening the stable court behind. A similar device is used at Knockdrin Castle. Interestingly, the plan is that of a circle within a square, like Francis Johnston's

Townley Hall, only here the scale is much more intimate. A small Gothic vestibule leads to a domed circular stairhall, flanked by the drawing and dining rooms at the front and sides and bounded by three large rooms at the rear. The interior plasterwork detail is a quirky amalgam of acorns, oak-leaves and Gothic pendant motifs. The tradition that Lisnabin is a castellation of an C18 house is unsupported except by a number of raised six-panel doors in the basement. The plan would be extraordinary before the 1790s.

HUNTINGDON. 2.5 km NW. Solid, well-built gentleman farmer's residence, built by the Purdon family in the second half of the C18, probably *c.* 1770. Two-storey, five-bay front built over a basement of limestone rubble. Formerly harled and crowned by a substantial hipped roof with central chimneystacks. A central blocked and pedimented doorcase with side-lights frames a fourteen-panel door. The plan is of the old-fashioned single-pile type, with a simple central stair flanked by a drawing room and dining room.

ST BRIGID, RAHARNEY: KILLUCAN CHAPEL OF EASE. 3 km NE. Simple mid-C19 T-plan church, with lancet windows to the nave and transepts and a triple lancet E window in the chancel. Timber cross-braced roof and stencilled decoration in the sanctuary. – STAINED GLASS. E window: Crucifixion in a primitive High Victorian style 'erected to the glory of God by Raharney Rovers, New York'. – MONUMENTS. The Rev. Eugene O'Rourke †1874. The Rev. Eugene O'Keefe †1898.

HYDE PARK. 3 km SE. Attractive mid-Georgian gentleman's farmhouse of 1775. Built by the Darcys of Killucan. Two storeys over a basement, harled, with a low hipped roof, no eaves cornice and now curiously no chimneys. Ample plain façade with sash windows, twelve panes to the ground floor, nine above, set in a rhythm which gives a broader expanse of masonry to the central bay. The doorcase has a Gibbs surround, fanlight and side-lights. The house is one room deep, with a drawing room and dining room flanking the hall. These have pretty plasterwork cornices with rococo flower-baskets and garlands to the friezes.

KILMESSAN

ME *8050*

KILMESSAN PARISH CHURCH (C of I). Plain three-bay gabled hall, with a bellcote and porch at the W end and twinlight geometric windows lighting the nave. First built in 1731; renovated in the early C19 with a grant from the Board of First Fruits. – MONUMENT. Major General Preston †1788 by *Edward Smyth*.

CHURCH OF THE NATIVITY OF MARY. First erected *c.* 1820; practically rebuilt in 1895 by *William Hague*, and recently modernized. Small T-plan chapel, cement-rendered, with a rubble entrance gable pierced by a round window with a pattern of quatrefoils and trefoils flanked by two tall cusped lancets. –

ALTAR FURNITURE. *Pearse & Son.* – MONUMENT. The Rev. Thomas C. Dunne † 1851 by *J. Farrell.*

KILMESSAN GLEBE. *c.* 1800. A small, simple and perfectly charming glebe-house, reminiscent in its proportions of nearby Galtrim House and very likely from the hand of *Francis Johnston.* At three bays and two storeys over a semi-basement, it is a small building and has been enlarged in later years by the addition of single-bay, single-storey wings on each side. Shallow hipped roofs throughout and one central chimneystack. The entrance front is simple, with sash windows and a projecting central bay, which has a sash window set in a segmental-headed recess above a wide elliptical fanlit doorcase in an elliptical arch. Thin Adamesque Ionic shafts frame the side-lights. However modest, this is one of the most elegant country houses in the county.

SWAINSTOWN. 1 km SE. An intriguing house of *c.* 1750, built or reconstructed by Nathaniel Preston, a brother of the Irish M.P. John Preston, who was then building Bellinter, less than 10 miles N of here. Local tradition relates that Swainstown was built from materials left over from Bellinter and, while this cannot literally be true, there is, both within and without, a tendency to improvisation, which suggests both that Mr Preston was something of an architectural magpie and that Richard Castle may have had a hand in the design. Certainly there are oddities to be explained, though the initial impression of Swainstown, set in broad acres of parkland with the land falling away to the W beyond the house, is of text-book mid-C18 architecture. Indeed it could almost be taken from a plate in James Gibbs' *Book of Architecture*: a long regular block flanked by detached rectangular pavilions and linked to the house by quadrant wings. The formula is familiar, and the façade also conforms to conventional patterns: a wide two-storey block, set on a semi-basement, with the central three bays slightly advanced and approached by a broad flight of steps – as wide as the centre three bays – held between solid retaining walls. The house is decorated with quoins, at the corners and at the breaks on the façade, a continuous frieze, eaves cornice and blocking course and a segmental pediment over the doorcase. It has a hipped roof and two symmetrical chimneystacks. The wings are each two-storey, three-bay blocks with parapets and hipped roofs behind.

All this is perfectly routine for a substantial country house of *c.* 1750. It is in the detail that things start to go wrong; nothing lines up properly with anything else. The pavilion wings were probably added after the main block was built and are linked very loosely to it. The walls that tie them to the house look odd, as they are exactly the same height as the pavilions – not lower, as would be more usual – and the plan they follow is not a quarter circle or even a segment but a vague and ill-defined curve. Near the centre each is decorated by a blind niche with a lanky Ionic pilaster on either side. There is no entablature, just a broad course of exposed limestone; and it is similar courses of limestone, or interrupted courses, that trim the main façade. A problem design: how and why was it built the way it is? Looking at the house today, it does seem that Nathaniel Preston got hold of a spare set of window lintels, thirteen in all, and was determined to use them. Each has a raised keystone carved in the centre and trapezoid ends, as if the lintel were to form the top part of a blocked or Gibbs surround, though the sides of all these windows have no stonework but plain undecorated plaster reveals.

What is even odder is that, once the lintels were in place, the masons promptly put another course of exposed limestone above them, but could not manage the work with sufficient care for this second course to be built at the same level, between the first and second floors, so that it would line in with the cutstone of the quoins at the corners and centrepiece of the façade. Classical architecture depends for its effect on scrupulous care in these matters, and any half-competent architect would have insisted that the course lines of the quoins and of these string-courses should coincide. At Swainstown they collide, and the different levels are not reconciled one with the other until the main cornice is marked. The front doorcase is also a very odd design, a narrow segmental pediment with fine dentils on top of an attenuated architrave frame. It is really too tall for this front and its proportions would be more normal in a building of 1710 than one of 1750. Perhaps, like the lintels, it was picked up cheap in some mason's yard!

The interior of the house also contains surprises. It looks like a straightforward double-pile design and in so far as it is two rooms deep it lives up to expectations, but the layout of the rooms is once again idiosyncratic. The basement is the most usual plan, a long rectangular block with a central corridor running across the house from end to end. Its windows at the front are circular and the staircase occupies an odd position at the extreme N end of this corridor, filling the last bay of the entrance front. (It is also odd that it is the only staircase in the main house and that the long spinal corridor, so common in a double-pile plan, is not repeated on the main floor.) Here the original plan seems to have set two ranges of rooms back to back in such a way that no single wall ran through the house from one side to the other. The entrance front of seven bays had, reading from l. to r., a two-windowed room (the present dining room); a two-windowed hall, with the front door opening into one side and two doors facing it on the internal wall; then a second separate two-windowed room; and finally, taking up the space of the last window, the stair. Exactly the same sequence of rooms existed on the garden front but in the reversed order, so that behind the stair was a room two windows wide, then a second and a third – the present library – which has a single-bay cabinet opening off it. This is not an easy plan to describe and it is made the more difficult to discern today because in both fronts two rooms have been thrown into one. The hall has absorbed the room next to it before the stairs, creating a uniquely lop-sided entrance hall, 30 ft 6 in. (9.3 m) wide and 20 ft (6 m) deep, while the present drawing room has been created out of the two rooms at the back, next to the library, where the old arrangement of two back-to-back corner fireplaces has been replaced by a late Georgian flat chimneypiece on the internal wall. The dining room and library retain their original corner fireplaces and generous wainscotting, which rises in three fielded panels to a timber room cornice. The library also preserves what is probably another of Nathaniel Preston's bargains: three exceptionally tall and narrow oak doors, 8 ft (2.5 m) high, and made of unusually thin sections of timber. These cannot be coeval with the rest of the house; they seem to have been cut down in their upper section and can only be explained as materials adapted, like so much else in this house, from another building. Certain other idiosyncrasies throughout the house, like the incorporation of varied turned and fluted balusters in the stair and a diversity of mouldings to the joinery in the hall, point either to a mish-mash of building materials from the start, as tradition suggests, or alternatively to much wilful reworking and adaptation since the C18.

KILCARTY. 2 km S. Modesty and simplicity are the qualities of this handsome building of the 1770s (*see* pp. 46–7), erected as a 'hobby-farm' for a professor of anatomy, Dr Cleghorn, to designs by *Thomas Ivory*. A compact and practical house, Kilcarty is as elegant an instance as one will find of vernacular classicism in domestic architecture: a five-bay, two-storey gabled farmhouse with low lean-to wings and curtain walls screening a large office court behind. The courtyard is bordered on each side by tall shed ranges, whose gable ends, embellished with simplified pediments and oculi, serve as the terminal pavilions at each end of the entrance front. The buildings are rough-cast, with brick trim to the circular shed windows and a limestone blocked surround to the central doorcase. The windows of the house have twelve sash panes on the ground floor, six on the upper storey and six to the squat lean-to wings. Symmetrical plan, with two reception rooms flanking a small central stairhall: a rear corridor recently enlarged was accommodated across the back in a lean-to.

CHURCH OF THE ASSUMPTION, KILTEALE. 3.5 km S. 1882. Gothic, in rubble limestone with ashlar trim. Gabled lancet hall and chancel, with a bellcote and side porch so positioned that the side wall serves as the entrance front: a welcome change of siting from the ubiquitous triangular gabled façade. A small building nicely detailed. The porch, an unusual cusped opening, has a handsome moulded rere-arch springing from polished stone colonnettes with foliated capitals, hood-moulding and carved head label stops. Buttresses with offsets to the angles and pretty surrounds to the windows, like strip-cartoon eyelashes. Triple-light window with geometric tracery to the chancel. Bright interior, with a cross-braced timber roof, exposed rafters and purlins.

KILSKYRE

ME *6070*

Country parish with a church and school at a crossroads.

ST ALPHONSUS LIGUORI (AND ST SKYRE), KILSKYRE PARISH CHURCH. 1847–68 by *J. J. McCarthy*. A rural parish church in the heart of Co. Meath which was to become a touchstone for the success of the Gothic Revival in Ireland. Here, according to *The Catholic Directory* of 1849, was 'no barn of overgrown dimensions' but a church of 'true and ancient Catholic type', a harbinger of the proper ecclesiological medievalism that was to replace the thin decorative Gothic of late Georgian country chapels. Kilskyre stands at the beginning of McCarthy's celebrated career in the service of Irish Catholicism; within five years he was appointed to complete Duff's work at Armagh Cathedral, and innumerable commissions for Catholic parish churches followed. Kilskyre is thus a McCarthy prototype church. The style is a hard-edged C13 Gothic: a tall gabled nave with lean-to aisles, a gabled chancel, vestry, side chapel and a porch to the S aisle. A tower N of the entrance gable is crowned by a thin pinnacled spire, not completed until 1887. The church is built of limestone rubble masonry, has stepped buttresses and hoodmouldings of crisp limestone trim. All clear-cut, simple and skilfully massed, with steep slated roofs.

The interior is tall, though of modest proportions. The nave has a six-bay arcade of chamfered arches carried on alternating round and octagonal shafts, built of pale Ardbraccan limestone with E.E. capitals. Cusped twinlight windows to the aisles, with a large four-light window to each gable. A typical instance of the minuteness of Victorian criticism was *The Ecclesiologist*'s remark that it 'did not like the cinquefoils of the lights of the eastern window nor the trefoil on the head of the west'. A cross-braced roof with exposed rafters and purlins provides a dark foil to the whitewashed walls and limestone trim. One mark of McCarthy's youthful practice is the treatment of the clerestory, ample on the interior but cramped outside, with a narrow band of masonry looking as if its base had been chopped off by the aisle roofs. Nonetheless this is a charming building that fits perfectly into its rural setting.

In a field opposite McCarthy's church are the ivy-grown ruins of a medieval church. – MONUMENT. Part of a handsome C17 monument to Hugh O'Reilly dated 1686. Set into the wall, carved armorial bearings in a provincial classical style. Beneath, a stone sarcophagus with three primitive figures along one side and a skull and crossbones at one end.

KILSKYRE NATIONAL SCHOOL. 1836. Attractive two-storey, five-bay building, crowned by a wide hipped roof. Built of limestone rubble with cutstone jambs, lintels and raised corner quoins. Doorcase at each end for girls and boys respectively.

5040 KINNEGAD WM

In September 1748 Patrick Higgins of Kinnegad publicly advertised his reopening of the 'great inn at Kinnegad', which he claimed to have put into 'extraordinary good order … new furnished with stables in proper condition and with additional stalls'. He also claimed to hold 'a large stock of the best wines'. Today Kinnegad is still a stopping post, one long main street lined by two-storey lounges and cafés, with a plethora of large and unpleasant neon signs.

OUR LADY OF THE IMMACULATE CONCEPTION. 1904–9 by *T. F. McNamara.* A cruciform church of pale rock-faced limestone. Nave, transepts and chancel, with a tower and broach spire on the E side of the entrance table. A broad, even dumpy design, the church has all of McNamara's usual features, cusped lancets, quatrefoils, pointed arches, label mouldings and twinlight geometric windows. Though nowhere 'wrong', this is dry and lifeless Irish Catholic Gothic. The interior is equally conventional but more successful, flooded with light from paired lancets in the nave and triple-light windows in the transepts. Satisfying too in the authenticity of its fittings, altar-rail, reredos, altar and stained glass, all of a piece and hopefully to stay. – STAINED GLASS. *Mayer of Munich.*

KINNEGAD NATIONAL SCHOOL. 1893 by *A. Scott.* Picturesque single-storey school building with advanced and gabled end bays, each expressed as three graded lancets set into a round-headed relieving arch. Built of limestone rubble, with orange brick trim. Decidedly an addition to the street.

GRIFFINSTOWN. 3 km NW. Two-storey classical villa of *c.* 1820. Built of squared and coursed punched limestone, with a tetrastyle Greek Ionic porch in fine ashlar work. Regular sash windows throughout, with a three-bay front and four-bay back. Built by John Fetherston-Haugh, who developed the whole estate by laying a railroad through it, to help drain the surrounding boglands. The plan of the house – two rooms deep with a large central entrance hall, two rooms at the back, one each side and a bowed stairwell in the centre of one flank – is remarkably similar to Rockview (*see* Dysart), also built by the Fetherston-Haughs. Good ample proportions and fine-quality joinery also characterize both houses, though the hall doors here are of walnut rather than mahogany.

RATTIN CASTLE. 5 km WSW. Massive and imposing tower house. One of the largest and plainest isolated towers in Midhe, now ruinous, with little or no surviving cutstone detail. Four storeys rise from a battered base and the thick walls are honeycombed with mural chambers, stairs and passages, especially on the E side, where a number of separate and substantial long vaulted rooms remain. Here some traces of wickerwork centering survive. One C17 source claimed that Rattin had originally several towers and five hundred rooms! The usual lack of sound documentary references prevails, though it is known that by the C17 the castle was in the hands of Nicholas D'Arcy of Platten in Co. Meath. The manor of Rathwire had been granted to John D'Arcy of Platten in 1336, and the lands of Rattin may well have been part of the same grant; so the castle may be of the mid-C14, though whether it was built by the D'Arcys or by their Westmeath tenants is not clear.

CORALSTOWN CATHOLIC CHURCH, KINNEGAD CHAPEL OF EASE. 6 km NW. Long, routine Gothic Revival hall, designed by *J. P. Davis* in 1870. Six bays with a chancel and a three-stage pinnacled tower and spire offset on the N flank. Two twinlight geometric windows above a pointed arch to the entrance gable. The nave has cusped lancets with buttresses between. Davis intended the tower to be freestanding, joined by a cloistered porch to the chancel; lack of funds presumably determined the present more conventional arrangement. The tower gained its spire in 1954, when the steeple from the ruined Church of Ireland in Kinnegad was taken down and re-erected here. Inside, big plain hall and apsidal chancel; timber cross-braced roof.

KNOCKBRIDGE

LO *9000*

ST MARY. *c.* 1830. Large rectangular block, box-like, with a shallow hipped roof and more like a Nonconformist than a Catholic church. Remodelled *c.* 1870 by *John Murray*, who added a three-stage, battlemented and pinnacled belltower to the centre of the long E side. Refitted by *Ralph Byrne* in 1937. Cement-rendered and horizontally channelled, with long round-headed twinlight windows throughout. A pleasant airy interior with a gallery around three sides – once again a Nonconformist plan. A striking Hiberno-Romanesque sanctuary by Byrne fills the entire W wall. Three round arches carried on broad piers with nook shafts and panels of Celtic interlacing. More Celtic detail in the altar furniture and ceiling plasterwork. – STAINED GLASS. The Virgin and Child, and St Patrick, on the altar wall and belltower by *Harry Clarke*. SCULPTURE. In the belltower, statue of the Virgin by *P. Bell*, 1949.

STEPHENSTOWN HOUSE. 1.5 km SE. *c.* 1790. Large, square mansion hcuse of plain clear lines. Two storeys over a basement, five windows wide on each front, with a shallow hipped roof. Adjoining on the N, a single-storey Regency addition. Cement-rendered, with limestone trim, continuous eaves cornice, blocking course and corner quoins. Regular sash windows with pediments on the ground floor and flat entablatures above. A continuous string-course links the first-floor sills. The large single-storey Tuscan porch on the entrance front looks *c.* 1840. A nice feature of the house is the basement, enlivened by rusticated door and window surrounds. This is an elegant house, too large for modern rural life, empty in 1985 and likely to become derelict.

CORDERRY. 3 km S. Large rectangular single-storey villa, built on a deep basement, described as 'modern' in 1823. The principal elevation has three bays, with four to the side. Of Regency character, with the usual shallow hipped roof, bracketed eaves and big sash windows. The entrance, approached by a tall flight of broad steps, is framed by a timber entablature carried on Tuscan corner piers with two plaster columns *in antis*. – STABLES of 1841, mixing classical architecture with picturesque rubble building. The shed ranges have narrow slit lights, flat-headed doors and windows with heavy jambs, lintels and quarry glass. The main gateway is crowned by a mini temple-front with an Italianate cupola and weathervane.

4050

KNOCKDRIN CASTLE

WM

0.5 km E of Portneshangan

The gate lodge of Knockdrin Castle, a battlemented Gothic archway flanked by a dummy turret on one side and a solid and taller octagonal tower with a machicolated parapet on the other, leaves the visitor in no doubt as to the neo-medieval pretensions of this house. The castle was built by Sir Richard Levinge (1785–1848), who succeeded his father as sixth Baronet when he was eleven years old. The mansion house he inherited, High Park, was described as old and in poor repair, and when Sir Richard came of age he decided to replace it with a more romantic and more convenient type of property. There was on the estate the ruin of an old castle. Romantic fancy thought it might have been built by King John, and this no doubt provided the impetus to build in a castle style. It seems probable that Sir Richard would not have embarked on the rebuilding until after his marriage in 1810 or the birth of his eldest son in 1811, so a date for the new house somewhere in the mid-1810s seems most probable.

The architect chosen to design the new house was *Sir Richard*

Knockdrin Castle, from Sir B. Burke's *Visitation of Seats* (1855)

Morrison. Two copies of the front façade as designed by him survive, one at the house, the other in the Irish Architectural Archive. These propose a massing which is essentially the same as the castle has today, but neither is a proper match for the façade as it was built. Morrison proposed an irregular front which was evidently to be three rooms wide, with a battlemented wing on the l. screening a court of offices and ending in a flat two-storey tower. The hall, in the centre of the façade, was entered through a high archway similar to one that Morrison had built at Moydrum Castle, with a large mullioned window recessed within the arch above the front door. A pair of round turrets flanked this archway, with a taller and more substantial tower squashed in irregularly on one side.

Knockdrin as built creates a different effect from Morrison's drawn medievalism. It is a more ambitious house, with a centrepiece that is quite symmetrical, two flat turrets flanking a wide three-storey elevation with wide Gothic windows set one above the other and a charming tripartite Gothic doorway topped by a wide four-centred arch which contains a Gothic fanlight. The house is an essay in the type of architecture pioneered by James Wyatt, where a surfeit of almost accurate Gothic detail and a conscious avoidance of symmetry somehow create a regular and a rational effect. Thus on the entrance front the rooms on either side of the central symmetrical section are arranged as two-storey blocks, two windows deep, with a square corner turret on one side, and one window deep, with a round turret, on the other. On the garden front three reception rooms are laid out as three distinct parts: a corner turret adjoining a two-storey range of three windows; a projecting canted bay window treated as a three-storey tower – with the drawing room behind it – and then another two-storey section ending in another corner turret. The courtyard screen wall is much more emphatic than what was proposed in Morrison's drawings, with tall buttressed pinnacles marking out its length and a substantial two-storey gatehouse with turrets and an octagonal corner tower at its end. Built of a sombre grey limestone rubble and peppered with pretty white-painted Perp windows, Knockdrin appears to be an architectural stage-set, but its mood is one of civilized entertainment and not of melodrama.

The symmetry of the entrance tower and certain details are much closer to the castles of Francis Johnston, or perhaps even more his assistant James Shiel, than they are to Sir Richard Morrison's designs. Though there are no documents to confirm the suggestion, it seems possible that Levinge decided against the Morrison proposal and used the basic plan as the starting-point for a new design prepared by a second architect. If this were the case, then it seems likely that his choice fell either on Johnston or on Shiel, whose vigorous, and at times almost coarse, interpretation of Gothic matches much of the work at Knockdrin.

In keeping with the rational irregularity of the entrance front the interior is developed on a logical plan not far removed from standard late Georgian prototypes. A rectangular entrance hall, roofed with a pattern of three shallow lierne-vaults in plaster, leads to an enchantingly pretty triple-arched Gothic screen, with cluster-shafted columns and open cusp work, just where a pair of regular columns might be expected in a classical country house. Within the screen the roof is vaulted as a cross-corridor opening r. to the library and l. to a lobby outside the dining room and the back stairs of the house. Up to this point, only the neo-medieval detail would have been unfamiliar to a late Georgian visitor, but beyond the hall and on its axis there is not, as might be expected, a saloon but a theatrical top-lit Gothic stairhall, with a grandiose oak stair, cusped Gothic banister arches (of a type employed by Johnston at Charleville Forest, Co. Offaly), spiral fluted newel posts, crocketed and cusped ogee-headed niches, and, at first-floor level, a gallery colonnade of fluted shafts. The richly ornamented plaster ceiling has Shiel's favourite flattened geometrical Gothic panels.

In the grounds are a GOTHIC LOGGIA, a romantic TOWER and a CONSERVATORY. This is a pretty Regency design, with cast-iron antefixae of 1812 made by *G. Maliphart*. – The ruins of a small TOWER HOUSE (King John's castle?) are W of the modern castle. Built of limestone rubble with a slight batter at the base. A mural stair, loop windows and an ogee-headed window on the S face suggest the late C15 or C16. This was probably a residence of the Tuite family, who held these lands from the C12 until the C17 and the Irish rebellion of 1641.

0060 LANESBOROUGH LF

An important bridging point on the river Shannon, Lanesborough occupies the site of the medieval borough of Áth Liag – the ford of the stone – and the site of successive bridges between Midhe and Connacht. The Anglo-Normans quickly recognized the strategic significance of Áth Liag, and it was occupied throughout the C13 by de Lacys, de Mariscos and de Verduns. In the later Middle Ages Athlone became the more important centre and little is known of the place until the late C17, when it was granted at the Restoration to Sir George Lane. Lane proceeded to build 'fine stone houses and a very fair church with a tall steeple'. The stone bridge he erected in 1667 was described in 1682 as 'in length and breath the largest in the Kingdom'.

ST JOHN, RATHCLINE PARISH CHURCH. 1856–61 by *Joseph Welland*. A classic example of this architect's Puginesque work on a small scale. Nave, chancel, S porch and gable bellcote, all of snecked limestone rubble. Three-bay hall lit by paired lancets with quarry glass. Now utterly dwarfed by the great power station behind it.

BLESSED LADY OF THE ROSARY, LANESBOROUGH PARISH CHURCH. 1859. Mid-Victorian hall and tower church which has been reworked in the early C20. Three-bay gabled hall, with a square battlemented tower rising from the centre of the entrance front, flanked by flat-roofed two-storey vestibules, giving the front a boxy appearance. A curious mixture of quoins and hoodmouldings, with big octagonal pinnacles to the tower. Inside, big plain hall with an apsidal sanctuary. – STAINED GLASS. Pictorial saints in Gothic niches, 1913–19.

RATHCLINE CASTLE. 2 km S, on the E shore of Lough Ree. This late medieval castle, partly contained by and partly forming a large rectangular enclosure, was built by the Quinn family. Enlarged and provided with a fortified yard in the early C17, it was attacked by Cromwell, then restored *c.* 1666 by Sir George Lane, the patron of Lanesborough, only to be destroyed once again during the Williamite wars. Lane seems to have planned to rebuild the house entirely. He held a powerful position as secretary to the Duke of Ormond, the first Irish Viceroy of the Restoration period. No doubt he was influenced by the Duke's taste for classical architecture. At any event he is known to have procured plans and estimates for building a new house from an English architect. At Kilkenny the Duke had sought the advice of Hugh May and of Christopher Wren; Lane followed suit by employing another, if less prestigious, heir of Inigo Jones, the gentleman amateur *Dr John Westley*, who had married a daughter of Jones' pupil John Webb. Nothing, however, seems to have come of Dr Westley's proposals, or nothing survives, beyond the terraces and ditches of a rectangular water garden laid out at about this time to the SE of the old castle.

Given such illustrious associations the ruins of Rathcline are scanty and disappointing. Only the long E wall and a short N wall of the castle survive, with perimeter walls to the S and W. From the E the castle appears to be of two distinct building periods: at the S end is a substantial three-storey tower with a battered base, built of limestone rubble. Adjoining this is a longer three-storey range, rough-cast, with string-courses defining each floor, several large blocked-up cross-mullioned windows and, at the N end, a projecting rectangular three-storey turret. What appears to have happened is that an early C17 building was accommodated between two late medieval Quinn towers. An archway in the centre of the S perimeter wall is also of the first half of the C17. This evidently was once flanked by freestanding classical columns of a primitive character as traces of the pedestal bases and salient entablature blocks remain in the walls. The corners of the courtyard wall had low two-storey flanking bastions with loops for artillery fire. So Rathcline was clearly done up, perhaps *c.* 1630. The interior of the courtyard is a disappointment; virtually the whole of the castle has been dismantled and there is now little more than the line of high walling which is seen from the exterior. A moulded limestone chimneypiece is on the N wall, limestone embrasures survive in the tower and the charred holes for the roof timbers. – The shell of a range of mid-C19 FARM BUILDINGS with segmental window heads is inside the enclosure.

FERMOYLE. Another C17 mansion, now demolished, which stood a short distance S of Rathcline. It was built in the middle of the century by the Newcomen family, Cromwellian settlers.

8060 LISCARTON ME

3 km NW of Kells

Set in fields between the Boyne and the Kells road, the remains at Liscarton are extensive and deserve to be better known and better conserved. They offer a fascinating view of many of the structures found in an Irish late medieval manorial community. The ruins of two castles extend in a long range, parallel to the road, with a fortified entrance tower at the SE end and farm buildings and a detached manorial church to the N. Tall, rectangular and swathed in ivy, at the time of writing, the ruins could pass for a derelict industrial mill; their bulk is as extensive but their interest is far greater.

CASTLE RUINS. Records of Liscarton begin with the arrival of the Normans in Ireland, when Jocelin de Angulo, a Welsh knight, was granted the place with other townlands in the barony of Navan. Soon after, *c.* 1185, de Angulo confirmed an earlier grant of the Liscarton land (made by its previous owners, the O'Rourkes) to the Augustinian abbey in Navan, which made returns for the property in the Papal taxation of 1302–6 and remained responsible for the church at Liscarton until the Dissolution in the C16. The de Angulo family, also known as Nangle and de la Corner, retained responsibility for the security of the area and probably built the fortified buildings here.

In the Civil Survey of 1641 the townland of Liscarton is listed as being 292 acres in extent, with two castles, a church, a mill and a weir. It then belonged to Sir Robert Talbot of Carrtown and Adam Minott of Bellewstown. In the Cromwellian period the property changed hands once more when it passed to the Cadogan family, who retained it until the C19. It is probably a mistake to refer to this group of buildings as one unit. The entrance tower, a segmental vaulted passage, with a room above and a stair on its E side, is quite separate from all the other buildings and, like the similar tower at Newhaggard near Trim, may once have protected a relatively large enclosure.

The castle itself is really two independent and very substantial tower houses. That to the N, nearest the church, is possibly the earlier of the two structures. It is a grand building, with all its walls standing entire for a full three storeys, lacking only the battlemented parapets and turret tops that once completed its design. The scale is impressive, for this late medieval house contains a huge central hall, 17 ft (5.1 m) wide and some 40 ft (12 m) in length, set above two large vaulted chambers. The hall is approached by a dog-leg stair accommodated in a separate tower at its SE corner; two further square towers extend from its longer N side. Each of these towers has a separate spiral stair to give access to a succession of rooms set one above the other. The NE tower retains most of its vaulting, with the top two floors closed by almost flat vaults of huge slabs of stone, where lovers of picturesque decay can enjoy a giddy view through one floor to the ceiling of the next. The NW tower has no vaulting and may possibly be a little later in date. It preserves characteristic stone recess window seats on the upper floors and a perfect cusped two-light mullioned window at the top of its W wall. The wall-heads are corbelled inward to provide a footing for the timbers of the roof. More small chambers, with windows decorated with cusped heads, are accommodated in the SE stair tower. The stair itself, once the level of the hall is reached, converts to a spiral form, but a generous one with treads $4\frac{1}{2}$ ft (1.4 m) wide.

The second castle stands 44 ft (13.2 m) to the S and is a similar large tower house with the remains of a rectangular great hall at its centre to which smaller square towers are attached, one on the NE corner and two on the S at either end of the long side wall of the hall. This second castle is more ruinous and bears traces of extensive alteration in the C18, with many large square-headed brick openings and an C18 vaulted room filling the space between the two towers on the S. Three spiral stairs are set in the corners of rooms along the W wall. That at the N is as ample as the main stair in the first castle, though now partly fallen away. Pointed stone door openings with single-chamfered reveals and some fireplaces remain at the E end of the hall. Piles of rubble fill most rooms and impede access to the basement of the great hall.

CHURCH. Like the gate tower, the church is entirely detached from the rest of the ruins, standing on its own in a different field to the N. It is a narrow rectangular structure, still in use in the C18, when three large segment-headed windows were made in the side walls. It preserves a very perfect two-light mullioned window, with cusps and elaborated tracery, in the N gable, and another over the entrance door. Carved label stops of a lord and lady wearing coronets and a mitred abbot have been interpreted as portraits of John Nangle, his wife, Eleanor Dowdale, and Richard Nangle, Abbot of Navan in the late C15. The interior was divided into nave and chancel, with traces of a rood loft and stair at the junction. – Between the church and the castle ruins are extensive ranges of C18 or early C19 STABLING, BYRES and a square FARMYARD. Some of these buildings have architectural pretensions and make use of oculus lights to the upper storey.

LOBINSTOWN

ME *9080*

CHURCH OF THE HOLY CROSS. 1984 by *Noel MacAree*. Basically a rectangular gabled hall, rough-cast, with a narrow tower flanking the S gable. The church is given interest by stepping in the nave roof-level to provide a V-shaped clerestory in the centre, and by bringing the slating of the taller section over the eaves as a deep border, not unlike the effect of a mansard roof. The long E and W elevations have low walls with entrance porches and large panels of abstract stained glass.

CHURCH OF THE NATIVITY OF THE BLESSED VIRGIN. 1.5 km E, at Heronstown. Erected in 1857 by the Rev. James Lynch. A big gabled hall with that type of cutstone Gothic façade made popular by Thomas Duff during the 1830s and repeated well into the Victorian period in country parishes throughout North Leinster: three Y-traceried windows in pointed arches, with pinnacled buttresses defining each bay. Inside, the church is arranged as a four-bay nave and a single-bay chancel, divided by a broad two-centred arch.

KILLARY CROSS. 1.5 km W. The shaft of a lone cross, 6 ft (1.8 m) high and standing near a featureless ruined church. The cross is decorated with panels of interlace and carved with figure subjects. These are, reading from the base up, on the E face, the Fall, the Flood, the Sacrifice of Isaac and an unidentified figure between two rampant animals. On the W face, two unidentified figures, the Baptism of Christ and the Presentation in the Temple. On the N side are two figure carvings, now largely illegible; otherwise the sides are decorated with panels of plait-work, spiral patterns, interlacing and bosses.

ST DAVID, SYDDAN PARISH CHURCH (C of I). 2 km N. 1881 by *J. F. Fuller*. A small, pleasantly massed church consisting of a tall four-bay nave, a lower chancel flanked by gabled vestry rooms, a tower and porch at the W end of the N elevation and an apsidal baptistery projecting from the W gable. Built of rock-faced limestone, with smooth limestone dressings. E.E. detail, with triple-light windows to nave and chancel and a simple rose window at the W end. The tower and spire, complete with pinnacles and lucarnes, is C13 French in character. Pleasant bright interior, with an open kingpost roof and a timber reredos containing decorative brass panels. – MONUMENTS. Two nice thinly detailed memorials from a former church: Charles Adams †1815; the Rev. Brabazon Disney †1831.

CHURCH OF THE NATIVITY OF OUR LADY. 3.5 km NE, at Newtown. Plain early Victorian T-plan church, nicely set behind a symmetrical wall with paired gates to its precinct. Cutstone gable with tiny pinnacles and a narrow Y-tracery window with hoodmoulding. Pointed arches in the transepts.

1070

LONGFORD

LF

Historically Longford pales in contrast with frontier towns like Athlone and Dundalk or great military and religious centres like Trim and Kells. Physically it is also unremarkable, neither quaint in a medieval sense nor planned like a Georgian square. And yet the place is not without atmosphere: it has the charm of a bustling

C19 market town, its streets lined with fancy stone and stucco façades and its skyline dominated by one of the largest and finest Victorian churches in the country. The tradition that this was the site of a Patrician monastery is unsubstantiated, and of the C15 Dominican monastery founded by the O'Farrells nothing now survives. These reputedly stood at the N end of the town near the river in present-day Bridge Street. Here also, on the site of the modern Seán Connolly Barracks, stood Longford Castle, built *c.* 1627 by Francis Aungier, Lord Longford, whose family resided here until the late C18, though by then the aristocratic title had passed to the Pakenhams. During the course of the C17 and C18 and beginning in 1619 the Aungiers secured several royal grants of markets and fairs and duly built beside the castle a large and spacious markethouse. This building, which in 1774 was sold with the castle to the Royal Commissioners of Barracks, is the oldest surviving in Longford town.

By the 1780s the town could be described as 'clean and tidy', 'large and well built'. With the arrival of the Royal Canal in the 1820s it improved rapidly and soon became one of the leading markets for grain, pork, bacon and butter. In 1836 its public buildings included churches, a barracks, a courthouse, gaol, schools and a branch of the Bank of Ireland. Modern-day Longford presents a very long main street, wide and high at its centre, but shunning its principal churches. The Church of Ireland building is marooned in a quiet oasis round a corner at the top of the town, where its spire can make little contribution to the townscape, while the great Catholic Cathedral, a building of quite exceptional bulk, is lost down a side road in the outskirts to the SE, approached through narrow streets of C19 terraced houses.

ST MEL'S CATHEDRAL. This huge, plain building, begun in 117
1840, can probably best be read as an act of faith in stone. It is the work of three architects: *John B. Keane*, who had supervised the construction of the Pro-Cathedral in Dublin as clerk to Sir Richard Morrison and who made the original designs; *John Bourke*, who designed the campanile tower (1863) and continued the construction after Keane's death in 1859; and *George C. Ashlin*, who built the entrance portico in 1889–93.

St Mel's is a very metropolitan design dropped down on the edge of the countryside and looking incongruous here. Its orientation is roughly S–N rather than E–W, and the long E side, even today, looks out on fields of browsing cattle and the tree-lined avenue which leads to the cathedral Seminary. On the W are little streets of low houses, while the front, beyond its handsome Victorian gates and cast-iron railings, faces a confused intersection of roads and a sloping car park. In terms of formal architecture Keane's church should occupy the centre of one side of a square, or preside over a marketplace at the end of a street. It requires – and deserves – such a setting, yet landowners and the denominational politics of early Victorian Ireland denied the building a proper site.

Keane's design is remarkable for its scale and for the originality of the interior. On the exterior the high limestone walls seem too large for the almost unarticulated architecture of which they are built, with little more than shallow rustication and a thin eaves entablature to differentiate their surfaces (Ralph Byrne, ninety years later, was to grapple with the same problem of a long flat nave wall at Mullingar, and demonstrates there a far richer manipulation of the wall surface.) Short rectangular transepts, framed at the corners by shallow Doric pilasters, project from the sides at the N end. The back of the cathedral block contains offices beyond the church and has a surprisingly domestic, symmetrical three-storey façade. What all this looks like is a church whose sides were intended to be hidden by the surrounding buildings of a centre-city site, as is the case with many of the early C19 classical churches in Dublin which Keane knew – St Andrew's, Westland Row, St Audoen's, Thomas Street, St Paul's, Arran Quay, and Keane's own Jesuit church of St Francis Xavier in Gardner Street.

The Doric pilasters suggest that Keane's portico would have been Doric too, but, soon after St Mel's was begun, the Famine intervened, halting the building's progress, and when John Bourke was employed to finish the work the church was given a plain gabled front surmounted by the present octagonal belfry. This is a good design, in three stages with an excellent silhouette, enhanced by four Ionic aedicules which project boldly, a little like the arrangement used by Gandon at the Dublin Customs House, from the slanted sides of the second storey.

A curved indentation of the wall entablature at each end of the nave, just before the portico, marks the junction between Bourke's work and Ashlin's. An angry correspondent to *The Irish Builder* in 1893 maintained that the massive six-column Ionic portico was not Ashlin's idea but was due to the County Surveyor James Bell. Ashlin certainly drew up the plans and supervised the work – an odd job for the leading Gothic architect of his generation – and it is perhaps the portico, with its wide intercolumnation and massive ashlar wall in blue-grey limestone, which, more than anything else, makes the cathedral seem out of place in its setting. In itself it is a finely executed piece of academic classicism. The pedimental sculpture, showing St Mel enthroned as first bishop of the diocese, is by *George Smyth*.

The dullness of St Mel's side elevations is fully compensated
118 by Keane's interior, which is one of the most beautifully conceived classical spaces of Irish architecture. The church is planned as a nave and aisles, separated by a continuous Ionic arcade which flows without interruption into the walls of an apsidal sanctuary, where the order changes to that of an Ionic pilaster respond, not unlike the Doric of the exterior. The side walls of the aisles repeat the pattern of the pilasters in the sanctuary and are carried across the transepts as a freestanding three-bay arcade of Ionic columns, identical in scale and detail to those of the nave. Niches filled with statues on high plinths

alternate between the windows of the side walls and fill the blank arcading of the sanctuary apse. The simple coherence and logic to this design are completed by a high semicircular ribbed vault over the nave and by flat coffered ceilings to the aisles. Much of the inspiration for this interior seems to come from the church architecture of early C 19 France (particularly the work of Chalgrin) and from the first scheme for the Pro-Cathedral in Dublin, preserved in the form of a model, which was to have employed a feature which Keane also uses here, lunette windows located at the base of the vault immediately above the entablature of the arcades. These windows have also an Irish ancestry in Sir William Chambers' Chapel at Trinity College, Dublin, so the sources of Keane's inspiration were evidently complex. What is beyond doubt is the success of his solution, matched by craftsmanship of great quality in the dressing of the stone columns, the carving of the capitals and the modelling of the plaster angels in the spandrels above them. The bronze screens to the transept chapels and electric light standards in the nave are by *Ralph Byrne*. The furniture in the sanctuary dates from the 1970s; the original high altar has been dismantled.

The entrance to the cathedral is through a central octagonal lobby added by Bourke. A stairway off this leads to the organ gallery, an upper gallery under the vault, and echoing empty spaces of bare boards and plain walls which seem never to have had much use.

ST JOHN TEMPLEMICHAEL PARISH CHURCH (C of I). A pleasant, big Georgian church with a good site closing a short vista at the E end of Bridge Street. The church was founded in 1710, and that building's fabric may well be incorporated in the existing church, which is, however, late C 18 in character; the Rev. D. A. Beaufort, visiting Longford in 1787, remarked upon the 'very handsome new church'. In 1812 the building was further renovated and enlarged to accommodate the town garrison. The W front now presents the familiar hall and tower pattern of a Protestant church: a central three-stage tower and needle spire flanked by parapeted vestibules. Yet the ample proportions of the tower are quite different from the usual thin Board of First Fruits work, and this is probably part of the 1780s building. The C 18 church consisted of a large rectangular hall with a tall hipped roof, round-headed windows and a W entrance tower. In the nave, fielded panelling from this church survives to sill level. In 1810 an apsidal sanctuary was added to the centre of the long S wall, and opposite that a large N transept was built to accommodate the larger congregation. A gallery was inserted at the W end of the nave and another in the new transept. The decoration in this bright airy interior is neoclassical in feeling, with gilded garlands and masks to the galleries and, in the apse, a Greek-key impost course and pleated fan decoration to the apex of the arch. Without its round-headed stained-glass window the chancel would look not unlike a shallow end recess in a Francis Johnston drawing room. – MONUMENT. The Rev. James Sterling, Rector, † 1691 and his wife, Helen Maxwell, † 1709; plain white marble plaque.

128 ST MEL'S DIOCESAN SEMINARY. 1863 by *John Bourke*. Prosaic institutional classicism on a grand scale, relieved to some extent by an attractive tree-lined approach. Bourke's college is a sixteen-bay, three-storey block redeemed from dullness by a shallow manipulation of the surface, which breaks in and out, with each step emphasized by corner quoins. There are four projecting bays at the centre, two at each end, and the middle two of the centre four are further advanced and crowned by an eaves pediment and a short Italianate lantern typical of Bourke's style. In the central block a freestanding Tuscan porch is flanked by Adamesque Venetian windows in relieving arches, and a pedimented niche occupies the space between the two first-floor windows, creating a central focus in an historic Irish way that goes back to Richard Castle. In the recessed four-bay block on each side, round-headed ground-floor sash windows take up the arch theme. The plan of the college (since much altered) is an extended U-shape, of which the entrance block formed the base. The college architect in the early C 20 was *T. F. McNamara*. – STATUE. John Kilduff, Bishop of Ardagh and founder of the college (1820–67).

CONVENT OF MERCY. 1872–4 by *John Bourke*. Two-storey, nine-bay block with a central gabled projection and pointed twinlight windows. Of limestone rubble with polychrome brick trim. The convent chapel is relatively large and richly decorated. Cruciform, with an off-set tower, cusped geometric tracery and carved wooden stalls arranged in collegiate fashion. – Seven-bay school building with blue and red brick trim, 1886.

MARKETHOUSE. Within the precinct of Seán Connolly Barracks. The oldest building in Longford and one of the earliest and best-surviving markethouses in Leinster. 1619 is the traditional building date, but this seems much too early for such a neat and classically inspired structure; a date in the early C 18 is more probable. However, given the lack of documentary evidence, the standard character of markethouse arcades from the later C 17 throughout the C 18 makes accurate dating difficult. What we do know is that the building was erected by the Aungier family and was sold by them to the barrack commissioners in 1774, so that it was presumably in use for a long period of time before that. Longford Markethouse differs from the usual Irish form in having only one storey, with no fenestrated assembly rooms above it. It is a large rectangular building, of brick and rubble, and was originally arcaded throughout. The exterior clearly expresses the structure in a series of ample round-headed arches, four to the E and W elevations and two to the N and S. The building is roofed by a series of brick groin vaults spanning the spaces between the arcade piers and a row of five piers which runs down the centre of the building. It is still floored with limestone cobble stones.

One intriguing aspect of its design is the treatment of the external arches of the arcade, which are framed by almost primitive rusticated borders made up of curious rough pebble-filled stones. This is the so-called pudding stone, a mixture of sandstone, quartz and limestone found at Slieve Caldragh near Ardagh, which is used extensively in the late medieval tower house of Castlerea in that area. Its use here at Longford suggests perhaps an early date and certainly the presence of a sophisticated designer willing to use natural local materials in a remarkably expressive way.

COURTHOUSE. 1791; remodelled and enlarged in 1859. A tall ungainly building, like an overscaled Georgian town house, which dominates the W side of the main street. Modern shopfronts and offices obscure the ground-floor level, which was formerly a basement bridewell. In the centre, a massive Doric porch with freestanding columns, full triglyph frieze and pediment reinforces the authority of the law. It is flanked by two very tall round-headed windows and surmounted on the floor above by a regular Venetian window. So the original courthouse presented a standard five-bay, two-storey front to the street, with semi-basement lock-ups below. It has stone quoins at the corners and stone architraves to the window. The mid-Victorian enlargement added two top-lit courtrooms at the back of the building and an extra floor on the front. Here the detail changes slightly: the windows are segment-headed and a clumsy Italianate double-light window under an eaves pediment is placed over the Venetian window. Dull Victorian glazing does little for the original design.

SEÁN CONNOLLY BARRACKS. A cavalry barracks was established at Longford in 1774 on land leased to the Barracks Commissioners by Lord Longford. The site included the former Longford Castle and the old Aungier Markethouse. During the C18 the markethouse was used as stables for 28 troop horses. New barrack buildings were constructed between 1808 and 1843. The most impressive of these is a large and handsome building of 1815 by *John Behan*, whose drawings survive in the military archives at Cathal Brugha Barracks. Close to the institutional idiom of Francis Johnston, this has a three-storey, five-bay central block with a low hipped roof, flanked by two-storey, six-bay ranges with advanced and gabled end blocks. Horizontally channelled basement to the centre and end blocks. Sash windows throughout except on the first floor of the end blocks, which have large Wyatt windows. The building was designed to accommodate the officers' mess and sleeping quarters.

ULSTER BANK. 1863 by *James Bell, Junior*. The best façade on Longford's main street: good solid Victorian architecture. Three-storey, four-bay palazzo-style block flanked by narrow single-storey curtain walls, all in crisp limestone ashlar. A tall and deeply moulded arcade across the banking hall front has sandstone keystones carved with the faces of rivers, which link to a corbelled first-floor string-course; segmental pediments above the first-floor windows and smaller windows in moulded surrounds to the top floors. Wide roof cornice with a bold modillion course. One of the earliest buildings constructed in the southern counties by a Belfast bank.

BANK OF IRELAND. *c.* 1860. *William Caldbeck*'s standard large design for the National Bank Co.: Italianate three-storey, five-bay street frontage with advanced and pedimented outer bays. Limestone rusticated arcade to the banking floor, with pedimented windows to the first floor and simple plate-glass windows on the top storey. Renovated by *Millar and Symes*, 1901.

OTHER BUILDINGS. At the N end of the town, the METHODIST CHURCH, 1895, is a four-bay gabled hall of limestone rubble with yellow stone trim, paired lancets and gabled porch. MASONIC HALL. 1886. Attractive two-storey, three-bay redbrick house with terracotta details. Brick pilasters between each bay, string-courses and miniature machicolation at eaves level. CLONGUISH NATIONAL SCHOOL. Late C19. Low two-storey redbrick building, with big slated roofs in a sober picturesque idiom.

7040

LONGWOOD ME

CHURCH OF THE ASSUMPTION. 1841. Built by the Rev. John Hackett, Parish Priest of Longwood from 1842 to his death in 1854. Three-bay lancet hall, with a bellcote, battlemented parapet and triple-light Perp window to the entrance gable. Nice limestone holy-water stoups inside the entrances.

LIONSDEN. 3 km N. A two-storey late C18 house which appears to have been radically remodelled. The proportions of the entrance front, now of two bays, are exceedingly odd, with inordinately large expanses of masonry. Rough-cast, with a blocked cutstone doorcase and a radial fanlight above the door. A bowed and slated extension adjoins the gable end. Vaguely reminiscent of Roristown near Trim.

BALLINDERRY HOUSE. 2.5 km SE. Boxy two-storey, five-bay Georgian block, not unlike Newhaggard House, a short distance N from here (*see* Trim). Both are harled, with a parapet that entirely hides a low hipped roof. Pain-type Doric doorcase.

NEWCASTLE. 5 km SE. Built into a C19 farmyard, a modest C15 tower house comprising two storeys and a roof-walk above a tall vaulted basement, with chimneys in the W wall and a garderobe at the SE corner. The building's most remarkable feature is its unusual stair arrangement, a circular turret located in the centre of the E wall. C18 and C19 window openings.

JORDANSTOWN AND KILL PARISH CHURCH. 5.5 km SE, at Kilcorney. Tall mid-C19 five-bay lancet hall, with a bellcote over the W end. Renovated in 1907 by *T. F. McNamara*, who faced the entrance gable with snecked limestone rubble and inserted a new Ruskinian chancel arch and a triple-light window in the altar wall.

LOUGHCREW

ME *5070*

LOUGHCREW CHURCH. A late medieval manorial church built by the Loughcrew branch of the Plunkett family, the ancestors of St Oliver Plunkett, who was born here in 1629. Although by no means as ambitious or as richly ornamented as the other Plunkett churches in Meath (Dunsany, Killeen and Rathmore), Loughcrew is a well-preserved and evocative building in a charming rural setting. It shares one characteristic with the other Plunkett churches, a substantial residential tower, here situated at the W end of the nave. The plan is otherwise straightforward: a long nave, with a small chapel projecting from the middle of the S wall. The floor level rises at the chancel end; otherwise there is no marked break between the two parts of the church. Entrance is gained through the tower, a squat three-storey structure, 25 ft by 27 ft (7.5 m by 8.1 m), with a straight stair to first-floor level and a spiral stair to the upper storeys. Traditional tower-house appearance; the regularity of the window voussoirs and the pocked surface of the dressed stonework suggest a mid- to late C15 date. The body of the church, 94 ft 10 in. by 21 ft 7 in. (28.9 m by 6.57 m), is relatively plain and classical in feeling, with deep round-headed windows on each side and a large E window set into a round relieving arch, all probably the result of an C18 remodelling. The only cutstone detail to survive is a window in the S chapel, which now appears as two pointed lights, the central mullion gone, and surmounting the central spandrel a carved coat of arms and a hoodmoulding. The arms are those of the Naper family, who came to Loughcrew in the late C18; as the carving seems earlier, it may have been brought from another site. The church continued in use into the modern period. In the 1640s it was described, together with a castle, as in 'tolerable repair', and by 1818 it had been renovated and re-roofed. It was abandoned only in 1843, when a new church was built. – MONUMENT. Grave slab in the tower with raised lettering (now illegible) commemorating Mrs Elizabeth Duddel (the Duddel family became the owners of Loughcrew after the Plunketts were dispossessed). – CHURCHYARD. Two headstones of interest. S side of church, row 5, a plain stone to Alexander Cremer †1754 aged sixteen; 'erected by Hugh Cremer Mason in the parish of Loughcrew in the year 1759'. N side of nave, headstone to Alexander Duggan, stucco plasterer and artist, †1831 aged forty-five; 'This monument was erected by a few of his admiring friends as a small testimonial of their regard for his personal merits and professional abilities of which the congruous mansion of Loughcrew abounds with many brilliant specimens'.

ST KIERAN, LOUGHCREW PARISH CHURCH (C of I). *c.* 1840 by *Joseph Welland*; an early work, designed before its architect had absorbed Pugin's ideas. Small, four-bay hall of punched limestone with round-headed lancets. Gabled W porch, diagonal buttresses, w bellcote and quarry glass. The original interior had a flat plaster ceiling with a cornice band of linked rings. New chancel by *J. F. Fuller*, 1904.

Loughcrew House. One of Ireland's major architectural losses, demolished in 1968, though the estate is still announced on the main road by a charming and unorthodox classical gate lodge – Inigo Jones' St Paul's, Covent Garden, done over in neo-Greek detail. The house itself is now reduced to one low range with terminal pavilions, a painted illusionistic façade and one gaunt two-storey side of the original main block open to the elements. Formerly an austere, neoclassical complex, Loughcrew was built in 1823 for J. L. Naper to designs of *C. R. Cockerell*. It was an ill-fated house: burnt three times and twice rebuilt within the space of one century. The courthouses of J. B. Keane come to mind in considering Cockerell's design, which was a large and austere limestone cube with a two-storey Greek Ionic portico and an Italianate pedimented centre to the side elevation. The masonry was of exceptional quality, finely droved limestone ashlar; some of it has been imaginatively reused in paving the West End Arcade at Drogheda. The house, perhaps because it has now gone, exerts a continuous influence on the imagination of architectural historians, yet Cockerell's own verdict should be recalled: 'the proportions seem just but very plain, too bald. After all it is but a square house, admirably executed.'

Newtown House. Rectangular three-storey block of five bays, with a lower two-storey, two-bay wing. Of mid-Georgian proportions, though evidently reworked in the early Victorian period, when a castellated porch, label-mouldings and small gablets over the top-floor windows were added to the front: cut-price romanticism, common in Ireland at this date.

9000 LOUTH LO

Quiet crossroads village with a group of fine medieval ecclesiastical remains. The centre of a royal manor and borough during the C13 and C14, Louth was once one of the most important settlements in the region and gave its name to the county of Louth.

St Mochta's House. Although of a relatively early type of Irish church construction, St Mochta's House owes nothing but its name to the C5 saint and disciple of St Patrick who established a monastery at Louth. Of that foundation nothing survives beyond a few historical references: that the monastery was plundered by Danes in 830 and 839 and that its round tower was blown down *c.* 980. The 'house' is a simple gabled oratory with a steeply pitched roof, built of local Silurian stone with limestone quoins, the external roofing made up of thin flags horizontally bedded. Inside, a ground-floor chamber; above it an inner barrel-vault taking the thrust of the roof slopes and leaving a small roof-croft above it. Such structures have been built in Ireland since the early C 9 – St Colmcille's House at Kells and St Kevin's Church at Glendalough, Co. Wicklow, are examples – but St Mochta's House is not as old as these, having a more sophisticated form of vault construction and a stone stair, however tortuous, leading to the upper chamber. Both of these argue for a later date; earlier oratories, as at Kells, have simply a trap door in the roof of the vault approached by a ladder. At Louth, the roof-croft must have been used regularly, perhaps as a sleeping chamber, whereas in earlier churches its function was principally structural. St Mochta's House may be compared to St Flanan's Church at Killaloe, Co. Clare, and may be dated to the C 10 or C 11.

LOUTH ABBEY. At the dissolution of the monasteries Louth Abbey consisted of a priory, a rectory, a church, two castles, a dormitory, a bakehouse, a pigeonhouse and a granary. All that survives of this extensive complex is the roofless abbey church, with no trace of the buildings which once adjoined it. The abbey was the Augustinian Priory of St Mary, founded in 1148 by Donnchad Ua Cerbaill, King of Airghialla, and Aidan O'Caellaidhe, Bishop of Louth. Destroyed by fire in 1312, the monastic buildings were rebuilt in the early C 14, perhaps before 1325, when a general chapter of Augustinian canons was held here. A valuation in 1400 estimated the abbey to be one of the richest monasteries in Ireland. Today there is little here that is redolent of wealth, but the few remaining fragments of cutstone detail suggest at the very least a church of some grandeur.

The fabric of the church is a mixture of slate and limestone rubble, with dressings of limestone and sandstone. Both gables are fully standing, and the long S wall of the church is largely intact. The N wall is largely a modern rebuilding. The articulation of the long S wall explains the interior arrangement of the building. At its W end, tiers of joist holes, a doorway and a single tall, narrow window bespeak a short, dimly lit nave, with residential buildings originally abutting on the S. Two broad buttresses interject between the nave and a much longer five-bay chancel, lit originally by large traceried windows, though these are now mostly walled up. At 154 ft by 26 ft (46.9 m by 7.8 m) internally, the church was once a grand structure, with nave and choir divided by a rood screen, of which a fragment survives inside, E of the existing doorway in the S wall of the church. A vaulted and still plastered recess in the angle made by the screen and the chancel wall probably housed a stair to the rood loft.

In contrast to the small and dimly lit nave, the scale and luminosity of the chancel must have been a striking feature of this interior. The apertures which once provided such abundant light are broad, triple-light windows with large roll-moulded mullions rising to form deeply layered and foiled intersecting tracery. The E window in particular preserves enough cutstone to suggest the remarkably plastic, almost sculptural, quality of the masonry work. Originally the gable windows were even larger in profile, as is demonstrated by an over-scaled internal hoodmoulding above the E window and by an excessively long apron to the W window. These must once have been filled by groups of tall, plain lancets. The new windows, which were inserted in the C14, were further embellished by moulded rere-arches with carved label stops.

The finest surviving carved ornament at Louth adorns not one of the larger traceried windows but rather the tall single-light opening in the S wall of the nave. This is framed on the interior wall by a moulded rere-arch terminating in two wonderfully crisp limestone bell capitals carved with filleted rolls, dogtooth and foliated ornament. It is usually ascribed to the C13, but in a provincial Irish setting such as Louth such ornament would not be out of keeping with an early C14 date. Similar delicate carving would presumably have ornamented the sedilia which occupied one of the easternmost bays in the wall of the chancel, now merely a gaping recess, a shadow of its former self.

LOUTH FORMER PARISH CHURCH (C of I). Erected in 1807 to designs by *Francis Johnston*; enlarged in 1828. Now a ruin completely hidden from view among trees, thorns and nettles.

CHURCH OF THE IMMACULATE CONCEPTION. 1890–1904 by *W. H. Byrne & Son*. Large Gothic church on an elevated site; the tall broach spire is a prominent local landmark. A typical work of this firm, which specialized in robust, no-nonsense architecture. The entrance gable is generously designed, with a pair of ample twinlight windows above an arched door flanked by colonnettes and thin lancets. Buttressed three-stage NE tower with statue niche, double-louvred belfry and lucarnes to the spire. The interior is bright and spacious, a four-bay nave opening through an arcade into shallow transepts. Paired lancets in the nave and triple lancet windows to transepts and chancel. Pink polished granite shafts support the transept arcades, with polished grey granite colonnettes and Caen stone angel corbel stops to the chancel arch. – STAINED GLASS. The Virgin, St Joseph and St John the Baptist by *Mayer of Munich*.

MONVALLET HOUSE. 1.5 km N. 1872 by *Robert McArdle*; built for the Neary family. Modest Italianate three-bay house, the front two storeys on a sunk basement, with a shallow roof, brick chimneys and bracketed eaves. A clumsy Tuscan porch now hides a tripartite door with fanlight and console brackets. Corner quoins, string-course and ornamental window surrounds. Columnar screen in the hall.

STONETOWN CATHOLIC CHURCH. 3.5 km NW. A charming rural church, built by the Rev. P. Banàn in 1837. Tiny, T-plan with a bellcote over the entrance gable. Harled with corner quoins and Y-traceried windows. Plain interior with modernized reredos.

KILLANY OLD CHURCH. 6 km W. Simple barn-style Catholic chapel of 1789, now used as an outbuilding. Gabled and lime-washed, with a pointed entrance and external stair at one gable end. Typical of the modest country chapels which were constructed throughout Ireland during the last decades of the penal code.

MELLIFONT ABBEY

LO *0070*

If Mellifont is seen in late summer, bathed in a warm golden light, it is not hard to imagine it as it once was, the Fountain of Honey which its name still recalls. This was the first of the Cistercian foundations in Ireland, harbinger of tendencies in the C12 church towards a more disciplined and a more resolute monastic life. Set across the shallow valley of the river Mattock, little more than a deep stream, few places could be better suited both to meditation and to industry. Even though the ruins are fragmentary, enough survives to allow the visitor to reconstruct a picture of the abbey's medieval life.

Though Mellifont was not founded until 1142, its real beginning could be dated two years earlier, when St Malachy, *en route* for Rome, visited the Cistercian mother house at Clairvaux and left four companions behind him to learn the Cistercian rule. Two years later, together with Donough O'Carroll, King of Oriel, he founded the abbey of Mellifont with a community of monks sent by St Bernard from Clairvaux. A strong French influence pervaded every aspect of the abbey's foundation, from the conventional Cistercian design, reputedly supervised by the French builder-architect *Brother Robert*, to the Caen stone imported from Calvados in Normandy for the mouldings and fine members of the building. The continental influence was to be short-lived, however, for it soon transpired that the Irish wished to assert a degree of independence and were disinclined to observe all the statutes of the Order. In a short time the French founder brothers returned to Clairvaux, leaving Mellifont's affiliation to the general Cistercian chapter strained at least until 1228, when Stephen of Lexington made a visitation to Ireland which included this abbey and had some success in initiating reforms.

The first abbey took fifteen years to complete and was consecrated in 1157, by which time seven colonies had been sent out by the community to found other abbeys in Ireland. By 1170 there were 100 monks and 300 lay brothers living at Mellifont alone. On the invasion of King Henry II, the Norman administration in Ireland favoured the abbey and from 1228, when Mellifont had become a solidly Anglo-Norman establishment, its church was reconstructed in a more fashionable style. Evidence of a great fire in the early C14 explains the extensive rebuilding at that time, and the style of this work and of later C15 additions reflects the prosperity of a very wealthy community which was by then peopled with an exclusively Anglo-Irish stock.

With the exception of the late medieval gatehouse, the parish church, the chapter house and the lavabo, the remains of the abbey today hardly rise more than 8 ft (2.5 m) above foundation level. If the walls are mostly low, they are extensive, and a

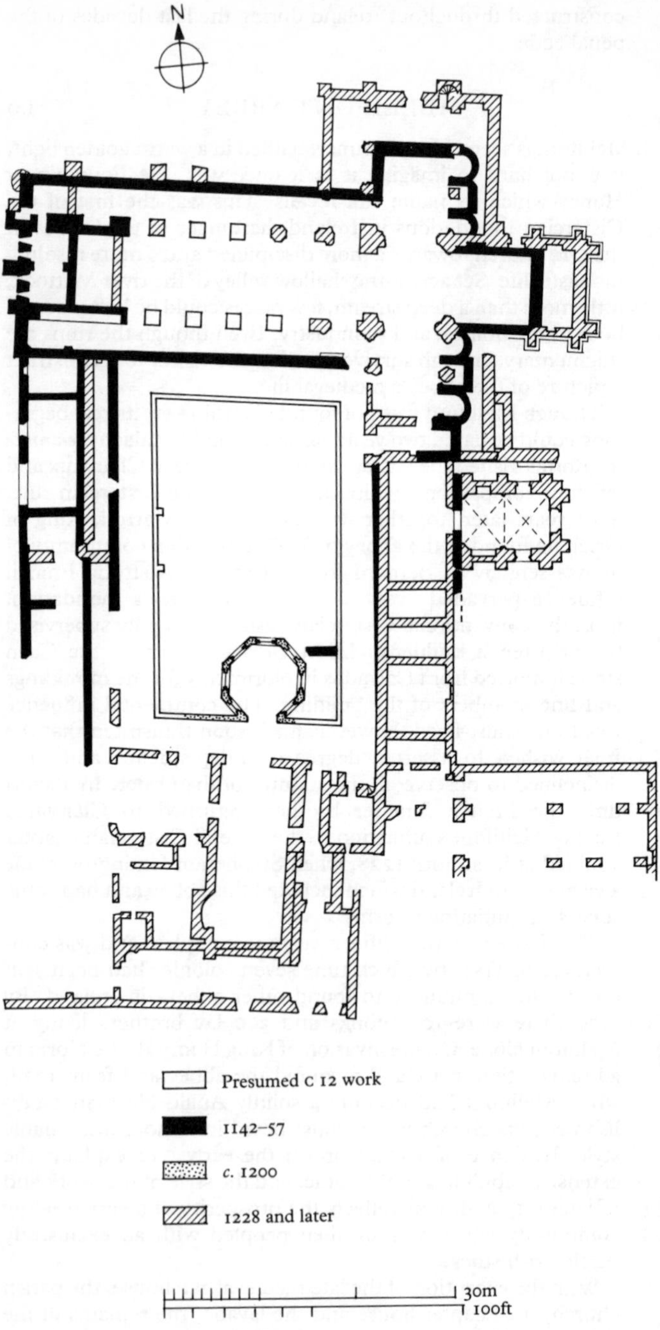

N
Presumed c 12 work
1142–57
c. 1200
1228 and later
30m
100ft

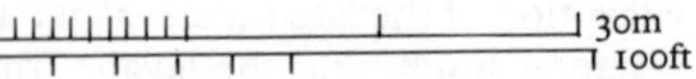

Mellifont Abbey. Plan

very complete plan of the building, and its different phases, can be made out from them. A terrace at the S end of the car park allows the layout to be seen from above, and it is worth pausing to understand the over-all plan from this level. The foundations of the abbey church are immediately below, with the chancel and E end cut into rising ground on the l. The N transept is immediately below, opening towards the crossing, which is marked by the stumps of four heavy piers, and the nave and aisles of the church are represented by very low walls which extend r. towards the line of the river. Beyond, S of the nave, is the cloister, marked by a rectangle of grass, with the lavabo – the monks' wash room – rising at its farther end. The cloister is surrounded by ranges of building, now marked by further low walls and gravel. The only other substantial structure, the chapter house, rises on the E side of the cloister. These ruins are of different dates and it is important to understand that in the abbey church the plans of two separate buildings are superimposed one upon the other. The first church, begun in 1142, was much smaller than in its final form, and, at its E end, its walls are contained *within* the outline of the later building. It had a square chancel, whose end is marked by the change in level in the chancel today; both transepts were short, with an unusual sequence of side chapels – alternately semi-circular and square-ended – set along the E walls. There were no aisles in the transepts. Only the outside line of the nave walls and the basement at the W end – which was a practical piece of building to raise the floor level of the church and does not appear to have been used for liturgical purposes – remain from the plan of the first church.

Visitors descend the staircase from the car park and enter the ruins through the remains of the doorway which stood in the centre of the N transept. This doorway must always have been the principal entrance to the abbey, as the W end of the building extended almost to the bank of the river and could never have been developed satisfactorily as a major approach to the church. The transept was rebuilt about the mid-C 13; at the same time the chancel was enlarged and both have characteristic E.E.-style detailing. The doorway has a deeply chamfered reveal, in three registers with attached shafts, and immediately l. inside is the base of a spiral mural staircase which must have led to a clerestory passage and to the roofs. That this was the grand entry to the church is made clear by the monumental character of the transept, which gained aisles on both its E and W sides, so that an arcade of three arches conducted the visitor to the centre of the church at the crossing.

The square piers of the arcades have slender shafts carved at their corners and, on the inner face opposite the aisle wall, attached shafts with fillets which suggest that the side aisles were rib-vaulted. On the W side delicate PISCINA stoups, partly corbelled out from the side of each pier, indicate an unusual arrangement under which the openings of the arcade were blocked by side altars which can only have been approached from the W aisle. Rectangular stones projecting from the piers suggest the line on which the reredos of each altar was constructed. The foundation wall, which crosses the transept at the level of the first pier, marks the original extent of the N transept. After this the foundations of the three side chapels of the first church may be noted on the E, with the second pier of the C 13 transept built in the middle of the earlier square-ended chapel. (As part of the modern work of consolidating the ruins, the walls of these earlier chapels have been built up, so that they now appear to rise above the level of the moulded bases of the later piers; obviously when the building was excavated the old walls stopped below the level of the floor of the second church.)

Beyond the crossing, the S transept was remodelled *c.* 1320 in the Dec period, which saw the introduction of huge diamond-shaped piers with attached multiple shafts set, once again, in the centre of an earlier side chapel. Because of the monastery buildings immediately to the S, this transept could not be extended further as had happened on the N side. The rough area of rock in the SW corner would have been covered in the finished building by the night stair which led down from the monks' dormitories into the church at this point.

In the chancel to the E, the rise in the level of the floor was made necessary by the closeness of the bed rock to the soil level. The E end of the church had virtually to be excavated out of the rock and for this reason its high altar must have been approached by an impressive flight of steps starting after the line of the crossing. The chancel was lit by a large E window of three lancets, of which the base moulding survives on the E wall. In the N wall of the chancel a doorway indicates the level of the floor in the finished building. This was the *porte des morts*, the door through which, after a requiem, the coffins of dead monks were carried for burial. Immediately outside this door, and round the E end of the chancel, are the bases of massive rectangular buttresses with sloped steps, E.E. in style and similar in detailing to the buttresses of the Lady Chapel at St Patrick's Cathedral in Dublin, also of the mid-C 13.

The one roofed part of the ruins, S of the chancel, is the
37 CHAPTER HOUSE. It preserves three C 14 windows, with robust curvilinear tracery, on its N, E and S sides. These date from a later remodelling and have been inserted into an earlier building of *c.* 1220, which was itself an addition to the original chapter house of the first abbey. The location of the building is in the traditional place for a monastic plan, immediately S of the church and entered directly from the E side of the cloister. The long rectangular area, two squares in plan, which lies at right angles across its axis marks the location of the original C 12 chapter house, which was apparently rib-vaulted, with two columns to support the vault on the central line of the room. One modest little round-headed window, splayed on the interior, survives from the first chapter house in the wall immediately S of the present building. After the new chapter

house was completed its predecessor must have formed an outer lobby for the new room. The monks' dormitories were accommodated above.

The C 13 chapter house had a rich E.E. doorway, with cluster-shafted reveals, three colonnettes on each side and an arch of five registers alternating moulded and carved sections. This survived until the C 18, when it was removed to form part of a private house now long demolished. The doorway is known

Mellifont Abbey, chapter house. Door, from Thomas Wright's *Louthiana* (1748)

today only from an engraved drawing made by Thomas Wright in the C 18. Internally the chapter house is roofed by two ribbed vaults rising from clustered wall shafts. The nailhead decoration and trumpet-scalloped capitals suggest a date in the first quarter of the C 13. A large collection of moulded ribs and tracery fragments is now kept in the building.

As first built, the cloister was square in plan. It was extended to its present rectangular shape *c.* 1200, when the octagonal LAVABO, the most original and also the most sophisticated 24
structure of the whole monastic complex, was built. Nothing can better illustrate Mellifont's lack of commitment to the austere discipline of the Cistercian Order than the architectural elaboration and magnificent decoration of the lavabo, which

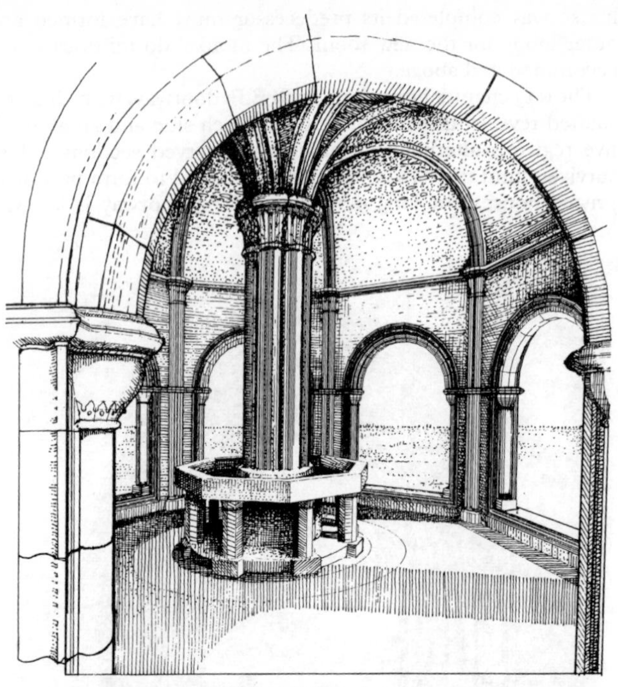

Mellifont Abbey, lavabo

was put up at a time when adherence to Cistercian precepts was at its weakest. Clearly a symbol of the abbey's importance and prestige, the lavabo had no doubt a deeper symbolic significance, suggestive perhaps of the power of baptism and of Divine Grace. It was designed as a freestanding structure of two storeys; an octagonal cistern to supply the water was located at the upper level over the wash room itself. An octagonal barrel-vault, strengthened at each corner by transverse ribs with triple roll mouldings, linked the outer walls to a central pier of masonry, now gone, which supported the weight of the water above. Wash basins were arranged around this central pier.* The character of the architecture is monumental and in striking contrast to the more delicate scale of the cloister arcade, part of which has been re-erected S of the lavabo. Here the arches are supported on pairs on slender shafts as a series of narrow round-headed openings, with an unusually complex grouping of clustered shafts, whose bases remain, just at the opening to the lavabo. The lavabo itself, in its geometry and its detail, is very much an ideal structure, with identical round-headed

* Carved fragments from a frieze set at the level of the waterspouts have recently been identified (March 1993) which suggest that the water supply did not come from an upper cistern and prove that the central shaft was a single circular column, not compound as shown here.

arches opening on each side, framed by generous roll and beak mouldings – early Gothic in spirit if not in form – with an inner arch supported on half-column shafts, set into the reveals, and given delicately carved leaf capitals.

Other remains at Mellifont are fragments from the C14 and C15. The labyrinth of the refectory and infirmary buildings at the S end of the abbey is the confusing product of several rebuildings, now lacking in any detail. All trace of these buildings had been lost by the C18, when the soil level was higher and the river regularly flooded this section of the site. The W range, also fragmentary, accommodated the lay brothers' dormitories and probably the latrines, which were most likely positioned over the river, as was the normal practice. The fire which destroyed the church in the early C14 led to the reconstruction of the S transept; the piers at the crossing were rebuilt in the C15 to enable them to support a central tower. Fragments of twenty-seven different types of floor tile were unearthed during the excavation, giving some indication of the richness of the interior of the church.

Surrounding the entire monastery was a defensive wall of stone, still discernible in the hills E of the abbey and to the N of the site. Above the abbey ruins to the NE is the shell of the medieval PARISH CHURCH. C15; a small rectangular hall, with a double bellcote on the W gable and a two-light E window. The GATEHOUSE, N of the abbey, marks the limit of the precinct. Rubble-built and now lacking in any detail, it is a tower of three storeys built over a barrel-vaulted archway. Like the protective walls it serves as a reminder of the less tranquil aspects of medieval Irish monasticism. After the dissolution of the monasteries Mellifont was acquired in 1540 by William Brabazon, vice treasurer of Ireland, and passed later to Sir Edward Moore, who established a fortified house within the ruins *c.* 1560. His descendants lived there until 1727, after which the house, like the abbey, fell into disrepair.

MOATE

WM *1030*

The Norman motte which gives this town its name was erected during the 1190s by Richard Tuite, whose principal stronghold stood at Ballyloughloe. In 1365 the last Sir Richard Tuite died without issue, leaving his lands open to attack by the O'Melaghlins, who by then controlled most of S Westmeath, having established themselves at Moyelly, Ballinderry, Clonloan and at Moate. For two centuries the O'Melaghlins held this country, despite recurrent family feuds and constant threats from the O'Donnells, O'Carrolls and O'Connors. In the C16 their obedience to the Tudor monarchy was rewarded by a patent of royal protection and the peerage of Lord Clancolman. Then in 1596 the clan rose in revolt against the Crown, an act which cost it the bulk of its property in the ensuing Protestant plantations. The most significant influence in the development of the town came with the Cromwellian plantation, when the lands of Moate were used to pay arrears of wages to disbanded soldiers. For many of these, the midlands of Ireland held little appeal; they could not afford to develop their estates and sold them at give-away prices to the few who chose to remain. Prominent among these was Captain John Clibborn, who acquired the lands of Coole prior to 1656 and later bought the former O'Melaghlin castle at Moate from a departing soldier. By the 1680s the Clibborns possessed an extensive estate in the area and, together with the Homan family, had become Moate's principal landowners. The family converted to Quakerism in the late C17 and established a meeting house in the town in 1692.

The strict disciplined lifestyle of Moate's Quaker community had its physical expression in what all C18 visitors regarded as an exceptionally neat and well-built town. In 1709 Dr Thomas Molyneux described the place as 'a pretty clean-built town of a different air from the generality of Irish villages in this part of Ireland', and John Wesley on his visit here in 1782 found it 'the pleasantest town' in all of Ireland. Grain, sheep, linen and tanning were the town's principal resources, owned and regulated by the Clibborns and Homans. In the 1790s and early 1800s many new buildings were erected on the main street and in a new suburb at the NE corner of the town, known as Newmarket or Newtown. With the end of the Napoleonic wars, however, and the resultant fall in demand for Irish agricultural produce, Moate began to decline. Despite some public building activity during the mid-C19, the place never recovered the prosperity of the late C18.
10 Today Moate still wears a late Georgian appearance – one long and exceptionally broad main street lined by neat two- and three-storey houses with sash windows, fanlit doorcases and some first-floor windows arranged in a simplified Venetian pattern. Newtown is a charming enclave of late C18 Ireland. Here too are elegant two- and three-storey houses, with symmetrical façades, sash windows and fanlit doorcases; they were built in the immediate aftermath of the Union by William Handcock, the newly created Lord Castlemaine.

MOATE CASTLE. The original late medieval castle of the O'Melaghlins, now embedded in C17 and C18 building work. Situated on an elevated site on the N side of the main street, the castle now appears as a tall and plain three-storey pile, roughcast and gabled, with irregular fenestration and broad expanses of bare masonry. It is a large and bulky building, clearly of two distinct periods: a very broad, three-bay block on the W adjoining a more square two-bay, three-storey block which, in turn, has a smaller and lower block of curved profile at its SE corner. The O'Melaghlin tower is the two-bay section, now thoroughly altered, though fragments of cutstone detail survive in the office courtyard at the NE of the building. A cusped lancet with dished spandrels, a decorative ventilator circle and a moulded arch, with chamfered edges tapering down to a base point, are all probably of late C15 or early C16 date. The tower preserves corner quoins with pocked tooling. Above the arch is a crudely represented *sheila-na-gig*. The large three-storey house which adjoins the former tower house on the W shows its rear elevation to the street. The principal N-facing entrance front is of three bays, with a central doorcase and windows on each storey in the outer bays. The proportions and general aspect of the building suggest an early to mid-C 18 date, as does the symmetrical tripartite plan and the fielded panels of the joinery.

When Captain John Clibborn acquired Moate Castle in 1659 the place was described as 'in ruins but nearly habitable'. He repaired the old castle and rebuilt the stable yard, incorporating in it the cutstone fragment from the tower. (The first good modern stone house to be built at Moate was that of the Homan family in 1683.) The Clibborns seem to have contented themselves with the existing castle until the 1730s, when James Clibborn (1710–84) erected the present building beside it.

QUAKER MEETING HOUSE. In the garden behind the castle are the gable and plaque from the former meeting house first built in 1692 by John Clibborn, rebuilt in 1768 and taken down in 1924.

MOATE VIEW. Built in 1762 by James Clibborn at a cost of £35. A nice two-storey, five-bay gabled house of single-pile tripartite plan. Regular sash windows with exposed sash boxes, a stone eaves cornice and a moulded limestone door surround with a central scrolled keystone, now screened by a C 19 porch. The inscribed plaque above the door bears witness to an illiterate mason or a careless scribe, proclaiming to posterity that 'James Clibborn Biult This House an° dom' 1762'.

ST MARY, KILCLEAGH PARISH CHURCH. 1782. Big, plain church built of limestone rubble. Nave, transepts and a rounded chancel, with a thin battlemented tower adjoining the W entrance gable. Nice curved finish to the slating over the chancel end. Bright interior, lit by large pointed sash windows with intersecting tracery. Moulded ceiling cornice and remnants of fielded panelling. – MONUMENTS. Joseph Morgan Daly of Castledaly † 1838; William Henry Robinson † 1884; both draped urns by the firm of *Coates*.

SS PETER AND PAUL. 1867 by *William Caldbeck*. Designs for this church were first commissioned in 1861 from *John Bourke*, but there was a disagreement between priest and architect, and the project was shelved until 1867, when *William Caldbeck* was brought in. The result is an attractive essay in E.E. Gothic, built of yellow-coloured snecked rubble with limestone trim: a small cruciform church with a two-stage tower and broach spire flanking the entrance gable. Windows of two and three lights, with simple geometric tracery. Inside, the nave opens through paired pointed arches into shallow transepts, the arches carried on octagonal limestone shafts with E.E. capitals.

CHURCH OF THE IMMACULATE CONCEPTION. 1863 by *J. J. McCarthy*. The chapel of Moate's Carmelite monastery is a neat symmetrical building in an E.E. idiom. A crisp pointed design built of snecked limestone rubble. Nave, aisles and an apsidal chancel, with a three-storey tower and broach spire fronting the entrance gable – very much the same arrangement as McCarthy had used at Cookstown, Co. Tyrone, in 1853. The tower is embellished with clasping corner buttresses, offsets, lancets, hoodmouldings and lucarnes to the spire. Inside, the nave is carried on an arcade of five arches springing from cylindrical limestone shafts with plain bell capitals. Paired cusped lights to the aisles and trefoil windows in the clerestory, two to each arch of the arcade. Polygonal chancel, roofed with exposed braced trusses. A recent renovation preserved the bones of McCarthy's design but has destroyed the church's Victorian ambience, replacing it with a weak brand of C20 modernism.

COURTHOUSE. 1828 by *John Hargrave*. Attractive and unusual bow-fronted building in pale blue-grey limestone ashlar. A shallow three-bay, two-storey bow with a giant order of Tuscan pilasters supporting a frieze, cornice and parapet. Sash windows to the first floor, with plain doorcases below. A string-course incorporating the first-floor sills links the main block to the parapets of a carriage arch on each side. These have arches of curious stilted profile, the upper part designed as a half-octagon. As always with Hargrave, the impression is one of a personal, quirky approach to classical design.

BANK OF IRELAND. 1854–6 by *William Caldbeck*. The classic banking formula. Tall three-storey, five-bay block flanked by carriage arches. Horizontally channelled limestone ashlar on the ground floor, with rendered upper storeys. Eaves cornice and Italianate detail. Advanced end bays with relieving arches to the upper-floor windows. The banking floor has two Italianate doorcases in the outer bays, with three round-headed windows between. The upper storeys are more plainly expressed as square-headed plate-glass windows.

NEIGHBOURHOOD

ST KIERAN, CASTLEDALY. 5 km SW. 1875. Small aisled church built of dark snecked rubble with redbrick trim: unusual building materials in such a rural context. A very nice and unexpected interior, ambitious for its diminutive scale, with a six-bay arcade of broad pointed arches carried on round shafts with curious bracketed capitals. Open kingpost roof and lancets to the aisles and clerestory. The aisle windows have lovely polished wood sills to deep embrasures and exposed brickwork surrounds.

KILCLEAGH HOUSE. 5 km SW. Formerly known as Castle Daly, this house was built *c.* 1780 by Thomas O'Daly, High Sheriff of Co. Westmeath, whose family had settled at Kilcleagh in the C17. Castle Daly was a substantial and conventional late Georgian house: a two-storey rectangular block with a hipped roof, a continuous eaves cornice and a pediment over the middle of a five-bay entrance front. Sash windows, with a central fanlit doorcase, a Venetian window to the first floor and a tiny semicircular window in the eaves pediment. Symmetrical plan of two rooms deep, with a bowed projection on the S front facing the garden.

In May 1852 Kilcleagh Estate was sold in the encumbered estates court. It was later acquired by Thomas Scruton Odell, who in 1880 built a N extension to the house, replaced the sash bars with plate glass and added an Italianate loggia-like porch to the entrance front. The house is now a hotel.

MOLYSKAR

WM *4040*

A parish of beautiful countryside, on the E shore of Lough Ennell, and remarkable for a quantity of noteworthy C18 houses. Distances are given from Molyskar Parish Church.

TUDENHAM PARK. 1 km SW. If Belvedere presents the architecture of *Richard Castle* to advantage, Tudenham Park (formerly Rochfort House) exhibits a more prosaic mind. Now a derelict shell, this house was built *c.* 1743 by George Rochfort, brother of Castle's patron at Belvedere (q.v.), some time before the two men fell out. Envy of the scale of Tudenham is sometimes given as the cause of the brothers' quarrel, and if this is the case then Robert Rochfort was clearly no critic, a man more impressed by scale than by quality. In contrast to Belvedere, Tudenham was a full-scale country house: a big rectangular block of three storeys over a basement, with seven-bay elevations on each side. Built of cut limestone and clumsily repointed after 1836, when the house was sold to Sir Francis Hopkins. The one common denominator between Belvedere and Rochfort is the use of bowed side projections. Here three-bay semicircular bows project from the centre of the two side elevations. The entrance front is also of seven bays, with plain rectangular openings diminishing to the top storey; eaves cornice, first-floor cornice, raised corner quoins and simple moulded window frames. The three centre bays follow a pattern which is standard in much of Castle's work and which provides the basis for the firm attribution of Tudenham to him. First a pedimented tripartite Doric doorcase; above it a round-headed niche flanked by sash windows in a Venetian window motif; on the top storey, a circular bracketed niche flanked by squat sash windows. It is an effective and economical way of giving a big plain house a central visual focus. 67

The plan is symmetrical, with a large central entrance hall flanked by reception rooms, and had formerly a galleried and domed two-storey upper hall, with the stairs and back stairs screened by an arcade at the far end. In 1773 Sir James Caldwell of Castle Caldwell considered the place to be 'the largest house in Ireland and the offices quite a town'. The gardens he described as 'immense', commenting specifically on the 220 pounds of grapes cut from the conservatories in the previous year. In contrast to Belvedere's opulence Caldwell records that at Rochfort House breakfast was served at eight sharp, after which psalms were read.

ANNEVILLE. 1 km E. The proximity of Anneville to Belvedere (q.v.), together with the similar character of its interior detail, clearly suggests that this smaller and more modest building was built in conjunction with Robert Rochfort's lakeside villa. In 1786 Anneville was the property of one John Smith, though occupied by the Rev. Robinson, curate of Molyskar. Indeed, in its simple farmhouse idiom the house might almost have been built as a glebe. It is of two storeys over a basement, with a tall hipped roof; rough-cast, with limestone trim. In the five-bay principal entrance front the centre three bays project in a deep canted bow. Broad, flat limestone surrounds frame the windows on the main floors, with a gentle segmental curve to the tops of the frameless basement windows. On the upper storey the windows preserve thick early Georgian glazing bars with square blocks at the intersections. The entrance has a simple limestone blocked surround supporting a flat entablature and is approached by a short flight of steps arched over the basement area.

The plan of Anneville is tripartite and one room thick, with the bowed central entrance and stairhall flanked by large drawing and dining rooms. The stair (now altered) was originally a half-turn with two landings. Here are the same elongated classical balusters as at Belvedere. The canted bow has an especially charming effect in the first-floor hall. Original fielded panelling with lugged door and window surrounds. The basement is elaborately vaulted throughout.

BELVEDERE LODGE. 1.5 km N. Early C19 two-storey house looking W to Lough Ennell. Nine bays, with broad three-bay bows at either end and a flat three-bay centre. Harled, with miniature battlements in place of a parapet. A limestone Tuscan porch screens a fanlight and tripartite door behind. Modern bay above. Inside, simple neoclassical detail, with reeded borders, scalloped panels and oval ceiling garlands. Now a hotel, the house has been extended eastward and much altered internally.

CARRICK HOUSE. 2.5 km S. Substantial early to mid-C18 house built by the Fetherston family. Long two-storey block, one room thick, with a tall hipped roof and narrow early Georgian proportions to the sash windows. The narrow canted projection, with the door not quite in the centre of the entrance front, and three bays on one side and four on the other, is possibly an improvement of *c.* 1770. Harled, with a limestone pedimented doorcase complete with a blocked surround and a pulvinated frieze. Fielded shuttering throughout.

MOLYSKAR PARISH CHURCH (C of I). In September 1787 the Rev. D. A. Beaufort drew up plans for improvements to Molyskar Church for the Rochfort family. Nothing of that building survives and the present church was built in 1877 by

Mrs Tottenham of Tudenham Park. It is absolutely typical of Church of Ireland architecture in the later C19; a small gabled hall of snecked limestone rubble with a dumpy three-stage tower and spire adjoining the W gable and a S gabled porch. The W gable contains a geometric wheel window recessed in a pointed arch, and the chancel is lit by triple lancets.

GAINSTOWN CATHOLIC CHURCH. 2 km NE. 1853. Small gabled three-bay hall, lit by round-headed windows. A top-lit chancel, porch and freestanding belfry were added *c.* 1950.

MONASTERBOICE

LO *0080*

The name Monasterboice derives from Mainistir-Buite, the monastery of St Buite, who founded a Christian community here in the early C6. In 551 St Columba visited the place to consecrate both the church and the remains of St Buite. The community continued to thrive throughout the early Middle Ages but began to decline in the C12 with the establishment of the Cistercian abbey at nearby Mellifont. The principal monuments at Monasterboice date to about the C10, when the monastery was a particularly wealthy institution. One of the contenders for the builder of the famous Muiredach's Cross was an early C10 abbot of Monasterboice, visiting abbot of Armagh and chief steward of the southern O'Neills, which if nothing else gives some idea of the status and prestige of the monastery during this period.

Documents record the burning of the round tower here, with many books and treasures, in 1097. Clearly the most eloquent statement of Monasterboice's former glory is its splendid crosses. For the lover of sculpture, the pilgrim or the student of Irish history, it is a wonderful place. Here is monumental sculpture of a quality not surpassed anywhere in Europe at this date; an evocative ancient graveyard, fringed by trees and with cawing rooks; and, in the undulations in the field to the S, traces of the circular earthen ramparts that once enclosed the monastery. An architectural enthusiast may feel some disappointment; apart from a good round tower, there is little here to engage the admirer of buildings. The two surviving churches, though they incorporate masonry from as early as the C13, are dull roofless boxes with no features or ornament of interest. Much more endearing are the charming miniature versions of early Christian churches which surmount both the South and the West Cross. These represent narrow single-cell structures with steeply pitched shingled roofs and heavy timber gables running up to form X-shaped finials.

ROUND TOWER. Probably C10. It is perhaps too easy to be blasé 17
about round towers. Because of their homogeneous shape and their familiarity in the Irish landscape, one imagines that to see one is to see them all. There is not much scope for casual exploration in a round tower inside or out, and therefore natural human curiosity promptly relegates the monument to the status

of digested knowledge. Understandable as this may be, it is unfair to the masons who produced these marvels of medieval workmanship. The tower at Monasterboice is particularly noteworthy. A vertical accent on the skyline for miles around, this is a masterful column of stone worked from the hard intractable slate of the surrounding hills laid in flat beds to produce a perfectly cylindrical curvature. Built with many tightly packed rubble courses – not of ashlar blocks – with a base 31 ft (9.3 m) in circumference and a height of 110 ft (33 m), it is a truly remarkable achievement. A discriminating eye may detect minor bulges here and there in the circumference as the tower rises, and the true line, probably not an original mistake, is deflected near the top. Only a portion of the conical stone roof remains. The entrance door is keyhole-shaped, with the inclined jambs typical of early Irish monastic building, and it is set, for defence, some 6 ft (1.8 m) above the ground. It has a moulded frame in a reddish stone. Above is a small window with a primitive triangular lintel formed from two stones. Inside, rings of projecting stones mark the position of five former floor levels. The top stage of the tower has been consolidated by the Office of Public Works, who also installed the present system of timber floors and ladders. The line of the surrounding earthwork ramparts is particularly well seen from the platform at the top.

HIGH CROSSES

The great scriptural crosses at Monasterboice are amongst the most remarkable and aesthetically satisfying monuments of all Irish art. There are three crosses: two High Crosses – the South or 'Muiredach's Cross' and the West Cross – both elaborately worked with a mixture of abstract designs framing sculpted biblical scenes; and a third, North Cross, which is almost plain. Beside this last cross is a sundial marked with the canonical hours.

To a modern visitor much of the meaning of a High Cross may now be obscure, and it is important in deciphering, or attempting to decipher, the subjects represented in the various sculpted panels to bear in mind the thematic or theological links that were commonly understood to exist between apparently different scenes. Around the central facts of Christian belief – the sin of mankind, the divinity of Christ, his sacrifice to redeem the world, and the Day of Judgement – other incidents from the Old and New Testament are grouped, to illustrate the concept of God's continuing bounty towards his people; events such as Moses striking water from the rock in the desert (which is a sustenance from God); the three young Hebrews in the furnace (an instance of divine deliverance); or Abraham's sacrifice of Isaac (which prefigures Christ's own sacrifice in the Crucifixion). Similarly scenes from the life of King David are an instance of the power of God to deliver the faithful, as when he kills a lion, and an allegory, as he wrenches the lion's jaws apart, of the breaking of the gates of Hell by Christ. A rich variety of meanings and of interrelated religious ideas is set forth in the sculptural scenes of Monasterboice's two great scriptural crosses.*

MUIREDACH'S CROSS. This, the first monument which a visitor to Monasterboice encounters, takes its name from an inscription on the W side carved into the background of the lowest part of the shaft, which is decorated with two seated cats, one licking a kitten and the other holding a bird. Behind and around these domestic pets the inscription reads: OR DO MUIREDACH LASDERNAD IN CHROS ('A prayer for Muiredach for whom this cross was made'). Muiredach has for many years been assumed to be the second abbot of that name, Muiredach mac Domhnaill, who died in 923, which would place the cross comfortably in the early C10. There is, however, an argument to be made for dating it to the period of the first Abbot Muiredach, who died in 844, which would place the cross almost 100 years earlier in the first half of the C9.

Muiredach's Cross is made of two pieces of stone, the shaft and its base. It stands 18 ft (5.5 m) high, with a truncated pyramidal base supporting a shaft surmounted by an open ring-headed cross which is completed by a house (or church-shaped) cap. If the pattern is familiar from other Irish high crosses, subtleties may be noted in the balance between high-relief sculpture in the figural scenes and shallower abstract patterns elsewhere. The designer displays a sophisticated awareness of the effects of different planes, so that the front face of the sculptural panels is actually projected beyond the edge of the corner moulding which contains them, while the nimbus, or ring, of the cross is cut back and recessed behind the surface of the arms, making it seem a separate element which runs through and interpenetrates the arms themselves.

The SCULPTURAL SCENES on the cross are identified as
follows. On the W face, above the inscription, the bottom panel 18
shows the arrest of Christ, who holds a staff and is restrained by two men with swords. Second panel: the incredulity of St Thomas. Christ is the central figure; Thomas is shown on the l. sticking his hand into Christ's side; the figure on the r. is thought to be St John, whose Gospel alone records this post-Resurrection incident. Third panel: Christ flanked by St Peter, to whom he gives the keys, and St Paul, who receives a book of the Gospels. The Crucifixion is shown in the central part of the cross, with a young Christ whose hands are nailed but whose feet are tied together with the heels touching. Two angels minister to him above, while soldiers pierce his side and offer the sponge dipped in vinegar. Above the soldiers' knees are two human heads which may represent the thieves crucified with Jesus. – Soldiers present at the Crucifixion appear on the l. arm of the cross, while the r. side shows the Resurrection

*An excellent and very complete account of the crosses and their interpretation is given in Helen M. Roe, *Monasterboice and its Monuments* (County Louth Archaeological and Historical Society, 1981). All the identifications given here are taken from Miss Roe's work. *See* also the footnote on p. 330.

with two soldiers kneeling on either side of the tomb. – The scene on the 'house' at the top has not been identified.

23 On the E face, bottom panel: the Fall of Man, with Adam and Eve and the serpent and the consequences of their disobedience, with Cain killing Abel. Second panel: the story of David and Goliath, showing, from l. to r., King Saul armed with sword and round buckler; then David, the shepherd boy with crooked stick over his shoulder and his sling hanging in his other hand; then Goliath, a giant who would not fit into the panel unless the sculptor showed him, as he is here, crumpling on bent knees, with his head twisted round looking back to David. The last figure is Goliath's armour-bearer, dumbfounded at what has happened. Third panel: Moses striking the rock on the l., while the Children of Israel sit in two rows each holding a drinking horn. The top scene shows the Adoration of the Magi: the Virgin is seated on the l., holding a rather large and boisterous Christ child, while St Joseph, old and venerable, with a long beard and moustache, leads in the Three Wise Men, whose curving bodies and bent knees suggest a proper reverence.

The head of the cross is devoted to a spirited depiction of the Day of Judgement, which centres on the splendid figure of the risen Christ. Immediately below, the Archangel Michael is weighing a soul in a pair of scales and fights a small devil who is trying to pull the scales down on his side. On the l. arm (Christ's right-hand side) are the elect of God, led by King David (nearest to Christ), who is playing his harp, while the Dove of the Holy Spirit perches on its frame. On Christ's left-hand side (the r. arm of the cross), the Archangel Gabriel sounds the trumpet to call the dead to rise, and the damned are herded into hell by the Devil, with a three-pronged fork, and two assistants who kick the lost souls. Above Christ is an eagle, the symbol of his Resurrection, then Christ between two winged figures, and, on the side of the 'house' at the top of the cross, a scene showing two figures, which also appears at Duleek Cross, but which cannot be identified.

The sides of Muiredach's Cross are mostly decorated with sophisticated abstract patterns of interlace and bosses. On the N side the cross end carries a scene from the Passion, probably the Flagellation or Mocking of Christ, and the gable end of the 'house' above shows St Paul and St Anthony, identified by their croziers, being fed in the desert by a raven which flies down between them with a loaf of bread in its beak. Underneath the arm of the cross is a remarkable illustration of the *Dextra Dei*, the hand of God. On the S side, the cross end shows Pilate washing his hands: Pilate sits on the l. while a steward pours water over his hands; three armed guards look on in the background. The gable end of the 'house' above shows the opening scene of the Passion, with Christ riding into Jerusalem.

WEST CROSS. This is the tallest of the northern group of high crosses, standing almost 23 ft (6.9 m) high. Only the high crosses at Arboe, Co. Tyrone, and at Clones, Co. Monaghan (were that complete), come near to the dramatic elongation of this lofty sculptural shaft and cross. Whereas on Muiredach's Cross there is room for only three or four scenes on the height of the shaft, here the sculptor has accommodated no fewer than six on each face, with an additional block of abstract decoration set in at the top of the shaft before the ring and arms of the cross. The greater scale of the monument forced its designer to construct his cross out of four pieces: a truncated pyramid base, the shaft, the cross head, and the cap-stone, which once again is in the form of a miniature house or church. The arrangement of the cross head follows the pattern of Muiredach's Cross quite closely, with the same recessed nimbus and the same use of half-round lobes of stone – volutes or billets – set on the curved intersections of the cross to give variety to its silhouette, which the extra height of the West Cross seems to enhance. The sculpture here has weathered unevenly and in places is so badly eroded that some scenes are no longer identifiable. Its forms are, if anything, more expressive than the monumentally passive figures of Muiredach's Cross, while the programme of illustration is highly individual and in some cases unique in Irish art.

The SCULPTURAL SCENES on the West Cross are identified as follows. On the bottom panel, the soldiers at Christ's tomb. The second panel shows a large figure on the l. holding a book with two little figures rising from box-like tombs, with a second figure higher up on the r. and a bird, a symbol of the soul. This appears to represent the resurrection of the dead. Third panel: three figures, possibly apostles. Fourth panel: Christ giving the keys to St Peter and a book to St Paul. Fifth panel: possibly the incredulity of St Thomas. Sixth panel: the arrest of Christ.

The Crucifixion occupies the centre of the cross head and is a development of the arrangement seen on Muiredach's Cross: the figure of Christ is here displayed in a more pathetic pose, with elongated arms, the palms of his hands turned outwards to display the nails and the head twisted awkwardly to one side. Once again the soldiers pierce his side and offer the sponge of vinegar; his feet are bound by a rope, and two more soldiers, dressed in Roman armour (?), prop up the scene from below. The heads of the crucified thieves are set beneath Christ's hands, but what is unique here are the little genre scenes immediately beyond the hands, showing a shepherd milking on the l. side and another slaughtering a sheep on the r. side, which refers to Christ's role as both good shepherd and suffering servant, passing mute to his death like a lamb to the slaughter. The scene on the l. arm of the cross is Judas's kiss; at the top St Peter with his sword, having cut off the ear of the high priest's servant, and on the r. the mocking of Christ. The side of the 'house' cap-stone may possibly represent St Mark with his winged lion.

On the E side the scenes are as follows. Bottom panel: David 17
killing the lion. Though much eroded, King David can be made

out kneeling on the lion's back and, like Hercules, wrenching its jaws apart. Second panel: the Sacrifice of Isaac. Abraham, a tall figure on the l., thrusts his son's head down towards an altar, while an angel and the ram which will be sacrificed instead of the boy are in the corner above Isaac's head. Third panel: the worship of the Golden Calf, with Aaron on the l., a horned monster in the centre and the misguided Israelites in two rows. The fourth panel contains two scenes: on the r., the anointing of David by Samuel; on the l., David with Goliath's head. On the fifth panel Goliath appears as a giant with long hair and beard, brandishing a huge spear and threatening three rows of the Israelite army. The sixth panel, only half the height of the others, appears to show a chariot.

At the centre of the cross head, a large figure with sword, spear and shield represents Christ's second coming, with an army of the faithful behind him. Abstract patterns of bosses separate this scene from the four that surround it in each arm of the cross. The bottom scene shows the three young Hebrews – Shadrach, Meshach and Abednego – protected from the heat of the furnace by the wings of an angel, while soldiers on either side carry extra faggots on long forks and blow through horn-shaped bellows to increase the heat of the fire. The scene at the top also illustrates deliverance, only now it is the New Testament story of St Peter, who left the boat to walk over the water to Jesus and, lacking faith, began to sink. Christ stands on the r., helping Peter, while four disciples stay rowing in the boat. The right-hand scene shows the fall of Simon Magus, a pagan magician who flew with the help of the Devil and was brought crashing down through the united prayers of St Peter and St Paul. He is shown here tumbling upside-down to the l. of the two saints. The left-hand panel shows a central figure 'caught' by two grotesque beasts with animal heads and human bodies. This has been interpreted as the temptation of St Anthony in the wilderness, though Helen Roe suggests it may represent the deadly sin of avarice, with a miser being taken off to hell. The figure on the cap-stone 'house' may represent St Luke with his bull.

The scenes on the S side of the cross are much weathered and have not been identified. The lower scene, showing two people walking and one carrying a child, may be the Flight into Egypt, though the Virgin and Child are nowhere else in Christian art shown as walking. On the N side are two remarkable Old Testament scenes. The lower shows King David armed and enthroned like a Roman consul on a chair; the upper is Daniel in the lions' den, with the heads of two lions at his feet and one leaping creature on either side.

NORTH CROSS. A plain sandstone cross, re-erected on a new lower shaft, and standing about 10 ft (3 m) high. The cross head is well proportioned and here, in contrast to the other two crosses, it is the recessed nimbus which bears the stone lobes, to add variety to the silhouette. Incised borders, single on the nimbus and double on the arms of the cross, provide the principal decoration. The E face of the centre of the cross has a pattern of low bosses with triple spiral decorations; on the W face is a simplified Crucifixion scene reduced to the figure of Christ and soldiers with the sponge and spear.

MORNINGTON

ME *1070*

A small sea-side village at the mouth of the river Boyne which gave the titles of Earl and Baron to the Wellesleys of Dangan Castle near Trim. The lands at Mornington were leased to the Brabazon family. In 1816 James Brabazon was in possession of 'a substantial elegant spacious mansion, seated on a lawn, a short distance from the sea with offices of all descriptions'. Nothing now survives of the house or estate buildings.

MORNINGTON CATHOLIC CHURCH. 1841. A chapel of ease to St Mary's Church in Drogheda. Simple four-bay cement-rendered lancet hall, with a prettier Gothic frontispiece of coursed rubble and limestone trim. Advanced central bay with a pointed arch and lancet, flanked by blind outer bays with corner quoins and pinnacles. Tenders for masonry work were invited by the Rev. Mr Donellan in June 1839. *Hammond* of Drogheda was the building contractor.

THE MAIDEN TOWER. 1.5 km E, beside the sea-shore. A tall slender beacon or lighthouse tower. Some 12 ft (3.6 m) square in plan and 62 ft (18.9 m) in height, it tapers to a battlemented parapet. Limestone rubble, harled over and originally lime-washed. Inside it is simply a spiral stair lit by loops in deep embrasures, with a pair of windows near the top on the E and W sides. Originally a trap door provided access to the platform and parapet. Though it was evidently built to guide ships entering the Boyne estuary, nothing is known of the tower's history. Isaac Butler visited it in 1744 and left an accurate account of the building, which has remained substantially the same today. While the battlemented parapet is clearly C19, the fabric of the tower, built with the typical Irish masonry technique of tapering the stair to a fine rising point instead of a newel, may well be several centuries earlier.

DONACARNEY NATIONAL SCHOOLS. 1 km S. 1873. Plain but pretty building in a simple Gothic idiom. Matching gabled classroom blocks, each with three graded lancets and a flanking lean-to porch nicely blended with the roof-line. These are joined by a more modest horizontal range to give a broad H-shaped plan. Brick, with tall steep slated roofs. – Beside the schoolhouse is the fragment of a late medieval TOWER HOUSE, with just the hint of its former barrel-vault and a chimneypiece in the S wall.

EASTHAM HOUSE. 3 km SE, at Bettystown. Attractive late C18 house. Five bays wide, three storeys high and two rooms deep. The windows to the upper storeys are unusual in having exposed sash boxes, and the entrance is framed by a timber pedimented doorcase with fluted Tuscan columns. Possibly built by the Shepheard family, who were the proprietors of Bettystown in 1835.

0040 MOYDRUM CASTLE WM

Moydrum Castle, from J. P. Neale's *Views of Seats* (1823)

Part of the estates granted to William Handcock during the Cromwellian plantation, Moydrum, like Waterstown (*see* Glassan), was settled in the early C18 by one of the Handcocks' two sons. Thomas Handcock of Moydrum died in 1783 and was succeeded for a short space of time by the Rev. Richard Handcock. In 1791 William Handcock inherited the estate. An M.P. for Westmeath, William Handcock was an opponent of the Union who resisted all financial inducements but ultimately succumbed to the offer of nobility, taking as his title Lord Castlemaine. To celebrate his new status Handcock transformed the mansion house at Moydrum into a theatrical Jacobean castle. The work was given to *Sir Richard Morrison* and was completed in 1814. Neale's *Views of Seats* (1823) described the old house as 'nothing more than an ordinary farmhouse, contracted in its dimensions, mean in its external form and inconvenient in its interior arrangements'. Morrison incorporated this house within the new building, which was burned down in 1921 and is now a scanty but picturesque ruin.

The best-preserved feature of Morrison's design is the

E-facing entrance front: a long asymmetrical façade of two storeys, with octagonal turrets at each end and an offset twin-turreted entrance bay resembling a Tudor-Gothic gate-tower. The idiom is very much that of William Wilkins in England and of early William Burn in Scotland. The gate-tower is flanked by one very wide single bay on the N and by five regular bays on the S. The masonry is cement-rendered and decorated with battlements, hoodmouldings and crossed loops. Though this can never have been great architecture, it was and is impressive in a fairytale stage-set fashion. The rest of the building was largely destroyed by the fire and all that survives is the outline of the entrance hall, with an octagonal inner vestibule leading to a large stairhall on the S, both decorated with round-headed niches and recesses. Three rooms flanked the hall on the S, with one larger room on the N.

MOYDRUM CHURCH (C of I). 0.5 km N. Small roofless lancet hall of *c.* 1860. Three bays, built of rock-faced limestone rubble, with a bellcote over the W gable and a polygonal chancel end. Inside the W gable, a plaque commemorates a former church 'built by contributions of Dean Handcock, Robert Handcock and other well disposed persons in the year one thousand, sevenhundred and forty'.

CORPUS CHRISTI, MOUNT TEMPLE PARISH CHURCH. 5 km E. 1932 by *Martin McGuire*. Small, white stuccoed church in a continental Romanesque idiom. Gabled hall and transepts, with a four-stage campanile flanking one side of the nave and an apsidal E end. The entrance front is a gable with a round window of simple petal-like tracery above a round-headed entrance arch with three orders of arch rings, lancets each side and a band of blind arcading at gallery level. Inside, the nave is lit by paired round-headed lancets and has an open kingpost roof. Paired round-headed arches open into shallow transepts, carried on shafts of polished grey limestone with stylized Romanesque capitals.

BEALIN CROSS. Erected on a little hill in Bealin Twyford Demesne, 1 km E of the ruins of Moydrum Castle. Early C9. A high cross of modest proportions, some 7 ft (2.1 m) high. The bottom panel on the W side carries an Irish inscription in raised letters – 'Pray for Tuathgall who caused this cross to be made' – thought to record an Abbot Tuathgall who died in 810 at Clonmacnoise (some 14 km SW in Co. Offaly). The arms and head of the cross are now much weathered and only one section of the ring, on the lower S side, survives. There is no cap-stone.

Unlike the magnificent scriptural crosses at Clonmacnoise, Kells and Monasterboice, the decoration of Bealin Cross is worked principally in intricate, abstract patterns of Celtic interlace, executed to two quite different scales. On the E face three spiral scrolls, of a bold scale, are superimposed above each other on the shaft. The centre of the cross is marked by a more delicately scaled knot within a square frame, with another three-point knot above. A shallow relief of a beast is on the S arm. The lowest panel on the N side also has traces of animals in relief; otherwise the sides have each three panels of abstract patterns. On the shaft of the W face is the Prayer, a square panel of four round interlace knots and a more boldly scaled section of interlace weaving which 'flows' round a flat circular boss beneath a larger circle marking the centre of the cross on this side. Flat bosses mark each end of the arms. The ring of Bealin Cross is unusually narrow in relation to the width of the shaft, which seems to be an 'early' feature in the Irish high crosses.

9040 MOYGLARE ME

A parish and a crossroads on the borders of Counties Meath and Kildare just a few miles from Maynooth.

ST PAUL, MOYGLARE PARISH CHURCH (C of I). 1866 by *Edward McAllister*. The typical product of mid-Victorian ecclesiology: a small, three-bay gabled nave and lower chancel, stone Y-tracery windows to the nave and a triple lancet window to the chancel. Paired lights to the W gable. The church is entered on the N by a buttressed porch with an octagonal belfry above, crowned by a small spire. – STAINED GLASS. E window: SS Paul, James and Peter. W window: Evangelists, by *William Wailes* of Newcastle.

MOYGLARE CASTLE. In February 1558 E. Balfe of the Cregge, Co. Meath, received parliamentary assistance to build a border castle at Moyglare. Unfortunately, given the scarcity of datable tower houses, all that survives of Moyglare Castle is a part of the gatehouse. Two tall N- and S-facing ivy-grown walls, with a chimney corbelled out on the N wall and a crisp portcullis groove.

MOYGLARE HOUSE. 1.5 km N. Perhaps *c.* 1780. Large and handsome house, three storeys over a basement and two rooms deep. Five bays to the entrance front, the centre three advanced in a canted bow rising the full height of the house. Regular sash windows and a nice pedimented limestone doorcase with Scamozzian Ionic columns, taken exactly from William Pain's *Builder's Companion* (first published 1758). Raised limestone corner quoins and a low parapet which partially conceals a high hipped roof. The garden front is six bays wide, with the windows diminishing in height up the façade. A substantial home, simply but elegantly expressed, but dull in its limitation. Masonry-box style of architecture, with no attempt to develop the ends of the building or to create any architecture beyond the two fronts (*see* p. 45). Fine neoclassical cornices in the principal rooms; stairs as in a double-pile plan.

MOYGLARE GLEBE HOUSE. 1 km N. 1803. Diminutive Regency villa of exceptionally pleasing proportions. Three bays and two storeys, yet a little different from the normal glebe-house in having a boldly advanced and pedimented centre bay and a wide hipped roof with emphatic eaves. Limestone doorcase with consoled architrave above a rectangular fanlight.

MOYGADDY CASTLE. 1.5 km ESE. Tiny tower house in a field near the river Rye on the border of Meath and Kildare. At only 10 ft by 11 ft (3 m by 3.3 m) internally, Moygaddy is even smaller than the unrealistic measurements specified by the £10 castle-building grant of 1429; one can only presume that it was a subsidiary of a large property elsewhere, perhaps the Fitzgerald fortress at Maynooth. A section of low curving wall attached to the SE corner was probably part of an adjoining enclosure. The building has two storeys but is very low, with a battlemented roof-walk and a narrow spiral stair at the SE corner. The ground floor is barrel-vaulted, while the upper chamber is roofed by a flat corbelled ceiling of immense, thin slabs of limestone.

KILLARKIN HOUSE. 4.5 km E. Long, low country house in the Regency cottage idiom. The building began in the late C18 as a two-storey, three-bay house with a hipped roof and large sash windows. This now constitutes the back of the building; *c.* 1820 it was enlarged by adding a new range, nine bays long, across the front, with a corridor between. The whole was made more picturesque *c.* 1880 by the addition of gables, canted bays, windows and diamond panes to the windows.

KILLARKIN CASTLE. 4 km E. In a cow yard, the stump of a tower house, consisting of a vaulted basement, 16 ft by 11 ft (4.8 m by 3.3 m) inside. Round-headed recess in the S wall and a ruined stair at the NW corner.

KILLARKIN GLEBE HOUSE. 4 km E. Three-bay, two-storey, early C19 house, with a hipped roof, an advanced centre bay to the entrance front, fanlit doorcase and tripartite windows.

DOLANSTOWN OLD CHURCH. 2.5 km NW. On a slight mound, surrounded by trees, the ruin of a rubble-built and rough-cast mid-C18 church. Two-bay hall, 54 ft by 21 ft (16.2 m by 6.3 m) inside, with a shallow segmental apse, round-headed windows and a bellcote over the W gable. No details survive in this carcass of a church, ivy-grown and thick with sapling trees.

DOLANSTOWN HOUSE. 2.5 km NW. Large L-shaped house, early C18 in part, though now much altered and entirely rebuilt inside. Two storeys, with a tall hipped roof and a modillion eaves cornice. The principal front is of seven bays, with tall and narrow sash windows flanking a Venetian window and pedimented doorcase in the centre bay. Five-bay garden front, again with narrow windows, here set in flat recessed rectangular panels. On the ground floor, a large Victorian bay window. In 1786 the seat of a family called Jones.

BRIDESTREAM HOUSE. 3.5 km WNW. Miniature Palladian country house built *c.* 1750 (*see* pp. 46–7); in 1786 the seat of Mr Hill. The design has been attributed to *Nathaniel Clements*. In a sense this is the mid-Georgian forerunner of Galtrim House in Co. Meath. Although similar in scale to a substantial glebe-house, Bridestream adheres to the formal Palladian arrangement of a central block with quadrants linking it to end pavilions and archways giving access to small courtyards at the rear: a neat plan that is charming in its scale, if a trifle plain in elevation. Central four-bay block of two storeys over a basement, the two central bays breaking forward under an eaves pediment. The roof has a tall, almost pyramidal profile that serves to reinforce the form of the pediment, with thin chimneystacks at each end. The door, just fitting between the two bays on the ground floor, is framed by a plain limestone blocked surround. The building is harled, with moulded limestone cornices and a continuous string-course to the quadrants and pavilions. Aediculed niches ornament the sides of the pavilions facing the forecourt. Fragments of the C18 GARDEN survive: behind the house a horseshoe-shaped pond, and a little way to the S a lake, now dry, with a circular wooded island. A belt of trees forms a boundary to the estate.

CALGATH HOUSE. 4 km WNW. Mid-C18 gentleman farmer's residence. Double-gabled end elevations, with a five-bay, two-storey front. Two rooms deep, with relatively small windows, broad expanses of masonry and a plain limestone door surround with fanlight and side-lights.

LARCHHILL HOUSE. 5.5 km NW. Plain two-storey house facing S over a miniature park which contains an amusing collection of rustic follies and garden buildings, probably of the late C18. These include a BATTLEMENTED TOWER with pebble mosaics decorating the interior, an OCTAGON of rubble columns (an Irish 'Druids' Temple'?), a RUSTIC SHELTER built against a curving wall, three heavy stone stumps supporting a stone slab with a rubble mound above, and, oddest of all, the FOX'S EARTH, a vaulted grotto with three pointed windows in a relieving arch, surmounted by a symmetrical earth mound with another primitive rubble structure above: rubble piers supporting a flat hexagon of stone with a rubble dome above. A belt of trees encloses these architectural oddities. Who built them, for whom, when and why are all unknown. A STATUE OF NIMROD stood on an island in the now dried-up lake S of the house. This also contains the walls of an elaborate pentagonal FORT (known as 'Gibraltar'), of low profile and marked by round towers with Irish stepped battlements at its corners. In 1836 Larchhill belonged to a Mr S. E. Watson.

KILMORE CHURCH RUINS. 7 km NW, at Kilmore crossroads. An ancient ecclesiastical site, now occupied by the ivy-covered ruin of a church finished and consecrated in 1686 and destroyed by the Irish in 1689. Fragments of mouldings and ogee-headed windows strewn about are the remnants of a late medieval building. – MONUMENT. The most notable feature at Kilmore is a large funerary slab dated 1575 bearing the outline of a plain cross, with a primitive figure of Christ down the centre, and on either side an inscription in raised letters in Irish and in English. The latter carries the reassuring homily 'No one ought to be grieved at death since in living there is labour and danger, while in dying there is peace and assurance of resurrection. Pray for the soul of Rory McMahon who made me'.

MOYMET

ME *7060*

4.5 km NW of Trim

Moymet is a rare microcosm of late medieval life in Ireland. A complete C16 manor survives: a gatehouse, castle, outbuildings and manorial church erected by the Dillons, a powerful Meath family which had close connections with the borough of Newtown Trim where many of its members were priors of the Victorine Abbey and Cathedral. In the C15 the Dillons established themselves at Tara and Skryne and built the castles of Newtown and Proudstown. Sir Lucas Dillon, a son of Robert Dillon of Newtown, was the builder of Moymet Castle. In 1570 he became Chief Baron of the Exchequer in Ireland; his marriage, at about the same time, to Jane Bathe suggests that it would be in this period that Moymet was built. Later, in the 1580s, Chief Justice Drury is recorded as bringing some Germans from Strasbourg to visit Dillon's house at Moymet. Today Sir Lucas and Jane Bathe lie buried in the parish church within the cathedral precinct at Newtown Trim. Moymet is therefore no secluded provincial manor, as it might now appear, but the seat of one of the most powerful magnates of the Elizabethan Pale.

MOYMET CASTLE. An imposing three-storey gatehouse at once announces Lucas Dillon's wealth and prestige. As large as many an entire tower house, the building consists of a great roomy archway – formerly vaulted, with two rooms above – and a chimney in the E wall. This is adjoined on the W by a narrow vaulted chamber lit by loops, with a spiral stair at the SE corner. The ruins of the castle proper, S of the gatehouse, are now sadly reduced, although they present an impressive silhouette when seen from the S. What survives is the S wall, with a great fissure up the centre where windows once were, and an entire side wall with a square garderobe turret at its N end. The castle was of three storeys over a vaulted basement; the masonry was of crisp limestone rubble with punched stone quoins and corbels and chiselled limestone mullions to the windows. Some windows have bar-holes, pocked margins and hoodmouldings. Immediately W of the castle is the stump of a long barrel-vaulted structure with thick walls and deeply splayed windows, crudely executed, with surviving remnants of the wickerwork centering. Although larger, the building is similar to the long low vaulted range built in 1590 at Balsoon (*see* Bective Abbey). It probably served as a farm or office building.

CHURCH OF ST BRIGID. The late medieval church of Moymet is now ruinous and ivy-clad. Long, rectangular building of limestone rubble, housing a nave and chancel, and entered through two pointed arches at the W end of the building. The nave is broader than the chancel; a mural spiral stair in the NE angle between the two gave access to a gallery or rood screen. The nave was lit by single cusped lights with trefoils carved in the spandrels and emphatic plastically rendered hoodmouldings. The chancel has a plain rectangular window in the

N and S walls, and in the E gable are three charming cusped ogee lights set in a rectangular frame and crowned by a hood-moulding. All of this carved work, together with the wave-moulded jambs of the entrance arches, is mid-C 16 in character, and there is a marked resemblance between the E window here and the window of the ruined chancel at St Patrick's Cathedral, Trim (q.v.). At Moymet, however, the mullions are not carried up to the lintel as they are at Trim, creating a pretty openwork effect.

7080

MOYNALTY ME

A pretty village, charmingly set in rolling green fields beside the Borrora River. Neat colour-washed estate houses with dormer windows, gables and quarry glass, all laid out and built during the 1820s by an improving landlord, John Farrell. At the time of the Cromwellian plantation the lands of Moynalty were granted to the Betagh family; early in the C 18 they became the property of the Farnham family, who sold them in 1790 to James Farrell of Merrion Square, Dublin, a successful brewer and moneylender. He gave Moynalty to his son John on his marriage in 1820. Work on rebuilding the village began in 1826 and was largely completed by 1837.

ST MARY, MOYNALTY PARISH CHURCH (C of I). 1819. Simple two-bay hall with Y-tracery windows and a battlemented three-stage tower. Sited at the crossroads in the middle of the village, with the churchyard sloping downhill to the river. – MONUMENT. Claudius Wm Cole Hamilton † 1822 and his wife, Nichola Sophia, † 1863; erected by their son Richard Chaloner of Kingsfort.

OUR LADY ASSUMED INTO HEAVEN. T-plan chapel of 1820 with lancets, pointed arches and hoodmouldings; rough-cast, with limestone trim. Originally a single-bay nave; extended to two bays in 1976. Gothic chancel of 1910. Pretty freestanding Gothic belfry of 1909 in stone and timber with decorative cast-iron cresting to the slated roof.

MOYNALTY LODGE. Charming Regency-style house built for John Farrell during the 1820s. The design would be ordinary – a two-storey, three-bay house with the usual shallow hipped roof and oversailing bracketed eaves – were it not for the simple yet extremely effective device of four low-relief giant pilasters extending across the front and three to the sides, all notionally supporting a blank frieze at eaves level. Limestone Doric porch, of excellent masonry and reminiscent of Johnston. Pretty gate lodge, a whitewashed four-bay cottage with a tall slated roof, dormer windows, hoodmouldings, quarry glass and picturesque timber bargeboards.

WALTERSTOWN HOUSE. 2 km N. Pleasant late Georgian house. Two-storey, three-bay front. Rough-cast, with sash windows of twelve and fifteen panes and a very elegant limestone Tuscan doorcase with side-lights and a segmental fanlight.

KINGSFORT. 4 km S. A big regular house, set in pleasant rolling countryside and built in the mid-C18 by the Chaloner family. Although now ruinous, Kingsfort is of interest for its unusual quality as a structure and on account of the vivid picture of life here left to us in the early C19 journal of Richard Chaloner. The house had a S-facing two-storey, seven-bay entrance front. As a shell it is reminiscent of a plate from Gibbs' *Book of Architecture*, with the three centre bays advanced, and built of exceptionally crisp masonry, in red brick with dark limestone trim. There were raised corner quoins to the centre and ends, keystones, a deep first-floor string-course and an eaves cornice. The house stood on a limestone basement, with segment-headed windows. Its sides are now covered in ivy. Inside, Kingsfort was equally sophisticated and must once have possessed a remarkably elegant interior. The plan is reminiscent of Richard Castle's Dollardstown (*see* Donaghmore), three rooms wide and two rooms deep, with the stairhall in the centre directly behind the entrance hall; but here the scale is much smaller and the character infinitely more feminine. One distinctive departure from the usual alignment of hall and stairhall is that the hall here occupies only two bays, as a third of the space was absorbed into a longer dining room E of the hall. Ultimately this large room was lit only by one large window at the E end, so that there were three blind windows on the entrance front, an unusually large number for such a small house, which suggests a remodelling in the early C19, perhaps in 1813. Inside, the hall and all of the ground-floor rooms are brick-vaulted, with a long coved vault to the dining room. Fragments of cornices, wall panels, pineapple corbels and flower-baskets bear witness to what was once a remarkably pretty decorative scheme. In 1813 Richard Chaloner added a long plain two-storey extension at the rear of the house, to designs by an architect named *Keegan*. About the same time he whiled away many hours planting and laying out 'the Glen', some miles from here at Cherrymount, a wooded retreat beside a stream with a miniature house, a waterfall and a cenotaph to his favourite dog, all now overgrown and accessible only to the most intrepid traveller. Despite his enthusiasm for rustic garden retreats, Chaloner was no misanthropist, but a man who loved company and disliked the periodic isolation of rural life. 'Solitude is far from being so pleasant as certain dismal people represent it' is a thought confided to his journal on a dull day in May 1811; by then he was 'quite sick of it'!

CHERRYMOUNT. 4 km SW. A much altered early Georgian gentleman's house, originally the seat of the Chaloners after they had purchased the estate from Captain Stopford in 1704. The proportions suggest a date in the 1730s or 1740s, certainly before the family built Kingsfort, when Cherrymount became their dowerhouse. Single-pile and gable-ended. Five-bay entrance front, the windows set in an a–b–a rhythm, with a squat castellated tower at the W end and a gabled wing at the rear giving an L-shape plan. The original house is of tripartite plan, with a central stairhall, six-panel doors, a dentil cornice and moulded ceiling panels to the hall, and a Corinthian cornice in the drawing room.

NEWTOWN CHURCH RUIN. 5 km SE. The ivy-grown shell of a simple C18 classical hall, which had been recently repaired in 1810. Four bays long and gable-ended, with round-headed windows, blind in the N wall, a square-headed entrance and semicircular window to the W gable and what looks like the remains of a Venetian window at the E end. Newcastle was not a viable living and owed its origins to the fact that in Norman times Newtown had been a village in its own right.

NEWCASTLE CATHOLIC CHURCH, CHAPEL OF EASE TO MOYNALTY. 11 km NW. Built by the Rev. Philip Farrelly in 1844. Plain three-bay hall, with timber Y-tracery windows, corner quoin strips and an early C20 Gothic chancel. – STAINED GLASS. Triple-light E window, the Crucifixion, in a Clarke-like palette of vivid blues, mauves and pinks but inferior draughtsmanship. Erected to the memory of his parents by Thomas Mulraney, Bishop of Meath, 1939. – Freestanding Gothic BELFRY with diagonal buttresses, slated roof and pretty cast-iron cresting, like the one at Moynalty of 1909.

MOYHILL CHURCH (C of I). 16 km N. Late C19 rubble hall with red and yellow brick trim, lancet windows and a gabled S porch crowned by a slated bellcote. Dinky architecture.

4050 MULLINGAR WM

Mullingar, a large inland market town laid out on the familiar main street pattern, is set amongst flat fertile lands at a crossing on the river Brosna between Lough Owel and Lough Ennell. The significance of agriculture to the area and the early Irish monastic tradition of N Westmeath combine to give Mullingar its unusual title, An Muileann gCearr, the left-hand mill. The story, deriving from the C12 life of a C7 saint, Colum Mac Luachainn, relates how the saint as a young man performed a loaves-and-fishes-type miracle by causing a corn mill to turn backwards and produce enough flour – indeed, a sack that never emptied – to pay his parents' dues to the King of Meath. A more recent and less sublime vernacular tradition celebrates the flourishing livestock industry of the area, in the common Irish definition of rotundity as 'beef to the heels like a Mullingar heifer'!

With the coming of the Normans, the richer lands of the northern midlands were incorporated into De Lacy's kingdom of Meath. In 1227 De Lacy granted the lands of Mullingar, as the Manor of Magheradernon, to William de Petit, a brother of Ralph de Petit, the powerful Anglo-Norman Bishop of Meath. De Petit erected a castle in the town and within a decade endowed two monastic foundations, the Augustinian Priory of St Mary, founded in 1227, and a Dominican Priory, founded in 1237. He also established a parish church, which he impropriated to the Canons Regular of Llanthony in Gloucester. Of these, Mullingar's three principal medieval churches, not a trace survives, though the belltower of the parish church remained intact until the early C 19, when it was demolished to make way for the new Church of All Saints. In the Cathedral Museum is a conjectural model of the tower based on C 18 and C 19 accounts.

Mullingar, like Dundalk and Longford, is essentially a modern town whose fabric dates for the most part to the C 18 and C 19. In 1682 Sir Henry Piers found here some 'old fashioned castles' and also 'some demolished', with 'better or at least more commodious houses built in their room'. A new gaol had also been erected and a large courthouse was then in progress. Some of this development must have been effected by Sir Arthur Forbes, second Earl of Granard, who received a grant of the manor of Mullingar upon the restoration of Charles II. By 1786 the town could be described as 'large and well-built', and many of the houses which now line the principal streets date to the mid-C 18. The extension of the Royal Canal to Mullingar in 1806 greatly increased the town's prosperity, and in the first half of the C 19 several important new public buildings were constructed, including a courthouse and gaol, two large parish churches and a lunatic asylum. In 1863, however, *The Dublin Builder* was 'surprised' to report that a recent visit to the town had shown, with the exception of the newly erected Hevey Institute, 'literally nothing doing by way of local improvements'. Momentum soon picked up and within a decade of this assessment much of the centre of Mullingar received a stuccoed Italianate face-lift, probably at the hands of *William Caldbeck*, who designed a new markethouse for the town in 1867 and a hotel and hunt club room in 1869. In 1858 Lord Greville purchased part of the Granard estate together with the town's market rights.

Over a hundred years later Mullingar has still the appearance of a mid-Victorian commercial centre, one long main shopping thoroughfare running eastward from Dominick Street on the W, through Oliver Plunkett Street to Pearse Street. Welcome breathing-space is provided by the small market square at the junction of Plunkett and Pearse Streets and also at the junction of Plunkett and Dominick Streets, where the latter broadens out into a square of sorts, bounded by the town's two principal C 19 banks. The main C 20 addition to Mullingar, and undoubtedly its most conspicuous landmark, is the Cathedral of Christ the King, whose assertive twin-towered silhouette dominates the skyline for miles around.

CATHEDRAL OF CHRIST THE KING, R.C. DIOCESE OF 137
MEATH. 1932–6 by *Ralph Byrne*. Massive and grandiose church in an eclectic and triumphalist classical mode; an Irish version of the Roman classical revival prevalent in a Europe dominated by Hitler, Mussolini and Franco. Stark and yet richly finished, this is a building which relies on opulence and scale for its effect: it is impressive only in so far as it is designed to be so. A rival in pomp and scale to St Mel's Cathedral, Longford, and perhaps deliberately so; there is here a greater

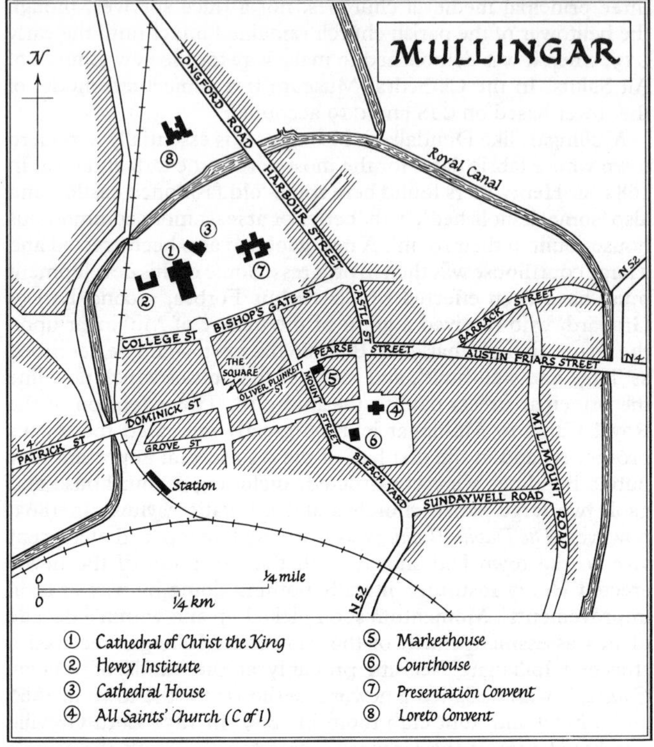

articulation of the wall surface, evident particularly in the complex arrangement of the transepts with colonnaded loggias set across their ends.

Byrne's unabashed eclecticism, if not quite a success, is nevertheless an intriguing amalgam of Roman, Palladian and baroque elements. The church is essentially a great rectangular hall with adjoining aisles and transepts, a dome over the crossing – not expressed internally – and two tall campanile towers crowning the entrance front. The front is a remarkable composition in horizontally channelled granite ashlar; a pedimented two-storey central block, with open colonnades on both levels, marks the end of the nave. It is flanked by two broad single-storey blocks with shallow attics which support two four-storey campanile towers a little recessed behind the main front. The central pedimented block, with its open colonnades, derives ultimately perhaps from Palladio's two-storeyed villa designs, such as the Villa Pisani, though in the centre bay of the ground floor the entablature is broken by a huge round-headed arch to create the classic tripartite Venetian opening in an unexpected place and to a greatly exaggerated scale. This is not now Palladian but the freewheeling classicism of Lutyens, Baker or

Webb. Flanking this huge Venetian opening, the single-storey outer bays employ a motif popularized by James Gandon, a flat-headed recess with a doorway in the centre flanked by two columns *in antis*, while the twin stacked and arcaded belfries are rooted in the baroque tradition of central Europe. The union of these disparate elements, knit together by a skin of horizontally channelled granite, with reiterated cornice lines, results in a façade which, if not beautiful, clearly manifests its imperial pretensions. The sea of undifferentiated asphalt filling the forecourt of the church today is an unworthy approach to Byrne's ambitious design, and unworthy of the care lavished on the building which even in the 1930s cost over quarter of a million pounds.

Like St Mel's in Longford, Mullingar Cathedral has a fine sculptural pediment. This one, carved in Portland stone by *Albert Power*, reflects the cathedral's change in dedication from the Immaculate Conception to the new concept of Christ the King. Here the kneeling Virgin offers a model of the old Tudor-Gothic Cathedral (*see* Cathedral House, below) to the crowned Christ flanked by St Peter and St Patrick on the l. and by the kneeling figures of Pius XI (at whose request the dedication was changed), Cardinal Thomas Mulvany, Bishop of Meath, and Cardinal MacRory, Archbishop of Armagh. The head of Moses on the keystone of the main arch and the sculpted panels on the façade are by *H. Thompson* of Dublin.

The side elevations are not entirely satisfactory. Here the dome over the sanctuary is particularly weak, too small and dwarfed both by the tall W towers and by the bulkiness of the transepts, which though rich with classical references appear almost as a series of later additions to the core of the church. There is too an uncomfortable shift in scale between the different parts. The aisle walls are expressed as flat rusticated piers supporting round-headed windows, with carved panels below, while the transepts, buttressed by freestanding porches, have colonnaded screens which reflect the loggia of the entrance front.

The interior combines the styles of the great early Christian 138
basilicas of Rome – S. Maria Maggiore, St John's Lateran or St Paul's Outside the Walls – and of Italian late C16 classicism – the work of men like Vignola, Alessi or Pellegrino Tibaldi. Byrne's invention here is admirable and wonderfully well contrived. The cathedral can seat 1,800 people. Its nave is a great rectangular space, and to provide a vault over this area would have been quite beyond the means of the cathedral authorities. The exterior may seem to call for a high barrel-vault, but instead Byrne provided a flat ceiling divided up into coffered panels, a solution he took from the Roman basilicas. The apse in the sanctuary and the two round-headed arches opening into the transepts are also hints taken from the basilicas, and so too is the arrangement of the walls as a colonnaded ground floor with flat-headed windows in a clerestory above.

The C16 is evoked in the arrangement of the columns

between the nave and the aisles. Byrne adopts a pattern, much favoured by Pellegrino Tibaldi, of arcades supported not on single columns but on groups of two, with a flat entablature linking alternate pairs of columns. This results in a wall elevation that looks like a series of Venetian windows or arches laid end to end and it gives a variety of rhythm to the aisle arcades as the columns are alternately close together and wide apart in an a–b–a–b pattern. Now these two dimensions – a and b – provide the core to the positioning of every element in the interior. The pilasters of the clerestory follow this rhythm; so too the square returns at the entry into the sanctuary area, which is narrower than the nave, take their size from the interval of the columns. Some may interpret the narrower space of the sanctuary as a memory of Palladio's famous arrangement at the church of the Redentore in Venice; others may recall Giulio Romano's cathedral in Mantua on stepping into the vaulted aisles, which contrast so emphatically with the flat ceiling of the nave. Romano-like, Byrne even repeats the Doric columns of the aisle arcade against the outer wall to enhance the classical grandeur of his church. This is an interior that demonstrates a wonderfully well-stored and articulate mind and there is real pleasure in watching the architect at work. Unlike so many post-modernist *pasticheurs* Ralph Byrne thoroughly understood the discipline of classicism.

The stone of the aisle columns is Rochambeau marble, with Irish marble bases and capitals. In the MORTUARY CHAPEL the fresco of the Resurrection is by *Fr Aengus Buckley O.P.* and the mosaics in the CHAPELS OF ST PATRICK and of ST ANNE are by *Boris Arwep*, 1948 and 1954. – FURNISHINGS. The lavish gilt and marble fittings in the sanctuary are by *Early & Co.*, *Gunning Smyth's*, *J. & C. McGloughlin* of Dublin, and *Oppenheimer* of Manchester.

CATHEDRAL HOUSE. E of the Cathedral. Built in 1871 as the result of a competition for an 'Episcopal Residence' won by *William Hague*, with J. J. O'Callaghan in second place. Irish institutional Gothic, robust if gaunt. Three-storey block in squared rubble limestone, with dressed quoins and window surrounds, granite colonnettes and yellow brick chimneystacks. The centre bay is slightly advanced over a heavy porch with a deep Gothic archway and high gable at eaves level. The Bishop's Chapel, linked to the house by a square tower chamfered to an octagonal roof, is a gabled hall, nave and chancel with a Dec three-light E window.

This house is a reminder of the Gothic phase of the earlier Mullingar Cathedral, a large T-plan church with a pretty Gothic façade and short sanctuary, dedicated in 1836 and said to have accommodated 6,000 people. This church replaced the parish chapel of 1730.

ALL SAINTS, MULLINGAR PARISH CHURCH (C of I). 1813. A Board of First Fruits church with a W tower and spire, nicely sited at the end of a short cul-de-sac. Lancets in the nave; Perp windows to the transepts and chancel added in 1861 as part of an extensive refitting by *Welland and Gillespie*. In 1878 the chancel walls and arch were altered and heightened to designs of *Thomas Drew*. The interior is dark, owing to an abundance of Victorian stained glass and the recent ill-advised removal of the plaster from the walls. – MONUMENTS. S transept: Hugh Bowen †1724; a marble and slate classical aedicule. Rebecca Dobson †1787; an elegant neoclassical plaque.

PRESBYTERIAN MEETING HOUSE. 1825. Tiny and very simple church built by the united congregation of Mullingar and Tyrrellspass, which was established in 1821. Three bays, with a lower chancel and a diminutive three-stage tower at the W end. Harled; round-headed windows. Among the properties sold by the Earl of Granard in 1859.

HEVEY INSTITUTE/ST MARY'S COLLEGE. By *John Bourke*, 1854–6. The Hevey Institute was built as a free school with funds from the bequest of Mr James Hevey, a successful Mullingar brewer who died in 1837. Since its foundation the College has been administered by the Christian Brothers. A handsome Italianate building of snecked limestone rubble with ashlar trim and broad bands of quoin pilasters marking the principal elements. Eleven bays and two storeys, the three centre bays advanced, with a gable treated as an open pediment and crowned by the short pedimented Italianate belfry so typical of this architect. The centre is answered at each end by advanced and gabled end bays of equal breadth. Between are flat three-bay elevations with round-headed sash windows. The gabled ends are grandly scaled, with pedimented tripartite windows on the main floor and Venetian windows in relieving arches above. This, the principal residential block of the College, returns at each end to give two schoolroom ranges at the rear. The nine-bay side elevations have pedimented centrepieces and central Tuscan porches.

PRESENTATION CONVENT. 1869 by *William Caldbeck*. Dull three-storey, eleven-bay gabled block, cement-rendered, with plate-glass windows and minimal Gothic detail. The three centre bays are advanced and gabled, with a broad four-centred entrance arch and tripartite Venetian-like windows on the upper levels. The convent chapel was added in 1873 to designs by *John P. Davis*.

LORETO CONVENT. Built in 1881 and many times enlarged. The original building is a nine-bay, two-storey block with a tall slated roof, the entrance projecting as a dumpy canted bay with three graded lancets above. Regular Victorian institutional Gothic with irregular fenestration. Stone Y-tracery below, sash windows above. 1920s additions by *W. H. Byrne & Son*.

ST FINIAN'S COLLEGE. 1902–8 by *J. J. O'Callaghan*. Enormous 130
classical-cum-Gothic institutional block, built as a minor seminary for the diocese of Meath to replace the old seminary of St Finian at Navan of 1802. The sheer scale of this building, announced by a grandiose classical gateway and approached by a sweeping avenue, is a testament to the confidence of the Catholic Church at the turn of the C19. In contrast to its

assured stage management, however, the architecture of St Finian's is sadly uninspired, impressive only in its scale. The seminary is a vast block, three storeys over a tall basement, twenty-one bays long to the central block, flanked by advanced and pedimented three-bay wings. In the principal range the three central bays are slightly advanced and are crowned by a steeply pointed eaves pediment. The entrance, approached by a grand flight of limestone steps, is screened by a big porch with a Ruskinian Gothic three-bay arcade. As at the Hevey Institute the main block returns at each end to give two substantial ranges at the rear. E of the College is a freestanding E.E. Gothic CHAPEL with graded lancets in its gable ends.

129 ST LOMAN'S HOSPITAL. An impressive essay in picturesque institutional Gothic, built in 1855 as a lunatic asylum, to designs by *J. S. Mulvany* (*see* p. 75). Remodelled 1890–6 by *Joyce and Parry*. Long and tall three-storey range with a steeply pitched roof and a series of shallow gabled projections at front and rear. The pattern of projection and recession lends interest and variety to the façade, as do the occasional canted bay windows, clasping buttresses, tall chimneystacks with diagonally placed chimneys and windows of two and three lights. The masonry is of crisp grey limestone rubble, all starkly impressive. The HOSPITAL CHAPEL, 1886, is a seven-bay lancet hall with an apsidal chancel and an open kingpost roof inside.

ST MARY'S HOSPITAL. The former Union workhouse, built in 1841 to one of the standard designs of *George Wilkinson*. In front, a five-bay, two-storey governor's house with advanced and gabled end bays, dormer windows, curly bargeboards and minimal Tudor-Gothic detail; behind, the usual long range, here two-storey and thirteen bays long, ending in three-storey double-gabled blocks at each end. All of limestone rubble with yellow and red brick trim.

84 COURTHOUSE. *c.* 1824. Large and accomplished courthouse in the distinctive Italianate classicism of *John Hargrave*, who in 1821 had designed the new Mullingar gaol (now long since demolished). The courthouse is an elegant seven-bay, two-storey building, the centre five bays making an emphatic projection from the main block. The façade is conceived as two superimposed blind arcades, all of limestone ashlar, rusticated in the lower storey. In the advanced central block, which houses offices, entrance hall and main staircase, the first-floor arcade is 'carried' on Doric pilasters and frames five regular sash windows. Below, the arcade forms an open porch in the three centre bays, flanked by round-headed sash windows in the blind outer arches. The recessed wings, originally the Crown and Record Courts, are lit from the side elevations. The courthouse has a shallow hipped roof behind a continuous eaves cornice and blocking course. A horizontal tablet flanked by volutes is set centrally above the façade. Hargrave's elegant design does not seem to have much impressed the local populace; a few years after its completion, in the summer of 1830, the Westmeath Grand Jury books report the courtyard to be in

'... an extremely filthy state with a large dunghill in one corner ... a stable or cowhouse erected against the front of the wing wall; a pighouse erected and a turfstore converted into a washhouse ...'

MARKETHOUSE. 1867 by *William Caldbeck*. Large rectangular two-storey building with a rather awkward eight-bay façade. Lord Granard's markethouse at Mullingar was described in 1815 as a 'two-storeyed block with eight large gateways'; in 1858 that building, together with all Mullingar market rights, was purchased from the Earl of Granard by Lord Greville. Several years later the new landlord dutifully provided a new market building. Designs were commissioned from Caldbeck and work began in 1867. Judging from the existing façade it is likely that Caldbeck was requested to remodel the earlier building. Principal elevation of eight bays, the two centre bays advanced and crowned by an eaves pediment supporting the Greville arms and with a louvred clocktower on top. The main block is arcaded in the two flanking bays on each side and has segmental-headed windows at each end. On the first floor, square-headed windows are set in large segmental-headed surrounds. Discrepancies abound, such as the cramped proportions of the central projection and the assorted levels and sizes of the first-floor windows. Recent restoration removed an ugly cement-rendering, and the paved area in front greatly enhances the building.

COUNTY BUILDINGS. Early C20 academic classicism housing Westmeath County Council's offices. Asymmetrical Italianate façade of limestone ashlar: a six-bay mish-mash which looks rather like two distinct halves. On the r., a three-bay, two-storey house with a central attic and pediment and a roof-line balustrade. Here the central bay is articulated as a Venetian window set above a projecting semicircular porch carried on freestanding columns and crowned by a balustrade. Square-headed windows in the outer bays, with segmental-headed pediments on the first floor. Adjoining this on the l., the second two-storey, three-bay block, also with roof-line balustrade, has pedimented doorcases on the ground floor, pedimented windows above and giant pilasters between.

COLUMB MILITARY BARRACKS. Mullingar has a long history of military occupation; in 1641 the Confederate army used the town as a food and munitions base and in 1690 General Ginkel made camp here before the siege of Athlone. The existing barrack is, however, a relatively modern complex, built in 1814 with the unavoidable title of Wellington Barracks. Enclosed within an extensive curtain wall this is a large U-shaped court of harled three-storey Georgian ranges, with fanlit doorcases and sash windows with lintels and jambs of punched limestone. ST COLMAN'S CHAPEL, 1855, is a nine-bay lancet hall with a chamfered belfry projecting from the entrance gable. Built of dark limestone rubble with ashlar trim and quarry-glass windows. 'A new ablution house, workhouse and baths' were added in 1896, and married soldiers' quarters were built in 1909.

PAROCHIAL HALL. 1888 by *J. F. Fuller*. Beside All Saints Church, a six-bay gabled hall of rock-faced limestone rubble in a Tudor idiom. Mullioned windows to the entrance gable, clasping corner buttresses and a chimney surmounting the entrance gable.

FORMER NATIONAL BANK (now BANK OF IRELAND). 1858 by *William Caldbeck*. Tall freestanding block, three storeys by five bays, with advanced end bays. Rusticated limestone ashlar basement and rendered upper storeys with a limestone eaves cornice. Three round-headed windows light the banking floor, flanked by flat-headed architraved doorcases in the outer bays. The upper storeys have plate-glass windows, set in a tall segmental-headed relieving arch in each of the outer bays.

BANK OF IRELAND. Dominick Street. 1874 by *Sandham Symes*. Two-storey, four-bay palazzo-style design. Limestone ashlar ground floor and a tall brick upper storey designed to appear as a *piano nobile*. Two segmental-headed windows light the banking floor, flanked by a doorcase at each end. Four tall architraved windows light the upper storey, which is crowned by an emphatic eaves cornice.

ULSTER BANK. 1911 by *Blackwood & Jury*. Three-storey, six-bay façade with a stuccoed banking floor and coursed limestone upper storeys. Advanced end bays with decorative shaped gables. Shallow projection to the central bays on the upper storeys, and a wide canted bay window beneath. Eclectic classical ornament.

OTHER BUILDINGS

The GREVILLE ARMS on PEARSE STREET is presumably the 'new hotel' for which *William Caldbeck* made designs in 1869; a five-bay, three-storey rendered terrace with a big limestone consoled architrave to the central door. Two doors E of this is a nice row of three three-storey, two-bay commercial façades built of flint and limestone rubble, with big sash windows and broad elliptical arches – now shop windows – probably of the mid-C 19. On the opposite side of the street, No. 48, established in 1875, has large plate-glass windows alternated with timber colonnettes and fluted fans in the spandrels.

W of the Markethouse, in OLIVER PLUNKETT STREET, the MULLINGAR CREDIT UNION has an attractive pale limestone façade. Early C 20 cosmopolitan classicism with two tall doorcases flanking a tetrastyle Scamozzian Ionic banking floor; above, a pair of two-storey gabled and canted bay windows. Nos. 14–16, also on the N side, are noteworthy for the proportions of their upper storeys, with small early to mid-C 18 window openings, some with fielded shuttering inside. The shop façades have pretty carved foliate consoles. In contrast to the two handsome C 19 banks at the E end of DOMINICK STREET (*see* above), the C 20 BANKS on Plunkett Street leave much to be desired. The BANK OF IRELAND building in PEARSE STREET is a pleasant Victorian design; five-bay, three-storey block, *c.* 1860, with segmental-headed plate-glass windows to the upper storeys and one broad segmental-headed window to the banking floor, flanked by round arches with over-emphatic Ruskinian colonnettes. At the W end of the town, the RAILWAY STATION, built in 1848 to designs of *J. S. Mulvany*.

NEIGHBOURHOOD

PORTLOMAN ABBEY. 5.5 km NW, on the W shore of Lough Owel. A monastery and centre of learning founded in the C6 by St Loman. About 597 a eulogy of Colmcille was written here by Dallan Forgaill, chief poet of Ireland. Portloman's site and associations are of more interest than the surviving building – the dilapidated ruin of a rectangular church and priest's residence with no architectural detail remaining.

WALSHESTOWN CHAPEL. 5 km NW. Small T-plan chapel of mid-C19 appearance. Harled, with punched limestone quoins. Timber Y-tracery windows to the chancel and transepts; lancets in the nave. – MONUMENT. The Rev. Patrick Kane † 1863 by *Farrell & Son*.

BELMONT. 4.5 km SW. The dowerhouse to the now demolished Ledestown. A two-storey, five-bay house with a wide hipped roof and typical Regency detail. Sash windows to the two outer bays, with a bowed semicircular porch and a tripartite window to the broad central bay. This architecture is deceptive, for Belmont was not built until 1860. The interior decoration is more directly eclectic, with gilded neoclassical doorcases and pilasters brought here from Killua and a chimneypiece with strapwork-like motifs from Leixlip Castle. The box hedge arrangements in the garden were inspired by Lutyens' work at Howth Castle, Co. Dublin.

MULTYFARNHAM ABBEY

WM *4060*

Like Ballintubber in Co. Mayo, Multyfarnham is a restored medieval church once more in use, and in this case it is the home of a monastic community as well: a happy outcome made possible only by the heroic tenacity of the Westmeath Franciscans. The abbey was first founded on the banks of the river Graine in the late C13. Patronized by a soldier-landowner, William Delamer of Street, the abbey church of St Francis was brought to completion and dedicated in 1306. By the C15 the monastery had grown in size and wealth, adding a central crossing tower and a large S transept in 1450. In 1540 the abbey was suppressed but instead of the more familar pattern of disintegration and demolition the community here withstood successive raids, retiring and returning on each occasion to the abbey. Thus in 1583 Captain Piers had to report that 'the Franciscan friars had crept into the old friary in Westmeath and begun their superstition afresh'. As a result the abbey was

Multyfarnham Abbey, from J. N. Brewer's *Beauties of Ireland* (1825)

raided at least five times in 1590, 1601, 1604, 1613 and 1618; yet the friars always returned. Only the Cromwellians in 1651 succeeded in scattering the community. Soon after this final and most effective raid, monastic life was re-established at nearby Knightswood, and the community remained there until the 1820s, when once more it returned to Multyfarnham and began the work of restoration.

In 1682 Sir Henry Piers described the abbey buildings as 'rather neat and compact, than sumptuous or towering, having in the midst between the body of the church and the chancel a handsome straight but very narrow steeple'. When the Franciscans returned in 1827 this basic fabric had survived, with the exception of the chancel, of which only the foundations remained. A modest restoration followed whose achievement was to secure the existing nave, tower and S transept; the cloister range N of the church was by then in ruins, and a plain C 19 three-storey block was built in its place.

The present appearance of the church, with its neat gables, crisp coursed masonry and pointed Gothic windows, owes much to this early C 19 renovation and to a subsequent refurbishment, which would appear to be of the late Victorian period. Today the tower is almost the only authentic feature of the building: a thin, two-storey structure, characteristically slender and, like so many Irish friary towers, straddling the ridge of the roof of the church. In the body of the church itself only the E wall of the transept remains from the original building, and the sole surviving medieval window is that in the transept's gable end: a pointed triple-light opening with shallow ogee-heads and lobed reticulated tracery. The other windows are mid- to late C 19; paired cusped lights with trefoil or plain round heads.

The most recent restoration, of 1975, has reconstructed the chancel, so that, in plan at least, the church once more resembles its medieval predecessor, with a nave and chancel of almost equal length. The modern building, however, has copied the Gothic Revival of the mid-C 19 rather than attempting any accurately revived medieval style. Indeed the E window is taken from the Victorian Tully Presbyterian Church, now disused (*see* Edgeworthstown). Unlike Ballintubber or Holycross, Co. Tipperary, where the interiors of medieval abbeys have been reinstated with white-washed and partly plastered walls, Multyfarnham suffers from the mistaken modern predilection for stripped walls, a taste which removes all finishings from the building regardless of the original architects' intentions. With a modern sanctuary located at the crossing, bare rubble walls, a Victorian panelled pine roof in the transept, a mean modern one in the chancel and some monuments from the old chancel, the interior is now a disappointing mess. – MONUMENTS. S wall of the nave; brought here from the old chancel. An inscribed plaque: 'Wm Delamer erected this tomb for himself and his family AD 1684 whose predecessor Wm Delamer of Streete a soldier founded and built this monastery AD 1306.' N wall of the nave: a horizontal stone panel with armorial bearings and raised lettering to Christopher Nugent and his wife, Anne Cusack, 1629.

NEIGHBOURHOOD

MULTYFARNHAM PARISH CHURCH. *c.* 1840. On the village main street, a tall T-plan chapel with a three-stage tower and slated spire flanking the central projecting gable. Tall Y-tracery sash windows and pointed arch entrances. Large bare interior with three classical-cum-Gothic niches to the altar wall, round-headed with colonnettes, ogee-headed frames and crocketed finials. – MONUMENTS. The Rev. Michael Duff † 1869 by *Farrell & Son*. The Rev. B. Moore † 1862.

KILLINTOWN CHURCH (C of I). 2.5 km SE. Small hall and tower church with a chancel. Harled, with a blank N wall and pointed windows. Pinnacles and battlements to a three-stage tower.

BALLINAFAD NATIONAL SCHOOL. 2.5 km S. By *James Carroll*, 1841. Single-storey schoolhouse of snecked limestone rubble with sash windows and an advanced and gabled central bay.

CLANHUGH POLICE STATION. 2 km S. Limestone rubble building of *c.* 1840. Two storeys with a hipped roof and small mullioned windows with quarry glass. Lop-sided two-storey porch with its own roof. Odd.

BUNBROSNA INN. 3 km SW. Handsome early C 19 coach inn, situated on a crossroads on the main Mullingar–Longford road. Two-storey, three-bay building, with a half-hipped roof, like many farmhouses in Co. Fermanagh, a central fanlit door and regular sash windows. Random flint and limestone rubble masonry, with brick window surrounds.

FARRAGH CHARTER SCHOOL. 3.5 km SW. A bulky pile, high up on the slope of a hill overlooking Bunbrosna crossroads. Farragh School is a neighbour, a contemporary and a relative of Wilson's Hospital. It was founded in 1758 with a bequest from the will of the Rev. William Wilson, the nephew and heir of Andrew Wilson, the benefactor of Wilson's Hospital. While the latter was designed for almost 200 inmates, Farragh School boarded about 60 children and is in consequence both smaller than Wilson's Hospital and much plainer in its design. It began as a two-storey block with a hipped roof, a five-bay S front and four-bay sides. The centre three bays of the front are advanced with a stepped pediment, like Michael Priestley's work at Prehen, Co. Derry, and indeed the front is very like a smaller country house. The masonry is the same mixture of local flint and limestone rubble seen at Bunbrosna Inn. At a later date, perhaps in the early C19, three ranges in a plain Georgian style were added at the back to create a central courtyard. Recent renovation has entirely obliterated any C18 interior detail which might have survived, and the eaves pediment over the entrance front, now coated in cement, has assumed a post-modernist appearance.

113 CLONHUGH LODGE. 3.5 km SW. 1867 by *William Caldbeck*. Attractive Italianate villa in a beautiful wooded setting on Lough Owel. Built to Caldbeck's designs by *Francis Nulty* of Kells for Colonel F. S. Greville. Handsome rectangular two-storey block of punched limestone rubble with a broad hipped roof broken by a shallow pediment over the central entrance bay. Five-bay entrance front with big plate-glass windows to the outer bays and three narrow round-headed lights above an Ionic entrance porch. Italianate interior, with a range of three rooms along the garden front, two flanking the entrance hall, and, in the centre of the house, a grandiose stairhall lit from the W by a large Venetian window of the Corinthian order.

MOUNT MURRAY. 3.5 km SW. Handsome late C18 house, built, as its title makes plain, by the Murray family, who have lived here on the E shore of Lough Owel since 1646. The field between the house and the lough was the site of a castle. The present house was probably built *c.* 1780 by Alexander Murray, who was living here in 1786. Two storeys over a basement, with a low hipped roof; this was a simple rendered block with regular sash windows and a limestone blocked surround to the doorcase. The plan is two rooms deep, of tripartite arrangement, with a central entrance and a stairhall flanked by reception rooms on each side. The only mid-Georgian detail to survive inside is one six-panel door beneath the stair; the house was thoroughly remodelled *c.* 1820, when a deep semicircular bow was added at the SW end of the front, with tripartite windows to the NE side. The interior was brought up to date with simple neoclassical decoration.

LENY OLD PARISH CHURCH (C of I). 3 km SW. 1817. Small, plain hall and tower church, in a beautiful location overlooking Lough Owel. Four-bay hall, harled, with wide Gothic windows.

Triple-light geometric E window. Later C19 aisle, chancel and vestry built of snecked limestone rubble.

LENY CHAPEL. 2.5 km W. Harled T-plan chapel built *c.* 1840 with thin lancets, pointed arches and buttresses to the entrance gable. Inside is a charming kingpost roof decorated with open trefoils. The E window is also pretty: later C19, three double cusped lights with daggers. Restrained Gothic altar fittings of 1915. – STAINED GLASS. E window: Sacred Heart and Saints, *Clarke Studios*, 1923.

CARRICK CASTLE. 3.5 km W. Rectangular three-storey tower house with distinctively rounded corners and curious pointed windows, and gables both probably late C18 in origin. The tower preserves a barrel-vault over the lower storeys, flanked by a straight mural stair in the E wall. The entrance was located at the E end of the S wall.

LACKEN CHURCH RUINS. 2.5 km NW. The fragment of a small late medieval nave and chancel church standing on the site of an abbey founded in the C7 by St Cruimmin, a contemporary of St Fechin of Fore. The *Four Masters* record obituaries for the C8, C10 and C12. In 1836 John O'Donovan visited Lacken Church and was 'much pleased with its antiquity', believing it to be contemporary with the Church of St Fechin of Fore. O'Donovan found the ruin as it is today: part of the S side wall standing intact to the wall-head, with an ogee-headed window and a lintelled entrance. The window, crisply wrought with dished spandrels, is probably of C15 date. – MONUMENT. Near the door is a coffin-shaped cross slab whose inscription is now illegible.

NAVAN

ME *8060*

Described in the C19 variously as 'delightfully situated on the west bank of the Boyne' and 'a dirty, ill-built straggling collection of houses', with scarcely a glimpse of the river 'from any of its narrow streets', Navan today falls half-way between these extremes. Although it is hardly the most inspiring of Irish towns, the scathing views of Sir William Wilde are unfairly dismissive. Navan is at the centre of a rich agricultural region and developed first and foremost as a market town. It was utilized by the landed families of rural Meath but never became a significant residential centre. The Georgian appeal of places such as Slane or Kells results from the presence of a wealthy and resident magnate, the Marquis Conyngham or the Taylours of Headfort. Navan benefited from no such patronage. The four principal estates in and around the town were owned by absentee landlords: the Duke of Bedford, the Earl of Essex, Lord Howth and Lord de Ros. Although there are several fine houses in the vicinity, the place itself remained a modest country town, so has little to remark beyond the usual collection of public buildings that such a community requires.

Navan town was founded during the Norman period when

Hugh de Lacy assigned the barony of Navan to the Nangle family. Jocelin Nangle (de Angulo), first Baron of Navan, founded an Augustinian abbey dedicated to the Virgin in 1189. Ruinous in 1641, it has left no trace today. By the late Middle Ages Navan was a walled town; in the C16 an act of Henry VIII ordered that every plough-hand in Meath or Westmeath should contribute a subsidy towards rebuilding the walls. But again nothing of the walls survives. By the C17, the place had become a thriving market centre, with a charter of incorporation and a tholsel which accommodated administrative and marketing activities. A mid-C18 map includes a large five-storey granary, a church, a session house and the still existing county infirmary. The extension of the Boyne navigation to Navan after 1800 further improved the market, though landlord investment was still negligible. Even in mid-Victorian times the agent for the Bedford estates could lament that this 'town of very considerable traffic' had never been given 'the least encouragement'.

ST MARY, NAVAN PARISH CHURCH (C of I). 1813–17 by the *Rev. Daniel Augustus Beaufort*. Not as distinctive as his church at Collon, because St Mary's began as a work of adaptation and piecemeal alteration rather than a new church. It is nonetheless a welcome variation on the usual Board of First Fruits Gothic design. Broad three-bay nave with a short chancel, a small entrance block projecting from the centre of the N wall, and a tower at the W end. Built in primitive Regency Gothic, of coursed limestone rubble with ashlar trim, the church has diagonal pinnacled buttresses at every angle, four-centred arches and big Perp windows with the thin pattern-book tracery seen elsewhere in Beaufort's work.

Plans to enlarge the late medieval church, last restored in 1683, were made in 1752, when it was said to be too small. All that was done, however, was to add a vestry room and the tower at the W end to the designs of a local mason, *Edward Morgan*, who in 1764 was given a present of 3 guineas for his care in building the belfry. The tower incorporates part of the earlier belfry, built by Morgan and a second local mason, *Robert Price*. Beaufort 'beautified' it in 1807–13 with corner pinnacles and a rebuilt upper stage.

Inside, plaster corbels support an unconventional star-shaped rib-vault in both nave and chancel. – STAINED GLASS. Dark strongly coloured; early C19. – MONUMENTS. A handsome array. Joseph and James Preston, who both died in the wreck of the Thames steamer, 1841; plaque with mourning figures, urns and a stormy sea. – William Morgan †1881 by *Gaffin & Co.*; Corinthian aedicule in white marble. – First Earl of Ludlow †1803 by *Colles* of Dublin. Richard Ruxton Fitzherbert of Blackcastle †1840.

ST MARY. A good instance of post-Emancipation triumphalism, begun in 1836 and completed ten years later, when it was described as 'an elegant Grecian edifice'. Today St Mary's presents a strange amalgam of early and later Victorian taste:

Roman classicism overlaid by Hiberno-Romanesque. It is a very large rectangular church, the two end walls acting as entrance fronts, with the altar in the centre of the long W wall. The siting of the church in the very centre of Navan, between two busy streets, makes the churchyard a hub of activity, adding vitality where there is usually splendid but silent isolation. The original appearance of the church can be sensed from the side elevations. Here giant blind arcades frame large rectangular windows, with small semicircular lights above. The interior preserves much of the original classical design. The altar wall is articulated by a giant arch framing the high altar, with minor arches on each side, and the early C 19 arrangement of plastered and panelled galleries survives on the other three sides.

Within fourteen years of the completion of the church doubts were expressed as to the safety of the hugh span of its roof. In 1858 *John Bourke* was called on for advice. Bourke's proposals went far beyond structural requirements; besides the division of the span into nave and aisles, he suggested the addition of an apse and side chapels at the W end, the reshaping of the façades with arcaded windows and, as the *pièce de résistance*, the building of two 100-ft (30-m) towers to the entrance front, to be connected by an open arcade. Of all this only one tower was built, in Bourke's characteristic Italian Gothic idiom, though the main façades were extensively altered in 1885 to give the church its present Hiberno-Romanesque appearance. FURNISHINGS. THE FOUR EVANGELISTS by *Richard King*. CRUCIFIX by *Edward Smyth*, 1792. – MONUMENT. Memorial bust of the Rev. Eugene O'Reilly, builder of the church, † 1852 by *T. Farrell* of Dublin.

LORETO CONVENT OF ST ANN. Beside the churchyard, a simple three-bay, three-storey house of 1830. Adjoining the house, the two-storey gabled hall erected *c.* 1850 houses the CONVENT CHAPEL, a charming room upstairs on the first floor. A four-bay hall, lit by round-headed Y-traceried windows, each complete with its C 19 oil-painted canvas blind bearing pictures of the saints. Despite the Gothic windows the decoration of the chapel is classical. The walls and ceilings are panelled and abound in egg-and-dart mouldings, Greek key, fruits and anthemia. The reredos, screening a narrow Gothic window, has an open timber pediment carried on paired Corinthian columns, and is repeated on a smaller scale in the side altars. All told, a rare and charming survival from mid-Victorian Ireland.

ST MICHAEL'S LORETO CONVENT AND SCHOOLS. In 1896 the Bishop of Meath gave to the Loreto community a house and an extensive demesne on the S side of Navan. The house, known as BOYNE COTTAGE, is a small mid-C 19 Greek-revival building; five bays by three with a hipped roof, eaves cornice, sash windows and a Greek Ionic limestone porch. Opulent Greek-revival interior detail. The CONVENT CHAPEL AND RECREATION HALL, by *W. H. Byrne*, 1929, is an impressive two-storey, nine-bay building with a rusticated basement, broad round-headed french windows and, on the first floor, long narrow round-headed openings. Inside, the chapel is a large barrel-vaulted hall with giant-order Corinthian pilasters framing the window bays. It culminates in a sanctuary framed by Corinthian pilasters, now bleak and bare following the removal of Byrne's high altar.

THE ROYAL SCHOOL. *c.* 1810. A truly startling design of which any post-modernist architect might be proud. Lying derelict on a low hill S of Navan, this neglected building must be one of the most unusual pieces of historic architecture in the country – a good instance of the experimental spirit abroad in the Regency period. In plan, an elongated oval with a gently curved hipped roof and the usual pegged eaves. The long curved side walls are of six bays, with big tripartite windows set over round-headed doorcases or squat geometric windows on the ground floor. The bays are defined by simple tapering buttresses, which are themselves decorated with two round-headed niches. Stripped of any Gothic connotations these buttresses are probably the most curious element in the design.

COUNTY MEATH INFIRMARY. Situated on an elevated site above Bridge Street. 1754. Large three-storey, seven-bay block, now much altered, with a big hipped roof; originally a two-storey, five-bay building with high pitched roof. Limestone surrounds to sash windows and a central square-headed entrance. A text from St Mark's Gospel inscribed above the door well ('I was sick and you visited me') reflects the ethos of mid-C 18 charitable foundations.

ST BRIGID'S HOSPITAL. The former Union workhouse, built in 1840 to designs of *George Wilkinson*. Intended to house 500 poor. A standard design, here consisting of three long ranges, one behind another. The principal building is a long two-storey gabled range with dormer windows, exposed rafters and tall chimneys; at each end, a more decorative gabled four-storey block, with big mullioned windows, loops and decorative bargeboards. Rubble, with limestone quoins and redbrick surrounds.

FORMER COURTHOUSE. Situated on a narrow hill street but set back from the pavement behind railings. 1801. A slim two-storey gabled building with an eaves pediment; built of squared rubble with smooth sandstone trim. Three tall round-headed windows, with a blank oculus in the eaves pediment, a broad string-course at first-floor level and raised corner quoins. The building, now a savings bank, has recently been crammed with mock Georgian doors and windows on the ground floor.

TOWN HALL, POST OFFICE etc. *See* Other Buildings, below.

BLACKCASTLE. On the N bank of the Boyne. Large early C 19 house built as a shooting lodge by the Fitzherbert family. Simple unpretentious architecture. The entrance front has a plain two-storey, three-bay façade with a low roof and eaves cornice. Multi-paned windows, and a columnar porch. The garden front is larger: six bays, the centre two projecting forward. Symmetrical plan, with two entrance halls, a top-lit stairhall and a dining room in the middle of the house flanked by large reception rooms on each side. The interior is more ornate than the façades would suggest, with neoclassical plasterwork by *Richard Eason* and Greek-revival motifs to the joinery.

LEIGHBROOK HOUSE, now the CONVENT OF MERCY. Five-bay, three-storey house of *c.* 1770; the upper storey was added or altered in 1857. Once part of the Ludlow estate. Cement-rendered, with a square-headed doorcase and sash windows in moulded frames. Inside, a robust late C18 staircase, with three Tuscan balusters per tread, fielded wainscotting and six-panel doors in lugged surrounds.

NAVAN RAILWAY STATION. 1885 by *N. A. Mills*. Similar to Dunleer Station, but of yellow brick with blue- and redbrick strings. Single-storey, nine-bay range; segmental-headed windows with strings at sill and impost level. Big limestone rubble engine shed with blocked-up arch and oculus.

OTHER BUILDINGS

The TOWN HALL, formerly a police barracks, is an attractive two-storey block of *c.* 1850, well sited above a clearing at the lower end of the town near the river. Five-bay front, of rubble limestone with dressed quoins. The central bay breaks forward with a Diocletian window over an Egyptian-style porch and an eaves pediment. Any advantage the site might provide is unfortunately destroyed by an enclosed car park in front of the building. The Italianate BANK OF IRELAND, by *Sandham Symes*, 1879, has a three-storey, four-bay façade of granite ashlar, square-headed windows with scrolled keystones lighting the banking hall, flanked by a door at each end. The HIBERNIAN BANK, also Italianate, is smaller: two-storey, four-bay façade. The POST OFFICE of 1908 is by *George William Crowe* of the Board of Works. An attractive two-bay gabled building of brick and stone; segmental-headed windows, with lugged architraves and keystone blocks. Tall chimneys capped by finials.

Navan is a cramped town, with tight terraces hugging the street line, mostly cement-rendered and mostly of two storeys. The houses grow in stature towards the MARKET SQUARE, where more regular three-storey Georgian buildings are common. The best is the CENTRAL HOTEL, a large five-bay, gabled block with a limestone pedimented doorcase. LUDLOW STREET, a narrow street running downhill from the square, has some nice houses, early C19, with fanlights and good iron railings. One aspect of Wilde's criticism (*see* p. 427) is true: like many Irish towns, Navan turned its back on its rivers. The new bypass at least gives motorists a concrete-bounded view of the Boyne and the Blackwater, which meet here.

NEIGHBOURHOOD

MILLBROOK HOUSE. On the Blackwater River, immediately N of the town centre. This was the millhouse for a paper mill operating from the early C18; owned in the early C19 by the McDonnell family. A handsome three-storey house of *c.* 1770, rendered, with an eaves parapet, corner quoins and moulded window surrounds. Oddly for this date the house is only one room thick. Pain-style Doric doorcase with finely droved limestone columns, now painted. The interior detail of the house looks *c.* 1810. The mill buildings, early C19, are at the back: two three-storey rubble-built blocks of four and five bays forming an L-shaped plan. Large horizontal-axis mill wheel.

RATHALDRON CASTLE. 3 km NW, on the E bank of the Blackwater. Miniature battlemented country house, approached by a grand avenue and an impressive castle-style gateway with high octagonal towers, possibly by *James Shiel*, which marks the entrance to the estate. The core of the castle is a late medieval four-storey tower house, built apparently in the C14 for a branch of the Cusack family, Lords of Gerardstown. It has a square tower on the NW corner and a spiral stair diagonally opposite on the SE. The castle was extended in the classic way of Irish tower houses, with an additional narrow wing, two storeys high and three bays long, built out from the S side. Subsequently, probably *c.* 1800, this wing was gothicized, in a delicate late Georgian manner, with shallow pointed sash windows under label mouldings. At the same time the tower house gained some dummy arrow slits, stepped battlements and two large Gothic sash windows framed between flat turrets which create the effect of a two-storey oriel projected from the centre of the castle wall. In 1843 new owners, called O'Reilly, added two floors of larger rooms across the end of the wing and projecting slightly from it. The architecture here is harder, with precise early Victorian masonry and large mullioned windows under flat label mouldings. The centre of the house is occupied by a three-bay Gothic vaulted hall, with the principal staircase behind it. A yard, N and W of the tower house, is screened by a battlemented wall and entered through a four-centred Tudor archway.

KILCARN BRIDGE. 2.5 km S, up-river from Navan and visible from the main Navan–Dublin road. Among the finest late medieval bridges to survive in North Leinster. The earliest record of a bridge at Kilcarn is a description of 1599, and modern authorities place its construction between 1550 and 1594. Built of random limestone rubble, the bridge now comprises four central arches with spans of 20–22 ft (6–6.6 m), flanked (looking up-river, i.e. S) by three arches of 11–12 ft (3.3–3.6 m) and four of 10–12 ft (3–3.6 m). When first constructed the bridge would have comprised four central arches, with two on each side. The width of the bridge has also been extended, from an original 9 ft (2.7 m) to its current 21 ft (6.3 m). This extension was made to the up-river side of the bridge, so that now only the N-facing down-river elevation preserves its authentic late medieval aspect. Here the original triangular cutwaters are preserved, one being carried up to form a pedestrian refuge.

Kilcarn Bridge was retired from service in 1977, when a new concrete bridge was opened to traffic, an event which will hopefully secure the survival of this important late medieval structure.

BELMOUNT. 1 km SE. Charming Regency-style house of *c.* 1820 set on a hill-top overlooking the Boyne. In 1836 the residence of Mr James Goggan. Single storey over a basement, with a wide hipped roof, central chimneystacks and bracketed eaves. Large sash windows flank a fine limestone Doric doorcase.

ST COLUMBAN'S COLLEGE. 6 km SE. 1934–43 by *Jones and Kelly*. Hiberno-Romanesque and on the grandest scale. A massive, not to say daunting, complex of symmetrical institutional buildings, laid out in long three-storey ranges and built on an axial plan around a series of internal courtyards. The entrance front stretches the Romanesque idiom to breaking point! Long façade of cold smooth limestone, with a projecting gabled centrepiece and advanced gabled ends. The windows are all round-headed, either single or in pairs. Details have the stripped appearance so characteristic of 1930s classicism, and two geometric lamp holders flanking the Romanesque entrance arch might have served equally well outside a cinema. Inside, vast barrel-vaulted corridors, lit by round-headed sash windows and with squeaky parquet floors, provide an effective arterial system for the plan.

The COLLEGE CHAPEL is set centrally within the first 140
courtyard, on an axis with the hall, but can be approached only via the corridors. If this means that the symmetry of the façade must disappoint the visitor, it also establishes the chapel as very much the focus of its own community. It is a complete church: cruciform in plan and emphatically Hiberno-Romanesque in style, with a barrel-vaulted nave that seems to echo the proportions of Cormack's Chapel at Cashel, Co. Tipperary, though the scale is quite different. The nave arcade, of six bays, is carried on stocky quatrefoil shafts of polished limestone with vigorous zig-zag decoration to the fascia and soffit of the arches. Each pier continues visually across the ceiling of the vault in a series of broad transverse ribs which bind the design together. Paired round-headed lancets light the clerestory between each rib, while a relieving arch above, in emphasis of the plastic nature of the design, cuts into the curve of the vault. The chancel arch is supported on paired Romanesque shafts with cushion capitals and is enriched with revived C12 detail, said to be derived from the chancel carvings at St Saviour's Priory, Glendalough, Co. Wicklow. The altar is framed by quatrefoil Connemara marble shafts supporting a massive Byzantine baldacchino. Though the spirit of this architecture may seem remote today, its design is skilful and intelligent and creates a memorable space. Detailing is impeccable; the choice of marbles, grey-green, pink and black, is calculated to emphasize the forms and give a sense of enrichment. The quality of materials in the chapel and the sheer scale of the college, with its monotonous repetition of standard units – bay after bay –

bespeaks both the confidence and the conservatism of the Catholic Free State in early and idealistic days.

In the grounds a short distance S of the college buildings is a small BURIAL GROUND with rows of limestone crosses and a curious pavilion-like structure which was constructed from fragments of the great ruined mansion at Summerhill (q.v.). It is a tall seven-bay, single-storey loggia with a dominant central block crowned by an attic storey. The loggia is articulated as an arcade of tall round-headed arches with rusticated lintels and recessed rusticated frames. An advanced central block frames a wide central arch with an inappropriate metal canopy. The arch is contained within a Doric frontispiece and surmounted by a pedimented attic storey, with large console brackets flanking a blank oculus. While the central bay appears to derive largely from one of the towers which flanked the main block at Summerhill, this is a composition of fragments rather than an attempt to reconstruct part of the former building. The most striking feature of this odd little structure is the quality of its masonry, whose crisp pale limestone ashlar provides a stark contrast to the machined limestone of the modern tombstones nearby.

125 DOWDSTOWN HOUSE. 5 km SE. The mansion house of the estate purchased by the Columban Fathers for their seminary. An extensive Baronial design by *Lanyon, Lynn and Lanyon*, possibly with the assistance of *S. P. Close*, *c.* 1870. Mostly of two storeys and in an idiom made fashionable by the Belfast practice of Lanyon and Lynn, with tall gables, a round turret room at one corner with a conical slate roof, a bowed projection for the drawing room, and a tall 'Elizabethan' tower with classical balustrade, a columnar loggia and a 'Jacobean' Corinthian porch, offset and projecting from its base. Built of rock-faced limestone, with paler polished stone trim and large plate-glass windows, many of them vaunting the new luxury technique of a curved surface. The house is attached to the S end of a range of early C19 office buildings and has two main fronts: the entrance façade, facing W, and the garden front, facing S. Seen from an angle that includes both, it masses well as a picturesque object. The design has similarities to the former Gerardstown Castle, which stood some miles from here.

BOYNE HILL HOUSE. 3.5 km SE. Small and severe late Georgian house of cubic proportions. Two storeys with a squat attic. Three-bay entrance front with plain sash windows on both floors, a continuous string-course joining the first-floor sills, and a small semicircular window lighting the attic, leaving broad expanses of bare masonry. Square, enclosed Tuscan porch. Five-bay side elevation with horizontally channelled ground floor. The rear elevation, overlooking the Boyne, may once have been the entrance front. Here the ground-floor windows are framed by relieving arches, and the attic storey is screened by an eaves pediment with an armorial crest.

ARDSALLAGH. 5.5 km SE. The demesne of Ardsallagh, laid out by the Ludlow family and situated on the winding S bank of the Boyne, was the object of much admiration during the C18. Swift and the Delanys were among the most frequent visitors, and many descriptions of the house and its gardens survive. In 1748 Mrs Delany found the house 'a good one, with some good pictures, the gardens fine'. She was particularly delighted with the gardens nearest the river, planted in 'a wilder way ... dug down so low (in a former quarry) that the rocks as you walk are a considerable way above your head, ... and so well crowned with trees of all kinds that nothing can be more wilder or romantic'. In the early C19 the property passed from the Ludlows to the Duke of Bedford, who in the mid-1840s erected the present house, accounts and drawings for which survive in the Bedford Estate Office. This is a substantial Tudor-revival design in the manner of *Edward Blore*. Built of dark grey limestone with silver-grey trim; steep gables, tall chimneys, dormers, oriels and mullioned windows.

ATHLUMNEY CASTLE. 1.5 km ENE, set on high land above a 55
broad curve in the river Boyne. Athlumney Castle is both an impressive and an evocative ruin. Built in two periods, it marks in its own structure the change from medieval to modern Ireland. At the N end is a bulky three-storey tower, rectangular in plan, with the square corner turrets common in late medieval domestic architecture in Ireland. The turrets project on the E front, but line in with the N and S walls. Much of the wall-head is substantially intact, with the string-coursing and weep-holes of Irish late medieval construction clearly visible and one gable of the roof surviving on the N side. The interior preserves a spiral stair, built to a generous scale, with little chambers opening off it. Holes for floor beams remain at first-floor level and there are corbels for the wall-plate of the roof structure at the wall-head. The castle, which is comparable to larger houses like Liscarton and Dunsany, dates from the C15 and formed the focus of the manorial village of Athlumney, which included a motte, a souterrain and a medieval parish church, whose walls survive in the graveyard W from the castle.

The second part of the building, a long range, one room thick, which extends from the S side, dates from *c.* 1600 and is either late Elizabethan or early Jacobean. It is of three storeys, with four sets of widely spaced mullioned windows facing E (the mullions all robbed from the ground floor but largely intact above) and four tall triangular gables set across the front, with a modest four-centred doorway at ground-floor level directly between the second and third gables. The door is of ashlar limestone with chamfered reveals and has a curved hoodmoulding which matches the long label mouldings over the windows. There is an oriel window at the S gable end of the range. The W wall, which is much more solid, has a turret at the S end and is broken by two massive chimneystacks which end in diamond-shaped chimneys, all built in stone. From the E front this new façade seems almost symmetrical, though the arrangement of the interior as two rectangular rooms does not match the expectations of the visitor. A bawn wall creates a courtyard on the E side, which may explain the relative lack of window openings on the other sides. The addition of a long wing was the standard way to enlarge a tower house at the end of the medieval period. The same type of addition was made to Carstown in the same period. It is interesting to note, however, that here no attempt was made to build in the new classical idiom of the Tudor renaissance. The plan and the airiness of the new wing are modern, but the detail remains Gothic. The house has been a ruin since 1649, when it was fired by its owners, the Maguires, so that it should not fall into the hands of the Cromwellian army. A similar policy adopted by both sides in the Irish Civil War ruined many more houses in the early years of this century.

1070 NEWTOWNFORBES LF

Simple street village which grew up around Castle Forbes (q.v.), the estate of the Earls of Granard.

ST PAUL, CLONGUISH PARISH CHURCH (C of I). Not the 'good-looking large church in the form of a cross' seen by the Rev. Daniel Beaufort in 1787, but a pretty Gothic rebuild of 1829 designed by *John Hargrave*. Small harled cruciform building with crowstepped gables and Perp windows. Patronized by the Forbes of Castle Forbes and the Achmuty-Musters of Brianstown, the church, though small, is quite different from the usual Board of First Fruits offerings, consisting of a nave, chancel and transepts, with a low two-stage tower now unsym-
101 pathetically reroofed. The interior has charmingly vague Perp detail: plaster cusped rib-vaulting, cusped panelling and decorative braces to the transept galleries and clustered colonnettes framing four-centred arched entrances. A single quadripartite rib-vault in plaster spans the crossing. The transepts are nicely arranged, with a small vaulted vestibule at each end. Large Perp window to the chancel. – Handsome two-tiered timber PULPIT consisting of two flat, panelled desks for clerk and reader flanking a tall cylindrical carved pulpit. BOX PEWS are a rare and happy survival, though puzzling in that they consist of fielded panels in the nave and plain flush panels in the transepts. This suggests a number of possibilities: either the C 18 nave was incorporated in the new church, or the old box pews were simply reused, or an old-fashioned joiner worked here in 1820 and the transepts were added later. – MONUMENTS. In the chancel, Sir George Forbes, Earl of Granard, †1765. A white marble tablet inscribed with a full account of Sir George's eventful life as a seaman, soldier and statesman. In 1738 he declined the governorship of New York and became instead governor of Longford and Westmeath. – In the churchyard, a C 20 miniature temple with two Doric columns *in antis*: Beatrice, Countess of Granard, †1972.

ST MARY, CLONGUISH PARISH CHURCH. 1864 by *J. J.*

McCarthy. Remodelled in 1974; an uninspiring modernization of what was once a decent Victorian Gothic church. Originally the typical McCarthy format of a nave, aisles and chancel, with the nave arcade carried on limestone shafts with E.E. capitals. Owing to structural difficulties the nave was lowered almost to aisle level and the arcade inside taken down, creating a wide gabled hall with structural braces down each side. Lighting is provided by the aisle windows and by triangular clerestory windows in the roof. The chancel has three graded lancets and also modern top-lighting. The exterior of snecked rubble is better, and the N elevation, with an expansive slated roof, is quite effective.

BRIANSTOWN HOUSE. 3 km SW. Built in 1731 for Samuel Achmuty, whose arms and motto are in the tympanum over the door. Formerly a two-storey house, Brianstown was gutted by fire in the early C20 and became a single-storey house on a basement, with a shallow hipped roof. Five-bay front, with a narrow entrance set between two small windows and held together by a border of raised limestone quoins. Similar quoins frame the windows of the outer bays. Before its demolition the first floor continued this window pattern, with a niche between the two central windows. A high hipped roof was pierced by two dormer windows. A strong resemblance to Barretstown in Co. Kilkenny has been remarked by Maurice Craig; both these early C18 Georgian houses stand Janus-like between the C17 Dutch-inspired Beaulieu tradition and the C18 Palladian classicism then becoming current through the influence of James Gibbs and William Kent.

NEWTOWN TRIM ME *8050*

The consolidation of Anglo-Norman power in Ireland was greatly assisted by the invaders' purposeful infiltration and gradual domination of the Irish church. Newtown Trim was both the symbol and one of the first fruits of their victory, founded in 1206 by Simon de Rochfort, a Lord of Parliament, who in 1192 had himself elected as the first Norman Bishop of Meath. Clonard was then the principal see in Meath, but when that town was destroyed by the Irish in 1200, de Rochfort used the event to his advantage and transferred the see to Trim, thereby securing a site under the protection of Trim Castle. The new foundation was to be called Nova Midia and consisted of a priory for Canons Regular of St Victor and a Hospital Priory of Crouched Friars. No cathedral as such was included in the scheme; the church of the Victorine Abbey served this purpose throughout the Middle Ages. The abbeys are located on opposite banks of the Boyne with clear views across open fields to the castle and towers of Trim (*see* p. 510 for a map).

VICTORINE ABBEY and CATHEDRAL OF SS PETER and PAUL. 26
The abbey church or cathedral at Newtown Trim was

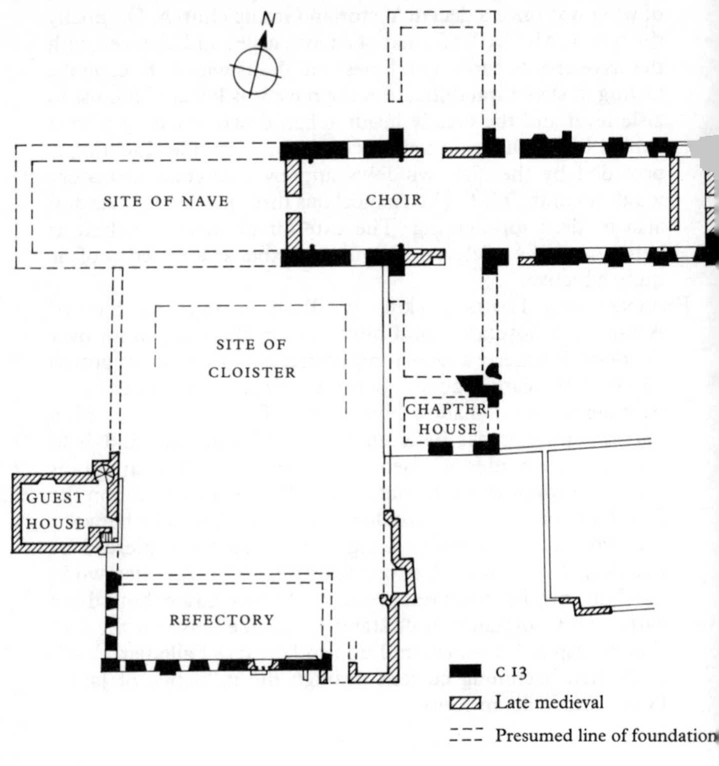

Newtown Trim, Cathedral and Abbey. Plan

celebrated during the Middle Ages as a church of exceptionally large dimensions. It was also one of the few large-scale stone-vaulted Irish churches outside Dublin, and from what can be construed from the present ruins was intended to be splendid. The cathedral ruins are approached today across a small stream and stand as great chunks of rubble masonry in an elevated graveyard. Sticking up here and there without any clear connection one to the other they are more like giant grave slabs than parts of a coherent medieval structure symbolic of Norman ecclesiastical power. The visitor must work hard to make a picture of the church as it once was, but fortunately enough remains for the effect of the building to be described. A long gravelled rectangle, on an E–W axis, marks the chancel and part of the nave of the church. Nave and chancel are both the same width, 30 ft (9 m) across, and neither had any aisle. The W end of the church is today closed by a heavy gable wall, liberally peppered with putlock holes, with a central door, a large rectangular window opening and a small lancet one above the other. From one end of the church to the other is 136 ft (41.4 m), but this gable does not mark the W extremity of the original cathedral: that stood a full 50 ft (15 m) further W, as the gable, and the broad flat buttresses which support it outside, were built only after the dissolution of the abbey *c.* 1542, when the church had to be reduced in size. The complete cathedral was 186 ft (56.4 m) long from W door to high altar, and to walk down its length in the C13 must have been an extraordinary experience. The proportion of the plan is longer than six squares laid end to end and, as the tops of the nave and chancel walls are nowhere more than 35 ft (10.5 m) high, the spatial effect must always have emphasized this great length. No wonder contemporary records spoke of the size of Newtown Trim.

Medieval churches usually began building at the E end and worked W. The choir at Newtown Trim is no exception and details display an early Gothic manner, in fact a fusion of Norman and early Gothic styles. The focus of the choir was of course the high altar and E window. Their place today is occupied by a vertical gash in the masonry with a view through to yew trees and a C19 Celtic cross. Only the corners of the E gable remain attached to the chancel walls, of which two and a half bays stand on the N and one bay to the S. The window openings here are the high broad lancets typical of early English Gothic design. Their sides splay inwards, so that the glazed

Newtown Trim, Cathedral, choir

area was narrower than the opening, and the point where the splay joins the interior wall is marked by a moulded roll in stone. What is fascinating about these mouldings is that they alternate from one window to the next. The two lancets furthest E, flanking the now vanished E window, were framed by a comparatively elaborate triple roll, in which two plain rolls framed a richer central section made up of four short lengths of stone – colonnettes – held in place by rings of stone built into the wall. The colonnettes (perhaps made of some rich marble and polished) have of course long disappeared, but the rings that held them in place are still to be seen, and so are some of the plain wide capitals carved out of black basalt that stood above the top colonnette before the moulding turned into the arch at the top of the window. The second lancet on the N side of the chancel is of a plain type, and though only part of the third lancet is left it clearly was of the elaborated type with colonnettes. This type of alternating pattern, rich–plain–rich–plain, is typical of early Gothic taste, while colonnettes framing window openings may be seen in the Norman nave of Christ Church Cathedral, Dublin, which was building at the same time.

The evidence for a reconstruction of the E window is complicated by the fact that it seems to have been rebuilt as one large opening, perhaps in the C16 at the same time that the nave was shortened. There is space for three lancets side by side, the sort of arrangement seen in endless C19 Gothic Revival churches, and one that survives at Cashel Cathedral in Co. Tipperary, at Inch and Grey Abbey in Co. Down, and elsewhere in Irish C13 work. Part of one built-up lancet can be seen clearly in the SE corner of the chancel. The ledge on which it stood is about a foot (0.3 m) higher than the level of the side windows, and part of the moulded arch that framed the top of the window is still in position. At the N side of the chancel only the splayed reveal remains as evidence of the matching lancet on this side. All the moulded stone at its edge has gone; so of course has the central lancet, but there can be no doubt that three lancets originally stood above the altar here.

To complete the picture of the chancel in its original state the visitor must imagine a ceiling vaulted in stone. Once again there is just enough evidence to indicate how this was arranged, for the line of the shape of the vault is clearly cut into the stonework of the walls above and between the lancet windows on the N wall, and may be detected even in the E corners of the chancel, where it appears to have been linked to the lower walls by a small round shaft running down the internal angle. Otherwise the vault floated across the chancel without any visual connection to the lower parts of the church.

The Gothic system of building is more accommodating, and can be adapted to suit specific needs more readily, than the classical rules of architecture allow. In this respect it may be noted how the builders of the abbey church moved the last two windows of the chancel side walls nearer the altar end: they do not stand in the centre of the vaulting arch but are to the E of it, presumably to increase the flood of light on the altar itself. At ground level the wide space between the two windows accommodates a recess in the N wall – now filled with a sculpted tomb figure and, in the S wall, a double SEDILIA. Both the recess and the sedilia have old-fashioned round-headed arches. Those of the sedilia are carried on a central shaft and although the mouldings are now badly eroded they appear to have been much broader and bulkier than Gothic work, rather like the sandstone arches in the central keep at Trim Castle, so the style of the building developed as it grew. Fragments of glass and patterned tile found around the site indicate that this was once a richly ornamented interior, though the building was quite plain outside, with only broad unstepped buttresses breaking the wall surface between the window openings.

At the W end of the gravelled area a portion of the nave remains. Here it is the S wall that provides most evidence of what the church looked like. The first and most obvious feature to note is the hollow wall construction; in contrast to the solid masonry between the lancets of the chancel, the nave walls, N and S, had two narrow corridors, one above the other, incorporated in the thickness of the wall at triforium and clerestory level. This is the classic hollow-wall construction of early English Gothic, developed in the C12, in conjunction with rib-vaulted systems, where the thrust of the vault, instead of relying on a series of flying buttresses, as in French Gothic architecture, was more evenly absorbed by a hollow wall. The corridors, which often ended in small chambers, were also practically useful in providing easy access to all parts of what could be a very tall building. At the same time as Newtown Trim was under construction this system of superimposed passages was also being used in the choir and transepts of St Patrick's Cathedral in Dublin.

Unlike the chancel lancets no moulded stone remains in the nave to give a detailed guide to how the windows were arranged. The side walls were clearly divided into three horizontal bands: a ground floor of plain wall, the level of the first passage and the level of the second passage. The nave was richly vaulted and, once again in contrast to the chancel, employed a system that linked the vaulting visually with the walls of the church. On either side of the one remaining complete window opening are two stone shafts which rise for the full height of the first passage level. They end in small capitals from which the ribs of the cross vaulting spring just above the level of the floor of the upper passage. So the interior treatment of the nave walls increased in richness with their height: a plain surface; a regular succession of vertical shafts; and a pattern of ribbed quadripartite vaults. What is uncertain is how the nave was lit. The top passage level must have had windows. The lower passage may possibly have been lit as well, or, more likely, was treated as a triforium (a passage with small arcaded openings looking into the church and a blank wall on the outside). The mouldings of the ribs and the capitals look to be later C13, suggesting that the church was not completed for some considerable time after the abbey's foundation in 1206.

There is no reliable evidence today on how the transition from nave to chancel was managed. A chancel arch providing a visual stop to the length of the nave may be assumed, however, and perhaps also a belfry tower, whose collapse might have given rise to the complete lack of any wall between the fragments of the nave and chancel that remain. Certainly the nave, with its great length and lesser illumination, must have provided a dramatic prelude to the climax of the church in its rich chancel.

PARISH CHURCH RUINS. E of the Cathedral chancel, the fragmentary ruins of a late medieval parish church. Undivided nave and chancel of coursed limestone with entrances at the W end of the nave. A featureless building worthy of note only for its location within the Cathedral precinct and the unusually
59 elaborate DILLON MONUMENT, an altar tomb of 1586 with recumbent effigies of Sir Lucas Dillon and his wife, Jane Bathe, both of Moymet. Carved from grey limestone, the figures lie on a large tomb-chest, their heads resting on rectangular stone cushions and their hands joined on their breasts. Sir Lucas is splendidly dressed in ornate Italian embossed armour. On the long W side of the chest, a family group at a lectern, presumably depicting the Dillon household. The scene on the E side is now illegible. On the N and S ends of the chest, framed by fluted pilasters, strapwork, swags and putti, are the arms of the Dillons and the associated families of Barnewall, Bathe and Sharl. A handsome monument, quite up-to-date in its Mannerist sculptural detail, though relying for its basic form on a tried-and-true late medieval pattern.

VICTORINE ABBEY RUINS. The abbey church, described above, marked the N boundary of the monastic complex, whose other buildings were located to the S and W on ground sloping gently towards the Boyne. The layout of these was traditional, with the CHAPTER HOUSE on the E, the frater to the S, and a structure of tower-house type, perhaps for the accommodation of guests, on the W, facing towards Trim. Of the chapter house all that survives is the base of a very fine limestone entrance arch, carved with a series of moulded colonnettes between filleted roll mouldings. Opposite this, on the W, is the ruin of a three-storey rectangular tower, with a ruined circular stair turret at the NE angle and an oven in the S wall. In the N wall is a small window with some pocked dressing, suggesting a late C15 or even C16 date.

26 The REFECTORY, the last building before the river at the S end of the side, was built against a steep fall in the ground, which gave space for storerooms below with access to the Boyne, and provided an elevated site for the refectory itself, at the same level as the other monastic buildings. Only the W gable and a length of the S wall remain. From the river side, the building almost has a fortified appearance, with a pronounced

corbel course and part of a wall-head above. The architectural details that remain are of two dates: C13 windows, the lower section of a pair of lancets in the gable and three more in the S wall. The outline of two more may be detected in the masonry of the S side, but the insertion of a fireplace and chimney in the lower room has altered the upper arrangement of the wall, and a small C15 two-light window with cusped heads and dished spandrels occupies their place. E from this window the projecting block of stone marks the location of the reader's pulpit or gallery. The refectory was a large room, some 60 ft by 20 ft (18 m by 6 m), with presumably a roof of exposed rafters and trusses.

HOSPITAL PRIORY OF ST JOHN THE BAPTIST. The hospital 27 priory for crouched friars, founded in the early C13 by Simon de Rochfort as part of his new ecclesiastical centre of Nova Midia, is a short distance E of the Victorine Abbey, picturesquely located beside a hump-backed bridge on the opposite bank of the Boyne. Although it has certainly been rebuilt, part of the existing four-arched bridge is late medieval. The priory is a confusing complex, for the most part reduced to foundation level, with two castle-like blocks, an E window and a variety of walls. It follows no contemporary norms for the layout of monastic buildings. In contrast both to the Cathedral of SS Peter and Paul and to the Augustinian Church in Trim, where the church occupied the usual position N of the claustral buildings, here the river forms the northern boundary, with the church closing the group on the S. The site, a narrow flat strip on the S bank of the Boyne, seems to have dictated this unusual plan, as the river was diverted into a channel which ran inside part of the N (presumably service) range. The priory enclosure, 245 ft by 180 ft (74.6 m by 55 m), was surrounded by high boundary walls on the other three sides, with round defensive towers located at the NE and SW angles. The masonry is of a pale yellowish limestone rubble and is so crisp and regular, with a good deal of punched dressing, as to suggest a date later than the C13. An indulgence granted for the repair of the hospital in 1402 may have prompted extensive rebuilding.

The largest building in the priory was the church, a long aisleless building, originally 119 ft by 24 ft (36.3 m by 7.2 m) internally, now reduced to its E gable, the S boundary wall and a confusing number of ruined cross walls, one of which is the base of a rood screen. The W end of the nave seems to have been narrower than the chancel. The E gable contains a group of three lancets in widely splayed embrasures with the fragments of thin sandstone shafts between. The curious elliptical profile of the arch above is the legacy of a C19 restoration. Built onto the NE corner of the chancel is a small low C15 sacristy, roofed over by three groin vaults that spring from carved pillars and corbels. This opened N into an external porch. At the W end of the enclosure, on axis with the body of the church, is a four-storey tower house with diagonally opposite square towers, the usual barrel-vaulted hall, spiral stair, garderobe chute and two chimneys corbelled out from the W wall. The most complete building in the priory, this is clearly of C15 date and probably remained in use long after the Dissolution, when the priory buildings were granted to Robert Dillon, attorney general to Henry VIII. It later passed to the Ashe family, who made alterations for domestic purposes. Adjoining this on the N, the W wall of the N range is pierced by a single round-headed door with an external elevation of two wide blind arches – also round-headed.

The N range, though now largely ruinous, may once have risen to three storeys. The most complete building on the river front is the N half of a three-storey tower of C15 appearance; a perfect cross-section of the barrel-vaulted hall and two upper floors, with a NE spiral stair, corbels for roof timbers and press recesses, remains. W of this are the remains of three adjoining rectangular chambers with traces of barrel-vaulting and a water-race which brought the river water through the two rooms at the W end. Running water was always a prerequisite of the monastic site and was obviously of special importance here in a building dedicated to medicine and the care of the sick.

8080 NOBBER ME

Small village of one broad main street; birthplace in 1670 of the famous blind harper Carolan, the last of the native Irish bards, whose memorial is in St Patrick's Cathedral, Dublin.

NOBBER PARISH CHURCH (C of I). Small gabled C18 hall with a bellcote over the entrance gable. Round-headed, Y-traceried windows in simple blocked surrounds; a bolder blocked surround to the main entrance. Recently purchased as a private dwelling and not improved by the addition of an ugly chimney and modern glazing. The tall ivy-covered wall nearby is of a late medieval church tower, ruinous since 1641. Mounted on a wall near the church is the CRUISE MONUMENT, a recumbent effigy which once stood in the chancel of the medieval church. The inscription, now barely legible, reads 'Here is buried the body of Gerard Cruise of Brittas and Margaret Plunkett his wife, which Gerald did build this monument and is here lineally descended from Mauritius Cruise who died the 1st year of Henry III, AD 1216.'

ST JOHN THE BAPTIST. 1976. Small tent-like octagon, with a conical lantern and glazed porch. Whitewashed walls and narrow windows. Like several contemporary churches in Co. Meath, this presents an awkward amalgam of post-modernist features.

FORMER RECTORY. 1 km SE. Handsome mid-C19 house of coursed limestone rubble. Two storeys over a basement, with a wide hipped roof and oversailing bracketed eaves. Three-bay entrance front, with a central fanlit doorcase set in a blocked surround, with the flanking windows set in shallow segmental-headed relieving arches.

Cruicetown Church. 3 km SW. A ruined medieval parish church in a lonely rural setting. Well-preserved nave and chancel of *c.* 1200, with several round-headed lancet windows in deeply splayed embrasures and an early baptismal font. The footing for a W bellcote survives. Cruicetown's main attraction is the much later **Cruise Monument**, set into a broad roofed recess inside the chancel. This, erected by the local landowners who gave their name to the locality, consists of the recumbent effigies of a man and a woman, Walter Cruise and his wife, Elizabeth Cruise, who both died in the 1660s. The monument was erected in 1688 by their son Patrick. The figures, carved in wooden doll-like fashion with a band of cherubs hovering above their heads, have a naive charm. On the base of the monument are three squat pilasters, with panels between, carved with flowers and decorative patterns. Set into the wall over the monument are the armorial bearings of husband and wife: that both were members of the one family testifies to the close-knit character of contemporary ascendancy life. In the churchyard is a large limestone ringed cross, also 42
late C17 and again the work of a naive sculptor, here one with a very strong plastic sense whose carvings of the Crucifixion and Virgin and Child, although crude, are not without charm.

Cruicetown House. 3 km SW. A long, two-storey gabled house of *c.* 1845. Set in a forecourt with battlemented walls and a castellated porch. The house replaces an earlier building of 1735. The battlement improvements and folly-like gates are the work of Sir Lionel Alexander, who owned Cruicetown after 1874.

Moydorragh. 3 km S. Nice Georgian farmhouse erected by the Cruise family in 1790. Two storeys, with a simple gabled roof and an entrance front of five bays whose features include a tiny semicircular window above the central first-floor window, a tripartite limestone doorcase and corner quoins.

Julianstown House. 3.5 km E. Big rubble farmhouse, probably of the early C19, with a low gambrel roof and big central stone chimneys. Two storeys, with an attic at the side and a basement at the rear. Broad expanses of masonry and narrow sash windows, three bays in the principal elevation.

Thomastown Catholic Church. 4.5 km SW. Small early C19 T-plan chapel, with a round window and a pointed arch to the entrance gable and pointed double Y-tracery windows throughout. Blocked window and door surrounds. – MONUMENT. The Rev. James Dillon P.P. † 1858 by *Farrell & Son.*

Brittas. 1.5 km W. The seat of the Bligh family since the C17, Brittas is surrounded by mature woods planted in the early C18 by General Thomas Bligh, whose magnificent portrait by James Latham is so well-known. The existing house is, however, predominantly of the C19. Its core is a rectangular two-storey building with a wide hipped roof, two rooms deep, with a central hall flanked by stairs and reception rooms and behind it a large bowed drawing room with smaller rooms on each side. The interiors are simply decorated, with dentil cornices and neoclassical friezes. The joinery has thin applied mouldings, all of *c.* 1800. Though Brittas is by no means as sophisticated as Francis Johnston's Galtrim House, there is an unmistakable resemblance to it, especially in the attractive rough-cast garden front, which has a two-storey central bow, here with long eighteen-pane sash windows extending to the ground and squat six-pane windows above. A four-bay ballroom with similar fenestration was added to the E side of the house, apparently not long after it was built. Although the garden front preserves its early C 19 appearance, the entrance front was thoroughly reworked in the later C 19, when it gained a sandstone rubble facing, a Tudor recessed porch and large mullioned windows with leaded glass and square label mouldings. It is an overblown picturesque cottage in appearance now.

0070 OLDBRIDGE LO and ME

The bridge at Oldbridge is modern but it marks the site of the battle of the Boyne, and here, at its N abutment, a grateful 'Protestant nation' erected a monumental obelisk to record the achievements of 1690. The obelisk has gone now but the pedestal of its base remains, sitting high over the road on a piece of rock. In 1744 Isaac Butler recorded the gilded inscriptions as follows. On the N side:

Sacred to the Glorious Memory of King William III who on the 1st July 1690 passed the river near this place to attack James II at the head of a popish army advantageously posted on the south side of it and did on that day by a successful battle secure to us and to our posterity our liberties and our religion. In consequence of this action James II left this Kingdom and fled to France. This memorial of our deliverance was erected in the 9th year of the Reign of King George II, the first stone being laid by Lionel Sackville, Duke of Dorset, Lord Lieutenant of the Kingdom of Ireland, MDCCXXXVI.

The inscriptions on the other three sides were, on the E, 'Marshal the Duke of Schomberg in passing this river died bravely fighting'; on the S, 'In defence of Liberty, July 1st MDCLXXXX'; on the W, 'This monument was erected by the grateful contributions of several protestants of Great Britain and Ireland'.

OLDBRIDGE HALL. *c.* 1750 and *c.* 1832. Long three-storey house with a plain ashlar frontage of seven bays, the centre three widely spaced and slightly advanced. Wide and flat in its appearance, like a second-generation Palladian house in England. Quadrant walls link the house to its park, with boldly rusticated doors. The interior was completely refitted in the Victorian period, with standard four-panel doors and a new stair running across one of the windows of the front.

Despite the monolithic and rather dull appearance of the façade, the house is of two quite different dates. Originally it was designed as a three-bay, three-storey block, with low

Oldbridge, obelisk, from Thomas Wright's *Louthiana* (1748)

single-storey wings, more like a suburban villa or town house than a country property. Early C19 additions of two floors to each wing, apparently by *Frederick Darley*, made the house look more dull and *retardataire* than it ever was in the C18. Affinities to Dowth Hall nearby and to Dunboyne Castle suggest the involvement of the earlier *George Darley* in the original design.

ROSSIN/MONKNEWTOWN MILL. 3.5 km E. An attractive group of industrial buildings situated on the river Mattock close to Dowth and the Boyne. The mill produced flax and was powered by a water wheel on the Mattock. These are simple buildings of local rubble and red brick, modest by comparison with Slane's grand C18 mill but nevertheless excellently built and now most picturesque. The principal block is a crisp seven-bay, four-storey structure of slate and limestone rubble, with cutstone door and window surrounds. Flanking this to the W is a redbrick chimney, like that at John MacNeill's Mountpleasant Flax Mill (*see* Ballymascanlon), and then a further four-storey gabled range. MacNeill's Mountpleasant complex was completed in 1851, and this building is most likely of similar date.

CHURCH OF THE ASSUMPTION OF THE VIRGIN MARY, MONKNEWTOWN. 3.5 km E. 1837. Simple T-plan country chapel. Rough-cast, with round-headed entrances and windows. Recently refurbished. In 1837 the Rev. Duff invited tenders for 'raising walls and reroofing the Chapel of Monknewtown and Dowth'.

CHURCH OF THE NATIVITY OF MARY IMMACULATE, DONORE. 3 km S. A charming little church of squared limestone rubble. Four-bay lancet hall with an unusual frontispiece: instead of the standard gabled façade, a narrow gabled block is set lengthways across the front with an advanced and gabled central bay and lancets on each side. Inside, an attractive timber Gothick reredos with turret-like canopies and foliated pinnacles. A rare and happy survival. – Outside, on the S side of the church, is a stone cross inscribed 'Mission of the Jesuit fathers Rev. N. Power P.P.'.

5080

OLDCASTLE ME

Small market town in the hills of N Co. Meath just W of the great hill of Loughcrew, famous for its megalithic monuments and a spectacular view S across the flat central plain. Rolling hills, lichen-covered drystone walling and everywhere the bleating of sheep evoke the landscape of western Ireland. It is not surprising that Oldcastle developed during the C18 as the largest yarn market in the country. The town and surrounding lands were then the property of the Naper family, whose improvements contributed much to its present appearance. The town plan reflects Oldcastle's traditional market role, built as it is around an irregular central 'square' with a large markethouse in the middle. In character the town is substantially Georgian, two- and three-storey late Georgian houses, some with stuccoed Victorian commercial façades. A Norman motte S of Oldcastle, the site of a Tuite stronghold, is thought to have given the place its name.

ST BRIDE, OLDCASTLE PARISH CHURCH (C of I). 1816. Rebuilt on the site of an earlier church which was a dependency of the Abbey of Fore. Small three-bay hall of coursed limestone rubble with a squat pinnacled tower and spire at the entrance gable; the spire was a gift of J. L. W. Naper of Loughcrew. Unsympathetic modern clock to the tower. Inside, a bright boxy hall with Y-tracery and quatrefoil windows and a pretty timber Gothic organ installed in 1926, perhaps purchased from an older church elsewhere. – STAINED GLASS. Copy of *Holman Hunt*'s Light of the World.

ST OLIVER PLUNKETT MEMORIAL CHURCH. 1899–1904 by *W. H. Byrne*. Gothic. Tall cruciform church, boldly textured, with coursed limestone rubble and ashlar trim. Big Dec window, pointed arch and lancets to the entrance gable, which is flanked by a tall new belltower and thin broach spire added in 1930. Bright airy interior, the nave lit by four pairs of lancets and opening through paired two-centred arches into shallow transepts. Elaborate and satisfying complete sanctuary, with polychrome marble panelling and cusped niches on Ruskinian colonnettes to the walls and reredos. The altar rail is a cusped arcade on miniature polychrome marble shafts. Mosaic to Sacred Heart and Lady Chapels. – STAINED GLASS. Triple-light E window: Assumption and Saints, pictorial in pinnacled niches and good of its type. S transept: angels bearing emblems. Lancets in W gable: Martyrdom of St Lawrence and St Oliver Plunkett. All in vivid jewel-like colours in the manner of the Harry Clarke studio's late work.

GILSON ENDOWED SCHOOL. 1823. One of the nicest surprises 85
of Co. Meath, and certainly from the hand of *C. R. Cockerell*, who in the same year designed Loughcrew House for J. L. Naper. Naper was one of the trustees of the school's bequest, made by a native of Oldcastle, Laurence Gilson, who had returned to Meath after amassing a large fortune in London. Not as severely neoclassical as Loughcrew, the Gilson School is, properly speaking, a Palladian design, although a lot more austere in character than authentic C 18 Palladianism. It follows the classic formula of a large central house with lower links and wings, all executed in wonderfully crisp grey limestone ashlar. The house in this case was a residence for headmaster and headmistress, with the hall and boardroom appropriately dividing male and female quarters; the wings house boys' and girls' schools respectively. The house is of two storeys over a semi-basement, with a five-bay entrance front, the centre three bays advanced, with a shallow eaves pediment. Crisp limestone cornice to the outer bays, raised corner quoins to centre and ends. Shallow segment-headed windows light the basement, with round-headed windows to the principal storey and short six-pane sash windows on the first floor. The most consciously neoclassical element in the design is the central porch, approached by a short flight of steps with a plain entablature and cornice carried on two panelled limestone monoliths. The links between house and schools are short and flat. Each has a simple fanlit doorcase. The schoolrooms consist of two broad three-bay, single-storey halls set end on to the façade and expressed as single-bay blocks, with a broad projecting central section filled with a tripartite segment-headed window. The articles of agreement for building the school survive, including pages of detailed building specifications outlining every aspect of the construction, from the precise measurement of nails to the method of chiselling to be employed.

MARKETHOUSE. Now much altered and not improved by a flat roof, shallow battlements and modern picture windows. Originally a three-bay, two-storey markethouse with a triple arcade in the central bay of the ground floor and windows above. A map of 1778 indicates a markethouse on this site, which may be the nucleus of the surviving building. The property of the Naper family, it was converted into a barracks during the 1790s. In 1797 William Naper received the sum of £7 9s. od. from the Leitrim Militia 'on account of the repairs to the markethouse . . . at the time they were quartered there'.

OTHER BUILDINGS

On the N side of THE SQUARE, a large Victorian stuccoed façade of 1862. Six-bay, three-storey, with plate-glass windows, shell tympana and moulded continuous string-courses. Spoilt by its ground floor. On the W side, a five-bay, three-storey hotel. Provincial classical architecture, with horizontally channelled ground floor and projecting Tuscan porch. Giant pilasters at the corners and centre bay with the windows grouped as 2, 1 and 2. LAGAN STREET has a nice two-storey, three-bay Georgian block, with a carriage arch and a C19 shopfront. Next door, a good Victorian house, three-bay, three-storey front with a pretty brick and terracotta façade above the shopfront. Further W, several attractive late Georgian houses. In OLIVER PLUNKETT STREET, the NORTHERN BANK is a two-storey late C19 Italianate building of punched limestone with ashlar trim; three-bay first floor; four-bay asymmetrical banking hall. Next door, an attractive cream-rendered manager's house with an emphatic stone eaves cornice. The central block of OLDCASTLE RAILWAY STATION, *c.* 1880, is a two-storey, three-bay building with a wide hipped roof and oversailing eaves, in an Italianate idiom, with moulded lugged window surrounds.

NEIGHBOURHOOD

KILLEAGH CATHOLIC CHURCH. 3.5 km W. Ugly modern gabled hall and a freestanding belfry, built in the 1960s to replace a chapel erected in 1825 with the aid of J. L. Naper and E. Rotheram. Angular lancet windows, cement buttresses and a stagy interior.

CROSSDRUM HOUSE. 1.5 km SW. Derelict. Dull and ill-proportioned Georgian house of late C18 or early C19 date, built by the Rotheram family. Rectangular plan, two rooms deep, with a wide hipped roof and central chimneystacks. Five-bay entrance front of grey limestone ashlar: corner quoins, moulded window surrounds and a tripartite fanlit doorcase with an ungainly Tuscan porch.

MOYLAGH CHURCH and CASTLE. 4.5 km S. Fragmentary limestone rubble ruins situated on the low but steep Moylagh ridge, which runs N–S for a quarter mile (400 m). All that survives of the castle is the heavily buttressed stump of an E gable. Foundations stretching N, E and W bear witness to a long rectangular structure built into the W slope of the hill, looking like the remains of a relatively late fortified house. A castle was certainly here in 1470; Roger Rockford was granted assistance in that year to build a tower 'near Moylagh Castle'.

The church, traditionally of C14 date, preserves only the stump of the E gable, fragments of the S wall and, the most interesting feature, a three-storey residential tower which adjoined the S side of the nave and from which access was provided to the rood-loft. It is a relatively tiny tower, some 14 ft by 12 ft (4.2 m by 3.6 m) inside, with a vaulted basement, two storeys above and a roof-walk. A rounded SW corner contains the spiral stair. Two corbels on the N face mark the nave roof-line, and built into the SE corner are two carved medieval heads. The masonry is somewhat crude, with massive stones forming the jambs of simple loops, but the regular treatment of the window voussoirs suggests a late date, perhaps C15. The earliest tombstones visible date to the C16.

ST MARY, MOYLAGH. 4.5 km S. Traditional T-plan church in a pleasant tree-lined churchyard. Built in 1834 by the Rev. George Leonard. Cement-rendered, with limestone trim, pointed arches, inscribed plaques and late C19 cusped twinlight windows.

OMEATH

LO *1010*

Small linear village, little more than a straggle of souvenir shops, in a pleasant situation on the S shore of Carlingford Lough.

ST ANDREW (C of I). 1838. Harled tower-and-hall-type church. Three-bay lancet hall, with quarry glass, quoin surrounds and a three-stage battlemented tower. The late C19 chancel is by *Welland Gillespie*. Inside, funerary monuments to the Woodhouse family of Omeath Park.

ST ANDREW'S NATIONAL SCHOOL. Next door to the church and probably of similar date. A plain whitewashed T-plan building with sash windows and a gabled entrance front.

ST LAWRENCE. Early C19 T-plan chapel, with later C19 porches, chancel and sacristy. Cement-rendered, with shallow moulded corner quoins. Plain interior with gallery and confessionals at the base of the T. The chancel is more accomplished, with a broad Tudor arch framed by colonnettes; Perp tracery and four-centred arched doorways to the sacristy.

OMEATH PAROCHIAL HALL. Whimsical early C20 classical hall. Single-storey, three-bay, with a projecting pedimented centrepiece, elaborately treated for such a rural setting, with Edwardian baroque window surrounds and door.

DRUMULLAGH. Small mid-C18 gentleman's house, single-storey over a basement, with a broad hipped roof and a tripartite doorcase. Regency-style porch. Tripartite windows and dormers.

PROSPECT HOUSE. Early to mid-C18 T-plan farmhouse on an elevated site immediately above the village. Remarkable for its old-fashioned four-gabled frontage, and reminiscent of Piedmont House further S on the Cooley peninsula (*see* Gyles Quay). A single-pile plan, with a central entrance hall, rooms either side and a staircase behind forming a T. Early C19 windows throughout, with primitive classical entablatures on the ground floor.

4060 PORTNESHANGAN WM

A parish N of Mullingar on the E side of Lough Owel, containing some curious churches and some of the most interesting country houses in Co. Westmeath. Distances are calculated from Portneshangan Parish Church (C of I) in the townland of Knockdrin.

PORTNESHANGAN PARISH CHURCH (C of I). 1824. A good hall and tower church in a correct late Gothic idiom by *John Hargrave*. The site and a large proportion of the building costs were donated by James Gibbons of Ballynegall, with additional funds from Sir Richard Levinge of Knockdrin. A small but highly finished building, comprising nave – with low gabled projections in the centre of each side for family pews – tower and neat octagonal spire. Built of limestone rubble with ashlar trim. English Perp in style, with windows of three lights to the nave and belfry and a big five-light E window. Continuous battlemented parapet, hoodmouldings and pinnacles to the base of a slender needle spire. A beautiful late Georgian Gothic church unroofed by the Church of Ireland in 1989.

34 ST MUNNA, TAGHMON. 5 km NE. In its striking plastic impact, Taghmon Church is as much a sculptural monument as a building. A simple structure, built of local limestone rubble, and yet possessed of a memorable quality of stockiness and solidity. It is a rectangular single-cell church, $42\frac{1}{2}$ ft by $19\frac{1}{2}$ ft (12.95 m by 5.94 m), with a deep continuous parapet of Irish battlements, joined at its W end by a plain rectangular, four-storey tower. Although the appearance is of one build, the tower was evidently added to the existing church. The latter is probably of mid- to late C15 date and the tower is presumably not much later, completed as a fortified dwelling for the parochial clergy. What gives the building its distinctive profile is the pronounced inward slope of its walls both in the nave and even more so in the tower. This, together with the very small window openings – mere loops in the tower and cusped single-light windows in the nave – creates an impregnable fortress-like impression. The doorway is a pointed arch in the N wall, formerly matched by a second on the S. The jambs of the arch are chamfered and tapered to a base point in characteristic C15 fashion, and the windows, two in the N and S walls, are single cusped lights with dished spandrels, tapering hoodmouldings and vine-leaf label stops. The E window is an insertion by *Joseph Welland*, who restored and refitted the church in 1843. The door is surmounted by a carved head of an ecclesiastic, and one of the lower windows has a grotesque imp above it.

The interior of the church is remarkable in having a flat stone vault, whose weight pushed out the S wall in 1755. The interior is plain, relieved only by its windows and aumbry niches. It is now an ancient monument, and all traces of its early Victorian furnishings have gone. Gravel covers the floor, and green algae discolour the vault. Two arches communicate with the tower, which has stone vaults over two floors, a spiral stair at the NE angle and window seats, fireplaces and slop stones in each of the principal rooms.

PARSONSTOWN CATHOLIC CHURCH, CHAPEL OF EASE TO MULTYFARNHAM. 2 km N. 1844. A highly unusual arrangement of a church and parish priest's residence under one roof, and as such a neat modern parallel of Taghmon Church with its residential tower at the W end. Here there is no structural distinction between church and dwelling, as both are housed together in one long gabled hall. Three narrow lancets light the body of the church, and beyond them at the S end is the three-storey, single-bay end of the priest's house, clearly expressed as three sash windows. Inside, the church is similar to Multyfarnham, a big plain gabled hall with three large round-headed altar-cum-statue niches at the chancel end. Like Multyfarnham these have clustered colonnettes, foliated borders and several orders of arch rings.

BALLYNEGALL. 0.5 km NW. The fate of this elegant house by *Francis Johnston* – now a gutted shell, roofless, its floors sawn out for their timber and all fittings gone – is one of the most tragic consequences of the laissez-faire attitudes of successive governments towards the architectural inheritance of the State. Here was a most delightful villa by one of Ireland's most refined designers – a man of European stature – and in its place today is perfect, inexcusable waste. There can be little satisfaction in contemplating the lacerated fragment of a Fragonard and still less pleasure in a visit to Ballynegall as it is now.

The house was built in 1808 for James Gibbons. An ample, broad design of Regency character verging on the Italianate palazzo manner (made fashionable in the 1840s by Charles Lanyon), and indeed Ballynegall was to beget a Victorian Italianate relative in George Papworth's Middleton Park (*see* Castletown Geoghegan), which copies its external arrangements closely. The house was of two storeys, astylar, apart from a four-column Greek Ionic porch set across the front door, and an emphatic mutule cornice in stone – one of Johnston's favourite motifs – which ran all round the house at eaves level. The entrance front was of six bays, with an extra bay for the main door at ground level, and the central two bays were slightly advanced. On the garden front, large tripartite windows on both floors flanked a broad segmental bow. Johnston articulated this bow carefully: it does not, as it were, slide out of the flat walls beside it but is projected cleanly as a square corner from which the bow springs, a conscious architectural decision which is emphasized by the stone frieze and mutule cornice above. On the plain three-bay S side stand the ruins of a cast-iron conservatory by *Richard Turner*, with characteristic glazed pilaster shafts and lotus capitals. This presumably replaced an earlier conservatory by Johnston, as it is screened, on the entrance front, by a low single-storey, single-bay wing which is part of Johnston's scheme. The interior of Ballynegall possessed all the spacious sobriety, all the satisfaction of details minutely resolved, that is typical of Johnston at his best. Large well-lit rooms with restrained rectangular panelling and immaculate neoclassical detail in shallow relief, guilloche and palmette friezes, dentil and foliage cornices. The stair area, set at right angles, N of the entrance axis, and screened from the hall by a pair of Ionic columns, made sustained use of Johnston's favourite elliptical forms, with a bow-shaped landing lit by an elliptical-headed window and further elliptical arches breaking the length of the bedroom corridor above.

LEVINGTON PARK. 3 km SW. A charming and unusual house of 1748, built for Sir Richard Levinge (1724–86) on the occasion of his marriage. The present nine-bay, two-storey entrance front disguises its early origin, as it was renovated *c.* 1810, when the three centre bays were given a shallow eaves pediment with a fanlight window inside it, an overscaled Doric porch and a first-floor Wyatt window. Before these improvements the house was simply a long gabled block of limestone rubble, two storeys high, with nine sturdy sash windows with exposed sash boxes. The plan is of the old-fashioned single-pile type with a long vaulted corridor set across the back. This is returned at each end as two four-bay gabled ranges, creating a three-sided court at the rear of the house. The projecting ranges connect with outhouses to form a long narrow enclosed court. The principal stair is at the junction of the main block and one wing, and is framed by a charming twin-arched screen. The original plan consisted of four modest-sized rooms across the front, two on each side of the hall. The 1810 alterations created one large room S of the hall and added a bowed extension to the room at the N gable end. Now only the small room N of the hall retains its early Georgian character, with a frieze of flower-baskets, swags and squirrels and a large purple marble fireplace. The most charming part of this house today is its rear garden court, whose long narrow proportions and narrow rectangular lily pond create the ambience of a manor house.

Sir Richard Levinge was a celebrated eccentric. Among many whimsical projects was a scheme to train vines along the S wall of the house and introduce them through the holes of the ceiling joists into his bedroom, where he might pluck the fruit at his leisure. This was foiled when the vines would not grow. A second notorious venture was his placing of a large mirror on the ceiling above the dining-room table, so that in resting between courses the host might contemplate the 'natural beauties' of his female guests! Sir Richard's experiments in the cult of Venus met with no more success than his bedroom Bacchic fantasies: when the mirror was installed, steam rising from the food at table fogged its surface!

RATHKENNY

ME 8070

Rathkenny crossroads is a perfect illustration of C20 developments in Catholic church accommodation. A large modern church of brick, glass and steel stands diagonally opposite the remnant of its modest Victorian predecessor – a limestone Gothic façade, retained as the entrance to an enlarged cemetery and reflected in the glass doors of the new church. Some interesting minor 'seats' are in the area.

RATHKENNY PARISH CHURCH. A little way N of the crossroads. The ivy-grown remnant of an early C19 church. Rectangular two-bay hall with apsidal chancel and a handsome rusticated limestone doorcase. – MONUMENT. Classical limestone niche on the S wall of the nave; the inscription was illegible at the time of visiting.

ST LOUIS, OLD CHURCH. This now largely demolished church was described in 1837 as 'a large chapel just built, the front faced with hewn stone'. Renovated in 1853–7 and again in 1878.

ST LOUIS, RATHKENNY PARISH CHURCH. 1973–4 by *David Duignan & Associates*. Octagonal steel-frame church of brick and cement-rendered concrete, with a widely splayed hipped roof. Pagoda-like, with pairs of long narrow mullioned lights decreasing in size towards the angles of the façade. Tall brick tower with a glazed belfry and a cone-like crown.

RATHKENNY CASTLE. 0.5 km N. The overgrown ruin of what appears to have been a large C17 fortified house, perhaps incorporating part of an earlier tower house. Built by the Hussey family, Barons of Galtrim, who intermarried with the Petits of Rathkenny in the C15. Now largely ruinous, but part of a vaulted basement survives, together with press recesses and stone corbels for the roof timbers.

RATHKENNY HOUSE. 1.5 km N. Handsome and sophisticated house built in two stages during the C18 by the Hussey family. Now a seven-bay, two-storey gabled block with quoins, parapet and blocking course, it was originally five bays wide, as is made plain both by the location of the three chimneystacks and by the hall door, which, as it retains its position at the centre of the older block, is now asymmetrically placed on the whole façade. The narrower proportions of the windows of the earlier part, particularly those on the first floor, similarly betray the house's composite history. Built most probably for Stafford Hussey, *c.* 1750, the original house was a single range with a central stairhall flanked by two large rooms on each floor. On the principal floor the dining room to the l. of the hall retains a fine wainscotted interior, now stripped back to the timber to suit modern taste. An early basket-grate with scalloped border is framed by a neoclassical polychrome marble chimneypiece. The latter may well date from the time of the extension of *c.* 1780, which added the extra two bays to the W. Though now broken into one continuous space, this was originally a two-storey wing, lit by ample twelve-pane sash windows on each floor. In the later C19 major extensions were made at the back.

CAUCESTOWN HOUSE. 4 km S. A plaque at Caucestown records a foundation date of 1748 and a reconstruction in 1845 by a Mr Grainger. Of the former building nothing is now evident, and Caucestown appears today as an emphatically Victorian stuccoed Tudor-Gothic house. One possible legacy of the C18 is the symmetry of the entrance front: three bays and two storeys, with an advanced and gabled central bay. The latter has an elaborate turreted frame to the entrance and an oriel window to the first floor. Square-headed windows, hood-mouldings and miniature decorative gables to the flanking bays. An element of asymmetry was gained by the addition of an oratory to the N – not unlike the contemporary convent oratory, a plain gable with a triple-light Perp window. The house's rear elevation is more wilfully picturesque – five bays here, with tall gables and bay windows.

FIRMOUNT. 4 km S. Charming mid- to late C18 gentleman farmer's house; sympathetically reconstructed in 1984. The classic five-bay, two storey gabled roof formula, with sash windows and a blocked door surround. The whole is flanked by curved quadrants screening farm offices behind. Familiar, modest and elegant architecture.

STACKALLEN GLEBE HOUSE. 5 km S. 1815. Handsome square house, smooth rendered, with a shallow hipped roof and plain eaves. Three-bay by two storeys over a semi-basement. The doorcase of cut stone, with a wide sweep of steps, may have been reused from an earlier building and looks *c.* 1770. Possibly brought from the older part of the house, which overlaps the main block at the back.

TANKARDSTOWN HOUSE. 2.5 km E. Built by the Townshend family in the early C19. An odd building whose principal front has more the appearance of a markethouse or an elegant stable block than of a house. This may, however, have much to do with the masonry, exposed limestone rubble, which tends to transform reticent Regency classicism into a more utilitarian idiom. A facing of stucco would no doubt reinstate an elegant Johnston-like restraint. Of two storeys and three bays, it is a simple composition; a central doorcase and flanking windows framed by three shallow segmental-headed arches, three square-headed windows above, a first-floor string-course and eaves cornice. In plan the house is a cubic three-bay block with a very wide central hall and two staircases at the rear. In the late C19 a narrow rectangular block was built across the back housing a grandiose Jacobean stairhall. In the house proper the interior detail presents a mixture of early C19 neoclassicism with later, more gross classical details. The plan too seems to have been altered later in the century. The avenue gates, stamped 'Paris 1890', may indicate the date of these alterations, which were carried out for the Blackburn family.

RATHMORE

ME *7060*

This late medieval manor, the property of the Plunkett family, is represented today by the ruins of a church and a tower house.

RATHMORE CHURCH RUIN. Like its contemporaries at Dunsany and Killeen, Rathmore was presumably a manor church, built to serve the spiritual needs of the Plunkett family of Rathmore Castle. The builder was most probably Thomas, third son of the first Sir Christopher Plunkett of Dunsany and Killeen, who acquired the manor of Rathmore some time after his marriage to Mary Cruise in 1423, and certainly before 1440. The armorial carvings of the Rathmore altar constitute a vital *Who Was Who* of the northern Pale, reflecting clearly the political implications of marriage in late medieval Ireland. Contained in ogee-headed niches, besides angels and ecclesiastics, are the impaled arms of Plunkett and Hollywood; Fitzgerald and Talbot; Bellew and Bermingham; Plunkett and Cruise.

Rathmore Church is an evocative building that recalls the civilizing forces at work in late medieval Irish society. Similar in many aspects to the churches at Killeen and Dunsany, it is nevertheless a lower structure, less complete and less distinguished. It was a long, low gabled building, built of limestone rubble, with one stocky tower at the SW corner, now a hollow pigeon shaft. Hardly anything survives of the battlemented parapets which originally finished the wall-heads, and only the loops at the W end tell of the church's defensive aspects. The plan consists of a nave and chancel of equal length, with a three-storey tower, adjoining the chancel on the N, which housed a sanctuary with rooms above for a priest or sacristan. As at Dunsany, entrance to the church was by two pointed doorways, which face each other across the W end of the nave. A stone stair set into the N wall of the nave formerly led to the rood-loft and, further up, to the parapet walk. On either side of the chancel arch, beneath the rood-loft, were two small chapels, again like those at Killeen and Dunsany, now deep recesses lit by low windows.

Several features in the chancel place the church firmly in the C15. These are the twinlight window with pointed and cusped heads on the N wall and the triple SEDILIA, on the S wall, which, though much restored, retains its original ceiling, decorated with an oddly diagrammatical fan-vault which recalls the carving of the font at Dunsany Church. The E window is a handsome triple light with cusped curvilinear tracery which would not be out of place in the C14, so that only the conservatism of Irish taste can explain its occurrence here. The label stops on the exterior wall are charming carved heads of a queen and king, with all the refinement of late International Gothic work. Beneath the window the ALTAR, with its shallow ogee-headed niches and figures, is a mistaken modern reconstruction using the sides of the Plunkett altar tomb now in the sacristry: note especially St Lawrence, the patron of the church, with his grid-iron, between two angels with censers. The FONT, near the nave door, is an octagonal limestone bowl, set on a central shaft, with scenes and figures set in niches round the sides. These include the Baptism of Christ, St Thomas, Christ displaying his wounds, St Peter and St Paul, an abbess and a bishop. The font is thought to have been presented to the church by Lady Catherine Plunkett, either on her marriage *c.* 1490, or on her husband's accession to the manor of Rathmore in 1503. A ruined N porch and a rather crude cross, near the chancel, were also erected by this couple. – MONUMENT. Reconstructed in the sacristy, the double altar tomb of Sir Thomas Plunkett † 1471 and his wife, Marion Cruise. Much defaced effigies of a knight and his lady, his feet resting on a little dog, hers on a cushion. The knight's head lies on a pillow. He wears a suit of plated armour with a chain-mail collar (a pisane) and skirt. There are circular bosses (besagews) on his shoulders and elbows. The female effigy is headless. It is dressed in a very full pleated skirt, with a belt, delicately decorated with S's in relief. There is a fragmentary inscription round the edge of the slab. – A LABYRINTH carved in limestone is on the N wall of the nave; there is also a classical limestone aedicule on the S wall to Thomas Bligh † 1770.

RATHMORE CASTLE. NE of the church. Large square tower house built by the de Verduns. Probably early C14; in the possession of the Plunketts by the end of the century. Now covered in ivy and in dangerous condition.

RATHMORE CHURCH. 0.5 km NE. Built in 1844 for the Rev. J. Rickard P.P. Large three-bay lancet hall, with a porch against the W gable, finials, and intersecting Y-tracery in a Tudor arch. High Victorian STAINED GLASS and *Mayer* statuary.

ATHLUMNEY CHURCH. 4 km N. Built in 1837 for the Rev. Michael Reid P.P. Tall four-bay rendered hall, with a three-stage tower projecting from the entrance gable; this is now stripped back to expose limestone rubble masonry. Pointed entrance arch and pointed windows with hoodmouldings. FONT. C16. Marvellous Tudor work: octagonal limestone font, carved as a range of four-centred arches with foliated tops framing emblem-bearing figures and a scene of the Coronation of the Virgin.

7040

RATHMOYLON ME

RATHMOYLON PARISH CHURCH (C of I). Rectangular gabled hall built in 1797 and enlarged in the C19 by the addition of a substantial N transept. In 1862 *Joseph Welland* added an entrance porch, octagonal belfry, tower and spire, into the angle between the transept and nave. Effective but economical. The interior is Victorian Gothic in character, with paired and triple cusped lights in the nave, Y-tracery windows in the transept, quarry glass and carved oak pews. A chamfered four-centred arch marks the junction of nave and transept. – MONUMENTS. In the nave: Sir Richard Levinge † 1747; a large and impressive Tuscan aedicule in grey-black marble framing an inscribed tablet. N transept: S. Conway Bennine LLD, Vicar of Rathmoylon, † 1823; a reticent neoclassical plaque by *T. Kirk*.

KILBALLYPORTER FORMER CATHOLIC CHURCH. 1.5 km W. Large early C19 T-plan church, harled, with bellcote, buttresses and lancets, remodelled for factory purposes. Empty and neglected in 1984. Immediately N of the church is an attractive early C19 farmhouse, a gabled, two-storey house with sash windows, fanlit doorcase and corner quoin strips.

TRAMMONT. 2 km NW. Small early Victorian, Hansel-and-Gretel-style house built by *James Williams*, who died in 1853 and is buried at Rathmoylon. A modest single-storey building with a steeply pitched roof, incorporating four tall pointed dormer gables with decorative bargeboards; casement windows and nice red and yellow brick patterning.

TOBERTYNAN HOUSE. 3 km W. Straightforward Georgian house, castellated in the early C19. Two storeys over a basement, with a three-bay entrance front, sash windows and a tripartite fanlit doorcase which looks *c.* 1780. During the C18 Tobertynan was the property of the Nugent family, although in 1786 it was described as the seat of a Mr Donellan. About 1800 it was purchased by Francis McEvoy, one of the founders of the College of Surgeons in Dublin, and it was his family who added four round rubble towers to the corners, a battlemented parapet and two-bay kitchen wing at the rear. The McEvoy arms and motto, 'Bear and Forbear', are carved on a plaque over the central window in the main front.

RATHCORE PARISH CHURCH (C of I). 4.5 km SW. Low, three-bay hall with an apsidal chancel, built in 1788 and altered in 1864 by the addition of a new vestry, a W porch and a bellcote over the W gable. The original entrance has a pointed arch framed by a Gibbs surround. Cement-rendered, with timber Y-traceried windows.

RATHOWEN

WM *3060*

RATHASPIC PARISH CHURCH (C of I). In the village of Rathowen. A gabled hall and tower church, built in 1814 and enlarged in 1821. Rough-cast, with Y-tracery windows and quarry glass. Late C19 E window of three cusped lights with geometric tracery. Three-stage pinnacled tower flanked by side vestibules.

ST MARY, RATHOWEN PARISH CHURCH. 1 km SE. Substantial and well-built cruciform church of snecked flint and limestone rubble. Built in 1846 by the Rev. James O'Reilly on a site donated by the Bonds of Ardglass. More ambitious than the usual T-plan country chapel, this is quite a tall building, with a large and square two-stage tower projecting from the entrance gable. The proportions of the church are curiously solid, as transepts and nave are all of identical dimensions and each two bays long with lancet windows. Battlements and pinnacles to the tower, which cleverly avoids the C of I image by missing out the usual intermediate storey between the entrance and belfry stage. Inside is an open kingpost roof, a moulded two-centred chancel arch carried on colonnettes with bell capitals, and a triple-light geometric window lighting the chancel. The chancel has been tastefully adapted to modern liturgical requirements by *Dan O'Riordan*. – STAINED GLASS. E window: Sacred Heart, St Joseph and the Virgin by *Mayer of Munich*. Abstract glass to new porch in the W transept: 1986 by *Pascal Fitzpatrick*.

NEWPASS. 2 km W. Large mid-Georgian house of three storeys over a basement, made dull in the C19 by too much cement-rendering and plate-glass windows. Three-bay entrance front articulated as a central fanlit doorcase with side-lights, a Venetian window to the first floor and a flat-headed tripartite window on the top storey. This was flanked in the outer bays by sash windows at each level. The plan consists of two large receptions rooms flanking a central entrance hall, with two smaller rooms flanking the stairhall behind. The interior is now C19, though the room S of the hall preserves a big polychrome marble chimneypiece and fielded joinery in the shuttering. Newpass was built by the Whitney family, who had received a grant of the town of Rathowen in 1684. In 1786 the Whitneys were still living here, but by 1836 the house was the property of the Fetherston-Haughs.

CROMLYN. 2.5 km SW. Three-bay, two-storey house over a semi-basement. Sash windows and square projecting porch. Built by the Crawford family in 1795, but much reworked.

0050

RATOATH

ME

Small village in S Meath which derives its name from an earthwork now standing in the grounds of the Catholic church. This is a motte with a crescentic bailey on the E side, through which the drive to the presbytery was cut. In the C12 Hugh de Lacy granted the Holy Trinity parish church to the Abbey of St Thomas in Dublin, and throughout the Middle Ages Ratoath remained an important manor.

RATOATH PARISH CHURCH, HOLY TRINITY. Tall five-bay hall and chancel church begun by the Rev. Richard Carolan in the early C19 and completed in 1874, when the chancel was added. Attractive cutstone entrance front of 1868; three bays with pointed arches, traceried twinlight windows and a central canopied niche and bellcote. Twinlight windows with hood-mouldings to the side elevations and pinnacled buttresses with offsets. Inside, a shallow four-centred chancel arch is carried on clustered colonnettes with foliated capitals. Reredos of 1869.

RATOATH FORMER PARISH CHURCH (C of I). 1817. All that survives is the tower and the base of the church walls. The former is the usual three-stage structure with pinnacles and a battlemented parapet. – MONUMENTS. On the W face of the tower and presumably from the C18 church, a handsome classical wall monument in the manner of James Gibbs. An inscribed plaque flanked by scrolled consoles and above it a flat aedicule framing a circular bust niche. The bust, of Jane Lowthe † 1764, has long since gone. – In the churchyard near the tower is a late C13 or early C14 sandstone effigial tomb; coffin slab with the figure of a knight wearing a belted round-necked coat and holding a sword, his legs broken off from knee level. Incised Lombardic inscription.

THE MANOR HOUSE. Long seven-bay, two-storey house of late C18 appearance. Rough-cast, with a central Ionic doorcase and windows with exposed sash boxes. The ground-floor windows are set in segmental-headed relieving arches. Inside, late Georgian joinery with thin applied mouldings. More recent additions to the side and at the rear. Seat of J. I. Corballis in 1836.

RATOATH GLEBE HOUSE. 1813. Gabled five-bay house of two storeys over a semi-basement. Sash windows and a tripartite fanlit doorcase.

HOLY TRINITY PAROCHIAL HOUSE. 1869. By *William Hague*. Built for the Rev. Fr Fulham with a loan of £1,000 from the Board of Works; completed in 1874. A High Victorian three-bay, two-storey house of brick and stone with Gothic detailing.

HERBERTSTOWN HOUSE. 5.5 km S. 1916. Built by Captain H. Whitworth. Long low classical house with a tall hipped roof in a vaguely Queen Anne idiom. Five-bay, two-storey entrance front, with corner quoins in dressed limestone and an emphatic eaves cornice carried up as a pediment over the central bay. Elaborate Ionic porch flanked by mullioned bay windows. Slated bow windows to narrow side elevations. Tripartite plan, with a C17-style oak staircase in a large central hall and reception rooms on each side. Kitchen wing at the rear. Pretty redbrick gate lodge, square, with a pyramidal slate roof and a central chimney.

CRICKSTOWN CHURCH RUIN. 1.5 km N. The ruin of a late medieval church built by the Barnewall family of Kilbrew and Crickstown. Rectangular building of approximately 50 ft by 25 ft (15 m by 7.5 m) internally, with a stair to the rood-loft in the N wall and a two-storey sacristy N of the chancel. A carved C16 font from Crickstown Church is now in St Andrew's Church at Curragha (*see* below).

ST ANDREW, CURRAGHA. 3 km N. 1898–1904. By *G. C. Ashlin*. Gabled Gothic hall of limestone rubble, the nave flanked by an octagonal belfry crowned by a diminutive spire. The entrance gable has two twinlight windows with geometric tracery and a pointed arch flanked by lancets. Five paired lights with reticulated tracery to the nave. Inside, the sanctuary is framed by three moulded two-centred arches carried on polished granite shafts. The chancel is lit by five cusped lancets with geometric tracery of trefoils and cinquefoils. The original group of early C20 Gothic furnishings is preserved complete. –

MOSAIC. 1932. – FONT. Transferred here in 1904 from the ruined medieval church of Crickstown (*see* above). A very fine C16 octagonal font now inexplicably painted white. The upper register is carved with figures of the Apostles, two to each panel, together with a scene of the Annunciation and another of the Crucifixion. On the sloping underside of the basin a central boss marks the junction of each panel. On the shaft are standing figures set in niches: St Catherine of Alexandria; St Margaret of Antioch; an abbess; an archbishop; an abbot; John the Baptist; St Michael and the dragon. The base is decorated with grotesque animal heads. The figure carving on this font is most accomplished, particularly on the shaft. There is a certain naivety in the handling, for instance, of the Crucifixion scene, but the poses of the figures and the treatment of the draperies show that the sculptor had clearly imbibed the influence of contemporary European classicism.

KILBRIDE CATHOLIC CHURCH. 6.5 km SE. By *Ashlin & Coleman*, 1929. A chapel of ease to the Church of SS Peter and Paul at Dunboyne. Nicely located on a hill site that overlooks the ruin of old Kilbride Church. Small gabled hall of rock-faced granite with an octagonal bell turret flanking the entrance gable. Five-bay nave with a timber cross-braced roof, lit by lancets in the side elevations, a triple-light E window and a rose window in the entrance gable.

0010 RAVENSDALE LO

Small village with some pretty picturesque estate buildings. The big house nearby, Ravensdale Park, was formerly the estate of the Fortesque family, Lords Clermont. Its demesne is now a forest park.

RAVENSDALE PARK. A rambling Italianate mansion by *Thomas Duff*, later extended by *Lanyon and Lynn*, was burned in 1921. Much of the masonry was later used in the building of the Catholic church at Glasdrummond in Co. Armagh. All that survives in Ravensdale itself is the Gothic stable block, probably also by Duff. A square courtyard of granite ashlar, with flat-headed windows and doors along three sides and, opposite the main entrance, a two-storey house with Tudor-arched porch. The centrepiece of the entrance, pierced by loops, is now missing, leaving plain buttressed walls which terminate in gabled ends. N of the stables is the former estate SCHOOLHOUSE, a small picturesque cottage, L-shaped, with quarry glass, hoodmouldings and decorative bargeboards. A new house of 1974, S of the stables near the site of the old mansion, is by the Omeath architect *Brian O'Neill*.

ANNAVERNA. In Ravensdale Park. Plain two-storey, five-bay Georgian house designed *c.* 1790 by *Thaddeus Gallagher*. Good cast-iron gates with Greek-key pattern.

In RAVENSDALE VILLAGE proper is a tiny mid-C19 COURT-

HOUSE, now derelict. Cement-rendered, with lugged door surround, eaves pediment and royal coat of arms. Also a number of picturesque mid-C19 estate houses. A two-storey house, with a bracketed central gable, decorative bargeboards and hoodmouldings, was once the DISPENSARY and DOCTOR'S RESIDENCE. Next to it, a very pretty cottage, with tall chimneys, bargeboards and quarry glass, for the schoolmaster.

READYPENNY CROSSROADS

LO *0090*

KILINCOOLE CASTLE. 0.5 km NW. A welcome change from the normal straight-sided Irish tower house with round or square corner towers; the walls of Kilincoole are all gently curved. This, together with a pronounced batter at the base of the walls, makes for a very distinctive mass, with profiles reminiscent of abstract sculpture. In plan, the castle is roughly rectangular, with two round stairtowers diagonally opposite each other at the NW and SE angles. It is of four storeys. There are two entrances: one high up in the SW turret and a second at ground-floor level on the N elevation. Inside this, two murder holes await the intruder. Inside, the ground-floor barrel-vault is well preserved and bears traces of wickerwork centering used in its construction. The first floor, also vaulted, is intact, but the floors above are gone, leaving a cavernous upper chamber where fireplaces and window openings punctuate the walls. Judging from the wholly defensive nature of its curved masonry – much more difficult to achieve than sharp arrised corners – Kilincoole is very probably one of the earlier strongholds of the Pale, dating perhaps to the mid-C13. The castle and surrounding lands were the property of the Gernon family from the reign of Edward II to the C18.

KILINCOOLE PARISH CHURCH (C of I). 0.5 km W. 1799. Three-bay rubble hall with a bellcote over the W end. Additional lower chancel and a porch at the W end. Remodelled *c.* 1880.

GLEBE-HOUSE. *c.* 1800. Attributed to *Francis Johnston*. Neat two-storey gabled house built on a semi-basement. Simple symmetrical plan of a central hall with a staircase at its rear, flanked on each side by a single large room. Principal elevation of three bays, with a projecting centre bay under a plain eaves pediment. Square-headed doorcase, approached by a short flight of steps with elegant cast-iron handrails. Sash windows throughout. Pretty staircase with straight fluted balusters and a mahogany handrail that changes to oak on going down to the servants' quarters.

DARVER PARISH CHURCH. 1 km SE. 1905. Broad, gabled four-bay hall with a lower chancel. Small three-stage belltower with slated needle spire flanking the entrance gable. Built of coursed rubble; the tower and entrance front of rock-faced granite with limestone trim. The gable façade, though reminiscent of W. H. Byrne & Son, is awkward. A central window in the shape of a spherical triangle with an eight-foiled circle inside is set above a tall row of blind arcading. Beneath, stumpy buttresses and lancets flank a gabled door. Inside, three sets of paired lancets light the nave, which is framed by a blind arcade carried on wide nook-shafted pilasters, also reminiscent of Byrne. Triple-light plate tracery window in the chancel.

DARVER CASTLE. 0.5 km SE. A much altered four-storey tower house, with an adjoining two-storey dwelling house of modest Regency appearance with tripartite windows throughout. Battlemented yard behind. The tower house has a projecting round tower at the NE angle and a square one at the NW angle. When Thomas Wright visited Darver in the 1740s he recorded very unusual and fanciful battlements on the tower house. These have now been replaced by early C19 battlements in cement, and the castle has four tripartite windows like the rest of the house. A CHURCH (C of I) erected in the grounds in 1840 has been demolished. – Opposite the entrance to the castle are DARVER CHURCH RUINS. A foundation dating to the C14 or C15. All that survives is the base of the walls and a section of the E gable.

7080 ROBERTSTOWN CASTLE ME

Like Athlumney Castle or the domestic additions to Bective Abbey, the ruins of Robertstown Castle offer, for North Leinster, a rare survival of C16 domestic building. In contrast to these other houses Robertstown is very much a Scottish building. Baronial in character, if of an angular sort, it lacks the multi-gabled roof-line and expansive mullioned windows of Elizabethan houses and is a much more closed structure, with broad expanses of rubble masonry punctuated by relatively small window openings. Though a marked development from the Irish tower-house formula, patently this is still a defensive structure. Essentially the building is a large rectangle, some 75 ft (22.5 m) long, with end gables. Originally of four storeys, it is now reduced to two, except at the W gable, which stands to its full height. The plan is not strictly a parallelogram but rather the union of two rectangular gabled blocks, both roughly of equal length, but with one 25 ft (7.5 m) wide and the other some 6 ft (1.8 m) narrower and, as a result, checked back on the S elevation. The junction of the two is marked, above basement level, by a square turret or oriel supported on four tiers of continuous cornice corbelling. For the modern visitor this front is Robertstown's most impressive elevation. It is built of coursed rubble masonry, with cutstone trim, and is pierced only by loops on the ground floor, with tall window openings, now robbed of all detail, and one surviving mullioned window near the W end. At the NW corner of the gable end is a shallow square turret, corbelled out, once more, on continuous cornices with a two-light mullioned window and label moulding above and the remains of an upper window.

Entrance to the building is by two openings on the N front. The basement has four substantial barrel-vaulted rooms, with lintelled entrances, press recesses and musket loops. A spiral stair, located near the middle of the N wall, leads to three large rooms on the upper floor, now featureless, with the significant exception of a finely wrought arch leading into the S turret. Executed in grey limestone, this is a moulded two-centred opening with a rolled and tapering chamfer and pocked tooling to the surround. Robertstown is maintained as a National Monument and neatly illustrates the transition of the late medieval castle in Ireland from tower to fortified house.

ROCHFORTBRIDGE

WM *4040*

CASTLELOST PARISH CHURCH. Miniature tower and hall church of 1815. Harled two-bay hall and three-stage tower in squared rubble with clasping buttresses. Y-tracery windows with quarry glass and a triple-light Perp E window.

MEEDIN PARISH CHURCH. *c.* 1840. Cement-rendered gabled hall, with miniature octagonal corner turrets to the entrance gable, a large elliptical window and a square porch. Later C19 limestone tower tapering to an octagonal belfry crowned by a slated spire.

CONVENT OF MERCY. 1896 by *Scott and Son*. A five-bay, two-storey essay in plain institutional Gothic. Gabled and cement-rendered, with lancet windows and an advanced central bay with a hipped gable over the entrance. Gabled school range to the S and N, a pleasant classical chapel built in 1822 to designs by *T. J. Cullen*. Pedimented, with four Diocletian windows down each side.

CASTLELOST. 1.5 km NW. Formerly one of the principal castles of the Tyrrells, this important stronghold is now reduced to the basement storey of a tower, ruinous and strewn with fallen stones. Once a large rectangular building, roughly 40 ft by 20 ft (12 m by 6 m) internally, with windows in the base of the S wall and deep recesses on the W and E. Near it is the motte built *c.* 1186 by Hugh Tyrrell and a large curious amphitheatre-like formation that has been interpreted as a bull-ring.

CASTLELOST CHURCH, NW of the castle, has been ruinous since the early C19, when much of its cutstone work was removed, some to be incorporated in Meedin Chapel (*see* Tyrrellspass). The church was probably erected during the mid- to late C16 by Sir John Tyrrell.

ROKEBY HALL

LO *0080*

3 km SE of Dunleer

This large square house, built from *c.* 1785 for the Protestant Archbishop of Armagh, Richard Robinson, is the work of two men. It was begun to designs of *Thomas Cooley*, but he died in

1784 and the building had to be supervised by the young architect from Armagh, *Francis Johnston*, whom the Archbishop had encouraged to study in Dublin under Cooley. Johnston then became the Primate's architect, and Rokeby is often described as his first house. Robinson, whose later career was spent in beautifying and reconstructing the city of Armagh, had building in his blood. He was the sixth son of William Robinson of Rokeby in Yorkshire and a brother of Sir Thomas Robinson, the amateur architect and connoisseur who finished the W wing of Castle Howard for the Earl of Carlisle. Richard Robinson chose the name of his family's property in Yorkshire for his new house at Marley in Co. Louth when he succeeded to the English estate in 1785.

At the Irish Rokeby, the collaboration of two architects must explain the mixture of traditional, indeed rather tame, classicism with up-to-date free detail. As a basic design the house appears routine: a seven-bay, two-storey front above a basement, with the centre slightly advanced and emphasized by a miniature temple front grafted onto the upper storey. Four shallow Ionic pilasters support a pediment, and a cornice and blocking course surround the house at eaves level. The sides and back are absolutely plain.

80 Inside, a rectangular hall with a screen of two Doric columns opens l. and r. into the front reception rooms. All this is standard, but beyond the columns the plan is more unusual; instead of three rooms, with a central saloon set on axis with the hall, Johnston has provided just two rooms, side by side across the rear of the house, each three windows long and built to a grander scale than the front would seem to indicate. Another unusual feature is the arrangement of the main and service stairs, which are grouped together on one side of the entrance hall. This improves the 'flow' of the rooms on the main floor and also allows Johnston to design an elegant circular lobby at the bedroom-floor level – a motif which seems to anticipate the magnificent staircase rotunda at Townley Hall – and a second, top-lit circular lobby at attic level. Both spaces are nicely detailed: an arcade of round-headed arches frames doorcases with oculi above on the bedroom floor, while the attic floor is simpler, with thin pilasters defining the circular space.

What is not traditional about Rokeby is the house's reticence and refinement of detail. The entrance front has none of the usual texturing, no rustication or V-jointed masonry, no heavy cornices or architectural emphasis but only clean unadorned limestone ashlar. Although a certain grandeur of scale characterizes domestic architecture throughout the Georgian period, the very ample, even lofty proportions of the rooms – all the ceilings on the main floor are 15 ft (4.5 m) high – place Rokeby firmly in the late C18. So too does the treatment of detail: for example, the Doric entablature in the hall, which simply omits the frieze, to accommodate the lower ceiling level behind the screen of columns; or the tops of the door surrounds, where miniature pine-cones alternate with dentils on the cornices. Both of these are instances of the neoclassical penchant for refining and refreshing traditional motifs.

MARLEY FARM. 1 km NE. Small farmhouse and office yard designed in 1786 for the Lord Primate by *Francis Johnston*. The drawing for the scheme, which survives in the Albert Murray Collection, bears the inscription 'Drogheda 1786', in which year Johnston was engaged in redesigning the spire of St Peter's Church in the town and preparing designs for Drogheda Cornmarket, which he submitted to the town corporation in 1787. The Marley design, though much more modest, does relate to the markethouse commission, both in its functional storage requirements and in its form as an enclosed office yard with gate entrances and a more formal building at the centre of the front curtain wall. Essentially what Johnston proposed was a central three-bay, two-storey farmhouse, two rooms deep, with a central stair and symmetrical plan, flanked by single-storey curtain walls with gate entrances to the office yards behind. At the rear of the house a stable and barn range extended perpendicularly, bisecting the courtyard to give two separate yards for livestock and storage. The rear wall of the enclosure comprised arcaded or colonnaded shed and cow-house ranges. Clearly Robinson requested a simple utilitarian structure, and Johnston's design is absolutely plain in its detail, the only concession to ornament being loops and lintelled windows to the barn and stable range. In its present state Marley is a very ordinary derelict farmhouse. While the bones of Johnston's plan survive, the more promising rear ranges are now part demolished, part nondescript, while the house has been much reworked. The stables and barn do, however, retain punched limestone lintels, sills and jambs.

SAINTS ISLAND

LF *0050*

Accessible by road from the E shore of Lough Ree, Saints Island still has an aura of watery isolation, particularly at the lovely monastery site near the island's N shore. Established before 1244 by Sir Henry Dillon of Drumraney, this small Augustinian foundation now consists of no more than the shell of the modest monks' church and the outline of the N cloister; but the ruins are truly evocative and charming. The place is lent further significance and atmosphere by the fame of Augustin Magraidin († 1407), a monk of All Saints, who compiled an important collection of the lives of Irish saints and an historical chronicle which was drawn upon by the Four Masters. Yet, despite its fame as a place of learning, contemporary references to the priory are few. Those that survive refer to the appointment of Prior Kinnane O'Ferral in 1410 and Maolseachlainn O'Ferral in 1425. At the Dissolution, the priory lands were granted to Sir Patrick Barnwell, though it seems that the community maintained a precarious existence until the C17, when the Magraidin manuscripts were acquired directly from here.

The monastic church is a long rectangular aisleless structure,
28 best preserved at the E end, where the S wall contains three tall round-headed lancets set in deep and widely splayed embrasures. The E gable also survives, but here the window is a C15 insert, three pointed lights with simple intersecting tracery set into the old widely splayed embrasure and no doubt replacing a group of C13 round-headed lancets like those at Ballintubber, Co. Mayo, or Fore. Beneath the lancets in the S wall are single- and twin-arched piscina and aumbry recesses. All of the window embrasures are defined by borders of limestone quoins, which contrast well with the rubble masonry. Here, in the choir and in the refectory of the priory, Magraidin's *Lives of the Saints* were read to the community on their respective feast days.

Adjoining the nave at a right angle, towards the centre of the S wall, is a short ruined section of wall, pierced by a finely wrought C15 window, formerly of two lights, with curvilinear tracery and crowned by a hoodmoulding which tapers to an elegant curved point. Whether this represents the E wall of a transept, chapel or porch is not clear. Unlike Cistercian foundations, Augustinian priories did not adhere rigidly to one plan type, and at All Saints Priory the cloister was located on the N of the church rather than the more usual position to the S. Foundations of this survive, together with part of a ruined vaulted range W of the church and a curious garderobe-like tower in the SW angle of the perimeter wall. Cutstone fragments collected from the site include both C13 and C15 features – bell capitals with multiple rolled abaci and sections of square-headed openings with trefoils hollowed out of the spandrels, which may relate to the cloister arcade.

9060 SKREEN ME

ST COLUMBA'S CHURCH RUINS. A church founded and dedicated to St Columba during the C11 when the saint's shrine was brought here for safety from England. Despite all precautions it was carried off by the Norse of Dublin in 1127 but was returned to Skreen a month later. About 1175 Adam de Fergo, Lord of Skreen, founded a church here, and in 1341 an Augustinian abbey was established nearby by Adam's descendant, Francis
40 de Fergo. The present church ruin, formerly confused with the abbey, is that of the parish church of Skreen, built in the late C15. It stands on a splendid hill-top site, a long rubble-built nave, with an imposing four-storey tower at its W end. The tower, which pre-dates the nave, is a plain rectangular building with few complete features: the usual pointed barrel-vault, a spiral stair in the SE corner, slit windows and formerly paired pointed lights at belfry level. The nave is more satisfying: an entrance on each side, four tall pointed windows in the S wall

and in the N wall a large alcove and a remnant of the rood stair. Enough cutstone detail survives of an early Perp character to place the building *c.* 1500. Both the N and S entrances preserve fragments of moulded limestone frames, alternated colonnettes with broad bell-like bases and a lone bell capital to the N door. Fragmentary grape and vine-leaf label stops and a *fleur-de-lys* mason's mark adorn the windows of the S wall. The most complete cutstone feature is the pointed entrance arch to the rood stair, with the classic C15 device of the chamfered edge tapering to a point at the base. Mounted on the walls of the church are fragments of cusped lights with dished trefoil spandrels. BISHOP STONE. Set into the wall over the S doorway is a C14 sandstone panel carved with the effigy of a bishop holding a book. THE MARWARD STONE, E of the church. A large, rectangular limestone slab, now much eroded. Carved upon it are the arms of William Nugent and those of his wife, Janet Marward, the arms of Walter Marward and his wife, Margaret Plunkett, and the arms of Walter's father, James Marward. The inscription, now illegible, formerly read 'This monument, William Nugent the younger son of Richard Baron of Delvin and Janet Marward heiress and only daughter, set up as an ornament for the church to Walter Marward Baron of Skryne and his first wife, Margaret Plunkett, and to Matilda Darcy in truth are buried here. I, *John Cusack*, the brother germane of Walter by the same mother carved with mine own hand for an everlasting memorial – the year of our Lord 1611'.

SKREEN CASTLE. The lands of Skreen were granted by Hugh de Lacy to Adam de Fergo, who in 1172 held a motte and castle here. The present Skreen Castle is a later medieval tower house, now much altered and adjoined by a three-storey mid-Georgian house. The tower was a rectangular structure, internally 23 ft by 13 ft (6.9 m by 3.9 m), with a barrel-vault and a circular corner stair turret. In the mid-C19 the vault was removed when a new stair, a great chimneystack to the front wall, a porch, battlements and Gothic windows were all added to make the whole more picturesque.

ST COLUMCILLE, SKREEN PARISH CHURCH. 1 km S. 1827. A hall and tower church that looks not unlike a typical Board of First Fruits structure, except that the hall is too big and the tower and spire too small. Three-bay gabled hall with a three-stage tower to the entrance front, crowned by a short slated spire. Cement-rendered, with limestone trim. Diagonal buttresses, pinnacles and a louvred belfry to the tower, with unusual octagonal corner buttresses to the nave – perhaps they are meant to give a 'Roman' air – and three big pointed doors to the entrance front. Inside, a typical Catholic country church with deal panelling to sill level, lancet windows, a panelled ceiling and two big stone holy-water stoups on each side of the main entrance. Attractive three-bay Victorian Gothic chancel of 1868 by *M. B. Moran*.

THE CUSACK MONUMENT. A charming sculptural altar or tomb monument, formerly in Trevet graveyard, erected together with others at Staffordstown and Trevet, Co. Meath to commemorate Sir Thomas Cusack of Lismullin, Lord Chancellor of Ireland and Speaker of the House of Commons, who died in 1571. A naive monument, which yet displays an acquaintance with European Renaissance art, it has been attributed to Sir Thomas's son, *John Cusack*, an amateur stone-carver who was responsible for the Marward Stone at Skreen Church. The decoration of this monument is a large rectangular limestone panel carved in low relief, with the kneeling figures of Sir Thomas and his second wife, Margaret Darcy, with their thirteen children kneeling on each side in step-like fashion, the tallest at the centre and the smallest at each end, the girls alongside their mother and the boys flanking their father. Carved in the top right-hand corner is a figure of a mermaid, the Cusack crest. Above the figures, a canopy of five round-headed arches ending in pendants provides a frame for the composition, rather like the loggia device prevalent in C15 Italian painting. The respective ages of the children date the monument to *c.* 1559. Although the frieze-like layout and conventional poses of the figures are quite old-fashioned, aspects of the piece are strikingly up-to-date: the carrying of personal attributes by the figures, and the inclusion of a memento mori, devices common to contemporary European portraiture. Here the girls carry symbols of their father's office, a judge's mace and the Lord Chancellor's purse, while a third child blows bubbles to illustrate the fleeting character of human existence.

CORBALTON HALL. 2.5 km SE. 1801 by *Francis Johnston.* Charming two-storey, three-bay country house, originating as an addition to the home of Elias Corbally, a wealthy Co. Meath miller. Perhaps this extension was prompted by the new-found prosperity of the Irish corn market during the Napoleonic campaigns. The existing C18 house was remodelled by Johnston and, although less elegant, it looked not unlike the addition, a harled three-storey, three-bay block with an advanced centre bay. Wyatt windows and, rising behind in the centre, an Italianate octagonal lantern which lit a spiral stair. Johnston's new front almost doubled the floor space of the house and was designed, as at Cloncarneel (*see* Kildalkey), to cover completely the bulk of the older building. Today the old house has gone, demolished in 1970, leaving a gap between the 1801 design and the stable court of the old house. The new block was carried out on a characteristic Johnston formula, a two-storey rectangular house of tripartite plan. The centre consists of a spacious entrance hall with a bowed projection at the rear, housing the stair well. Large and lofty drawing and dining rooms on either side. Three-bay entrance front, the centre bay advanced, with a freestanding Ionic porch and a tripartite window above. The outer bays have the very wide rectangular sash windows beloved by Johnston. At ground-floor level these are set into shallow recesses with raised impost courses and fluted semicircular motifs above each window. The first-floor sills are incorporated into a moulded string-course, and the low hipped roof is partially screened by a modillion cornice and blocking course. The masonry is of the finest droved limestone ashlar. Inside, charming profile to the stair and pretty plasterwork to the drawing room, combining a Greek-key motif with garlands of cherries. The joinery employs the elegant circular panels found also at Castlecoole, Co. Fermanagh, and Townley Hall. – OFFICES. At the rear, a pretty five-bay, two-storey stable range, the three centre bays advanced. Vernacular markethouse classicism, with segmental-headed arches on the ground floor and six-pane sash windows above. Rough-cast with limestone quoins and eaves pediment to the centre bays. Castellated fancy-dress cornerstone in the yard behind.

BELVIN HALL. 1.5 km E. Modest late Georgian block, perfectly proportioned. The two-storey, three-bay entrance front has sash windows and a limestone Doric doorcase with an elliptical fanlight. A limestone string-course incorporates the first-floor sills, and as at Kilmessan Glebe the central window is set in a shallow segmental-headed recess. Burnt and completely refurbished *c.* 1984.

KILLEEN GLEBE. 4.5 km SW. *c.* 1810. Two storeys over a basement, with a low hipped roof and an irregular L-shaped plan. Asymmetrical entrance front with the door in the re-entrant angle and big Wyatt windows on each floor in the projecting end. A spacious and unusual design.

SLANE

ME *9070*

A perfect instance of the formally planned C18 estate village. Not 4
quaint or pretty, like later examples such as Castlebellingham or Castlepollard, but solidly built and charming in a sober way, with four identical mansions and outhouses facing each other diagonally across the main crossroads. Slane, however, is not as modern as it might first appear, as references go back to early Christian times and, through mythology, even further. According to the *Dinnshenchas*, Slaine, king of the Fir Bolg, died at Slane and was buried there with a mighty mound erected over him. The hill of Slane is also central to Christian accounts of the place which claim that here in 432 St Patrick lit the paschal flame in defiance of pagan taboo. Having established a monastery, Patrick then appointed his local disciple Erc as first Bishop of Slane, a see which later merged into that of Meath. A monastery survived throughout the Middle Ages despite successive Viking raids. In 948 the round tower of Slane is recorded as being burnt by the 'foreigners of Ath Cliath' – Danes from Dublin.

Nothing survives of the early foundation, and the existing monastic buildings both near the river and on the hill of Slane date largely to the C15 and C16. A Norman motte near the W foot of the great hill was the site of a castle built in the 1170s by Richard Fleming, Baron of Slane, whose last descendant, Christopher Fleming, twenty-second Lord Slane, died without male heir in

1726. Incorporated in the present Slane Castle (*see* pp. 478–83) are parts of a later Fleming castle which was forfeited by the Fleming family in 1641 and later in the century.

It was the Conynghams, a military family rising to prominence at the time of William III, who created the Georgian village of Slane. The centre of the village, known as the 'square' (actually an octagon), was laid out during the 1760s on land leased to private individuals by Viscount Conyngham. The same spirit that guided the planning of Georgian Dublin informed each of the Conyngham leases. The plot on the NE corner of the square was granted to one Henry Fischer with the stipulation 'House to be built within five years, same plan as new inn opposite recently built, also the other houses same plan as laid down for building in the said town of Slane'. The four big houses which stand on the square clearly fulfilled the requirement of uniformity. Each is of three storeys, with a hipped roof and gable chimneystacks, built of squared limestone, with blocked window surrounds and each linked by a low curtain wall to a small gabled pavilion, articulated as two blind arches. Not what might be described as handsome houses, but substantial and as a group impressive.

Individuality was confined to the doorcases. Following the example of the NW corner house, Henry Fischer chose a Gibbsian blocked surround, while the inn-keeper opposite, on the SE corner, decided on an odd pedimentless Pain-style doorcase, and the proprietor of the SW corner house chose two simple pilasters, a fanlight and keystone. The streets emanating from the square are lined with terraces of two-storey houses, of squared limestone or cement-rendered, some with blocked surrounds, fanlight doorcases and the occasional carriage arch. The village's commercial premises are largely quiet C19 façades which merge gently with the streetscape.

SLANE ABBEY. Sited high above the village, on the hill of Slane, this is the place where St Patrick is reputed to have lit the paschal fire; the magnificent prospect, N to Slieve Gullion, E to Drogheda, S as far as the Sugar Loaf and W to the midlands, makes plain the reason for choosing such a site. Nothing survives from early Christian times, and the ruins on the hill-top
1 are the remains of a small Franciscan monastery or college and a later parish church, built in 1513 by Christopher Fleming, Lord of Slane, and his wife, Elizabeth Stuckle.

The FRANCISCAN COLLEGE housed four priests, four lay brothers and four choristers. Two friars found living in the ancient hermitage of Erc were removed from there and installed in the new abbey. The building consists of three ranges grouped around a central courtyard and enclosed on the W by a curtain wall. The entrance, in the centre of the S range, has a moulded four-centred arch and, above, a sandstone plaque bearing the arms of England and France quartered (thought to have been inserted by order of Richard Plantagenet, Duke of York and Lord Lieutenant of Ireland between 1447 and 1460). W of the
53 entrance, a low range, now partially ruined, presents two small

windows on the first floor – originally there were four – which are worthy of note. A central mullion and single crossbar form four lights with shallow four-centred heads above and three-centred heads below, all plastically treated and surmounted by a hoodmoulding ending in foliated label stops. The detail, with applied roll mouldings, is forceful if gross, and the striking similarity of this late Gothic idiom to much of the C 19 Gothick work of Francis Johnston and his circle, given the fact that Johnston worked extensively in Slane and throughout Meath, suggests that these windows may have been the source for many early Gothic Revival details in Ireland. In the college they lit a long two-storey range, perhaps a refectory or reading room, of which two fireplaces with massive limestone lintels remain. At the W end, projecting from the gable wall, is the carving of a bird or griffin. E of the entrance is the largest building in the college, a three-storey rectangular block, formerly with two corner towers at its E end, housing stairs and garderobe. The barrel-vaulted ground-floor chamber houses a collection of fragments of cutstone windows. The remaining N section of the E wing is now largely ruinous, with the base of a stair tower at its NE angle. In contrast the outer wall of the N range is in a remarkably good state of repair, with a double-garderobe annex at the centre and four chimneypieces with big limestone lintels. Set into the W boundary wall of the courtyard are the Fleming arms, a mortarpiece casting out a bomb with flames.

THE PARISH CHURCH, SW of the college, consists of a long nave and chancel, S aisle and a tall W tower and belfry. The body of the church is now featureless, apart from three deep pointed arches which divide it from the aisle, a slightly later addition. The tower is a tall square tapering structure of limestone rubble, with a battlemented roof-walk and round-headed twinlight window at belfry level with loops below. Its finest features, apart from the view from the top, are the elegant masonry of the upper sections of the spiral stair and the W window at the base of the tower. This is of three fully cusped lights with decorated tracery of a type prevalent in the second half of the C 15. It jars stylistically with the four-centred arch below. Pretty old-fashioned if it was erected in 1513, but pretty anyway!

ST ERC'S HERMITAGE. In the wooded grounds of Slane Castle, near the Boyne and just W of the village. Dedicated to Erc, first Bishop of Slane, who died in 514. A neglected microcosm of Irish monasticism, comprising a small late medieval church tower with adjoining anchorite cells and a later, probably C 15 nave and chancel which use the tower as a chancel arch. The cells, complete with fireplaces and garderobes, were arranged on two storeys adjoining the S side of the tower. Surviving cutstone detail is confined to the chancel and suggests, for it at least, a C 15 date: particularly two square-headed twinlight windows with ogee heads and flowers and leaves carved in the spandrels. Until the late C 19 the nave had a fine pointed entrance arch with a decorated hood. – MONUMENTS. In the chancel, a large box-tomb of Ellenor Barnewell, first wife of Randal Fleming, Baron of Slane, †1667. The APOSTLES STONE, NW of the church, a solid coffin-shaped monument with figures of the Apostles carved on each side and the Crucifixion at one end; apparently brought here from the old abbey cemetery of Navan in the late C18 by William Burton-Conyngham, the antiquary. The cover slab, which depicts a recumbent bishop, is now set into a yard wall at Slane Castle; authorities agree on a late C14 or early C15 date.

ST PATRICK, SLANE PARISH CHURCH (C of I). Simple and elegant church of late Georgian appearance. Barn-like, with a low gabled roof, a S transept and a thin Gothick belfry in the centre of the N entrance front. The fabric may date to 1712, when a new church was built on this site to replace the old church on the hill of Slane. In 1773 the vestry was built at the W end, and in 1797 the clocktower was added to designs by *Francis Johnston*. Four-stage tower with clasping corner buttresses rising to pinnacles and a long pointed belfry with timber louvres and Y-tracery. Between 1805 and 1809 the vestry minutes record successive consultations with Johnston concerning alterations to the windows and seating arrangements and the insertion of a gallery for Lord Conyngham. The windows, which formerly were probably broad round-headed openings, were transformed by building up the sides below springing level to give the more neoclassical shape of a semicircle set above a rectangle. A similar motif, often employed by Johnston, is a sash window set in a round relieving arch with a decorated impost course. The gallery is a pretty design in stained timber, carried on four clustered shafts, stepping forward at the centre and decorated with cusped panels. Colonnettes rising from the handrail support a thin three-bay Gothick arcade with quatrefoils in the spandrels, more cusped panelling and rope-like borders. S transept added in 1830. The chancel, with three deeply moulded round-headed arches and aedicules, is by *P. J. Dodd*, 1890. – STAINED GLASS. Brought here in 1958 from the demolished Painestown Church (near Beauparc) and inserted in the transept; erected by Mary Harriet Bourke, decorative. *M. & R. Sillery*, 1862, Dublin.

MONUMENTS. Vestry: Mrs Anna Lambart †1820. Transept: four memorials to the Bourke and Connemara families; classical aedicules in green and white marble by *C. W. Harrison & Sons*. – CHURCHYARD. Attached to the outer wall of the church is a stone doorcase and three monuments, all brought here from St Collan's Church, Stackallen, when it was demolished in 1958. The doorcase is a moulded four-centred arch with a crowned head keystone and a hoodmoulding with vine-leaf label stops. On one side, the DEXTER MONUMENT, a coffin slab to the memory of Sir Richard Dexter, *c.* 1300; a cross and sword carved in relief. Apart from the first two words the inscription is in French and cut in Lombardic letters; the latter half is carved back to front. One explanation for this is that the original drawing given to the stonecutter may have been visible on both sides of the paper and, being ignorant of French, he copied the reverse side. On the other side is a simple slab with incised cross and border. The BARNEWALL MONUMENT, above the door, is a rectangular panel framed and recessed, flamboyantly carved in high relief with the Barnewall arms, a shield, helmet and crest with a falcon sitting on a plume of five ostrich feathers. A Latin inscription incised in Old English characters reads in translation 'the escutcheon of Sir Barnaby Barnewall Knt, second justice of the Kings bench [†1495], Margaret Plunkett was his wife'.

Set into the S wall of the vestry is a monument of late C12 or early C13 date, brought here in 1958 from Painestown Church; it is a coffin slab with a high-relief carving of a recumbent ecclesiastic.

ST PATRICK, SLANE PARISH CHURCH. Tall T-plan church and freestanding belfry, erected between 1798 and 1802 by Dr Michael O'Hanlon on a site donated by Earl Conyngham. According to tradition, Conyngham gave the site as a mark of gratitude to Fr O'Hanlon, who while living at the Irish college in Paris had obtained his release from a Parisian military tribunal in 1796. The freestanding rubble round tower, with its unusual ogee top, is reputedly the first belfry to be erected at a Catholic church in the diocese of Meath after the Reformation; it is also the earliest, if a rather unorthodox, example of a Celtic Revival round tower in Ireland. The church has a three-bay entrance front articulated as three thin pointed arches framing arches below and lancets above. The punched limestone finish may be a Victorian refacing. The body of the church is roughcast, with lancets and a triple-light E window. Simple interior, with a gallery in each arm of the T. Big plaster rectangular panels to the ceiling with moulded frames, guilloche borders and early Victorian Greek-revival detail.

SLANE BRIDGE. The medieval bridge of Slane is an impressive and picturesque structure which dominates the southern approach to the village. Over 500 ft (150 m) long, the bridge comprises thirteen arches, seven of which, on the down-river section, have pointed segmental intrados in the style of Trim's C14 bridge. Five of these arches are built in the river, and two are flood arches. The bridge was widened by 8 ft (2.5 m) on the up-river side during the C18 or C19. A bridge at Slane was destroyed by flood in 1330, and the earliest mention of a second bridge is a reference to 1599, when Hugh O'Neill planned to send his army across it into the Pale. However, the demise of Babe's Bridge, several miles up-river, *c.* 1500 and the absence of a bridge at Drogheda between 1472 and 1506 suggest that Slane would have been an important crossing point in the late C15. Similarities between the original down-river elevation and that of the bridge at Trim have prompted a late C14 attribution. As at Kilcarn (*see* Navan), the original up-river elevation is now obscured by a later extension, and the best view of Slane Bridge is to be had from the SE.

108 SLANE MILL. Below the village to the SE. A monument to the 'improving' spirit of the C18 Irish landowner. The desire to harness and exploit available natural resources to their full potential manifests itself in the innumerable mills, navigation schemes and market buildings which survive throughout the country, here in particularly impressive form. In early Georgian Ireland, livestock farming had predominated, and 'improving' efforts were largely concentrated on developing a market network of roads and canals. As the century progressed, however, grain- and flour-milling became more significant, especially from the 1780s onwards, with the protection of Grattan's Parliament and with increased demand for corn during the Napoleonic wars. Slane, thanks to its position on the Boyne and at the heart of a rich corn-growing area, provided the ideal site for a large mill. Since the beginning of the C18 a group of neighbouring landowners from Counties Louth and Meath had been involved in a navigation scheme to open the Boyne to traffic from Drogheda inland as far as Trim. David Jebb, Engineer to the Board, who superintended the canal works between Drogheda and Carrickdexter, was responsible for building and running the mill at Slane; most of the capital was provided by Townley Balfour of Townley Hall. When in 1785 Jebb had completed building a guard lock above Slane bridge, he was acting for the navigation board in the capacity of engineer, treasurer, secretary, toll collector and paymaster. The mill was completed long before this, in 1766, at a cost of £20,000.

Slane Mill is a large and very handsome building, a tall five-storey gabled block of squared and dressed limestone. The W elevation, which faces the bridge, is a regular nine-bay façade, the centre three bays projecting forward and crowned by an eaves pediment. It has raised quoins to ends and centre and moulded window surrounds throughout. The rear elevation is simpler and more fine. Eleven bays with no incident but the larger scaled windows in the central bay. Gibbs surrounds to the basement windows; sash windows in moulded surrounds on the upper storeys diminishing in size to the top. In 1776 Arthur Young dined with David Jebb and viewed the mill, which he described as 'a large and handsome edifice such as no mill I have seen in England can be compared with. The corn upon being unloaded is hoisted through doors in the floors to the upper storey of the building by a very simple contrivance, being worked by the water wheel and discharged into spacious granaries. From thence it is conveyed during seven months of the year to the kiln for drying. From the kiln it is hoisted again to the upper storey from thence by a small sifting machine into the hoppers to be ground and is again hoisted into the bolting mills to be dressed into flour, different sorts of pollard and bran ... it employs constantly 10 to 12, the flour is sent to Dublin and the manufacturing country to the north about Newry etc.' The MILLHOUSE where Young dined is presumably the small two-storey, three-bay house of coursed rubble behind the present millhouse, with a long W wing flanking the N wall of the latter building; a two-storey limestone block of cubic proportions, with a hipped roof and big 1790s sash windows.

SLANE GLEBEHOUSE. Erected in 1807 by a local architect, *Charles Henry Sillery*. Simple Georgian house of two storeys over a basement with a three-bay entrance front.

FENNOR CASTLE. 1 km S, on a rocky elevated site above the 57
Boyne. The ruin of a big early C17 house, incorporating in its fabric part of a late medieval tower house. Although often branded as fortified houses, this type of building is quite different from its predecessor the tower house and is in fact the first Irish dwelling type of any size to approach the modern conception of a 'house'. Fennor is a three-storey rectangular structure with big end chimneystacks and large square-headed windows. The N-facing elevation projects forward at the centre in the form of a narrow square tower, part of the old tower house, with a steeply battered base, pierced by a loop, and regular window openings above. This more than likely functioned as the stair well. Defence considerations are in evidence in the principal elevation, with its six square-headed windows all ranged along the first floor.

CARRICKDEXTER. 2 km W, in a charming but surely indefensible setting on a low fertile bank of the Boyne. Late medieval tower house with a later, probably C17 fortified house extension, erected, as its name suggests, by the Dexter family. Four-storey tower house, with the principal entrance on its N face and two square corner towers opposite each other at the NE and SW angles. Inside, the usual barrel-vaulted basement, two spiral staircases and a murder hole over the main entrance. Adjoining the tower to the E is a three-storey extension, with access to the tower on all floors. Three-bay front to the river, with a deep central projection on the N face, reminiscent of nearby Fennor, though this is on a smaller scale. Inside, some large chamfered limestone chimneypieces.

ROSNAREE CHURCH. 3 km SE. An early C19 chapel which contains a simple funerary monument that powerfully evokes the spirit of this rural parish during the Famine period. A large plain limestone slab set into the aisle before the sanctuary is simply inscribed in large plain letters 'Rev. Denis Walsh P.P. Died of cholera 1849'. The rigours of parochial service in the face of famine and epidemic are here graphically evoked. A marble monument on the wall of the church records that Denis Walsh was fifty-one years of age in 1849 and had been parish priest of Rosnaree and Donore for thirteen years. The church is a simple T-plan structure with panelled timber galleries in the arms and the sanctuary in the centre of the long S wall. The interior is unusual in having a pretty plaster groin vault throughout. STAINED GLASS. In the sanctuary, highly coloured pictorial glass by *P. X. Zettler*, Munich.

ROSNAREE HOUSE. 3 km SE. Small late C19 Italianate villa on a wonderful site S of the river Boyne and a short distance W from Newgrange. According to tradition, Rosnaree was the burialground of Cormac, high king of Ireland during the C3. The modern house is a rectangular two-storey block with a hipped roof, bracketed eaves and an advanced and gabled entrance bay. Cement-rendered, with stone corner quoin strips, a first-floor string-course and plain segmental-headed windows. A simple but elegant house.

YELLOW FURZE CHURCH. 4 km SW. The new brutalism in rural Co. Meath. A rectangular flat-roofed church in an aggressive modernist idiom. The entrance front is a blank rough-cast elevation with two registers of rectangular clerestory windows, flanked at one end by a pier-like masonry band, at the other by an entrance porch and tower. The tower and porch are the most effective elements in the design – a boxy geometric tower rises above a massive lintelled porch which is carried on three monolithic slabs radiating from the entrance – all in concrete formwork. Inside, the sanctuary is located diagonally opposite the porch, illuminated by long narrow lights cut back, concertina-like, from the corner of the building.

GERNONSTOWN CHURCH RUIN. 3 km NW. The ruin of a late medieval single-cell church with a barrel-vaulted chamber adjoining the E end of the N wall. Remnants of a large traceried W window.

9070

SLANE CASTLE* ME

3 km W of Slane

The view from the Bridge of Slane – water meadows, a weir, the slow, long curve of the dark waters of the Boyne, and a great house perched high above the river and backed by mature woodlands – offers an enduring image of much that was admirable in C18 Ireland. The weir improved the view from the house but was useful as well, providing the power that drove Slane Mill (*see* Slane), downstream below the bridge. The lush fields were created by new methods of farming recently introduced, and the banks of hanging woods – now sadly reduced by too much clear felling – spoke of a confident world that planted with an eye to improvement and profit in the future. Across the bridge, on the N bank, a theatrical battlemented gateway, over-scaled and over-simple, like the backdrop of a romantic opera, proclaims the presence of a lordly demesne. The gateway is by *Francis Johnston*: a tall round arch, flanked by attenuated hexagonal towers and battlemented screen walls ending in smaller turrets, one round and one square. The demesne wall runs up-hill to the 'square' in Slane village and after a few houses reappears on the S side of the Navan road. The Protestant church is behind the wall in the demesne for, as at Birr in Co. Offaly, the castle is very much a

*The mansion house was badly damaged by fire in 1991. The rooms in the E section were entirely gutted and the central section containing the hall and saloon survived only in part; the W section is largely unspoilt. A temporary roof was placed over the central and W section.

part of the township. After a further stretch of wall comes a second gate, also presumably by Johnston, with a lodge, and a square room with an oriel built over the entrance arch. This is the principal entrance to Slane Castle today.

When Arthur Young visited Slane in June 1776 it struck him as 'one of the most beautiful places', with grounds 'very bold and various, rising around the castle in noble hills'. At that time the castle was an old house built on the site of an earlier structure which had belonged to the Flemings, Lords Slane, who forfeited their estate in 1641. In the late C17 it became the property of the Conyngham family, descended from Alexander Conyngham, a Protestant clergyman in Mount Charles, Co. Donegal, who had twenty-seven children and died in 1660. His grandson, General Henry Conyngham, who brought a troop of 500 men from King James's army into the service of William III, was the first of the family to live at Slane. The house he built, Conyngham Hall, was constructed on the foundations of the Fleming castle between 1703 and 1709 and was built by a master mason called *George Garret.* This work survived until the 1770s. Drawings and a view of *c.* 1773 show that it was built on an L-shaped plan in a curious style that is a mixture of Anglo-Dutch motifs, with a hipped roof, cupola, central pediment and modillion eaves cornice sandwiched between four turrets with concave pyramid and bell-cast slate roofs arranged across the front. (A fragment of one window surround of this house still survives at half-basement level on the E side of the present house.) It was General Conyngham's grandson, William, the first Lord Conyngham, who owned the estate when Arthur Young visited Slane.

Lord Conyngham rarely resided at Slane but he spent huge sums of money on agricultural improvement and some time in the mid-1770s asked the celebrated English landscape gardener *Lancelot 'Capability' Brown* for designs for the layout of the estate, new stable buildings and a new castle. It is unlikely that Brown visited Slane (when offered £1,000 by the Duke of Leinster as soon as he should set foot in Ireland, he is said to have excused himself with the remark that he could not come as 'he had not yet finished England'), and all that was built according to his design was a long STABLE BLOCK in a weak Gothick idiom with a crenellated pediment in the centre and ogee label mouldings. The woods seem to have been planted and laid out to designs of the Irish gardener *John Sutherland.* In 1773 and 1775 *James Wyatt* provided a scheme for the decoration of the old hall in the house, but, whatever was planned for the house, nothing was completed by the time of Lord Conyngham's death in 1781. The castle that exists today was begun by Lord Conyngham's nephew, Francis Burton, who succeeded his uncle as second Baron, and the interior was completed by his son, third Baron and first Marquess Conyngham, *c.* 1800. As two men built the house, so two architects are largely responsible for its design: the shell of the building is by James Wyatt, who returned to Slane to work for

Slane Castle, from J. N. Brewer's *Beauties of Ireland* (1825)

the second Baron in 1785, after an interruption of ten years; and some of the interiors are by *Francis Johnston*, who completed the house for the first Marquess.

Slane Castle is an important monument in the history of Irish taste, as it is one of the earliest picturesque houses in the country built in a consciously neo-medieval style. The buildings which precede it, Moore Abbey at Monasterevan, Co. Kildare, and Castle Ward at Strangford, Co. Down, are tame by comparison with what is attempted here. On the river side, Slane has a bold silhouette, with a battlemented round tower breaking forward in the centre of the S front, two round turrets rising behind it, and broad square turrets securing the corners at either end. Seen from below it rises up as a tall four-storey block, with two big rooms, one above the other, in the round tower. The side elevations are less striking, three-storey Georgian blocks with plain windows, a battlemented parapet and square towers at each end; the entrance front, facing N, is a long, dull design with pairs of square turrets flanking a flat façade. Wyatt at the time of this design was certainly not the inspired Gothic Revivalist of Fonthill Abbey or Ashridge, and his early castle-style house at Slane seems a little dour.

It is perhaps unfair to blame Wyatt for all this dullness, as his schemes were restricted by two factors: first, by the determination of Lord Conyngham to use part of the foundations and upper walls of the older house, and second, by an earlier unsuccessful attempt at rebuilding which seems further to have limited the scope of his proposals. The earlier rebuilding was the work of an architect called *Robinson*, one of whose plans is scathingly endorsed by Wyatt 'of no use whatever'. It seems possible that this Robinson was Robert Robinson, one of Capability Brown's principal draughtsmen in the 1750s, and it may be that, as Brown would not come to Ireland, a younger designer who had been associated with him came in his place. If this were the case, then the long flat front of Slane with its four towers may derive ultimately from Brown's own designs for the house. A survey of the castle drawn by Thomas Penrose in 1783, long after Robinson's work had stopped, shows the L-shape of the old house, lying along the line of the E and N fronts of the present castle; it had classical Gibbs surrounds to its windows (though it is not clear whether these were Garret's work of 1703 or Robinson's remodelling) and square tower-like extensions at each corner – a motif not unknown in early C 18 houses in Ireland, occurring at the original L-shaped house at Borris, Co. Carlow. Every architect who made proposals for Slane converted these square rooms into turrets and filled out the plan to make a regular rectangle. In 1783 *James Gandon* produced a design very like what Wyatt was to build, and Wyatt's work was carried out in 1785 and 1786. He took down the front of the rebuilt house to basement level and the other parts to the level of the main floor.

Perhaps from an employer's point of view, the skill of the English architect lay in his ability to bring order out of confusion. The plan of Slane today offers no hint of its messy and protracted genesis, for Wyatt contrived a regular late C 18

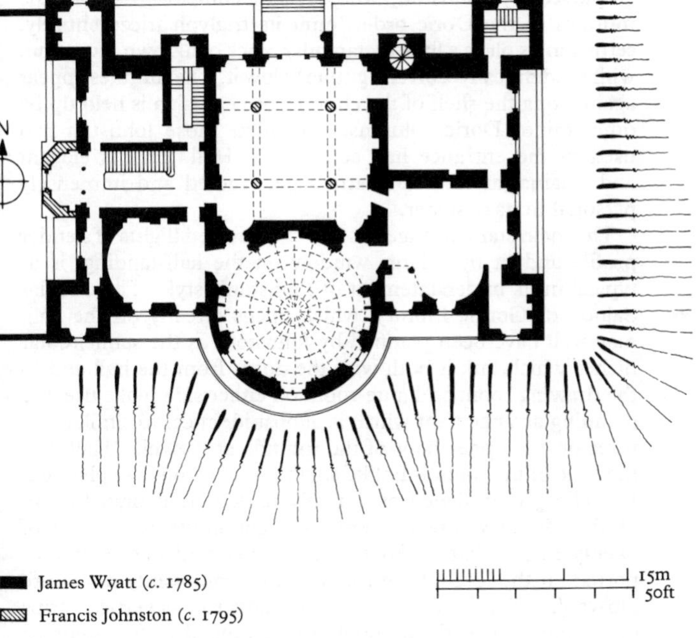

Slane Castle. Plan

country-house plan out of the old foundations. It is in effect an up-date on the well-tried double-pile plan: a central hall with a round saloon behind it and two rooms on either side, divided on the W by the principal staircase. Wyatt had made careful designs for elaborate neoclassical plasterwork of an Adamesque character for the old building, but the interiors of the new house were finished in an understated way, with reticent six-panelled doors with narrow beads and mouldings, shallow room cornices and plain flat ceilings. One wall of the ante-room was built in a shallow segmental line, and the drawing room was planned as a rectangular room with a semicircular apse on the longer side. Otherwise the rooms were plain. Only the hall, the main staircase and the Gothic Saloon depart from this norm. The first two are the work of Francis Johnston, who came to work at Slane in 1795. Johnston's hall is a characteristic piece of work in which the shallow surface and deliberate contrast of plan and decorated areas – so much a part of early neoclassical taste – are skilfully employed. Four baseless fluted Doric columns support shallow and cleanly defined plaster beams which divide the ceiling into nine parts: the central one is square with a flat rosette and circular fan in the middle. Recessed rectangular panels and arches overlaid with ropes of oak leaves alternate along the walls, and big mahogany doors are set within the arches in each corner of the room. The room cornice picks up but only hints at the Doric of the columns, for it is one of those elided designs, so much employed by Johnston, who is here content to quote the mutules of the Doric order, omit its triglyph frieze entirely, setting in its place a little rectangular block of his own invention, with academically 'correct' guttae below it. The mutules appear again along the shelf of the chimneypiece, which is held up by other minor Doric columns, not unlike those Johnston had used in the entrance hall at Townley Hall. This is elegant and original architecture; articulate, studied and immensely personal to its designer.

The main stair, arranged as two cantilevered flights of slender profile and lit by a large window on the half-landing, is as typical in its understatement of Johnston's style. The circular
88 Saloon or Gothic Library, which opens directly off the hall, may well have been planned by Johnston, as the semicircular niches which link it both with the doors from the hall and to the drawing room and ante-room on either side make use of a planning arrangement which is almost identical to similar features on the upper floor of the rotunda at Townley Hall; but the style of the room is unlike anything Johnston ever planned. Its ceiling is designed as a richly undercut, if unhistorical, Gothic dome whose plasterwork accommodates a series of twenty ribs, radiating from a central pendant boss and supported, at the level of the room cornice, on twenty miniature fan-vaults. Slender cluster-column shafts run as vertical strips down the wall, with the bookcases arranged in four-centred Tudor archways, surmounted by miniature pinnacles and

cresting. Only the wide and low chimneypiece, a tripartite design supported by caryatid herms, survives from an earlier arrangement of the room. The Gothic decoration is probably by *Thomas Hopper* and was carried out in 1813. The arrangement of the elements of the room, including the ceiling, closely resembles his Norman library at Gosford Castle, Co. Armagh, building from 1818. A rather incongruous Gothic arcade was cut into one side of the apse in Wyatt's drawing room about the same time; this too is presumably by Hopper. The kitchen offices are served from a recessed yard on the W of the house. The lower hall, under the entrance hall, has four elephantine columns in limestone to support the paved floor above.

STABANNAN

LO *0090*

STABANNAN PARISH CHURCH (C of I). The ruined tower of a Board of First Fruits church erected here in 1826. Of two stages, harled, with limestone trim, pointed window and clasping buttresses rising to tall finials.

STABANNAN CATHOLIC CHURCH. 1884–7 by *W. H. Byrne & Son*. Regular Gothic church, comprising a five-bay lancet hall with steeply pitched roof and lower chancel. A three-stage belfry tower, nicely detailed, with a solid little broach spire, flanks the entrance gable. Of rock-faced limestone, with limestone ashlar trim. Triple lancet windows to each gable. Inside, a pointed chancel arch carried on colonnettes with bishop's head corbel stops. Gothic reredos. – STAINED GLASS. In the chancel: the Crucifixion, St Nicholas and St Patrick, by *Mayer* of Munich.

ST MARY MANSFIELDSTOWN CHURCH RUINS. 3 km N. A delightful little ruined church set in a small wooded cemetery. Architectural history and great events are intermingled here, for the church is a monument both to the enduring taste for Gothic forms in Irish ecclesiastical architecture and to the impact that an event like the battle of the Boyne creates at local level. In 1690 Mansfieldstown Church had been ruinous since the 'warrs' of the 1640s owing to the poverty of a parish which contained only two Protestant families. In the year after the battle of the Boyne the church was extensively rebuilt at a cost of £140. A visitation of 1692 commented favourably on the parish and recorded that the church had a 'decent pulpit, a good communion table, a decent carpet and also a font of stone'. The walls date from 1691 and, like many C17 churches, it is a simple, single-cell structure built of rubble stone. What gives it special interest is its beautifully preserved E window, not C17 but 200 years older, a late Dec three-light window, with narrow octagonal mullions, double cusps and dagger lights in the intersecting tracery at its head. Here is a case of conscious preservation, or what might be called Gothic survival, in the classical age. The window was removed here from the previous church, and the corbel heads and label moulding which protect it outside are of 1691. Two twinlight cusped windows, one on each side of the nave, are C19 inserts. At the E end of the church, a memorial slab marks the Tisdall family vault, opened in 1702.

BRAGANSTOWN HOUSE. 3 km N. Attractive Tudor-Gothic house of the 1840s by *Thomas Smith*, perhaps incorporating the earlier Georgian residence of the Tisdall family, as suggested by the difference in the window levels on the garden front. All of two storeys, with label mouldings and cross-mullioned windows. Regular five-bay entrance façade, with a battlemented parapet, a modest central *porte cochère* and a gabled two-storey, bay-window corner turret at each end. The garden front is fashionably irregular, with a gable and large bay window as an asymmetrical incident. Corbelled turret shafts at each corner. Inside, the staircase is at right angles to the entrance hall, set behind a shallow Perp arcaded screen. STABLEYARD, SE of the house, erected in 1824; vernacular architecture in rubble stone with ashlar trim.

DRUMCASHEL HOUSE. 1.5 km W. Boxy little castellated house built in 1851 for Richard Macon. Two storeys and squarish in plan, three bays by five, with a small three-storey tower, also square, set back in the centre of the entrance front. Castellated porch protected by crossed arrow loops. Regular battlements entirely hide the roof, and hoodmouldings decorate every window. Dinky is the only word for this small castle: stylistically forty years out of date when it was built, and now derelict.

52 ROODSTOWN CASTLE. 2.5 km W. Neat small tower house, probably mid-C15, well preserved by the Board of Works. Of crisp rubble masonry, with finely chiselled limestone trim. Four storeys, with a barrel-vaulted basement and two square turrets set asymmetrically at the NW and SE corners of the plan. The NW tower houses garderobes, and the SE contains the stair, which as usual is spiral and communicates directly with the door, here located on the castle's E face. The staircase is protected by a murder hole directly over the door, and when Thomas Wright sketched the castle during the 1740s a machicolated box projected from the wall-walk above. This has now gone. The corner turrets have plain loopholes. Five trefoil-headed windows, either single or paired, and one cross-mullioned windown on the S face lit the main rooms. The wall-walk provides a fine view over the flat lands of Louth.

DROMIN CHURCH RUINS. 2.5 km S. The site of a C6 monastery founded by St Finian, the saint who quarrelled with St Columba in the famous argument over manuscript copyright, resulting in a war between Leinster and Connaught and Columba's self-imposed exile in Iona. The present ruin is much more recent, and the surviving cutstone details can be no earlier than C15 in date. Ruinous by 1539, the church was repaired in 1622. In the churchyard are some early C19 tombstones, with naive carvings of the Crucifixion, angels and cherub heads.

ST JOSEPH, DROMIN. 2.5 km S. 1826. Early C19 harled T-plan church with Y-traceried windows. At the E entrance end, a four-stage Gothic tower of 1843. Coursed rubble with extensive limestone trim and a slated needle spire, added in 1877, when the church was partially rebuilt. A pleasant building.

RICHARDSTOWN CASTLE. 1.5 km SW. A complicated battlemented house of at least four periods. Rather bulky and messy at the back. The oldest part is a four-storey tower house, not unlike Smarmore (*see* Ardee), but taller and with four circular corner towers where Smarmore has two. Perhaps C14 or C15 in origin. Immediately N of the tower house, and attached to it, is a substantial Georgian block. Ample in its proportions, with a bland three-bay, three-storey front of *c.* 1770. By early in the next century such a frank conjunction of castle and country house offended against good taste. The Georgian block was then given battlements and the tower house was tidied up, with the same battlements as the house and lancets in the round towers filled with quarry glass to give it a picturesque and cosy look. Turrets and further picturesque lights were added to the walls about the house at this time. By perhaps 1860, taste had changed again: the early C19 castellation seemed too tame, so the Victorian proprietors rebuilt the back of the Georgian house in a bigger and more aggressively castle style. Their additions have large stone mullioned windows and a heavy square bay projecting from a battlemented gable on the N front. They also added a castellated porch to the front door. The entire house has recently been covered in an unsympathetic render of rough-cast cement and gravel, giving a homogeneous furry look to the place.

STACKALLEN HOUSE ME *9070*

Gustavus Hamilton, the builder of Stackallen House, was a man 60
very much at the centre of Irish Protestant affairs in the later C17. His mother was the daughter of Sir John Vaughan, governor of the city and county of Londonderry; he became a captain in the army in the reign of Charles II; attended the Duke of Ormonde as Chancellor of Oxford University, and there took the degree of D.C.L. in 1677. On the outbreak of the Williamite wars he was chosen to be governor of Enniskillen. He defended Coleraine and Enniskillen against Jacobite attack in 1689, commanded a regiment at the battle of the Boyne – when his horse was shot from under him – and, in leading his troops, waded through the Shannon at the capture of Athlone. On the conclusion of the war, Hamilton received large grants of lands out of the forfeited estates in Co. Meath. Under Queen Anne he became a Privy Councillor and rose in the army to the rank of major general. He took part in the wars against Louis XIV and in 1715, on the accession of George I, when he was already seventy-six, was raised to the peerage as Baron Hamilton of Stackallen. Two years later he was advanced to the dignity of Viscount Boyne. He died in 1723 at the age of eighty-four.

Stackallen is one of the few surviving early classical country houses in Ireland. On the assumption that Lord Boyne would only have built such a grand house after he had been raised to the peerage, the date is usually given as *c.* 1716, yet his age at that time and the style of the building both suggest an earlier period. Certainly this is the house of a victorious military commander, U-shaped but designed to appear as a massive cubic block, with two main fronts facing S and W, each of three storeys and crowned by the steeply pitched roof of French and Dutch C17 houses, with a projecting eaves cornice of enlarged dentils and a broad eaves pediment in the middle of each front. The centre three bays are slightly advanced on both façades, with seven windows across the S and nine on the W, which was originally intended to be the entrance front. The architecture here is slightly more elaborate: the corners and the breaks in the façade are marked by quoins, which are missing on the corners of the other front; the windows are bound together by a continuous full cornice, extending the length of the façade, and the sills are of an early moulded type. On the S front the sills and the cornices are just flat bands, and there is an open basement area, which is not exposed on the other side. Gustavus Hamilton's coat of arms, halfed with that of his wife, Elizabeth Brooke of Brookborough, is set in an oculus in the pediment of the W front.

Somewhat old-fashioned for 1716, this architecture is the culmination of a type of C17 house based on the example of Sir Roger Pratt, Robert Hooke and other Restoration builders, of which Eyrecourt, Co. Galway, Ballyburly, Co. Offaly, Beaulieu (q.v.), not twenty miles from here, and the Red House at Youghal, Co. Cork, are noted examples. The arrangement of the windows in all these houses differs significantly from buildings of the Georgian period and is marked by the fact that the ground-floor and first-floor windows – and therefore the storeys – are of equal height. At Stackallen they are all sash windows with fifteen panes of glass, and only the top floor reduces in size to sashes of nine panes. From a stylistic point of view there is no reason why Stackallen should not have been built quite soon after Hamilton was granted his Meath estates in the early 1690s, and a successful figure in public life might be expected to build on his new property in his middle age rather than wait until much later. As neither the coat of arms on the façade nor the one on the ceiling of the staircase in the house incorporates a nobleman's coronet it would seem that they were put in place and the house was completed before its builder became a lord, and since a dated gutter head of 1712 has been found, the years 1710–12 seem the most likely date.

The interior of Stackallen is dominated by one of the largest staircases in the whole of Ireland, one broad, long flight rising within a deep rectangular well and entirely surrounded by a
63 timber landing at first-floor level. The ceiling above is a vast flat area, richly ornamented with heavy plasterwork: pulvinated

oak-leaf borders, whose corners are cut as convex quadrants and filled with daisy-like flowers, trophies of musical and martial instruments, trombones, trumpets, cannon, a medieval helmet and powder charges. The Hamilton crest of an oak-tree, with a cross-saw through the trunk and the motto 'Through', and Gustavus Hamilton's and Elizabeth Brooke's coats of arms are joined in the centre of the ceiling.

A show staircase is very much a feature of English late C 17 houses; Lord Boyne must have known many, and his own great stair, though unique in its plan, takes its place logically, in point of scale, beside many other examples in Britain. It is not clear, however, how far the present arrangement matches what was originally planned. The stair has a pair of banisters to each tread, some fluted and some plain, Corinthian column newel posts, and a swept handrail. But the changes in pattern are illogical and not part of a clearly explained design, so it may be that the stair was reworked later in the C 18. When the entrance was moved from the W to the S front, a pair of Ionic columns was introduced as a screen wall to open the new hall directly into the staircase space. Other alterations no doubt took place at this time. It also seems likely that the full plan for Stackallen was never finished: the house reads as a great cube, and would logically have been designed as a suite of three rooms on the E and W fronts, set back to back, with the present entrance hall and the deep staircase between. As built, the house lacks a full range of rooms on its E side, so that the r. side of the present entrance front is no more than one room deep.

STAMULLEN

ME *1060*

Small and unpretentious village, noteworthy for two fine sculptural monuments in the ruined medieval parish church.

STAMULLEN FORMER PARISH CHURCH. On a small grassy hill at the heart of the village is the ruin of a substantial late medieval church. Documents record that in 1183 Hugh de Lacy granted the parish church of Stamullen to the Augustinian abbey of Colpe near Duleek. The existing ruinous church appears to date to the C 15. A long nave-and-chancel structure, with two pointed-arch entrances at the W end of the nave. In the E window are fragments of limestone mullions, and in the S wall of the nave the remains of an ogee-headed twinlight window. In the S wall of the chancel, two large round-headed relieving arches which formerly housed monuments. Adjoining the chancel on the S is the Preston Chantry Chapel, dedicated to St Christopher. Stamullen was the burial place of the Prestons of Gormanston Castle. Also ruinous and now roofed by corrugated plastic, this room houses two of the most interesting funerary MONUMENTS in North Leinster. Double slab altar 41
tomb of a Preston knight and his lady, *c.* 1540. The knight

wears an unusual suit of foreign 'white armour', whose forms have been highly stylized and mannered by the sculptor. Notice particularly the headpiece, with jewelled cheek flaps, and the bordered plates at the shoulders, elbow and knees. Indeed this heavily protected C16 figure looks not unlike an American footballer of the C20! He carries a loose sword and a dagger tucked into his belt, and his feet rest on a lion. The Preston lady wears a jewelled coronet set on a spotted veil. She wears a long gown with a tight bodice, wide turned-back cuffs and a loose, full skirt, gathered at the centre to show a pleated underskirt. Her feet rest on a dog. Devilish imps pluck at the cushions placed under both figures' heads. – The tomb cover of a CADAVER MONUMENT, probably of mid-C15 date, and as such one of the earliest cadaver tombs in Ireland. No fragments of the tomb-chest survive and therefore no inscriptions that might identify the monument. However, it is clear from the size of the slab and its elaborate carving that it was originally an impressive tomb. The slab is carved with a life-size female skeleton enfolded in a vermin-infested shroud. This lurid depiction of man's mortality is characteristic of continental funerary sculpture in the wake of the Black Death and indeed throughout the C15. The monument closely resembles an effigy at Beaulieu (q.v.).

ST PATRICK, STAMULLEN PARISH CHURCH. Very tall T-plan church, begun by the Rev. Patrick Nowlan in 1831 and dedicated in 1835. Major renovations were carried out in 1961, when a new sanctuary and baptistery were built. Harled, with limestone quoins, it retains its early C19 roof of graded slates. Square-headed entrance. Lancet windows. Inside, a decorative plaster rib-vault. – REREDOS. Large painting of the Crucifixion, hung in a massive and very ugly frame. The painting, which is in the manner of the C17 Bolognese classicists, was the gift of Lord Gormanston, who also contributed to the construction of the building. – STAINED GLASS. Transepts: 1928; vivid jewel colouring in the manner of Clarke studios. – MONUMENT. The Rev. Patrick Nowlan †1863 by *Farrell & Son.*

STEDALT HOUSE. 1 km W. In 1836, several decades before the erection of the present house, Stedalt was the seat of W. Walsh Esq. Later it became the home of the Tunstall-Moore family. It is a large two-storey house in the Italianate idiom favoured by railway architects and engineers during the 1860s and 70s. A seven-bay, two-storey block with an asymmetrical entrance front, the two northernmost bays advanced, with a heavy Gothic porch filling the angle made with the main block. The house is rendered, with rock-faced limestone quoins and string-courses. Regular segmental-headed plate-glass windows, a bracketed eaves cornice and Italianate chimneys. The garden elevation is symmetrical, with broad canted bay windows at either end on the lower storey. Near the village, the entrance to the Stedalt CARRIAGE YARD is an attractive three-bay rubble-built elevation with a central carriage arch.

STREET

WM *3070*

Two mottes in the village of Street recall a Norman presence here, as does the name of Delamer, the principal local landowners until the C19. About 1270 William Delamer, a soldier of Street in Co. Westmeath, endowed and founded the Franciscan abbey of Multyfarnham.

STREET PARISH CHURCH (C of I). Simple hall and tower church with flanking rooms around the tower and a late C19 interior. Three-bay hall, lit by round-headed Y-tracery windows, with a round chancel arch and three round-headed graded lancets at the E end. – MONUMENT. Miss Thomazin Crofton †1767, aged nineteen.

ST MARY, STREET PARISH CHURCH, BOHERQUILL. 2.5 km N. Gabled T-plan church, cement-rendered, with lancet windows and modern porches. Built in 1812; the chancel and sacristy were added in 1869 by *William Hague*, and the entire building was renovated and reroofed in 1932 by *Michael Grace*.

DARAMONA. 0.5 km N. Early to mid-C19 classical villa built as a rectangular block across the front of an earlier house. The older has been demolished, leaving a surprisingly neat villa with a three-bay front and two-bay sides. Cement-rendered, with horizontal channelling to the ground floor, an emphatic eaves cornice and solid parapet. The windows have early Victorian architraves and shallow cornices. A massively detailed Tuscan porch, with coupled columns at each corner, dominates the front. This does not line in with any of the rest of the classical architecture on the façade and is presumably earlier. S of the house is an attractive screen wall terminating in a rusticated Italianate pavilion reminiscent, in some sense, of nearby Kildevin. Daramona was built by the Delamer family.

KILDEVIN. 2 km N. This curious house was built in 1833 by Robert Sproule, a fact proclaimed by a plaque above its entrance. Sproule was perhaps a member of the family of architects of that name. The house is a rectangular block of two storeys over a basement, built of squared local limestone rubble, with a shallow hipped roof and an emphatic eaves cornice supported on paired brackets. It has sash windows, wide three-bay front and rear elevations, and shorter three-bay sides. The house rises cleanly from its site without the clutter of other buildings beside it, but what makes it unique is the extraordinarily narrow centre bay, which is thrust forward as a light semicircle and rises to an attic storey with a classical balustrade at the top. This 'classical' tower occurs on both fronts, and the balustrade runs at roof level from the front to the back of the house. The effect is very odd and vaguely naval – as if someone wanted to remember a quarter-deck while pacing across the roof of his house – but there is no known story to explain the design. Semicircular balustrades flank the house at ground-floor level, yet despite these and the low windows there is something sombre and vaguely institutional in this design. The decayed state of the house in 1986 reinforced these impressions.

BOHERQUILL CASTLE. 2.5 km N. Ruined late medieval tower house with the foundations and part of the wall of a large bawn, built on a long low earthwork. The tower is rectangular in plan, approximately 27 ft by 10 ft (8 m by 3 m) internally, of three storeys over a now ruined vaulted basement. Built of limestone rubble masonry laid on regular courses and battered at the base. A spiral stair was located at the NW corner and a chimney in the N wall. What cutstone detail survives is crisply executed and probably C16 in date: an ogee-headed angle loop, a cusped single-light window and some pocked tooling to the chimneypiece corbels. The crease-line of a tall pointed gable indicates the former presence of an addition to the tower within the bawn.

COOLAMBER MANOR. 3 km NE. A late example of Regency classicism, built by Major S. W. Blackhall *c.* 1830 to designs of *John Hargrave*. Two features of Coolamber are of interest: its style and its plan. Hargrave is noted for a thin, somewhat reticent type of late classical architecture which frequently avoids the use of any identifiable order. His buildings are given a certain visual structure by shallow giant-order pilasters – Moate Courthouse is an example in Co. Westmeath – but often these pilasters have no proper capital and no proper entablature. This is the case at Dungannon Courthouse, Co. Tyrone, and also here. Coolamber is an elegant, rather low-looking house with the air of a marine villa. Two storeys high, with a three-bay front and five-bay side elevation broken by a shallow segmental bow at its centre. Giant-order pilasters divide each bay on the front but do not appear to support anything, as Hargrave – and this is his handwriting – checks back the eaves cornice and blocking course round each pilaster and checks back the pilasters themselves from the end of the façade, so that each corner becomes an elaborately stepped play of lines. This delicate architectural idiom is somewhat at variance with the size of the house, for Coolamber is built on an ample plan. For a start, it has an entire basement storey hidden below ground, and in contrast to the usual late C18 plan of three rooms built back to back with three more, the plan here is half as large again, three rooms long by three rooms deep. This gives rise to an interesting proto-Victorian country-house plan, as there is necessarily a central vestibule space in the very middle of the house, which Hargrave lights not by opening it up into an enormous two-storey hall, as Sir Charles Barry or Charles Langan would do, but by placing a large double-return staircase in the middle of one side, lit by a huge tripartite window. The ceiling here is decorated with a Greek key pattern and simple foliate motifs. The entrance hall has a curved wall with niches flanking its inner door, though the porch outside is modern. In the later C19 all the architect's care in devising this subtle plan was spoilt by the addition of two lumbering stone-built blocks of bedrooms at the NW corner of the house. A two-storey courtyard of stables with pedimented archways stands N of the house.

SUMMERHILL

ME *8040*

The inhabitants of Summerhill may well either thank or damn fate for their charming but sleepy environment. What might have been Ireland's answer to Blenheim or Versailles rarely sees the clamour of coach and camera; instead Summerhill preserves the quiet leisured ambience of an Irish country village. The great mansion built at Summerhill in the 1730s and twice burnt in the C 19 and C 20 is now entirely demolished. Its dramatic central avenue, a vista designed to dominate the village, now focuses absurdly on a modern bungalow. Indeed the village itself, one long wide street with a narrow tree-lined green running down the centre, on axis with the avenue, functioned as a punctuation mark in this great baroque layout. The existing three-storey Georgian houses and single-storey estate cottages date to the late C 18 and early C 19.

Summerhill was designed *c.* 1730 for Hercules Langford Rowley, probably by *Sir Edward Lovett Pearce*, and was completed by *Richard Castle* (*see* pp. 41–3 and 50). The design owed much to the spirit of Vanbrugh, in whose office Pearce had trained and whose sense of drama he inherited. The house consisted of a large two-storey, seven-bay block with a Corinthian giant order framing the three centre bays, two massive square towers at each end, and great arched chimneystacks. This was joined by curving two-storey wings to end pavilions with shallow domes. Beyond the house, on the extreme l. and r., two grandiose pedimented archways are all that now survive of Ireland's grandest classical house. At a width of 30 ft (9 m) each, more than half the frontage of a modern bungalow, these fragments give some idea of the massive scale of Pearce's design. They are boldly treated in rusticated limestone, each with a tall round-headed arch, flanked by circular niches on two levels, and crowned by a massive pediment. Summerhill never failed to provoke comment from discerning visitors: the English classical architect C. R. Cockerell considered 'few sites more magnificently chosen' and sketched the house in his journal; Mrs Delany, whose Palladian tastes are well known, admitted its splendour while finding it 'large but not pleasant'. Perhaps it was too baroque, but its qualities evidently appealed to the Empress Elizabeth of Austria, who rented Summerhill for two hunting seasons in 1879 and 1880. The house was burnt accidentally *c.* 1800, remodelled in the C 19 and burnt again in 1922. Its spectacular ruin was demolished in the 1950s.

In the demesne NW of the site is the GOTHIC MAUSOLEUM. A dedication tablet, now gone, read 'This beautiful building was designed and executed by the Right Honorable Hercules Langford Rowley in 1781 when he had it dedicated as a general burying place for his Langford Rowley family at Summerhill and any or all of his attached friends who lived respected and useful lives'. Long hall, 40 ft by 110 ft (12 m by 33 m), of brick and stone, with a semicircular apse in the centre of the long N wall and a naive Gothic arch to the entrance front. A nice instance of the mid-Georgian layman's understanding of 'Gothic'. A broken ornament lying near the entrance is a weird and grossly simplified adaptation of a crocketed pinnacle. The roof of the mausoleum had a plaster groined vault, and the windows were filled with variegated glass. Inside, at the E end, niches were provided for the busts of those interred. The mausoleum also boasted a fountain with a weeping female figure designed by *Thomas Banks* in 1791. Vault, busts and Banks' fountain have long since disappeared.

LYNCH'S CASTLE. E of the entrance avenue to Summerhill. An intriguing ruin of at least two distinct building periods. Begun in the late C 16 by the Lynches of the Knock, feudal tenants of the Wellesleys at Dangan, and repaired as a residence after the Cromwellian wars by Bishop Jones. The Lynches' original work is well preserved: a rectangular four-storey tower house, vaulted at second-floor level, with the entrance on its W side. The spiral stair is located in the NW angle, a mural passage and garderobe at the NE, and several large fireplaces in the S wall whose big chimneystack survives. The castle is a strikingly late example of a tower house and one of exceptional quality. Details in the construction are quite unlike C 16 work in Ireland and are closer to Scottish models. The spiral stair, for instance, is built to provide a round newel instead of the usual Irish arrangement of bringing each step slab to a sharp point, and the stonework of the windows is surely the most sophisticated in the northern Pale. Remarkably elegant are, on the N face, a thin round-headed loop splayed externally towards the bottom, and a crisp arrow loop cut into the corner stones at the upper SE corner of the tower. On the upper storeys are several pointed windows with dished spandrels, hoodmouldings and pocked tooling to the frames.

Adjoining the tower at the SW angle is a second, large four-storey tower, its own SW angle adjoined by a third tower, giving a step-like plan. Both towers, now very much ruined and ivy-grown, were gabled and had large mullioned windows of two and three lights. The southernmost tower, some 15 ft (4.5 m) square, contained a timber stair rising round an open wall. Whether the two towers were built at the same time is unclear. *The Civil Survey* of 1652 indicates three square towers, two of them unroofed, which would suggest that Bishop Jones made the original tower his residence and that the two additional towers had been added by the Lynches some time between 1600 and 1640. A plaque attached to the N wall may or may not be misleading: it bears the O'Neill arms and commemorates Luke Wye, priest, with the date 1636. Wye was apparently a chaplain to the Co. Down O'Neills, who spent some years skirmishing in the neighbourhood. Their relationship with the Lynches is not known, but the date 1636 and the presence of a mason at the castle may provide some key to the date of the later buildings. Large and spacious stairhalls were common in England from the late C16, but not in Ireland, and, allowing for the usual delay in stylistic developments, 1636 would seem a reasonable date for the two towers. Conjecture aside, the castle illustrates neatly the departure of Irish architecture from the medieval models into the Jacobean age.

CHURCH OF OUR LADY OF LOURDES. 2km N. 1911 by *W. H. Byrne & Son.* Cruciform church of rock-faced limestone. Tower and broach spire with lucarnes, flanking the entrance gable. Four-bay nave opening through paired round-headed arches into shallow transepts and terminating in an apsidal sanctuary. Byrne's brand of minimal Romanesque, with round-headed lancets to the nave and entrance gable and geometric windows to the transepts. Nice open kingpost roof with a border of pierced quatrefoils. The FORMER CHAPEL, cruciform, with Y-tracery windows, stands in a field S of the church.

COOLE CHAPEL. 2.5km S. Plain harled four-bay lancet hall, with a four-centred entrance arch and lancet windows. Built *c.* 1840 to replace the former T-plan thatched and mud-walled building. According to tradition, the chapel was opened on the day of the great Repeal meeting at Tara, 15 August 1843, after which the congregation walked the twelve miles to Tara.

CHURCH OF THE NATIVITY, MOYNALVEY. 3km E. 1901 by *W. H. Byrne & Son.* Small bellcote hall of rock-faced limestone rubble, with lancets and buttresses to the side elevations and the classic Byrne motif of a circular window within a relieving arch, to the entrance gable. – CROSS. In the churchyard is the head of a cross, carved with the Sacred Heart at the centre, surrounded by instruments of the Passion; a naive work, probably of the C17.

AGHER PARISH CHURCH (C of I). 3km SW. Small church in a secluded setting. Two-bay hall, harled, with limestone trim and a steep slated roof, erected in 1804 by the Winter family of Agher House and rebuilt by them in 1902, when a four-stage tower of limestone rubble was added to the W end. The latter has clasping corner buttresses to the lower stages with remarkably accentuated offsets at the angles, a square twinlight belfry and stepped battlements to the parapet. – STAINED GLASS. E window, brought here from the private chapel at Dangan Castle: St Paul preaching to the Athenians, in greys and brown by *Gervaise* after Raphael. – MONUMENT. C18 slate slab with armorial crest, to the Pratt family of Agher.

In the churchyard, the WINTER FAMILY CRYPT is a charming miniature Gothic building, like one of the designs from Thomas Wright's *Arbours and Grottoes* of the mid-C18, though clearly much later: the first interment was in 1804. Barrel-vaulted room with a three-bay battlemented frontispiece, the centre bay projecting with a pointed arch flanked by a pointed window on each side, a recessed quatrefoil above each opening.

AGHER NATIONAL SCHOOL. 3.5km S. Built in 1876 by the Winter family. A charming essay in the cottage picturesque.

Red brick, with yellow brick trim, and a steep slated roof. Brick gables, projecting porch, carved bargeboards and mullioned windows.

RAHINSTOWN HOUSE. 4 km SW. Designed by *Sandham Symes* *c.* 1870. Large and grandiose Italianate house, impressively sited at the end of a tree-lined avenue. Built to replace a Georgian Gothic house destroyed by fire, and thus flattered by mature planting. The estate was developed by Robert Fowler, Bishop of Killaloe (1725–1801), and has remained the home of the Fowler family since then. The existing house, built for another Robert Fowler, is a conservative design which marries late Georgian patterns with an up-to-date Italianate idiom of rectangular plan, tall, with three storeys over a basement, crowned by a shallow hipped roof with central chimneystacks and oversailing bracketed eaves. Rendered in Roman cement with sandstone dressings. The three-bay entrance front has sash windows, raised corner quoins and an emphatic first-floor string-course. A central emphasis is provided by a big square Tuscan porch with paired columns *in antis* and a bracketed pediment to the window above. The house is much deeper than it is wide, with a five-bay garden façade to the side, breaking at the centre into a shallow bow, expressed as a large tripartite window on the ground floor and sash windows above. In plan the house has a central spine, with three large reception rooms on the garden side, a vestibule, stairhall, library, back stair and gun room looking onto the office court. A columnar screen divides the vestibule from the stairhall, which has an elaborate cast-iron stair rail. The drawing room has a pretty Adamesque ceiling, chimneypiece and neoclassical joinery. Classical aedicule doorcases throughout and cornices filled with heavy moulded plasterwork.

9090 TALLANSTOWN LO

Small estate village situated at a crossroads beside the Glyde river. The centre of the village is an open triangle, bounded by rows of cottages which housed Lord Louth's estate workers. They are of the early C19, with steep slated roofs and large redbrick chimneys. The house at the NW corner beside the bridge was the Manor Court. Beyond the bridge the row of rubble cottages was erected in 1851 for the tenants of Rathbrist.

SS PETER AND PAUL, TALLANSTOWN PARISH CHURCH. Small low T-plan church, rendered, with limestone dressings. Originally a single-cell longitudinal church. Late C18, as suggested by two fanlit round-headed doorcases in the transepts. This was converted to a T-plan *c.* 1830 (*see* p. 64) and given a nice Gothic frontispiece at the bottom of the T with a triple-light Perp window, and paired buttresses at each end – almost like pilasters – with finials on top. The interior preserves a good timber Gothic reredos, 'recently erected' in 1855.

TALLANSTOWN CHURCHYARD (C of I). Flamboyant mid-Victorian Gothic gateway erected by tenantry in memory of William Filgate †1868. Thin pointed arch set in an exceptionally tall gabled hood, flanked with octagonal piers and pinnacles on either side.

LOUTH HALL. Set high on a bare hillside, an impressive castellated mansion whose long battlemented outline dominates the N approach to Tallanstown. The home of the Plunkett family, Lords Louth, from the later Middle Ages until early in the C20 and as such a rare instance of continuity of tenure in a country of successive confiscations. In the mid-C17 Lord Louth was a resolute supporter of St Oliver Plunkett, his kinsman, who as a Catholic Archbishop of Armagh stayed at Louth Hall.

The hall physically displays this continuity, consisting of the original Plunkett tower house, perhaps C14, a large mid-C18 house, and a new suite of late Georgian reception rooms added in 1805, all knit together by a rough-cast and battlemented skin. The Georgian house looks *c.* 1760. Long three-storey range, one room deep, with a scale-and-platt stair placed centrally on an axis with the entrance hall, forming a T on the rear elevation. The nine-bay entrance front is arresting but undistinguished, with an over-abundance of windows and a plain pedimented doorcase. Above the door are the Plunkett arms and motto, '*Festina Lente*'.

Inside, some delicate rococo plasterwork adorns two niches in a room at the NE corner, and the stair well has crisp neoclassical plasterwork. The tower house at the W end of the building was joined to the main residence and largely remodelled *c.* 1805, when it was given pointed windows throughout. Account books for the period 1805–8 record numerous payments for mason work and decorating materials for the 'new room', which were designed by *Richard Johnston*, elder brother of Francis Johnston. The first floor of the tower constitutes an elegant Gothic drawing room, roughly 25 ft (7.5 m) square, decorated with delicate plasterwork of oak garlands and acorns and with nice details such as fluted borders to the doors and chair rail. The bowed two-storey extension tucked in at the back between the stair well and the SE corner of the main house has similar Gothic features and is probably part of the same remodelling by Richard Johnston. The spiral stair which leads to the battlements of the tower is evidently a late C19 rebuilding, and the battlements of the main block appear to have been given a more exaggerated profile about this time. Two profiles can be traced in places at the top of the walls. At the rear of the house is a pretty artificial lake and to the W a regular stable court. All near-derelict at the time of writing.

GLYDE COURT. 2 km SE. Originally a seat of the Foster family, and known in the C18 as Rosy Park. In the C19 it became the home of the Upton family but was repossessed by the Fosters before 1868. A rambling two-storey house consisting of two very long narrow ranges joined at the N end by an entrance hall, an adjoining stair well and a small bridge of service apartments, giving an extended U-shape plan. The E wing, probably of late C18 or early C19 date, is plain, with fanlit doorcases and sash windows; the entrance front and W wing, which have tall curly gables and cement mouldings (architectural scenography, as there is no ridge or visible roof behind the gables), date from a mid-C19 Jacobean remodelling begun by the Upton family in 1843 and completed by the Fosters in 1868. The entrance front has a three-bay recessed centre screened by a three-arched porch – a little like one side of a cloister – flanked by the blank end gables of the E and W ranges. The W garden front is the house's most attractive feature: a long regular façade with a five-bay centre flanked on each side by deep three-light bows for the dining and drawing rooms and continuing for a further three bays on either side. Sash windows throughout, with blocked surrounds and decorative keystones on the ground floor. Shaped cement gables over the bows – but flat with the line of the front, not curved – and dormer windows lend picturesque interest to a roof-line which must previously have been plain. Inside, the principal rooms face W, flanked by a long corridor running N–S. At the S end of the range, the library, dining room and gallery pre-date the mid-C19 rebuild and are probably *c.* 1790. Otherwise the interior is almost entirely C19 in character, with four-centred arch openings, strapwork overdoors and a big Italianate pattern-book fireplace in the entrance hall.

RATHBRIST HOUSE. 1 km N. *c.* 1870. A minor Italianate villa: three-bay, two-storey over a basement, cement-rendered, with a shallow hipped roof, bracketed eaves and a pediment over the central bay. Corner quoins, central Tuscan porch and tripartite window above.

PHILIPSTOWN CHURCH RUIN. 1.5 km N. A simple and attractive church of the C15 or C16. The walls survive to eaves level and are built of uncoursed rubble. Opposing pointed arches in the N and S walls and a handsome cusped twinlight window of punched-dressed limestone in the S wall. Inside the doorway in the S wall is a limestone holy-water stoup with a carved human head on its outer face.

LISRENNY. 2 km S. Eight-bay, two-storey house with a N-facing entrance front, whose early C18 date is indicated by the narrow proportions of the first-floor windows. As is suggested by the chimneys, one at each gable and a third close to the E end, the building grew from a modest three-storey house. Remodelled in the C19, when two large mullioned bay windows were added to the later five bays. Between 1788 and 1798 William Filgate added a most impressive three-storey, seven-bay Georgian house to the gable end of the existing building, making the early house the stem of a great T-plan. Sadly this very substantial part of the house was demolished in 1974.

THOMASTOWN CASTLE/KNOCK ABBEY. 2.5 km NW. A typical union of house and castle, which supposedly marks the site of an abbey founded by Donough O'Carroll and Edward Kelly in 1148. The castle is a large keep built by the Bellew family during the C14 which later became the seat of the O'Reilly family. Adjoining the castle is a plain C18 three-storey house of seven bays, with extremely long sash windows on the lower storeys, diminishing abruptly to small rectangular windows on the top floor.

In 1858 the keep was castellated and extended by Miles O'Reilly to designs by *William Caldbeck*. The extension, which contained a library, oratory and living rooms, is a four-bay, two-storey block of coursed rubble, with a square corner tower at its N end, a battlemented parapet and pointed windows: all rather like a toy fort. The castle and its extension, but not the old house, were gutted by fire in 1923 and rebuilt by *W. S. Barber*.

TARA

ME *9050*

A place enveloped by legend and myth, Tara requires more of the imagination than the eye. A site of sustained settlement from the Iron Age through to the C11 A.D., this was the seat of the Irish High Kings and also one of the sites chosen by St Patrick to preach the gospel of Christianity. Today, although the hill, great in its breadth rather than its height, still commands spectacular views of the flat lands of Meath, the evidence for its royal and saintly past is scant. All that survives is a small passage grave and a series of low and much damaged ring forts. The evocative nomenclature – 'The Mound of Niall of the Nine Hostages', 'The Rath of the Synods', 'The Banqueting Hall' etc. – reflects C19 romantic antiquarianism rather than sober scholarly analysis. Nevertheless the combination of this elevated site with remembered myth and legend makes Tara for many people a place of powerful atmospheric character. Seen on a summer evening when a low sun points up the earthworks and promises the viewer the exhilaration of long and clear prospects across Meath it is indeed magical.

ST PATRICK (C of I). 1822. Small plain three-bay hall and three-stage tower, harled, with Y-tracery windows and quarry glass. Remarkable only for the range of blind windows which makes an attractive camouflage on the usual windowless N-facing wall, and for the late medieval window built into the W face of the tower. This has reticulated tracery and a hoodmoulding with paterae and label stops.

RIVERSTOWN CASTLE. 2 km W. Large C16 castle built by the Dillons. Now reduced to a great ivy-grown mass standing in a farmyard. A four-storey rectangular tower house with two big square turrets projecting from the S face and a circular stair turret projecting at the NE angle. Inside, the rooms were 15 ft (4.5 m) square, with the usual barrel-vaulted lower chamber subdivided by a timber floor. An extensive single-storey range stands to the W. Reputedly this was the birthplace in 1717 of the Irish antiquarian and classical scholar Robert Wood, whose publications on Baalbek and Palmyra were to play a significant part in establishing neoclassical concepts of architecture throughout Europe. It is intriguing to consider that classicism might spring from this bleak castle and that the development of the cult of Antiquity in England could owe some measure of its spirit to the ghosts of Tara.

ODDER CASTLE. 1.5 km SW. Not a castle but rather a modernized fortified house, probably of the early C17. Five bays and three storeys, a single gable-ended range with chimneystacks set diagonally at either end. Greatly altered *c.* 1880, when a large central stairhall was created. A slight dichotomy in the window proportions on each side of the doorway, with larger, more ample windows in the two right-hand bays, suggests that the modernization proceeded at different dates. Odder was originally the property of the Barnewells, who established an Augustinian convent here. In the grounds are some cutstone fragments of cusping with dished spandrels suggestive of the C15.

1080 TERMONFECKIN LO

Today, there is little in Termonfeckin to suggest that this was once a place of ecclesiastical significance. Its history begins in the C7 as the site of a monastery dedicated to St Fechin; later, in the C12, it gained an abbey of nuns dedicated to the Virgin, and in the later Middle Ages it was famous for the palatial seat of the Anglo-Irish Archbishopric of Armagh, sited here after the archbishops had found themselves estranged from the native primatial see in Armagh. The last resident primate was James Ussher, who died in 1656.

TERMONFECKIN CASTLE. Not the former residence of the archbishops, of which no trace survives; this building is a modest C15 tower house, extensively repaired by the Brabazon family in 1641. Of three storeys, crowned by a battlemented roof-walk, with one spiral stair in the NW corner and an octagonal garderobe turret at the SE angle. Each floor has one large chamber, with a smaller room adjoining it on the E, possibly an addition of 1641. The main feature of the castle is a remarkable corbelled vault in the upper chamber.

ST FECHIN'S CHURCH (C of I). A small church, rebuilt to designs by *Francis Johnston* in 1792, with a tower and broach spire of 1904 by another Armagh architect, *Samson Jervis*. The church is barn-like. A harled, four-bay hall, with timber Y-traceried windows in the S wall and a short gabled chancel added in 1862. The tower is of rock-faced limestone with diagonal buttresses, double-louvred belfry and a pinnacled broach spire of limestone ashlar. Inside, four monuments to the Brabazon and McClintock families are set neatly along the blank N wall. The doorway at the E end of the church is narrow and elegant and has a pointed tympanum with the distinctive trefoil division favoured by Cooley and Johnston, also seen at nearby Ballymakenny. Plaster rib-vaulting and Perp window to the chancel.

In the churchyard, affixed to a ruined gable, a classical aedicule to the memory of Christophilus Jenney † 1741.

HIGH CROSS. In St Fechin's Churchyard, NW from the church tower. By comparison with those at Kells and Monasterboice, Termonfeckin Cross is modest in scale, being no more than 9 ft (2.7 m) tall. Though the sandstone is worn in parts and the base is sunk in the ground, the cross is still complete, retaining an unbroken nimbus ring and cap-stone in the form of a miniature church. In contrast to the other crosses of North Leinster, the shaft has a pronounced taper and is decorated entirely with cord interlace and abstract patterns, contained by a double roll border which also surrounds the arms of the cross. The E face shows the Crucifixion, with a spear- and sponge-bearer; Christ in Glory is in the centre of the W side.

CHURCH OF THE IMMACULATE CONCEPTION. Designs were prepared for this church by the Drogheda architect P. J. Dodd in 1878, but the commission went to *William Hague*, who completed the building in 1883. A substantial and not unattractive church of rock-faced limestone situated on a wooded hill at the S end of the village. Tall, four-bay hall with shallow transepts and a lower chancel resulting almost in a T-plan. NW tower and octagonal spire beside the entrance gable. Plain Gothic in style, with corner buttresses, lancet windows and a big plate-tracery rose window in the gable. – ALTAR FURNITURE. In Caen stone, with yellow and white marble, by *W. H. Byrne*, with *Edmund Sharp* as sculptor. STAINED GLASS by *Mayer & Co.*

RATH HOUSE. 0.5 km N. An attractive mid-to late C18 gentleman's house. Of two storeys over a basement and double-pile in plan, the house has a five-bay entrance front with an advanced and gabled centre bay. Switch-back glazing to the fanlight and a lunette window in the eaves gable. Sash windows have been replaced by plate-glass.

NEWTOWN HOUSE. 1 km SE. Large rectangular mansion. Stuccoed, with Italianate detailing and a coherent architectural character. Two storeys throughout, with a shallow hipped roof, modillion eaves cornice and corner quoins. The two principal fronts are on adjacent sides. The entrance, W, is of three bays, with the centre slightly advanced and marked by a four-columned Ionic porch with a triple-light window above. Single-storey canted bay windows flank the porch. The garden façade, S, is simpler: a seven-bay, two-storey elevation with the central bay slightly advanced and supporting an eaves pediment. On ground-floor level a glazed porch in freestone, with a tripartite window above, fills the entire width of the central bay. It may be noted that on this front the three windows to the E are more widely spaced than those to the W of the porch, and this provides the key to the architectural history of Newtown House.

Despite appearances the building is of two dates. A survey of 1774 illustrates a two-storey, seven-bay house with a recessed three-bay centre and advanced gabled ends. This house belonged to the McClintock family, who sold it in 1852 to a Mr Ralph Smith. The Victorian Italianate house is Mr Smith's work, but a portion of the McClintock building survives at the E end of the S front. Inside this part of the house, which also has a basement from the C18, there is a handsome Georgian room with elegant proportions, six-panel doors, a modillion cornice and a rococo plasterwork centrepiece, all of later C18 character. The detail of the rest of the house, also classical, is heavier and clearly early Victorian. A large top-lit stair on a line with the hall is its best feature. Newtown is now a college of the Irish Countrywomen's Association, An Grianán.

BALLYMAKENNY CHURCH (C of I). 4 km W. 1785–93. Thin late Georgian Gothic, executed by the young *Francis Johnston* but to designs which *Thomas Cooley* had made for Primate Robinson, whose nearby seasonal residence was at Rokeby Hall. The Robinson coat of arms and the archiepiscopal insignia are set over the entrance. Although a prototype for the ubiquitous early C19 tower-and-hall-type church, Ballymakenny has a sparing elegance that surpasses all but the very best of its successors. A charming little building, which boasted one of the most authentic C18 church interiors to survive in Ireland. The attenuated proportions of the Gothic tower and spire make the church a prominent vertical accent in the surrounding countryside.

The plan is of a type much favoured by Cooley, found at Cappagh in Co. Tyrone (1768) and elsewhere: the entrance tower is flanked by small vestries with lean-to roofs that continue the line of the roof of the church itself. Thus the tower is contained within the main bulk of the building and is not freestanding as in the early C19 churches. On the side elevation, vestry and church appear as one four-bay unit, though within there are of course only three windows to the church – answered by blind niches on the N wall. The walls are of punched blue-grey limestone, with chiselled limestone trim. Windows have double Y-tracery, hoodmouldings and quarry glass. The interior is a simple hall, panelled to sill level, complete with plain box pews and a canopied three-tier pulpit and reading desk. Against the altar wall, a stuccoed Gothic reredos; five cusped niches framing the Lord's Prayer, the Ten Commandments and the Creed in gold Gothic characters on a black background. Decorative elements are minimal but effective. A simple drop motif forms a continuous cornice and also a border just above the timber panelling. Two slender ogee-headed niches flank the door, whose tympanum is decorated with a trefoil device repeated also on the outside door.

CARNTOWN CASTLE. 5 km W. Two storeys of a small and probably quite late tower house which now adjoins a modern farmhouse. Built of local slate and limestone, it was originally a three-storey tower. The entrance was formerly at the S end of the W wall and the stair was located at the SW angle of the tower. Twinlight window of punched-dressed limestone at first-floor level in the N wall. Fine triple-light window in the E wall with carved head corbels. The round-headed profile of the windows and the quality of stonework suggest a late C17 date.

SANDPIT CHURCH. 6 km W. 1846. To the passer-by, Sandpit Church will appear a very dull building: a six-bay gabled hall with tall four-centred windows and a squat E entrance tower, all rendered in cement. Hardly, it would seem, worth the bother of stopping. Step inside and all is transformed by a charming and beautifully preserved early Victorian interior, just as good 104
in its way as the Georgian elegance of Ballymakenny. A succession of the most slender clustered shafts, with leafy stylized capitals, steps down the church carrying pointed keel-like vaults over a broad nave and narrow aisles. The transverse ribs and rectangular panelling of the plaster vaults, all painted blue and white, create an effect of iced confectionery and focus the eye on a spiky pinnacled reredos against the altar wall. This is a nice example of mid-C19 joinery, with inset panels of painted mirror and glass intended to simulate inlaid brass. – The ALTAR is itself a regular late Victorian High Gothic design, as are the majority of the windows which now contain STAINED GLASS; the window immediately inside the entrance on the l. is the only one to retain its original pattern and clear glazing. The architect of this highly original design is not known.

TINURE CROSS

LO *0080*

ST MARY IMMACULATE. 1886–94 by *P. J. Dodd.* Cruciform Gothic church of rock-faced limestone with polished trim. Hard and brittle in its effect, with a tall slated roof and big geometric wheel window in the entrance gable. Cusped lancets to the nave, transepts and apse. Dodd had included a tower in his plan, but the thin three-stage belfry tucked in between the nave and E transept was added in 1914 by *J. V. Brennan.* The interior has a four-bay nave and paired two-centred arches opening into shallow transepts and an apsidal sanctuary. It is very dark owing to the quantity of stained glass.

MONASTERBOICE HOUSE. 2.5 km S. It was not possible to visit this house, which appears to incorporate a medieval tower house in its fabric. The house proper is of early C19 appearance, with twelve-pane sash windows and a shallow hipped roof. Regency-style bowed garden front. Three-bay glazed and arcaded porch to the entrance front, which sits awkwardly between two castellated bays on the l. and two standard sash bays on the r. Rubble folly tower and arch in the demesne.

TULLYALLEN PARISH CHURCH (C of I). 5.5 km S. First Fruits hall and tower church of 1814. Two-bay lancet hall, roughcast, with a three-stage battlemented belltower. The church was repaired in 1837 and received new seatings by *Joseph Welland* in 1857. Renovated in 1900 by *J. Brown* of Newry.

MELLIFONT PARISH CHURCH, TULLYALLEN. 5.5 km S. Tenders for a new front and bell turret at Tullyallen Church were invited in the summer of 1873. Presumably these referred to a proposed remodelling of an older chapel. The existing church is of 1898 and by *W. H. Byrne*. Modest Hiberno-Romanesque in style: a cruciform structure composed of a broad nave with shallow transepts and a wide chancel. Round-headed entrance arch and a sexfoil window to the entrance gable, which is flanked by a squat unfinished belltower. Rock-faced limestone masonry. Bright and attractive interior, lit by lancets and a round-headed E window. Timber panelled ceiling. Paired round-headed arches opening into transepts. Reredos, altar and side altars all of 1900–5. STAINED GLASS. Nativity by *Mayer & Co.*, Munich. MONUMENT. Rev. Richard O'Sullivan P.P. † 1861; slate and marble. CHURCH RUIN. The ivy-grown ruin of a late medieval church, now featureless but for the fragment of a cusped sandstone E window of C15 or C16 date.

1080 TOGHER LO

ST COLUMKILLE. 1 km NE. 1866 by *John Murray*. Handsome Gothic Revival church of coursed limestone rubble, with a slender pinnacled broach spire that is visible for miles. Undoubtedly this is Murray's most accomplished design. Its architecture is steeped in the tradition established by A. W. N. Pugin twenty years before. Each element is lucidly expressed; there is a substantial, handsome character to the choice of mouldings and details and, inside, a Puginesque gradation of richness towards the sanctuary of the church. This is a manner first developed in Ireland by the architect to the Ecclesiastical Commissioners, Joseph Welland, and, in the Catholic Church, by J. J. McCarthy and John O'Neill. The antecedents of this church in other men's work need not diminish Murray's achievement; St Columkille's is a fine building worthy of the age and the religious enthusiasm that produced it.

The church has a tall nave with flanking, lean-to aisles, a shallow sanctuary and an off-set four-stage belfry tower on the W side of the sanctuary. Paired lancets light the aisles with a quatrefoil clerestory – derived from Irish medieval architecture as at Bective (q.v.) or Gowran in Co. Kilkenny – and a big geometric window in the entrance gable on the N. The masonry, by *Hammond* of Drogheda, is of particularly good quality, with very crisp limestone dressings. Inside, the short five-bay nave is carried on arcades of chamfered two-centred arches supported on limestone columns with big E.E. capitals. There is an open timber roof with braced trusses to the nave and aisles and satisfyingly deep embrasures to the clerestory and aisle windows. Single-bay chancel with triple-light window and a pinnacled reredos.

TOGHER/DUNANY PARISH CHURCH (C of I). 2.5 km NE. Harled hall-and-tower-type church erected in 1813, although the tower remained incomplete until 1889. Remodelled in a Tudor-Gothic idiom, probably *c.* 1840. Five-bay hall, with Y-traceried windows on both long walls, buttresses rising to pinnacles between each bay, and a battlemented parapet. A rural version of the chapel in Dublin Castle. Inside, two small vestry rooms precede the church proper, a pleasant late Georgian Gothic interior with a timber gallery carried on clustered shafts, coombed ceiling with large central flat area and a four-centred chancel arch.

DUNANY HOUSE. 3.5 km NE. Early C18 two-storey house with a steeply pitched roof. Much altered and extended in the later C18 and further enlarged and superficially castellated in the C19, so that the old house now forms the S arm of a rambling U-shaped building. A Tudor-Gothic screen, somewhat in the manner of Francis Johnston, is placed across the open end of the U and encloses a square forecourt. Bolection-moulded chimneypiece in the hall. In the grounds, a featureless ivy-grown CHURCH RUIN of a pre-Reformation foundation.

CLONMORE CHURCH RUINS. 0.5 km W. The site of a monastery founded *c.* 550 by St Columba, now containing the ruins of two churches. The best-preserved of these, originally C14, was extensively repaired in 1692. Nave walls and gables stand entire. Narrow round-headed window above the door in the W gable. A low arch in the E gable was perhaps for a chancel, though nothing of the chancel itself remains. The second church, now entirely overgrown, was erected in 1794 by Archbishop Robinson and abandoned after Disestablishment in 1869. Part of a de Verdun CASTLE, C13, stood beside the graveyard in 1910; no trace survives today.

CLONMORE GLEBE. 1.5 km SW. An unobtrusive early design by *Francis Johnston*, built in 1782. Elegant two-storey gabled house. The principal elevation of four bays, the centre two projecting and crowned by a low eaves pediment. Sash windows throughout. Central round-headed doorcase, with blocked surround flanked by thin side-lights and approached by a flight of steps with stone handrails. Low single-bay wings (added later?). All typical of the plain, understated elegance favoured by the established church during the late C18.

TOWNLEY HALL

LO *0070*

This house is *Francis Johnston*'s master work, a building where his preference for minimalism and understatement is celebrated both in the precision of the detail and in the absolute accomplishment of the craftsmanship which brought it into being. In many ways Townley Hall is the perfect neoclassical house: ideal in conception; severe in execution; lucid and uncluttered in its interior spaces. Its effect, when it was first completed for Blayney Townley Balfour some time *c.* 1798, must have been utterly novel.

There is a monumental simplicity in the design of the house, which sits as a square block of grey limestone on the crown of a shallow hill. Behind the house, and a little to the N, the land continues to rise, yet the view from the drive is carefully contrived so that the hall appears to dominate its gentle eminence, drawing into one unified effect both the site and the perfect geometry of the architecture. There is much that is ideal in this building. Its plan is a pure square, with a domed and circular stairhall at its centre. It has three fronts which, with the exception of a Doric porch at the entrance, all have identical façades; seven windows long and two storeys high, with a tall cornice and blocking course carried up above the first-floor windows to minimize the impact of the roof and to obscure completely the dormer windows of the attic storey. The basement is in a sunk storey, and the kitchen offices are hidden below ground level, opening into a broad yard at the back of the building. This is a house that is chaste, severe and consciously limited in its architectural articulation; self-denial is a conscious precept of its design, and it cannot be seen, or *should* not be seen, as monotonous, gaunt or dull. The architecture is pure. It is the purism of an international neoclassical taste, and, since such sophisticated ideas are hardly to be expected in the 1790s in rural Co. Louth, the design requires some explanation.

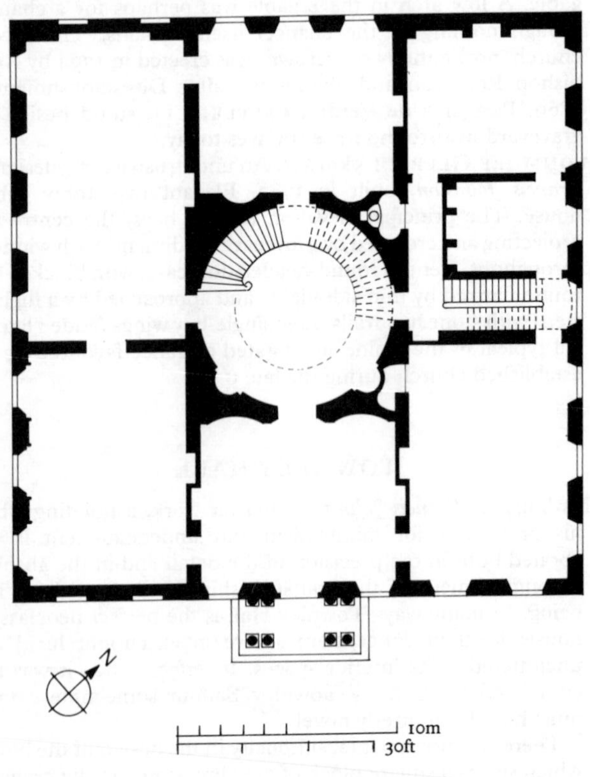

Townley Hall. Plan

Townley Hall is the product of a most fruitful collaboration between its builder, Blayney Townley Balfour, his family and his architect, Francis Johnston. Johnston had not travelled, but Mr Balfour had; he had made a tour through Europe as a young man and had returned to France, accompanied by his mother and two sisters, in 1791, when he was twenty-two. From Nice he had gone to Italy alone, to Florence and Rome, where, between April and July 1792, he discussed his intention of building a new house in Co. Louth with the Scottish architect and sometime assistant of Robert Adam, *James Playfair*. After his return, in February 1793, he received three separate designs for houses from Playfair, all of which proposed an architectural solution of a distinctly ideal character, together with a sunk basement and kitchen wing detached from the main block. These plans, and no doubt the ideas Balfour had discussed with Playfair in Rome, provide the starting-point for the architectural novelties of Townley Hall. They are the seed for new ideas, but no more than that, for none of Playfair's drawings was used for the house Balfour began to build in 1794.

Not long after his coming of age in May 1790 – and before he had gone abroad – Balfour had approached Francis Johnston for a design for the house. Johnston's proposal, dated 30 November 1790, was for a tall pedimented block very much like his recently completed design for Rokeby. After a gap of three years, and particularly to a client just returned from Rome, this scheme would have appeared old-fashioned. It was apparently at this stage that *Balfour* himself and his sister *Anne*, an accomplished architectural amateur, took to designing for themselves. Their drawings suggest that brother and sister worked together, and it is from their sheets that the notion of a circular stair at the centre of the plan, the dimensions for the stair at a diameter of 30 ft (9 m), and the overall size of the house as a square of 90 ft (27 m) first emerge. In January 1794 Johnston sent 'an abstract of my estimation of your plan', and by July the principal contractors *James Reay* and *Andrew Kindelan* were at work on the excavations for the basement storey.

There is one other personality who was possibly involved in the design of the house, Mr Balfour's wife, *Lady Florence Cole*, a daughter of the Earl of Erne from Florence Court, Enniskillen, Co. Fermanagh, whom Balfour married in 1796. This link with Fermanagh proved important, as it brought Balfour into contact with the supremely elegant architecture of James Wyatt, who had been building the magnificent neoclassical house of Castlecoole for the Earl of Belmore, also near Enniskillen, from 1790. The sophisticated joinery employed at both houses certainly suggests that a knowledge of the one inspired standards at the other, while details at Townley Hall, such as the central circular panel in the drawing-room doors or the plasterwork of the drawing-room ceiling, are taken directly from Castlecoole. After her marriage Lady Florence seems to have shared her husband's architectural interests (as his sister had done before) and it was certainly B. T. Balfour and his wife who designed the piers of the main entrance gates, erected in 1810, and probably the GATE LODGE, put up in 1819 as a primitive temple, perhaps to prepare the visitor for the radical austerity of the house. Built in an unorthodox Tuscan order, its portico has baseless columns with smooth shafts, primitive blockish capitals and a deeply overhanging eaves cornice supported on elongated mutules – a miniature version and neo-classical up-date by talented amateurs of Inigo Jones' famous design for St Paul's, Covent Garden.

The interplay of characters and influences giving rise to the main ideas for the house (admirably discussed by Professor Frank Mitchell) should not detract from the achievement of Francis Johnston as the architect of the building. It is he who acted as the inspired professional, responsive to the concepts his client proposed, ready to develop his plans and prepared to provide the knowledge and expertise that brought them to a successful conclusion. The taste of the architecture is Francis Johnston's entirely: the big spare proportions of the windows, which give the house an alert, almost a surprised look; the blocks of Sheephouse limestone, beautifully dressed in droved ashlar; the precise fluting of the Doric columns set in pairs at the entrance porch, and the logical disposition of the panelled soffit above – each element is a considered expression and conscious choice on the part of this most exacting architect.

The interior too is full of a subtlety called into being by Johnston's discerning eye. The scale of the house is generous, and its big rectangular rooms have a refreshing clarity and airiness. Proportions are important: the principal rooms all have a ceiling height of 18 ft (5.5 m), and the drawing room and dining room, both exactly the same shape, are 24 ft by 36 ft (7.3 m by 11 m) – that is, a proportional ratio of 3:4:6. The rightness of these ratios is felt within each room and is enhanced by the clean lines of the room cornices and the integrity of shallow planes which is a distinctive feature of the detailing of all the ceilings, doors, architraves and shutters in the house. Townley Hall is a building to delight the connoisseur of Georgian craftsmanship. Its doors in polished mahogany do not hang on ordinary hinges; as at Ardbraccan, by Johnston's master Thomas Cooley, they turn on steel pivots at top and bottom, and the inside edge is gently curved so that a door left standing open presents nothing but a clean line of polished hardwood to the view. In the dining room, the windows are designed to allow a section of the reveal to be opened before the shutters are closed and then folded back again when they are once in place, leaving the joinery of the window opening perfect, a self-sufficient and fully panelled section of the room which needs no curtain.

The same craftsmanship distinguishes the interior stonework: the pair of Doric chimneypieces in the entrance hall, with squat baseless columns so typical of Johnston's taste, the Portland stone floor and, most wonderfully, the shallow

cantilever of the main stair and radiating pattern of angular lozenges which make up its floor. The stairhall is the cul- 81
mination of Johnston's architecture: another pure space, now a broad domed cylinder, whose ample and uncluttered volume communicates, as is always the case with a rotunda, a sense of perfect repose at the centre of the house. Here the ideals of Roman neoclassicism, Playfair, Mr Balfour and Francis Johnston meet: this is a space which seems to have survived the passage of time and to express for ever the values of another age.

If the rotunda theme of the stairhall is timeless, Johnston manages both the space and its decoration in an individual way. Four doorways open into the room. They are set within relieving arches on the cardinal points and alternate with shallow blank niches set in similar arched recesses. The doorway from the hall, a double door, is broader than the rest 82
but has been accommodated within the full width of its relieving arch so that its extra size does not disrupt the flow of the architectural patterns round the wall. The stair rises as a shallow line of stone round half of the perimeter of the wall, breaking once to form a landing, directly opposite the hall doorway, which provides a section of flat ceiling, exactly where it is needed, immediately above the W door which opens into the billiard room at the back of the house. It is never easy for an architect to carry a stair across a wall which has been architecturally enriched, as a collision between the line of the rising steps and other patterns in the architecture is inevitable. At Townley Hall Johnston manages these problems with considerable skill; although, just as it starts, the lower flight cuts across a niche, and, near the top, the soffit of the stair decapitates part of the frame of a relieving arch, the final effect is one of poise and architectural clarity. At first-floor level these problems disappear. Here the wall is articulated as a succession of eight shallow arches, tied by enlarged keystones to a deep frieze decorated with ox skulls set between swathes of fringed drapery, while the soffit of the dome is panelled in light diagonal coffers in a pattern that was popular in the later C18 and which architects and Grand Tourists who visited Italy copied from the apses of the Temple of Venus and Rome. Johnston's version is prettier and more delicate, however, and indeed the character of all the plasterwork in the stair is lighthearted and consciously anti-academic. Most regular classicists, and certainly the architects of the previous generation in Ireland, would have wanted to use a strong cornice and frieze to emphasize the change from ground- to first-floor level in the well of the staircase; a common pattern much used in Irish houses was the Vitruvian scroll. But Johnston does not want a heavy line to cut across the upward flow of his cylindrical space, and he devised a bold yet shallow pattern of a simple stepped Greek key, interwoven with a foliated tendril and decorated with five 'acorns' which hang from the alternating lower sections of the key. The result is a suitable enrichment which holds the eye but traps so little

shadow that the volume of the stair well still reads as one. Informed visitors to Mr Balfour's house must have enjoyed the wit of this pattern. Certainly it hints at the triglyphs and guttae of the formal Doric frieze and thus makes sense of – or provides an intellectual context for – the ox skulls Johnston places in the frieze below the dome.

The lower hall built below the stairhall which it supports reflects another aspect of the architect's personality. To carry the weight of the Portland stone pavement, Johnston had thought of building a circular load-bearing wall in the centre of the room, but in the house as built this is replaced by a nicer detail, a robust quatrefoil Gothick shaft which is plumbed to carry water to four stone basins at the base of the shaft. In his castle-style buildings, his additions to churches and in the design of the Chapel Royal at Dublin Castle, Johnston was to demonstrate an early interest in a rather wispy form of Gothic architecture; here he seems to derive his idea from a famous local antiquity, the lavabo at Mellifont Abbey, one of the most famous pieces of Romanesque architecture in Ireland and not three miles distant on Mr Balfour's estate. As with the ashlar blocks of which the house is built, the tooling of the masonry for this Gothic shaft, executed by a mason called *Glover*, is admirable in its craftsmanship and gives a true sculpturesque quality to this practical piece of design.

A broad passage leads from the lower hall to a sunk kitchen yard on the W side of the house. Only here does Townley Hall appear as the four-storey building it really is. This bald façade is Johnston in unorthodox mood and towers above the single-storey wing (roofless at the time of writing) which was built to accommodate the kitchen offices. The wing is surprisingly self-conscious as a piece of architecture intended to be buried at the back of a country house. It has more of the primitivism of the gate lodge; an arcade of three round-headed windows in ashlar stonework, which lit the kitchen, is flanked by end rooms whose elevation is a curious arrangement of a low segmental arch spanning the breadth of the room and cut by a beam, at the level of the impost of the kitchen arcade, and supported by a pair of baseless, smooth-shafted columns. W of this wing a service road curves up from the level of the sunk yard into the woodlands behind the house.

8050 TRIM ME

Now a charming enclave of late medieval Ireland, Trim was once the most important manor of the northern Pale, the centre of the Lordship of Meath, granted by Henry II to Hugh de Lacy in 1172 in return for the service of fifty knights. The ruins of de Lacy's great castle with its massive perimeter wall built during the first half of the C13 still dominate the centre of the town, while Trim's skyline is a collage of church towers, medieval and modern: the tower of the C15 cathedral, the Yellow Steeple and the spire of St

Patrick's Church. A belt of green fields stretching along the banks of the Boyne to Newtown Trim lends an aura of quietude and enhances Trim's medieval character.

Across the fields from the Yellow Steeple to the E stands the Sheep Gate, the only surviving gate of the town's medieval defences. The earliest murage grant dates to 1290, followed by two more in 1316 and 1393. The wall had a circumference of over one and a quarter miles and was entered through five principal gates: the Athboy Gate (N), the Navan Gate (NE), the Sheep Gate (E), the Dublin Gate (S) and finally the West Gate. Two large monasteries stood within the medieval town, and a third was located just beyond the Athboy Gate. The earliest of these, reputedly a Patrician foundation, was St Mary's Abbey, N of the town, later to be colonized by Augustinian canons introduced by de Lacy. The site of the present Courthouse was occupied by the Grey Friary, founded in the early C14 and dedicated to St Bonaventure. At the Dissolution its buildings were destroyed and the church was taken over by the Corporation for use as a tholsel. The Dominican Friary, whose ruins were mostly destroyed in the mid-C18, is, in the context of Trim's history, the most interesting of the three. It was founded in 1263 by Geoffrey de Genneville, who had acquired the Lordship of Meath through his marriage to Matilda, the grand-daughter of Walter de Lacy. In 1308, then an old man, Geoffrey entered the monastery as a friar and entrusted the Lordship to Roger Mortimer, husband of his grand-daughter Joan. Trim remained in the hands of the Mortimers throughout the C14 until 1427, when Edward de Mortimer bequeathed it to Richard Plantagenet, Duke of York, upon whose death in 1460 it reverted to the Crown.

By the C16 Trim was a substantial and well-fortified city, so much so that in 1584 the parson, Robert Draper, felt moved to recommend it as the best site for an Irish university. In his memorial to the Lord High Treasurer he described the place as 'full of very faire castles and stone houses builded after the English fashyon and devyded into fyve faire streetes'. For the college accommodation Draper recommended either St Mary's Abbey or the Dominican Friary, adding that provisions might be brought by river from the coast, stone and slates from a nearby quarry, and corn and cattle from the countryside around. Nothing came of this proposal, and although the C16 street plan does survive, the many castles and houses do not.

In the C18 Trim functioned as the county town of Meath, seat of the assizes and a thriving market centre, but in the C19, Navan developed into the more successful commercial centre and eventually displaced it as the administrative capital of the county. Given Trim's unique heritage, this was perhaps no bad thing.

TRIM CASTLE. This spectacular building is undoubtedly the 43
most impressive Norman castle in the country, the first great stone structure to be built in Ireland by Henry II's barons. Situated on the S bank of the river Boyne, the castle stands at the centre of an extensive three-acre (1.2-ha) bailey, surrounded by

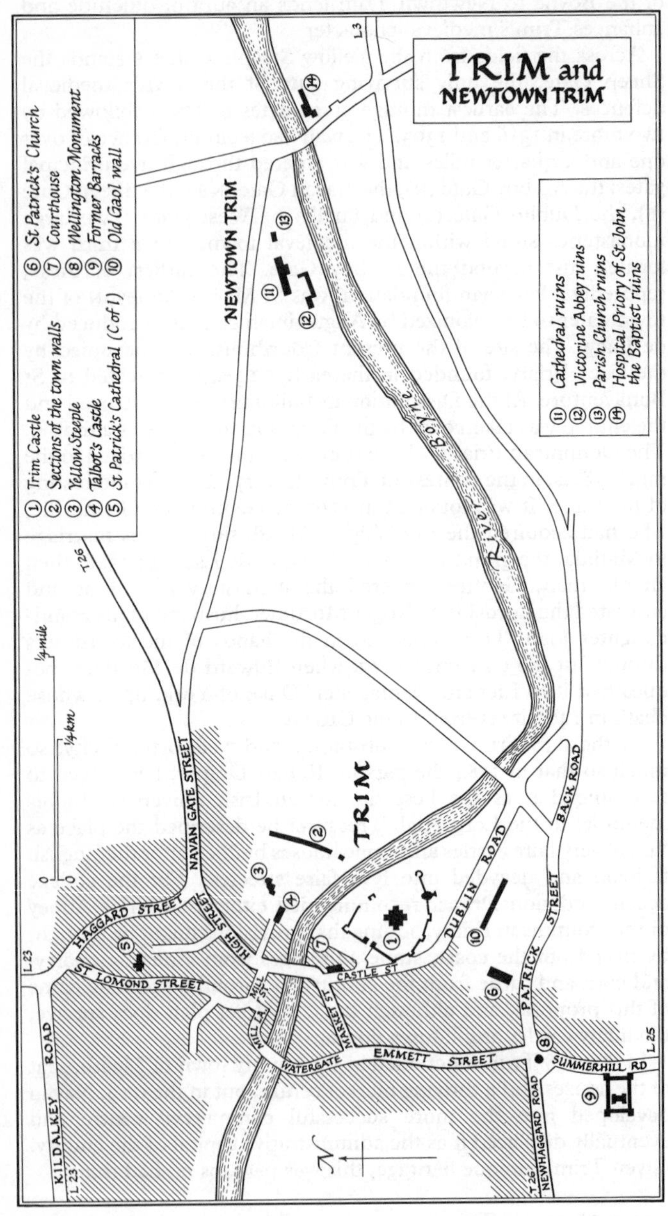

TRIM and NEWTOWN TRIM
① Trim Castle
② Sections of the town walls
③ Yellow Steeple
④ Talbot's Castle
⑤ St Patrick's Cathedral (C of I)
⑥ St Patrick's Church
⑦ Courthouse
⑧ Wellington Monument
⑨ Former Barracks
⑩ Old Gaol wall
⑪ Cathedral ruins
⑫ Victorine Abbey ruins
⑬ Parish Church ruins
⑭ Hospital Priory of St John the Baptist ruins
NEWTOWN TRIM
TRIM
River Boyne
¼ mile
¼ km
N
T26
L3
L23
L25
KILDALKEY ROAD
HAGGARD STREET
ST LOMOND STREET
NAVAN GATE STREET
HIGH STREET
MILL LA
MILL ST
MARKET ST
CASTLE ST
WATERGATE
EMMETT STREET
SUMMERHILL RD
NEWHAGGARD ROAD
PATRICK STREET
DUBLIN ROAD
BACK ROAD

a defensive perimeter wall which marked the SE corner of the town's defences. On the opposite bank of the river are the remains of the Sheep Gate, from which pieces of the wall continue N forming the eastern boundary of St Mary's Abbey. Green fields stretch northward beyond the Yellow Steeple and eastward to the ruined cathedral at Newtown Trim.

The curtain wall of the castle is fortified on the S and E by a series of semicircular open-back towers which are especially impressive when seen from the S approach. Trim had two principal entrances: one, beside the modern car park, is located in the centre of the W wall and is flanked by a gatehouse; the other, in the S wall, provides Ireland's only complete surviving example of a barbican gate and tower. A ditch cut round the castle on the S and W sides could be flooded from the Boyne, which flows past the other two sides in a tight curve. Both the keep and its defences are of local limestone rubble, mixed with a small amount of sandstone. Ornament is minimal, and the effect is the characteristic one of massive strength.

The building history of Trim Castle has been the subject of much debate. While documentary sources clearly establish the construction of a castle at Trim by Hugh de Lacy in 1172, that building was believed to be a motte-and-bailey structure which preceded the existing castle and was destroyed in the year after its erection by Rory O'Connor, King of Connaught. When exactly the present keep was built has been a matter of conjecture. One argument suggests that it was begun by De Lacy soon after the destruction of his motte castle and that the building was probably complete *c.* 1215. Another view places the inception of the building *c.* 1200 and its completion over fifty years later.

Fascinating new evidence is being assembled by Kevin O'Brien of the Office of Public Works, who is conducting an exhaustive structural survey of the keep and to whom we are greatly indebted for access to new and most interesting findings. This work is still in progress, but discoveries have already necessitated a thorough review of the building's chronology. The survey has focused on alterations and additions to the keep, together with dendrochronological evidence from timbers at various levels throughout the structure. While a conclusive history of the keep at Trim awaits documentation, Mr O'Brien has suggested that the entire keep was constructed within a forty-year period in three successive stages.

The most exciting discovery of the new chronology is that the keep dates from very soon after the granting of the Lordship of Meath to Hugh de Lacy in 1172. It is also interesting that the second principal phase of construction, during the 1190s, coincides with the accession of de Lacy's son Walter.

The timbers which have provided new evidence are of two types: rough uncut scaffolding timbers in putlock holes and squared timbers set more deeply within the wall at regular intervals and at continuous levels around the building. Kevin O'Brien has shown that the latter supported an enclosed timber hoarding which provided both circulation and an archers' platform at a high level around the entire keep.

What cannot be fully explained by any of the historical or physical evidence to date is the very unorthodox plan of the castle: a great three-storey keep, with four square corner turrets and a substantial square four-storey tower projecting from the centre of each side (the N tower is now demolished). This intriguing variant of the usual Norman keep is found in no previous or contemporary structure in Britain and remained unique until Warkworth Castle was built in the early C 16. Two analyses of the keep's unusual plan are worth noting. The first maintains that the requirement for many rooms within the castle dictated the complex Greek-cross plan; the second argues that the shape of the building was as much an architectural statement as an expression of functional requirements.

Perforated by mural stairs and passages, the walls of the castle are never more than 13 ft (3.9 m) thick, and this, coupled with the twelve sharp arrised corners (instead of the usual four), results in a design which from a defensive point of view was certainly outmoded. At a time when strategic considerations encouraged the increasing use of circular walls Trim's rectangular architecture is remarkable indeed.

Inside, the castle follows the pattern of C 12 keeps in having a great N–S cross-wall dividing the space into two large chambers. Also common is the location of the entrance and of a chapel on the floor above in a projection to the E, which is exemplified by Trim's E tower, with the entrance arch on the first floor of the N wall and a chapel on the floor above, as indicated by a double-arched piscina. Mural passages and stairs lead off both principal chambers, giving access to the S, W and former N tower. Surviving cutstone detail is concentrated in the central keep, with heavy red sandstone mouldings to the large round-headed arches which are similar to the sedilia in the cathedral of Newtown Trim (begun in 1206).

On the exterior, the N, E and W sides of the keep present sheer masonry faces, whereas on the sloping S side there is a coarse limestone rubble plinth, also found on the outer side of the curtain wall. This battered plinth was added during the construction of the outer defences, probably in the mid-C 13. Unlike the angular plan of the castle, the towers and gateways of the perimeter wall are technically advanced, the type of open-backed D-shaped structures set at intervals along the wall which came into use generally in the middle of the C 13. These towers are fortified with many arrow loops, which appear as mere slits on the exterior but open within the walls into broad embrasures that allowed a bowman a wide field of cover and also, as the slits sloped steeply downwards, the possibility of shooting directly into the ditch or moat. Well-preserved arrow loops remain at two levels in the SE corner tower and in the next tower along the S section of the walls, the Barbican Gate.

The BARBICAN GATE represented the most up-to-date type of medieval fortification: not in this case a dramatic twin-

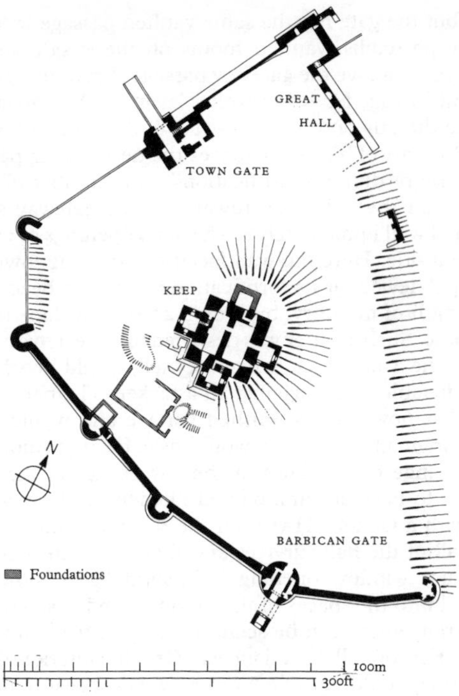

Trim Castle. Plan

towered barbican like St Laurence's Gate at Drogheda, but a squat tower, oval in plan and pierced by a vaulted passageway, with the barbican, a narrow passage held between two battlemented walls, carried on a bridge across the moat to join a turret on the opposite side. The purpose of a barbican was to force an attacker into a restricted space before the weakest point of any fortification, the gate. A barbican meant that the enemy could be trapped between walls and picked off with fire from above. The Barbican Gate at Trim was a fully developed piece of fortification, with mural passages for archers set on the E and W sides of the gateway passage and a portcullis, whose channelled groove remains in the masonry, just before the front face of the tower. A guard room at first-floor level was located above the main passage. The portcullis was operated from here, and the room also gave access to the tops of the barbican walls. On its W side a doorway leads to a first-floor mural passage with an arrow-loop embrasure and a lavatory for the men. The second interval tower W from the Barbican Gate houses a small water-gate at its base.

The TOWN GATE, about the middle of the W wall, is now approached by a steeply ramped roadway and would originally have been protected by a drawbridge. There is no barbican here, but the gate has the same vaulted passage with a groove for the portcullis, vaulted rooms on the N side and another guard room above the gateway passage. From this guard room a mural passage led N to another lavatory. A doorway on the S opened directly onto the wall-walk of the outer walls.

In this part of Trim's defences the designers appear to have made use of dummy fortifications, as a number of the arrow loops – on the polygonal tower S of the gateway and in the length of wall immediately N – have no openings or embrasures on the inside. Here the wall faced towards the town, and the principal device for its fortification must have been the extensive length of masonry, built on a 45-degree slope (or batter), at its base. Such a batter was designed to deflect missiles thrown against the walls which, when they fell, would ricochet back at unpredictable angles against an attacker. The battered wall at Trim has now lost its finished surface and would no longer work: originally its surface would have been of smooth stone.

The range of buildings at the NW corner of the enclosure appears to have accommodated kitchens and servants' quarters, with a GREAT HALL on the N wall, running E–W. Only one wall of the hall survives and that has been much rebuilt, with later window openings of paired lights, now blocked, inserted into the spaces of the original windows. Traces of the first arrangement can be seen, outside the wall on the N side, as a series of tall thin lancets. On the interior the yellow sandstone mouldings of a Norman window seat remain in one window recess.

Although the castle continued to be used periodically throughout the C14, C15 and C16 when trouble flared in the northern provinces, the archaeological evidence suggests that permanent occupation largely ceased after 1350. Repairs were carried out twice in the C14 and also *c.* 1450, when the Lord Lieutenant, Richard, Duke of York, held court here. By the mid-C17 most of the town's defences were in decay, and although Cromwell is reputed to have attacked Trim there is no reliable evidence for this. An earthen mound thrown up to the height of the outer wall between the W gate and the third flanking tower is probably a C17 cannon base.

ST PATRICK'S CATHEDRAL (C of I). A church with Patrician associations, reputedly entrusted by St Patrick to St Loman, the first Bishop of Trim. Bishops and abbots are recorded here from the C8 to the C12, although all the surviving medieval remains date to the post-Norman period. The existing church is an unexceptional small building of 1801, renovated and refitted in 1869 by *Thomas N. Deane*. Gabled hall of snecked limestone rubble, with a four-light Dec window in each gable. Of more interest is the tower, which adjoins the N side of the W gable, through which the church is entered. This is a five-storey C15 structure with a square stair turret at the NW corner, plainly ornamented, with a single string-course dividing the tower storeys from the belfry level and a battlemented parapet. The arms of Mortimer and Burgh are built into the upper W face of the tower. A fragment of wall jutting out from the E face may suggest the presence of an E aisle in the medieval church. The only other remains of the medieval fabric are the N and S walls of the C15 chancel, which stand immediately E of the existing church. Here the S wall contains a C16 window which clearly replaced an earlier pointed opening. This is close in style to the E window of the nearby Moymet church (q.v.) and consists of three cusped ogee-headed lights set in a rectangular frame and divided by slender limestone mullions which continue up to join the lintel, with delicate open trefoils in the spandrels above each light. A hoodmoulding frames the window on the outer wall and is decorated with a double-billet design, rather like a miniature castellation. The label stops are the carved heads of a king and bishop with the thin delicate features characteristic of International Gothic. Both the tower and the chancel belonged to a church erected here in the middle of the C15 which has long been associated with Richard, Duke of York, who inherited the lands of Trim in 1427 and resided here for a time in 1449. The tradition that he contributed to the building of Trim Cathedral is supported by the arms of de Burgo impaling those of de Mortimer, the Duke's personal emblem, which is built into the tower.

A number of MEDIEVAL SCULPTURAL FRAGMENTS have been gathered together in the vestibule in the tower. These include a double-headed slab with the Crucifixion, second half of the C14; a sandstone slab carved with the heads of a man and his wife and below them Christ crucified, flanked by Mary and John and censing angels, with a twin-bodied beast and floriated scrollwork at the base. – At the back of the nave is the bowl and shaft of a C15 piscina/font which was brought here in the C19 from the ruined chancel and set into a large sandstone capital with trumpet scallops. The bowl is carved with a three-dimensional frieze of fantastic creatures resting on a broad band of semicircular mouldings. The shaft has three large panels carved with angel shield-bearers. The coats of arms are those of James Butler, the White Earl, and the Royal Arms of England impaling those of de Burgo and de Mortimer, Richard, Duke of York's personal device. Traces of red and blue paint are still discernible in the panels. – STAINED GLASS. E window: the Last Supper by *Heaton, Butler and Bayne*, 1901.

ST MARY'S ABBEY. A monastery famed for its miraculous statue of the Virgin, which drew huge numbers of pilgrims to Trim throughout the C14 and C15. Founded in Patrician times, the abbey was destroyed in 1127 and rebuilt in the C13 by Hugh de Lacy, who colonized it with Canons Regular of St Augustine. A great fire in 1368 destroyed the church and monastic buildings, and the process of rebuilding continued well into the C15, as suggested by the style of the surviving buildings. An indulgence was granted towards repairs in 1423, although it is
not clear how extensive these were. The Yellow Steeple, even 32
in ruin a magnificent structure, is all that survives of the abbey church. The tallest of Trim's medieval buildings, it is the most

dramatic feature of the town's unique skyline. The site too is memorable, located above the Boyne to the N and looking across to the castle on the opposite bank. The W face of the tower has vanished totally, so that what stands today is only the E wall, seven storeys high, a portion of the N wall, no more than a return, and the ruined S wall, which rises to five storeys. Built of punched and squared limestone blocks, the walls rise vertically, with only a slight base batter. Two clasping corner buttresses run to the very top of the E face, greatly enhancing its verticality. The building is clean and sheer, broken only by a series of moulded string-courses where the buttresses step back and interspersed with small loops and square-headed windows. The most elaborate feature is the belfry window, a generous pointed opening with two pointed lights bisected at the centre by a cross-mullion, with a flowerlet formed in the tracery pattern above. The tower clearly relied for its effect not on ornament but on the elegance of its shape and scale. Similar elegance may be remarked in the spiral stair at the SW corner, a remarkable piece of masonry, with each step brought to a sharp point so that there is no newel but in its place a gentle spiral line. The Rev. Daniel Beaufort, visiting Trim in 1787, noted another refinement here, that 'the winding stairs in the Yellow Steeple are bevilled off underneath which is very neat and rare'. The S wall provides the key to the position of the tower in relation to the abbey church. Clearly this wall, which in places is built of rubble, was never intended to be exposed as exterior architecture. In one part it seems to have accommodated a structure with a high pointed profile, a canopied funerary monument perhaps, which would have been located on the N side of the church – or even in a N aisle. It is tempting to suggest from this that the Yellow Steeple stood perhaps in a line with the chancel gable of the abbey or else, as at Fountains Abbey in Yorkshire, half-way down the N side. Certainly the abbey church stood S and W from here.

TALBOT'S CASTLE. It has long been assumed that the Yellow Steeple is the only part of the abbey to survive and that the large building to the SW, popularly known as Talbot's Castle, is a domestic residence erected in 1415 by the Irish Lord Lieutenant, Sir John Talbot, whose coat of arms is set into the N wall at the W end of the building. Yet whatever Talbot's involvement here, and he undoubtedly had some connection, this large building, of two storeys over a vaulted basement, is simply too big (80 ft by 15 ft – 25 m by 4.5 m – internally) and quite the wrong shape to have been merely a private residence. There are too certain internal features which suggest that this might well have been the refectory of the Augustinian abbey. After the building had become the Diocesan School in the C18, a report of the Commission for Irish Education of 1827 described it as 'a very old building forming part of the quadrangle of St Mary's Abbey'. Today the building has very much a manorial appearance, imposed upon it *c.* 1909 by the then proprietor, Archibald Montgomery, who added an attic storey with yellow-brick gables to the W end and retained a mish-mash of pointed C18 sash windows and Gothic-French windows throughout the rest of the building. On close examination it becomes clear that the W end of the building with the Talbot arms is in fact distinct from the rest of the range, a tower 15 ft by 30 ft (4.5 m by 9 m), of two storeys over a vaulted basement with a square turret at the NW angle. The punched limestone rubble and big square embrasures still visible in the basement are similar to the Yellow Steeple and support an early to mid-C15 date. Adjoining the tower on the E is a longer (50-ft, or 15-m) range, again of two storeys over a vaulted basement, with two straight flights of stairs leading from the basement to the upper storey. Above the long vaulted undercroft are large panelled dining and drawing rooms, created in 1909. In the drawing room at the E end of the building is a remarkable and very rare medieval survival, an oriel window or gallery opening off the room at the SE corner, roofed over by two bays of quadripartite vaulting, springing from octagonal shafts, all of punched grey limestone. One has only to look at the refectory building at Newtown Trim to recognize that this is the characteristic position of the reader's desk or gallery from which scripture was read while the monks ate their meals. On the floor above, some of the windows incorporate fragments of C15 cusped lights with angel shield-bearers in the spandrels, presumably found and reused in the reconstruction of 1909. The rockery and garden which slope from the base to the river also incorporated cutstone fragments from the abbey. That Sir John Talbot built for himself a tower house attached to the monastic range seems most unlikely: it is much more plausible that he acted as a patron; 1415, the traditional date of Talbot's Castle, is just three years after reports of miracles worked at Trim, and such events might well have prompted patronage by the resident nobility.

In 1584 Robert Draper's memorial concerning the foundation of a university in Trim maintained that the town had 'one greate and large abbey, nothing thereof defaced but the church and therein great store of goodly roomes in meetly good repair'. Although the university was not established in Trim, the abbey was eventually appropriated to educational purposes. In the opening years of the C18 the Diocesan School of Meath, which was being run by Dean Swift's curate at Laracor, was without fixed accommodation. In 1713 Swift wrote to Stella on the matter, remarking how 'thin' the school had become. Three years later Stella bought 'St Mary's Abbey' from John Blakeley for the sum of £65 and in the following year she either sold or gave it to Swift, whereupon it became the home of the Diocesan School, which remained there until the C19. The first floor of the W tower house is the only C18 interior to survive, a large square room, wainscotted throughout with shallow fielded panelling, with a dentil cornice and four timber Corinthian pilasters adorning each of the side walls. The doors have lugged architraves, and the windows are large pointed openings, set in deep embrasures, with a charming view of the garden, castle and river.

W of the house, bordering Abbey Lane, was NANGLE'S CASTLE, now a mere limestone rubble shed with a galvanized roof and no datable features. E of the Yellow Steeple is the ruin of the SHEEP GATE, one of the five principal gates of the medieval town. This was formerly a two-storeyed limestone gatehouse, with one principal chamber arched over a barrel-vaulted passage reached by a spiral stair in the NW corner.

134 ST PATRICK. 1891–1902 by *William Hague*. Large and ambitious cruciform church, not without grandeur. Richly ornamented in terms of its surface pattern and of its structural embellishments. Textured local limestone rubble, with generous ashlar trim. The church consists of the usual nave, chancel, aisles and transepts and follows the example of J. J. McCarthy in placing a large tower on the axis of the nave across the entrance gable rather than set off to one side. The tower, which is flanked by tall gabled vestibules, dominates the entrance front. From a distance, it has a fine silhouette; closer to, the tower shows a change in scale and style that is not altogether satisfactory. It starts as a large, square two-storey structure with a portal at the ground-floor level and a geometric window above to light the nave. At this point McCarthy would have had a massive belfry and broach spire, but Hague (or *W. H. Byrne*) changes the design to a minor and more delicate key. Four spirelets smooth the transition from the tower to a slender octagonal belfry, which has tall cusped louvred lancets and is crowned by a delicate octagonal spire, complete with string-courses and lucarnes.

The interior is large and impressive with a busy cross-braced hammerbeam roof. The nave arcade has moulded two-centred arches with tall plinths and plain E.E. capitals. Cusped lancets light the aisles, with triple lancets in the clerestory and a big five-light geometric window to the chancel. The chancel arch stands on pink granite colonnettes and is elaborately decorated with a Celtic-cum-Art-Nouveau mosaic. – Rich white marble REREDOS of 1901 by *Pearse & Sons*. The matching SIDE ALTARS and arcaded COMMUNION RAIL are of 1902 from the office of *W. H. Byrne*, who took over the project on Hague's death. – STAINED GLASS. Highly pictorial, Mayer-style glass. E window: Crucifixion.

ST JOSEPH'S CONVENT OF MERCY. 1858–67 by *William Caldbeck*. Attractive limestone rubble building in an institutional Gothic idiom. Quadrangle of two-storey gabled ranges, adjoined at the SW angle by a small chapel with a miniature spire at its W gable. The principal front is of seven bays with advanced gabled ends, diagonal, stepped buttresses, a gabled porch and a variety of single, paired and triple lancet windows.

CHRISTIAN BROTHERS SCHOOL. E of the town centre. The former District Model School, erected in 1847 to designs by *Frederick Darley*. Asymmetrical two-storey Tudor range with advanced gabled ends, mullioned windows and tall chimneys.

ST JOSEPH'S HOSPITAL. The former Union workhouse, designed by *George Wilkinson*; erected in 1841 to accommodate 600 poor. Only the largest range survives. It is a standard design: a fifteen-bay, two-storey block ending in higher six-bay, three-storey blocks with paired gables.

WELLINGTON MONUMENT. Corinthian column surmounted by a statue of the Duke. The column seems rather too small for the heavy square base on which it is set, which reduces its effect, but it is a distinctive local landmark and a nice alternative to endless commemorative obelisks. Erected in 1817 by the inhabitants of Co. Meath, the monument was designed by a local man, *James Bell*, who subsequently became County Surveyor for Longford. The figure is sculpted by *Thomas Kirk*. Wellington's family home was originally at Dangan Castle (q.v.), three miles S from here.

FORMER GAOL. 1827 by *John Hargrave*. To tackle the commission for a new gaol on a site directly opposite one of the country's most imposing Norman strongholds would be a daunting experience for any architect. The challenge seems to have fired Hargrave's imagination, and what remains of Trim Gaol is arguably the most powerful of his surviving buildings. Set on an elevated site above the castle (and now partially hidden by the modern Garda barracks), the great formal façade of the gaol is all that survives of Hargrave's design. Behind it, where once stood five radiating cell blocks and a central governor's house, there is now a modern school. Hargrave's gigantic screen wall, roughly 200 ft (60 m) long and 25 ft (7.5 m) high, now encloses nothing more dramatic than a school yard. It is a happy survival, and long may it remain so.

Though the site of the gaol was level with the street on the S side, a conscious decision seems to have been made to exploit the great slope towards the river to provide a formal entrance front. This can hardly have been for practical reasons, given the ramps and platforms necessary to negotiate the sleep incline. It seems therefore that both the building committee and their architect were eager to cash in upon the dramatic possibilities of an elevated façade overlooking the castle and the river. Hargrave was wise enough not to produce a castellated design, and the building, though fortress-like in effect, is ancient and vaguely Egyptian in feeling. Set above two tiers of stone ramps and platforms, the façade proper is an extended horizontal composition, expressed as one gigantic single storey, vigorously rusticated in deep horizontal bands of punched limestone and pierced only by a central entrance arch and doorcases in advanced end-bays. Ornament is limited to a continuous stone eaves cornice, with ashlar frames to the three entrances, which have blank neoclassical plaques above.

What contributes most to the Egyptian quality of Trim Gaol are the massive pylon-like supports which buttress the façade at each end, the terraced arrangement of ramps, platforms and steps leading to the entrance and the deeply inclined jambs of the central arch and doorways. All is aggressive, monumental and, if perhaps overstated for refined palates, one of the best examples of expressionistic establishment architecture to survive from late Georgian Ireland.

COURTHOUSE. *c.* 1810 by *Richard Morrison*. A dull building for this architect, though presumably the fault lies in the parsimony of the Grand Jury who commissioned it. The entrance front, at the E end of Market Street, is a two-storey, seven-bay design, the three centre bays advanced and marked by an eaves pediment. Cement-rendered finish, with lugged window surrounds.

FORMER BARRACKS. Early C19. A rectangular enclosure with substantial limestone walls and an elliptical-arched entry. The two-storey barracks block in the centre is now much altered as a hotel.

TRIM BRIDGE. A bridge of four arches spans the river Boyne within the town of Trim and gives its name to Bridge Street. Recent research suggests that this is probably a structure of mid-C14 date. The arches have a pointed segmental profile, except for the E arch on the castle side, which appears to have been rebuilt at a later date. The arch spans are 16 ft (5 m) and the piers 8 ft (2.5 m), the same ratio as in the medieval Babe's Bridge near Slane. The width of the bridge is 21 ft (6.3 m), and it seems not to have been widened in the post-medieval period. The mid-C14 attribution is based upon stylistic evidence, in particular the bridge's resemblance to the former Baal's Bridge at Limerick, which is known to have been constructed in 1340.

OTHER BUILDINGS. S of the castle in CASTLE STREET is a row of ten picturesque early C19 estate cottages, with decorated bargeboards, quarry glass and canopied porches. Closing MARKET STREET at the N end, a once handsome five-bay, three-storey town house of a mid-Georgian idiom, the ground floor ruined by ugly modern shopfronts, and the sash panes replaced by plate glass on the upper levels. Particularly attractive is the advanced and pedimented centre bay with the classic Palladian formula of a Venetian window on the first floor and a tripartite segmental window above. In Bridge Street, the ULSTER BANK is a simple four-bay, two-storey gabled block, cement-rendered, with horizontal channelling to the banking floor and attractive recessed surrounds to the first-floor windows; 1863 by *James Hamilton*. In Market Street is the BANK OF IRELAND, built in 1909 by *L. A. McDonnell* in a redbrick Tudor-Revival idiom, with advanced gables and mullioned windows.

NEIGHBOURHOOD

NEWHAGGARD HOUSE. 2 km W. Substantial late C18 Georgian block: two rooms deep and two storeys high, on a sunk basement. 'Block' is the right word, as the roof of this house is completely hidden by the façade parapet. Harled five-bay entrance front, with fifteen-pane sash windows to the ground floor, twelve panes above. Scamozzian Ionic columns framing a simple fanlit doorcase. There is something odd about the proportions here – rather as if a third storey had either been removed or was intended but not built. Newhaggard Mill was established *c.* 1760, but a description of the place in 1786 makes no reference to a house. All of the interior detail looks *c.* 1790, with thin applied mouldings to the joinery, simple neoclassical plasterwork and marble chimneypieces.

NEWHAGGARD FLOUR MILLS, referred to in 1786, are no doubt incorporated in the existing grandiose ruin. Large vernacular building of limestone rubble. Six-storey and of five main bays, with irregular extra windows on the lower floors. A battlemented parapet rises to each gable end, and there is a great brick chimney in the centre of the W wall facing the Boyne. Although this is irregular architecture, the scale is grand and the silhouette impressive.

NEWHAGGARD CASTLE GATE HOUSE. Standing E of the house and mill in a field. Ruined four-storey tower; the upper walls are now shrouded in luxuriant ivy, but that does not quite obscure the remarkable machicolated course which carries the upper floors on the S wall, a good 2 ft (0.6 m) in front of the lower wall face. The machicolation is set on six corbel brackets which support five shallow four-centred arches with voussoirs of rubble stone. The central arch is narrower than the rest. A stair tower projects at the SE corner, and the interior preserves the remnants of a high vault. The stonework of the S face of the castle, which has two clear vertical joints splitting the front into three parts, does much to explain its history. Today there is a low square-headed door with a window above it; the line of a four-centred archway may be detected above the window which is level with the vault inside, suggesting that the tower originally had a central arch (like the one at Audley's Castle, Co. Down), filled in at a later date. As such, the building represents a rare variant on the usual late C15 castle form.

HARCOURT LODGE. 4 km W. *c.* 1760? Small and very charming two-storey gabled house of the mid-C18. Harled five-bay entrance front, the centre bay slightly advanced with an eaves pediment, pierced by a tiny semicircular window. Finely dressed limestone pedimented doorcase. The plan is the old-fashioned single-pile with a corner chimneybreast at each end and lean-to additions. The rooms are simple with fielded joinery, six-panel doors and egg-and-dart cornices. One narrow door has the round-topped panel motif which was fashionable during the 1750s and 60s.

WATERLOO LODGE. 4 km W. Built presumably *c.* 1815, when Trim basked in the pride of Wellington's achievement. Different to the usual three-bay, two-storey house in having the outer bays gently advanced, a pyramidal hipped roof and a Tuscan doorcase with a lantern incorporated in the fanlight. The hall has a timber Tuscan arcade framing the doorcases and a pretty neoclassical boss to the ceiling.

BOYNE LODGE. 4 km SW. A house built *c.* 1730 by the Barnewell family and remodelled by the O'Reillys *c.* 1810. Two storeys with end chimneystacks, a tall hipped roof and three-bay entrance front with narrow sash windows whose proportions recall the house's early date. Inside, white marble neoclassical chimneypieces with reeded pilasters and Empire-style grates. Oak garlands, lyres and foliated bosses to the plasterwork, with Wyatt windows on the side elevations. All that survives from the early Georgian period is one six-panel door and some fielded shuttering in a room at the rear.

ST BRIGID, BOARDSMILL. 5 km SW. Harled early C 19 gabled hall lying parallel to the Trim road. A tall C 20 tower adjoins the centre of the E wall, crowned by an open canopied belfry. Simple interior lit by lancets, with nice plaster cherubs over the sanctuary and a pretty gilt and wrought-iron altar rail.

TULLYARD. 2.5 km N. Charming Regency villa which in 1836 was the residence of a Mr Samuel Winter. Possibly by *Sir Richard Morrison*. A crisp two-storey, rectangular block (painted white, over what appears to be finely tooled limestone masonry), with a low hipped roof and oversailing eaves. The style is minimal but the proportions are good. A three-bay front and two-bay side with twelve-pane sash windows below and only six panes above. All the ground-floor windows are set in shallow round-headed relieving arches. The porch projects as a square box with baseless Doric half-columns framing a large Wyatt window.

KILCOOLY HOUSE. 3 km NE. Handsome gentleman farmer's house of *c.* 1780. Three-storey, five-bay, gable-ended block, built of limestone rubble, with sash windows of twelve and six panes and a simple moulded doorcase and fanlight. Inside, a symmetrical tripartite plan, two rooms deep; central staircase with Tuscan balustrade.

RATHNALLY. 3 km NE. A modest country house on the gently sloping W bank of the river Boyne, built in the early C 18 for Thomas Carter, Master of the Rolls. His town house in Henrietta Street was designed by *Sir Edward Lovett Pearce*, and inevitably Pearce's name has been associated with Rathnally. The house certainly displays the robust classicism of the Pearce–Castle school, but any more specific attribution seems merely speculative.

Rathnally was much altered in the C 19, and it is difficult to imagine the appearance of the early C 18 house. As one approaches the building it now appears as a tall three-storey, three-bay block, cement-rendered, with a hipped roof, Italianate chimneys and a square rusticated porch. In fact the N-facing entrance block is a Victorian remodelling of the original house, whose C 18 character may be discerned only in the garden front and in the river elevation. Here the plan of the house is distinguished by an emphatic canted bow which projects eastward towards the river from a three-bay rear or garden elevation. At the back the house is of two storeys, with squat attic-like windows to the upper floor and generous windows on the ground floor, all in crisp limestone blocked surrounds. The windows are set close together on the garden front, divided by a broad band of masonry from the river bow but ending abruptly in a narrow quoined pilaster at its western end. One imagines that part of the house has either been demolished or was never built.

Behind this puzzling façade are two substantial reception rooms divided by a central corridor. To the W, the dining room is a large and elegant interior, 21 ft by 16 ft (6.3 m by 4.8 m), with fielded joinery to the windows, an C18 room cornice and Victorian ceiling and frieze ornament. The canted bow at the E end of the façade constitutes part of a large octagonal drawing room, 20 ft by 20 ft (6 m by 6 m), with a coved ceiling, classical soffit ornament and a polychrome marble chimneypiece. In the basement beneath is a vaulted room of similar dimensions.

FOSTERSTOWN HOUSE. 1.5 km S. Plain three-bay, two-storey house with a hipped roof, sash windows and a columnar fanlit doorcase which has the date June 1843 carved on the base of one column. Reputedly the temporary home of the future Duke of Wellington while his father was in the process of selling Dangan in the 1790s; if so, either greatly altered in 1843 or completely rebuilt. Nice thatched gate lodge.

LARACOR OLD PARISH CHURCH (C of I). 3 km S. 1855. By *Joseph Welland*. Small Victorian gabled hall of snecked limestone rubble, with a lower chancel, a S porch and a bellcote over the W end. Coupled lancets to the W end and single lancets lighting the nave. Adapted for use as a dwelling.

RORISTOWN. 3 km SW. Two-storey, five-bay house with a charming situation on the Boyne, built in 1787 by Cornelius Drake and given semicircular bowed ends in the late C19. Harled, with plate glass replacing the original sash bars. Handsome Adamesque Ionic porch. Inside, the plasterwork is a curious blend of late Georgian classicism and early Victorian Gothic. Fluted borders, animal masks and neoclassical foliage motifs, together with plaster rib-vaulting and clustered shafts to the upstairs door frames. This mixture suggests a remodelling of *c.* 1840. In the late Victorian period the two large rooms flanking the entrance hall were entirely remodelled and extended to give the house its distinctive curved profile. These rooms are perfectly preserved examples of late Victorian decorative ideas, almost uncanny in their authenticity.

TRIMLESTOWN CASTLE

ME *7050*

Set in fields on the E bank of the Trimlestown River, a tributary of the Boyne, 3 km W of Trim, are the imposing ruins of a large, late medieval castle built by the Barnewell family, probably in the C15. The castle has surprising bulk, rising for a full three storeys, with a big corner tower and extensive battlemented wall-heads that give it a distinctly romantic silhouette. It is a long range of buildings, 114 ft (34.7 m) in extent and some 40 ft (12 m) deep at the widest part. At this sort of size Trimlestown was clearly an important feudal base, one of the great castles of Meath like Dunsany, Liscarton and Killeen. Most of the ruins, despite late Georgian improvements, are medieval.

48 The core of the castle is a long two-storey barrel-vaulted hall, 52 ft by 17 ft (15.8 m by 5.1 m), now partly filled with rubble and with recesses at ground-floor level down each long wall. A straight mural stair in the E side may have connected with an upper level in the room, which was possibly divided by a timber floor. The upper storeys of this range of building were not vaulted and are now overgrown with ivy. The rooms were 22 ft (6.6 m) wide and have four large window openings along the SE side. The end of the hall, facing SW towards the river, is strengthened by three massive clasping buttresses, square in plan and tapering as they rise. These stop well below the wall-head and have solid stone roofs. Attached to the NW corner of the end of the hall is a square tower, barrel-vaulted at first-floor level, with a garderobe accommodated in the corner buttress. High on its SE face the tower carried a shield, coupling the arms of Barnewell and Nugent (the two families often intermarried), with a crest of a pelican and a helmet above.

The ruins at the other end of the castle are less easily read. Here it would appear that there was once another square tower, set at the other end of the castle and on the opposite side to protect the NE and SE walls. This was largely demolished *c.* 1800, when Trimlestown was modernized, and only its base remains, projecting forward from the SE side, with a segmental squinch arch, some 6 ft (1.8 m) from ground level, introduced to support a splayed section of wall where the principal spiral stair of the castle was placed. At the top of this splayed wall is a circular bartizan, which is probably mostly original. Beyond the bartizan, later Georgian romanticism takes over and medieval masonry is replaced by the gaunt perforated stonework of a broad bay window, three storeys high, with miniature battlements at the top. Beyond the bay window, lower ruinous sections of wall seem to be partly medieval, with C17 and C18 window and door openings. A round-arched doorway at the N end of the NW side is possibly Jacobean and has a deep bolt-hole in the depth of the reveal.

Neither the date of the modernization nor the name of the architect is known, though the style of the remodelling recalls the work of *Richard Johnston* at Louth Hall (*see* Tallanstown). The Barnewell family came from Crickstown Castle, Co. Meath, and in 1461 a younger son, Sir Robert Barnewell, was raised to the peerage by Edward IV as Baron Trimlestown. The eighth Lord served in the army against Cromwell and for his loyalty was banished 'from his rich grazing and fattening grounds in Co. Meath to a sheep walk in Co. Galway'. Under an Act of Settlement part of his lands was restored, but it was not until 1795, when the thirteenth Lord conformed to the Church of Ireland, that the Trimlestown title was acknowledged; several members of the family either lived or found military service abroad.

This history may account for the unaltered state of much of the medieval house. A probable date for the modernization must be soon after 1797, when the fourteenth Lord, who was already seventy and had inherited the estate only the year before, took, as his second wife, a girl of twenty-four. Perhaps she got a new house to compensate for an old husband, though, like an old dog with a young puppy, Lord Trimlestown enjoyed a new lease of life and survived to his eighty-eighth year! Soon after, the estate was united with that of Turvey House, Co. Dublin. The castle seems to have fallen into decay in the 1890s.

TRIMLESTOWN CHAPEL. N of the castle, in an old graveyard. Small rectangular, stone-built chapel containing the tomb of Margaret Dungan, fourth daughter of Sir John Dungan and wife of Robert, the ninth Baron Trimlestown (who is cited on the tomb, however, as the thirteenth Lord). It was this Lord Trimlestown who built up the estate after the Cromwellian forfeiture. 'There is now only a good house wanting', he wrote to his son in 1686, 'which I leave to you to do at your own leisure, without incommoding yourself of the fortune I leave you'. Unfortunately the Williamite wars followed almost immediately. A large sandstone piscina with bulky roll mouldings is built into the W wall. Lady Trimlestown died on 5 November 1680, and the tomb and chapel were built in her memory. The inscription has a heavy classical moulding and deeply undercut armorial carving. Now much defaced.

TULLYNALLY CASTLE

WM *4070*

In 1655 the lands of Tullynally were granted to Henry Pakenham, 89
a captain of a troop of horse who, having served with the army in Ireland, accepted the grant of lands in Wexford and Westmeath in lieu of his arrears of pay. For the next three hundred years the estate was to be known as Pakenham Hall, and it has reverted to the older name of Tullynally only in recent times. The house at Tullynally acquired by Captain Pakenham survived, no doubt in a modernized form, at least until the end of the C18. In 1737 it was described as an old building, 70 ft by 90 ft (21 m by 27 m), and when Arthur Young visited the estate in 1776 he noted that the house was 'pleasantly situated with much old wood about it'. The Pakenham family had been raised to the peerage in 1756 as Barons of Longford (later Earls), and with the succession of the second Earl in 1794 the time seemed appropriate to build a new mansion or at any rate to give the house a new look.

An architect, who is recorded in the accounts as *Mr Myers*, is known to have carried out improvements to the house *c.* 1780; a drawing of Pakenham Hall by *Francis Sandys*, which presumably records its appearance before the early C19 remodellings, shows it as a reticent, if solid, rectangular house, with tripartite windows on the entrance front. Of the earlier work, only some doorcases in the upper rooms and a small study in the NW corner of the house survive. The study has a handsome early C18 dentil room cornice and an imposing black marble chimneypiece, with an ogee-scrolled transom and large keystone of *c.* 1740.

What Myers and Sandys may have done has now been obscured by later additions, first by *Francis Johnston*, then by *James Shiel* and finally by *Sir Richard Morrison*. Tullynally today seems a perfect expression of the Irish Romantic castellated house, sprawlingly irregular, picturesque and yet preserving at its core – and still just visible – the remnants of an earlier symmetrical house. The old house, at the S end of the present castle, still accommodates the principal rooms and is distinguished from the rest of the building by being rendered and colour-washed on its S and W fronts. Its overall dimensions are close to those recorded in 1737, and it appears to have been a three-storeyed block, with the principal fronts each seven windows wide. In the centre of the entrance front a high two-storeyed hall seems, at least as a space, to have survived from the earlier plan. Front halls of two storeys are common in the grander houses of the early Georgian period, and this room may even have an earlier origin: the *Parliamentary Gazetteer of Ireland* of 1846 describes the house as 'the only mansion in the country which contains anything like *The Hall* in its original arrangements', which perhaps records a family tradition that the hall itself was very old.

Johnston's drawings for the building are on paper watermarked 1794 and 1798, and some other designs, for the addition of round towers, are dated to 1806. In April that year he approved the accounts of Samuel McNabb who had acted for two seasons as Clerk of Works at the house, by which time some £1,172 had been spent on the work. What Johnston did amounted to little more than a Gothic face-lift for the earlier house. On the S front he added two round towers projecting from the very corners of the main block; thin label mouldings were placed over all the windows and the eaves and edges of the lead flat in the centre of the roof were each given battlemented parapets. At the entrance he altered the ground-floor windows, as a pair of segment-headed designs with timber mullions, and he built a new central porch. On an axis with the main block and to the N, a rectangular stable court was built behind low battlemented walls.

None of this work could be described as adventurous, and though Maria Edgeworth considered Lord Longford's additions had made the castle 'a mansion fit for a nobleman of his fortune', Johnston's discreet battlemented box, with its office court beyond, must soon have seemed a little tame. The castles John Nash was building about this time in Ireland – Killymoon, Co. Tyrone, Loughcutra, Co. Galway, and Shanbally, Co. Tipperary – had far more swagger, and so by 1820 it was decided to alter the house again. Lord Longford had been married in 1817 and the decision to make further alterations may well have been an expression of Lady Longford's advanced tastes. In January 1820 an architect, *R. Richards*, made proposals to build out a bow window on the E front behind the hall, and though his scheme was not adopted it formed the basis for alterations undertaken in the same year to a design by Johnston's former clerk, James Shiel, who added a broad canted bay window towards the N end of the E front, with bartizan turrets in the re-entrant angles and wide mullioned windows under label mouldings in the new bay. The architecture of this addition was still in the idiom of Johnston's castle style, though the asymmetrical bay and curved link to a new round tower to the N introduced a greater variety of outline. There is also greater vigour in the interior decoration which dates from this period. Shiel had a liking for plasterwork with plain roll mouldings on a large scale and for simple geometrical shapes such as squares and octagons on a ceiling. The dining room, drawing room and library are all decorated in this style, while the hall has an uncompromising ceiling of prismatic fan-vaults, angular and overscaled, with the same dowel-like mouldings marking the intersection of the different planes. In contrast to the thin refinement of Cooley, Gandon or Johnston, Shiel's interiors have the weight – even the grossness – that marked the taste of the new generation in the 1820s. The hall is indeed in a very curious taste, theatrical like an Italian Gothick stage set, and rendered especially strange by the smooth wooden wainscot which completely encloses the space and originally masked all the doors which opened off it. Shiel's Gothic interiors normally use a type of Perpendicular-revival door with rich cusped panels, and this smooth style is untypical of his manner. Indeed the Gothic panelled doors are used throughout the other main rooms of the house, so it would appear that the treatment of the hall – and the dining room, where the same smooth wainscot is introduced – is a later, and most unusual, alteration. There is more of Shiel's Gothic taste in the long vaulted corridor that runs through the house at first-floor level.

The final phase in the development of Tullynally took place between 1842 and 1845, when Sir Richard Morrison added two long wings in polished ashlar limestone to link the house to the stable court. On the entrance front the new work appears as a Tudoresque family wing, six bays by two storeys, marked off by tall octagonal turrets, with a lower section ending in an octagonal stair tower which joins the stable court. This was refaced and gained a battlemented gateway in the manner of the towers that Morrison had previously built as gatehouses at Borris House, Co. Carlow, and Glenarm Castle, Co. Antrim. The entrance porch, a wide archway in ashlar stonework, with miniature bartizans rising from the corners, was also rebuilt at this time. Though Morrison provided a link between the old house and the family wing by building a tall octagonal tower, very much in the manner of Johnston's earlier work at Charleville Forest, Co. Offaly, the succession of façades from S to N hardly adds up to a coherent whole. The kitchen wing, which forms an extension of the E front, is much more convincingly massed, with a variety of stepped and pointed gables breaking the skyline and a large triple-light, round-headed window to light the kitchen in the middle of the façade. The detail of this work breaks new ground for this architect, and it seems unlikely to be the initiative of such an elderly practitioner (at the time of the completion of the wing, Sir Richard was already seventy-eight years old). Perhaps he had recently taken on a new clerk, such as someone trained in the office of Daniel Robertson, whose style is closely imitated in the kitchen wing.

Early in the C18 the grounds of Tullynally were celebrated for an elaborate water garden laid out about a long canal to the S of the house, with cascades, fountains and symmetrical basins. These disappeared in the later C18, when the demesne was landscaped, though a fragment of all this artifice survives in the RUSTIC GROTTO set into the side of a hill, with views over Lough Derravaragh. The grotto is a domed octagon, built of tufa blocks and rough stones collected from a river-bed. It has flanking rustic walls, and its back, which is tucked into the hill-side, has a continuous seat to allow visitors to enjoy the view. The castellated arched GATE LODGE, a two-storey, three-bay rubble block with central entrance arch and circular corner tower, is by *James Shiel.*

4030 TYRRELLSPASS WM

The modern route from the E to the W of Ireland, which runs through Tyrrellspass, follows the same line as the medieval roadway: a strip of dry passable land which in the Middle Ages was of strategic importance on account of the marshiness of the entire central midlands. Before the Shannon navigation developed in the later C18, the water-level in this area of Ireland was more than 8 ft (2.5 m) above its present level. Command of such a significant routeway could clearly be turned to profit, and the Tyrrell family held this position from the C15 until the middle of the C17. Their castle still stands beside the pass at the W edge of
7 the village. The modern Tyrrellspass is essentially a Georgian village, patronized in the C18 and C19 by the Rochforts, Lords Belfield and later Earls of Belvedere. The most distinctive feature of the place is the charming crescent and village green which were laid out in the opening decades of the C19 by Jane, Countess of Belvedere.

CASTLE. The fate of the Irish tower house is usually a sorry one; the countryside is strewn with fragments of long-forgotten towers, while many more, though ruinous, are still in a retrievable condition. Even so, in the entire area of North Leinster only two such structures have been reclaimed from dereliction and adapted for modern habitation. The castle at Tyrrellspass is the finest of these, painstakingly restored over the past two decades by Laurence Ginnell. Unlike the majority of Irish tower houses, this castle has been dated precisely; dendrochronological tests on a cross-section from an oak beam in the ground-floor chamber have shown that the tree began to grow in 1280 and was felled in the autumn of 1410. Built by the Tyrrells, the castle was one of a chain of Tyrrell strongholds in S Westmeath (towers at Castlelost, Simonstown, Kilbride, Newcastle and Tyrrellstown). The family remained here until the middle of the C17.

The castle, an impressive battered five-storey tower, is crowned by a parapet of even-stepped battlements. It is flanked on the SE by one of the round angle turrets of the original bawn. A single-storey L-shaped extension is concealed at the rear. The entrance, through a pointed archway, is on the SE face, though, curiously, the tower's only machicolation protects the NW angle. The windows on the principal face are short, rather crudely dressed loops, one to the centre of each floor. On the SW face the surviving loops are more finely executed, and here there are several windows which were inserted during the restoration. Three mullioned twinlight windows were brought from the ruin of Kilbeggan Parish Church (C of I), and the ogee-headed lancets with pocked tooling came from Syonan Castle near Horseleap.

The internal arrangement of the tower is not dissimilar to Syonan, with a vaulted vestibule running the length of the SE wall, a spiral stair at one end and a door leading into the principal chamber. The pattern of one large room flanked by a small narrow chamber off the main stair and at intermediate levels is repeated on each of the upper floors. Above the second floor the spiral stair becomes a straight mural stair. A garderobe chamber is located on the top floor on the SW wall. The principal ground-floor room, now the dining room, was roofed with the massive oak beams of 1410, while the first floor has a pointed barrel-vault. The reconstruction of the principal roof of the tower was modelled on that of Clara Castle, Co. Kilkenny. – MONUMENT. At the rear of the castle, brought here from the ruin of Castlelost, is part of a broken effigy said to be of Richard Tyrrell.

THE CRESCENT. A school, courthouse, parish church and several neat two-storey houses are spaciously laid out as a broad crescent around a semicircular green. All of simple Regency style, these houses and public buildings were built in the first quarter of the C19 by the Countess of Belvedere. A survey of 1818 shows the scheme almost complete, with the exception of the schoolhouse and the courthouse, which were built in the 1820s. In 1818 the dwelling houses were leased to the families of Paine, Hall Jones and Parkinson. Richard Somers, the lessor of several houses, was the agent of the Belvedere estate in Tyrrellspass. The houses are neat two-storey blocks of three and four bays, rough-cast, with hipped roofs, fanlit doorcases, sash windows and corner quoins. Built in 1823, the SCHOOLHOUSE is a charming three-bay, single-storey block, faced with limestone ashlar. In a reticent neoclassical idiom, its outer bays project slightly and carry pediments. Shallow relieving arches frame wide round-headed sash windows. The former COURT-

HOUSE may not have been built for this function, as the public buildings listed in 1843 are a church, a Methodist meeting house, a schoolhouse, an infant schoolhouse and a dispensary. The building is a handsome five-bay, two-storey house, with a hipped roof, an eaves pediment set over the central three bays and a slender belfry dome above. Perhaps it was originally the principal schoolhouse. The idiom is that of a late Georgian markethouse, with sash windows on both floors, a round-headed fanlit doorcase and a clock in the pediment. The reticent classicism of both this building and the schoolhouse is reminiscent of Francis Johnston, and also of William Deane Butler, who in the 1830s had proposed a formal crescent layout for Dunleer (q.v.). – STATUE GROUP. Standing on the village green, a charming sculpture of three small schoolchildren by *Imogen Stuart*, 1970. Erected by the old I.R.A., 'in memory of the men of Westmeath and Offaly who died on Irish soil and in Foreign lands for the Independence of Ireland'. A welcome change from the more conventional commemorative sculpture. Catholic children were formerly barred from playing on the village green; Imogen Stuart's figures, innocent, vulnerable and creedless, are a sign of changed times.

ST SINIAN, CLONFAD PARISH CHURCH (C of I). Like all the buildings in the Crescent, this Protestant parish church reflects the patronage of the Rochfort family. Built for picturesque effect, it is tall and substantial, with an elaborate tower, spire and side vestibules, all in an early Gothic Revival style, new in 1832. The nave, a rendered and gabled three-bay hall, is lit by tall thin windows with two tiers of paired cusped lights and reticulated tracery. A wide Perp window fills the E gable. The tower, of cut limestone, is three storeys high and has a battlemented parapet, spiky corner pinnacles, with crockets and projecting carved heads, and a thin needle spire. The belfry has a tall Perp opening. Diagonal corner buttresses. In contrast, the interior is a simple Gothic hall, remarkable only for the Belvedere MONUMENTS. At the E end, George Augustus Rochfort, second and last Earl of Belvedere, †1814. An impressive neoclassical monument by *John Bacon the younger*. A full-scale sculptural group, with the Earl lying on his death-bed, supported by Faith and beckoned to Heaven by an angelic figure, while his young wife weeps at the end of his couch. An almost exact copy of a tomb designed by Bacon's father to the memory of Samuel Whitbread †1796 in Cardington Church, Bedfordshire. – Jane, Countess of Belvedere, †1836, 'gifted with a masculine understanding'; a simple monument with inverted torches. – George Augustus Rochfort Boyd, only son of Abraham Boyd and Jane, Countess of Belvedere (born 1817), †1887.

ST STEPHEN, TYRRELLSPASS PARISH CHURCH. 1858. An ugly remodelling of a mid-Victorian lancet hall. Tall angular window to the entrance gable, with geometric stained glass and a mosaic panel depicting the stoning of St Stephen. Single-storey gabled porch of coloured concrete bricks. Simple interior, with three graded lancets to the chancel and an open kingpost roof.

NEIGHBOURHOOD

LOW'S CASTLE. 3 km W. An unusual circular tower built on a high hill or earthwork. Called after the Low family, Cromwellian settlers in Co. Westmeath, and presumably built by them, though the pointed and double-chamfered entrance doorway looks earlier than the mid-C17. A circular building, with a circumference of approximately 160 ft (48 m), the tower is built of coursed limestone rubble, rough-cast, and has a bulky battered base. The entrance on the W leads to a central tunnel which branches off on the l. into a suite of three small rooms and on the r. to a mural stair. This winds upward inside the outer wall to the now ruined first floor. A large walled enclosure stood SW of the tower on the hill slope. In 1744 Isaac Butler described the building as 'a round castle in good repair, the dwelling place of Edmund Low Esq ... well improved by a fine grove and a large bogg to the eastward'. In the CHURCH RUIN, S of the castle, is a finely preserved armorial carving, deeply undercut and of flamboyant baroque character.

NEWTOWN PARISH CHURCH (C of I). 3 km W. Simple hall and tower church in a pleasant wooded churchyard. Described in 1810 as 'newly rebuilt', though Lewis gives the date of completion as 1834. Three-bay hall and three-stage tower, rough-cast, with limestone trim. Lancet windows with hood-mouldings, clasping corner buttresses and nice spiky pinnacles to the tower. Inside, a cast-iron braced roof, a timber panelled ceiling and a moulded E.E. chancel arch. – MONUMENTS. Richard Pilkington of Tore †1711; large plaque with a floral cartouche and armorial crest. Edward Lee of Cornaher †1876 by *C. W. Harrison*. John Vignobles †1843 by *R. Ballantine*.

NEWCASTLE. 2 km NE. Originally a McLaughlin stronghold, Newcastle was eventually granted in 1640 to James Stopford. In 1744, when Isaac Butler passed by, he found a 'large house enclosed with trees and a village called Newcastle, the habitation of a Mr North'. All that now survives from the medieval period is one long two-storey wall, with the fragment of a square corner tower; the W wall of what formerly must have been an extensive fortified structure. The new Newcastle is not the Georgian house of Mr North but a symmetrical castellated house of 1851, rendered, with plate-glass windows and an advanced tower-like central bay. Possibly by *William Caldbeck*, it is now roofless and derelict.

MEEDIN CHAPEL. 2.5 km NE. 1831. The usual rendered T-plan chapel with Y-tracery lancets, enlivened by some splendid fragments of late medieval masonry from the ruined C16 church of Castlelost (*see* Rochfortbridge). The principal doorway has a pointed and chamfered limestone arch with multiple thin mouldings and plait-like motifs, tapering down to a base point. It has a rich hoodmoulding ending in knot-like label stops.

Above is a mullioned and transomed window with two ogee-headed lights in a rectangular frame. Carved interlacing decorates dished spandrels. This window has a flat hoodmoulding with carved label stops curving out like horns.

The interior is more ambitious than the common country chapel, with a lanky Ionic aedicule of rococo character framing a crucifix set against a painted backdrop of a stormy sky over Jerusalem. The windows have internal hoodmouldings with plaster putti label stops. All these enrichments were made possible by the patronage of Richard Charles Coffey of Newcastle.

GUILFORD HOUSE. 1.5 km N. Handsome mid-C18 farmhouse built by the Reynolds family. Two-storey, five-bay block, built over a basement, with a gabled roof, end chimneystacks and a stair well projecting from the centre of the rear elevation. Rough-cast, with corner quoins. The sash windows have twelve panes on the principal floor and six panes on the upper storey. Central round-headed doorcase, with a limestone Gibbs surround and a broad flight of steps with stone handrails.

8080 WHITEWOOD LODGE ME

Designed in 1735 by *Richard Castle* as a hunting lodge for the Preston family, Whitewood is a perfect reflection of the sound practical sense of early Georgian builders. Substance and solidity are the qualities of this plain but handsome building. Unlike later Georgian country houses hidden away in the midst of picturesque wood and parkland, this house dominated an open vista from its main gate, framed on each side by broad bands of planting. At the rear the house overlooks Whitewood Lake. The lodge is a square limestone block of two storeys over a basement, with a shallow parapet partially screening a hipped roof and two large central chimneys. Both the principal and the side elevations are of three bays with small sash windows and broad expanses of masonry. A front stone staircase, finely worked, arches over the basement area to provide access to the main door, which like so many of Castle's minor works is understated, a simple opening with a small fanlight and plain surround. The house plan is symmetrical, two rooms deep, with a central entrance hall and staircase behind flanked by large rooms on each side. These have neat cornices, Kilkenny marble chimneypieces and fielded panels to all the woodwork. As a designer, Castle was often impatient with details, an attitude illustrated at Whitewood Lodge by the somewhat random alignment of the doors in the hall. All of the floors are stone-flagged, and the stairs too are of exposed solid limestone.

3060 WILSON'S HOSPITAL WM

69 Large and sophisticated Georgian building in the most unlikely of rural settings at the very NW extremity of Co. Westmeath.

The hospital was founded in 1759 with a trust fund set up by Andrew Wilson of Piersfield. Wilson's will of 1724 had stipulated that if there were no direct male heirs to his estate, which by 1743 was the case, then the estate and its profits should be transferred to the Church of Ireland hierarchy, to be used for building a hospital for aged Protestant men and school for poor Protestant boys. In 1762, after a family contest of the will, an Act of Parliament was passed to ratify the execution of Wilson's Trust. Meanwhile, in 1759, work had begun on the prospective hospital, which was completed in 1761. Although records do not survive, the design has been convincingly attributed to *John Pentland*.

Superficially the hospital is like a Palladian country house, given a commanding position on top of a grassy hill and dominating the landscape. It has flanking two-storey wings linked by low quadrant walls that curve back from the main block – a feature found in Nathaniel Clements' houses – but the mass of the main block itself is too complex and too extensive for the notion of domestic architecture to last very long. As a piece of architecture the hospital exhibits two concepts imposed one upon the other. Despite the showy painted ashlar elevation on the hill, the key to the building is its plan, which goes back to proven models for institutional architecture in Ireland, to Kilmainham Royal Hospital of 1680 and Dr Steven's Hospital in Dublin of 1720, both quadrangular structures with an open arcaded courtyard in the centre. Wilson's Hospital is the same, four ranges of functional stone buildings, each 112 ft (34.1 m) long, set round a courtyard with an arcaded ground floor and two 'square' corridors in the floors above. The courtyard is a wonderful piece of vernacular C18 architecture, tall and very distinctly enclosed, with a limestone pavement and ample rubble-built piers between the plain round-headed arches that line each side. On the N, the centre bay projects slightly and is carried up beyond the eaves to support a clock and octagonal bellcote cupola.

With the exception of this belltower cupola, the very symbol of discipline in a school, none of this plain architecture is seen from outside. Had the trustees been content with a simple workmanlike building the hospital might have appeared as an astylar square block with eight windows on each side, a tall hipped roof and regular chimneystacks. This is indeed what is seen on the side elevations, but for the façade ascendancy prelates expected more show, and this is what John Pentland gave them. The plain building of the sides is carried round to the front for one bay at the extreme ends of the façade. Then the architecture changes gear. Mr Pentland had evidently been consulting pattern books on Palladian designs, and an insouciant villa façade is grafted onto the front. The two do not fit well together, for the 'villa' part of the façade is designed to a larger scale, taller and altogether more self-conscious as architecture. In itself, however, it is a pretty design; a five-bay front, stepping forward at the junction with the main block and again for the centre three bays, which are crowned with a pediment. Blocked surrounds frame all the ground-floor windows, and rather over-large Venetian windows are set at first-floor level in the outer bays. The usual Palladian elements of string-courses, a central pediment and continuous cornice give the design a certain coherence within itself, yet it is never more than a façade and bears little relation to what goes on inside the building. The Palladian model suggests some major rooms at first-floor level; on inspection these are lacking, and the big Venetian windows are partly dummies inside.

To a modern taste the arcaded courtyard is the hospital's finer feature and it is one that enjoys an additional advantage – prized by aesthetic theorists in the age of Reason – the element of surprise. The hospital is set into the top of its hill, so that it is entered at first-floor level. The building is thus of two storeys on one side and three storeys on the other, and a visitor entering the wide square corridor behind the front hall looks *down* into the school courtyard. Across the yard in an axis with the entrance hall is the chapel. Two robustly detailed timber stairs are positioned in the side ranges half-way down each corridor. The plan is rational and works well, with kitchens, stores and offices at the arcaded basement level, the superintendent and inmates on the first floor, and the schoolmasters, hospital officers and superintendent's family on the upper floor.

77 The chapel is a two-storey room which projects as a central bow from the back of the building. It is lit by three large circular-headed windows with mid-Victorian 'Lombardic' mullions, and the sanctuary area has Victorian tiles. Otherwise this is a perfect mid-Georgian chapel, not dissimilar to Richard Castle's famous Rotunda Hospital chapel in Dublin, with a gallery or balcony down the sides and across the back. It is supported on widely spaced Doric columns with a full triglyph frieze and balustrade above. The columns stand on tall plinths which mark the level of the original box pews, now replaced by benches. Like the courtyard, the chapel is sensible rather than showy, though its details, for instance the rich modillion room cornice or the slender balusters in the gallery, are refined. The chapel stands above the Old Kitchen, now a classroom, which very sensibly, as cooking smells in a church would be offensive, is roofed with a groined vault. The vault springs from two rows of Tuscan columns which recall the stables of Richard Castle.

Throughout the C18 and C19 Wilson's Hospital was an emphatically male environment with old invalided men, young boys and a male teaching staff. Blue and orange uniforms were worn by both men and boys and a generous diet of food and drink was provided, so that the old men not infrequently were caught embezzling or hiding their food to sell it later! Inmates were required to attend chapel on every weekday, eat their meals decently and refrain from any immoral action. On 8 September an annual sermon was given by the chaplain in remembrance of Andrew Wilson's charitable intention. In the Rising of 1798 the hospital was taken over as a militia barracks. It was attacked on 6 September that year and, in 'the Battle of Wilson's Hospital', 150 rebels were killed and the rebellion in Westmeath ended.

GLOSSARY

Particular types of an architectural element are often defined under the name of the element itself, e.g. for 'dog-leg stair' see STAIR. Literal meanings, where specially relevant, are indicated by the abbreviation *lit.* Of the terms here defined, not all are necessarily used in this volume. The abbreviations E.E., DEC, and PERP, referring to stylistic subdivisions in English Gothic architecture, have little relevance to Irish medieval patterns. They are retained here principally because they provide a convenient shorthand with which to indicate the character of much C 19 Gothic Revival architecture in Ireland which, particularly in the first half of the century, was often based on English models.

ABACUS (*lit.* tablet): flat slab forming the top of a capital, *see* Orders (fig. 16).

ABUTMENT: the meeting of an arch or vault with its solid lateral support, or the support itself.

ACANTHUS: formalized leaf ornament with thick veins and frilled edge, e.g. on a Corinthian capital.

ACHIEVEMENT OF ARMS: in heraldry, a complete display of armorial bearings.

ACROTERION (*lit.* peak): pointed ornament projecting above the apex or ends of a pediment.

AEDICULE (*lit.* little building): term used in classical architecture to describe the unit formed by a pair of columns or pilasters, an entablature, and usually a pediment, placed against a wall to frame an opening.

AGGREGATE: small stones added to a binding material, e.g. in harling or concrete.

AISLE (*lit.* wing): passage alongside the nave, choir or transept of a church, or the main body of some other building, separated from it by columns or piers.

AMBO: raised platform or pulpit in early Christian churches.

AMBULATORY (*lit.* walkway): aisle at the E end of a chancel, usually surrounding an apse and therefore semicircular or polygonal in plan.

ANNULET (*lit.* ring): shaft-ring (q.v.).

ANSE DE PANIER (*lit.* basket handle): basket arch (*see* Arch).

ANTAE: (1) flat pilasters placed at the ends of the short projecting walls of a portico or colonnade, which is then called *In Antis*. *See* Orders (fig. 16). The bases and capitals of antae differ from, and are more simple than, the columns of the order that they accompany. (2) the side walls of a building projecting at the gables, typical of many early Christian churches in Ireland.

ANTEFIXAE: ornaments projecting at regular intervals above a classical cornice. *See* Orders (fig. 16).

ANTHEMION (*lit.* honeysuckle): classical ornament like a honeysuckle flower (*see* fig. 1).

Fig. 1 Anthemion and Palmette Frieze

APSE: semicircular (i.e. apsidal) extension of an apartment. A term first used of the magistrate's end of a Roman basilica, and thence especially of the vaulted semicircular or polygonal end of a chancel or a chapel.

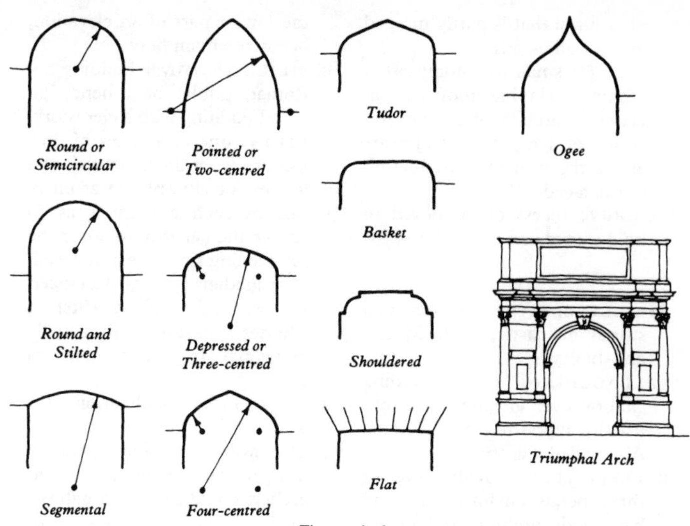

Fig. 2. Arch

ARABESQUE: type of painted or carved surface decoration, often with a vertical emphasis and consisting of intertwined foliage scrolls sometimes incorporating ornamental objects or figures.

ARCADE: a series of arches supported by piers or columns. *Blind Arcade*: the same applied to the surface of a wall. *Wall Arcade*: in medieval churches, a blind arcade forming a dado below windows.

ARCH: for the various forms *see* fig. 2. The term *Basket Arch* refers to a basket handle and is sometimes applied to a three-centred or depressed arch as well as the type with a flat middle. *Transverse Arch*: across the main axis of an interior space. A term used especially for the arches between the compartments of tunnel- or groin-vaulting. *Diaphragm Arch*: transverse arch with solid spandrels spanning an otherwise wooden-roofed interior. *Chancel Arch*: across the w end of a chancel. *Relieving Arch*: incorporated in a wall, to carry some of its weight, some way above an opening. *Strainer Arch*: inserted across an opening to resist any inward pressure of the side members. *Triumphal Arch*: Imperial Roman monument whose elevation supplied a motif for many later classical compositions. *See also* Rere-arch.

ARCHITRAVE: (1) formalized lintel, the lowest member of the classical entablature (*see* Orders, fig. 16); (2) moulded frame of a door or window. Also *Lugged* (Irish) or *Shouldered Architrave*, whose top is prolonged into lugs (*lit.* ears).

ARCHIVOLT: under surface of an arch or the moulded band applied to this curve. Also called Soffit.

ARRIS (*lit.* stop): sharp edge at the meeting of two surfaces.

ASHLAR: masonry of large blocks wrought to even faces and square edges.

ASTYLAR: term used to describe an elevation that has no columns or other distinguishing stylistic features.

ATLANTES: male counterparts of caryatids, often in a more demonstrative attitude of support. In sculpture, a single figure of the god Atlas may be seen supporting a globe.

ATTACHED: description of a shaft

or column that is partly merged into a wall or pier.

ATTIC: (1) small top storey often within a sloping roof; (2) in classical architecture, the top storey of a façade if it appears above the principal entablature of the façade.

AUMBRY: recess or cupboard to hold sacred vessels for the Mass.

BAILEY: open space or court of a stone-built castle; *see also* Motte-and-Bailey.

BALDACCHINO: free-standing canopy over an altar or tomb, usually supported on columns. Also called Ciborium.

BALLFLOWER: globular flower of three petals enclosing a small ball. A decoration used in the first quarter of the C 14.

BALUSTER (*lit.* pomegranate): hence a pillar or pedestal of bellied form. *Balusters*: vertical supports of this or any other form, for a handrail or coping, the whole being called a *Balustrade. Blind Balustrade*: the same with a wall behind.

BARBICAN: outwork defending the entrance to a castle.

BARGEBOARDS: projecting inclined boards, often decoratively pierced and carved, fixed beneath the eaves of a gable to cover and protect the rafters. Common in C 15 and C 16 architecture and revived by Picturesque designers in the C 19.

BARROW: burial mound.

BARTIZAN (*lit.* battlement): turret, square or round, corbelled out from a wall or tower of a castle, church, or house. Frequently at a corner, hence *Corner Bartizan*.

BASE: moulded foot of a column or other order. For its use in classical architecture *see* Orders (fig. 16). *Elided Bases*: bases of a compound pier whose lower parts are run together, ignoring the arrangement of the shafts above. Capitals may be treated in the same way.

BASEMENT: lowest, subordinate storey of a building, and hence the lowest part of an elevation, below the main floor.

BASILICA (*lit.* royal building): a Roman public hall; hence an aisled building with a clerestory.

BASTION: one of a series of projections from the main wall of a fortress or city, placed at intervals in such a manner as to enable the garrison to cover the intervening stretches of the wall. Post-medieval and developed for use with artillery (first at Rhodes), bastions are usually polygonal or semicircular in plan.

BATTER: inward inclination of a wall.

BATTLEMENT: fortified parapet, indented or crenellated so that archers could shoot through the indentations (crenels or embrasures) between the projecting solid portions (merlons). After the invention of gunpowder had made them obsolete, battlements continued in use as decoration until at least the C 17. *Irish Battlements*: a system where the up-and-down rhythm of merlons and embrasures is interrupted at the corners, which are built up in a series of high steps, typical of late medieval architecture in Ireland.

BAWN (*lit.* ox fold): defensive walled enclosure attached to, or near, a tower house or Plantation castle.

BAYS: divisions of an elevation or interior space as defined by any regular vertical features (arches, columns, windows, etc.).

BAY WINDOW: window of one or more storeys projecting from the face of a building at ground level, and either rectangular or polygonal in plan. A *Canted Bay Window* has a straight front and angled sides. A *Bow Window* is curved. An *Oriel Window* projects on corbels or brackets from an upper floor and does not start from the ground.

BEAKHEAD: Norman ornamental motif consisting of a row of bird or beast heads with beaks biting usually into a roll moulding.

BELFRY (*lit.* tower): (1) bell-turret set on a roof or gable (*see also* Bellcote); (2) room or stage in a tower where bells are hung; (3) bell-tower in a general sense.

BELL-CAST: *see* Roof.

BELLCOTE: belfry as (1) above, with the character of a small house for the bell(s).

BILLET (*lit.* log or block) FRIEZE: Norman ornament consisting of small blocks placed at regular intervals (*see* fig. 3).

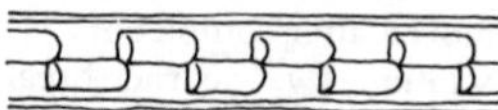

Fig. 3. Billet Frieze

BLIND: *see* Arcade, Balustrade.

BLOCKING COURSE: plain course of stones, or equivalent, on top of a cornice and crowning the wall.

BOLECTION MOULDING: convex moulding covering the joint between two different planes and overlapping the higher as well as the lower one, especially on panelling and fireplace surrounds of the late C 17 and early C 18.

BOND: in brickwork, the pattern of long sides (stretchers) and short ends (headers) produced on the face of a wall by laying bricks in a particular way (*see* fig. 4).

BOSS: knob or projection usually placed to cover the intersection of ribs in a vault.

BOW WINDOW: *see* Bay window.

BOX PEW: pew enclosed by a high wooden back and ends, the latter having doors.

BRACE: *see* Roof (fig. 22).

BRACKET: small supporting piece of stone, etc., to carry a projecting horizontal member.

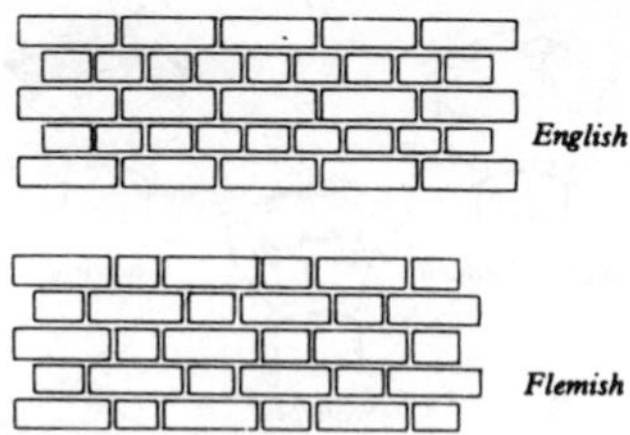

Fig. 4. Bond

BUCRANIUM: ox skull, used decoratively in classical friezes.

BULLAUNS: boulders having an artificial basin-like hollow. Now frequently regarded with superstition, they are found at early monastic sites and killeens and were probably used for pounding and grinding grain.

BULLSEYE WINDOW: small circular window, e.g. in the tympanum of a pediment. Also called *Œil de Bœuf*.

BUTTRESS: vertical member projecting from a wall to stabilize it or to resist the lateral thrust of an arch, roof, or vault. For different types used at the corners of a building, especially a tower, *see* fig. 5. A *Flying Buttress* transmits the thrust to a heavy abutment by means of an arch or half-arch.

CABLE MOULDING or ROPE MOULDING: originally a Norman moulding, imitating the twisted strands of a rope.

CAMBER: slight rise or upward curve in place of a horizontal line or plane.

CAMPANILE: freestanding bell-tower.

CANDLE-SNUFFER ROOF: conical roof of a turret.

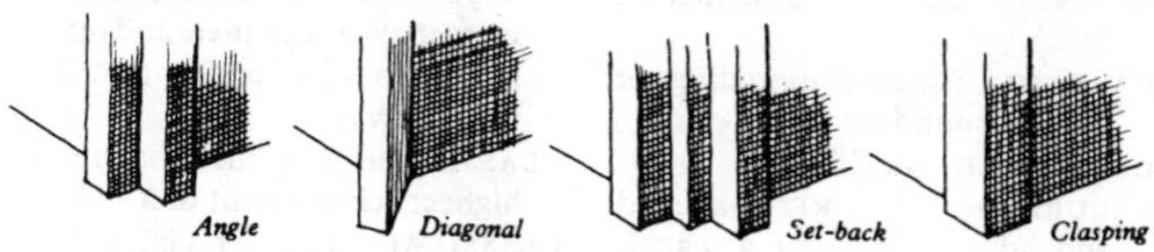

Fig. 5. Buttresses at a corner

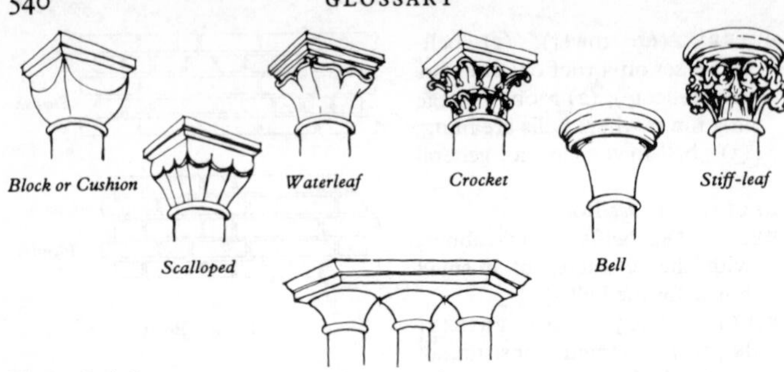

Fig. 6. Capitals

CANES: *see* Quarries.

CANOPY: projection or hood over an altar, pulpit, niche, statue, etc.

CANTED: tilted, generally on a vertical axis to produce an obtuse angle on plan, e.g. of a canted bay window.

CAPITAL: head or top part of a column; for classical types *see* Orders (fig. 16); for medieval types *see* fig. 6. *Elided Capitals*: capitals of a compound pier whose upper parts are run together, ignoring the arrangement of the shafts below.

CARRIAGE ARCH: *see* Pend.

CARTOUCHE: tablet with ornate frame, usually of elliptical shape and bearing a coat of arms or inscription.

CARYATIDS (*lit.* daughters of the village of Caryae): female figures supporting an entablature, counterparts of Atlantes.

CASEMATE: in military architecture, a vaulted chamber, with embrasures for defence, built in the thickness of the walls of a castle or fortress or projecting from them.

CASEMENT: (1) window hinged at the side; (2) in Gothic architecture, a concave moulding framing a window.

CASTELLATED: battlemented (*q.v.*).

CAVETTO: concave moulding of quarter-round section.

CELLURACH: *see* Killeen.

CELURE or CEILURE: panelled and adorned part of a wagon roof above the rood or the altar.

CENTERING: wooden support for the building of an arch or vault, removed after completion.

CHAMFER (*lit.* corner-break): surface formed by cutting off a square edge, usually at an angle of forty-five degrees.

CHANCEL (*lit.* enclosure): that part of the E end of a church in which the altar is placed, usually applied to the whole continuation of the nave E of the crossing.

CHANTRY CHAPEL: chapel attached to, or inside, a church, endowed for the celebration of masses for the soul of the founder or some other individual.

CHEVRON: zigzag Norman ornament.

CHOIR: (1) the part of a church where services are sung; in monastic churches this can occupy the crossing and/or the easternmost bays of the nave, but in cathedral churches it is usually in the E arm; (2) the E arm of a cruciform church (a usage of long standing though liturgically anomalous).

CIBORIUM: canopied shrine for the reserved sacrament. *See also* Baldacchino.

CINQUEFOIL: *see* Foil.

CLAPPER BRIDGE: bridge made of large slabs of stone, some built up to make rough piers and other longer ones laid on top to make the roadway.

CLASSIC: term for the moment of highest achievement of a style.

CLASSICAL: term for Greek and Roman architecture and any subsequent styles inspired by it.

CLERESTORY: upper storey of the nave walls of a church, pierced by windows.

COADE STONE: artificial (cast) stone made in the late C 18 and the early C 19 by Coade and Sealy in London.

COB: walling material made of mixed clay and straw. Also called *Mud Wall*.

COFFERING: sunken panels, square or polygonal, decorating a ceiling, vault, or arch.

COLLAR: *see* Roof (fig. 22).

COLONNADE: range of columns supporting an entablature.

COLONNETTE: small column or shaft in medieval architecture.

COLUMN: in classical architecture, an upright structural member of round section with a shaft, a capital, and usually a base. *See* Orders (fig. 16).

COLUMNA ROSTRATA: column decorated with carved prows of ships to celebrate a naval victory.

COMPOSITE: *see* Orders.

CONSOLE: ornamental bracket of compound curved outline (*see* fig. 7). Its height is usually greater than its projection, as in (*a*).

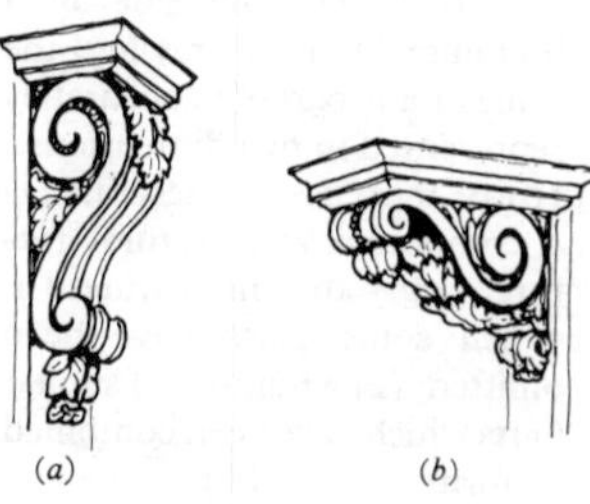

Fig. 7. Console

COPING (*lit.* capping): course of stones, or equivalent, on top of a wall.

CORBEL: block of stone projecting from a wall, supporting some feature on its horizontal top surface. *Corbel Course*: continuous projecting course of stones fulfilling the same function. *Corbel Table*: series of corbels to carry a parapet or a wall-plate; for the latter *see* Roof (fig. 22).

CORINTHIAN: *see* Orders (fig. 16).

CORNICE: (1) moulded ledge, decorative and/or practical, projecting along the top of a building or feature, especially as the highest member of the classical entablature (*see* Orders, fig. 16); (2) decorative moulding in the angle between a wall and ceiling.

CORPS-DE-LOGIS: French term for the main building(s) as distinct from the wings or pavilions.

COURSE: continuous layer of stones etc. in a wall.

COVE: concave soffit like a hollow moulding but on a larger scale. A *Coved Ceiling* has a pronounced cove joining the walls to a flat surface in the middle.

CREDENCE: in a church or chapel, a side table, often a niche or recessed cavity, for the sacramental elements before consecration.

CRENELLATION: *see* Battlement.

CREST, CRESTING: ornamental finish along the top of a screen, etc.

CROCKETS (*lit.* hooks), CROCKETING: in Gothic architecture, leafy knobs on the edges of any sloping feature. *Crocket Capital: see* Capital (fig. 6).

CROSSING: in a church, central space opening into the nave, chancel, and transepts. *Crossing Tower*: central tower supported by the piers at its corners.

CROWSTEPS: squared stones set like steps to form a skew; *see* Gable (fig. 9).

CRUCK (*lit.* crooked): piece of naturally curved timber combining the structural roles of an upright post and a sloping rafter, e.g. in the building of a cottage, where each pair of crucks is joined at the ridge.

CRYPT: underground room usually below the E end of a church.

CUPOLA (*lit.* dome): small polygonal or circular domed turret crowning a roof.

CURTAIN WALL: (1) connecting

wall between the towers of a castle; (2) in modern building, thin wall attached to the main structure, usually outside it.

CURVILINEAR: *see* Tracery (fig. 25).

CUSP: projecting point formed by the foils within the divisions of Gothic tracery, also used to decorate the soffits of the Gothic arches of tomb recesses, sedilia, etc.

CYCLOPEAN MASONRY: built with large irregular polygonal stones, but smooth and finely jointed.

DADO: lower part of a wall or its decorative treatment; *see also* Pedestal (fig. 17).

DAGGER: *see* Tracery (fig. 25).

DAIS: raised platform at one end of a room.

DEC (DECORATED): historical division of English Gothic architecture covering the period from *c.* 1290 to *c.* 1350.

DEMI-COLUMNS: engaged columns, only half of whose circumference projects from the wall.

DIAPER (*lit.* figured cloth): repetitive surface decoration.

DIOCLETIAN WINDOW: *see* Thermae Window.

DISTYLE: having two columns.

DOGTOOTH: typical E.E. decoration applied to a moulding. It consists of a series of squares, their centres raised like pyramids and their edges indented (*see* fig. 8).

Fig. 8. Dogtooth

DONJON: *see* Keep.

DORIC: *see* Orders (fig. 16).

DORMER WINDOW: window standing up vertically from the slope of a roof and lighting a room within it. *Dormer Head*: gable above this window, often formed as a pediment.

DORTER: dormitory; sleeping quarters of a monastery.

DOUBLE-PILE: *see* Pile.

DRESSINGS: features made of smoothly worked stones, e.g. quoins or string courses, projecting from the wall which may be of different material, colour, or texture. Also called *Trim*.

DRIPSTONE: moulded stone projecting from a wall to protect the lower parts from water; *see also* Hoodmould.

DRUM: (1) circular or polygonal vertical wall of a dome or cupola; (2) one of the stones forming the shaft of a column.

DRY-STONE: stone construction without mortar.

E.E. (EARLY ENGLISH): historical division of English Gothic architecture covering the period 1200–1250.

EAVES: overhanging edge of a roof; hence *Eaves Cornice* in this position.

ECHINUS (*lit.* sea-urchin): lower part of a Greek Doric capital; *see* Orders (fig. 16).

EDGE-ROLL: moulding of semicircular or more than semicircular section at the edge of an opening.

ELEVATION: (1) any side of a building; (2) in a drawing, the same or any part of it, accurately represented in two dimensions.

ELIDED: term used to describe (1) a compound architectural feature, e.g. an entablature, in which some parts have been omitted; (2) a number of similar parts which have been combined to form a single larger one (*see* Capital, fig. 6).

EMBATTLED: furnished with battlements.

EMBRASURE (*lit.* splay): small splayed opening in the wall or battlement of a fortified building.

ENCAUSTIC TILES: glazed and decorated earthenware tiles used for paving.

ENGAGED COLUMN: one that is partly merged into a wall or pier.

ENTABLATURE: in classical architecture, collective name for the three horizontal members (architrave, frieze, and cornice) above a column; *see* Orders (fig. 16).

ENTASIS: very slight convex deviation from a straight line; used on classical columns and sometimes on spires to prevent an optical illusion of concavity.

ENTRESOL: mezzanine storey within or above the ground storey.

ESCUTCHEON: shield for armorial bearings.

EXEDRA: apsidal end of an apartment; *see* Apse.

FERETORY: (1) place behind the high altar where the chief shrine of a church is kept; (2) wooden or metal container for relics.

FESTOON: ornament, usually in high or low relief, in the form of a garland of flowers and/or fruit, hung up at both ends; *see also* Swag.

FIELDED PANELLING: panelling, or wainscot, characteristic of the late Stuart and early Georgian periods (1690–1770), in which each panel is bordered by a sloping chamfered edge, creating a flat panel or 'field' in the centre.

FILLET: narrow flat band running down a shaft or along a roll moulding.

FINIAL: topmost feature, e.g. above a gable, spire, or cupola.

FLAMBOYANT: properly the latest phase of French Gothic architecture, where the window tracery takes on undulating lines, based on the use of flowing curves.

FLÈCHE (*lit.* arrow): slender spire on the centre of a roof.

FLEUR-DE-LYS: in heraldry, a formalized lily as in the royal arms of France.

FLEURON: decorative carved flower or leaf.

FLOWING: *see* Tracery (Curvilinear; fig. 25).

FLUTING: series of concave grooves, their common edges sharp (arris) or blunt (fillet).

FOIL (*lit.* leaf): lobe formed by the cusping of a circular or other shape in tracery. *Trefoil* (three), *Quatrefoil* (four), *Cinquefoil* (five), and *Multifoil* express the number of lobes in a shape; *see* Tracery (fig. 25).

FOLIATED: decorated, especially carved, with leaves.

FOSSE: ditch.

FRATER: refectory or dining hall of a monastery.

FREESTONE: stone that is cut, or can be cut, in all directions, usually fine-grained sandstone or limestone.

FRESCO: painting executed on wet plaster.

FRIEZE: horizontal band of ornament, especially the middle member of the classical entablature; *see* Orders (fig. 16). *Pulvinated Frieze (lit.* cushioned): frieze of convex profile.

FRONTAL: covering for the front of an altar.

GABLE: (1) peaked wall or other vertical surface, often triangular, at the end of a double-pitch roof; (2) the same, very often with a chimney at the apex, but also in a wider sense: end wall, of whatever shape. *See* fig. 9. *Gablet*: small gable. *See also* Roof.

GADROONING: ribbed ornament, e.g. on the lid or base of an urn, flowing into a lobed edge.

GALILEE: chapel or vestibule usually at the W end of a church enclosing the porch; *see also* Narthex.

GALLERY: balcony or passage, but with certain special meanings, e.g. (1) upper storey above the aisle of a church, looking through arches to the nave; also called tribune and often erroneously triforium; (2) balcony or mezzanine, often with seats, overlooking the main interior space of a building; (3) external walkway projecting from a wall.

GARDEROBE (*lit.* wardrobe): medieval privy.

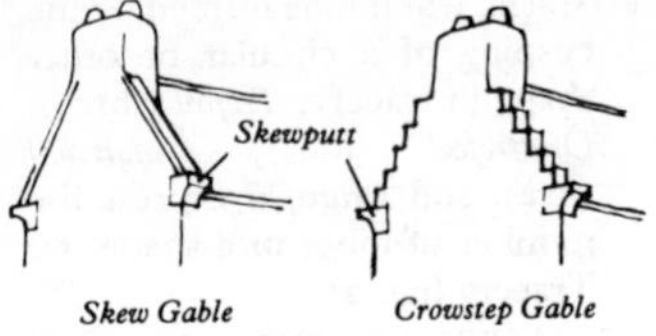

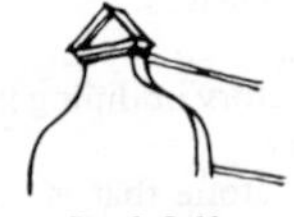

Fig. 9. Gables

GARGOYLE: water spout projecting from the parapet of a wall or tower, often carved into human or animal shape.

GAZEBO (jocular Latin, 'I shall gaze'): lookout tower or raised summer house overlooking a garden.

GEOMETRIC: historical division of English Gothic architecture covering the period *c.* 1250–90. *See also* Tracery (fig. 25). For another meaning, *see* Stair.

GIB DOOR: doorway flush with the wall surface and without any visible frame, so that the opening appears to merge with the wall of the room. It often has the skirting board and chair-rail carried across the surface of the door.

GIBBS SURROUND: C 18 treatment of door or window surround, seen particularly in the work of James Gibbs (1682–1754) *see* fig. 10).

GLACIS: in military architecture, a bank, extending in a long slow slope from a fort, on which attackers are exposed to fire.

GLEBE-HOUSE: a house built on and counting as part of the portion of land going with an

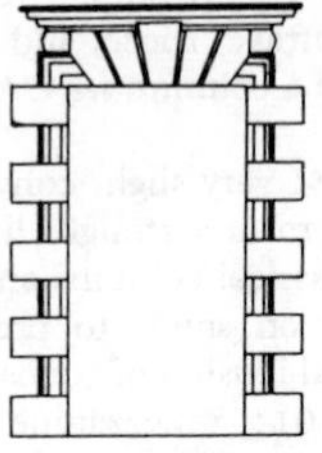

Fig. 10. Gibbs Surround

established clergyman's benefice.

GNOMON: vane or indicator casting a shadow on to a sundial.

GRC: glass-fibre reinforced concrete.

GROIN: sharp edge at the meeting of two cells of a cross-vault; *see* Vault (fig. 26a).

GROTESQUE (*lit.* grotto-esque): classical wall decoration of spindly, whimsical character adopted from Roman examples, particularly by Raphael, and further developed in the C 18.

GUILLOCHE: running classical ornament formed by a series of circles with linked and interlaced borders (see fig. 11).

Fig. 11. Guilloche

GUN LOOP: opening for a firearm.

GUTTAE: *see* Orders (fig. 16).

HAGIOSCOPE: *see* Squint.

HALF-TIMBERING: timber framing with the spaces filled in by plaster, stones or brickwork.

HAMMERBEAM: *see* Roof.

HARLING: *see* Rendering.

HEADER: *see* Bond.

HERM (*lit.* the god Hermes): male head or bust on a pedestal.

HERRINGBONE WORK: masonry or brickwork in zigzag courses.

HEXASTYLE: term used to describe a portico with six columns.

HOODMOULD: projecting moulding above an arch or lintel to throw off water. When the moulding is horizontal it is called a *Label*.

HUNGRY JOINTS: *see* Pointing.

HUSK GARLAND: festoon of nutshells diminishing towards the ends (*see* fig. 12).

Fig. 12. Husk Garland

IMPOST (*lit.* imposition): horizontal moulding at the spring of an arch.

IN ANTIS: *see* Antae, Orders (fig. 16), and Portico.

INDENT: (1) shape chiselled out of a stone to match and receive a brass; (2) in restoration, a section of new stone inserted as a patch into older work.

INGLENOOK (*lit.* fire-corner): recess for a hearth with provision for seating.

INTERCOLUMNIATION: interval between columns.

IONIC: *see* Orders (fig. 16).

JAMB (*lit.* leg): one of the straight sides of an archway, door, or window.

KEEL MOULDING: *see* fig. 13.

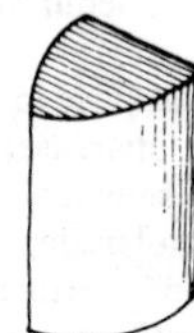

Fig. 13. Keel Moulding

KEEP: principal tower of a castle. Also called Donjon.

KEY PATTERN: *see* fig. 14.

Fig. 14. Key Pattern

KEYSTONE: middle and topmost stone in an arch or vault.

KILLEEN or CELLURACH (*lit.* a cell or church): a walled enclosure, used until recent times for the burial of unbaptized children. Often near old monastic sites.

KINGPOST: *see* Roof (fig. 22).

LABEL: *see* Hoodmould. *Label Stop*: ornamental boss at the end of a hoodmould.

LADY CHAPEL: chapel dedicated to the Virgin Mary.

LANCET WINDOW: slender pointed-arched window, often in groups of two, five, or seven.

LANTERN: a small circular or polygonal turret with windows all round crowning a roof (*see* Cupola) or a dome.

LAVATORIUM: in a monastery, a washing place adjacent to the refectory.

LEAN-TO: term commonly applied not only to a single-pitch roof but to the building it covers.

LESENE (*lit.* a mean thing): pilaster without base or capital. Also called pilaster strip.

LIERNE: *see* Vault (fig. 26b).

LIGHT: compartment of a window.

LINENFOLD: Tudor panelling ornamented with a conventional representation of a piece of linen laid in vertical folds. The piece is repeated in each panel.

LINTEL: horizontal beam or stone bridging an opening.

LOGGIA: sheltered space behind a colonnade.

LOUVRE: (1) opening, often with lantern over, in the roof of a building to let the smoke from a central hearth escape; (2) one of a series of overlapping boards placed in a window to allow ventilation but keep the rain out.

LOZENGE: diamond shape.

LUCARNE (*lit.* dormer): small window in a roof or spire, often capped by a gable or finial.

LUGGED: *see* Architrave.

LUNETTE (*lit.* half or crescent moon): (1) semicircular window; (2) semicircular or crescent-shaped surface.

LYCHGATE (*lit.* corpse-gate): wooden gate structure with a roof and open sides placed at the entrance to a churchyard to provide space for the reception of a coffin.

LYNCHET: long terraced strip of soil accumulating on the downward side of prehistoric and medieval fields due to soil creep from continuous ploughing along the contours.

MACHICOLATION: in medieval military architecture, a series of openings at the top of a wall head, made by building the parapet on projecting brackets, with the spaces between left open to allow missiles or boiling liquids to be dropped on the heads of assailants.

MAJOLICA: ornamented glazed earthenware.

MANSARD: *see* Roof (fig. 21).

MARGINS: dressed stones at the edges of an opening.

MAUSOLEUM: monumental tomb, so named after that of Mausolus, king of Caria, at Halicarnassus.

MERLON: *see* Battlement.

METOPES: spaces between the triglyphs in a Doric frieze; *see* Orders (fig. 16).

MEZZANINE: (1) low storey between two higher ones; (2) low upper storey within the height of a high one, not extending over its whole area.

MISERERE: *see* Misericord.

MISERICORD (*lit.* mercy): shelf placed on the underside of a hinged choir stall seat which, when turned up, provided the occupant with support during long periods of standing. Also called Miserere.

MODILLIONS: small consoles at regular intervals along the underside of some types of classical cornice. Typically a Corinthian or Composite element.

MOTTE: steep earthen mound forming the main features of C 11 and C 12 castles.

MOTTE-AND-BAILEY: post-Roman and Norman defence system consisting of an earthen mound (motte) topped with a wooden tower within a bailey, with enclosure ditch and palisade, and with the rare addition of an internal bank.

MOUCHETTE: motif in curvilinear tracery, a curved version of the dagger form, specially popular in the early C 14; *see* Tracery.

MOULDING: ornament of continuous section; *see* the various types.

MUD WALL: *see* Cob.

MULLION: vertical member between the lights in a window opening.

MUNTIN: post forming part of a screen.

MURDER HOLE: small rectangular trap in the ceiling of an entrance passage in a castle or tower house.

NAILHEAD MOULDING: E.E. ornamental motif, consisting of small pyramids regularly repeated (*see* fig. 15).

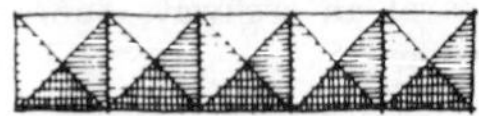

Fig. 15. Nailhead Moulding

NARTHEX: enclosed vestibule or covered porch at the main entrance to a church; *see also* Galilee.

NEWEL: central post in a circular or winding staircase; also the principal post when a flight of stairs meets a landing.

NICHE (*lit.* shell): vertical recess in a wall, sometimes for a statue, and often round-headed.

NIGHT STAIR: stair by which monks entered the transepts of their church from their dormitory to attend services at night.

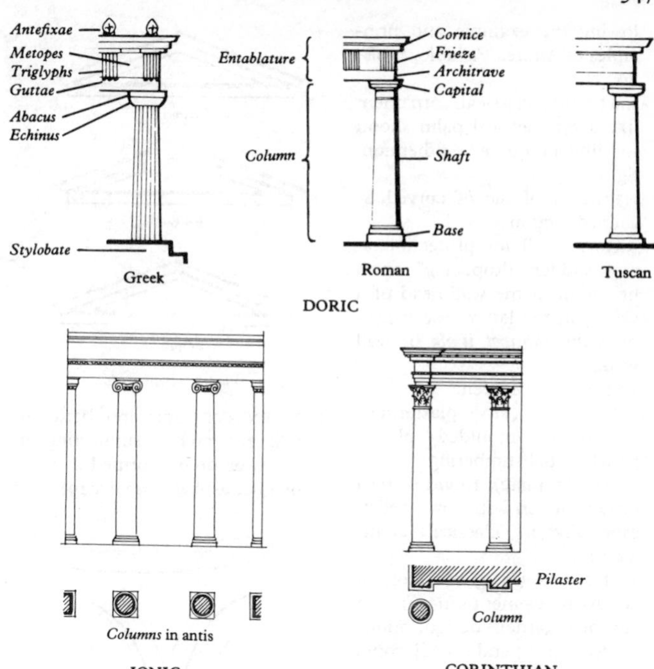

Fig. 16. Orders

NOOK-SHAFT: shaft set in an angle formed by other members.

NORMAN: *see* Romanesque.

NOSING: projection of the tread of a step. A *Bottle Nosing* is half-round in section.

OBELISK: lofty pillar of square section tapering at the top and ending pyramidally.

OCULUS: circular or oval window or other opening, used to create a conscious architectural effect.

ŒIL DE BŒUF: *see* Bullseye Window.

OGEE: double curve, bending first one way and then the other. *Ogee* or *Ogival Arch*: *see* Arch (fig. 2).

ORDER: (1) upright structural member formally related to others, e.g. in classical architecture a column, pilaster, or anta; (2) one of a series of recessed arches and jambs forming a splayed opening. *Giant* or *Colossal Order*: classical order whose height is that of two or more storeys of a building.

ORDERS: in classical architecture, the differently formalized versions of the basic post-and-lintel structure, each having its own rules of design and proportion. For examples of the main types *see* fig. 16. Others include the primitive Tuscan, which has a plain frieze and simple torus-moulded base, and the Composite, whose capital combines Ionic volutes with Corinthian foliage. *Superimposed Orders*: term for the use of Orders on successive levels, usually in the upward sequence of Doric, Ionic, Corinthian.

ORIEL: *see* Bay window.

OVERHANG: projection of the upper storey(s) of a building.

OVERSAILING COURSES: series of stone or brick courses, each one projecting beyond the one below it; *see also* Corbel Course.

PALLADIAN: architecture following the example and principles of Andrea Palladio, 1508–80.

PALMETTE: classical ornament like a symmetrical palm shoot; for illustration *see* Anthemion, fig. 1.

PANTILE: roof tile of curved S-shaped section.

PARAPET: wall for protection at any sudden drop, e.g. on a bridge or at the wall-head of a castle; in the latter case it protects the *Parapet Walk* or wall walk.

PARCLOSE: *see* Screen.

PARGETING (*lit.* plastering): usually of moulded plaster panels in half-timbering.

PATERA (*lit.* plate): round or oval ornament in shallow relief, especially in classical architecture.

PATTE D'OIE (*lit.* goose foot): a common element in French baroque garden design, much copied in C 17 and C 18 Europe, where three radiating avenues focus on a single point.

PEBBLEDASHING: *see* Rendering.

PEDESTAL: in classical architecture, a stand sometimes used to support the base of an order (*see* fig. 17).

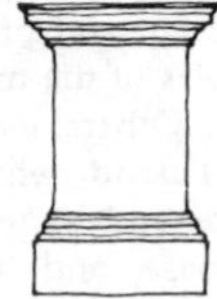

Fig. 17. Pedestal

PEDIMENT: in classical architecture, a formalized gable derived from that of a temple, also used over doors, windows, etc. For the generally accepted meanings of *Broken Pediment* and *Open Pediment see* fig. 18.

PEND: covered archway passing through a terraced building to give vehicular access to gardens or yards behind. Also called a *Carriage Arch*.

PENDANT: hanging-down feature of a vault or ceiling, usually ending in a boss.

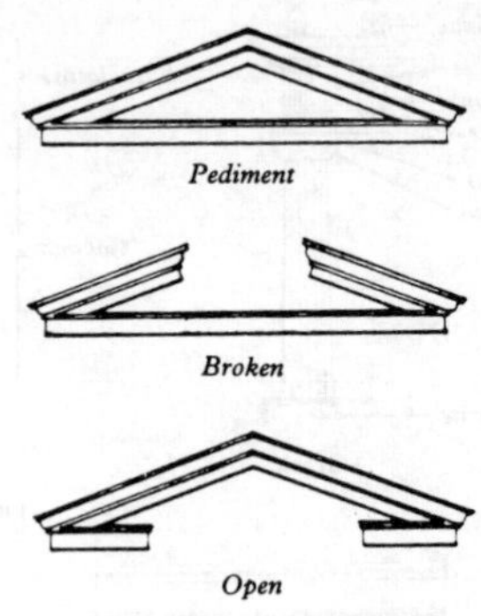

Fig. 18. Pediments

PENDENTIVE: spandrel between adjacent arches supporting a drum or dome, formed as part of a hemisphere (*see* fig. 19).

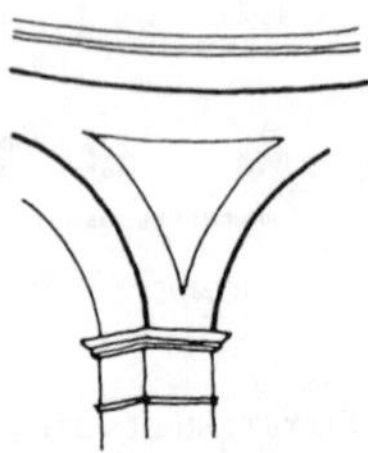

Fig. 19. Pendentive

PERISTYLE: in classical architecture, a range of columns all round a building, e.g. a temple, or an interior space, e.g. a courtyard.

PERP (PERPENDICULAR): historical division of English Gothic architecture covering the period from *c.* 1335–50 to *c.* 1530.

PERRON: *see* Stair.

PIANO NOBILE: principal floor, usually with a ground floor or basement underneath and a lesser storey overhead.

PIAZZA: open space surrounded by buildings; in the C 17 and C 18 sometimes employed to mean a long colonnade or loggia.

PIER: strong, solid support, frequently square in section. *Compound Pier*: of composite section, e.g. formed of a bundle of shafts.

PIETRA DURA: ornamental or scenic inlay by means of thin slabs of stone.

PILASTER: classical order of oblong section, its elevation similar to that of a column. *Pilastrade*: series of pilasters, equivalent to a colonnade. *Pilaster Respond*: pilaster set within a loggia or portico, or at the end of an arcade, to balance visually the column which it faces. *Pilaster Strip*: *see* Lesene.

PILE: a row of rooms. The important use of the term is in *Double-pile*, describing a house that is two rows thick, each row consisting of three or more rooms.

PILLAR PISCINA: free-standing piscina on a pillar.

PILOTIS: French term used in modern architecture for pillars or stilts that carry a building to first-floor level, leaving the ground floor open.

PINNACLE: tapering finial, e.g. on a buttress or the corner of a tower, sometimes decorated with crockets.

PISCINA: basin for washing the communion or mass vessels, provided with a drain; generally set in or against the wall to the S of an altar.

PLATBAND: deep, flat string-course, frequently employed between a rusticated lower storey and ashlar work above.

PLINTH: projecting base beneath a wall or column, generally chamfered or moulded at the top.

POCKED TOOLING: hammer-dressed stonework with a pocked appearance characteristic of Irish masonry from the C 14 to the C 16.

POINTING: exposed mortar joints of masonry or brickwork. The finished form is of various types, e.g. *Flush Pointing, Recessed Pointing. Bag-rubbed Pointing* is flush at the edges and gently recessed in the middle of the joint. *Hungry Joints* are either without any pointing at all, or deeply recessed to show the outline of each stone. *Ribbon Pointing* is a nasty practice in the modern vernacular, the joints being formed with a trowel so that they stand out.

POPPYHEAD: carved ornament of leaves and flowers as a finial for the end of a bench or stall.

PORCH: covered projecting entrance to a building.

PORTAL FRAME: a basic form of pre-cast concrete construction where walls and roof are supported on a series of angled concrete beams which, meeting at the ridge of the roof, form 'portals'.

PORTCULLIS: gate constructed to rise and fall in vertical grooves at the entry to a castle.

PORTE COCHÈRE (*lit.* gate for coaches): porch large enough to admit wheeled vehicles.

PORTICO: roofed space, open on one side at least, and enclosed by a row of columns which also support the roof (and frequently a pediment). A portico may be free-standing: more usually it forms part of a building, often in the form of a projecting temple front. When the front of the portico is on the same level as the front of the building it is described as a *portico in antis*.

POSTERN: small gateway at the back of a building.

PREDELLA: (1) step or platform on which an altar stands; hence (2) in an altarpiece the horizontal strip below the main representation, often used for a number of subsidiary representations in a row.

PRESBYTERY: the part of the church lying E of the choir. It is the part where the altar is placed.

PRINCIPAL: *see* Roof (fig. 22).

PRIORY: monastic house whose head is a prior or prioress, not an abbot or abbess.

PROSTYLE: with a row of columns in front.

PULPITUM: stone screen in a major church provided to shut off the choir from the nave and also as a backing for the return choir stalls.

PULVINATED: *see* Frieze.

PURLIN: *see* Roof (fig. 22).

PUTHOLE or PUTLOCK HOLE: putlocks are the short horizontal timbers on which during construction the boards of scaffolding rest. Putholes or putlock holes are the holes in the wall for putlocks, and often are not filled in after construction is complete.

PUTTO: small naked boy (plural: putti).

QUADRANGLE: inner courtyard in a large building.

QUARRIES (*lit.* squares): (1) in stained glass, square or diamond-shaped panes of glass supported by lead strips which are called *Canes*; (2) square floor-slabs or tiles.

QUATREFOIL: *see* Foil.

QUEENPOSTS: *see* Roof (fig. 22).

QUIRK: sharp groove to one side of a convex moulding, e.g. beside a roll moulding, which is then said to be quirked.

QUOINS: dressed stones at the angles of a building, usually alternately long and short.

RADIATING CHAPELS: chapels projecting radially from an ambulatory or an apse.

RAFTER: *see* Roof (fig. 22).

RAGGLE: groove cut in masonry, especially to receive the edge of glass or roof-covering.

RAKE: slope or pitch.

RAMPART: stone wall or wall of earth surrounding a castle, fortress, or fortified city. *Rampart Walk*: path along the inner face of a rampart.

RANDOM: *see* Rubble.

RATH: circular or near-circular enclosure consisting of one or more earthen (or occasionally stone) banks with ditches outside, classified as univallate, bivallate, or trivallate. Most date from early Christian times and housed single farms or served as cattle enclosures for the farms. Also called *Ring Forts*.

REBATE: rectangular section cut out of a masonry edge.

REEDING: series of convex mouldings; the reverse of fluting.

REFECTORY: dining hall (or frater) of a monastery or similar establishment.

RENDERING: the process of covering outside walls with a uniform surface or skin to protect the wall from the weather. *Stucco*, originally a fine lime plaster finished to a smooth surface, is the finest rendered external finish, characteristic of many late C 18 and C 19 classical buildings. It is usually painted. *Cement Rendering* is a cheaper and more recent substitute for stucco, usually with a grainy texture and often left unpainted. Shoddy but all too common in Ireland. In more simple buildings the wall surface may be roughly *Lime-plastered* (and then whitewashed), or covered with plaster mixed with a coarse aggregate such as gravel. This latter is known as *Rough-cast* or, in Scotland and the North of Ireland, as *Harling*. A variant, fashionable in the early C 20, is *Pebble-dashing*: here the stones of the aggregate are kept separate from the plaster and are thrown at the wet plastered wall to create a decorative effect.

RERE-ARCH: archway in medieval architecture formed across the wider inner opening of a window reveal.

REREDOS: painted and/or sculptured screen behind and above an altar.

RESPOND: half-pier bonded into a wall and carrying one end of an arch. *See also* Pilaster Respond.

RETABLE: altarpiece; a picture or piece of carving standing behind and attached to an altar.

RETROCHOIR: in a major church, an aisle between the high altar and an E chapel, like a square ambulatory.

REVEAL: the inward plane of a jamb, between the edge of an external wall and the frame of a door or window that is set in it.

RIB-VAULT: *see* Vault.

Fig. 20. Rinceau

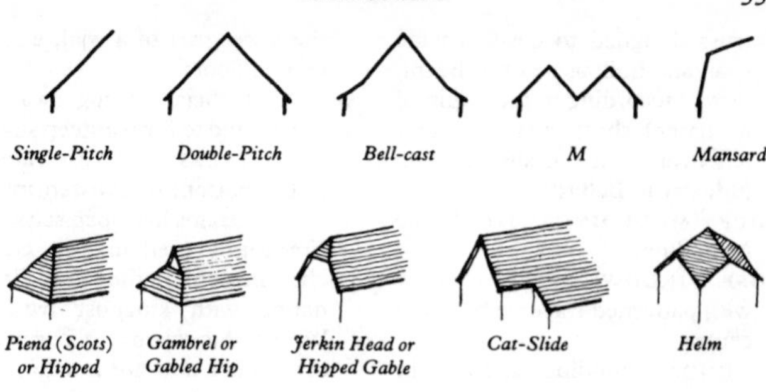

Fig. 21. Roof Forms

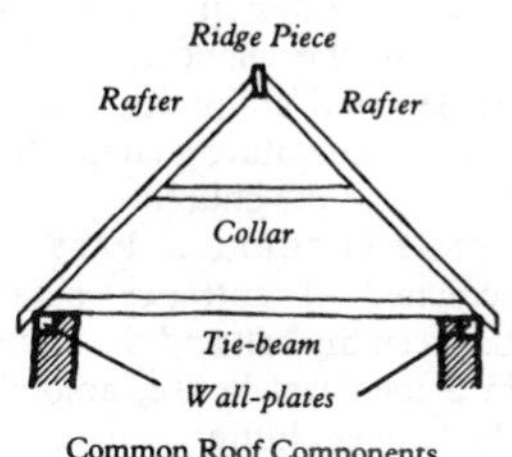

Common Roof Components

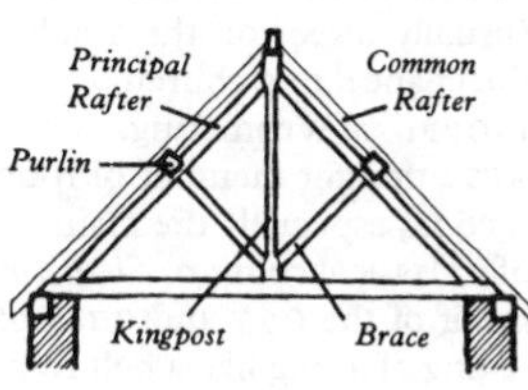

Roof with Kingpost Truss

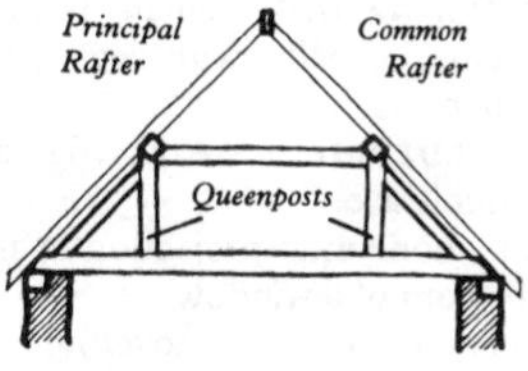

Roof with Queenpost Truss

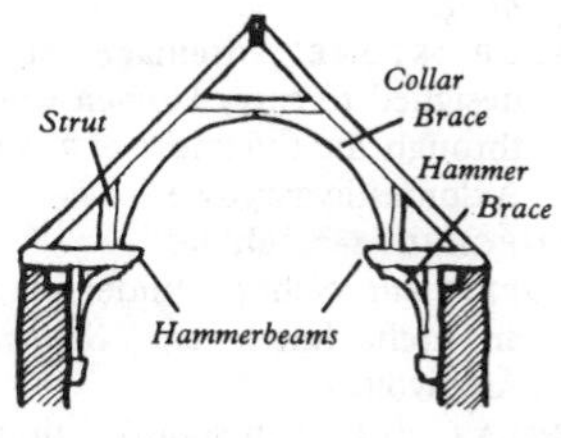

Hammerbeam Roof

Fig. 22. Roof Construction

RINCEAU (*lit.* little branch) or antique foliage: classical ornament, usually on a frieze, of leafy scrolls branching alternately to left and right (*see* fig. 20).

RING FORT: *see* Rath.

RISER: vertical face of a step.

ROCK-FACED: term used to describe masonry which is cleft to produce a natural, rugged appearance.

ROCOCO (*lit.* rocky): the light-hearted last phase of the baroque style, current in most continental countries between *c.* 1720 and *c.* 1760, and showing itself in Ireland mainly in light classical elements and scrolled decoration, especially in plasterwork.

ROLL MOULDING: moulding of semicircular or more than semicircular section.

ROMANESQUE: that style in architecture which was current in the C 11 and C 12 and preceded the Gothic style (in England often called Norman). (Some scholars extend the use of the term Romanesque back to the C 10.)

ROOD: cross or crucifix, usually over the entry into the chancel. The *Rood Screen* beneath it may have a *Rood Loft* along the top, reached by a *Rood Stair*.

ROOF: for external forms *see* fig. 21; for construction and components *see* fig. 22. *Wagon Roof*: lined with timber on the inside, giving the appearance of a curved or polygonal vault. *Belfast roof truss*: segmental roof truss designed to cover a wide span and built as a lattice beam, using (according to the origin of its name) short cuts of timber left over from the shipbuilding industry in Belfast.

ROPE MOULDING: *see* Cable Moulding.

ROSE WINDOW: circular window with patterned tracery about the centre.

ROTUNDA: building circular in plan.

ROUGH-CAST: *see* Rendering.

RUBBLE: masonry whose stones are wholly or partly in a rough state. *Coursed Rubble*: of coursed stones with rough faces. *Random Rubble*: of uncoursed stones in a random pattern. *Snecked Rubble* has courses frequently broken by smaller square stones (snecks).

RUSTICATION: treatment of joints and/or faces of masonry to give an effect of strength. In the most usual kind the joints are recessed by V-section chamfering or square-section channelling. *Banded Rustication* has only the horizontal joints emphasized in this way. The faces may be flat but there are many other forms, e.g. *Diamond-faced*, like a shallow pyramid, *Vermiculated*, with a stylized texture like worms or worm-holes, or *Glacial*, like icicles or stalactites. *Rusticated Columns* may have their joints and drums treated in any of these ways.

SACRAMENT HOUSE: safe cupboard for the reserved sacrament.

SACRISTY: room in a church for sacred vessels and vestments.

SANCTUARY: area around the main altar of a church (*see* Presbytery).

SARCOPHAGUS (*lit.* flesh-consuming): coffin of stone or other durable material.

SCAGLIOLA: composition imitating marble.

SCALE-AND-PLATT (*lit.* stair and landing): *see* Stair (fig. 24).

SCARCEMENT: extra thickness of the lower part of a wall, e.g. to carry a floor.

SCARP: artificial cutting away of the ground to form a steep slope.

SCISSOR TRUSS: roof truss framed at the bottom by crossed intersecting beams like open scissors. Frequently used in C 19 churches in conjunction and alternating with kingpost trusses. Where the scissors occur with each rafter and are not formed into separate trusses the structure would be called a scissor-beam roof.

SCREEN: in a church, usually at the entry to the chancel; *see* Rood Screen and Pulpitum. *Parclose Screen*: separating a chapel from the rest of the church.

SCREENS or SCREENS PASSAGE: screened-off entrance passage between the hall and the kitchen in a medieval house, adjoining the kitchen, buttery, etc.

SEDILIA: seats for the priests (usually three) on the S side of the chancel of a church.

SET-OFF: *see* Weathering.

SHAFT: upright member of round section, especially the main part of a classical column. *Shaft-ring*: motif of the C 12 and C 13 consisting of a ring like a belt round a circular pier or a circular shaft attached to a pier.

SHEILA-NA-GIG: female fertility figure, usually with legs wide open.

SHOULDERED: *see* Arch (fig. 2), Architrave.

SILL: horizontal projection at the bottom of a window.

SLATE-HANGING: covering of overlapping slates on a wall, which is then said to be *slate-hung*.

SLOP STONE: drainage stone designed to carry kitchen waste through the thickness of a wall. A domestic gargoyle.

SNECKED: *see* Rubble.

SOFFIT (*lit.* ceiling): underside of an arch, lintel, etc. *See also* Archivolt.

SOLAR (*lit.* sun-room): upper living room or withdrawing room of a medieval house, accessible from the high table end of the hall.

SOUNDING-BOARD: horizontal board or canopy over a pulpit; also called Tester.

SOUTERRAIN: underground stone-lined passage and chamber.

SPANDRELS: surfaces left over between an arch and its containing rectangle, or between adjacent arches.

SPIRE: tall pyramidal or conical feature built on a tower or turret. *Broach Spire*: starting from a square base, then carried into an octagonal section by means of triangular faces. *Needle Spire*: thin spire rising from the centre of a tower roof, well inside the parapet. *Helm Spire: see* Roof (fig. 21).

SPIRELET: *see* Flèche.

SPLAY: chamfer, usually of a reveal.

SPRING: level at which an arch or vault rises from its supports. *Springers*: the first stones of an arch or vaulting-rib above the spring.

SQUINCH: arch thrown across an angle between two walls to support a superstructure, e.g. a dome (*see* fig. 23).

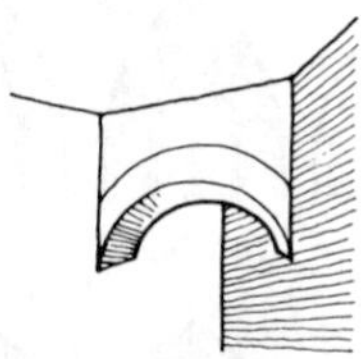

Fig. 23. Squinch

SQUINT: hole cut in a wall or through a pier to allow a view of the main altar of a church from places whence it could not otherwise be seen. Also called Hagioscope.

STAIR: *see* fig. 24. The term *Perron* (*lit.* of stone) applies to the external stair leading to a doorway, usually of branched or double-curved plan as shown. *Spiral* or *Newel Stair*: ascending round a central supporting newel, usually in a circular shaft. *Flying Stair*: cantilevered from the wall of a stairwell, without newels. *Geometric Stair*: flying stair whose inner edge describes a curve. *Well Stair*: term applied to any stair contained in an open well, but generally to one that climbs up three sides of a well, with corner landings.

STALL: seat for clergy, choir, etc., distinctively treated in its own right or as one of a row.

STANCHION: upright structural member, of iron or steel or reinforced concrete.

STEEPLE: a tower together with a spire or other tall feature on top of it.

STOUP: vessel for the reception of holy water, usually placed near a door.

STRAINER: *see* Arch.

STRAPWORK: C 16 and C 17 decoration used also in the C 19 Jacobean revival, resembling interlaced bands of cut leather.

STRETCHER: *see* Bond.

STRING-COURSE: intermediate stone course or moulding projecting from the surface of a wall.

STUCCO (*lit.* plaster): (1) smooth external rendering of a wall etc.; (2) archaic term for plasterwork.

STUDS: intermediate vertical

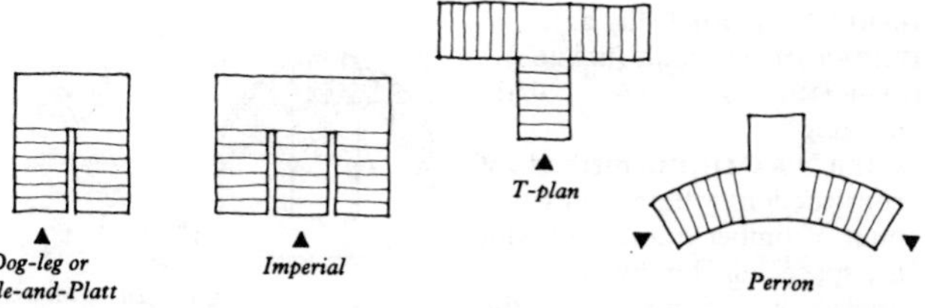

Fig. 24. Stair

members of a timber-framed wall or partition.

STYLOBATE: solid base structure on which a colonnade stands.

SWAG (*lit.* bundle): like a festoon, but also a cloth bundle in relief, hung up at both ends.

TABERNACLE (*lit.* tent): (1) canopied structure, especially on a small scale, to contain the reserved sacrament or a relic; (2) architectural frame, e.g. of a monument on a wall or free-standing, with flanking orders. Also called an Aedicule.

TABLE TOMB: raised memorial tomb in the shape of a table or altar, often with recumbent effigies on the table top.

TAS-DE-CHARGE: stone(s) forming the springers of more than one vaulting-rib.

TERMINAL FIGURE or TERM: upper part of a human figure growing out of a pier, pilaster, etc. which tapers towards the bottom.

TERQUETRA: *see* Triquetra.

TERRACOTTA: moulded and fired clay ornament or cladding, usually unglazed.

TESTER (*lit.* head): bracketed canopy, especially over a pulpit, where it is also called a sounding-board.

TETRASTYLE: term used to describe a portico with four columns.

THERMAE WINDOW (*lit.* of a Roman bath): segmental or semicircular window divided by two mullions. Also called a *Diocletian Window* from its use at the baths of Diocletian in Rome.

THOLSEL: exchange or market-house.

TIE-BEAM: *see* Roof (fig. 22).

TIERCERON: *see* Vault (fig. 26b).

TILE-HANGING: *see* Slate-hanging.

TIMBER FRAMING: method of construction where walls are built of timber framework with the spaces filled in by plaster or brickwork. Sometimes the timber is covered over with plaster or boarding laid horizontally.

TOMB-CHEST: chest-shaped stone coffin, the most usual medieval form of funerary monument.

TOURELLE: turret corbelled out from the wall.

TOWER HOUSE (Scots and Irish): compact fortified house with the main hall raised above the ground and at least one more storey above it. A C 15 type continuing well into the C 17 in its modified forms.

TRACERY: pattern of arches and geometrical figures supporting the glass in the upper part of a Gothic window, or applied decoratively to wall surfaces or vaults. *Plate Tracery* is the most primitive form of tracery, being formed of openings cut through stone slabs or plates. In *Bar Tracery* the openings are separated not by flat areas of stonework but by relatively slender divisions or bars which are constructed of voussoirs like arches. Later developments of bar tracery are classified according to the character of the decorative patterns used. For generalized

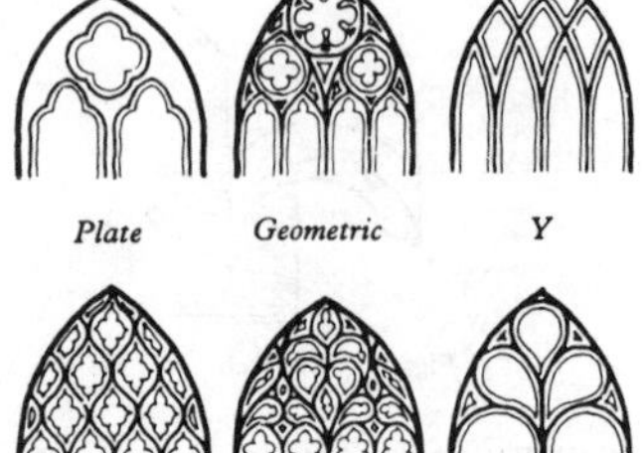

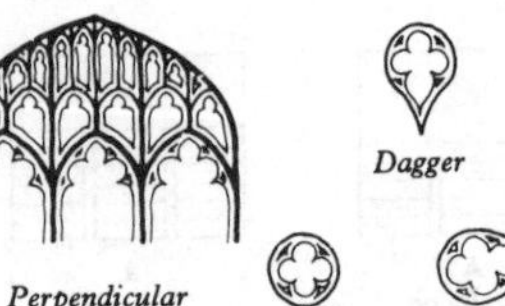

Fig. 25. Tracery

illustrations of the main types *see* fig. 25.

TRANSEPTS (*lit.* cross-enclosures): transverse portions of a cross-shaped church.

TRANSOM: horizontal member between the lights in a window opening.

TREFOIL: *see* Foil.

TRIBUNE: *see* Gallery (1).

TRIFORIUM (*lit.* three openings): middle storey of a church treated as an arcaded wall passage or blind arcade, its height corresponding to that of the aisle roof.

TRIGLYPHS (*lit.* three-grooved tablets): stylized beam-ends in the Doric frieze, with metopes between; *see* Orders (fig. 16).

TRIM: *see* Dressings.

TRIQUETRA: a symbolic figure in the form of a three-cornered knot of interlaced arcs, common in Celtic art. Hence also *Terquetra*, a knot formed of four similar corners.

TRIUMPHAL ARCH: *see* Arch.

TROPHY: sculptured group of arms or armour as a memorial of victory.

TRUMEAU: stone mullion supporting the tympanum of a wide doorway and dividing the door opening into two.

TRUSS: *see* Roof.

TURRET: small tower, often attached to a building.

TUSCAN: *see* Orders (fig. 16).

TYMPANUM (*lit.* drum): as of a drum-skin, the surface between the lintel of a doorway or window and the arch above it.

UNDERCROFT: vaulted room, sometimes underground, below the main upper room.

VAULT: ceiling of stone formed like arches (sometimes imitated in timber or plaster); *see* fig. 26. *Tunnel-* or *Barrel-Vault*: the simplest kind of vault, in effect a continuous semicircular arch. *Pointed Tunnel-Vaults* occur in Irish late medieval castles but are

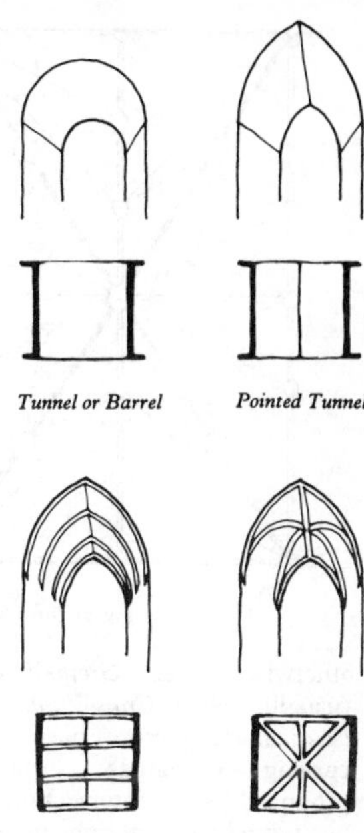

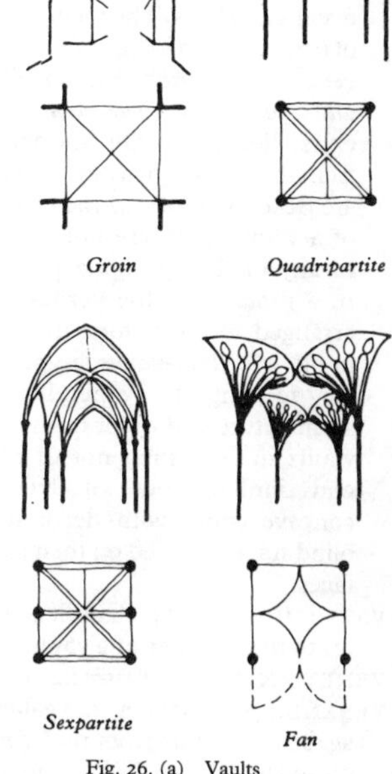

Fig. 26. (a) Vaults

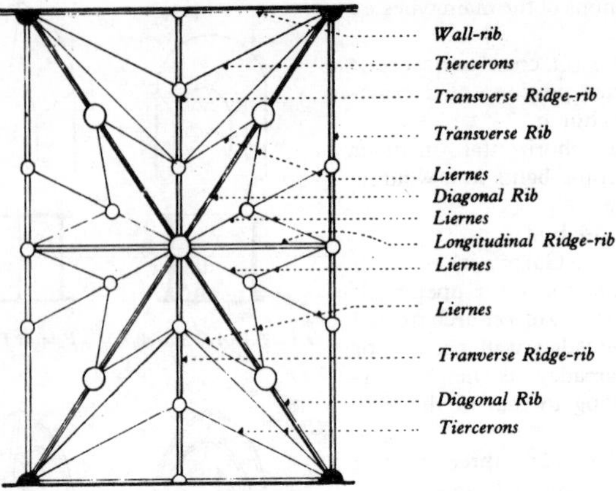

Fig. 26 (b). Ribs of a late Gothic Vault

otherwise rare. *Groin-Vaults* (usually called *Cross-Vaults* in classical architecture) have four curving triangular surfaces produced by the intersection of two tunnel-vaults at right angles. The curved lines at the intersections are called groins. In *Quadripartite Rib-Vaults* the four sections are divided by their arches or ribs springing from the corners of the bay. *Sexpartite Rib-Vaults* are most often used over paired bays. The main types of rib are shown in fig. 26b: *transverse ribs, wall ribs, diagonal ribs, and ridge ribs. Tiercerons* are extra, decorative ribs springing from the corners of a bay. *Liernes* are decorative ribs in the crown of a vault which are not linked to any of the springing points. In a *stellar vault* the liernes are arranged in a star formation as in fig. 26b. *Fan-vaults* are peculiar to English Perpendicular architecture and differ from rib-vaults in consisting not of ribs and infilling but of halved concave cones with decorative blind tracery carved on their surfaces.

VAULTING-SHAFT: shaft leading up to the springer of a vault.

VENETIAN WINDOW: *see* fig. 27.

VERANDA(H): shelter or gallery against a building, its roof supported by thin vertical members.

Fig. 27. Venetian Window

VERMICULATION: *see* Rustication.

VESICA (*lit.* bladder): usually of a window, with curved sides and pointed at top and bottom.

VESTIBULE: anteroom or entrance hall.

VILLA: originally (1) Roman country-house-cum-farmhouse, developed into (2) the similar C 16 Venetian type with office wings, made grander by Palladio's varied application of a central portico. This became an important type in C 18 Britain, often with the special meaning of (3) a country house which is not a principal residence. Gwilt (1842) defined the villa as 'a country house for the residence of opulent persons'. But devaluation had already begun, and the term implied, as now, (4) a more or less pretentious suburban house.

VITRIFIED: hardened or fused into a glass-like state.

Fig. 28. Vitruvian Scroll

VITRUVIAN SCROLL: running ornament of curly waves on a classical frieze. (*See* fig. 28.)

VOLUTES: spiral scrolls on the front and back of a Greek Ionic capital, also on the sides of a Roman one. *Angle Volute*: pair of volutes turned outwards to meet at the corner of a capital.

VOUSSOIRS: wedge-shaped stones forming an arch.

WAGON ROOF: *see* Roof.

WAINSCOT: timber lining on an internal wall.

WALLED GARDEN: C 17 type whose formal layout is still seen in the C 18 and C 19 combined vegetable and flower gardens sometimes sited at a considerable distance from a house.

WALL-PLATE: *see* Roof (fig. 22).

WATERHOLDING BASE: type of early Gothic base in which the upper and lower mouldings are separated by a hollow so deep as to be capable of retaining water.

WEATHERBOARDING: overlapping horizontal boards, covering a timber-framed wall.

WEATHERING: inclined, projecting surface to keep water away from wall and joints below.

WEEPERS: small figures placed in niches along the sides of some medieval tombs; also called mourners.

WHEEL WINDOW: circular window with tracery of radiating shafts like the spokes of a wheel; *see also* Rose Window.

WYATT WINDOW: early C 19 term for the type of large tripartite sash window made popular by the Wyatts.

ACKNOWLEDGEMENTS FOR THE PLATES

We are grateful to the following for permission to reproduce photographs:

Aerofilms Ltd: 13
Bord Fáilte Photo: 3, 4, 16, 116
Country Life: 88
Hugh Doran: 60, 61, 62, 63, 67, 70, 78, 79, 80
Irish Architectural Archive: 55, 57, 64, 65, 68, 71, 72, 73, 74, 75, 76, 81, 82, 85, 87, 102, 108, 109, 115, 124, 125, 127, 132, 135, 141
Office of Public Works, Ireland: 1, 2, 14, 15, 17, 18, 19, 20, 21, 22, 23, 24, 25, 26, 31, 32, 33, 34, 37, 38, 43, 44, 45, 46, 47, 49, 50, 52, 53, 54, 56, 59

All remaining photographs are copyright The Buildings of Ireland Record.

The plates are indexed in the indexes of artists and places, and references to them are given by numbers in the margin of the text.

INDEX OF ARTISTS

INDEX OF PATRONS AND RESIDENTS

Indexed here are the names/titles of families and individuals (not of bodies or commercial firms) recorded in this volume as having owned property and/or commissioned architectural work. The index includes monuments to members of such families, but not those to other individuals. Minor differences in the spellings of names are disregarded.

INDEX OF PLACES

Principal references are in **bold** type; demolished buildings not described in the Gazetteer are shown in *italic*. The counties are abbreviated as LF = Longford, LO = Louth, ME = Meath, WM = Westmeath.